In Prai

MW00616401

"*Drug War* is an amazingly entertaining read, and the most comprehensive look yet at the biggest mystery of our culture: why drugs are illegal, who profits, and who benefits... a tour de force of intellectual courage and honesty on a subject which encourages neither. In *Drug War*, author Dan Russell convincingly demonstrates that the current CIA-Drugs debate is part of a larger societal struggle between the forces of freedom and those of repression, and that the phony 'drug war' is really just a 'trojan horse' in the creation of what has been called 'friendly fascism.'" **Daniel Hopsicker, *Drug Money Times*:madcowprod.com; author of *Barry and the Boys***

"An important, strenuously argued contribution to the case against our nation's scandalous narcotics policies and laws. Particularly valuable are the encyclopaedic historical and anthropological perspectives which the author brings to bear on our cultural crisis. His scathing review of today's unjust confiscation and sentencing statutes is balanced by encouraging and badly-needed statistics about the successes of alternatives, such as the Dutch decriminalization program." **Peter Dale Scott, English Department, University of California, Berkeley, author of *Cocaine Politics, Deep Politics, Crime & Cover-Up, Coming To Jakarta*, etc.: http://socrates.berkeley.edu/%7Epdscott**

"Russell provides a vibrant, detailed history of drug use and drug policy. This book should be studied by anyone working to develop a policy that works. It is obvious that we are currently repeating mistakes we have made in the past — hopefully this book will be widely read and more sensible approaches can be pursued."
"Russell's review of history shows that drug prohibition enforced by a war on drugs will not only fail, it will make health, crime and other drug-related policies worse. By learning from history we can break the spiraling cycle of extremist policies and enact more cost-effective approaches that create a safer and healthier America." **Kevin Zeese, Esq.,President, Common Sense For Drug Policy: www.csdp.org**

"A very impressive piece of work! Your anecdotes are enjoyable, your breadth is magnificent, and the data are well-supported...A hard-hitting account that will disturb many of its readers, but may also expand their perspective by offering alternative options to what has become a no-win situation." **Stanley Krippner, PH.D., co-author of *The Mythic Path*, co-editor of *Broken Images, Bro-***

ken Selves

"Dan Russell is a paradigm shifter of the first order. In the twenty-two years that I have been living the seemingly intractable problem of drugs, the economy, government and ethics I have found myself being compelled to answer ever larger and larger questions.... With a sixteen page bibliography and more than 1300 footnotes, Russell has gone outside 'the box' to provide explanations that resonate with my life's journey and the better parts of the human spirit as I have found them. As a recovering alcoholic who, as part of his spiritual life, uses no mind altering chemicals of any kind, the historical truths of shamanic pharmacology and their implications ring totally true. The race has been cut off from itself. Dan Russell has expanded my consciousness. Out of hundreds of books I have read there are only fifteen on my top reference shelf, *Drug War* is now one of them. Anyone who wants to understand the real issues raised by drugs and the drug war cannot afford to bypass this seminal work." **Michael C. Ruppert, former LAPD narcotics investigator; anti-CIA activist; publisher/editor - *From The Wilderness*: www.copvcia.com**

"I just finished *Drug War*. Wow! I have learned so much and enjoyed this read tremendously. Your book was a watershed event for me. It helped me 'see the world whole' and understand the drug business and the war on drugs in an important new way. We are all pressed for time, but reading your book was the ultimate time saver for me. There is nothing more powerful than understanding the chaos when you are in it....Your book is a monumental achievement....for goodness sakes this needs to get out asap. Excellent is excellent!" **Catherine Austin Fitts, Federal Housing Commissioner, 1989-90; President, Solari, Inc.: Community Resource Toolkits: www.solari.com**

"Dan Russell's *Drug War* goes to the heart of the so-called 'drug-problem', really a 'prohibition-problem':extra-curricular drug- and gun-running by numerous governments, with that of the United States at the head of the list, its cynical and duplicitous 'war on drugs' notwithstanding - nought but a racist war on the poor and disenfranchised, both nationally and internationally, and withal a 'war on the drug competition'; nor ought we to forget who invented modern money laundering shell-games, nor who profits the most from them. I urge you to read Dan Russell's shocking *exposé* - may it serve as a much-needed wake-up call!" **Jonathan Ott, author/co-author of *Pharmacophilia Or The Natural Paradises, Pharmacotheon, Persephone's Quest, The Road To Eleusis, Hallucinogenic Plants of North America, The Age of***

***Entheogens**, etc.

"The best book I ever read on the Drug War." **Celerino Castillo III, lead DEA agent in Guatemala and El Salvador, 1985-90, who developed much of the Contra cocaine evidence; author of *Powderburns***

"*Drug War* epitomizes such books as Alexander Cockburn's *Whiteout*, Alfred McCoy's *The Politics of Heroin*, and Gary Webb's *Dark Alliance* all together, with riveting photography throughout. Written in an easy to read, flowing style that is entertaining while at the same time amazingly detailed, concise, and to the point, *Drug War* covers one hell of a lot of ground. With a sixteen page bibliography, and a copious amount of footnotes, this is a very in-depth look at the current state of affairs, the whys and wherefores of the Drug War." **Preston Peet, High Times Magazine**

"Dan Russell's sequel *Drug War* is on par with Howard Zinn's *People's History of the United States*. This historical account needs to be in every educational institution, beginning with high school, to tell the other side of the story of our loss of earth-based ecstasy. *Drug War* brilliantly shows how our healing relationship with plant allies came to be replaced with the prevailing political agenda of drug propaganda. I recommend this great book, which I personally couldn't put down as it engages like a historical/political novel, for all schools of free thinkers. It is the central text in our homeschool for my teenagers this year!" **Jeannine Parvati Baker, author of *Hygieia:A Woman's Herbal; Conscious Conception:Elemental Journey Through the Labyrinth of Sexuality; Prenatal Yoga & Natural Birth*: www.freestone.org**

"*Drug War* is a sometimes glittering tale of how corrupted drug control and global politics are soul mates. As long as this war lasts, Russell's book is an encyclopedic weapon for drug policy reform intellectuals and soldiers." **Peter D.A. Cohen Ph.D, Director, Centre for Drug Research, University of Amsterdam: www.frw.uva.nl/cedro**

"Dan Russell's *Drug War* is one of the more comprehensive studies of the real life truth of the real drug war and the lies that have been told to the American public. I recommend it to anyone who wants to understand how American 'politics' plays an important role in this political lie called the 'Drug War'. The American public should be informed and make immediate changes to the American political structure before it is too late. Otherwise, we will become like our own worst enemies. I am afraid that it is a current reality."

John Carman, former Senior Customs Agent: amerikanexpose.com/customs1.html

"*Drug War*'s sickening hypothesis unfortunately makes intuitive sense once articulated, and has the broad power not only to tie together a vast array of seemingly unrelated geopolitical events, but explain the otherwise unexplainable drug war. This book should be required reading for anyone who is puzzled by the seeming irrationality of current drug policy, concerned with the steady erosion of civil liberties...or simply seeks to understand the history of the 20th century from a new angle. I highly recommend it." **R. Andrew Sewell, M.D., University of Massachusetts/Memorial Health Care**

"Russell's *Drug War* is an excellent antidote to the drumbeat for ever increasing incarceration and punitive drug policies. We can learn a great deal from *Drug War* about how our society got into the self-destructive mess we are in, and how we can work our way out." **Rick Doblin, President, Multidisciplinary Association For Psychedelic Studies: www.maps.org**

"Although I am not an expert in many of the areas covered, I find this general history to be well written, easy to read, and fascinating. I believe it will be one more nail in the coffin of the Drug War." **Lester Grinspoon, M.D., Department of Psychiatry, Harvard Medical School**

"A penetrating examination of the host of forces currently supporting the modern Drug War...sure to become an essential addition to the Drug War library." **Richard Glen Boire, Esq., in *Journal of Cognitive Liberties*: www.alchemind.org**

"Mr. Russell has produced a work of careful scholarship that will interest not only the participants in the drug wars, but the drug-gang victims as well. This piece of contextually multidimentional history is academic in the finest tradition, and, realistically, should be required reading for junior high, high school, and college students as a rational substitute for the 'Just Say No' ditty. Teachers, by reading and discussing this volume with their students, might derive an attitude adjustment. The rationale is to drive home the point that while not all illegal substances are harmful as officially alleged, uninformed substance abuse is not innocuous."

"A fascinating tapestry of nineteenth and twentieth century history weaves highly informative pictures of medicine, racism, security agencies, and popular political movements such as neocolonialism. Some of the materials are usually excluded from current history books, and the author pulls no punches. And gives names, dates, and places accurately. Many of our best youth will recognize *Drug War*, the book, as the product of a writer who is shining a light on the subject of substances rather than shining them on in the customary way of often-uninformed society."

"*Drug War* is heady, irreverent stuff because the reader is confronted with a huge succession of inescapable facts that challenge one's views of the use and abuse of substances, both natural and synthetic. As in many other arenas of life, attitude is everything. 'Pharmaco-shamanism' as laid out in great detail in Russell's previous book, *Shamanism and the Drug Propaganda*, is reified in *Drug War* as one meaningful and sensible path between the extremes of a 'fixation on sobriety' and some cultural acceptances of constant, purposeless intoxication. Legitimate medical information and roadmaps and systems of consciousness such as meditative practices help the potential substance abuser to steer a clear path between the extremes of drug abuse and drug-phobic sobriety to a healthy spiritual life facilitated in part by culturally-defined sacraments. The politico-historical element of substance use/abuse is partly summarized by Russell when he says, 'since it prefers to finance physicians rather than drug-gangs, Holland has virtually eliminated drug-related crime.' **Marshall F. Gilula, M.D., EEG/ Epilepsy Fellow, Department of Neurology, University of Miami School of Medicine: www.mindspring.com/~mgilula**

Photograph from Charles K. Moser

THE AUCTION BLOCK, WHERE THE ARAB BUYS HIS DAY'S SUPPLY OF KHAT

"How much! How much! will you give for this flower of paradise? 'Tis sweet as a maiden's eyes; 'tis like bees' breath for fragrance; 'tis——"

National Geographic, 8/1917

THE
NARCOTIC PERIL
AND HOW TO MEET IT

BY
Richmond Pearson Hobson
BULLETIN NO 5
International Narcotic Education Association
Los Angeles, California.

Drug War

Covert Money, Power & Policy

Dan Russell
Kalyx.com

Publisher's Cataloging-in-Publication (Provided by Quality Books, Inc.)

Russell, Dan, 1945-
    Drug war : covert money, power & policy / Dan Russell. - 1st ed
    p. cm.
    Includes bibliographical references and index.
    LCCN: 99-94065
    ISBN: 0-9650253-4-9

    1. Narcotics, Control of--United States--History. 2. Racism--United States--History. 3. Race discrimination--United States--History. 4. Discrimination in law enforcement--United States. I. Title.

HV5825.R87 1999   363.45'0973
                  QB199-249

Book design by Dan Russell

Kalyx.com
P.O. Box 417
Camden, NY 13316
www.kalyx.com
www.drugwar.com

Manufactured in the United States of America

Contents

Illustrations

Illustrations

A Bolivian *coquero* sucking a quid of coca, *Natural History*, 2/1947

Drug War

Euroamerica

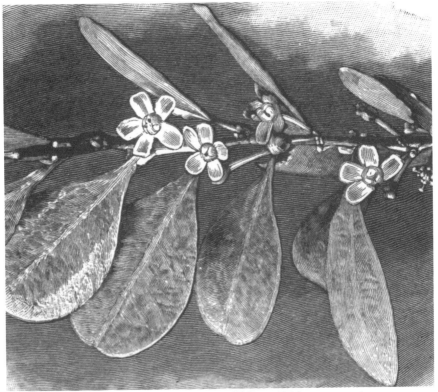

Mortimer: *History Of Coca*, 1901

The central sacrament of Incan culture, coca leaf, a medicinal chew and tea leaf, was determined to be *un delusio del demonio* by Pizarro's priests, who proceeded to save Incan souls by working them to death as beasts of burden under the lash.

There is nothing whatever dangerous about whole coca leaves; they are as harmless as orange pekoe tea. Cocaine, which wasn't isolated until 1860, comprises about ½ of 1% of the weight of a coca leaf. It takes a ton of coca leaves to make 5-20 pounds of cocaine. There are far more dangerous compounds in potatoes, tomatoes, celery and fava beans, all of which are perfectly safe to eat.

Traditional sacramental plant-foods can't be equated with poisons, and poisons can't be equated with naturally-occurring plant isolates. Some plants are poisonous, and some plant isolates are as safe to use as corn. This book is largely the political history of that intentional confusion, a confusion rooted in the *unconscious* contents of our political culture. That is, in the planted axiom that "the drug problem" can be discussed in terms of modern politics. The Drug War can't be separated from the cultural compulsion of our conquistador history. Nor can it be separated from the evolutionary function of inebriative behavior.

The industrial process has been as successful in burying conscious knowledge of the archaic techniques of ecstacy as it has been in burying the wolf, and those that understood it. Unconscious knowledge, on the other hand, is a tad more difficult to manipulate, as the neurotic lurching of so many of our public figures demonstrates; "just say no," after all, was promulgated by an alcoholic.

We are no longer overtly racist, in our public laws at least, but we are still brutally anti-tribal, in many ways institutionally unloving, structurally violent, to millions of our children, our tribal primitives, and to our shamanic adults. This is a *psychological* inheritance from our conquistador past, as well as a legal one.

This internalized industrial fascism, this proscription, *causes* drug problems, in the same way that violent sexual puritanism causes sexual problems. The ancient tribal wisdom prevents them. There are many cultures, both tribal and industrial, the Vicosinos of Peru and the Dutch, for instance, that don't have anything like our current disaster, and they all apply prescription rather than proscription.

The ancient tribal wisdom was the prescription of John Wesley, author of colonial America's most popular medical book, *Primitive Physic*, first published in London in 1747. The book went through more than forty editions over the next hundred years, becoming the basic home health guide of the era.

The populist evangelist worked in Georgia from 1735-37, and was deeply impressed by Native American health and medicine. An enemy of venal practitioners who used high-falutin language to hide their obvious ignorance, Wesley pointed out in his preface that "It is probable Physic, as well as Religion, was in the first ages chiefly traditional; every father delivering down to his sons what he had in like manner received."

"It is certain this is the method wherein the art of healing is preserved among the American Indians to this day. Their diseases indeed are exceeding few; nor do they often occur, by reason of their continual exercise, and (till of late) universal temperance. But if any are sick, or bit by a serpent, or torn by a wild beast, the fathers immediately tell their children what remedy to apply. And it is rare that the patient suffers long; those medicines being quick, as well as generally infallible."

But after our expulsion from this Garden of Eden, "Physicians now began to be in admiration, as persons who were something more

Primitive Phyſick:

O R,

An Eaſy and Natural METHOD

O F

C U R I N G

M O S T

D I S E A S E S.

By *J O H N W E S L E Y*, M.A.

Homo ſum; humani nihil a me alienum puto.

THE SEVENTEETH EDITION.

L O N D O N; Printed by R. HAWES,
And Sold at the Foundry in *Moorfields;* and at the
Rev. Mr. *Weſley's* Preaching-Houſes, in
Town and Country. 1776.

than human. And profit attended employ as well as honor; so that they now had two weighty reasons for their keeping the bulk of mankind at a distance, that they might not pry into the mysteries of their profession.... Those who understood only how to restore the sick to health, they branded with the name Empirics. They introduced into practice an abundance of compound medicines, consisting of so many ingredients, that it was scarce possible for common people to know which it was that wrought the cure;....chemicals, such as they neither had skill, nor fortune, nor time to prepare; yea, and of dangerous ones, such as they could not use without hazarding life, but by the advice of a physician. And thus both their honor and gain were secured, a vast majority of mankind being utterly cut off from helping either themselves or their neighbors, or once daring to attempt it."[1]

His book then goes on to prescribe "a single plant or fruit duly applied" for the common ailments. Wesley's ideas reflected the American psyche and became permanently imbedded in it. Thomas Jefferson shared Wesley's egalitarian medical views, expressing his respect for "an abandonment of hypothesis for sober facts, the first degree of value set on clinical observation, and the lowest on visionary theories."[2]

When Jefferson talked of "visionary theories" he was referring to the "regular" physicians of his day. At the time of the Revolution the colonies had about 3500 regular physicians, of which about 400 had medical degrees "that were no guarantee of empirical knowledge or manual dexterity."[3]

Their founding father was the minister of the North Church in Boston, Cotton Mather (1662-1728), a Puritan theocrat who became famous for his support of the 1692 Salem witch trials. Mather wasn't a bloodthirsty man, and he refused to condemn people on the "spectral" evidence of "possessed" people, but he did truly believe in possession by the devil - and in the political utility of the witch hunt. His world was full of demons. He saw European education as a proof against the "Creolean degeneracy" that threatened to "deprave the children of the most noble and worthy Europeans when transplanted into America."[4]

As a lecturer at Harvard College he read his Galen, Bacon, Boerhaave, Sydenham, Plater, Le Boe, Harvey, Culpeper, Kircher, Leeuwenhoek and the other founders of "regular" medicine. He had a theoretical understanding of blood circulation, herbalism, chemistry, anatomy, physiology and even Leeuwenhoek's primitive microbiology, but very little clinical experience; nonetheless, he was a prolific medical writer. Disease was a consequence of Original Sin, therefore the Heavenly Remedy was *The Great Physician*, which was the title of his 1700 book.

Mather was perfectly well aware that the Great Physician was an herbalist, and willingly acknowledged that the "diabolical" Indians wrought "cures many times which are truly stupendous." He was, nonetheless, relieved that "the woods were almost cleared of those pernicious creatures, to make room for a better growth."[5]

A

DISCOURSE

UPON THE INSTITUTION OF

MEDICAL SCHOOLS

In AMERICA;

Delivered at a Public ANNIVERSARY COMMENCE-
MENT, held in the COLLEGE of PHILADELPHIA
May 30 and 31, 1765.

WITH A

PREFACE

Containing, amongst other things,

THE AUTHOR's

APOLOGY

For attempting to introduce the regular mode of
practising PHYSIC in PHILADELPHIA:

By JOHN MORGAN M.D.

Fellow of the Royal Society at LONDON; Correspondent of the Royal Academy of Surgery at
PARIS; Member of the Arcadian *Belles Lettres* Society at ROME; Licentiate of the Royal Colleges of
Physicians in LONDON and in EDINBURGH; and
Professor of the Theory and Practice of Medicine
in the College of PHILADELPHIA.

PHILADELPHIA
Printed and sold by WILLIAM BRADFORD at the
Corner of *Market* and *Front-Streets*, MDCC,LXV.

American Journal of Pharmacy, 1/1904

Mather's epic contribution to the development of inoculation was taught him by his captive African, "my Negro-man Onesimus," whom he had the good sense to heed, and the humility to credit. "Onesimus" (Philemon) learned it as a boy when he was inoculated by his shaman. Mather was well-read enough in the current medical literature to recognize that Onesimus was describing the technique recently published in the *Philosophical Transactions of the Royal Society*. Inoculation, first recorded in India, c.1500 BC, had recently been publicized by two Italian physicians who had learned it in Turkey.[6]

Despite rejection by Boston's medical establishment, Mather and his "inoculation-ministers" cut the death rate of the 1721 Boston small-pox epidemic from 12% to 2% among those few hundred they were able to inoculate.[7] This contributed to Jenner's discovery of preventive inoculation and to all modern vaccination.

The leading regular physician of Jefferson's day was Benjamin Rush (1745-1813), the New England Federalist who signed the Declaration of Independence and was a member of the Pennsylvania legislature. Rush equated Jefferson's Republicans with the vice-ridden French Jacobins, insisting that distilled spirits were "anti-federal...companions of all those vices that are calculated to dishonor and enslave our country."

He drew up a *A Moral and Physical Thermometer* that went from Health & Wealth to the Gallows, and from Water & Milk to Whiskey.[8] Rush is a founder of the American Temperance movement. His temperance tracts were widely distributed in 19th century America. When Jefferson took office Rush sadly reflected that "Nothing but the gospel of Jesus Christ" could save the country now.[9]

Rush was a graduate of the aristocratic Edinburgh College of Medicine, where he absorbed the regular tradition promulgated by his contemporaries Cullen and Brown, with whom he studied. As Wesley intimated, the regulars, having exterminated the carriers of Europe's herbal traditions, the midwives, in the Inquisition, were left with nothing but their own wild speculations. They combined these with a working knowledge of anatomy and a blind faith in industrial solvents like mercurous chloride, "calomel," and antimony and potassium, "tartar emetic." Certainly no midwife would claim intimacy with the mysteries of calomel and bloodletting.

Rush's standard cure for emotional problems, the accepted regular treatment, included heavy bloodletting, calomel to evacuate the bowels, tartar emetic to induce convulsive vomiting, physical restraint, chastisement, physical shock and terror.[10] He is the founder of American psychiatry, disseminated from his influential Philadelphia College of Medicine, where he taught for 44 years. His primitive brutality and his rationalizations were identical to the ethereal idiocy of the worst of the medievals. His psychiatric treatment became the basis of the Towns-Lambert method, the standard AMA treatment for drug abuse in the 1920's.

Rush authoritatively declared: "We have no discoveries in the materia medica to hope for from the Indians in North America. It would be a reproach to our schools of physic if modern physicians were not more successful than the Indians, even in the treatment of their own diseases." "a belief in specific remedies is the sedative of reason." "It is by no means necessary to know how to class epidemics in order to cure them, any more than it is individual or solitary diseases."

The physician should beware of "an undue reliance on the powers of nature in curing disease." "The time, I hope, will soon come, when the rejection of the powers of nature in acute and chronic diseases, and greater simplicity in pathology and the materia medica, will enable us to reverse the words of Hippocrates, and to say 'Ars brevis, vita longa.' That is, our short, or speedily acquired art, prolongs life."[11] Rush was, unquestionably, the leading shortcut artist of his day; he pioneered the chemical diploma mills of the nineteenth century.

There was, declared Rush absolutely, only one cause of disease: "arterial excitement" or "venous congestion." He somehow reconciled this with his belief that lying on damp brick pavement in hot weather caused tetanus.[12] In 1799 Rush told the American Philosophical Society that Blacks had dark skin as a consequence of an ancestral epidemic of leprosy caused by the intense African heat.

When faced with the 1793 Philadelphia yellow fever epidemic, Doc Rush had the answer: copious bleeding, mercurous chloride ("calomel") and jalap pills. Mercurous chloride is mercury and chlorine, the toxic metal found in thermometers and the mineral base of WW I's poison gases and many insecticides. The idea was to bleed until unconsciousness approached, at which the fever was said to break, then unclog the "venous congestion" with calomel, a violent purgative, and jalap, producing "copious watery stools."[13]

Rush claimed he had the sense to stop the calomel when the patient's tongue turned brown and he began to salivate, an outcome he desired (symptoms of acute poisoning). He then prescribed such common-sense pick-me-ups as wine, roast beef and opium. It was Rush who popularized calomel, with which the incompetent did the gullible to death.

This violent caustic poison was given orally. It caused softening of the gums, loss of teeth, ulceration of the mouth, death of the bone tissue of the lower jaw, lockjaw and permanent disfigurement. Rush's advocacy made it official in the early pharmacopeias, one of the most frequently prescribed medicines in the country. Early nineteenth century America was full of children who had been so badly poisoned with calomel that they had permanent lockjaw, and had to suck their food through a straw inserted through the holes in their lower jaw caused by the caustic poison.[14]

Rush's Aristotelian dream-world, combined with a genuine knowledge of anatomy, made him truly dangerous - his "visionary theory" being that "capillary tension," the "bad humor" reduced by bleeding, was the universal culprit. Following ancient hepatoscopy, Rush declared that since the liver "suffers more or less from all general, and many local diseases," then calomel, since it acted on the liver, deserves "its usefulness and fame in all general and chronic diseases." Calomel was "the Sampson of the materia medica." Rush doesn't seem to have noticed that calomel acts on the liver by destroying it.

Plant medicines compared to his "modern" chemicals as "a company of Indians, armed with bows and arrows, against the complicated and deadly machinery of fire-arms."[15] One can understand the force of this logic for Rush. There were about 40 million Native Americans in the New World when Columbus found it. By Rush's time, 90% of South America's 30 millions had been wiped out, and a century later North America could boast the same achievement.

By some wild stretch of the imagination, Rush classed calomel, bleeding and tartar emetic right alongside opium, alcohol and Peruvian bark as standard empirical remedies. "Tartar emetic," antimony and potassium, is so poisonous that it is used today as an insecticide. It does indeed produce convulsive vomiting. Rush's "general remedies," bleeding, calomel, tartar emetic, cold baths, cold drinks, enemas, blisters, quinine, opium, wine and a few selected European herbs, were prescribed in different combinations for everything from toothache and hemorrhoids to heart disease and smallpox.

Rush's ideas about the blood date to Galen (129-210 CE), the canonical, as it were, Graeco-Roman physician, whose unempirical faith in Aristotle's humors helped the pinheaded medievals count their angels. Galen had simplified the subtle herbalist Dioscorides, and Rush simplified Galen. Galen's "science" consisted of "manipulating" Yellow Bile, Black Bile, Blood and Phlegm. "Drugs" of whatever kind were either warm, cold, wet or dry in their bodily actions, designed to coax the humors into the proportion proper for a given age or sex.

Galen got his bloodletting ideas from the Egyptians, who used bleeding and cathartics to evacuate the pus and bad blood they assumed, from their observation of infection, was the "universal cause" of disease. Some bleeding actually does, sometimes, lower a fever, but when Galen said bleed a little, Rush bled a lot. "A few required the loss of a hundred ounces of blood to cure them" reported the astute Rush, his subtle reasoning being that the more severe the disease, the more blood should be drawn.

GEORGII WOLFFGANGI WEDELII,
MED. DOCTORIS, PROFESSORIS PU-
BLICI, ET MEDICI DUCALIS
SAXONICI,

OPIOLOGIA

ad mentem
Academiæ Naturæ Curioforum.

JENÆ,
SUMPTIBUS JOHANNIS FRITSCHII,
Bibliopolæ Lipfienfis.
TYPIS SAMUELIS KREBSII.

ANNO M. DC. LXXIV.   3

Needless to say, he lost patients by the truckload, especially when the treatment was repeated, as it often was, but the epidemics, and his handle on politics and advertising, kept him well supplied. Rush argued that blood was quickly manufactured from the bodyfat, and that therefore copious bleeding did no harm. In his 1789 *Defense of Bloodletting* he insisted that four-fifths of a patient's blood could be drained without ill effect.[16] Amputations were said to require the loss of an amount of blood estimated to circulate in the limb to be amputated, lest the patient suffer from "plethora," too much blood for the reduced body mass; that is straight out of Galen.[17]

Rush thought it particularly important to bleed toddlers when fever struck, "three to five times in the ordinary course of their acute diseases."[18] He let three year-olds watch their own blood spurt out of their slit veins into an open bucket. Rush made the bleeding of young

children and infants official in early nineteenth century medicine, causing countless deaths from convulsion and blood loss. Because their
small veins were hard to locate, infants were bled from the jugular
vein.

His medical critics called him "the remorseless Master Bleeder."
One of Rush's peers, Dr. Hutchinson, was so outraged by his "murderous" bleeding and poisoning that he threatened to flog him. Dr.
Hodge called him a "horse doctor."[19] William Cobbett of Philadelphia founded a monthly journal detailing Rush horror stories, calling
his therapeutics "one of those great discoveries which are made from
time to time for the depopulation of the earth."[20] Modern medicine
still peddles this egotistical idiot as an heroic founding father. My
local profit-making, heavy-advertising "drug-treatment" facility is
called The Benjamin Rush Center.

James Adair, a trader among the Indians in the southern U.S. in
the 1760's, expressed a typically American attitude when he wrote,
"For my own part I would prefer an old Indian before any chirurgeon
whatsoever, in curing green wounds by bullets, arrows, &c. both for
the certainty, ease, and speediness of cure."[21]

Europeans were amazed at the superiority of Native American
trauma treatment. Indians from Peru to Canada understood the use
of arboreal oleoresins, antiseptic and healing herb juices, honey and
egg whites. William Wood, in 1639, wrote, "Some of them have been
shot in at the mouth, and out of the ear, some shot in the breast; some
run through the flank with darts, and other desperate wounds, which
either by their rare skill in the use of vegetatives, or diabolical charms,
they cure in a short time."[22]

Bossu, in the 1750's, reported the progressive use by Choctaw shamans of an antiseptic powder on a wound, a regular antiseptic wash,
and drying and healing agents. Dr. Pitcher, in the mid-nineteenth century, reported that the Michigan Indians began the treatment of a gun-
shot wound using a powdered puffball as an effective hemostat. A
bladder and quill syringe was then used to inject a mild antiseptic
wash into the wound, guarding against premature closure with a
drainage straw of slippery elm bark - firm enough to sink in, soft
enough not to damage the wound.[23]

In 1929, Dr. Harlow Brooks in the *Bulletin of the New York Academy
of Medicine* declared: "In frontier medicine much, one may even say
most, of the settlers' knowledge in regard to the treatment of trau-
mata has been bodily copied from the Indians."[24]

The Indians "developed a splint for legs, which, in their time, was superior to those used by whites."[25] The Ojibwas would put liniment on and warm a broken limb until it was relaxed, then jerk the dislocated bone back into place, setting it with wet clay or rawhide in conjunction with herbal poultices and elastic splints made of cedar or cactus ribs.[26] The techniques of the Ojibwas, Pimas and Mescaleros for resetting and immobilizing broken bones with form-fitting splints are now the standard techniques of modern medicine. In his 1887 report on "The Medicine-Men of the Apache," Bourke described an Apache curandero administering an enema with an animal bladder and a hollow leg bone; that's how "modern" medicine was invented.[27]

Two nineteenth century historians wrote that "For a century, French *voyageurs* and *coureurs du bois* had preferred the Indian treatment of wounds and chronic sores with poultices and herbs to that of whites. Native medicine men also doctored many other ills with concoctions of herbs, drinks, sweatings, and rubbings, usually accompanied with ceremonials, incantations, ghost shooting in the night, and similar aids. They even sucked out manitous, or evil spirits. In some western communities in the earlier years there were Indian doctors who were held in quite as high repute as regular white doctors."[28]

When William Bent, the legendary trader of Bent's Fort, was being choked to death by a throat infection, "the medicine man strung a sinew with sandburs and dipped it in hot buffalo tallow. This he forced down Bent's throat with a peeled stick. When the tallow melted, he jerked the string out, pulling the infected membrane with it. Bent survived."[29] An old Sioux shaman, Baptiste, was so treasured at the Winnebago agency, that when his tribe was moved west the government built Baptiste a clinic and kept him on at the agency, where he treated Red and White alike, "finally dying respected by both races."[30]

Bossu described the "steam cabinets" of the Choctaws "in which are boiled all sorts of medicinal and sweet-smelling herbs. The vapor filled with the essence and salts of these herbs enters the patient's body through his pores and his nose and restores his strength."[31] Spruce noted in the 1850's that "the domestic medicine of the South American Indian is chiefly hygienic, as such medicine ought to be, it being of greater daily importance to preserve health than to cure disease."[32]

In 1812 Peter Smith, author of the popular *The Indian Doctor's Dispensatory*, explained, "I call myself an *Indian Doctor*, because I have incidentally obtained a knowledge of many of the simples used by the Indians; but chiefly because I have obtained my knowledge generally in the like manner that the Indians do.... I have by continued observation come to be of the opinion that our best medicines grow in the woods and gardens."[33]

THE

INDIAN DOCTOR'S

DISPENSATORY,

BEING

FATHER SMITH'S ADVICE

RESPECTING

DISEASES AND THEIR CURE ;

CONSISTING OF PRESCRIPTIONS FOR

MANY COMPLAINTS :

AND A DESCRIPTION OF MEDICINES,

SIMPLE AND COMPOUND,

SHOWING THEIR VIRTUES AND HOW TO APPLY THEM

DESIGNED FOR THE BENEFIT OF HIS CHILDREN, HIS FRIENDS AND THE
PUBLIC, BUT MORE ESPECIALLY THE CITIZENS OF THE WESTERN
PARTS OF THE UNITED STATES OF AMERICA.

BY PETER SMITH,
OF THE MIAMI COUNTRY.

Men seldom have wit enough to prize and take care of their
health until they lose it—And Doctors often know not how to get
their bread deservedly, until they have no teeth to chew it.

CINCINNATI .
PRINTED BY BROWNE AND LOOKER,
FOR THE AUTHOR.
. 1813.

In 1822 Samuel Thomson published his *New Guide to Health, or Botanic Family Physician* and *A Narrative of the Life and Medical Discoveries of Samuel Thomson*. They began a national movement. The *Thomsonian Recorder* began publishing as Friendly Botanic Societies sprang up everywhere. The Botanico-Medical College of Ohio was chartered in 1838, and the Southern branch opened in 1839.[34] Retailing his franchises for $20 each, Thomson claimed 100,000 sales by 1839.[35] The Thomsonians, with their steam baths and all-purpose herbalism, operated their own clinics, pharmacies and distribution centers. States began to recognize the equality of the Thomsonians with the regular physicians. The Thomsonians merged with, and eventually became known as the "Eclectics."[36]

In 1855 Daniel Smith, in *The Reformed Botanic and Indian Physician*, asked his readers to "Pause for a moment and view the Corner Stone of the Primitive Medical Edifice which is already laid, and no longer suffer yourselves to be cut to pieces by the lancet or the two-edge sword of the poisonous mineral drugs, which man's device has hatched up to pick your pockets and bear you to an untimely grave; for the God of Nature in early days supplied our ancient fathers with all the healing powers arising from the Vegetable Kingdom, to heal all the maladies they were afflicted with, when they broke Nature's unerring laws."[37]

Tribal cultures have always understood herbalism as a path to the powers of the Earth. And the Earth, as so many ecstatic Europeans realized, has a biological power over its immigrants. Carl Jung pointed to Franz Boas' 1911 U.S. Immigration Commission study showing that the cephalic index of American immigrants grows toward a common mean. The children of immigrants with a high cephalic index grew slightly smaller heads, those with a low cephalic index grew larger.[38] On his first trip to America Jung immediately noticed this "mysterious Indianization of the American people," and was able to demonstrate it analytically when he had the opportunity to engage quite a few Americans in deep psychoanalysis. "Remarkable differences were revealed in comparison to Europeans...."

He noticed not only the enormous influence of African America on American behavior in general, but the completely disproportionate influence of Native America, given their isolation and extremely small numbers in the 1920's. "....it was only in the course of very thorough and deep analyses that I came upon symbols relating to the Indian. The progressive tendency of the unconscious, as expressed for instance in the hero-motif, chooses the Indian as its symbol, just as certain coins of the Union bear an Indian head. This is a tribute to the once-hated Indian, but it also testifies to the fact that the American hero-motif chooses the Indian as an ideal figure. It would certainly never occur to any American administration to place the head of Cetewayo or any other Negro hero on their coins...."

He points out that American faith healing, spiritualism and Christian Science are derived from Native American shamanism. "Though the poverty of its spiritual content is appalling, Christian Science is a living force; it possesses a strength derived from the soil, and can therefore work those miracles that are sought for in vain in the official churches...."The American presents a "strange picture" of a European with African behavior and a Native American soul.

Some Native Australians insist that foreign soil can't be conquered, because the ancestor spirits that dwell within it reincarnate themselves in the newborn of the conquerors:

"There is a great psychological truth in this. The foreign land assimilates its conqueror. But unlike the Latin conquerors of Central and South America, the North Americans preserved their European standards with the most rigid puritanism, though they could not prevent the souls of their Indian foes from becoming theirs. Everywhere the virgin earth causes at least the unconscious of the conqueror to sink to the level of its indigenous inhabitants. Thus, in the American, there is a discrepancy between conscious and unconscious that is not found in the European, a tension between an extremely high conscious level of culture and an unconscious primitivity."

"Alienation from the unconscious and from its historical conditions spells rootlessness. That is the danger that lies in wait for the conqueror of foreign lands, and for every individual who, through one-sided allegiance to any kind of -ism, loses touch with the dark, maternal, earthy ground of his being."[39]

Prohibitionism and racism were the neurotic -isms of choice in the 1890's, and they are most definitely two sides of the same coin. A conqueror who lived Jung's psychological dichotomy was Captain John Gregory Bourke, who went up against Crazy Horse's Sioux and the Northern Cheyennes and was Crook's aide-de-camp when he penetrated the Sierra Madres to force the surrender of Geronimo. Although he spent the early part of his life killing Indians, he got to know not only his scouts but his adversaries personally, and became fascinated by their humanity and their shamanism, becoming their political defender in later life.

Bourke took up the study of anthropology with an eye toward recording the last of the Plains Indian hunting culture he was experiencing. His books and monographs earned him a worldwide reputation - even the great classicist Jane Ellen Harrison quoted him (see *Shamanism and the Drug Propaganda*). I just mentioned his 1887 monograph on "The Medicine-Men of the Apache." He was known as a "radical progressive" because of his desire not to torture the Indians once they were imprisoned on the reservations, but to treat them with honesty and compassion, as he saw it, and, literally, to put them in business.

But Bourke was no Dances-with-Wolves. The following letter,

published in *The Nation* on Dec. 4, was dated Nov. 28, 1890, exactly one month before the massacre at Wounded Knee. It will seem like a racist document to the modern eye, but it represents the liberal sentiments of the power elite of the 1890's. Bourke's fascination with shamanism turned into uncomprehending condescension. His equation of the religion of "our interesting savages" with medical quackery was accepted at the time as learned and compassionate, as was his proud advocacy of cultural genocide. Our contemporary drug laws are based largely on Bourke's equations.

The immediate cause of Bourke's letter is the concern of the authorities over a revolutionary shaman's prophesy that a Messiah was coming to save the Indians from their conquest - to resurrect those lost to the enemy on the coming Day of Judgement. Since this was an old story the Romans knew well, they knew just how to handle it:

THE INDIAN MESSIAH.

To the Editor of The Nation:

Sir: The recent excitement at the Sioux agencies on account of the " Ghost," or " Messiah " dances must have become a matter of grave consideration to every reflecting mind

within our boundaries. The settler seeking for lands upon which to plant his home; the capitalist on the look-out for new investments; and the taxpayer who will be called upon to foot the bill for the hurried massing of troops or the accumulation of supplies at the points supposed to be menaced by the concentration of excited dancers, will all feel a very natural desire to know what it all means. There have been numerous reasons assigned for the holding of the Messiah dance, but to none of them do I care to refer in this letter, which is written merely to call your attention to the immense influence still exerted upon the minds of the aborigines by the medicine-men, and to start the inquiry, Are there no means by which such an influence can be lessened or destroyed!"

"....These medicine-men, doctors, priests, or wise men - by whatever name they may be called - are of great importance to the aborigines. If a horse has been stolen, they consult the medicine-man; if a raid has been threatened by a hostile band, the medicine-man can sing and prevent it; have the rains failed, the medicine-man can make more; has scarlet fever carried off any of the children, has whooping-cough swept down upon young and old, has the measles seized upon infant boys and girls, the medicine- man knows the song, the charm, the amount of singing and bathing and painting and dancing requisite for driving them away - or, if his incantations cannot drive them away, then he can point out the wrinkled old crone who has rendered them all abortive, and whose death must expiate the crime of being a witch. He can talk in the depths of his stomach, he knows all the tricks of jugglery similar to those at which the heathen priests of Rome laughed in their sleeves in the first years of the Christian dispensation; he knows everything."

"We may shrug our shoulders and talk about quackery and lament the superstition of deluded men and women and children, but that will not bring the problem any nearer solution. We must break down the power of the medicine-men, and no effort is too great or too small to effect this. We must do just as the French were obliged to do with their tribes in Algeria, when they sent Houdin, the wizard, to work among them, and show that the medicine-men of the French could do more even than those of the Kabyles boasted of being able to do. Such a thing has already been done with excellent results among the Sioux themselves at their Sun Dance, in 1881, but as it was done by a volunteer and not under government auspices, perhaps the experiment did not meet with the fullest success. There was a strolling 'magician' who asked me to allow him to go with me to the Sun Dance at that time, as he thought it would do the Sioux good to see what a white 'medicine-man' was capable of performing. It is hardly worth while to say that when the Sioux warriors saw their biggest medicine-men smacked with full force on one cheek and a ten-dollar gold piece knocked out of the other - or saw a great warrior like 'Little Big Man,' wrenched violently by the nose and another gold piece pulled out of that important organ - they were amazed, and began asking themselves the question, Why couldn't their medicine-men do the same and make all the tribe rich?"

"The remedy suggests itself that we should take up the whole matter of the medicine-men with earnestness and intelligence, and do our utmost to remedy the mental condition which permits their existence, whether as a premeditated or unintentional menace to the frontier. At Carlisle and Hampton there should be introduced an elementary course which, if it did no more, should give an inkling of the advances made in electricity, chemistry, the use of the solar spectrum, microscope, telescope, and other instruments, the power of steam, and other forces which the white man has harnessed to do his bidding. For the more capable scholars, there should be a supplementary course in rudimentary therapeutics, or household medicine, so as to render them independent of the medicine-men of their own tribe. When a scholar returns from one of our Indian schools, he at present finds himself instructed in some handicraft, and able to read and write pretty well, but he is still no match for the vaunted pretensions of the medicine-men, who leave to him the knowledge of the material world, but retain for themselves the mysteries of the supernatural."[40]

But two medicine men Bourke knew well weren't charlatans, and Bourke knew it; the war shaman Crazy Horse and the war shaman Geronimo each outfought Bourke's divisions of the U.S. Army for years with a few hundred lightly armed warriors. Obviously they didn't need any lessons in military science, and when he got sick on the frontier, Bourke went to their healers.

Bourke was the son of an erudite, devoutly Catholic Irish bookseller. He was schooled by Jesuits in Gaelic, Greek and Latin, and at the age of sixteen, in 1862, joined the Fifteenth Pennsylvania Volunteer Cavalry. He won the Congressional Medal of Honor in his first battle, the vicious Battle of Stone River, in which his unit suffered 40% casualties. By the time he entered West Point, in 1865, he was a battle hardened veteran of 19 with a reputation for efficiency and coolness under fire.

With the Third Cavalry in 1870 he went up against the Apaches. "They knew how to disguise themselves so thoroughly that one might almost step upon a warrior thus occupied before he could detect his presence. Stripped naked, with head and shoulders wrapped up in a bundle of yucca shoots or 'sacaton' grass, and with body rubbed over with the clay or sand along which it wriggled as sinuously and as venomously as the rattler itself, the Apache could and did approach within ear-shot of the whites, and even entered the enclosures of the military camps....On such occasions he preferred to employ his lance or bow, because these made no sound, and half or even a whole day might elapse before the stiffened and bloody corpse of the herder or wagoner would be found..."[41]

The Apaches were "so keen that they can discern movements of troops or the approach of wagon-trains for a distance of thirty miles, and so inured are they to the torrid heats of the burning sands of Arizona south of the Gila and Northern Mexico, that they seem to care nothing for temperatures under which the American soldier droops and dies."[42]

The Apache war started as competition for the land with the Mexicans. By 1837 Mexico was offering a hundred dollars for the scalp of a man, fifty for a woman and twenty for the scalp of an Apache child. In the face of scalp-hunting Mexicans, trappers, traders and other Indians, the Apaches became awesome warriors: Bourke: "His powers of endurance and his knowledge of the country are so wonderful that he would sooner retreat for fifty miles than halt and fight and lose a single comrade unnecessarily."[43]

Apache warriors prided themselves on their slipperiness. Killing wasn't the objective of raiding, since status was gained by the acquisition of wealth, not by murder. Apache warriors rarely took scalps and disdained the Plains Indian "dog-soldier" ethos that valued standing one's ground against overwhelming odds.[44]

Their war parties were usually small *ad hoc* affairs formed to avenge a specific casualty. Their matrifocal family groups sometimes formed macrobands, really just extended families, but they never formed "tribes," that is, large coordinated political units. There were no generally recognized tribal leaders; the tribe was simply a diffuse cultural entity composed of independent extended families.[45]

When Bourke's commanding officer, Gen. George Crook, a Civil War hero and very experienced Indian fighter, came along in 1870 and offered those Apaches who would stop raiding a subsidized farmstead and military security, in exchange for the ruthless warfare he was then meting out, it split them politically.

Some of Crook's Apache scouts, Camp Apache, Arizona, 1871

Many Apaches came to resent their own hostiles, to whom they had no political ties, as an obstacle to a peaceful life. It was the hostiles who fueled the fires of racist genocide and mass deportation; Crook's policy was the only hope of holding on to Arizona land. For this reason, Crook was able to enlist as many as two hundred Apache scouts who became the terrifying spearhead of his unit.

By 1875 the Apache war was over, but it was to flare up again in the 80's as racist pressure grew to evict all the Apaches and steal their remaining land. In the meantime, Crook was sent to Red Cloud's war, in the Department of the Platte.

The land-dealing Colorado Governor John Evans had been using the murderous Col. John Chivington to drive the Plains Indians into oblivion. Chivington's regiments attacked the hopelessly outgunned Indians wherever they found them. Seeking to avoid disaster, the Cheyenne and Arapaho chiefs, led by Black Kettle, met with sympathetic army officers at Camp Weld, near Denver, September 1864. But the well-meaning Maj. Edward Wynkoop and Capt. Silas Soule couldn't control their own high command.

The Camp Weld Council, September 28, 1864. Standing third from left, John Smith, interpreter; to his left, White Wing and Bosse. Seated, left to right, Neva, Bull Bear, Black Kettle, One-Eye and an unidentified Indian. Maj. Edward Wynkoop is kneeling left, Capt. Silas Soule is kneeling right. The photographer is unknown.

Black Kettle, lulled into a false sense of security by Wynkoop's reliability, and required to remain in sight as a condition of not being attacked, parked most of his band of Southern Cheyennes at nearby Sand Creek. Wynkoop was then ordered to turn his hundred troopers at Fort Lyon over to one of Chivington's Colorado Volunteers, Maj. Scott Anthony. As November ended, Anthony, in the interest of military surprise, peacefully cooperated with the traders who were helping the Cheyennes at Sand Creek prepare for winter. Then Chivington arrived with 600 reinforcements.

The 700 heavily armed troops immediately bushwhacked Black Kettle's peaceful band on Sand Creek. They hit the place with mountain howitzers, leaving 105 women and children and 28 men dead. At this point, the Cheyenne, Arapaho and Sioux decided it would be better to die fighting.

During the winter of 1866, the frustrated Lt. Col. William Fetterman, bottled up by Red Cloud in Fort Phil Kearny on the Bozeman Trail, boasted that he could whip all the Lakotas with eighty men. The daring young Crazy Horse helped lure Fetterman's eighty men into a combined Sioux, Cheyenne and Arapaho ambush that left them all dead in the Wyoming snow. Bourke always insisted that a true gentleman never boasts.

Red Cloud's war chief Man Afraid of His Horses smoking the Peace Pipe in acceptance of the army's withdrawal, Fort Laramie, May, 1868; Alexander Gardner

By 1868 the U.S. Indian Peace Commission was reporting to Congress that "The result of the year's campaign satisfied all sensible men that war with Indians was both useless and expensive. Fifteen or twenty Indians had been killed, at an expense of more than a million dollars apiece, while hundreds of our soldiers had lost their lives, many of our border settlers butchered, and much property destroyed....it costs less to civilize than to kill."[46]

Red Cloud's 1868 victory, the Treaty of Fort Laramie, closed the Bozeman Trail and the forts on it and gave the Sioux, Cheyenne and Arapaho hunting rights in the Powder and Big Horn river region of Montana and Wyoming, and in the Dakotas.

But anti-Indian feeling was running high, especially after Quanah Parker's spectacular 1874 shoot-out with well-armed buffalo hunters at Adobe Walls, Texas. Here is Quanah's description of his preparations for battle:

"Tonkawas kill him [and] make my heart hot and I want to make it even. That time I little big man - pretty young man, but knew how to fight pretty good. I wait one month and go to Noconie Comanche camp on head of Cache Creek. Call in everybody. I tell him about my friend kill him [in] Texas. I fill pipe. I tell that man, 'you want to smoke?' He take pipe and smoke it. I give it to another man - he say I not want to smoke. If he smoke pipe he go on warpath - he not hang back. God kill him [if] he afraid."[47]

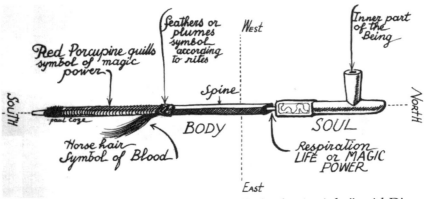

"There was never a more splendidly barbaric sight" said Dixon. "In after years I was glad that I had seen it. Hundreds of warriors, the flower of the fighting men of the southwestern plains tribes, mounted upon their finest horses, armed with guns and lances, and carrying heavy shields of thick buffalo hide, were coming like the wind. Over all was splashed the rich colors of red, vermillion and ochre, on the bodies of the men, on the bodies of the running horses. Scalps dangled from bridles, gorgeous warbonnets fluttered their plumes, bright feathers dangled from the tails and manes of the horses, and the bronzed, half-naked bodies of the riders glittered with ornaments of silver and brass. Behind this head-long charging host stretched the Plains, on whose horizon the rising sun was lifting its morning fires. The warriors seemed to emerge from this glowing background."

Quanah, who, by all accounts, was awesome in battle, always had the guts to pick real - that is really difficult - strategic targets. He never made war on women and children. Ultimately, of course, he was unable to overcome the advantage conferred at Adobe Walls by the hunters' telescope-mounted 50-caliber Sharp's canons. It was the publicity surrounding that spectacular shoot-out that interested one of the trapped buffalo hunters, Bat Masterson, in his future career, journalism.

Custer's trophy from Gen. Stanley's 1873 Yellowstone expedition; William Pywell

The month after Adobe Walls, the elk-hunting Col. George A. Custer advertised to the depression-torn West the existence of rich gold deposits on the sacred medicine grounds of the Sioux, the Black Hills of Dakota, 150 miles due east of Fetterman's last stand. This triggered a gold rush and government efforts to buy the land. On the collapse of those efforts, in December of 1875, under pressure from mining and railroad interests, the Indian Bureau ordered the Sioux (Lakota) and Cheyenne (Tsistsistas) onto the reservations, thus unilaterally abrogating the Treaty of Fort Laramie.[48]

In March of 1876 Bourke accompanied Crook in command of the nine hundred man Big Horn Expedition to break the power of the Sioux and Cheyenne. The campaign collapsed in a month after its only "battle," the completely unnecessary bushwhack by Col. Reynolds' column of a peaceful mixed Cheyenne and Oglala Sioux hunting village, at dawn on a bitterly cold morning.

Bourke, attached to the 300-man column, wrote that "Just as we approached the edge of the village we came upon a ravine... We got down this deliberately, and at the bottom and behind a stump saw a young boy about fifteen years old driving his ponies. He was not ten feet off. The youngster wrapped his blanket about him and stood like a statue of bronze, waiting for the fatal bullet; his features were as immobile as if cut in stone. The American Indian knows how to die with as much stoicism as the East Indian. I leveled my pistol. 'Don't shoot,' said Egan, 'we must make no noise.' We were up on the bench upon which the village stood, and the war-whoop of the youngster was ringing wildly in the winter air, awakening the echoes of the bald-faced bluffs."[49]

The shocked Indians put up such stiff resistance that none of them were killed in the firefight and, two days later, their reargaurd warriors were able to recapture most of their seven hundred ponies from the exhausted and freezing soldiers. The Cheyennes also drove off the army beef herd, collapsing the expedition.

The Cheyenne village, however, had been completely destroyed. "There was no great quantity of baled furs, which, no doubt, had been sent in to some of the posts or agencies to be traded off for the ammunition on hand, but there were many loose robes of buffalo, elk, bear, and beaver; many of these skins were of extra fine quality. Some of the buffalo robes were wondrously embroidered with porcupine quills and elaborately decorated with painted symbolism."

"The couches in all the lodges were made of these valuable furs and peltries. Every squaw and every buck was provided with a good-sized valise of tanned buffalo, deer, elk, or pony hide, gaudily painted and filled with fine clothes, those of the squaws being heavily embroidered with bead-work. Each family had similar trunks for kitchen utensils and the various kinds of herbs that the plains' tribes prized so highly."

"Of the weight of dried and fresh buffalo meat and venison no adequate idea can be given; in three or four lodges I estimated that there were not less than one thousand pounds. As for ammunition, there was enough for a regiment; besides powder, there was pig-lead with the moulds for casting, metallic cartridges, and percussion caps. One hundred and fifty saddles were given to the flames."[50]

Caught with nothing but their bed clothes, the freezing and wounded old folks, women and children had to trek upriver for days to Crazy Horse's camp, while the warriors covered their retreat; many died on the trail. Crazy Horse's Oglalas and the battered Cheyennes then went to Sitting Bull's powerful Hunkpapas, who called a rising of the tribes. This saw the formation, along the valley of the Little Bighorn in southern Montana, of some 1000-1300 lodges, 8-11,000 people, about a quarter of whom were the best light cavalry in the world. Thanks to the lively fur trade, they were well-armed enough to prove it.

The summer of 1876 saw the combined Bighorn and Yellowstone expedition, planned by General Sheridan. Lt. Bourke was aide de camp to Gen. Crook, in command of one of the three large columns, this time spearheaded by 175 Crow and 90 Shoshoni warriors out for revenge. Bourke rode and slept with the Indian scouts. He was fascinated by their hypnotic nightly dancing, and by their psychological and pharmacological preparations, extending so far as to give their surefooted, longlasting Appaloosas[51] special herbs before battle.

At the north fork of the Rosebud, before dawn on June 17, Crook found his whole column under attack by Crazy Horse's army. Crook was amazed to find Crazy Horse able to separate and pick his units apart one by one; the entire thousand-man column was fighting for its life over a five-mile area. Bourke joined the Shoshonis in a flanking counterattack that became a fierce hand-to-hand battle; he barely escaped with his life. The Crows hit the other flank. Crazy Horse broke off the all-day battle as Crook's crack troops began to exact too high a price.[52]

A pincer movement of Terry's, Gibbon's and Custer's columns was then aimed at the main Sioux encampment. It was to be initiated by Custer's Seventh Cavalry, followed immediately by Terry and Gibbon's combined thousand-man column.

Custer split his 750 troops into four small columns, just as he did in his successful surprise attack on Black Kettle's band of Southern Cheyenne on the Washita in 1867. Black Kettle had survived Chivington's 1864 Sand Creek attack only to die, with his wife, at Custer's hand in 1867. Custer killed about 90 women and children that day, but only eleven warriors. That established his reputation as an Indian fighter among Whites, and a murderer among Indians.

Just eight days after Crook's bloody near-disaster on the Rosebud, in which a tenth of his unit was killed, Custer led 240 men to their death by directly attacking the combined Sioux encampment on the Little Bighorn. He not only disdained to wait for Col. Gibbon's large column, but even mistimed his coordination with his own small columns. Bourke estimated that the Sioux and Cheyenne couldn't have lost more than fifty men.

Custer with his Black Hills grizzly, 1974. Bloody Knife, left, Custer's favorite Arickaree scout, died with him at the Little Bighorn. National Archives

The huge winter expedition of 1876-7 saw Bourke, expert in the intertribal sign language, in charge of 400 Indian scouts, many, like the Shoshonis, having just lost relatives to the enraged Sioux and Cheyenne. The army was unable to distinguish peaceful villages from hostile, so all Indian camps were attacked. The cruel winter fighting, the army's overwhelming resources and firepower, and, most of all, the Indian scouts, forced the surrender of most Lakota and Tsistsistas bands by 1878.

After the 1877 campaign Bourke had the run of the Red Cloud and Spotted Tail agencies. Bourke admired the "general courtesy of the savages to any strangers inside their villages," and was impressed when even the sullen Crazy Horse gave him a polite reception.[53]

"I saw before me a man who looked quite young, not over thirty years old, five feet eight inches high, lithe and sinewy, with a scar in the face. The expression of his countenance was one of quiet dignity, but morose, dogged, tenacious, and melancholy....All Indians gave him a high reputation for courage and generosity. In advancing upon an enemy, none of his warriors were allowed to pass him. He had made hundreds of friends by his charity toward the poor, as it was a point of honor with him never to keep anything for himself, excepting weapons of war. I never heard an Indian mention his name save in terms of respect."[54]

Bourke's unit, the Headquarters Staff for the Department of the Platte,1880. Crook is bottom center. Bourke is top, third from left. Nebraska State Historical Society

Many of the warriors enjoyed recounting their exploits to Bourke, including quite a few who helped Crazy Horse wipe out Custer. Over the years Bourke became close friends with one of Crazy Horse's chiefs, Little Big Man, whom Bourke insisted was "one of the boldest warriors who ever pulled a trigger."[55]

On Crazy Horse's death in 1877, Bourke noted: "...the United States will never again be forced to cope with an aborigine who is a match in the field for the whole miserable skeleton called its army and in the council for the shrewdest men civilization could pit against him."[56] Bourke ranked Crazy Horse with Tecumseh of the Shawnees and

Cochise of the Chiricahuas, whom he knew, as a giant who resisted with "science and daring."

One wonders why Bourke never connected the "scientific" powers of Crazy Horse with his shamanism, since he knew his reputation among his own people rested mostly on his status as a shaman, as did that of Sitting Bull, Gall, Geronimo, Cochise, Joseph, Corn Planter and many others. Bourke was humane and astute, but incapable of overcoming his conquistador prejudices; he never "went Indian."

The Indians' best friends included a few rare geniuses like Walt Whitman, Wharton James, William James, Franz Boas and James Mooney, and a few sympathetic agents like John Monteith, Tom Jeffords and John Clum, but these men had very little political clout. Bourke and his ilk were the only influential advocates the Indians had, and they wanted to exterminate their culture. Wrote Bourke, to "improve the condition of the Indians as tribes is simply an impossibility....They must first be crushed by the overwhelming forces of the Government, whose civilizing influences can then hope to find a free, perhaps fruitful field of labor among the new generations, treated as individuals but *never as communities.*"[57]

Bourke was willing to use force, but he preferred the carrot to the stick, advocating de-tribalization by reward and example. The Indian Bureau preferred the stick, but the philosophy was the same: "the tribal relations should be broken up, socialism destroyed, and the family and the autonomy of the individual substituted," said the Commissioner of Indian Affairs in 1889.[58]

Bourke's ethnology, the dominant school of its day, was the "Scot" school as explicated by Lewis Henry Morgan in his seminal 1877 book *Ancient Society*. Morgan saw humanity "progressing" through stages of culture from "Savagery through Barbarism to Civilization." That is from primitive hunter-gatherers to the likes of the Iroquois and early Greeks to contemporary Euroamericans. "A comparison of the Indian clan with the gens of the Greeks and Romans reveals at once their identity in structure and function."

Morgan's idea of the "experimental knowledge" necessary to make an orderly industrial society capable of "ethical progress" was simplistically mechanistic and ethnocentric, but it insisted on the great antiquity of man and his ascent from the animal kingdom. In a day when Creationists held sway in the culture, literally insisting that 4004 BC was the date of The Creation, the provision of a theoretical framework for the study of the biological evolution of culture was a seminal contribution.

No *shamanic* culture would have needed Morgan's prompting, of course, because humanity's relationship to the animal world is in-born knowledge, common knowledge in cultures that don't suppress instinctive emotions. Only a culture that has lost conscious contact with its own ancestors would need to be reminded that people are mammals. Black Elk would not have been offended to have been compared with a Black Elk.

MR. BERGH TO THE RESCUE.

THE DEFRAUDED GORILLA. "That *Man* wants to claim my Pedigree. He says he is one of my Descendants."

Mr. BERGH. "Now, Mr. DARWIN, how could you insult him so?"

Morgan provided Bourke with the theoretical structure on which to hang his fieldwork: "Rich as the American continent is known to be in material wealth, it is also the richest of all the continents in ethnological, philological and archeological materials, illustrative of the great period of barbarism. Since mankind were one in origin, their career has been essentially one, running in different but uniform channels upon all continents, and very similarly in all the tribes and nations of mankind down to the same status of advancement. It follows that the history and experience of the American Indian tribes represent, more or less nearly, the history and experience of our own remote ancestors when in corresponding conditions. Forming a part of the human record, their institutions, arts, inventions and practical experience possess a high and special value reaching far beyond the Indian race itself."[59] Bourke saw his own distant ancestors as "Indians" in need of some good industrializing.

It was Morgan, along with McLennan (*Primitive Marriage*:1865) and Bachofen (*Das Mutterrecht*:1861), who demonstrated, using his profound knowledge of Iroquois culture, that early human clan structures were largely matriarchal, thus throwing a whole new empirical light on the evolution of culture. "Descent is in the female line, which assigns the children to the gens of their mother. These are among the essential characteristics of the gens, wherever this institution is found in its archaic form."

The stages of culture were discernible through their defining associated technology. Thus the "Upper Status of Savagery" was defined by the bow and arrow and leads to the "Lower Status of Barbarism," pottery. This led to the "Middle Status of Barbarism," animal domestication, irrigation and adobe brick, which led to the "Upper Status of Barbarism," iron and the alphabet, that is, the birth of Civilization, culminating in "the electric telegraph; coal gas; the spinning-jenny; and the power loom; the steam-engine with its numerous dependent machines, including the locomotive, the railway, and the steam-ship; the telescope," and so on.

Morgan saw an immediate, so to speak, evolutionary impact of technological development: improved intelligence. "The achievements of savagery are not particularly remarkable in character, but they represent an amazing amount of persistent labor with feeble means continued through long periods of time before reaching a fair degree of completeness. The bow and the arrow afford an illustration."

"The inferiority of savage man in the mental and moral scale, undeveloped, inexperienced, and held down by his low animal appetites and passions, though reluctantly recognized, is, nevertheless, substantially demonstrated by the remains of ancient art in flint stone and bone implements, by his cave life in certain areas, and by his osteological remains."

"From the Middle Period of barbarism, however, the Aryan and Semitic families seem fairly to represent the central threads of this progress, which in the period of civilization has been gradually assumed by the Aryan family alone."

"The truth of this general position may be illustrated by the condition of the American aborigines at the epoch of their discovery. They commenced their career on the American continent in savagery; and, although possessed of inferior mental endowments, the body of them had emerged from savagery and attained to the Lower Status of barbarism; whilst a portion of them, the Village Indians of North and South America, had risen to the Middle Status."

"We have the same brain, perpetuated by reproduction, which worked in the skulls of barbarians and savages in by-gone ages; and it has come down to us ladened and saturated with the thoughts, aspirations and passions with which it was busied through the intermediate periods. It is the same brain grown older and larger with the experience of the ages."[60]

"The earliest inventions were the most difficult to accomplish because of the feebleness of the power of abstract reasoning."[61] "Savage" languages differed from "civilized" languages as the bow differs from the gun. This view, which of course is identical to Rush's view of "savage" medicine, was shared by most, but not all, of Bourke's many collaborators.

Among them Maj. John Wesley Powell, the heroic one-armed explorer who was director of the new Bureau of Ethnology, which was attached, as was the Bureau of Indian Affairs, to the Department of the Interior. Bourke's mentor, the influential historian Francis Parkman, to whom his famous book *On The Border With Crook* was dedicated, also shared these assumptions. So did the influential young Theodore Roosevelt, the English anthropologist E.B. Tylor (*Anthropology*:1881), Boston's powerful Rev. Edward Everett Hale, Congressman William McKinley, Charles Painter of the Indian Rights Association, Frederick Ward Putnam of the Peabody Museum - the entire progressive establishment.

Bourke boasted, quite honestly of Crook, that "If there was one point in his character which shone more resplendent than any other, it was his absolute integrity in his dealings with representatives of inferior races: he was not content with telling the truth, he was careful to see that the interpretation had been so made that the Indians understood every word and grasped every idea..."[62]

Theirs was a conscious rejection of racism, since all ethnic groups must pass through the same stages before they can reach the mental height of Euroamerican industrialization. It was also an unconscious affirmation of racism, since the planted axiom was that *they* have to learn from *us*, and not us from them. Progressive magazines, like *The Survey*, below, talked of "the Americanization" of the Indians, as if they had actually just come from India.[63]

COCHITI MAN, NEW MEXICO

His tribe was living on the western bank of the Rio Grande centuries before the earliest Spanish exploration. Formidable adversaries they proved, in 1680, to Spanish advance. They are still the most conservative of Indians, cherishing at heart the culture and religion of their fathers, viewing askance any Americanization of themselves. One of the few tribes not yet addicted to peyote, the Cochiti represent much that is best in Indian life and culture.

The Survey, 5/13/1916

"Savages," then, were children, our children, in need of "tough love," just as our children, today, are "savages" in need of "tough love." In fact, of course, it was the condescending paternalism of these pioneering anthropologists that was childlike. As both their art and material achievements indicate, Europe's Upper Paleolithic hunters could outfight, outrun and outthink most moderns with ease, just as Geronimo and Crazy Horse did against some very tough pony soldiers. Picasso was awestruck by the genius he found on the ancient cave walls of the Pyrenees.

We are not more intelligent and less mammalian than our forbears because we are more industrialized; mechanical evolution is a mechanical process. We eat, sleep, procreate, love our children, play, pray, sing, get sick and medicate ourselves, and our sophistication regarding these largely unconscious biological processes, the most important in our lives, is demonstrably inferior to that of many tribal cultures.

Herbal knowledge, like knowledge of animal ways, is instinctive, emotional knowledge, knowledge that connects us to our identity, our roots in the Earth. There is no distinction between plant biochemistry and human biochemistry. This is our food. Many human neurotransmitters are chemically identical to herbal isolates. Most sacramental herbs actually work by triggering or repressing our own neurotransmitters. Since we share our evolution with these sacred foods, their identity is dream-knowledge, accessible in cultures that foster such knowledge.

The shamanic state, the state of spirit-possession, often induced by sacred herbs, is often encyclopedic - super-conscious, not subconscious. That's why many shamans demonstrate uncanny memory. We know that *The Odyssey* and *The Iliad* were preserved, for hundreds of years before they were written down, by mnemonic power that very few moderns could match. The oral preservation of the *Vedas*, which weren't set into print until the 19th century, is even more spectacular. Imagine the power of the intellect that could sing *The Iliad* from memory. *Mnemosyne*, according to Hesiod, is the Mother of the Nine Muses. She could look forward as well as backward, that is, she 'remembered' how the world worked, so that she could prophesy as well as recall.[64]

When Jacques Cartier's crew, icebound in the St. Lawrence River near Quebec in 1536, were dying of scurvy, it was Domagaia, the local chief, who saved them. Cartier had already suffered twenty-five dead when the chief asked his women to gather "the juice and sapple of a certain Tree....boiling the bark and leaves for a decoction, and placing the dregs upon the legs....No sooner had they drunk than they improved in a manner truly and obviously miraculous....in six days a whole tree as large and tall as any oak in France was used up. And in those six days it worked more wonders than all the physicians of Louvain and Montpelier using all the drugs in Alexandria could have done in a year."[65]

The scurvy was stopped by Domagaia's white cedar, which Cartier called "the tree of life," and the explorer survived to write his name in the history books. It was Cartier's account of his rescue, two hundred years later, that caused Dr. James Lind of the Royal Navy to launch the experiments which "discovered" the dietary basis of scurvy. When Captain Cook went around the world in 1776-80, he carried a large supply of beer spiked with spruce, another traditional Indian remedy for scurvy. Eskimos have known for millennia that the adrenal glands of moose, rich in vitamin C, were a scurvy preventative, and made a ritual of sharing the glands among the family.

"Modern medicine" is as much a discovery of "modern science" as Hudson's Bay is a discovery of Henry Hudson. Galileo and Newton may have described acceleration mathematically, but they didn't invent the spear-thrower, the toggling harpoon, the bow or gun powder. Dr. Frederick Banting, the discoverer of insulin, credited tribal shamans with the "pharmaceutical spadework" that made his discovery possible. Fleming said the same thing about penicillin, and the same is true of digitalis, scopolamine, reserpine, ephedrine, atropine, quinine, curare and salycylic acid (aspirin), as well as of most basic medical techniques.

The Incas understood that kelp was a preventative for goiter, and used clay rich in kaolin for stomach upset and bacterial infections of the gut, just as modern medicine does. The birth control pill, in herbal form, is likewise a shamanic discovery. Hundreds of years before Withering discovered the cardiac stimulant digitalis in England, American Indian shamans were correctly using the American variety of foxglove, the source of digitalis, for the same purpose.[66]

A 1967 analysis of one billion prescriptions showed 50% containing active ingredients, vegetal, mineral, animal and microorganic, known and used by shamans, and it is fair to say that at least another 25% contained synthetic copies of the same.[67] A 1976 analysis came up with the same percentages.[68]

Pater dazzles us with the techno-trees so as to obscure the forest. There are only three historical epochs: *Prehistory*, which is the reptilian-mammalian spine and medulla oblongata; *Ancient History*, which is the advent of *Homo sapiens*, the Upper Paleolithic; and *Modern History*, which began with the industrial organization of human agriculture in the Neolithic.

If you think the Neolithic experiment in mammalian cybernetics isn't present and ongoing, just contemplate the industrial destruction of the ecosphere. The bacterial plagues seem to have been replaced by viral plagues, the uncontrolled burning of fossil fuels seems to be warming the ocean and the atmosphere at an evolutionarily suicidal rate, the destruction of the Earth's lungs, the rainforests, continues unabated, there is a massive die-off of species, an apparent change in the ratio of key atmospheric gases - the list goes on and on.

There is no guarantee, as the oceanographers and atmospheric scientists are warning, that a combination of these disasters won't careen out of control. If the poles heat up just a few more degrees, their cold water will cease to sink. It is this massive underocean river, which rises, heated, at the equator, that drives the ocean food chain. Imagine what a stagnant ocean will do to the atmosphere, and the life that depends on it.

Here is the evolutionary necessity to control industrial fascism - it won't control itself. Black Elk, or me, or you, smoking an inner peace pipe, communing with the vegetal source, refusing to make the assembly line a religion, ain't the problem. What killed Black Elk's people, and criminalized their shamanism, is. As Albert Szent-Gyorgi, the chemist who isolated vitamin C, puts it, we are still "the crazy ape."

As the renowned linguist David Crystal puts it, "Anthropologically speaking, the human race can be said to have evolved from primitive to civilized states, but there is no sign of language having gone through the same kind of evolution. There are no 'bronze age' or 'stone age' languages, nor have any language types been discovered which correlate with recognized anthropological groups (pastoral, nomadic, etc.). All languages have a complex grammar..."[69]

That grammar is the spontaneous geometry of mammalian perception and emotion. A co-worker of Bourke's in Powell's Bureau of Ethnology, the seminal anthropologist and linguist Franz Boas, in his 1911 *Handbook of American Indian Languages*, and Boas' student Edward Sapir, in his 1921 book *Language*, demonstrated that Amer-Indian languages have complex declensions, verbal tenses and concepts as abstract, and as difficult for a non-speaker to comprehend, as anything found in Latin, Greek or English.

"Snow" may be adequate for an industrial urbanite, but a hunting Eskimo, who has dozens of functional descriptions of snow, can use snow, and communicate its uses, in ways that would make most modern urbanites seem like amnesiac fools. Tribal languages, regarding the "biological technology," are *more* sophisticated than industrial language structures, not less.

No serious ethnologist missed the point that at least half the shamans were women with equal status in the medicine societies. I find myself pluralizing my sentences so as to find a pronoun, absent in English, or Spanish, that personalizes without specifying gender. The inanimate "it" is hardly a substitute for "he" or "she," although "they" or "them" does successfully personalize without specifying gender.

Edward Sapir's student Benjamin Lee Whorf called this linguistic inadequacy SAE, Standard Average European. That is, Whorf pointed out that conscious thinking is often relative to the language learned. He demonstrated that the Hopi can express time in more than twenty-five subjective ways, whereas in SAE English, well worked-over by the inquisitorial process, I have only a few impersonal tenses available to me, resulting in a far poorer ability to express or even conceptualize subjective states.[70] It follows that the attitude of the two cultures toward manipulating those states is equally different.

Very few mechanistic moderns can match the mnemonic power of a Hopi shaman ("spirit-person," no gender intended). Jane Ellen Harrison stressed the Greek origins of many SAE English words precisely to illustrate the buried shamanic roots of our culture. *Mnemosyne* may be the root of our word "memory," but its use in ancient Greek literature implies powers of vision, perception and automatic creativity that extend far beyond the recollection of past events.

Many things are unconscious for us simply by virtue of cultural inculcation. Fantasies and even political dialogue that would be acceptable in one culture can be unacceptable in another. That is, language often subliminally teaches self-censorship, the instant suppression of unacceptable content.

"Drug" is a medieval French word meaning "commodity no longer in demand and therefore valueless," as in our phrase "a drug in the market." It was put into the language by inquisitors and is a subtle piece of implicit propaganda, replacing the ancient "medicine" words, like the Greek *pharmakon*, with a put-down the speaker assumes to be subjective.

In France, in 1635, Cardinal Richelieu, a legendary inquisitor and slaver, established the *Academie francaise*, composed exclusively of priests, nobles and generals. He chartered them "to render it [the language] pure."[71] The Church founded the *Accademia della Crusca* in Italy in 1582 with the same object. The *Congregatio de propaganda fide*, "Congregation for propagating the faith," founded by Pope Gregory XV in 1622, gave us the word *propaganda*.

Put 'em all together and whaddya got? *Drug Propaganda*. Industrial fascists distort the meaning of history so as to destroy *mnemosyne*, because, as Plato said, "all learning is remembering." Slavers operate by co-opting the symbolism, and demonizing the sacraments, of the enslaved. It would have seemed very odd to Jesus, executed by Romans for resisting their military enslavement of Israel, to be told that Constantine, a Roman slaver, represented Jesus. That's sort of like naming the Chairman of the Joint Chiefs 'The Geronimo.' Constantine no more partook of the war shaman Joshua's actual sacraments than the Chairman of the Joint Chiefs partakes of Geronimo's - however many airplanes he jumps out of.

Industrialization, as Native American war shamans well understood, is largely the process of domestication and infantilization, submission to Augustine's industrial *paterfamilias*. Creativity and power are not its necessary results. Bourke thought it was the height of good sense for an Indian to walk away from his or her culture forever and "adopt the sacraments," as if they had none of their own.

Native American tribal geniuses were devalued right along with their means of creativity and communication. When a literate sensitive like John Neihardt bothered to record the words of a great Sioux shaman like Black Elk, Crazy Horse's cousin, what is revealed is a powerful healer with uncanny intellectual and spiritual powers. As the ecosphere itself proves, we are in the process of throwing out the baby with the bathwater. The herbs in the elk hide valises, Chiron's gift to Asklepios, were a gift from *Mnemosyne*. We reject gifts from the Earth at our peril.

Bourke's teacher, Lewis Henry Morgan, insisted that "the institutions of mankind have sprung up in a progressive connected series, each of which represents the result of unconscious reformatory movements to extricate society from existing evils." As the influential theologist John Fiske, in his 1902 *Studies in Religion*, put it: "From the general analogies furnished in the process of evolution, we are entitled to hope that, as it approaches its goal and man comes nearer to God, the fact of evil will lapse into a mere memory."[72] Herbert Spencer's "Social Darwinism" (*Principles of Sociology*:1876) left the White man with a hell of a burden.

This theocratic interpretation of evolution was as Protestant as it was Catholic, and was held by America's leading progressive lights. We can, I suppose, call it "scientific creationism," which, I am distressed to admit, is a force in contemporary Euroamerica. Bellowed Albert Beveridge, one of the Senate's leading Republicans in 1898: "It is God's great purpose made manifest in the instincts of the race whose present phase is our personal profit, but whose far-off end is the redemption of the world and the Christianization of mankind!"[73] Sounds contemporary, don't it?

Condescending as he was in victory, Bourke was completely honest, and sickened to the depths of his soul by the rapacity of the culture he fought to defend. "I am a strong Republican in my sentiments and sympathies but candidly concede that years of power had made it corrupt, avaricious and unscrupulous, and it should now be made to stand aside for some new party representing live issues and new principles."[74]

Noticing the health and sharpness of Indian children, Bourke complained, "We have too many stump-tailed monuments to George Washington and other corpses and not enough money spent in providing means of healthy recreation and amusement for our children in the big cities."[75]

God knows "tough love" is better than midnight basketball. We teach our cops so much "tough love" and "zero tolerance" that by the time they're fifteen many kids have been smashed in the face with nightsticks so often they're ready to start killing. Crazy Horse would understand, or Cinque, or Emiliano, all of whom preferred death in battle to life on the reservation with prohibitionist police.

In 1877 the Indian Bureau forced the Poncas, 710 people, to move to the Indian Territory in Oklahoma because their Nebraska reservation "unluckily for them, was arable and consequently coveted by the white invader."[76] (Bourke) Two years later, thanks to exhaustion, malnutrition, malaria and other diseases, the Poncas numbered 430.

When Crook was ordered to arrest Poncas peaceably walking back to Nebraska, he arranged lawyers for them and intentionally had his own orders challenged in court. The result was a legal landmark: the American Indian "is a *person* within the meaning of the *habeus corpus* act" and therefore had full legal rights.[77]

Between 1875 and 1880 Crook was preoccupied with the Sioux and Cheyenne in the Dakotas. The Indian Bureau, manipulated by "A 'ring' of Federal officials, contractors, and others...formed in Tucson, which exerted great influence in the national capital," took the opportunity to confiscate all the profitable Apache farmsteads Crook had set up. All the Western Apache groups, many of whom didn't get along with one another, were then "concentrated" on the San Carlos reservation.

Bourke: "The 'Tucson ring' was determined that no Apache should be put to the embarrassment of working for his own living; once let the Apaches become self-supporting, and what would become of 'the boys'? Therefore, they must all be herded down on the malaria-reeking flats of the San Carlos, where the water is salt and the air poison, and one breathes a mixture of sand-blizzards and more flies than were ever supposed to be under the care of the great fly-god Beelzebub."[78] The original Apache farmsteads on prime Arizona land were then sold by the Indian Bureau to "the boys."

Lied to, starved and cheated, the Apaches heeded Noch-ay-del-klinne, a White Mountain shaman, who announced the coming resurrection of all Apacheria and the imminent supernatural destruction of the Europeans. Even Apache army scouts were excitedly dancing to call up the Messiah, so his prophet was assassinated by the army in 1881. That, combined with the endemic corruption at San Carlos, was simply more than the Chiricahuas could take.

During the 1883 campaign, despite the help of 200 Apache scouts, Crook was unable to contact Geronimo after a month and a half in the Sierra Madres, although he was able to capture some of his women and children. Several of Geronimo's warriors later swore that on the day of their capture, Geronimo, 120 miles away, with no physical means of knowing, announced to the whole group that the army had captured their people and that they must go to the rescue. When Geronimo's party arrived on the scene, the disposition of the small army force was exactly as Geronimo had outlined.[79]

Unable to corner him, and uninterested in further warfare, both Crook and Bourke allowed themselves to be taken by Geronimo so as to talk him down without bloodshed. That speaks volumes about the stature of both men. Through the decades quite a few army officers risked their lives or careers to avoid going up against these extraordinary warriors, whom they deeply admired.

Once on the Turkey Creek reservation near Fort Apache, the Chiricahuas expected the contract made in the Sierras with Crook to be honored: they were to be allowed to develop their sheep herds and to pursue their own entrepreneurial ideas, for which they were famous.

Crook circumvented the cannibalistic military contractors by contracting directly with the Apaches for all the hay, wood, meat, corn, barley, produce, commodities and tools his troops could use, paying them directly in cash. This was a matter of honor with Crook, who did not give his word lightly, but it infuriated the contractors and their allies in the Army and Indian Bureau. Crook's ultimate objective was full citizenship for the Apaches, complete self-sufficiency and self-government, including the right to vote in general elections. This was an objective the land-grabbing Arizona governor did not share.[80]

The corrupt Bureau of Indian Affairs, attached to the Department of the Interior, not the War Department, ignored Crook's word, insisting that the Apaches give up herding altogether in favor of full-time farming. As Crook repeatedly pointed out, this was an impossibility on the grazing land at Turkey Creek.

Then the straightlaced Crook himself insisted that the Apaches give up *tizwin*, their favorite brew. This was universally regarded as an outrageous, and uncontractual, personal invasion. Apache paranoia was already at fever pitch due to constant genocidal threats from the Arizona authorities. The arrest of one young man for drinking *tizwin* only increased it, since he disappeared and wasn't seen again for months.

Tizwin-making was a trade of shamans, one of whom was the influential Pretty Mouth, a skilled midwife known to have powers from the lion and the lightning, Bourke's Apache interpreter. She convinced her husband Mangus to join Geronimo in yet another outbreak, thus ruining the whole peaceful arrangement.[81]

In 1885 Crook once again found himself in the field against Geronimo, whose few troops were succeeding in completely destroying Crook's political credibility in Arizona. With less than a dozen warriors, Ulzana covered 1200 miles through New Mexico and Arizona, killing 38 people, stealing and using up 250 horses, riding circles around thousands of troops, engaging in scores of close firefights, and returning to Mexico with the loss of only one man.

An Apache scout told Crook that they "could never catch the Chiricahuas because they could hide like coyotes and could smell danger a long way off like wild animals."[82] They could also travel forty to eighty miles a day[83] through the desert and broken precipices of the Sierra Madres under the blazing sun with little or no water: "No civilized army can do that," noted Bourke.

Ulzana, of course, left the field free for the advocates of wholesale deportation. Crook, pictured in Fly's famous photo below, desperately tried to talk Geronimo into another peaceful surrender - before the Apaches were left to the tender mercies of Brig. Gen. Nelson A. Miles, a politically ambitious racist murderer. The meeting failed for both Crook and Geronimo.

Gen. Miles replaced the politically defeated Crook in the field. Miles was utterly stymied and outfought by Geronimo, and eventually sent in an officer Geronimo knew with a generous deal.

Crook is far right. Bourke is immediately to Crook's right, looking at Camillus S. Fly's camera. Geronimo is seated left. His pistoleros ring the 3/26/1886 parlay.

Miles thought nothing of breaking his word, and as soon as Geronimo came in, he packed him and all the Chiricahuas, including his own and Crook's scouts, off to twenty years imprisonment. For the first few years the men were separated from their women and children. Both Bourke and Crook worked hard until their deaths, in the 1890's, to free the Chiricahuas. Bourke called Army Apache policy "the quintessence of idiocy; poppycock sublimed into madness."[84]

By the mid-1880's the Bureau of Indian Affairs had grown into a bureaucracy employing more than 2500 people, managing, with the help of the army, 250,000 Indians on 187 reservations.[85] The tribes had been stripped of the right to negotiate further treaties, and the chiefs were deprived of all legal power in favor of BIA courts. Rations were distributed to individual families rather than to the tribal organization, and Indians were legally subjected to White mores, the criminalization of polygamy, for instance.

The young were separated from their tribe and forced to attend trade schools, usually for nine months of the year. Most of those 200 boarding schools were run by churches or missionaries under government contract. The militaristic discipline, when not actually inhuman, was often quite harsh and unloving. Five and six year-olds, forced to separate from their families for most of the year, were

Drug War

marched around in uniform as if they were prisoners of war. They weren't even allowed to speak their own language among themselves. The objective, obviously, was cultural genocide. Even on the reservations, at the trading posts, if the adults didn't order in English, they didn't order. White dress and hairstyles were mandated. All shamanic rites, including sweat lodge and Sun Dance ceremonies, were prohibited by law and interrupted by the rudest personal intervention.[86]

Geronimo in the Sierra Madre; Camillus S. Fly, 3/1886

The General Allotment Act of 1887 broke up the tribally-held reservations into family plots of 160 acres each, the "surplus" land to be sold to settlers. The Sioux Act of 1888 carved up the Great Sioux Reservation into six small units: Pine Ridge, Rosebud, Cheyenne, Standing Rock, Crow Creek and Lower Brulé. Since the agencies contained just enough land to allot as farmsteads to the existing families, this device left 9 million "surplus" acres the Sioux didn't need anymore, which was sold to speculators at $1.25 an acre. In 1889 the beef rations were cut by several million pounds. Said Red Cloud, "We were prisoners, not in the hands of the army, but in the hands of robbers."[87]

1890 was yet another winter of hunger and bitter disappointment, to which measles, influenza and whooping cough added grief. The hunt and warfare were no more. The buffalo, the Sun Dance and the First Hunt were no more. Tribal elders were stripped of their power, and the traditional collective rites mercilessly suppressed. The medicine societies broke down as kinship ties disintegrated under the pass system, which prohibited traveling for visits.

Said Hunkpapa war shaman Sitting Bull, "The life of White men is slavery. They are prisoners in towns or farms. The life my people want is a life of freedom. I see nothing that a White man has, houses or railways or clothing or food, that is as good as the right to move in the open country, and live in our own fashion."[88]

It is ironic that an 1872 photograph of a Hunkpapa Lakota, a look-alike and relative of Sitting Bull, the strikingly handsome Running Antelope, was used as the frontispiece of the 1899 five dollar bill.[89] Many turn-of-the-century stamps and coins were stamped with Native faces.

Wovoka is above left, 1895. Gall, Sitting Bull's senior war chief, is right, 1886.

Emissaries were sent to the Paiute prophet Wovoka ("Cutter"), in Nevada, who prescribed the Ghost Dance of Resurrection for all Indians in preparation for the Messiah, who would cause a thick layer of fresh soil to cover the earth, burying the White world beneath a sea of sweet grass, tall trees, edible herbs, buffalo and game. All those who "made ready to join the ghosts" would be lifted up to watch the Earthly Resurrection and then set down to join their ancestors and loved ones lost in the wars.

Prayer-trees and medicine lodges sprang up on camp grounds throughout the Sioux lands as thousands danced and sang for hours, days, weeks, months. Indians forgot to cut their hair, to speak English, to go to church, to till their fields; the authorities panicked.

Sitting Bull predicted a warm winter that would enable his people to dance until Spring, the time of the expected Resurrection. General Miles issued orders to the Standing Rock agent to arrest Sitting Bull, who died in the ensuing firefight.

On hearing of the death of Sitting Bull, Big Foot's band of 350 Minneconjou dancers, gathered at Cherry Creek, quickly broke camp and headed for the protection of Red Cloud at Pine Ridge. Before they could reach the agency they were overtaken by Custer's old unit, elements of the Seventh Cavalry, led by officers Big Foot himself had humiliated at Little Bighorn. The tense Minneconjous were politely herded to Wounded Knee Creek, disarmed and counted: 230 women and children, 120 men.

Mooney's photo of Arapaho Ghost Dancers on the Cheyenne/Arapaho reservation, Oklahoma, 1891

When a follow-up search found Black Coyote's treasured new Winchester, the deaf young man made a show of giving it up, causing a shot to fire when he was unnecessarily jumped. As if on signal the entire force of 470 troopers, armed with repeating rifles and four Hotchkiss machine guns firing two pound explosive shells, one per second, opened up on the defenseless Minneconjous. Three of Bourke's old scouts, who rode out to Wounded Knee just after the massacre, told Bourke the soldiers had "murdered them wherever they caught up with them, in ravines, gulches, or other places to which they were retreating for safety."[90] The troops were so hysterical that they cut down most of their own 25 dead and 39 wounded.

About seventy Minneconjous survived, some because Black Elk, then 27 years old, led a party out while the shooting was still going on and scooped up the little ones.[91] Custer was avenged in an action that was typical of him: he did the same thing to Black Kettle's band of Southern Cheyenne on the Washita in 1867. It was Custer's commanding officer on that occasion, General Philip Sheridan, who told the captive Tosawi of the Comanches, who had protested that he was a good Indian: "The only good Indians I ever saw were dead."[92]

Little Crow, a Sioux leader in the 1862 war, photographed on his 1858 mission to Washington D.C. in an effort to avoid the war; James E. McClees Studio

The famous Kiowa peyotist Two Hatchet at the Trans-Mississippi and International Exposition, Omaha, 10/1898. He holds the ceremonial rattle and feather; Adolph F. Muhr

Quanah, flying with the eagle on the Kiowa-Comanche reservation in Oklahoma, 1892; Smithsonian Institution

Mescal

Like Two Hatchet, Tosawi's kin, the Comanche war shaman Quanah Parker, found a more successful path: "Lay down your arms, Quanah Parker. Your solution, as is the solution of all creatures, is personal. Turn your energies toward conquering the self.... Only through this will you and your people have a freedom that exceeds the white man's."

"I have planted my flesh in the cactus Pioniyo. Partake of it, as it is the food of your soul. Through it you will continue to communicate with Me. When all of those with the skin of red-earth clay are united by pioniyo, then and only then will they once again reign supreme. The white civilization will destroy themselves and the Indian will return to nature, master over himself and at peace with all."[1]

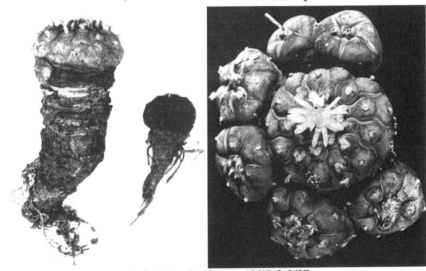

R.E. Schultes in *Nature*, 10/42 & 9/37

Péyotl is Náhuatl, Aztec, for "furry thing," used to describe a "cocoon," which is simply a description of the shape of the tuberous cactus, which is sliced to make the "buttons."[2] The ancient Huichol First Hunt equates peyote, Deer and Maize, the ecstatic ingestion of the "hunted" cactus unifying the world, bringing back the First Times.[3]

Peyote had always been used as a pain killer, febrifugue and hypnotic in healing ceremonies. Bourke reported in the *Journal of American Folk-Lore* in 1894 that army surgeons used it for those purposes when he was on duty. In 1978 Bruhn subjected thousand year-old peyote buttons found in a Southwest ritual site to chemical analysis, yielding mescaline, anhalonine, lophophorine, pellotine and anhalonidine.[4]

Indian shamans had *Claviceps purpurea*, the barley or rye mold sacred at Eleusis, *Amanita muscaria*, the Soma mushroom of the Rg Veda, *Sophora secundiflora*, the mescal beans of the shrub, the related *Erythrina flabelliformis*, the Arizona coral tree, *Sanguinaria canadensis*, bloodroot or puccoon, sharing opium alkaloids, *Datura, Lobelia,* morning glories, orchids, mushrooms and on and on. They taught western medicine most of what it knew about nervines, sedatives, tranquilizers, mood elevators and entheogens.

Quanah, Two Hatchet and the other leaders quietly resurrected the ancient shamanism, formalizing and communalizing the traditional peyote ceremony, making it an intertribal movement in the new post-tribal era.[5]

The peyote ceremony is an aesthetic all night vigil in which the communicants, after eating as many of the sacramental cactus buttons as they please, call on Peyote Woman to help them sing their spirit songs. Below, Peyote Woman nourishes the Earth.

Saskatoon Star-Phoenix in *Psychedelic Review* #9, 1967

The songs are sung in rotation, and then each communicant withdraws into deep contemplation, vision and revelation. Explained

Quanah: "The White man goes into his church and talks *about* Jesus; the Indian goes into his teepee and talks *to* Jesus." As the *Gospel of Philip* put it, 1700 years previously: "You saw the spirit, you became spirit. You saw Christ, you became Christ.... For this person is no longer a Christian, but a Christ."[6]

Saskatoon Star-Phoenix in *Psychedelic Review* #9, 1967

The Gnostic teacher Valentinus said that the search for *gnosis* begins with three sufferings: "terror, pain, and roadlessness (*aporia*)."[7] Magpie said: "Other religions teach men what to believe, but in this religion each man learns truth for himself. God has given the mescal to man that through it man might know. There is a word that comes at the end of the mescal songs and that word means 'the road.' Each man's road is shown to him within his own heart. When he eats the mescal he sees the road; he knows; he sees all the truths of life and of the spirit."[8]

The mescal, "sweet medicine," is the "balsam" of the Gnostics, though, of course, they used different "plants of truth."[9] A spontaneous Huichol peyote song, sung in a ceremony, goes like this: "climbed the blue staircase up to the sky/climbed where the roses were opening, where roses were speaking/heard nothing, nothing to hear, heard silence/I climbed where the roses were singing, where the gods were waiting, blue staircase up in the sky/but heard nothing, nothing to hear, heard silence, silence."[10] Many peyote songs are uncannily similar to the ecstatic poetry found in the Gnostic Nag Hammadi manuscripts, which date from 100 to 300 CE.

Peyote contains numerous psychoactive alkaloids, more than thirty, with mescaline accounting for 30% of the total alkaloid content. But "addiction" to peyote is medically unknown. Norepinephrine, the cerebrospinal neurotransmitter, is also a phenylethylamine derivative, very closely related to mescaline. By blocking norepinephrine receptors, commonly prescribed beta blockers combat anxiety and high blood pressure. Coca, cocaine and the amphetamines enhance both norepinephrine and dopamine reception.

Freud, who was fascinated by the uses of coca and cocaine, consciously based his invention of modern psychopharmacology on traditional shamanism. The neurotransmitter dopamine induces euphoria, epinephrine (adrenaline) speeds up the autonomic nervous system, and GABA functions as a downer.[11] Of the eleven undisputed neurotransmitters so far identified, most are either chemical or functional copies of plant compounds with which the primates share their evolution.[12]

"Communing with the vegetal source," or "visiting Peyote Woman" is neither a poetic metaphor nor a fantasy of babbling B-movie extras. It is a profound psychoanthropological reality. We eat vegetables to live because there is no difference between vegetal and human biochemistry - the vegetal world is literally our biological Mother. Just as all Native cultures insist, sacramental herbs are, to quote the Essene *Thanksgiving Hymn* found at Qumran, the "Plants of Truth."[13] Wine, a very ancient herbal inebriant, really *is* the Blood of Christ, just as Cretan flower wine, spiked with entheogenic herbs, was the Blood of Dionysos, 2000 years before Christ.

Serotonin, an essential neurotransmitter shown to be basic to the brain's ability to produce imagery, is a tryptamine derivative, structurally related to the mushroom alkaloid psilocybin and the related semisynthetic LSD.[14] The FDA-approved mood-enhancer Prozac works by gently blocking the reabsorption of serotonin, thereby increasing serotonin levels in the synapses. That is simply classic pharmacoshamanism. Coca leaf, the premier sacrament of Andean culture, works the same way with dopamine, and just as gently.

The body's basic painkillers are a family of peptides known as endorphins, which is short for endogenous morphines.[15] They cluster in various parts of the brain and spinal cord, and are designed to interact with human neuroreceptors. They have structural similarities to opiate alkaloids. Mammalian bodies also produce morphine, codeine and thebaine, also found in opium poppies.[16]

Of course, opium has more than three dozen alkaloids, including morphine, the most prevalent, and the body can perhaps do better than that.[17] This is a complex and technical biochemical mystery, but there is no doubt that the body produces opiate alkaloids, including some virtually identical to morphine and codeine, and that these bond to the brain's chemically-specific opiate receptor mechanisms.

Peyote produces a dreamlike hallucinatory state lasting from five to twelve hours. So far from being stultifying, the musical rhythm maintained in the peyote rite is very fast, 130-160 beats per minute. Everyone takes turns singing, drumming and rattling, and all pride themselves on the subtlety and accuracy of their musical performance.

By 1920 Peyotism was the dominant intertribal religious movement from the Rocky Mountains to the Great Lakes. Because the religion is shamanic, it attracted traditional Indians; because it is syncretistic, adopting compatible White values such as sobriety and industry, it attracted acculturated and marginal Indians as well, providing social roles compatible with the new way of life.[18] As an Onondaga shaman, a well-known musician, told me recently, "They did us a favor by isolating us that way. It helped us to preserve our traditions, which we never ceased to practice in private."

In 1888 an Indian Bureau agent named Clark reported this to the central office in Washington, calling peyote "Wokwave," which is close to the generic Comanche word[19] for cactus. "Four or five years ago, a Mexican, named Titcheestoque or Chewowwah, having been a captive of the Commanches and under their training having become equal to them in savage warfare escaped punishment by remaining with the Apaches in New Mexico. He returned to this reservation [Kiowa, Comanche and Wichita] during P.B. Hunt's term of office [1878-85], bringing with him quite a sack full of these opium buttons as I call them, and traded them to the Comanches."

"The Indian is supersticious by education. The influence of the Wokwave upon them I think is similar to that of large doses of chloral hydrate. It throws a person into a kind of trans, delema or like a dream, seeing or imagining all kinds of things. These visions, after the spell is passed off and the Indian sobers up, he does not consider his mental condition, but he thinks that all he saw and heard while in this condition is reality and that these things were communicated to him through the Wokwave and that they came direct from the Great Spirit."[20]

An 1890 BIA directive continued the tradition of pharmacological lucidity so brilliantly established by agent Clark: "It is the duty of the government peremptorily to stop the use of this bean by the Indians. You will direct the police of your agency to seize and destroy the mescal bean, or any preparation or decoction thereof, wherever found on the reservation. The article itself, and those who use it are to be treated exactly as if it were alcohol or whiskey, or a compound thereof; in fact it may be classified for all practical purposes as an 'intoxicating liquor.'"

In 1908 the BIA sent "Pussyfoot" Johnson, above, Chief Special Officer, Suppression of Liquor Traffic Among Indians, later a famous Anti-Saloon League spokesman, to Webb County in Texas, the national distribution center for peyote. Johnson bought and destroyed all the peyote on the market and threatened reprisals if dealers continued the trade in his absence. He also worked out informal, and illegal, agreements with the post office and mail order companies to refuse to ship it, and ordered customs to seize it at the Mexican border.

In a 1908 letter to the Secretary of the Interior, who was the head of the BIA, W.C. Roe of the Bureau of Catholic Indian Missions complained: "One of the worst results of its use is that it erects a very strong barrier in the way of the presentation of the Christian religion to any tribe that has adopted its use, and is an attempt on the part of the more enlightened of the Indians to establish a racial and tribal religion as against what they call the white man's religion.... I have been told repeatedly by those who have given up the practice that the so-called 'mescal feasts' were often scenes of unbridled libertinism."[21]

Scientific American, 9/1943

Rome's early Christian "love feasts" faced similar caricature under Septimius Severus: "It is reported that they worship the genitals of their pontiff and priest, adoring, it appears, the sex of their 'father.' ...the baby is killed... It is the blood of this infant...that they lick with thirsty lips.... On a special day they gather for a feast with all their children, sisters, mothers - all sexes and all ages. There, flushed with the banquet after such feasting and drinking, they begin to burn with incestuous passions.... By this means the light is overturned and extinguished, and with it common knowledge of their actions; in the shameless dark with unspeakable lust they copulate in random unions, all equally being guilty of incest..."[22]

The Rt. Reverend William Hughes reflected in *Commonweal* that "Every Catholic Indian missionary who has observed the effects of the drug has agreed with the statement of the Jesuit Father Jose Ortega, who, in 1754, wrote in his account of the Indians of the Nayarit that peyote is a 'raiz diabolica,' a diabolical root."

"In a handbook published in 1760 by Father Bartholome García for the use of the Franciscan missionaries to the Indians of San Antonio, Texas, appear the following significant questions for examination of conscience of Indians: 'Have you eaten human flesh?' 'Have you eaten peyote?'"

"In a very true sense the latter was worse than the former, because to eat the drug habitually was to destroy oneself, physically, mentally and morally."[23]

Padre García was using the standard inquisitorial rap; about a hundred years earlier Padre Nicolas de Leon was asking: "Art thou a soothsayer? Dost thou foretell events by reading omens, interpreting dreams, or by tracing circles and figures on water? Dost thou garnish with flowers the places where idols are kept? Dost thou suck the blood of others? Dost thou wander about at night, calling upon demons to help thee? Hast thou drunk peyotl, or given it to others to drink, in order to discover secrets, or to discover where stolen or lost articles were?" In Mexico City, on 6/19/1620, the Inquisition formally denounced peyote use as "opposed to the purity and sincerity of our Holy Catholic Faith." The next 250 years saw at least 90 *autos de fe* for peyote use.[24]

As the *Malleus Maleficarum* of 1484, the official legal and torture handbook of the Inquisition, put it: "Of Three Ways in which Men and not Women may be Discovered to be Addicted to Witchcraft...First of the Witchcraft of Archers....on the Sacred Day of the Passion of Our Lord, that is to say, on Good Friday, as it is called, during the solemnization of the Mass of the Presanctified they shoot with arrows, as at a target, at the most sacred image of the Crucifix. Oh, the cruelty and injury to the Saviour!"[25] Any sacrament other than the "presanctified" Host was "demonic." The intractable Incan shamans answered by applying that word, *Hostia*, to coca leaves.[26-28]

The "progressive" *Journal of the American Medical Association* continued to demonstrate that there really was no difference between science and religion: "Missionary workers in the Southwest are becoming seriously concerned over the spreading use of mescal buttons whether called peyote or by other name. In many Indian reservations, practically all the adults are addicted to the use of this agent. Commonly the buttons are chewed, but a tea is also brewed."

"Certain Sons of Belial [Judges:19:22], taking advantage of the tendency of the Indians to religious ceremonial, have been industriously spreading the word among the tribes that partaking of peyote enables the addict to communicate with the Great Spirit. It is true that certain Mexican tribes have long had a superstitious reverence for mescal buttons and have used them on occasion in religious ceremonials; and this old superstition gave the commercial dope vendor a great opportunity among the Indians in the United States. This has been carried so far that the 'Peyote Church' has actually been incorporated, the members being devotees, who gather for an orgy of frenzy, far worse than the cocain parties held among the negroes."

"The government has investigated the use of peyote and found its evil effects to parallel the Oriental use of cannabis. The addict becomes indolent, immoral and worthless. The great difficulty in suppressing this habit among the Indians arises from the fact that the commercial interests involved in the peyote traffic are strongly entrenched, and they exploit the Indian, even as similar interests exploiting morphin addicts are strongly entrenched. Added to this is the superstition of the Indian who believes in the Peyote Church. As soon as an effort is made to suppress peyote, the cry is raised that it is unconstitutional to do so and is an invasion of religious liberty. Suppose the negroes of the South had a Cocain Church!"[29] That is, a prison is a reservation for niggers, and a reservation is a prison for red niggers.

PEYOTE USED AS DRUG IN INDIANS' "CULT OF DEATH"

NEW 'RELIGIOUS' MOVEMENT

Incantations Once a Week That Last All Night

EFFECTS ARE VERY HARMFUL

One Person Prepares Small Mescal Pills and Passes Them to Others.

THE kind words that were said about peyote, the drug used by

In Northern Mexico. It is in the form of a prickly pear. The top, about one and one-half inches in diameter, very soft and green, is cut off and dried until it becomes brittle and hard. It has a bitter taste. It has been sold largely for commercial purposes by dealers in Laredo, Texas.

"It is generally eaten in this dry, brittle state, or made into a tea. In late years it has also been powdered and put in capsule form. More recently it has been put into peyote balls, made by an unpleasing process by which one person chews up a number of peyote buttons, rolls them into balls while moist and in that form passes them to others.

The Verdict of Science.

"From time immemorial peyote has been used by certain tribes in Mexico for the purpose of producing intoxication at religious ceremonies. From there it spread to the Kiowas of the Rio Grande, the Zunis of Arizona and others. In the early days it was always used for the purpose of producing intoxication at religious ceremonies. It is said that the Zunis selected a few of their number

described. The small gourd rattle, together with the small drum, furnishes the music. Gradually, after midnight, many present become intoxicated, enjoying the incessant and wonderful visions and music. Toward morning the company is generally in a stupor. The next day (sometimes days) is spent in sleep and lounging about or lying promiscuously on the floors to recover from the effects of the drug.

"An unceasing fighter against peyote was the late Rev. Walter C. Roe, whose service as a missionary among the Indians compels admiration and attention. Summing up the peyote cult Dr. Roe said:

"1. It is a drug habit producing pleasurable excitation of the imagination, ordinarily without immediate injurious effects.

"2. It is a religion which claims to be the Indian form of Christianity and therefore makes a strong appeal to the racial instinct.

"3. It is generally organized and promulgated by young educated Indians who thus find that pathway to ambitious prominence which is denied them under the old-time regime.

"The drug is also used by many during the week and is used in every form of sickness and disease by young and

The NY Times, 1/14/1923

The 1589 pamphlet showing the hanging of the Chelmsford witches succinctly put it in almost exactly the same terms as the *JAMA*, and for the same reason: the "witches" were midwives threatening the ecclesio-commercial medical monopoly: "Three feminine dames attached were,/Whom Satan did infect/With Belial's spirit, whose sorcery did/The simple so molest."[30]

The New York Times reported "INDIAN'S DREAM DIET REVEALED IN SENATE/Members Hear Peyote Flower Has a 'Kick' and Produces a 'Beautiful State of Mind'/ITS SUPPRESSION DEBATED."[31]

To help the Senators in their deliberations *The Times* followed up with the article above, "Cult of Death," 1/14/1923.[32]

The USDA's Harvey Wiley told the Senate: "It's a drug addiction, pure and simple."[33] But the BIA had badly underestimated the effect of the Indians' religious arguments on Congress. The Smithsonian's Bureau of American Ethnology, led by James Mooney, told Congress that peyotists were famous for their sobriety, moral rectitude and enterprise. Complained Mooney: "From the beginning it has been condemned without investigation...no agency physician, post surgeon, missionary, or teacher - with a single exception - has ever tested the plant or witnessed the ceremony." Congress saw no practical reason to suppress peyote.

James Mooney at Keam's Canyon Navaho trading post in Arizona, 1892

One of the most disturbing revelations of the inquiry into Wounded Knee had been the fact that an agent sent to investigate was ignored when he warned, weeks before the massacre: "If the Seventh-Day

Adventists prepare their ascension robes for the second coming of the Savior, the United States Army is not put in motion to prevent them. Why should not the Indians have the same privilege? If the troops remain, trouble is sure to come."[34] Progressive opinion would not tolerate any more violence aimed at the Indians, so the BIA had to drop its peyote suppression campaign "on instructions from Washington."[35]

The BIA thanked Mooney by expelling him from some of the reservations and continued its attempt to have peyote criminalized. But the racist precedent had been established that members of the Native American Church, legally incorporated in 1918 thanks to Mooney, either by virtue of their *ethnarchy* or simply by virtue of their *ekklesia*, could partake of peyote. Non-Indians, or nonmembers, however, if caught with peyote, could, since 1970, be sentenced to as much as fifteen years in prison, since peyote was listed in Schedule I of the Controlled Substances Act as one of the most "dangerous" "drugs."

Today the Native American Church counts 250,000 members, one quarter of the entire adult Indian population of North America.

Flathead mother, with a cradle on her pommel, and daughter, 1900

Mescal

57

A Siberian shaman, *Asia*, 1925, and Ulrich Molitor's caricature, 1489

Drug War

Inquisition

All illness may not literally be an alienation of the soul, but alienation of the soul is always an illness. The Church's medieval demons were animals who had lost their forest, projections of people grasping for their own roots in the earth, their own tribal memory. Ecstatic shamans, female and male, were able to unite the sexes, to bring back the first times, to make the world whole again. Theirs was powerful primal therapy.[1-3]

The Church wanted to exorcise the demonized animals, but the curanderas wanted to bring back the forest. In all pre-industrial cultures, medicine and religion are a unity, inseparable, just as "medicine" is considered a specialized type of food, "the food of your soul" as Quanah put it. These attitudes are instinctive; who ever heard of prohibiting food? If painkillers are illegal, doesn't that mean that pain is illegal? Who ever heard of criminalizing pain?

In Germany and Scotland, in the sixteenth century, midwives were burned alive for easing the pain of childbirth. The ostensible reason was that the pain was God's punishment for Original Sin, and so to interfere with it was heretical, causing great pain and hurt to Our Saviour (fascism is always maudlin). The real reason was that these shamans challenged the psycho-medical monopoly of the military-industrial theocracy.

Puritan Governor John Winthrop of Massachusetts plainly asserted as much in 1648, explaining why Margaret Jones had to be hanged: "she practising physic, and her medicines being such things as (by her own confession) were harmless, as aniseed, liquors, etc., yet had extraordinarily violent effects." Other accusations included an understanding "beyond the apprehension of all physicians and surgeons" and "some things which she foretold came to pass accordingly; other things she could tell of (as secret speeches, etc.) which she had not ordinary means to come to the knowledge of."[4] She sounds like a powerful shaman.

Susan Starr Sered, in *Priestess, Mother, Sacred Sister:Religions Dominated By Women*, discusses the contemporary religion of the Ryukyu Islands of Japan, Burmese Nat religion, Korean shamanism, Northern Thai matrilineal cults, West African Sande, Afro-Brazilian religions, Black Carib religion and North African Zar. All of these contemporary religions represent the more ancient cultural stratum and all are shamanic.

Even in circumstances of patriarchal conquest, women, because of their biological role as creators and primary childcare providers, tend to preserve the ancient shamanism, the ancient herbal medicine, as an aspect of their psychic wholeness, their evolutionary birthright. Women *remember* pre-industrial pharmacoshamanism more naturally, preserve it more easily, and so are the necessary last target of industrial cultural genocide - hence the Inquisition, which numbers women, especially midwives, as the overwhelming majority of its victims.

Late medieval Church-licensed male physicians, completely out of touch with the vast body of accumulated wisdom of the curanderas, would insert a "baptismal syringe" up the birth canal if it looked like the baby was going to die in utero. Native American curanderas had no military-industrial complex and no doctrine of original sin, and the reputation, at least, according to Professor Vogel, of rarely losing their babies in utero. "Evil, for them, is not sin. To the Tarahumara, there is no sin: evil is loss of consciousness," wrote Antonin Artaud.[5]

When the settlers called the Indians "the ten lost tribes of Israel," they usually meant that they reminded them of practical knowledge and powers long forgotten. Dr. Stone established that most Indians practiced Credé's method of expelling the placenta at least a century before Credé published it.[6] Dr. Engelmann, in 1883, described massage and manipulation techniques for the expulsion of the baby and the afterbirth that were just beginning to be adopted by White medicine: "Although constantly practiced by primitive people for thousands of years, these methods have been recently rediscovered by learned men, clothed in scientific principle, and given to the world as new."[7]

The Alabama-Koasatis induced contractions with boiled cotton roots. The Zunis eased labor with ergot. The Meskwakis used a decoction of wild yam root for the same purpose, and trillium was widely used to ease hemorrhage and promote parturition. All these ancient techniques became official in White medicine for the same purposes.

Indian mechanical tricks, both during and after birth, were sophisticated. Indian midwives understood infant medicine, and could herbally manipulate menstruation, lactation, conception and abortion. The Arikaras used chokecherry and mallow to stem postpartum hemorrhage. Red baneberry was used to dissolve blood clots and heal inflammation of the breast, and various herbs were used to eliminate the afterbirth. Most of today's birth control pills use diosgenin, from the Mexican wild yam, which also yields cortisone; it was a basic of the Aztec armamentarium.[8]

In 1848 the *Transactions of the American Medical Association* reported that "a very large proportion of regularly educated physicians are almost wholly ignorant of the plants, whether medicinal or non-medicinal, which exist in their own immediate localities."[10]

"Pregnancy," declared Dr. John Vaughan of Delaware, was "a diseased state" requiring - guess what - bleeding, emetics and cathartics, that is, chemical poisons.[9] That was the overwhelming regular medical opinion taught in the schools and advocated by the leading regular physicians of the first half of the nineteenth century.

Dr. Evory Kennedy, in the Lying-In Hospital in Dublin, prescribed "tartar emetic," antimony and potassium, for hundreds of women as a substitute for the official ergot to "relax the pelvic muscles," which it did by causing violent vomiting, something no midwife in her right mind would ever consider. It also, incidentally, poisoned the baby and prolonged the labor, the exact opposite of what ergot does.[11] Kennedy's procedures were brought across the Atlantic.

Due to the lack of aseptic conditions in many hospitals, something called "childbed fever," rare in home births, killed thousands of infants. Semmelweiss demonstrated in the 1860's that this was due to the exposure of the newborns to the contagious diseases in the hospital, but asepsis and segregation weren't effectively practiced in most hospitals until the 1900's. There were some famous exceptions, like New York Maternity Hospital,[12] but well into the twentieth century many hospitals treated new mothers to a high incidence of infant death and serious uterine infections.

Regular hospitals frequently used general anesthesia, which often proved damaging or fatal to the baby, and powerful sedatives, which interrupted the rhythm of contractions. Violent intravenous spasmodics, such as the now discredited ergotoxine, were then used when it became convenient to hasten delivery. If given to an undilated cervix, ergotoxine, or for that matter ergot, can crush the baby and rupture the uterus, as often happened.[13] Improperly used forceps often left permanent marks and even did brain damage. Regular hospitals to this day have a very high rate of unnecessary caesarians, an extreme trauma. The list of invasive hospital practices which horrified experienced midwives is a long one, including cutting the biologically active umbilical cord immediately on delivery and separating the newborn from the mother.

In the mid-nineteenth century Black women attended by midwives had a lower rate of infant death than White women attended by physicians.[14] In the 1860's the Viennese department of obstetrics at the University Hospital reported a death rate of 100 per thousand for its regular physicians, and 34 per thousand for the School for Midwives, in the same building; women literally begged in tears not to be sent into the regular obstetrical ward.[15] Midwives at the Royal Maternity Charity in England suffered only 4 deaths in 3,666 deliveries in 1872.

In 1909 physicians were responsible for 71% of the deaths from puerperal sepsis in Manhattan. Dr. Lobenstine, in 1911, said: "The poorly trained physician does far more harm than the midwife, as is abundantly shown by the various hospital records as well as by the records of the Board of Health."[16] Most experienced midwives had a far higher percentage of successful deliveries than most hospitals, and many people knew it.[17]

Tartar emetic - the chemical poisons antimony and potassium - continued wildly popular as a diaphoretic and emetic among some regular physicians, in that anyone who took it broke out in a cold sweat and started puking. The pustular eruptions that broke out all over the body were said to be a sign of healing. Because children were known to survive higher fevers than adults, some regular physicians reasoned that they required higher doses of their other favorite poison, calomel, that is, mercury and chlorine.[18]

In 1859 a regular doctor in the *St.Louis Medical Journal* proudly boasted that he had drawn more than one hundred barrels of blood in his career.[19] Physicians who didn't believe in copious bleeding often resorted to the more economical leeching. In the late 1890's Levene established experimentally that bleeding shortens the life of the patient. Nonetheless, bleeding remained regular practice until the twentieth century; it was official in Osler's *Principles and Practice of Medicine*, a basic textbook in 1912.[21] At that time Dr. Bedford Fenwick of the London Hospital for Women used bleeding in more than a thousand gynecological cases.[22] The motto of many regulars was "Bleed, blister, puke, purge and salivate."[23]

The very worst of the patent medicines contained the metallic and mineral poisons that were, or had been, official with the regular doctors. These included Chloro-Phosphide of Arsenic, Sulphur Compound Lozenges and Storey's [calomel] Worm Cakes. De Valagin's Mineral Solution was arsenious acid in dilute hydrochloric acid, and Donovan's was iodide of arsenic and mercury; strychnine was also popular.[24]

In 1863 the AMA stopped the Surgeon General from striking mercury from the pharmacopeia, citing eclectic and homeopathic prejudice. As late as 1885, the *Index-Catalogue of the Surgeon-General's Office* listed "cures" for rabies that included hydrochloric acid, hydrocyanic acid, lead acetate, mercury and potassium cyanide. Arsenic poisoning (from the patent medicine Fowler's Solution and others) was called "chronic dyspepsia" and "neurasthenia." In 1906 *Abbot's Alkaloidal Digest* recommended arsenic for 51 diseases.[25]

Obviously, the best of the regular physicians, and there were many, bitterly opposed bleeding and poisoning. Robert Bentley Todd, in the 1850's, treated his patients to the traditional roast beef, brandy and opium, without the poison, and no doubt did a great deal of good, but not nearly as much as an experienced herbalist could do. Bleeding and poisoning lost ground as American pharmacology became more sophisticated, and that sophistication was due largely to Native American herbalism, popularized over-the-counter. As Bourke's old comrade Buffalo Bill proved, the reputation and mystique of Native America was worth a fortune back East.

Bill with Sitting Bull, who liked the medicine-show man - 1885

Indian healers, or those who had known Indian healers, or those who had known those who had known Indian healers, or those who concocted Indian concoctions, were in great demand. Over the counter there was Pocahontas Bitters, War Paint Ointment, Comanche Blood Syrup, Zuni Stomach Renovator, Modoc Oil, Seminole Cough Balsam, Nez Percé Catarrh Snuff, Ka-ton-ka - the great Indian Medicine, Hiawatha Hair Restorer, Donald McKay's Indian Worm Eradicator, Wright's Indian Vegetable Pills, Indian Balsam of Liverwort, Osgood's Indian Chollogue and Kickapoo Indian Salve.

Doc Healy and Texas Charlie Bigelow's Indian Medicine Company, in the 1880's, had seventy-five Indian stage shows on the road at one time. They peddled Kickapoo Oil, Kickapoo Salve, Kickapoo Cough Cure and Indian Prairie Plant for Female Complaints.[26]

Today's prohibitionist cliché is that this was all bunk, an empty hustle. The actual fact is that many of these patent medicines were sophisticated herbal recipes. Kickapoo Oil was a masterpiece of composition; it contained ether, camphor, capsicum, clove oil, sassafras oil and myrrh.[27] It smelled sweet, tingled going on, felt hot, and got you good and happy, which is the best, usually, that the regular docs could do with most complaints; the soothing salve did a lot more good than harm.

In these days before regulation, of course, many patent medicines were worse than useless, especially those containing the chemical poisons of the regulars. Few of the herbal medicines were dangerous, but virtually all made absurd claims and refused to reveal their ingredients.

"Patent medicine" was an epithet of the prohibitionists. Since in order to patent a formula it was necessary to reveal it to the patent office, an agency not famous for its ability to keep trade secrets, most proprietaries simply "patented" their trademarks. "Patent medicine" is still very much with us: Midol, Doan's Pills and Bromo-Selzer were three turn-of-the-century standbys, and all over-the-counter cold remedies, painkillers, sleep aids and topical anesthetics are proprietary medicines; the only difference is content disclosure.

Wyeth's recurring ad, *American Journal of Pharmacy*, 1890's

Most physicians prescribed the same standard antiseptics, pain killers, fever reducers and herbal specifics prescribed by most druggists, midwives and herbalists. A sophisticated herbalist or midwife was a match for all but the greatest of physicians, and most of the great physicians were sophisticated herbalists.

Am. J. Ph.]   **16**   **[December, 1890**

SCHERING'S
CHLORALAMID

THE NEW HYPNOTIC.

The most popular patent medicines were alcoholic infusions of the most effective herbs. These included opium, cannabis, coca, mandrake, belladonna, henbane, datura, foxglove, lobelia, trillium, sassafras, black cohosh, skullcap, bloodroot and the many herbs called snakeroot. Soporifics like chloral hydrate ("Mickey Finn" - currently official as a sleep aid), ether and chloroform were also popular. Organized medicine positively drooled over the thought of a legal monopoly on all that, and the absurd claims of so many proprietaries, and their refusal to reveal their formulas, made it possible.

Bourke's favorite, Paine's Celery Compound, contained hops and coca leaves diffused in 21% alcohol. I don't know what was in it, but I particularly like the sound of Dr. Redwing's Mexican Herbs of Joy. Hostetter's Stomach Bitters, opiates diffused in 44% alcohol, was the official battlefield ration of the Union Army. The Southerners had Black Draught, fermented caffeine-rich cassina berries spiked with grain alcohol. The carton pictured a White woman standing next to a kneeling Indian maid, who pointed to a tall plant and said, "Take and Be Healed - The Great Spirit Planted It."[28]

In 1820 quinine was isolated from cinchona bark. Until WW II it was the only effective treatment for malaria, one of America's most common epidemic diseases. Its list of official uses in the 1918 *U.S. Dispensatory* covers "a large variety of purposes," including analgesia and local anesthesia, but its basic use was as one of the most effective febrifuges known, and as a malaria specific.

In 1832 Dr. John Sappington put his carefully manufactured "Anti-Fever Pills" on the market, composed of quinine sulphate, licorice, myrrh and oil of sassafras. Licorice was official in all pharmacopeias as a cough remedy, myrrh as a stimulant tonic and sassafras as aromatic flavoring that promoted perspiration. Sappington's army of drummers sold his pills, famous for their effectiveness, all over the country, marching straight into the most dangerous epidemic areas. When an area was hit by malaria, Sappington's drummers hit the area, taking three of his pills daily for protection; over the course of decades not one of them ever contracted the disease. His pills became an American standby, and were accepted as the official malaria treatment when Sappington formally presented his paper on the *Theory and Treatment of Fever*.[29] That, at its best, was patent medicine.

Dr. Kilmer's Swamp Root, another bestseller, contained an alcoholic extract (10%) of buchu, peppermint, rhubarb, mandrake, cape aloes, scullcap, colombo root, goldenseal, valerian, sassafras, cinnamon, oil of juniper, oil of birch, capiaba and tolu. All official or semi-official and a hell of an all-around tonic.[30]

The most famous of the bracers was Lydia E. Pinkham's Vegetable Compound For Female Complaints. Due to constant advertising and massive sales, it was said that, aside from Queen Victoria, Lydia Pinkham was the most famous woman of the nineteenth century.

Although a commercial superstar in later life, Lydia did indeed originally compound her compound on her Massachusetts farm. Her formula, diffused in 18% alcohol, included gentian, black cohosh, unicorn root, liferoot, pleurisy root, dandelion, chamomile, licorice and Jamaica dogwood.[31]

LYDIA E. PINKHAM'S
VEGETABLE COMPOUND.
Is a Positive Cure

For all those Painful Complaints and Weaknesses so common to our best female population.

A Medicine for Woman. Invented by a Woman. Prepared by a Woman.

The Greatest Medical Discovery Since the Dawn of History.

Gentian was used by the Indians for debility and stomach upset, and was official in the USP from 1820-1955. Black cohosh (squaw root or black snakeroot) was an Indian standard for irregular menstruation and was official in the USP from 1820-1936. Unicorn root (star root) was official in the USP from 1820-73 and in the NF from 1916-47 for stomach troubles and was used as a poultice for sore breasts. Liferoot (squaw weed, golden ragwort) was official in the

NF from 1916-36, and was used by the Indians as an emmenagogue and to hasten delivery. Pleurisy root (butterfly weed) was official in the USP from 1820-1905 as a diaphoretic and expectorant, and was used by the Indians for colic, hysteria and hemorrhage. Dandelion was official in the USP from 1831-1926 as a diuretic, tonic and laxative. Chamomile was official in the USP from 1863-1926 as a nervine, sedative and antispasmodic. Licorice is a tonic sweet herb that reduces hoarseness and contains estrogenic compounds, and Jamaica dogwood is a powerful sedative.[32]

A 1958 chemical analysis confirmed the estrogen content and the quality of the herbal extracts.[33] So far from being bunkum, Lydia Pinkham's Vegetable Compound was probably the best female tonic on the market, although Lydia did go a bit overboard in claiming to cure *all* female ills, and in advising customers to "write Mrs. Pinkham," avoid doctors altogether and just guzzle Compound.

The Rev. Andrew White, a former president of Cornell University who had offered Bourke's teacher Lewis Henry Morgan a job, summed up the progressive view of the evolution of patent medicine in the *Popular Science Monthly* of May, 1891: "Patent medicine had its origins in folk medicine. We are thus enabled to examine patent medicine as a magical practice and art of gradual development and of slow and subtle transformation. We shall argue that the blind, unthinking faith in a secret compound known as 'patent medicine' is, for the most part, a survival. Further, we shall be able to show how magical practices, as of the Indians, develop into remedies of the folk, of the people who share least in progress; how folk practices, in turn, in the hands of the mediaeval leech and alchemist, become 'occult science'; how, finally, out of leechcraft and quackery was evolved our curious system of patent medicine. The modern doctor is the heir of the leech, apothecary, and alchemist. He too seeks the elixir of life. He now makes a lymph more wonderful than the witches' ointment, which enabled people to sail through the air."

Actually, he was making a lymph that *was* the witches ointment that enabled people to sail through the air. The ointment applied to the broomstick was composed of various combinations of Thornapple (*Datura stramonium*), Deadly Nightshade (*Atropa belladonna*), Henbane (*Hyoscyamus niger*), Mandrake (*Mandragora*), Ergot (*Claviceps purpurea*) and Monkshood (*Aconitum napellus*), among others.

All but the ergot and aconite are closely related, bearing similar alkaloids: scopolamine, atropine and hyoscyamine. S c o p o l a m i n e was official in 1918 as a cerebral sedative, an aid for insomnia and delirium tremens, as a pain reliever, as a producer of surgical twilight sleep in combination with morphine, and as a *cure* for some types of insanity (!). Today scopolamine is official as a premedication for general anesthesia and as an antispasmodic for motion sickness, nausea and irritable bowel.

Atropine was official in 1918 to check secretion, stimulate circulation and respiration, overcome muscle spasm and as a local anesthetic. It is official today as a premedication for general anesthesia, to speed up an abnormally slow heart and as an antispasmodic. Hyoscyamine was official in 1918 as a substitute for many of the uses of atropine, and is official today as an antispasmodic. Aconitum was formerly official as a circulatory sedative.[34]

A Saxon shaman tripping on mandrake, from a thirteenth-century herbal in the British Museum; Mandrake, from an 1803 British herbal; Thompson

Ergot, the powerful entheogenic standby of ancient Greek, medieval European and Native American midwives, was official in the

1918 *U.S. Dispensatory* for the same thing it was official for in ancient Greece, shortening labor: "The effect of a small dose of ergot upon the uterus is to increase both the vigor of its contraction, and its muscular tone.... In the third stage of labor...many obstetricians recommend the routine use of egot...as a prophylactic against *post partum hemorrhage*.... Osborne...says that it had a powerful sedative effect upon the central nervous system and is useful in certain types of *asthma*, and *Graves's disease, hysteria*, and especially for the nervousness in the withdrawal of morphine."[35] That was the official medical comment, in 1918, on the entheogen of Eleusis, the central sacrament of Classical Greece.[36]

There is no reference to males assisting in birth prior to the seventeenth century, and no language has a masculine word for midwife, which in English means "with woman."[37] In Latin the word is *obstetrix* - "a woman who is present"; in French *sage-femme* - "wise woman"; in Danish *jordmoder* - "earth mother"; in Welsh *bydwraig* - "world woman." "Witch," with innumerable Old English and Norse antecedents, is related to "wise" and "divine."

Hans Baldung Grun, a popular sixteenth century illustrator, pictures the witches applying flying ointment to the absorptive membranes of the vagina.[38] The hanging of the Chelmsford witches, 1589, from a contemporary pamphlet in the Lambeth Palace Library.

The broomstick on which the curanderas were said to fly was Scotch Broom, the common plant whose stalks and leaves, tied in a bundle, were used as a household sweeper from time immemorial.

The word "broom" is related to "bush" and "bramble," and it is the plant that gave the sweeper its name. Smoked broom blossoms give a mild, calmative high; Canary Island Broom, the Mexican variety, is used the same way.

"Flying on a broomstick" has obvious sexual implications. The curanderas under examination also gave detailed descriptions of "anointing a stick" or "greasing a staffe" or "anointing themselves under the arms and in other hairy places."[39] "Antecessor gives us a horn with a salve in it, wherewith we anoint ourselves, whereupon we call upon the Devil and away we go!"[40] These happy curanderas were brutally slaughtered, by the hundreds of thousands, when trapped by the Inquisition. Late medieval Europe did not take kindly to powerful women.

Neither did nineteenth-century America. The first federal drug law in American history is aimed specifically at midwives, and the *zeitgeist* and legal language come straight out of the Inquisition. A sanctimonious Connecticut Congregationalist named Anthony Comstock joined the New York City YMCA's campaign against obscenity in 1868. Financed by powerful Puritan merchants and supported by leading Doctors of Divinity, Comstock was appointed to head the Y-connected New York Society for the Suppression of Vice.[41]

In 1873 Comstock engineered *An Act for the Suppression of Trade in, and Circulation of, obscene Literature and Articles of immoral Use* - "The Comstock Law": "That whoever...shall sell...or in any manner exhibit...or shall have in his possession...any obscene book, pamphlet...or other representation...or any cast, instrument or other article of an immoral nature, or any drug or medicine...for the prevention of conception, or for causing unlawful abortion, or shall advertise the same for sale...shall be deemed guilty of a misdemeanor...and on conviction thereof, he shall be imprisoned at hard labor in the penitentiary for not less than six months nor more than five years for each offense..."[42]

Comstock was made a special agent of the Post Office Department with the power to open the mail. His New York Society served as an army of private deputies.[43]

Comstock's language and assumptions can all be found in the *Malleus Maleficarum*, the official handbook of the medieval Inquisition. As Pope Innocent VIII put it, in 1484, in pharmacodynamic language, "...applying potent remedies to prevent the disease of heresy and other turpitudes diffusing their poison to the destruction of many innocent souls..." Does that sound like the Drug War to you? "Drug" "addiction" is a "plague," an "epidemic," a "scourge" of "poison"; all that comes straight out of the *Malleus Maleficarum*, which admits it's all really a "turpitude."

The most common evidentiary bust of the medieval Inquisition was the possession of prohibited substances, "witches' medicines." "Possession" was *de facto* proof of the ancient shamanic midwifery. The common phrase "addiction to witchcraft" meant "addiction to drugs," and, as today, simple possession was proof of "addiction."

The Pope's inquisitors, Kramer and Sprenger, are the original authors of the Comstock Law, and they got it from Cato of Utica, Caesar's aristocratic adversary, as they proudly point out: "And now let us examine the carnal desires of the body itself, whence has arisen unconscionable harm to human life. Justly may we say with Cato of Utica: If the world could be rid of women, we should not be without God in our intercourse."

"All witchcraft comes from carnal lust, which in women is insatiable. See Proverbs XXX: There are three things that are never satisfied, yea, a fourth thing which says not, It is enough; that is, the mouth of the womb. Wherefore for the sake of fulfilling their lusts they consort even with devils.... it is no matter for wonder that there are more women than men found infected with the heresy of witchcraft. And in consequence of this, it is better called the heresy of witches than of wizards, since the name is taken from the more powerful party. And blessed be the Highest Who has so far preserved the male sex from so great a crime; for since He was willing to be born and to suffer for us, therefore He has granted to men this privilege..."

"Now there are...seven methods by which they infect with witchcraft the venereal act and the conception of the womb: First, by inclining the minds of men to inordinate passion; second, by obstructing their generative force; third, by removing the members accommodated to that act; fourth, by changing men into beasts by their magic art; fifth, by destroying the generative force in women; sixth, by procuring abortion; seventh, by offering children to devils, besides other animals and fruits of the earth with which they work much harm."

"Witches who are midwives in various ways kill the child conceived in the womb.... The Canonists treat more fully than the Theologians of the obstructions due to witchcraft.... No one does more harm to the Catholic Faith than midwives."[44]

Isaac Jaspar's *Abomination des Sorciers*, c. 1560

Why, this almost rises to the theological heights of Augustine himself, who declared, in his *Liber de Fide ad Petrum Diaconum*, that he "most firmly holds and in no way doubts that not only every pagan, but every Jew, heretic, and schismatic, will go to the eternal fire, which is prepared for the Devil and his angels, unless before the end of his life he be reconciled with and restored to the Catholic Church." Pope Gregory IX, in his *Decretals*, used this "theology" to justify the worst horrors of the fifteenth and sixteenth centuries. "Finally, it benefits obstinate heretics that they be cut off from this life; for the longer they live, thinking their various errors, the more they pervert, and the greater the damnation they lay up for themselves."[45]

German midwives called the ergot of Eleusis *Mutterkorn*, possession of which, according to Bishop Peter Binsfeld, who wrote his *Commentarius* in 1622, was the most incriminating of the *indicia* of witchcraft.[46] Kramer and Sprenger detail how those who use "witches medicines" are to be stripped naked, carefully shaved of all bodily hair, and tied to "some engine of torture" for some good clean lascivious fun.[47]

Kramer and Sprenger, following a text originally penned by the Roman slaver Augustine,[48] promulgated *Reefer Madness*: "'and with our spells we kill them in their cradles or even when they are sleeping by their parents' side, in such a way that they afterwards are thought to have been overlain or to have died some other natural death. Then we secretly take them from their graves, and cook them in a cauldron, until the whole flesh comes away from the bones to make a soup which may be easily drunk. Of the more solid matter we make an unguent which is of virtue to help us in our arts and pleasures and our transportations; and with the liquid we fill a flask or skin, whoever drinks from which, with the addition of a few other ceremonies, immediately acquires much knowledge and becomes a leader in our sect.'"[49] So much for the *mutterkorn* of Eleusis.

In 1878 Comstock went to Madame Restell, a famous Cockney midwife established at 52nd & 5th in Manhattan for years. Although she was 67 and retired, she took pity on Comstock, who entrapped her by posing as a distraught husband whose hysterical wife was unable to sustain yet another pregnancy. On receiving medication, Comstock made his drug bust and threw the old lady in the Tombs. Facing a certain five years at hard labor, the distraught old woman cut her own throat.[50] Comstock proudly told the papers she was the fifteenth midwife he had driven to suicide.

Comstock then entrapped an unsuspecting Midwestern physician with two female decoys who begged for contraceptive protection from their uncontrollable husbands. The doctor answered by mail and was sentenced to ten years in Leavenworth; he was released after seven, a broken man.[51] When Emmeline Pankhurst came to America in 1913 Comstock promptly impounded all her copies of *Suffragette* and brought obscenity charges against her.

NYT, 10/24/1913; Sanger's first edition

Comstock's last case was his most famous. In 1915 he arrested Margaret Sanger for publishing her own magazine, *Woman Rebel* ("No Gods, No Masters"), which dealt explicitly with female medicine, sexual repression, labor organization and strike tactics.[52] She was charged on nine counts of obscenity, a possible 45-year sentence.[53]

Comstock also arrested Sanger's husband for distributing her famous pamphlet on *Family Limitation*,[54] dispensed at union meetings, which illustrated her research on the best of contemporary contraception. Growled Comstock, "In my opinion, this book is contrary not only to the law of the State, but to the law of God!"[55] Former President Roosevelt concurred, insisting that it was the "duty" of American women to bear large families in order to win the "warfare of the cradle" and prevent "race suicide."[56] Progressive magazines were full of dire warning about the superhuman capacity of the Japanese to reproduce.

That is, overpopulation forced wages down, since individual workers became expendable. When labor was scarce, its value and bargaining power increased. In 1913 Rosa Luxemburg from Germany and Anatole France in France called for an international birth strike, the refusal to bear children, as a nonviolent tactic the factory-slaves could employ to force humane working conditions. Sanger was particularly proud that *Woman Rebel* had drawn congratulatory responses, and subscriptions, from Rosa Luxemburg, Emmeline Pankhurst, Ellen Key, Olive Schreiner and other leading European feminists.[57]

Comstock; Margaret Sanger and Ethel Byrne on trial, Federal Courthouse, 1916

"Family Limitation" was what the AMA and Comstock had been calling "self-medication" for thirty years. Wrote Comstock: "Surely, such a mighty medium, power, and agency as the enlightened press of the nineteenth century in free America, ought not to become the tool of the villain, the vampire, nor the ghoul, to rob the simpleminded, honest laborer; or oppress, curse and destroy the sick and afflicted."[58] "Three feminine dames attached were,/Whom Satan did infect/With Belial's spirit, whose sorcery did/The simple so molest." The watchword of the "progressive" inquisitors was "social control."

Sanger was just the sort of uncontrollable ghoul Comstock hated most, a qualified obstetrical nurse who insisted that sexuality was "natural, clean and healthful...the creative instinct which dominates all living things."[59] In 1916 she had the guts to open the first birth control clinic in the U.S., in a Jewish and Italian neighborhood in Brooklyn. In 1917, in the absence of the recently croaked Comstock, using her connections with powerful society women, she forced the government to drop the obscenity charges against her. She is the founder of Planned Parenthood and the organizer of the first World Population Conference, held in Geneva in 1927.

In 1912 she went to Lawrence, Massachusetts to help bring 119 of about 300 strikers' children out of danger while their parents fought it out with the mill owners for the right to unionize. Lawrence had become an armed camp after company goons, that is city police, had shot a young girl as she picketed the factory gate. That's when the Italian socialists in the mill called in the IWW for the street fight.

Sanger and a few other people were then asked to get the kids out of the way. All the children were seriously undernourished: "Not a child had on any woolen clothing whatsoever, and only four wore overcoats. Never in all my nursing in the slums had I seen children in so ragged and deplorable a condition. The February weather was bitter, and we had to run them to the station."[60]

Lewis W. Hine, *Pittsburgh Survey*, c.1910

Sanger, who worked on New York City's Lower East Side, had repeatedly seen women she nursed die from pregnancies they couldn't support, or from the results of self-inflicted abortion. Manhattan alone was said to generate 100,000 illegal abortions a year. The horrifying inner city infant death rate was 200 per 1000. By comparison, the death rate for Guatemala in 1990, the worst in Central America, was 80 per 1000.[61]

Mulberry Street, 1900; Library of Congress

Given the unavailability, the illegality, of birth control information, contraceptive drugs or safe abortifacients, Sanger picked up her pen for *The Call*, the socialist weekly, and devoted herself to disseminating practical sex-related information:"What Every Mother Should Know," and "What Every Girl Should Know."[62] "No woman can call herself free who does not own and control her body."[63] This, of course, applies to men too, and to lungs as well as to wombs.

When Sanger got specific about gonorrhea, *The Call* was banned from the mails: "It was at this time that I began to realize that Anthony Comstock was alive and active. His stunted, neurotic nature and savage methods of attack had ruined thousands of women's lives. He had indirectly caused the death of untold thousands. He and a weak-kneed Congress, which, through a trick, in 1873 had given him the power of an autocrat, were directly responsible for the deplorable condition of a whole generation of women left physically damaged and spiritually crippled from the results of abortion. No group of women had yet locked horns with this public enemy. Women in far western states who had fought for the sacred privilege of the ballot and won it years earlier had never raised their voices against the Comstock laws. Their own shallow emotions had not yet grappled with so fundamental an issue as sex."[64]

The shallow women to whom Sanger refers are the doughty prudes of the WCTU and the more prohibitionist-minded of the Suffragettes, whose roots were in the old Rush-inspired Temperance movement. During the Civil War, Mother Stewart, a formidable paragon of Methodist rectitude from Ohio, organized what eventually became the American Red Cross, the Volunteer Women's Central Relief Committee. Her field hospitals were given official status during the war. Mrs. Annie Wittenmyer of Iowa, founder of the Methodist Home Missionary Society and editor of *The Christian Woman*, formed all-female field kitchens that worked so well Grant made them an official part of his western command.

In 1874 these Union heroines organized their hundreds of local groups into the national Women's Christian Temperance Union, solemnly declaring that "traffic in intoxicating liquors is a dishonor to Christian civilization."[65]

In one of history's funnier ironies, it was these proper ladies who popularized the epithet "pigs" applied to the police. The various statewide temperance laws of the 1850's and 60's prohibited the sale of alcohol, so the local saloons gave it away free, and charged the price of a drink to see the "two-headed turtle" or the "blind pig."

A Women's Crusade "praying band" beleaguering a saloon in Hillsboro, Ohio, *Harper's Weekly*, 3/14/1874

The WCTU's 1874 campaign, which was virtually nationwide, saw the bible-toting mamas actually burst into saloons and demand their closure on the spot. Police invariably took the bar owner's side. Thomas Nast's 1874 *Harper's Weekly* cover, next page, picked up the WCTU's snide retort, portraying the police as "blind pigs."

By the 1880's the WCTU was easily the most powerful women's organization in the country, with 150,000 dues-paying members in nearly two thousand local clubs.[66] They were ably coordinated with a

departmentalized national headquarters by Methodist educator
Frances Willard and her "Protestant nuns."

"Jewels Among Swine"; *Harper's Weekly*, 6/13/1874

Funky Frances saw woman "above on the hard-won heights of
purity that she may lead him upward into freedom from the drink
dominion...that he may learn...a chastity as steadfast as her own."[67]
Willard's Goals were "Preventive, Educational, Evangelistic, Social
and Legal."[68]

Like Bourke, she was a liberal in her time and place, but her milieu was exclusively "Native American," by which the ladies meant

White, Anglo-Saxon, and Protestant: "For God, Home and Native Land" was the motto of these immigrant granddaughters.[69] In the 1880's virtually every member of the WCTU was a churchgoing Protestant.[70]

Their antisacramentalism was firmly rooted in the Hundred Years War. Insisted Mary Livermore, president of the Massachusetts Union: "no Catholic should hold office in our country whose political allegiance is to the Pope, first. It is high time there was agitation."[71]

THE GREEK SLAVE.

Given that women had no vote or legal right to their own children or property in most states, it's understandable that these frustrated women fixated on the image of a drunken husband as the symbol of the evils of society. But the majority never understood their fixation, eventually rejecting Willard's broad social agenda in favor of a compulsive, theocratic prohibitionism.

Willard's agenda, strongly influenced by the Social Gospel of her friend Jane Addams, included the eight-hour-day, female prison reform, day-care centers, free public kindergarten, settlement houses, homeless shelters, free medical dispensaries, federal aid to education and animal rights.

But, like Bourke, Willard was of two minds: "Woman, who is truest to God and our country by instinct and education, should have a voice at the polls, where the Sabbath and the Bible are now attacked by the infidel foreign population of our country."[72] She asked Congress to "enact a stringent immigration law prohibiting the influx into our land of more of the scum of the Old World, until we have educated those who are here." But then she turned around and made a serious effort to educate the scum. By the time Willard died, in 1898, her ambivalent reformism had been rejected by her organization in favor of more reflexive compulsions.

It Pays to Obey
the new laws on teeth cleaning

Frances Willard; Toothpaste ad, 1920's

First, obviously, the women replaced the communion wine with grape juice in all Methodist, Baptist, Congregational, and some Presbyterian churches. The Episcopalians, Lutherans and Catholics stood their ground, insisting that Jesus' canonical Jews did *not* drink grape juice.[73] Logically, the ladies also engineered compulsory school prayer and sabbath laws.

They converted prostitutes to evangelical Christianity and temperance, and provided shelters for abused women. But they also worked for laws which criminalized them if they transgressed. They raised the legal marriage age in many states, creating a painful hardship for many pregnant young women, but also protected ten year-olds from rape.

Working *with* Anthony Comstock, the WCTU got obscenity laws in most states which criminalized the teaching of real sexual biology and contraception, even by physicians. They helped Comstock criminalize Sanger. The church ladies even acquiesced when the AMA engineered midwifery licensing tests in most states and then refused to test qualified midwives. Below is the comment of *The Masses*, "Your honor," says Comstock, "this woman gave birth to a naked child!"

The Masses, 9/1915

"The internal use of drugs will be discarded by all intelligent physicians," declared the ethereal Willard.[74] The WCTU pioneered "Scientific Temperance Instruction" (DARE) in the schools, creating a whole new class of textbook, which the WCTU wouldn't approve unless the "scientific" slant was just right.[75] Between 1892 and 1902 every state in the Union adopted the WCTU "physiology" texts.[76] The result was the canonization of such scientific pioneers as Benjamin Rush, who swore that he had seen a drunkard who belched near a candle instantly destroyed in the conflagration. Doc Gull insisted that, during autopsies, he could set the gassy corpses of alcoholics alight with a match.[77]

The WCTU's Department of Heredity lobbied for legislation that would restrict "the propagation of the vagrant and criminal classes." God knows what those farm girls had in mind. The WCTU even pushed for the closing of all canteens on military bases, and succeeded in getting military Prohibition in 1901.[78]

The church ladies were helped mightily by the mill owners, who turned their captive audiences over to the country's most popular fundamentalist evangelist, Baseball Billy Sunday, who pitched his slider for sobriety inside the factory gate.

Billy Sunday in Action; Ellis

The mill owners' major political action committee was the First Congregational Church of Oberlin, Ohio, home of the Rev. Howard Hyde Russell, founder of the far-right, evangelical Anti-Saloon League, which, like the WCTU, had enormous strength in Protestant churches. The League convinced itself that Prohibition was popular with all but "aliens of the lowest type."[79] "In God's name and with His help, we will enter upon a permanent good citizenship campaign which shall mean the victorious domination of Christian conscience, whose right it is to rule, in the politics of America."[80] Sounds contemporary, don't it?

The Anti-Saloon League was rolling in money from Ford, Cadillac, Packard, Dodge, Studebaker, S. S. Kresge, Vanderbilt, Morgan, Rockefeller and countless others. By 1918 Kresge had enrolled more than 14,000 business contributors to the League.[81]

"Whiskey is all right in its place," insisted the droll Billy Sunday, "but its place is in hell!"[82] Billy always managed to equate alcohol not only with inefficiency, but with unionism, that other unhealthy immigrant habit.

Rev. L. K. Peacock, one of Mr. Sunday's assistants, preaching in a machine shop in one of the noonday meetings that form an important part of all campaigns

Ellis

Business pressed for Prohibition laws wherever it could dictate, and then engineered selective antiunion enforcement. Divide (the issues) and conquer. Union leaders invariably discovered they had an alcohol problem; that's one of the reasons labor was bitterly opposed to Prohibition. Los Angeles, a few years later, discovered it had a terrible marijuana problem when the Mexicans started to organize; in fact, that's when "hemp" became "maria y juana."

The athletic and brilliantly glib Billy Sunday was hired to hold revivals in town after town where the League had a contest on the ballot: "The saloon must be destroyed!"[83]

The Anti-Saloon League, basically Republican, perfected the deadly art of "nonpartisan" bloc voting.[84] If the Republican was wet, the League didn't hesitate to swing its bloc vote to a dry Democrat. It had both parties quaking in their boots. By 1915, with 40,000 cooperating congregations, it was one of the most powerful forces in the country, controlling hundreds of small towns, dozens of cities, numerous state houses and a considerable portion of Congress.[85]

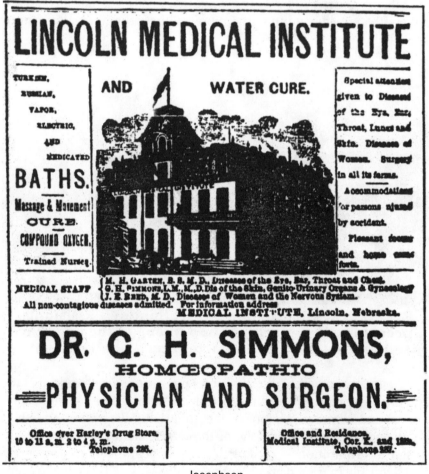

Josephson

Monopoly

Harvey Wiley, an Anti-Saloon League temperance fundamentalist, was the Chief Chemist of the Department of Agriculture. He also served as president of the A.M.A.-A.Ph.A. U.S. Pharmacopoeial Convention, the purpose of which was to draw up the legally official *U.S. Pharmacopeia*, on which the *U.S. Dispensatory* is based.

All of the articles in this department are written or indorsed by Dr. Harvey W. Wiley, formerly Chief of the Bureau of Chemistry, United States Department of Agriculture, who writes for this magazine exclusively.

Dr. Wiley cordially welcomes questions from GOOD HOUSEKEEPING MAGAZINE readers concerning the many phases of the great problem of Pure Food and its corollaries of sanitation and health. Persons seeking personal replies should send postage. Address

Dr. Harvey W. Wiley,
Director of the Good Housekeeping Bureau of Food, Sanitation and Health,
1120 Woodward Building, Washington, D. C.

10/1912

At the 1893 convention of the American Pharmaceutical Association one member called patent medicines "one of our great enemies - and that there are millions of dollars worth sold all over the country, thus diverting money which rightly belongs to the retail drug trade, in the way of prescriptions and regular drugs."[1] Wiley set out to rectify this injustice, aiming to engineer a teetotal AMA-APhA monopoly on all medically effective herbs and isolates. He did this by making no distinction between the two.

In 1903 he set up a government lab to publicize the contents of the patent medicines, making much of their use of the only effective solvent and preservative they had, alcohol. During AMA testimony for alcohol Prohibition, the docs, taking "an active part in the propaganda against drink," as the *Times* put it in 1918 - lying through their teeth - swore that alcohol "has no scientific value" in therapeutics.[2]

Alcohol was the standard battlefield disinfectant of the American army since the Revolutionary War, and the basic emergency anesthetic of the backwoods. The 1918 *U.S. Dispensatory* had it official as a germicide and surgical disinfectant, anesthetic, heart stimulant and "The purer forms of alcohol, whether strong or diluted, are employed almost exclusively in pharmacy; as in the preparation of medicines, such as ether, into the composition of which they enter; for the preservation of organic substances; in the extraction of the active principles of drugs, as in tinctures..."[3] Wiley didn't want no more Lydia Pinkhams.

Wiley also emphasized the presence of the opiates, coca, cocaine, cannabis, chloral or "other poisonous substances," completely ignoring mercury, chlorine, antimony, sulfuric acid and the many other real poisons. Wiley knew perfectly well that these "substances" were not only not "poisonous," but were the most widely prescribed medicines in the country - and that, of course, was the real point.

As Dr. David Macht, Instructor in Clinical Medicine and Lecturer in Pharmacology at Johns Hopkins University put it in 1915, in the *Journal of the AMA* no less: "If the entire materia medica at our disposal were limited to the choice and use of only one drug, I am sure that a great many, if not the majority, of us would choose opium; and I am convinced that if we were to select, say half a dozen of the most important drugs in the Pharmacopoeia, we should all place opium in the first rank."[4]

Wiley knew that opium sap was the safest and most effective herbal painkiller, febrifugue, sedative, hypnotic and antispasmodic on the market, official for these purposes, and that easy access to it was essential to the poor. Nonetheless, he led the propaganda campaign - from his bully pulpit in the Department of Agriculture and from his regular column in *Good Housekeeping* - that advertised opium as a baby killer when not dispensed by the hand of a licensed personage.[5] Opium's demonic image, pounded in decade after decade, is assumed to be reality today by the vast majority of people.

The 1918 *U.S. Dispensatory*: "Although capable of fulfilling all the indications for which morphine [one of opium sap's 39 alkaloids] is employed (above), when used as an analgesic or somnifacient, the alkaloid is usually preferred because of its lesser ability to disturb digestion. On the other hand, in *diarrhea* and *spasmodic colic* the whole drug is superior to the alkaloid. Opium is frequently a valuable remedy in *diabetes mellitus*. How it acts is uncertain, but the whole drug is to be preferred to any of its alkaloids. Because of its peculiar power in dilating the vessels of the skin opium tends to increase the sweat and is therefore useful in minor infections, such as *colds, grippe, muscular rheumatism*, and the like."

The legally official guide of organized medicine claimed, word for word, what the patent medicines claimed for opium; the entry for it is the longest in the dispensatory, nineteen pages.[6] Unlike the Dispensatory he helped to write, however, Wiley made no legal distinction between the herbal sap and Bayer's souped up refined morphine, heroin.

Am. J. Ph.]   7   [December, 1901

BAYER Pharmaceutical Products
HEROIN—HYDROCHLORIDE

is pre-eminently adapted for the manufacture of cough elixirs, cough balsams, cough drops, cough lozenges, and cough medicines of any kind. Price in 1 oz. packages, $4.85 per ounce ; less in larger quantities. The efficient dose being very small (1-48 to 1-24 gr.), it is

The Cheapest Specific for the Relief of Coughs

(In bronchitis, phthisis, whooping cough, etc., etc.)

WRITE FOR LITERATURE TO

FARBENFABRIKEN OF ELBERFELD COMPANY

SELLING AGENTS

P. O. Box 2160   40 Stone Street, NEW YORK

Likewise cannabis: "Cannabis is used in medicine to relieve pain, to encourage sleep, and to soothe restlessness.... As a somnifacient it is rarely sufficient by itself, but may at times aid the hypnotic effect of other drugs. For its analgesic action it is used especially in pains of neuralgic origin, such as *migraine,* but is occasionally of service in other types. As a general nerve sedative it is used in *hysteria, mental depression, neurasthenia* and the like."[7] Again, word for word what the patent medicines claimed.

Cardiologists prescribed wine because, like opium, it acts as a relaxant to reduce blood pressure. Marijuana was traditionally used the same way by European and American doctors. Queen Victoria, who suffered from migraine, was Victorian England's most famous pothead.

Cannabis, of course, as well as opium, was often bought unpackaged, generically, from the prescribing druggist, and the physicians fumed about the loss of a prescription fee. The druggists fumed when it was bought packaged in a general store, or, God-forbid, from a "dispensing physician."

Sanger worried about access to medicine, birth control and free clinics for the poor. Wiley worried about exactly the opposite: restricting access to the commercial interests he represented, criminalization of birth control, and the monopolistic domination of medical fees.

When a baby died of whooping cough or pneumonia, if it had been given an opiate to reduce the fever, stop the hacking cough and let it sleep, Wiley, in *Good Housekeeping*, attributed the death to the medicine. Given the lack of effective antibiotics and vaccines, opium was a great lifesaver; many a baby owed its life to opium, as Professor Macht indicated. The soothing syrups, like Parke Davis' Cocillana, or the tonic wines like Vin Mariani, were perfectly safe and healthful; they were effective medicine, and *that* was the point.

Wiley's crowning triumph, the Food and Drug Act of 1906,[8] is a great advance in medical monopoly and a modest advance in truth in labeling. Many over the counter proprietaries made absurd claims and refused to reveal their contents, which often were poisonous. The act, however, doesn't require content disclosure, even for poisons, and doesn't challenge absurd claims; it only mandates truth in content labeling, should the manufacturer care to disclose the contents.

Content disclosure was mandatory only for those drugs specifically listed under regulation 28, the most popular medicines in the country. Corrosive acids, poisonous metals and toxic minerals could all continue to be packaged without being listed. Only ten of the most commercially valuable medicines required listing, along with the percentage of their content, including gum opium, marijuana, coca leaves, "or any derivative or preparation thereof."

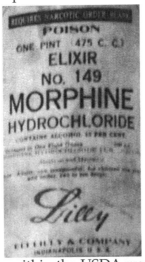

Wiley's police force within the USDA was then given unilateral power to decide what percentages were "poisonous," thereby requiring the manufacturer to label his product as "poison." When the USDA forced a poison label on a safe medicine, the manufacturer couldn't take it to court with evidence of medical safety, because the evidence was inadmissible. The law specifically stated that a dangerous drug was anything the USDA said it was. President Roosevelt called this "purposeful ambiguity." It is, in fact, a standard device of inquisitorial law - it's in Justinian's Code and the *Malleus Maleficarum*, and it's the law today.[9] *All pharmacological evidence is inadmissible in drug cases,*

which is the legal equivalent of saying that all forensic evidence is inadmissable in murder cases.

The Supreme Court threw out all the evidence regarding marijuana that Stephen Gaskin brought into court in 1973 without reading it. This included the reports of every major presidential, parliamentary, military and municipal commission over the past hundred years, and the opinions of the National Institute of Mental Health, today's AMA, the American Bar Association and a host of other reputable expert groups.

The Court's rejection automatically confirmed the Tennessee Supreme Court, which also didn't bother to read the evidence. Instead, it simply insisted that "the General Assembly of Tennessee presumably acted in the exercise of sound discretion and with adequate knowledge when it dealt with marijuana...[as a] dangerous drug or harmful substance."[10] Presumably? Isn't the purpose of a trial to "discover the facts"? The Supreme Court told Gaskin what it told Daniel Webster in 1833 when he challenged "no-license" - "majority rules" - regardless of the facts.

In 1915, an important Wiley ally, Dr. Oscar Dowling, President of the Louisiana State Board of Health and the Southern Medical Association, a member of the AMA's governing Board of Trustees, wrote in *Harper's* that "So called patent and quack medicines, if allowed to be sold and distributed many years longer, will undermine the health of America and in this contribute to the ultimate deterioration of the nation. I am not stating the case too strongly when I declare that the use of patent medicines is perhaps the greatest curse of the nation today."[11]

Not structural poverty, rampant disease or lack of access to medical care, but *access* to medicine. All day long on TV you can see "Drugs," "McGruff," "Let's Take a Bite Out of Crime," "Just Say No," "Frying Egg Brains," "Dr. Jekyll and Mr. Hyde," the "Junkie Werewolf," "Silence is Acceptance," "I Wasn't Tough Enough," "The Benjamin Rush Center" - and not one word about an effective national sweat-equity antipoverty program that would put real capital in the hands of poor folk, thereby eliminating the pain so many need to escape. The U.S. has the highest rate of child poverty in the industrial world, 22%. *The Economist*, 5/25/96: "One in five American children lives in poverty, more than double the rate in Germany or Britain."

The medical monopolists, instead, insisted that the problems were pharmacological, having to do with the improper use of herbs and isolates that only they were qualified to prescribe. This, of course, gave their industrialist allies one more way to sic the police on the unionists.

CONCENTRATED VICE, TORTURE AND DEGRADATION.

The photograph shows a million dollars worth of opium derivatives confiscated by agents of the Federal narcotics squad, which, but for the timely arrival of the agents would have been peddled to addicts all over the country.

The Literary Digest, 2/24/1923

Wrote an angry Henry Wood in the *Arena*, Nov. 1893: "Many are not aware of the fact, that if, in any one of a great majority of the states of this glorious, free (?) Union, one is healed of a disease by means of any treatment denominated 'irregular,' the person who has done him such service is liable to arrest, punishment, and classification as a felon."

"They dare not place their work upon the basis of the discrimination of an intelligent public, but ask that their 'sheepskins' be made *legal* tender. There is no other profession or occupation that expects to have a clientage furnished through governmental coercion. This is the class that have moved heaven and earth to have the business of healing 'regulated.'/Legislative monopoly makes it an offense to *practice* medicine *irregularly*. To cure is as much a violation as to kill."

Wiley's and Dowling's AMA was a commercial trade organization composed of an ascending pyramid of county, state and national associations. It was founded in 1847 to protect the regular physicians, the allopaths (Greek *alloion*, "different") against competition from the well-organized homoeopaths (*homoion*, "similar"), and from the not so well-organized but popular herbalists, eclectics and midwives.

The homeopaths pushed organized medicine in the right direction by relying on the body's own recuperative powers and insisting on the body's sensitivity to poisons and high dosages. Their quality schools taught careful symptomatic diagnosis. They also encouraged clinical drug experimentation on the healthy, and insisted on careful drug preparation. It was they who invented the sugarcoating of pills. They also pioneered gentle treatment of the insane.

Their "like-cures-like" microdosing, as well as their faith in hypnosis, were legally recognized, though only marginally by official institutions such as the army and major hospitals. The first women's medical college in America was the homeopathic New York Medical College and Hospital For Women, opened in 1863. Of the 14,000 practicing homeopaths in 1900, 1,158 were women, as compared to almost none for the regulars, who violently excluded women.[12]

Although many homeopaths were dogmatic about their infinitesimal doses, which supposedly cured by bringing on the symptoms of the disease itself, they had an empirical bias that helped to discredit cupping, bleeding, leeching and poisoning; inoculation, after all, is like-curing-like.

During the 1870's and 80's the homeopaths humiliated the regulars with their popular acceptance, and not all homeopathic prescriptions were in microdoses; dose judgments varied between practitioners. It was the homeopaths, whose technical anatomical knowledge rivalled that of the regulars, who forced many Native American botanicals into the pharmacopeia.

In the 1880's the more pragmatic homeopaths, which included most of the powerful hospital- and college-owning leadership, split with the radical microdosers in favor of union with the allopaths. They had 171 hospitals and dispensatories, 20 colleges and 35 medical journals.[13]

By the turn of the century the AMA had absorbed most of this structure, establishing itself as the most powerful medical lobby in the country. It rated medical schools for licensing, approved physicians for army and government appointments, fulfilled the medical requirements of workmen's compensation laws, passed on the value of all new drugs and licensed midwives.

The AMA estimated that a physician required a clientele of 2000 patients, minimum, to make a decent living. It complained bitterly about the overabundance of physicians being cranked out by the 160 medical colleges, 6000 a year, mostly from commercial diploma mills offering a *four month* course.[14]

Between 1888 and 1909, 72% of applicants, all with medical degrees, failed the Army Medical Corps' basic competence test.[15] Those reformers in the AMA who worried about standards had a point. Rallying around the famous 1910 Flexner Report,[16] they were responsible for a vast improvement in medical education and licensing, and so became the monopolists' best weapon. The power the AMA achieved over medical school licensing became a *diktat* of curriculum and even machinery from well-connected manufacturers.

By 1920 the AMA's Council on Medical Education and Federation of State Medical Boards, though merely extensions of a trade organization, achieved the legal power to either license or close medical schools.[17] Graduates of medical schools with a low AMA rating, regardless of their personal expertise, were barred from state licensing exams. This power was used to put the homeopathic schools, with their emphasis on pharmacology and symptomatology, out of business.[18]

At the turn of the century 75% of the births in St. Louis were home births attended by midwives, and in Chicago the figure was 86%.[19] 78% of Maryland's midwives were Black.[20] Not only was culture a factor, but the midwives' nominal fee, usually $15, including follow-up visits, was deeply resented by many regulars.

The AMA's midwife licensing system was based on the old Temperance "no-license" scam, the basis of all the seminal drug laws. In Daniel Webster's day it was taken as a constitutional given that any citizen could take any food, medicine or drink she or he pleased without interference from the police. Senator Webster, in 1833, argued before the Supreme Court that since state licensing powers were merely taxation devices they couldn't legally be refused to taxpayers. The state couldn't pass a tax on alcohol, refuse to collect it, and then prosecute citizens for nonpayment of the alcohol tax. But the Supreme Court upheld "no-license," saying simply "majority rules."

In 1896 the Illinois Board of Health instituted a pioneer program for the licensing of midwives which, once licensed, denied them legal access to medicines or instruments.[21] In 1913 Dr. Ziegler, in the *Journal of the AMA*, opposed "any plan which seeks to give [the midwife] a permanent place in the practice of medicine."[22] By 1925 the AMA got laws in most states which required a license to practice midwifery, and then refused to test any but hospital-connected graduates, thus putting independent midwives out of business, even if they could pass the test. The obstetrical training in, and access to, the regular hospitals improved, but at the cost of home birthing. By 1930 midwifery had virtually disappeared.[23]

Today in those states where attended home birthing is legal, not many, midwives, even if duly licensed RN's, aren't permitted access to any medically effective drugs, forcing almost all birth business into the hospital. Birth complications can usually be detected in preliminary exams, and it's reasonable to insist that home births involve only uncomplicated labors, but 98% of all labors are complication-free. If a little ripping occurs, a qualified midwife or RN is denied the local anesthetic needed to make three or four stitches. Commercial monopoly, not service to women, is at the back of that, since home births are far cheaper than hospital births, and the familiar surroundings conducive to a much calmer and safer delivery, as innumerable midwives have insisted for years.[24]

In 1882 the AMA agreed, for the first time, to allow the American Pharmaceutical Association to chair the U.S. Pharmacopoeial Convention, the purpose of which was to draw up the legally official compendium known as the *U.S. Pharmacopeia*, the basis of the *U.S. Dispensatory*. The *National Formulary* is the official guide of the APhA. In return for recognition of their right to be the only legitimate dispensers of medicines, the druggists wrote into their code of ethics not only a prohibition against the prescribing druggist, but a vow of secrecy, refusing to tell consumers the contents of, or alternatives to, the physician's prescription, even when asked.[25]

In 1899 the AMA was taken over by a brilliant medical hustler named George H. Simmons. Between 1899 and 1924 Simmons was Editor of *The Journal of the AMA*, Executive Secretary, General Manager, and Chief of the Council on Pharmacy and Chemistry. The two posts he held longest, Editor of the Journal and Chief of the Council on Pharmacy, were the two most powerful positions in the organization.

Simmons' medical career began in Nebraska in the 1880's, operating a massage parlor and abortion clinic as a licensed homeopath. In his ads in the Lincoln papers he claimed to be a "licentiate of Gynecology and Obstetrics from the Rotunda Hospitals, Dublin, Ireland."[26] Actually, the only regular medical degree he ever got in his life came from an unaccredited mail order diploma mill called the Rush Medical College of Chicago (apt name) in 1892. The prescription records in Lincoln proved that while "studying" in Chicago, Simmons was actually practicing in Lincoln. These facts came out in sworn testimony before a Senate committee in 1930 investigating the AMA's "practices in restraint of trade."

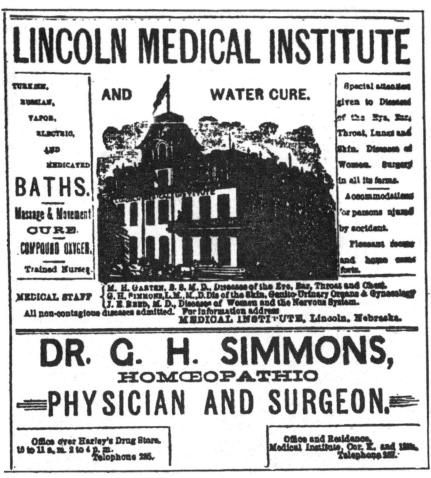

Josephson

The ophthalmic surgeon Emanuel Josephson was so infuriated by Simmons' behavior that he carefully catalogued the case against him in his 1941 book, *Merchants in Medicine*. Josephson points out that the phrase "a limited number of ladies can be accommodated at my residence," was the usual abortionist catchphrase.

But it wasn't service to women that made Simmons famous. Without approval from the AMA's Council on Pharmacy and Chemistry no new drug could advertise in *The Journal of the AMA* or in any other major journal or paper. Through kickback advertising contracts and truth in advertising laws which recognized only official AMA opinion as the truth, Simmons' Council on Pharmacy achieved enormous power. Harvey Wiley, while head of the USDA, was a member of the AMA's Council on Pharmacy.

G. H. SIMMONS, M. D.,

SPECIALIST.

Devotes special attention to the

Diseases of Women.

*

Have spent a year and a half in the largest hospitals of London and Vienna, and hold a diploma as Licentiate of Gynecology and Obstetrics from the Rotunda Hospitals, Dublin, Ireland.

Treats all Medical & Surgical Diseases of Women

A limited number of lady patients can be accommodated at my residence.

OFFICE, 1108 O ST.
RESIDENCE, 1310 G ST. } LINCOLN, NEB.
Telephones 661 and 887.

Josephson

The AMA rules stipulated that in order to win acceptance the manufacturer must agree: 1) Not to expect approval if any other preparation of the firm had not been submitted; 2) Not to use, in its literature or advertising, the work of any investigator who was not a member of the AMA or approved by it; 3) To submit all advertising copy in advance for approval; 4) Not to offer any prescription drug directly to the public and not to specify its uses on the label.[27]

Dr. Henry Rusby, Dean of the College of Pharmacy of Columbia University and an intrepid botanical explorer, recounted this story to Dr. Josephson: In 1913 Simmons had refused to approve the new radium line of Joseph Flannery, president of the Standard Chemical Company of Pittsburgh. Madame Curie herself had pronounced Flannery's radium up to standard, but Simmons adamantly refused to put it in his list of *New and Non-Official Remedies*, without offering any explanation. Flannery complained to his old friend Rusby that the rejection could cost him a fortune, whereupon Rusby told him to try bribery. After Flannery paid Simmons a hefty sum, the "analysis" department of the AMA's Council on Pharmacy and Chemistry endorsed Flannery's radium line.

But one of his products, a solution of radium salts for drinking, was highly toxic. With official AMA endorsement this "Radium Drinking Water" killed quite a few people before the USDA reacted. Another of Simmons' big winners was dinitrophenol, a lethal airplane glue approved by the Council on Pharmacy for weight reduction. Simmons' substitution of blackmail for medical analysis was standard AMA procedure, as Parke-Davis, Loesser and Abbot laboratories testified in court and before Congress.

It was this Council on Pharmacy that Congress went to for the basic pharmacological definitions that are the standing legal precedents of today's drug laws - and they are a tissue of overt empirical lies. The AMA and APhA wanted one thing only from The Food and Drug Act and The Harrison Act - complete commercial control of the most valuable medicines.

In 1914 Dr. Frank Lydston of the College of Physicians and Surgeons, a famous epidemiologist and theoretician, had this to say in his pamphlet *Why The AMA Is Going Backwards*: "The achievement of which the oligarchy of the AMA has boasted most vociferously has been its belated war on proprietaries, quack medicine manufacturers and impure food producers. When one recalls the nauseous array of proprietary fakes on the advertisements of which the oligarchy built its financial prosperity, its 'holier than thou' pose is sickening. It was fitting to its psychic constitution that after the AMA has for years done its level best to promulgate the interest, and fatten upon, fake manufacturers and professional poisoners of the innocent, it should bite the hand that fed it. Despotic powers such as the oligarchy wields over the drug and food manufacturers is dangerous, and human nature being what it is, that power might be expected sooner or later to be abused." Paracelsus penned the same warning 400 years earlier.[28-9]

With their powerful journals, the AMA and the APhA began a fierce coordinated campaign against "self-medication," demeaning the value of any household medicine not sanctified by the hand of a licensed personage. The Council on Pharmacy declared cod liver oil to be "a putrid oil of no greater value than any other fatty oil." A valuable source of vitamins A and D, cod liver oil has been given to infants for centuries to insure healthy skin and bones, and is official today for this purpose.

STEARNS' KOLA CORDIAL.

A New and Valuable Tonic Stimulant.

Each fluidounce represents 120 grs. of Kola (Sterculia Acuminata) whose agreeable odor and characteristic taste (without its acrid bitterness) are imparted to it in a marked degree.

KOLA owes its therapeutic value to Caffeine, Theobromine, and a principle peculiar to itself, called Kolanine. Its stimulating and sustaining effects on the nervous system are more prompt, powerful and of longer duration than that of Caffeine alone. It is also superior to Coca as a cerebro-spinal stimulant, with none of the objections which so frequently follow the continued use of the latter; hence this Cordial is recommended to those whose work subjects them to excessive mental or physical exhaustion. (Send for a copy of our MONOGRAPH ON KOLA.)

The two trade journals printed horror stories of cocaine abuse "by unfortunate women generally and by negroes,"[30] while simultaneously blurring the distinction between coca leaf and cocaine. Although the laws engineered by these monopolists equate the two, herbs, in practice, can be as different from their isolates as caps from grenades. That is, amateurs can experiment safely with most traditional plant-drugs, but refined isolates require training to measure and understand. When dosage is understood, natural isolates are not more dangerous than vegetables, and can, in fact, be safer, since some natural poisons can be filtered out during refinement.

Two thousand pounds of coca leaves, bathed in the right acid-alkaline wash, reduces, depending on the alkaloid concentration and process efficiency, to 5-20 pounds of cocaine. Cocaine is a natural isolate, artificial only in that it doesn't exist in nature in isolated form. The leaf's uses are well-taught in its native cultures, and it is largely this lack of cultural teaching that can make isolated cocaine dangerous. Intelligent adult users have no trouble learning proper alkaloid dosage, and unintelligent users can poison themselves with many herbs.[31]

Carcinogenic chemicals far more dangerous than cocaine can be extracted from celery, potatoes, beets, lettuce, pepper, common mushrooms, fava beans, mustard, horseradish, cottonseed oil, okra, alfalfa sprouts, spinach, radishes, rhubarb - in fact from most commercial fruits and vegetables.[32] Potato skins contain alkaloids, that is, nitrogenous compounds, dangerous enough to kill with one miniscule snort, yet it's perfectly safe and healthful to eat a potato.

Coca leaf, the traditional Andean chew and breakfast tea, a genuine health food, is as safe to use as orange pekoe tea, yet its possession in the U.S. will garner years in prison. One hundred grams of coca leaves actually satisfy the RDA for calcium, iron, phosphorus, vitamin A and riboflavin, and are higher in calories, protein, carbohydrates and fiber than most foods.[33] It is also empirically established that coca leaves are nonaddictive.[34]

There is nothing dangerous, in the legal sense, about most traditional inebriative herbs. In fact the Quechuan and Aymara coca chewers of the high Andes are famous as the *Centenarians of the Andes*, some of the most long-lived people on earth, despite the grinding poverty fascism has inflicted on them.[35] Obviously cocaine, the concentrate, is a newly-isolated (1860) surgical tool, a powerful local anesthetic capable of hypodermic injection. Hypodermic injection cannot be analogized with the traditional culinary uses of the whole leaf.

At the turn of the century, an alcoholic extract of whole coca leaves, mixed with good French wines, was the bestselling tonic wine in the world, Vin Mariani. It was happily lauded to the skies in Mariani's full-page ads by the likes of Thomas Edison, Jules Verne, Pope Leo XIII, Queen Victoria, Sarah Bernhardt, Emile Zola, Charles Gounod and Bartholdi, sculptor of the Statue of Liberty.

VIN TONIQUE MARIANI
A LA
COCA DU PEROU
LE PLUS AGRÉABLE ET LE PLUS EFFICACE DES TONIQUES ET DES STIMULANTS
PARIS, 41.B.^d Haussmann.

LE
VIN MARIANI
à la COCA
est garanti que par la
CAPSULE
ci contre
portier la signature
de Mr MARIANI

DOSE:
Un verre à Bordeaux avant
ou après les principaux repas.
pour les Enfants
un verre Madere est suffisant

MARIANI'S
TONIC
COCA WINE
is only guaranteed when
CAPSULED
as per
fac-simile beacime
Mons "MARIANI'S
signature

DOSE
One Claret-glassful
before or after the principal
meals, and for Children
half the quantity

Prix: 5 Francs.

Mariani said he used a traditional alcoholic infusion of whole coca leaves. He claimed never to have used isolated cocaine. Whether that is true or not, Mariani *was* world famous as a connoisseur of coca leaves. Their distinctions in the Andes were as sharp as the distinctions between French wines. Many of Mariani's imitators, of course, made no bones about adding indiscriminate amounts of refined cocaine and sugar to cheap wine.

This helped organized medicine to engineer a legal monopoly on the enormous tonic wine business. They were enabled to define the leaf, in law, as dangerous as an overdose of the alkaloid, and therefore available only by prescription.

Freud's 1884 essay *On Coca* popularized the use of cocaine for short-term stimulation, treatment of asthma, as an aphrodisiac, as a "maintenance therapy" in alcohol and opiate addiction, and as a local anesthetic.[36] Freud's colleague in Vienna, Carl Koller, reinvented eye surgery with it, since cocaine was the first surgically effective local anesthetic.[37] Koller's monumental 1884 discovery led to a revolution in general surgery the next year with the invention of spinal-block anesthesia using cocaine.

PERUVIAN WINE OF COCA.

A Genuine Rich Wine Imported by Ourselves and well known throughout Europe for its Strengthening and Nourishing Qualities.

It sustains and refreshes both the body and the brain, and has deservedly gained its excellent reputation and great superiority over all other tonics. It is more effective and rapid in its action. It may be taken for any length of time with perfect safety without causing injury to the system, the stomach and gastric juices. On the contrary, Peruvian Wine of Coca aids digestion, removes fatigue and improves the appetite, never causing constipation. For many years past it has been thoroughly tested and has received the endorsements of hundreds of the most eminent physicians of the world, who assure us of their utmost satisfaction with the results obtained by using it in their practice. They urgently recommend its use in the treatment of Anemia, Impurity and Impoverishment of the Blood, Consumption, Weakness of the Lungs, Asthma, Nervous Debility, Loss of Appetite, Malarial Complaints, Biliousness, Stomach Disorders, Dyspepsia, Languor and Fatigue, Obesity, Loss of Forces and Weakness caused by excesses, and similar Diseases of the Same nature. It is specially adapted for persons in delicate health and for convalescents. It is very palatable and agreeable to take and can be born by the most enfeebled stomach where everything else would fail.

Sears, Roebuck catalog, 1897

Freud, that is, used Niemann's "active principle" of the leaf rather as the Incas used the whole leaf.[38] Dr. William Hammond, former surgeon general of the army, announced cocaine as the official cure of the Hay Fever Association in the late 1880's.[39]

Am. J. Ph.]   15   [December, 1898

COCAINE DISCOIDS

A NEW, SAFE AND CONVENIENT MEANS OF
PRODUCING LOCAL ANAESTHESIA

It is certainly not a medical exaggeration to insist that concentrated isolates require some training in dosage, and can, therefore, be dangerous to that extent. Repeated cocaine overdose can drive the user crazy and can cause cardiac arrest, but that kind of compulsive behavior is a symptom, not a cause.

A correct dosage of pharmaceutical-grade cocaine can be used indefinitely, often to great personal advantage. Polluted street crap is a whole other story, having to do with the effects of Prohibition, not pharmacology.

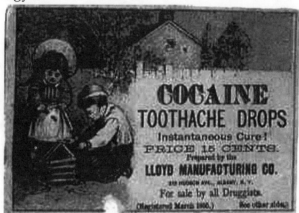

Cocaine, a powerful local anesthetic, made an excellent swab for teething pain. Rare indeed was the parent who made baby guzzle the stuff. But, seizing on the rare examples of hysterical or untrained overdosage, organized medicine proceeded to exaggerate the dangers of cocaine and to paint every other medically effective herb and isolate with the same brush. They had found, as *The American Journal of Pharmacy* put it in 1903, their "devil-drug."[40]

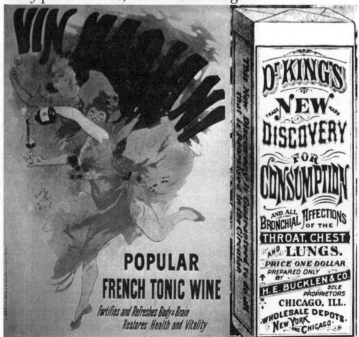

The intentional confusion between herbs and alkaloids supported the politico-commercial infantilization of the patient. The intentional confusion, combined with the artificial hysteria, enabled organized medicine to achieve a legal monopoly not only on the potentially dangerous refined concentrates, but on the perfectly safe bestselling herbs as well. That's why today's drug law contains no objective definition of "drug," just an irrational list of "substances," which can be either whole herbs, that is, vegetables, natural isolates or artificial compounds. Mariani's dilute alcoholic extract of whole coca leaves became as illegal as the refined cocaine in *Piso's Cure*, not that a correct, labeled dosage of *Piso's Cure* would have been dangerous. In no other area of law would such vagueness be tolerated. Of course, this was the era of "separate but equal," and that was no coincidence.

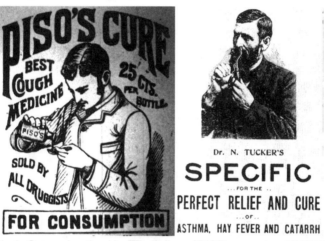

Piso's Cure, advertised in *The Indiana [PA] Progressive*, 1/9/1889

The Harrison Act taxed and licensed the sale and dispensing of coca leaf, cocaine, opium sap and most opium alkaloids. But Harrison turned into a "no-license" tax measure when actively administered by Treasury. What the medical monopolists hadn't foreseen was that the cops in the Treasury Department would end up with the legal power, confirmed by the Supreme Court in various decisions from 1919 through 1925, to throw the physicians and druggists themselves in jail for "nonmedical" prescribing - as defined by the cops in Treasury.[41] Today this power has devolved to the DEA and the FDA.

My use of the phrases "medical monopolists" and "organized medicine" shouldn't be misconstrued to mean "doctors." Most doctors are compassionate caregivers. Compassionate caregivers, however, tend to be preoccupied with giving care, not with achieving commercial control of trade organizations. Hustlers and power brokers tend to do that. Today, only 20% of doctors are members of the AMA, and some of the most effective criticism of contemporary drug law comes from anti-monopolistic physicians in search of clinical freedom.

Harrison had left consumers free to buy any non-opiate or coca medicine without a prescription, from the local druggist. This economic loophole was closed in 1938 by the FDA's Food, Drug and Cosmetic Act. Using Stalin's Russia as his model, Roosevelt's Assistant Secretary of Agriculture, economics professor Harry Tugwell, criminalized the purchase of any prescription medicine without a prescription. The AMA-APhA had long since forced manufacturers to define any effective new preparation as "prescription only," so Wiley's dream of a teetotal legal monopoly for his beloved licentiates finally became real. Tugwell also wrote into law the AMA's recommendation that prescription medicine labels "appear only in such medical terms as are not likely to be understood by the ordinary individual."[42]

Tobacco kills 400,000 Americans a year. Alcohol kills 150,000. Cars kill 20,000. All illegal drugs combined kill 6,000, and almost all of those deaths are due not to pharmacology, but to the effects of Prohibition, such as poisonous adulteration, ignorance, combination with alcohol or the unavailability of whole herbs. The hysteria about "drugs" is completely artificial, politico-economic. Tobacco leaf, another traditional shamanic herb, is far more dangerous than coca leaf, opium sap or marijuana leaves and flowers, and yet I can smoke it till I drop.

Commercial medicine, as opposed to compassionate medicine, is willing to torture all of Peru, and all of Detroit, forever, rather than admit that coca leaf is a safe, healthful chew and tea. To do so would be to readmit *curanderismo* into American culture, and that's just too dangerously tribal for the laity. Instead we got *The Saturday Evening Post*, in 1929, joyfully reporting that "Seventy-five years ago, there were no drugs to relieve headaches and similar pains, except dangerous, habit-forming opiates. Now, there are a wide range of relatively harmless drugs, such as coal-tar derivatives."[43] Since isolated coal tar derivatives can't be grown in anyone's garden, their permutations can be patented. That's why they're "safe."

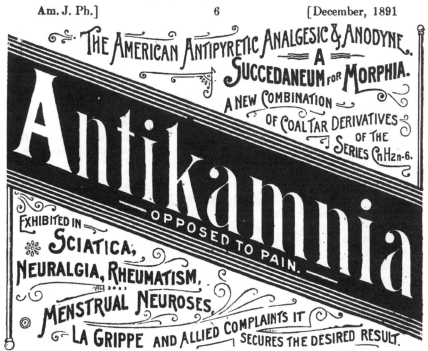

Am. J. Ph.]   6   [December, 1891

THE NEW THEATRE

THE NIGGER

A PLAY IN THREE ACTS BY
EDWARD SHELDON

PRODUCED BY GEORGE FOSTER PLATT

SCENES

ACT FIRST

JUNE 3D. EVENING AT "MORROW'S REST."

INTERMISSION — FIFTEEN MINUTES

ACT SECOND

APRIL 23D. THE GOVERNOR'S STUDY IN HIS CITY HOUSE.
ABOUT TEN O'CLOCK IN THE MORNING.

ACT THIRD

APRIL 26TH. THE GOVERNOR'S PRIVATE OFFICE AT THE
CAPITOL. EVENING.

PLACE: THE SOUTH.   TIME: NOW.

CHARACTERS

NAMED IN THE ORDER OF THEIR APPEARANCE

SIMMS, *Morrow's butler*   MR. REGINALD BARLOW
JINNY, *Morrow's "mammy"*   MISS BEVERLY SITGREAVES
CLIFTON NOYES, *president of the Noyes Distillery Works*
                                                  MR. BEN JOHNS
GEORGIANA BYRD   MISS ANNIE RUSS
PHILIP MORROW, *of "Morrow's Rest" and sheriff of*
        Westbury County   MR. GUY BATES
PURDY, *deputy sheriff of Westbury County* MR. ROBERT E. H   ANS
MRS. BYRD   MRS. H. OTIS DELLE AUGH
JOE WHITE   MR. OSWALD YORKE
JAKE WILLIS   MR. PEDRO DE CORDOBA
BARRINGTON, *the Governor's private secretary*
                                              MR. JACOB WENDELL, JR
CHIEF-OF-POLICE TILTON   MR. WILFRID NORT
COLONEL KNAPP, *of the 5th Militia*   MR. WILLIAM McV
THE GOVERNOR'S DOORKEEPER   MR. ROBERT VIV
SENATOR THOMAS R. LONG   MR. LEE BA
        MEMBERS OF THE GOVERNOR'S STAFF, REPORTERS, ETC.

First Production December 4, 1909

Black Fiends

| NEGRO COCAINE "FIENDS" ARE A NEW SOUTHERN MENACE |

Murder and Insanity Increasing Among Lower Class Blacks Because They Have Taken to "Sniffing" Since Deprived of Whisky by Prohibition.

screamed Dr. Edward H. Williams in *The New York Times*, Feb. 8, 1914, while Harrison was in committee. Old Doc Williams didn't let the facts stand in his way: "But I believe the record of the 'cocaine nigger' near Asheville, who dropped five men dead in their tracks, using only one cartridge for each, offers evidence that is sufficiently convincing."

"Nine men killed in Mississippi on one occasion by crazed cocaine takers, five in North Carolina, three in Tennessee - these are facts that need no imaginative coloring. And since this gruesome evidence is supported by the printed records of insane hospitals, police courts, jails, and penitentiaries, there is no escaping the conviction that drug taking has become a race menace in certain regions south of the line." At right, Williams' ally, Dr. Hamilton Wright, author of the Harrison Act.

It seems to me that, from the Black perspective, the achievements of the cocaine nigger were an endorsement of cocaine. *Obayi*, in the Akan language of Ghana, means witchcraft; it is counteracted with *myal*, spirit possession for the purpose of identifying and prescribing the curative herbs.[1] The captive African *obeah* and *myal* women and men of the West Indies teamed up to defend their enslaved culture. An 1891 *Scientific American* article, "Obeah Poisons and Poisoners," expresses the usual progressive compassion:

"There is probably no locality where Anglo-Saxon civilization is now waging so active a warfare in this direction as in the British West Indies. There the colonial governments are brought face to face with the Obeahman, whose skill with native poisons is supplemented by a certain rude acquaintance with the pharmacopoeia, and whose sway over his debased followers is practically absolute."

"Obeah, the worship and propitiation of the eternal snake as an emblem of evil, long ago degenerated into a series of obscene orgies among its West Indian followers.... it suffices to say that the result is to bring into great demand the services of the 'bush doctors,' as those uneducated charlatans are called who brew simples from the wild herbs at hand. This is not to be wondered at when we find that there is but one educated physician to every 12,300 of inhabitants, by far the greatest proportion of which are spread over stretches of wilderness, and what wonder that 'bush physic' is all that the ignorant, neglected negroes ever receive?"[2]

The medicine-man, dour and shriveled, sat on his three-pronged root of easy-chair and dipped his hand into his pot of food. He lived in the last hut at the end of the long street. Strangers he eyed grimly, malevolently

EAST AFRICAN BABIES
DOCTORED TO DEATH

British Explorer Found Great Mortality Due to the Use of Drugs.

reported *The New York Times*, Nov. 23, 1920: "The Daily Mail published further details this morning of the Rev. John Roscoe's expedition among East African tribes. Mr. Roscoe found that among the best tribes infant mortality was terrible, and that this was almost wholly due to the use of drugs. Out of sheer kindness babies were dosed with drug after drug, most of them prepared from crushed herbs given in water or milk."

Cannibal Witch

Look, 1938

The Literary Digest, in 1920, explained "The Cannibal's Substitute For Religion": "Religious consciousness is generally supposed to be innate among all races and tribes but Professor Richard L. Garner, a director of the Smithsonian Institution's recent expedition to the French Kongo, finds that the Pangwes, an incorrigibly cannibalistic tribe, acknowledge no deity and believe that everything which presents the least element of mystery is explainable by witchcraft. They are a purely materialistic people, without sufficient powers of abstraction to conceive of spirit as a thing apart from matter, nor of anything else that the natural organs of sensation fail to perceive. *Buiti* is the highest native conception of a beneficent being, says this authority in *The Forum*; but this being is only human, armed with the natural agencies of *monda* or 'medicine'; and *Nyakwa*, who is also human, is the most definite conception of an evil genius. The good services of the one are procured through a ritualistic ceremony which has no connection with any religious emotion, and tribute forestalls the malign influence of the other."

"Their belief in witchcraft has no religious aspect. It's secret knowledge. The wise men of the tribe know the medicinal and poisonous properties of certain herbs, and how to use them for a desired effect. The powers of a witch are limited only by the knowledge of such secrets and the ability to obtain the required ingredients of *monda*."[3]

The Bwiti religion of Gabon, Congo, Guinea and Cameroon, centered on the use of the Iboga root bark, was the African equivalent of the peyote religion, and is still a great intertribal force in Central Africa. There are between 1-2,000 Bwiti temples in contemporary Gabon, where it is virtually the state religion.

One "sees Bwiti" by "eating the Iboga."[4] The ancient legend says that deep in the Ituri forest a great Mbuti ("Pygmy") hunter was seized by Bwiti for killing too many wild boar, porcupines and gorillas. The hunter was cut into a thousand pieces and scattered throughout the jungle. Searching for her lost husband, the hunter's wife found flowering Iboga shoots growing from the scattered fragments of her husband's body, as if from seed. Bwiti told the widow that if she wanted to speak with the great hunter, all she need do was eat the Iboga. Thus was contact with Bwiti established for ever after.

Ibogaine, isolated from the root bark of *Tabernanthe iboga* bush, has been clinically shown to be of profound psychiatric value, in that it brings repressed memories to consciousness without inducing hallucinations. It is, therefore, a viable aid in the treatment of schizophrenia as well as neurosis and drug addiction. This is discussed by Dr. Claudio Naranjo in *The Healing Journey*, Dr. Stanislav Grof in *LSD Psychotherapy* and Dr. Arthur Janov, the founder of primal therapy, in *The Anatomy of Mental Illness*. Although under active investigation by NIDA's Medication Development Program because of its value to drug abusers, Iboga is *verboten* to us incorrigible Pangwes, who might, God forbid, see Bwiti.[5]

For those who think that the rationale of American drug law isn't inherently racist and anti-tribal, or that it's different than the industrial fascism of alcohol Prohibition, we have the KKK-supported Rep. Richmond P. Hobson of Alabama. In the 1920's Hobson was the most famous anti-heroin crusader in the country. In 1911 Hobson was the man who introduced what became the Eighteenth Amendment, Prohibition, in Congress. One of Rep. Charlie Rangel's favorite lies is that Drug Prohibition and Alcohol Prohibition are separate issues engineered by separate forces. They were, in fact, part and parcel of the same political program engineered by exactly the same individuals, most of them anti-Black racists.

The trouble with Prohibition was that the old Civil War Alcohol Tax had become the financial mainstay of the federal government, accounting for two-fifths of the federal budget. The solution, of course, was the one Temperance originally proposed in 1862, the other great constitutional rape, the personal income tax, which became the Sixteenth Amendment in 1913. The IRS, certainly the most intrusive government bureaucracy, is a *Republican* invention - originally conceived as a rationale for alcohol Prohibition.

Thomas Nast on the insanity of taxing work rather than dissipation, 1878

Since most state electoral districts were gerrymandered to give rural voters three times the voting power of urban voters, the only edge the cities had was their ability to act as the deciding bloc in an electoral fight. The Seventeenth Amendment, direct popular election of senators, undercut the power of the big city machines.

The Nineteenth Amendment, woman suffrage, would never have passed had it not been for the WCTU, although by this time the Woman Suffrage Association had become a major player, as had the less political but rich General Federation of Women's Clubs. The Southerners feared woman suffrage led logically to Black suffrage, and they had the votes to stop it. But the church ladies, who closed every WCTU meeting with their marching song, "All Around the World," sung to the tune of "Old Black Joe," argued that only the votes of educated "American" women could save the South now.

De Brewer's Big Hosses.

(SOLO AND CHORUS.)

H. S. Taylor.   J. B. Herbert.

1. Oh de Brew- er's big hoss - es, com - in' down de road,
2. Oh de lick - er men's act - in' like dey own dis place,
3. Oh I'll har- ness dem hoss - es to de temp-'rance cart,

Oh, de Brewer's big hosses, comin' down de road,
Totin' all around ole Lucifer's load;
Dey step so high, an' dey step so free,
But dem big hosses can't run over me.

CHORUS.

Oh, no! boys, oh, no!
De turnpike's free wherebber I go,
I'm a temperance ingine, don't you see,
And de Brewer's big hosses can't run over me.

Oh, de licker men's actin' like dey own dis place,
Livin' on de sweat ob de po' man's face,
Dey's fat and sassy as dey can be,
But dem big hosses can't run over me.—CHO.

Oh, I'll harness dem hosses to de temp'rance cart,
Hit 'em wid a gad to gib 'em a start,
I'll teach 'em how for to haw and gee,
For dem big hosses can't run over me.—CHO.

The church ladies were strong allies of the antilabor Anti-Saloon League. Southern factory owners and cotton planters hated unions at least as passionately as their Northern brethren, and they came to rely on the wholesome influence of the church ladies. Willard herself had stressed that the problem with labor was not so much "how to make higher wages" but "how to turn present wages to better account."[6] What that was supposed to mean to a sharecropper with starving children is beyond me. This ruthless bourgeois condescension was the prevailing attitude among the Southern Suffragettes and WCTU's. If they were what White female power was about, the South was all for it.

The KKK's Rep. Hobson of Alabama was the Anti-Saloon League's most popular and highest paid speaker. The assumptions of his astounding arguments are all written into today's drug law. Here are some excerpts from his Feb. 2, 1911 speech introducing what became, in 1918, the Eighteenth Amendment, Prohibition:

"History is a record of a sad procession of world tragedies. Nations and empires in turn have risen to greatness only to fall. Before the death blow was struck from without the evidence shows in every case the ravages of a titanic destroyer within, under whose operations the vitality and strength of the nation were submerged in a general degeneracy."

"For centuries the world's philosophers and historians have looked on appalled, overwhelmed. Only in the last few years has science taken up the question. Following her patient, rigid methods, under which nature and life have slowly yielded up their secrets, science has at last cleared up the mystery and identified the great destroyer as alcoholic poisoning."

HEROIN ADDICTION IN AMERICA IS APPALLING

Says Richmond Pearson Hobson, who is the leader of a movement to acquaint the youth of the country with the peril of the heroin habit. The hero of the *Merrimac* is shown here with his family at their home in Los Angeles.

The Literary Digest, 6/24/1924

"Exact laboratory, clinical and pathological research has demonstrated that alcohol is a dehydrating, protoplasmic poison.... under the microscope it was found that even a moderate drink of alcoholic beverage passing quickly into the blood paralyzes the white corpuscles. They behave like little drunken men. In pursuit they cannot catch the disease germs. In conflict they cannot hold the disease germs for devouring, and they cannot operate in great phalanxes, as they do when sober, against such powerful germs as those of consumption."

"If a peaceable red man is subjected to the regular use of alcoholic beverage, he will speedily be put back to the plane of the savage. The Government long since recognized this and absolutely prohibits the introduction of alcoholic beverage into an Indian reservation. If a negro takes up a regular use of alcoholic beverage, in a short time he will degenerate to the level of the cannibal. No matter how high the stage of evolution, the result is the same."

'IZZY' SEIZES 'NOZO,' 3% AT 20 CTS. A PINT

They Call It Beer, but It's Made of Bread and It Has More Kick Than Volstead Allows.

22 BARRELS CONFISCATED

Also 2,400 Bottles and Three Boilers With 450 Gallons—Kahn Calls Law a Harm Breeder.

Izzy Einstein and Moe Smith raided the store of Arcian Nazarewich, 430 East Eleventh Street yesterday. In the basement, they allege, they found three copper boilers in full operation, each containing 150 gallons of ingredients that make something stronger than Volstead allows. The agents seized 2,400 bottles and twenty-two barres of the stuff and ten bags of sugar, and gave a summons to the owner of the place to appear to-day before United States Commissioner Hitchcock.

The receptacles at the prohibition headquarters attracted much attention, and were viewed by all the officials. Ac-

FIGHT A NEGRO MOB FOR 5 DRUG CAPTIVES

Detectives Battle in San Juan Hill District Amid Rain of Missiles.

AMAZON WORSTS DETECTIVE

As Powerful Negress Finally Is Subdued Reserves Clear Path Through Rioters.

Reserves from the West Sixty-eighth Street Station, aided by half a dozen detectives from the west side yard of the New York Central, last night fought denizens of the San Juan Hill district to rescue four detectives of the Narcotic division who undertook to arrest two white men and three negresses for violating the narcotic law. In the fight started by the prisoners and their friends before the arrival of the reserves, sympathizers in nearby tenement houses showered the detectives with bricks, flower pots, boxes of coal and a large

Two articles side-by-side, *NYT*, 4/22/1922

"In our great cities like New York, Chicago, and Philadelphia the ravages upon the average character have been so great, so many degenerates have already been produced, that the degenerate and corruptible vote not only holds the balance of power between the two great political parties and can dictate to both, but actually holds a majority of the votes, so that honest and efficient self-government as a permanent condition is now impossible. Immigrants coming in vast numbers from abroad remained chiefly in the cities. As young as our Nation is, the deadly work of alcohol has already blighted liberty in our greatest cities."

"If America degenerates the yellow man will be on hand. Some may make light of the yellow man; so did Romans make light of the 'Barbarians.' The yellow man is not degenerating. He can shoot as straight as a white man now, and undegenerated he can live on one-tenth of what is necessary for the white men while they are in the field doing the shooting. A race of degenerates cannot occupy the American continent."

"In America we are making the last stand of the great white race, and substantially of the human race. If this destroyer cannot be conquered in young America, it cannot in any of the old and more degenerate nations. If America fails, the world will be undone and the human race will be doomed to go down from degeneracy into degeneracy till the Almighty in wrath wipes the accursed thing out!"

God, they loved him in Alabama. In the 1920's he founded the International Narcotic Education Association, with a board of directors of prominent industrialists and an advisory council of cabinet secretaries, governors, mayors, district attorneys, bishops and ambassadors, but not one reputable drug abuse expert. Having gotten his alcohol Prohibition, he decided that the fate of "the race" rested on defeat of the new "Great Destroyers" - all herbal and refined inebriants, advocating precisely the policies we now have in place, Draconian law enforcement combined with unrelenting propaganda:

"We need to preach the gospel of narcotic abstinence from the pulpit, to flash it on the screen, to enact it on the stage, to proclaim it from the public platform, to depict it in the press, and, above all, to teach it in our schools./All constructive social agencies will help in fighting this peril - in setting up in the minds of all the same abhorrence that is felt for a venomous snake..."[7]

All the measures Hobson advocated for the inner cities are now law. Our prisons are full of exactly the people Hobson thought belonged there. We don't say "nigger" anymore, of course, we say "drug dealer," so much more scientific; Hobson stopped saying "nigger" too. In *Good Housekeeping*, the progressive Dr. Wiley, below, worried about "Negro peddlers." In the yellow press the single most common synonym for "nigger" was "drug dealer" or "addict," as in the sharpshooter from Asheville; these words are racist code to this day.

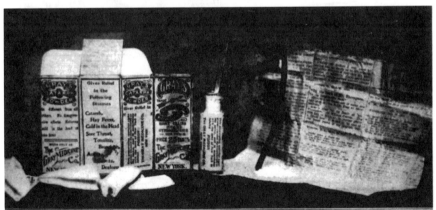

A deadly cocain-bearing catarrh powder, labeled poison in accordance with the New York law. The guarantee clause offsets the warning of the poison label, and the manufacturers cannot be prosecuted because the cocain is declared according to the law and a cure is not promised.—In the dirty newspaper is $2 worth of cocain. Negro pedlers of the drug conceal it in this way

Good Housekeeping, March, 1914

My old man grew up on the Lower East Side near Meyer Lansky and Benny Siegel, whom he knew as the big kids who put together the feared killers of the Bugs and Meyer Mob. They were the kids Grandma warned Dad to stay away from (Uncle Izzy didn't listen). While they were still teenagers, they teamed up with Charlie Lucania,

Frank Castiglia and their awesome collection of young Sicilians and Italians and built the organization that came to represent organized crime in America.

Prohibition made interstate and international cooperation the order of the day. Arnold Rothstein showed Lansky and Luciano how to use freighters hanging off the three-mile limit as wholesale warehouses servicing their fast crabs. God help the Fed who didn't shut up and take his cut.

The Wasp industrialists said it was all because of the Kikes and the Wops, and even the Micks, Krauts and Pollocks when they could sober up enough to put up a fight. Prohibition, of course, is still in force. Only the alcohol part has been repealed. Now it's all the fault of the Spics, Gooks and Niggers.

The racist hammering young Black men take behind the drug laws is intense and constant, driving many of them nuts with hostility. The schizophrenic Nation of Islam, of course, out-platitudes the platitudinous - and calls it prophesy. It supports escalation of the Drug

War, consistent with Islam's imperial hostility to tribal culture, while at the same time decrying the obviously racist enforcement. If the enforcement is incurably racist, as the Nation of Islam has always accurately insisted, why support escalation of the Drug War? Because racists, Black or White, thrive on hostility.

Racism relates to the Drug War exactly the same way it related to slavery. Racism didn't *cause* slavery, industrial fascism, the *economic* utility of slaves caused slavery, in ancient Sumer as in colonial Georgia. In fact *industrial fascism* can be defined as *the coercive use of people as industrial machinery*. It was inflicted on Native America and Native Polynesia by the Portuguese, Spanish, Dutch, French, English, German and American slavers in exactly the same way as on Native Africa, and plenty of Asians and Whites suffered from fascist brutality as well.

Sacramental Africa, *Asia*, c.1930

In Africa, of course, the European and American slavers had to deal through their military equals, the Moslem conquerors of North and Central Africa. The great Senegalese filmmaker Ousmane Sembene's film *The Cedo* is a good look at invading Islam from an African perspective. As Kenya's Gikuyu shaman Ngugi wa Thiong'o points out (*Decolonising the Mind*), Islam is no more a Native African religion than Christianity is a Native American religion. Nigeria's great Yoruba shaman Wole Soyinka, winner of the 1986 Nobel Prize for Literature, makes the same point. In Zimbabwe, Islam is virtually unknown; the predominant religions are those of the native Shona, Ndebele, and Tonga.

The Sufis of Islam, who preached against slavery and social injustice, often achieved their mystical communion, their detachment from the hypnosis of the official symbolism, through shamanism. They are remembered as the greatest poets Islam ever produced. Since they used, among other things, newly-popular coffee to focus their attention, coffee was criminalized. In Mecca, in 1511, all the Sufi coffee houses were closed. Istanbul's Murad IV, in 1625, put coffee drinkers to death, as did the Ottoman Grand Vizir Koprili in 1656.

"Our sovereign habit. O 'philosophe,' and one of the bounties of Allah"—thus was Ameen Rihani introduced to "ghat," the bitter-tasting shrub chewed everywhere in the Yemen. With it, at a ghat party like this gathering of Islamic dignitaries in Sanaa, inevitably go a jug of water and the tall water-pipe that is called "madaah" in this part of the world
Sacramental Yemen, *Asia*, c.1925

Koprili, a great slaver, was about as 'Moslem' as Charles V was 'Christian.' Anti-Black racism was an inevitable result of the economic and military utility of the African slave trade to the imperial powers. How can you militarize a culture without an enemy? From the fascist perspective, the police *need* a scapegoat. Detroit or Watts might as well be in Guatemala or Mexico. Every Nigger is a Zapatista.

The Nigger, a popular 1910 Broadway play, believe it or not, was typical of the traveling temperance shows that ran all over the country between 1880 and 1920. The scene is the deep South. Our hero is Phil Morrow, owner of the local big plantation and county sheriff. Our villain is Clif Noyes, owner of Noyes Distillery Works and Phil's childhood friend. There is a subplot of competition between the two for the hand of Miss Georgiana, but she rejects distiller Clif " as easily as I'd kick a niggah downstairs" and marries Phil after the first act.

THE NEW THEATRE

THE NIGGER

A PLAY IN THREE ACTS BY
EDWARD SHELDON

PRODUCED BY GEORGE FOSTER PLATT

SCENES

ACT FIRST

JUNE 3D. EVENING AT "MORROW'S REST."

INTERMISSION—FIFTEEN MINUTES

ACT SECOND

APRIL 23D. THE GOVERNOR'S STUDY IN HIS CITY HOUSE.
ABOUT TEN O'CLOCK IN THE MORNING.

ACT THIRD

APRIL 26TH. THE GOVERNOR'S PRIVATE OFFICE AT THE
CAPITOL. EVENING.

PLACE: THE SOUTH.   TIME: NOW.

CHARACTERS

NAMED IN THE ORDER OF THEIR APPEARANCE

SIMMS, *Morrow's butler*	MR. REGINALD BARLOW
JINNY, *Morrow's "mammy"*	MISS BEVERLY SITGREAVES
CLIFTON NOYES, *president of the Noyes Distillery Works*	
	MR. BEN JOHNS
GEORGIANA BYRD	MISS ANNIE RUSS
PHILIP MORROW, *of "Morrow's Rest" and sheriff of Westbury County*	MR. GUY BATES
PURDY, *deputy sheriff of Westbury County*	MR. ROBERT E. H ANS
MRS. BYRD	MRS. H. OTIS DELLE LAUGH
JOE WHITE	MR. OSWALD YORKE
JAKE WILLIS	MR. PEDRO DE CORDOBA
BARRINGTON, *the Governor's private secretary*	
	MR. JACOB WENDELL, JR
CHIEF-OF-POLICE TILTON	MR. WILFRID NORT
COLONEL KNAPP, *of the 5th Militia*	MR. WILLIAM McV
THE GOVERNOR'S DOORKEEPER	MR. ROBERT VIV
SENATOR THOMAS R. LONG	MR. LEE BA
MEMBERS OF THE GOVERNOR'S STAFF, REPORTERS, ETC.	

First Production December 4, 1909

The distiller has come to Phil's plantation to persuade its blueblood owner to run for governor against the progressive, niggah-lovin, carpetbagger prohibitionist who threatens to turn the state dry. Just as he accepts Clif's offer, a deputy runs breathlessly up to Phil to inform him that "it's a niggah, suh, the usual crime" - the rape-murder of a little White girl in the woods. The rapist, an habitual drunk, is one of Phil's plantation hands, so Phil gets his hands on him before the lynch mob, led by the murdered girl's father.

Law'n'order Phil adamantly refuses to turn the "black beast" over to the mob, insisting that he must be hanged legally. Distiller Clif warns that this action will endanger "the anti-niggah vote" but Phil refuses to relent. Just then the rapist bolts, the mob gets him, and the anti-niggah vote is saved at the end of a rope.

A KKK rally in Brunswick, Maryland, June 28, 1922; Brown Brothers

Once in the statehouse, Phil is confronted with a prolonged race riot down in the levee district. Explains Phil to the horrified distiller: "This volcano's helped me along considerable. We brought the niggahs ovah t' this country, Clif - an' I reckon we're responsible fo' them while theah heah. If we've kept 'em like children, we've got to treat 'em like children. An' we're not in the habit, Clif, o' pourin' liquoh down the throats of our infants. Why, day befo' yeste'day I had a count made an' theah were three thousand four hundred an' sixty-seven idle niggahs in the fifty-nine saloons o' the levee district! That was the end, Clif, an' the long an' the sho't of it is - we're goin' dry!"

As Rep. Edward Pou of North Carolina explained on the floor of Congress in 1914, the South prohibits Black voting not out of hatred, but "as the adult takes the pistol from the hand of the child."[8] We are all, of course, *The Nigger*, all children, too stupid to take herbs our Paleolithic ancestors knew how to use, all likely to "degenerate to the level of the cannibal" at the first toke (like Louis Armstrong?).

The KKK, "Defenders of Protestant Americanism," were violently Prohibitionist. Their "racial superiority" was *explained* in Prohibitionist, that is moral, terms. Prohibition was "Salvation," "Gospel" as Hobson called it. Fascism always masquerades as venial morality. In fact, the political confusion between venial morality and mortal morality is a defining characteristic of fascism, as if getting stoned too much were as evil as torturing people.

Fascism is always maudlin. Industrial fascists *need* a scapegoat to coalesce. Without the *pharmakos*, the Nigger, the Judas, the Witch, the Dealer, the Fiend, the Hippie who inflicts such grave hurt upon Our Salvation, there is no rationale for an ongoing *Inquisitio*, without which the structure of industrial fascism would be left standing naked. It ain't so much what they're *for*, it's what they're *against*.

Wide World photograph

The Temperance Tornado

Former Representative William D. Upshaw, of Georgia

The Literary Digest, 7/23/1932

The "White Hope" of Drug Victims

An Everyday American Fighter

HERE is an odd story of an odd man with odd ideals and odd adventures, whose virile personality to-day backs a nation-wide campaign in which not one individual in

morphine user Towns had ever seen. The man's condition was pitiable, his dependence upon the drug so absolute that he had to have a "shot" while the call was in progress, and Towns observed the operation curiously. The man was evidently

His specialty is the hardest job, whatever that happens to be. To cure the Chinese of the opium habit seemed a reasonable undertaking to him

White Hope

Charles B. Towns' cure, officially endorsed by the AMA, was famous throughout the country in the teens and twenties. It almost certainly would make anyone stop taking anything. It consisted of huge simultaneous doses of foxglove, belladonna, prickly ash bark and strong purgatives, coupled with constant prayer. Foxglove and belladonna are two of the most famous witchcraft herbs of Europe. Foxglove contains the cardiac stimulant digitalis, and belladonna contains the powerfully psychoactive scopolamine and hyoscyamine.

Towns claimed his cure was effective for opium, cocaine or alcohol addiction. His New York sanitarium charged between $200-$350 for a private room for the five-day course, and $75 for a double occupancy, big money in those days. Towns' theoretical and commercial partner was Dr. Alexander Lambert, chief of the AMA's Medicolegal Bureau during the fight to pass Harrison, later head of the AMA. Together they profitably administered the Towns-Lambert method.[1]

Lambert's entry on cocaine addiction in Osler's prestigious 1925 medical textbook, *Modern Medicine*, solemnly pronounced that "The most effective treatment is the Towns treatment and the method is the same as in dealing with an alcoholic, except that the cocaine should be cut off immediately. Strychnine, with or without some form of digitalis should be given from the beginning. The belladonna mixture and from 3 to 5 cathartic pills and 5 gr. of blue mass should be given simultaneously as the first dose. The belladonna mixture is continued every hour of the day and night, and twelve hours after the initial dose the patients are again given from 3 to 5 cathartic pills followed six hours later by a saline, and at the twenty-fourth hour after the initial dose they are again given cathartics and again at the thirty-sixth hour. After these last cathartics the bilious stool appears, and by the forty-fifth to forty-eighth hour castor oil is given."

That is, they pharmacologically kicked the shit out of their patients; they "puked and purged" 'em. They divined their success ratio by counting as cured all those who didn't return for further punishment.

Between 1893 and 1895 the British *Opium Royal Commission* produced three twelve hundred page volumes of expert notarized testimony concerning the use of opium in India. It made no attempt to exclude negative witnesses. Its only requirement was verifiable expertise on some aspect of the subject. One English missionary, who knew of no "hardier, thriftier or more careful people than the Punjabis," insisted regular opium use "seems to interfere neither with their longevity nor with their health." That was the overwhelming majority opinion of the hundreds of physicians, civil servants, merchants, missionaries and working people recorded by the Commission.

HISTORICAL NOTE on OPIUM and the POPPY in CHINA.—By DR. EDKINS, of the Chinese Customs Service.

Shanghai, May 1889

[This paper was cited by witnesses before the Commission; it is now out of print and unobtainable. The Commission therefore ordered it to be reprinted as an Appendix to the China evidence.]

Small amounts of opium produce a pleasant and energetic bodily lightness conducive to work and mental activity. Opium was used as a pre-battle stimulant by the Punjabis, and no British soldier wanted to face them. Larger amounts produce a dreamy reverie, "an aid to music composers" as one 1912 *New York Times* article had it.

An opium smoker's tools; *Scientific American*, 11/1921

Smoking opium sap is not analogous to injecting morphine or heroin. Dr. Brecher in *Licit & Illicit Drugs*: "Only about 10% of the morphine [5-15% of commercial opium by weight]...enters the vapor, and only a portion of the morphine in the vapor enters the human bloodstream when inhaled; there are no 'tars' or other carcinogens to cause cancer. The so-called 'opium-smoker' is actually a vapor inhaler. At a very rough estimate, a smoker would have to smoke 300 or 400 grains of opium to get a dose equivalent to the intravenous injection of one grain of heroin [diacetylmorphine]."[2] Smoked, all 39 of opium's alkaloids are delivered in concert, slowly and in minuscule doses, CNS exciters right along with the depressants. The most harm an opium smoker can do to himself is put himself to sleep.

Morphine, on the other hand, opium's major alkaloid, is a powerful CNS depressant, especially in conjunction with alcohol, and hypodermic injection makes absorption immediate and irreversible. But that, again, reduces to a question of dosage, expertise and public policy, not toxicity. As Jonathan Ott, the great entheobotanist and chemist, wrote to me: "So-called opiate overdose [overwhelmingly caused by anaphylaxis or toxicity of adulterants, as opposed to true overdose] results from respiratory, not cardiac, arrest, *via* a relaxant effect on the respiratory muscles, there's virtually no other toxicity at these dose-levels...morphine is one of the least-toxic drugs in the pharmacopoeia, and deaths from medicinal administration, also of heroin in Britain, even if from intravenous administration, are almost unknown, since known dosage and purity are givens."

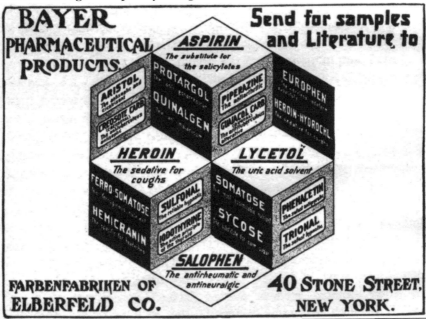

That is, you can get into trouble with morphine if it is a) adulterated, b) mixed with alcohol, or c) given in overdose. You can't overdose on the smoked sap. Alkaloids are more dangerous than herbs *when criminalized*, because: a) they are easier to adulterate; b) amateurs are untrained in concentrate dosage and administration; and c)

concentration and toxicity of unlabeled street alkaloids is unknown.

But the 1909-1914 criminalization of the safe sap automatically popularized the refined alkaloid, since it's far more profitable to smuggle. This was the conclusion of the official USPHS study conducted by Kolb and Du Mez in 1924. Prior to 1914 gum opium was favored by regular users, after 1914 the gum had been almost totally replaced by heroin and morphine.[3] As Professor Trebach pointed out, this substitution process repeated itself after WW II when American drug law was foisted on a supine world. Hong Kong, North Europe, Japan, Germany, Singapore, Thailand, Borneo and Turkey all found their opium smokers using the only available substitute - heroin.[4] Professor McCoy repeatedly makes the same point.

SAYS OPIUM CRITICS EXAGGERATE EVILS

Sir Richard Dane, Long in China, Reports Much Moderation in Use of Drug.

ADMITS DANGER TO NATIONS

But He Declares the Use of Alcohol Is Even More Serious for the Individual.

Special Correspondence of THE NEW YORK TIMES.

LONDON, Oct. 30.—"The abuse of opium is of course a serious evil, but the abuse of alcohol is also a serious evil. The two habits are comparable.

"The conclusions at which the Royal Opium Commission of 1893-95 arrived, with only one dissentient voice, on the subject of the opium habit as ordinarily practiced in India, merit reproduction," continued Sir Richard.

"That opium almost everywhere in India is the common domestic medicine of the people, that it is extensively used for non-medical and quasi-medical purposes and that the non-medical uses are so interwoven with the medical uses that it would not be practical to draw a distinction between them in the distribution and sale of the drug; that as regards the use of opium as a stimulant, the practice of taking the drug in pills or infusions is of old standing and is generally followed in moderation and without injurious consequences, and that as to the quasi-medical habit the evidence of medical witnesses leads to the conclusion that, in the circumstances of India in respect to climate, diet, modes of living and medical aid, this use is probably on the whole beneficial."

NYT, 11/7/1926

Is regular morphine or opium use "addiction" simply because it is regular? All genuine addiction experts agree that opiates do no physiological damage to the user at all - they do not damage liver, central nervous system, stomach, muscles, kidneys, glands, heart or brain. The most famous example of this is Dr. William Stewart Halsted, a clinical founder, chief of surgery, of Johns Hopkins University School of Medicine. Halsted injected morphine, or a combination of morphine and cocaine, every day for the last thirty years of his life and, simultaneously, was renowned as the greatest technical surgeon alive, "the father of modern surgery." He died at seventy, still operating.[5]

SAYS OPIUM AIDS MUSIC COMPOSERS

Jean Laporte Declares Many Owe Much of Their Fame to Smoking the Drug.

COLLEAGUES SUPPORT HIM

Two Well-Known Musicians Say a Few Pipes a Day Are No Worse Than Cigarettes—Doctors Contradict Them.

By Marconi Transatlantic Wireless Telegraph to The New York Times.

PARIS, Jan. 20.—"Opium as a Source of Musical Inspiration" is the title of a daring article by the well-known composer, Jean Laporte, which is attracting a great deal of attention. The writer affirms positively that the drug can and does act in this way, and quotes the conversations of some leading French musicians, who confess their indebtedness to its use for some of their best ideas.

To begin with, M. Laporte declares that opium smoking, if practiced in moderation, is no more harmful to the system than wine or tobacco; only its abuse is injurious. He protests against the vigorous campaign against the importation of opium now in progress in France.

A professor of music at the Conservatoire at Lyons, M. Mariotte, is quoted as declaring that his musical career was largely shaped in its early stages by opium smoking. He recounts that when under the influence of opium he used to see visually "processions of musical phrases."

M. Roussel of the Schola Cantorum, the famous Paris academy of singing, also owes his indebtedness to the drug, declaring at the same time that a few pipes of opium a day do no more harm than a few cigarettes. He describes an extraordinary composition, a "Patagonian Ballet," written by a friend from Brittany while under the influence of opium.

"Each time I hear it," he adds, "I experience again the exquisite impressions I felt when I was an opium smoker."

By a curious coincidence, both these professors were originally in the navy. Both first became acquainted with opium in the Far East, and both now regret that they no longer have the time or facilities to continue the habit.

Two French doctors, who have just published a work on literary genius, have come to the conclusion that such stimulants warp and, even destroy, the mind in the long run. It is asserted that the evidence collected by M. Laporte proves that this is by no means the case with musicians.

NYT, 1/21/1912

How then does one define "addiction." Is the word just an epithet? Halsted was a productive genius who *used* drugs. And the major "drug" he was using was the botanical version of a naturally-occurring human neurochemical. He was practicing psychopharmacology, to be sure, but to great advantage. The same can be said of a very long list of wildly productive contemporary geniuses, including some of our greatest novelists, filmmakers, songwriters, astronomers, physicists and entrepreneurs. Jonathan Ott, the entheobotanist taught at universities worldwide, publishes fluently in Spanish, German and English. He is one of the most powerful and productive scholars alive. And he has been a very active pharmacophile for decades. He tells me that my use of the word "pharmacoshaman" is a "pleonasm," a redundancy.

Prohibition, then, has very little to do with scientific pharmacology and its related disciplines, and much to do with the *politicization* of pharmacology. As Professor Alfred Lindesmith put it in the introduction to his 1947 classic *Addiction and Opiates*: "alcohol is addicting in approximately the same sense that heroin is...the fact that marijuana, cocaine, and heroin and other opiate-type drugs are covered in the same anti-narcotics legislation is a fertile source of confused thinking because it obscures the facts that the use of marijuana is totally unlike heroin or morphine addiction and that alcoholism...actually has very much in common with opiate addiction."

Alcohol, heroin and cocaine all show approximately the same ratio of addicts or abusers to users, 10% or less, hardly a proportion requiring mass hysteria. Cigarettes produce a rate of addiction higher than 50% in occasional users.[6]

Coca leaf and opium sap would be preferred by many to cocaine and heroin, were they available, but their legend is so terrifying, like Dracula's fangs, the mere mention of their phantasm brings shudders of fear, as if Dracula were real. In fact, neither opium sap nor coca leaf are a problem in their native cultures, where they're both religious sacraments and social inebriants.

Throughout southern Neolithic Europe, in the lakeshore villages of north Italy and Switzerland, for instance, opium was a major crop, and its association with Cretan and Greek ecstatic rites is certain.[7] Demeter's name is often used as a synonym for "poppy fields" in the Cretan palace records of 1600 BC, and she is often represented as "Opium Mother," either holding or wearing bulging poppy capsules. Inscribed Mycenaean Greek jars, full of an edible opium-containing "unguent," have been found in the earliest levels at Eleusis, c. 1300 BC.[8] Opium was a sacred symbol carved into the temple walls at Eleusis, a probable ingredient of the entheogenic "mixture" (*kykeon*) that was the central sacrament of Classical Greece. Opium continued to be a symbol of fecundity well into Roman times.[9]

Opium was cultivated by the Sumerians of 3500 BC, who called it "the Joy Plant." They had a thriving Asia trade. The Hindu surgeon Sushruta wrote of it in 300 BC. It seems likely that the Han dynasty scholars who compiled the pharmacopeia of Shen Nung around the time of Christ knew of opium, but the references are only suggestive. By the eighth century CE opium was a regular item in the Chinese herbals.[10]

In 970 CE Su Che, in his poem "The Cultivation of the Medicinal Plant Poppy," sang that opium's "seeds are like autumn millet; when ground they yield a sap like cow's milk; when boiled they become a drink fit for Buddha."[11] In 1057, Su Sung noted that the opium "poppy is found everywhere." Throughout China, for more than a millennium, honored guests were greeted with drinks or pipes full of opium.

Mr. Snow regards this scene as typical of hospitality in Anhwei Province—the guest provided with an opium-pipe instead of the traditional cup of tea

Asia, 1/1931

Of course, coolies under the lash in the turn-of-the-century colonial slave states could be expected to use opium, especially when it was substituted for their wages. It was literally the only escape they had. "Insufficient food, harsh work schedules, and beatings made most of the plantations slave labor camps with annual death rates higher than 20 percent."[12]

But whether coolie opium use was a function of pain or the need to escape, or whether there was, in fact, a high rate of opium use at all in the labor camps is open to question. As Ott points out, "when people *are* in intense pain, they are much *less* likely to fall under the thrall of opiates administered even in exorbitant doses to ameliorate it. This is simply because allaying the pain in some way detracts from the euphoria [which, in any case, only a minority of people perceive - for the majority, opiates are nauseating and so *aversive*, not *reinforcing, which is why opiates have never been and never will be majority inebriants*]..."[12] For a minority of users, then, opiates are euphoriants, and euphoria is, in a certain sense, analgesic. But one should not simplify the reasons people seek euphoria.

Opium, that is, is euphoriant enough for enough people to turn it into a demanded agricultural commodity worldwide. The European colonialists, and the Chinese Imperial slave states, then caricatured this large-scale use as "addiction," justifying their politically selective enforcement - and their need to monopolize the trade.

A British opium inspector in India, 1905. Scoring the seed capsules in Yunnan, *Asia*, 1/1931

The Chinese Opium Wars were about control of that trade, that is, control of China. Opium smoking was demonized as low-rent treason, "addiction," by the Chinese monarchy, and its American ally, only *after* the British cornered the global trade by conquering opium-producing India and taking control of major Chinese ports. Until that time, Chinese poets sang opium's praises. Under conditions of foreign monopoly, however, to smoke imported opium was to finance the British rape of China. It is finance and the attendant geopolitical power that Chinese Emperors worried about, not the health of their subjects.

This hypocrisy was epitomized by China's leading mandarin, Li Hung-chang, at the 1877 Shanghai Missionary Conference. Li declared that "China views the question from a moral standpoint; England from a fiscal."[13] But Li forgot to mention that he himself was a large opium producer. Since Li's Chinese opium contributed to the Emperor's exchequer, his was moral opium, not that evil British stuff.

Above, the raw sap drying in the Persian sun, 1925. Below, opium and sweet tea, Shiraz, Persia, 1925; *Asia*

Before the European attack on China's sovereignty, opium was a commonly accepted social inebriant and aid to meditation with a very long history as the most important painkiller, soporific, antispasmodic and febrifuge known. This medical respect for opium was accepted worldwide. As the 1918 *U.S. Dispensatory* put it: "It is at present more frequently prescribed than perhaps any other article of the materia medica."[14]

Nearly all the empirical research supports the conclusions of Dr. Marie Nyswander, the popularizer of the politically acceptable "methadone maintenance": "There is a pattern of self-limitation or restraint in opium smoking in countries where it is socially accept-able. It is common for natives in these countries to indulge in opium smoking one night a week much as Americans may indulge in alco-holic beverages at a Saturday night party.... families who accept opium smoking as part of their culture are mindful of its dangers much as we are mindful of the dangers of overindulgence in alcohol."[15]

Describing the high rate of opium or heroin "addiction" in Hong Kong in 1970, Professor McCoy stresses that "Most of the addicts were poor wage laborers who lived in cramped tenements and sprawling slums, which many social workers considered ideal breeding grounds for addiction."[16]

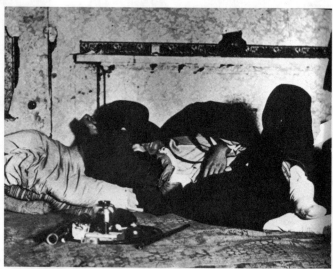

Police Commissioner Roosevelt's friend, the influential journalist Jacob Riis, took this shot on New York's Lower East Side, 1887

That is, it is the poverty that fosters the escapism, not the escap-ism the poverty. But of course, to acknowledge that politically would mean that public funds would start to flow *out* of police programs and *into* social programs.

Sociologists at the City College of New York in the early 1940's were astonished by the alcohol admission statistics of New York City's

Drug War

public hospitals, which then kept records by ethnicity. 25% of all admissions for alcohol-related problems were of Irish background, but only ½ of 1% were of Jewish background. On examination of other measures, they found that the same ratios held true. Alcoholism among Jewish Americans was one-fiftieth the rate of alcoholism among Irish Americans.[17]

Since no biological or psychological differences could be found, the answer seemed to lie in the attitude of the cultures toward alcohol itself. Jewish culture, like many Mediterranean cultures, teaches the sane use of alcohol to its young rather than simply prohibiting it. That is, as Dr. Nyswander says, acculturation is everything.

This same pattern repeats itself worldwide and can be found in completely unconnected cultures. The Vicosinos of Peru, who enjoy ritual and social inebriation as often as the Jews, and who also share sanctioned ritual inebriation with the children, likewise have virtually no alcoholism.[18] The Irish Catholic pattern is prohibition; even the sacramental wine is forbidden to all but the priest, producing a strong, alienated reaction in the pub. Those cultures that prescribe rather than proscribe don't have a drug problem.

Professor Charles Snyder: "Where drinking is an integral part of the socialization process, where it is interrelated with the central moral symbolism and is repeatedly practiced in the rites of a group, the phenomenon of alcoholism is conspicuous by its absence. Norms of sobriety can be effectively sustained under these circumstances even though the drinking is extensive. Where institutional conflicts disrupt traditional patterns in which drinking is integrated, where drinking is dissociated from the normal process of socialization, where drinking is relegated to social contexts which are disconnected from or in opposition to the core moral values and where it is used for individual purposes, pathologies such as alcoholism may be expected to increase."[19]

That is the general conclusion of empirical experts on drug abuse regardless of the inebriant. Polynesia has no problem with kava, Peru none with coca leaf, the Mbuti of the Congo none with marijuana, Yemen none with khat. Prescribing cultures, in which teaching and familial love and acceptance replaces proscription and ostracism, don't produce the stressful conditions in which inebriative behaviors become the focus of neurotic behavior. The "drug problem," then, is not one of pharmacology, but of public policy. Stress, alienation, pain, promotes the use of euphoriants and pain killers. Stress is the number one "gateway" to "abuse."

I heard Dr. Brown on NPR, 12/9/97, peddling "Dr.Brown's Home Drug Test Kit," recently approved by the FDA. Dr. Brown is in no doubt that parents must be on their guard for "gateway drugs," and that the best way to close the gate is with humiliating, and stressful, police procedures. The uncontrollable rage that being forced to urinate into a bottle will produce in many 16-year-olds should be feared a lot more than a little pot.

In the single most effective piece of Prohibitionist propaganda I have ever seen, a grief-stricken Carol O'Connor draws the conclusion from his son's tragic descent into drug abuse and suicide that he, O'Connor, wasn't *tough enough*. He prefaces the whole piece with the information that when he caught his 16-year-old son smoking some pot at home with his friends, he kicked them all out in a fit of rage. Of course, if it had been beer, the garrulous Irishman would have just joined the party. But, he makes it clear, he correctly equated marijuana with heroin. Alcohol, of course, would have been a better analogy, but the pharmacologically-challenged O'Connor seems oblivious to the distinctions. It never occurs to O'Connor that legal, loving pharmacotherapy could have saved his son's life. O'Connor prefers to insist that what that boy needed was a really good thrashing at the hands of the police. One can understand the son's alienation.

It is perfectly normal for a teenager on the verge of adulthood to reach for a cigar, or a beer, or a whiskey, or a joint, as the parents customarily do. The prohibitionists demonize the normal inebriative, that is, oral, behaviors of the young, and, rather than teaching the safe, traditional herbalism, make those herbs unavailable.

They therefore create a stressful atmosphere of ostracism and hostility which strongly favors wild, alienated inebriative behaviors. Those behaviors necessarily employ the only inebriants available - alcohol, tobacco, pot and the street alkaloids. The prohibitionists then point to those behaviors as a "pandemic" demonstrating the need for yet more institutionalized violence aimed at the young. That, of course, creates yet more "pandemic" - yet more stressed-out patients for the "substance abuse professionals" - who are very careful to confuse the safe traditional herbs with the profitable-to-smuggle, and prescribe, refined isolates.

It is the stress, the ostracism and hostility, that is the "gateway." That's why Holland, with legal pot and medicalized alkaloids, has one-seventh the U.S. rate of heroin "addiction," that is, neurotic abuse, and, apparently, half the pot use rate. O'Connor should have sent his son to Amsterdam, where loving pharmacotherapy is available.

Dr. Solomon Snyder, the current director of neuroscience at Johns Hopkins, explains that "while each drug acts on different receptors, 'all seem to funnel through one common reward pathway in the brain,' ...neural circuitry leading from lower brain regions to the nucleus accumbens in the forebrain. It seems to play a role in normal satisfaction-seeking behaviors involving food and sex but gets exaggerated in addiction..." That is, inebriative behavior is an instinctive oral behavior, physiologically, evolutionarily, related to eating and sex.

The "satisfaction" is achieved largely through the release of dopamine in the nucleus accumbens. Dopamine is an endogenous precursor of the cerebrospinal neurotransmitter norepinephrine. Peyote's major alkaloid, mescaline, also a phenylethylamine derivative, is very closely related to norepinephrine. Pure dopamine, chemically identical to the human catecholamine, is produced in large quantities by the *saguaro* cactus *Carnegiea gigantea*, used by the Seri Indians of Sonora to treat rheumatic pain. That is, just as the Seri say, the plant world is literally our biological mother.[20]

Continues the *JAMA*: "...scientific evidence supports the view of addiction as a chronic disease, says [NIDA Director Alan] Leshner [this country's *official* top drug expert]. Addicts have a disability and therefore are 'entitled to treatment,' the same as patients with any other disease."

That is, the "exaggeration" or neurotic abuse of heroin is defined by Dr. Leshner as a "disease," which is an odd description for a volitional behavior. Dr. Leshner does acknowledge that much heroin use is not "addiction." As Dr. Snyder pointed out, much heroin use, like most eating and sex, is rooted in "normal satisfaction-seeking behaviors" - "use," not "abuse." Dr. Leshner, of course, would argue that "abuse," "addiction," is a "disease" because it is not volitional, but his own research actually brings him to the assertion that most drug abuse is a "symptom," not a "cause."

Dr. Leshner: "Discerning when drug abuse is in fact an attempt to self-medicate for other disorders may also improve treatment efficacy. Some studies suggest that more than two thirds of patients with drug disorders also have mental disorder, and that almost a third of those with a mental disorder also have a drug problem."[21]

That is, people in pain turn to pain killers or euphoriants. The influential Dr. Mitchell Rosenthal, head of Phoenix House, a leading "substance abuse professional," turns this on its head, insisting that it's the drug-taking that causes the pain, not the pain the neurotic drug-taking.[22] That is, Rosenthal is engaging in a classic inquisitorial trick, insisting that the medicine is causing the disease.

There is a political dimension to this: fascism, the militarization of culture, feeds on the artificial production of stress. The exacerbation of stress, that is, is a traditional form of witchcraft: Dr. Jeanne Achterberg: "We have a thirty-year research effort from scientists such as Walter Cannon, Hans Selye, and many others, showing the potential for stress to hamper the immune function. There are series after series of animal trials from the most respected laboratories in the world showing that under stressed conditions, the compromised immune system can result in disease or even death. We even have growing acceptance for the notion that stress exacerbates the growth of cancer in humans, triggers flare-ups in patients with rheumatoid arthritis, and sends asthmatics off to the emergency room for oxygen. Stress is implicated as a factor in both onset and exacerbation of all the autoimmune diseases - those conditions where the immune system can no longer discriminate self from nonself, friend from foe."[23]

Stress is debilitating, confusing and painful, causing people, instinctively, to reach for whatever painkiller or euphoriant is available. Stress is the number one "gateway" to drug abuse, and there is no empirical doubt about that among the mainstream of addiction scientists, even those who have trouble distinguishing "use" from "abuse."

Rural India; *Asia*, c.1927

Biofeedback stress reduction has been shown to be medically effective in reducing hypertension, heart disease, speech disorders, arthritis, diabetes and many other maladies, and is one of the few ancient ecstatic techniques, mechanized, reimbursed by medical insurance companies.[24]

The proprioceptive, self-sensing, state induced by many herbal inebriants is an ancient form of biofeedback, since most traditional herbal inebriants employ or trigger the human body's own neurotransmitters. These traditional herbal sacraments are therefore a direct threat to the production of stress and hysteria in the culture.

In India marijuana has been famous as a relaxant and aid to meditation from time immemorial, and has always been considered a religious sacrament. The rebellious Rastas, stiff-necked Ethiopians, also meditate with ganja, refusing to forget their ancient sacrament - and the musical genius that goes with it. Musical ecstacy, admittedly, is useless in Babylon, on the assembly line, but it does help to hold an African tribe together. That's why slavers hate ganja. Creative geniuses make lousy, and dangerous, beasts of burden. They're "addicts" - a word originally used in Roman law as a synonym for "slave."

Below, a Nyabinghi Tabernacle in Ethiopia, where everyone goes automatic African. The Ethiopians of Jamaica found powerful allies in the East Indian Hindu saddhus brought to Jamaica in great numbers by the British during the nineteenth century.

Jake Homiak, Smithsonian Institution

There is no doubt that hysteria and depression are major reasons why people turn to inebriants for relief,[25] just as there's no doubt that stress is a major precursor to illness. Euphoria, *recreational pharmakon* use, can be profoundly healthful, in that mood improvement wards off stress. This is intuitive knowledge, rooted in oral instinct.

The millions who go to the local bar on Friday night to socialize and drink beer, this culture's most popular herbal inebriant, are practicing instinctive social shamanism. Obviously, if the traditional herbs were legal, the concentrated alkaloids, with which it's easier to get into trouble, would be a lot less popular. Prohibition *promotes* the use of alkaloids, as the difference in the alkaloid use rates between pre-scribing and proscribing cultures so easily proves.

Jidda, Saudi Arabia, 1927; Edward A. Salisbury, *Asia*

Hundreds of millions of people know from regular personal ex-perience the feeling of relaxation, balance and creativity given by the occasional use of a beloved herb. "The principal function of the sha-man in Central and North Asia is magical healing. Several concep-tions of the cause of illness are found in the area, but that of the 'rape of the soul' is by far the most widespread... If shamanic cure involves ecstacy, it is precisely because illness is regarded as a corruption or alienation of the soul."[26]

I, however, have no legal right to the traditional tribal sacraments. I can't even go to my "personal physician," apparently my Daddy or

Mommy, and ask for some pot to smoke because I'm feeling musically uncreative; the request will be deemed "nonmedical." I'll be told to wait until I'm good and sick, and then will be given Prozac, which ain't what I asked for. The jive term "habit-forming" will be applied to my "nonmedical" request, as if garlic, salt, oregano and coffee weren't equally "habit-forming."

JAMA:6/1/94: The AMA "discourages and condemns illegal drug use and encourages physicians to do all in their power to discourage the use of illegal drugs in their communities and to refuse to assist anyone in obtaining drugs for nonmedical use."[27]

Dr. James Todd, the Executive Vice President of the AMA, is no Doc Simmons. This is not corruption. Today's *Journal of the AMA* is a relatively open public health forum. This is genuine unconscious culture-centric bigotry, with just a touch of commercial self-interest. The good doctor automatically assumes Papal authority to decide for me what is and is not healthful. The AMA, apparently my legal guardian, tells me that my personal herbal *curanderismo* is "self-medication" and will not be tolerated. That is, organized medicine literally, legally, owns the medicinal lilies of the field.

The symbol of the AMA is the Caduceus, the healing snakes entwined on the living tree. "Caduceus" is Latin for *Kerykeion*, the magical staff of the Snake Nymph Korykia, the ancient "bulb-mother" of "underground" herbal ecstacy (from *krokus*, "bulb").

Korykia, also known as Persephone, is the archetypal Greek midwife. Ancient Greek midwives carried the *Kerykeion* as their power symbol (see *Shamanism and the Drug Propaganda*). Hippokrates of Kos, *fl.* 400 BC, the canonical "first physician" who carried the *Kerykeion*, learned to induce his healing dream-state, known as incubation, at the feet of Korykia, as he himself readily acknowledged.

That pharmacologically-induced dream state, which was conceived as a return to the womb, was also called *ekstasis*, ecstacy. Dr. Todd, claiming to have taken the "Hippocratic Oath," will tell you that *ekstasis* is "nonmedical," because it is "recreational." Hippokrates would have thought that was as stupid as saying that, since eating a good meal is recreational, it is, for that reason, "non-nutritive." You're on the Assembly Line whether you like it or not. You can remember your Bulb-Mother, your connection to the Earth, your birthright, when you're dead.

Dr. Christine Hartel, associate director for neuroscience in the Division of Clinical Research at the National Institute on Drug Abuse (NIDA), expresses the pharmacological sophistry very well: "It's a plant. We don't hand out opium pipes to test morphine, and we don't think about using marijuana in testing. We isolate the active compound and test that."[28] That is the precise logical equivalent of saying that "we don't hand out spinach for eating, we isolate the vitamins and hand them out."

Hartel's sophistry, by far the mainstream attitude, is designed to render my *pharmakon* unavailable to me by analogizing it with refined isolates, which can be controlled commercially. Dr. Hartel is actually saying that whole plants, which cannot be patented, have no place in the monopolistic synthetic compound distribution system she helps to manage.

Herbal *curanderismo* is sometimes self-medication, not that it's anyone's business, but more often it is simply the ingestion of soul-food. Ecstacy is nutritious, and, like eating, and sex, it's fun. Is eating a good meal "non-nutritious" because it's fun? Was Marvin Gaye wrong, is good sex not healing?

Pharmacological fun was outlawed in 1962, when Congress passed regulations requiring "drugs," meaning most sacramental herbs as well as natural isolates or artificial compounds, to be *disease-specific*. If their efficacy for a certain *illness* couldn't be demonstrated, they couldn't be sold or prescribed. Most people who take sacramental herbs aren't sick and don't want to be.

The Controlled Substances Act, part of today's blanket federal law, blithely insists, on pain of agonizing legal penalties, that marijuana, peyote, ibogaine, mescaline, psilocybin and heroin have "no currently accepted medical use." It is no coincidence that these are some of the most historically important tribal sacraments, or their isolates. All, in fact, have volumes dedicated to their medical usefulness.

Schedule II of The Controlled Substances Act, which allows unrefillable prescription but criminalizes unauthorized possession just as severely as Schedule I, defines opium sap and coca leaves as identical to "any salt, compound, derivative or preparation thereof" - just like Wiley wrote it.

Possession of coca leaves, probably the best and safest tonic leaf on earth, would subject me to more severe penalties than possession of a bazooka. And I can't go into court, evidence in hand, and prove that a coca leaf is not a bazooka; if the Attorney General says it's a bazooka, it's a bazooka. Senator Phil Gramm's grandstanding amendment to the 1988 Anti-Drug Abuse Act actually mandated twice the maximum penalty for bringing drugs into prison, 20 years, than for bringing in a bazooka.

As the California State Supreme Court told Yun Quong in 1911: "The validity of legislation which would be necessary or proper under a given state of facts does not depend on the actual existence of the supposed facts. It is enough if the lawmaking body may rationally believe such facts to be established."[29]

That is, it is sufficient if the California legislature, or the DEA, can *imagine* opium harming the health of Yun Quong; whether it actually does so is not legally relevant. Nor is Yun Quong's own opinion of his private behavior, nor that of his physician. That is the ancient Roman *prohibitio*; it shouldn't be current law.

It is absurd to insist that if opium and coca were legalized we'd all turn into junkies. Before 1914 opium, coca and their alkaloids were completely legal and widely available. The Kolb and DuMez study of 1924, which covered the years immediately preceding Prohibition, shows approximately ¼ of 1% of the population of 110 million regularly using opiates, as opposed to four times as many today.[30]

Between 1895 and 1904, before the propaganda campaign began, *The New York Times* had no call to run a single story about cocaine abuse, despite the fact that it was freely available over the counter.[31] That lack of publicity, of course, is part of the reason there was so little "abuse." The other part of the reason is that Vin Mariani and the original Coca Cola were also freely available, and, given the choice, most people prefer the herbal-strength dilution to the refined alkaloid. The only practical effect of the criminalization of Vin Mariani has been the popularization of refined cocaine, the covert trade in which is controlled by our client armies.

Good Egyptians and Bad Egyptians, caught with their ancient sacrament, hashish; *Asia*, 6/1930

That his might be a reign of indolent gaiety, King Kalakaua bar-
gained away rich Hawaiian sugar lands, opium licenses and valuable
concessions, in exchange for loans from his foreign friends

Drug War

Propaganda

Prohibition is about economic and military power, not health or science. It was the geopolitical utility of medical monopoly that saw it come to pass. The Harrison Act was conceived in China, at the 1909 Shanghai Opium Commission, the idea being that America should pass a model "no license" law it could then ask other nations to adopt. President Roosevelt had arbitrated the end of the Russo-Japanese War only to observe Russia and Japan dividing Manchuria, Mongolia and Korea between them. With China beginning to industrialize on a massive scale, all the imperial powers were delighted to have a "pro-Chinese" issue they could sell while competing for China.

America, with never more than 2500 troops in China, had the weakest military position, and so led the fight for an "open door" and an end to the opium trade. The Chinese leadership had grown to hate opium because the British controlled the nationwide trade, and had used it as a lever to control China. Industrialization, however, with its mills, mines and railroads, had created different stakes. For America, Chinese cooperation in the industrial competition was essential. The weaker the British position, the stronger the U.S. The Chinese government encouraged groups like the Foochow Anti-opium Society, below, to express their politically correct feelings for the foreign press.

A COLLECTION OF OPIUM PIPES GATHERED BY THE FOOCHOW ANTI-OPIUM SOCIETY AND DISPLAYED AT THE CELEBRATION OF THEIR THIRD ANNIVERSARY.
Current History, October, 1924

Secretary of State Root rammed through the 1909 Opium Exclusion Act "in time to save our face at Shanghai," even though the USDA's Wiley said he didn't need it to exclude opium. The State

Department then asked Dr. Hamilton Wright, a member of the Shanghai delegation, to draft a more general, model no-license law it could then ask other nations to adopt. This uniform international effort would force the British to give up an important element of their power. The Chinese staged opium burnings.

Asia, March, 1931

Wright criminalized unlicensed distribution of "opium or coca leaves or any compound, manufacture, salt, derivative, or preparation thereof."[1] Lobbying Congress in 1910 for his new bill, Wright fretted about cocaine's "encouragement among the humbler ranks of the Negro population in the South.... it has been authoritatively stated that cocaine is often the direct incentive to the crime of rape by the Negroes of the South and other sections of the country."[2] That was straight out of *The Nigger*. Here you have the geopolitical, the economic utility of racist pharmacophobia. Wright wrote the editor of the *Louisville Journal Courier* that "a strong editorial from you on the abuse of cocaine in the South would do a great deal of good - do not quote me or the Department of State."[3]

The 1912 Hague Opium Convention, which grew out of the Shanghai Commission, committed the U.S. by treaty to Wright's law, the 1914 Harrison Act, a domestic law controlling opium and coca products.[4] Below, *Hearst's Magazine* revivifies the 1880's pulp legend of the roué Clendenin, in time to support Harrison. Domestic drug propaganda is still the tool of imperial foreign policy. Today the operative treaties, also engineered by the U.S., are the 1961 Single Convention on Narcotic Drugs, the 1971 Convention on Psychotropic Substances and the 1988 Vienna Antitrafficking Convention.

"There, in a bunk, lay Clendenin. His slow and uncertain breathing told of his being under the influence of the drug. He lay on his back beside a layout with a half-cooked pill still in the bowl of his pipe"

Hearst's Magazine, 1/1913

Tobacco is the number one killer "drug" in the world, by far, and U.S. companies are among the world's premier purveyors. In fact, the U.S. moves against any country that tries to restrict tobacco imports. Wrote Peter Bourne, Carter's Director of Drug Abuse Policy, to Colombian president Virgilio Barco: "Perhaps nothing so reflects on Washington's fundamental hypocrisy on the issue as the fact that while it rails against the adverse effects of cocaine in the United States, the number of Colombians dying each year from subsidized North American tobacco products is significantly larger than the number of North Americans felled by Colombian cocaine"[5]

The Philip Morris Company, Brown & Williamson, Lorillard and the other great tobacco companies sponsor the flag-waving Partnership for a Drug-Free America, prime producer of anti-marijuana TV ads. Other sponsors include the alcohol and pharmaceutical giants, and the ad industry dependent on their advertising. You won't find The Partnership for a Drug-Free America worrying about the world's number one killer drug, or about number two either.

Hamilton Wright explained the situation. He wrote Bishop Brent, his fellow delegate to the Shanghai Opium Commission, that the new Secretary of State Knox was "only now grasping the fact that in this opium business he has the oil to smooth any troubled waters he may meet with at Peking in his aggressive business enterprises there."[6] The other delegate, future President William Howard Taft, the inventor of "dollar diplomacy," likewise worried about "one of the greatest commercial prizes in the world.... the trade with the 400,000,000 Chinese."[7]

America's "aggressive business enterprises" were challenged head-on by anti-prohibitionist Eugene Debs, leader of the powerful American Railway Union. Debs' moderate, libertarian Socialist Party was the electoral umbrella for scores of left-wing groups, including the industrial workers in the Northeast; German and Scandinavian enclaves in the upper Midwest; the radical populists of the Great Plains; Big Bill Haywood's tough miners and lumberjacks in the Western Federation of Miners - core group of the IWW; Margaret D. Robins' National Women's Trade Union League, and Alice Paul's direct action National Woman's Party - the radical spearhead that actually forced through woman suffrage.

Debs' constituency included the awesome scholar and cofounder of the NAACP, W.E.B. DuBois; the seminal young genius of the civil rights movement, A. Philip Randolph; Margaret Sanger and her mentor, the pioneering psychologist Havelock Ellis; muckracking novelists Upton Sinclair and Theodore Dreiser; the intrepid revolutionary reporter John Reed; the firebrand stump speaker Elizabeth Gurley Flynn; the great writer Howard Fast - author of *Spartacus*; radical publishers Carlo Tresca and Max Eastman; historian Will Durant; populist painter George Bellows; socialite Mabel Dodge; theatricians John Sloan and Robert Edmond Jones, utopian socialist Emma Goldman; pioneering sociologist Thorstein Veblen and muckracking journalist Walter Lippmann.[8]

Obviously, no tightly-held ideology bound this diverse group, but they all shared a libertarian fear of bureaucratic collectivism, finding William James and John Dewey more useful than Karl Marx. They also shared a respect for working folks, a disdain for racism and sexism, and a hatred of manipulative prohibitionism, which enshrined the values of the assembly line. Big Bill Haywood, the most radical of the lot, dreamed of a time when "experts will come together for the purpose of discussing the means by which machinery can be made the slave of the people instead of part of the people being made the slave of machinery."[9]

It was their ideas of the minimum wage, social security and unemployment insurance that helped stabilize capitalism during the

Great Depression.

And it was Lippmann who warned that "the manufacture of consent" by the corporate owners of the media was a deadly threat to real democracy. As corporate hit-man Edward Bernays, "the father of public relations" put it, in 1928, in *Propaganda*: "The conscious and intelligent manipulation of the organized habits and opinions of the masses is an important element in democratic society. Those who manipulate this unseen mechanism of society constitute an invisible government which is the true ruling power of our country... it is the intelligent minorities which need to make use of propaganda continuously and systematically."[10]

Propaganda during these years meant William Randolph Hearst, who owned the most powerful chain of yellow journals in the country. Hearst built its core circulation, the Chicago *Examiner*, using Moe Annenberg's gunsels to hijack delivery trucks, bomb newsstands and attack newsboys. Hearst literally fought for circulation city by city.[11]

In 1910 Annenberg branched out for himself in Milwaukee, although the connection to Hearst remained. By the mid-twenties Annenberg owned *Racing Form* and *American Racing Record*, the basic betting sheets, and the General News Bureau, the wire service that provided up-to-the-minute race results. Without Annenberg's wire, bookies were an easy target for those who did have the latest results. Annenberg's full partner was Al Capone.

Lansky, Rothstein and Luciano

It was the national implications of Annenberg's racing wire that caused Capone to invite him to the first great modern Syndicate confab, the 1929 Atlantic City Conference, necessitated by the lucrative interstate trade, now a hood monopoly, created by Prohibition.

The New York turf war between Joe the Boss Masseria and Salvatore Maranzano was then going at fever pitch, and the bloodshed was bad for business. The 'Castellammarese War' was finally settled by two very dangerous young Turks, Meyer Lansky and Lucky Luciano. They flank their early financier, the legendary gambler Arnold Rothstein. Lansky and Siegel's Jewish hitters, able to pose as G-men, walked right into Maranzano's well-guarded Grand Central Station office and blew him away. Luciano's button men had taken care of Joe the Boss six months earlier - April, 1931. Capone had been one of Luciano's New York hitters before he was sent to Chicago.

As the official mob wire, Annenberg's Nationwide News Service, by the mid-30's, enrolled more than 15,000 clients in 223 cities in 39 states.[12] Hearst tagged along, always able to count on mob goons for "circulation." Hearst, in turn, always peddled the mob's "anticommunist" political line.

Hearst also owned Kimberly Clark-St.Regis, the paper and lumber conglomerate that is still busy gobbling up the competition. A major Kimberly Clark-St. Regis customer was DuPont, which converted Kimberly's wood pulp into explosives and synthetic fiber. Hearst was very progressive. The progressive thrust was the orderly organization of industrial monopoly, that is, industrial fascism.

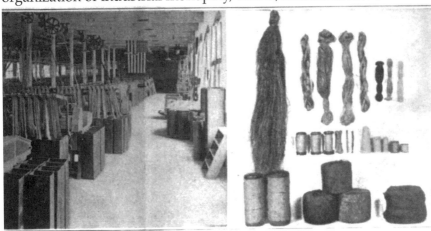

The products of a Michigan hemp mill; *Scientific American*, 6/4/1921

The economics of marijuana prohibition, brilliantly summarized by Jack Frazier in *The Marijuana Farmers* and Jack Herer in *The Emperor Wears No Clothes*, illustrate this fascism perfectly. Marijuana was one of America's most valuable crops in 1900. Much of the country's textiles, canvas, sails, rope, paper, paints, industrial solvents, lighting oil, machine oil, food oil and medicine was made from it. Marijuana was the raw material for fire hoses, ships rigging, fine linen, work clothes, good paper, candy, bread, bird seed and cheap energy.

The first American pot law, passed by the Virginia Assembly in 1619, actually required every farmer to grow it, since hemp rigging and caulking were deemed a strategic necessity. The Declaration of Independence and most of America's pre-Civil War books were printed on combination hemp/flax paper. Tens of thousands of acres were in regular production.

Scientific American, 6/4/1921

In the 1930's, the iconoclastic industrial genius Henry Ford had terrified his fellow industrialists by demonstrating that methanol from easy-to-grow hemp could replace gasoline. An acre of hemp yields 1000 gallons of clean-burning methanol, and it's far cheaper to make.[13]

Ford with his Hemp Car; *Popular Mechanics*, 12/1941

In *Popular Mechanics*, Dec. 1941, Ford's test car body itself was made from the tough hemp fiber.[14] The gasoline, sheet metal, synthetic fiber and plastics industries were not amused by the car Henry Ford "grew from the soil." They knew Ford was dangerous enough to invent them out of business.

Hemp, through ordinary pyrolysis, controlled burning, "cracking," yields charcoal, fuel oil, methanol and BTU gas, all without toxic emissions. The growing hemp consumes three times as much carbon dioxide as it emits during burning. This cheap, nonpolluting biomass is literally capable, now, of economically replacing most fossil fuels and eliminating much industrial pollution. As Herer puts it, "The plant is an annual that grows in all 50 states. It is the fastest growing sustainable biomass on the planet. It can produce paper, fiber, food and fuel."[15]

Not only could much coal and gasoline pollution be eliminated, so could the massive clearcutting of Alaska's forests for sale to Japanese paper mills. According to *Department of Agriculture Bulletin #404*, 1916, "Every tract of 10,000 acres which is devoted to hemp raising year by year is equivalent to a sustained pulp-producing capacity of 40,500 acres of average woodland." Hemp paper costs half of what tree-pulp paper costs to produce, and the production process is 80% less polluting.[16]

UNITED STATES DEPARTMENT OF AGRICULTURE

BULLETIN No. 404

Contribution from the Bureau of Plant Industry
WM. A. TAYLOR, Chief

Washington, D.C.   PROFESSIONAL PAPER   October 14, 1916

HEMP HURDS AS PAPER-MAKING MATERIAL

By LYSTER H. DEWEY, *Botanist in Charge of Fiber-Plant Investigations*, and JASON L. MERRILL, *Paper-Plant Chemist, Paper-Plant Investigations.*

Hemp cellulose was DuPont's original raw material for rayon, the first synthetic fiber. An extrapolation of the same process of nitrating cellulose was used by DuPont to produce its dynamite and TNT. DuPont supplied 30% of the explosives for the Allies during WW I, and is today's leading synthetic fiber manufacturer. Synthetic fibers, despite all the schmaltz DuPont puts on TV, are expensive, non-biodegradable, produced with polluting petrochemicals, patented, and capable of monopolistic control.

Hemp fibers and cellulose could economically, and ecologically, replace many synthetic fibers, building materials, insulations and plastic foams. As Henry Ford tried to make clear, there is no rational reason to be pumping millions of tons of toxic chemicals into the air each year. Biomass is here, now. The problem with hemp re-legalization is that the whole petrochemical and synthetic materials industry would be thrown open to massive small-scale competition, since high tech isn't needed to process hemp for many applications. The established chemical, plastics, lumber and paper giants are, to put it mildly, even more powerful than the established medical interests, so rationality won't prevail.

A DuPont operative, Hoover's Secretary of the Treasury, Andrew Mellon, engineered the legal destruction of the hemp industry. The first DEA, the Narcotics Division of the Prohibition Unit of the Treasury Department, was founded and funded by the Volstead Act of 1919, the enabling act of the 18th Amendment, Prohibition. The charter of the Narcotics Division, of course, was the State Department's Harrison Act of 1914, an original part of Prohibition's political package. The Harrison Narcotics Act was originally the responsibility of Treasury's Alcohol Tax Division, but went largely unenforced until the Volstead Act of 1919 funded the Prohibition Unit and its subdivision, the Narcotics Division.

The first chief of the Narcotics Division, Levi Nutt, held that job for ten years. But in 1930, Treasury Secretary Mellon appointed an Assistant Commissioner of Prohibition specializing in diplomacy, Harry Anslinger, to head Treasury's reorganized Bureau of Narcotics. Treasury's hopelessly corrupt Prohibition Unit was transferred to Justice.

"The Transfer"; Ireland in Columbus *Dispatch*

One of the straws that forced this reorganization reveals the actual dynamics of the situation: the indictment of Narcotics Chief Levi Nutt and most of his New York division by a New York Grand Jury, for being on the Rothstein/Lansky/Luciano payroll.[17] Nutt took over the Narcotics Division in 1920 under exactly the same circumstances: "Indict 3," below.

When the legendary gambler Arnold Rothstein was murdered by one of Dutch Schultz' hitters named McManus in 1928, his dying body was found with a small fortune in opium, morphine, heroin and cocaine - and all his carefully kept legal books, including the history of his relationship with Nutt.

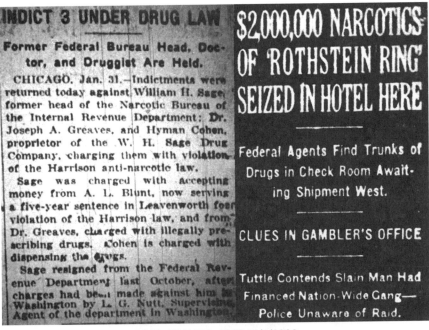

INDICT 3 UNDER DRUG LAW

Former Federal Bureau Head, Doctor, and Druggist Are Held.

CHICAGO, Jan. 31.—Indictments were returned today against William H. Sage, former head of the Narcotic Bureau of the Internal Revenue Department; Dr. Joseph A. Greaves, and Hyman Cohen, proprietor of the W. H. Sage Drug Company, charging them with violation of the Harrison anti-narcotic law.

Sage was charged with accepting money from A. L. Blunt, now serving a five-year sentence in Leavenworth for violation of the Harrison law, and from Dr. Greaves, charged with illegally prescribing drugs. Cohen is charged with dispensing the drugs.

Sage resigned from the Federal Revenue Department last October, after charges had been made against him in Washington by L. G. Nutt, Supervising Agent of the department in Washington.

$2,000,000 NARCOTICS OF 'ROTHSTEIN RING' SEIZED IN HOTEL HERE

Federal Agents Find Trunks of Drugs in Check Room Awaiting Shipment West.

CLUES IN GAMBLER'S OFFICE

Tuttle Contends Slain Man Had Financed Nation-Wide Gang—Police Unaware of Raid.

NYT, 2/1/1920; *NYT,* 11/8/1928

The rabid prohibitionist Nutt started his tenure as head of the Narcotics Division in 1920 with his son listed as Rothstein's attorney of record for tax matters with the Treasury Department, and his son-in-law operating as Rothstein's New York accountant and attorney.[18]

PICKS JUDGE NOTT TO TRY M'MANUS OCT. 8; BANTON ALSO PROMISES NEW EVIDENCE; TAMMANY MINIMIZES ROTHSTEIN ISSUE

La Guardia, Coudert and Enright to Be Called TRIAL PLANS ANNOUNCED
By Rothstein Estate Counsel to Bare Loans

It was Nutt's boss, Mellon, to the great benefit of Dupont, Hearst and their Syndicate allies, who ordered Anslinger to engineer the "Reefer Madness" campaign that criminalized marijuana. Mellon, through the Mellon Bank of Pittsburgh, was the major financial backer of DuPont and Hearst.

DuPont's 1937 *Annual Report* to its stockholders looked forward to "radical changes" due to "the revenue raising power of the government ...converted into an instrument for forcing acceptance of sudden new ideas of industrial and social reorganization."[19] From DuPont's perspective, that meant the replacement of the hemp industry with the synthetic fiber industry, the patents for which it owned. The "no-license" Marijuana Tax Act of 1937, enforced by Anslinger, criminalized the entire hemp industry, proving that the authors of DuPont's *Annual Report* knew precisely what they were talking about. Henry Ford's "car grown from the soil" had become virtually illegal.

MARIJUANA *Assassin of Youth*

Destroy It!

The American Magazine, 7/1937

The criminal-governmental symbiosis is a two-way street. If gambling were legal, who'd need Annenberg's gambling wire? If marijuana were legalized, the hood monopoly would be broken and marijuana would lose 95% of its value. The great hoods, geniuses at organizing street muscle, were *for* Prohibition, and Assistant Commissioner of Prohibition Anslinger was one of their major allies, operating the side of the street they couldn't independently run.

Alcohol and Drug Prohibitionist Anslinger, like his soul-mate J. Edgar Hoover, was in bed with the Mellon-Hearst-Annenberg-Syndicate hoods from the beginning. Anslinger always regarded Drug Prohibition as a tool for "social reorganization," fearing "communist" unions far more than Syndicate heroin gangs, who were, after all, Mellon's, DuPont's, Hearst's and Annenberg's patriotic strike breakers. They were also J. Edgar Hoover's most dangerous COINTELPRO operatives - right from the murderous Palmer raids of 1919, which Hoover organized.

J. Edgar Hoover pioneered the well-publicized destruction of "kingpins," brilliantly throwing a blanket of PR over his ineffectiveness and corruption. Hoover used the same ghost writer as Harry Anslinger, former circus press agent Courtney Ryley Cooper, the man who coined the phrase "Reefer Madness."[20] Cooper wrote flashy magazine stories dramatizing J. Edgar's fictitious personal encounters with "America's most wanted."

American Magazine, 1936

In 1939 Hoover decided that Lepke Buchalter was "the most dangerous man in America." This momentous decision was forced on J. Edgar when Lepke got himself indicted in 1937 for importing huge amounts of Japanese-KMT heroin from Tientsin.

Lansky, 1928, and Lepke, 1938, from NYC police files

Although the FBI had nothing to do with the investigation or the indictment, it asked Lepke's partners, Lansky and Luciano, to hand him over to Hoover personally, in the presence of Walter Winchell, no less, in exchange for anonymity and protection.[21] Lansky and Luciano wisely complied - it was good for business, and they were wise guys.

Lansky, Trafficante, Marcello, Giancana, Rosselli, Costello, Dalitz, Licavoli, Dragna, even the flamboyant Luciano never became FBI "Public Enemies" like John Dillinger or Pretty Boy Floyd, redneck pistoleros who never actually owned a Banana Republic. Of course, if Hoover's objective wasn't the suppression of organized crime but the suppression of political dissent, then he was, by his lights, acting correctly. Lansky was a dedicated "anticommunist."[22] Look how he helped Lepke "decommunize" the New York clothing industry. Look what he and Trafficante did for Cuba. Look how Luciano and Adonis helped clean the Reds out of Sicily. Look what Rosselli, Cohen and Siegel did for Hollywood's production unions. Look how Rosselli, a famous CIA contractor, cleaned up Guatemala. So far from going after the Syndicate or narcotics, Hoover's FBI consistently used hood dope dealers as red-baiting finks and antilabor street muscle.

Luciano's 1936 Arkansas capture; Bugsy Siegel, 1928, from NYC police files

The Red Menace wasn't just industrialist propaganda, it was Syndicate propaganda, as committed unionists knew all too well. One of the most menacing of the Reds, of course, was anti-prohibitionist Eugene Debs, who got 402,000 votes in the 1904 presidential election, coming in third to Roosevelt's 7,600,000. In 1912 he got 900,000, compared to 206,000 for the Prohibition Party, which started out as a postbellum Northern organization but ended up in bed with the KKK, strong vigilante enforcers of Prohibition during the 20's. By 1914 the Socialist Party had thirty members in twelve state legislatures, more than 300 city officials and one member of Congress, Victor Berger of Wisconsin.

The popular Debs stumped the country in opposition to the war, insisting that if industry supported the war it was only because it was to its tactical advantage to do so. This happens to have been the case. Corporate profits shot up 300% between 1914 and 1919, and leveled off at a spectacular 30% after the war.[23] Inflation, on the other hand, doubled between 1913 and 1920, completely wiping out the modest wartime wage increases. In 1919 a bushel of corn bought five gallons

Drug War

of gas; two years later it bought a half gallon.[24] Family farms went up for sale all across the country, gobbled up by gas companies. Eugene Debs, a farm boy, understood this.

Debs makes a whistle-stop campaign speech

The war created an administrative alliance between business and government that became institutionalized. Industry ran the War Industries Board, the Railroad Administration, the Food Administration, the Fuel Administration, the War Labor Board, the Committee on Public Information and the rest, setting national monetary, production, labor and propaganda policy. As Wilson said in 1917, "War means autocracy. The people we have unhorsed will eventually come into control of the country for we shall be dependent upon the steel, ore and financial magnates. They will run the nation."

Labor was treated to the Espionage Act of 1917, the Sedition Act of 1918 and a revitalized Immigration Act permitting the deportation of naturalized citizens. These were almost word-for-word repeats of the Federalist Alien and Sedition Acts of 1798. It became illegal to "utter, print, write or publish any disloyal, profane, scurrilous, or abusive language about the form of government in the United States, or the uniform of the Army or Navy." "False reports or false statements" which brought the government or military "into contempt, scorn, contumely or disrepute" became punishable crimes.[25]

In 1918, for his criticism of the war, Debs was thrown into prison for ten years. Prohibition's bitter enemy, the great libertarian lawyer Clarence Darrow, helped win a pardon from Harding in 1921.[26] Legally elected Socialists were refused their seats in Congress and the New York Legislature. The IWW was destroyed through imprisonment and assassination.

It was young J. Edgar Hoover, head of Attorney General Palmer's General Intelligence Division, who actually planned and executed the Palmer raids of 1919. Hoover netted more than 4000 Reds. Big Bill Haywood was sent to prison for twenty years, as were most of his surviving lieutenants. "America," said prohibitionist preacher Billy Sunday, "is not a country for a dissenter to live in."[27]

Sec. Daniels says: "The dry order helps shipbuilding."

Gen. Pershi

"BOOZE"
is the worst non-essential
STOP IT!

① Food   ② Fuel   ③ Labor   ④ Transportation

Brewers Waste Food   Brewers Waste Fuel   Brewers Waste Labor   Brewers Waste Transport

NYT, 11/3/1918

In 1919 there were 3600 strikes in the U.S. involving more than four million workers, and the strikers lost nearly every one.[28] The army and state police were used as strike breakers so often they became specialists in the job. In 1923 thousands of viciously abused coal miners in West Virginia staged the largest armed uprising in the U.S. since the Civil War. It took two divisions of the regular army to put it down. The great film *Matewan* accurately depicts the buildup to this short but bitterly fought guerrilla war. "You load sixteen tons and whatd'ya get, another day older and deeper in debt."

In 1920, Socialist Debs, from his jail cell, got nearly a million votes for president. His constituents considered Syndicate goons to be considerably more of a threat to society than coal miners on a Friday night binge.

The wartime head of the Committee on Public Information,

America's first official Propaganda Minister, was *Harper's* answer to *Good Housekeeping's* Harvey Wiley, George Creel, just before the war the most famous anti-patent medicine screamer in the country. Creel's 1913-15 series in *Harper's* is full of dragons, snakes and dead babies boiled in soothing syrup.

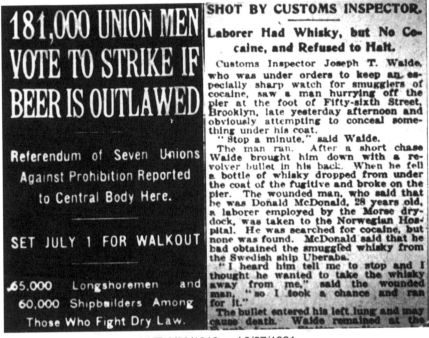

181,000 UNION MEN VOTE TO STRIKE IF BEER IS OUTLAWED

Referendum of Seven Unions Against Prohibition Reported to Central Body Here.

SET JULY 1 FOR WALKOUT

65,000 Longshoremen and 60,000 Shipbuilders Among Those Who Fight Dry Law.

SHOT BY CUSTOMS INSPECTOR.

Laborer Had Whisky, but No Cocaine, and Refused to Halt.

Customs Inspector Joseph T. Walde, who was under orders to keep an especially sharp watch for smugglers of cocaine, saw a man hurrying off the pier at the foot of Fifty-sixth Street, Brooklyn, late yesterday afternoon and obviously attempting to conceal something under his coat.

"Stop a minute," said Walde.

The man ran. After a short chase Walde brought him down with a revolver bullet in his back. When he fell a bottle of whisky dropped from under the coat of the fugitive and broke on the pier. The wounded man, who said that he was Donald McDonald, 28 years old, a laborer employed by the Morse drydock, was taken to the Norwegian Hospital. He was searched for cocaine, but none was found. McDonald said that he had obtained the smuggled whisky from the Swedish ship Uberaba.

"I heard him tell me to stop and I thought he wanted to take the whisky away from me," said the wounded man, "so I took a chance and ran for it."

The bullet entered his left lung and may cause death. Walde remained at the

NYT, 2/22/1919 and 2/27/1921

Three Babies Actually Killed by Soothing Syrups

Killed a Child in Seven Hours

"The child became peevish and cross. At eight o'clock A. M. the mother gave the child the first dose

Caused Twin Babies to Die

Two infants, twin babies, three months old, were given a dose of so-called soothing, sleeping "syrup"

LHJ, 4/1908

"Vin Mariani," wrote Creel dismissively, "ordinary Bordeaux red wine, strengthened by an alcohol preparation of coca leaves and sweetened with sugar."[29] In other words, after testing by its enemies, it proved to be exactly what Mariani said it was. The technique was to list the good with the bad, the invaluable herbal tonics right alongside the chemical shams, as if a high quality alcohol infusion of Mariani's selected coca leaves was as worthless as colored water.

The Ladies' Home Journal's answer to Wiley's commercial success was Edward Bok; *Collier's* was Samuel Hopkins Adams. In the early days of the propaganda campaign Bok and Adams would meet in Wiley's office to plan coordinated articles.[30] Subscription ads emphasized the importance of joining the anti-patent-medicine Crusade.

HELP!!!

The dog is valiant enough, no doubt. But he is a stuffed dog---stuffed with yard after yard of cunningly wound red tape---and what can a stuffed dog do?

It is all the more a pity, for the dragon isn't really unconquerable. He looks fierce, and he is fierce, but one growl from a dog with a real bite would terrify him back into his cave, where only the very foolish would venture. He's a coward at heart, and only stalks abroad because he knows the dog can't bite.

We Need a New Dog

So long as the present outworn, inadequate, sievelike Food and Drugs Act is our sole "protection"---the patent medicine fraud will go on exacting its toll of lives.

If you would like to know the remedy---read HARPER'S WEEKLY for the next few weeks.

2/1915

During the war Creel's Committee on Public Information launched the largest government-sponsored propaganda campaign in history, coordinating press and broadcast on both sides of the Atlantic, consistently portraying dissent as treason.

Incredibly, on Germany's surrender in 1918, Wilson and the Allies immediately rushed massive amounts of armaments to the Prussian militarists they had just defeated. The Spartacists had risen in Germany, taking Berlin, Munich, Dresden, Essen, Bremen and Dusseldorf, and the Allies knew they couldn't negotiate a reliable contract of reparations with them, so they backed the Prussians.

The revolt took the Prussians months to crush, and it is open to question whether they could have done it without Allied arms. Margaret Sanger's inspiration, Rosa Luxemberg, the birth strike advocate, died leading this revolt. Had we heeded the socialists and taken the opportunity to crush the Prussians once and for all, we would have saved ourselves the last great battle of World War I, World War II, as predicted in writing by Rosa Luxemberg on the eve of her execution by firing squad.

Chortled *The New York Times, á la* George Creel, December 12, 1918: "...in a few years more Germany would have been irresistible in war, for she would have made drug fiends of all the other nations of the world. Into well-known German brands of tooth paste and patent medicines - naturally for export only - habit-forming drugs were to be introduced; at first a little, then more, as the habit grew on the non-German victim and his system craved ever greater quantities."

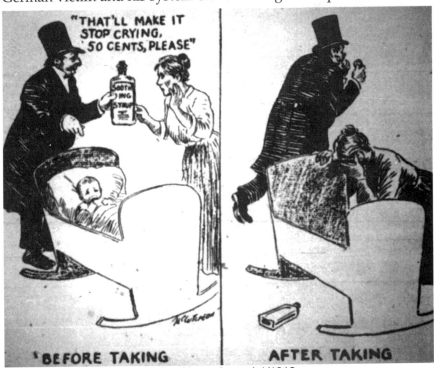

Ladies Home Journal, 1/1912

"Already the test had been made on the natives of Africa, who responded readily; if the General Staff had not been in such a hurry German scientists would have made their task an easy one; for in a few years Germany would have fallen upon a world which cried for its German tooth paste and soothing syrup - a world of 'cokeys' and 'hop fiends' which would have been absolutely helpless when a German embargo shut off the supply of its pet poison."

"But although the tale of this Teuton-all-too-Teuton scheme is probably a mere invention, Germany did concoct and spread through the world a habit-forming drug, and her leaders in this war have made good use of its ravages in other countries. More than half a century ago socialism was invented in Germany; and the rulers of the empire, foreseeing its vast possibilities in breaking down national morale, fostered its propagation abroad while they did their best to stamp out the habit at home.... Just as workmen in the tooth paste factories might have surreptitiously sampled the brands made for export only and found attractions not present in the products for the home market, so the Germans took to socialism and neosocialism. It is a rare poison that will not act on the system of its own inventor."

BOLSHEVISM AND BEER.

Even in dire extremes and amid the clash of arms, a German is still a German and a Bolshevik a Bolshevik. In the final hours of the collapsing Spartacist rebellion in Berlin, the last building to which the rebels clung with heroic tenacity was a brewery. Four or five hundred men sufficed for the garrison of police headquarters, the principal stronghold; as many held the Vorwärts office, but in the brewery the sons of Spartacus were massed by thousands, and many women among them. Heavy artillery was taken there from other positions, and supplies were banked up for a long siege. The Ebert Government

GERMANS SOLD DRUGS TO DEBAUCH SOLDIERS

Federal Authorities Arrest Two in Boston—Plot Included Many Cantonments.

BOSTON, Aug. 19.—A concerted attempt by German agents to supply soldiers in army cantonments with drugs has been discovered, Federal authorities here said tonight. Two men, Nathan Simalovitch and Jacob Schwanasky, were arrested at Brockton today, and more arrests are to follow, the authorities announced.

NYT, 1/16/1919, and 8/20/1918

That is almost exactly what Harry Anslinger told a Senate committee and the United Nations Narcotics Commission in 1951 about the Chinese Reds, holding up a bag of *Lions Globe* heroin he said they were shipping to our boys in Korea. This assertion was the basis of a major propaganda campaign that lasted for years.[31] Anslinger handled the press with the finesse of Creel himself. *Lions Globe* was actually the brand manufactured by our own Kuomintang allies, Chiang's boys, and the more entrepreneurial of the natives, also our allies, in the Golden Triangle, as our boys in Nam discovered, and as our own Bureau of Narcotics confirmed in 1972.[32]

In a famous 1959 case, Anslinger's top international agent, George White, an OSS/CIA operative, made a major heroin bust. It was Burmese Kuomintang heroin funneled through Hong Kong, bound for distribution by the American Syndicate. But by allowing the ringleader, a well-known member of San Francisco's KMT-organized Chinese Anti-Communist League to escape, White was enabled to claim that it was Red Chinese dope, "most of it from a vast poppy field near Chungking."[33]

SOUNDS WARNING: Harry J. Anslinger, U. S. Narcotics Commissioner, as he told Senate inquiry that Communist drug peddlers in South Korea and Japan had made addicts of undisclosed number of American troops. At right is David M. Key, an Assistant Secretary of State.

NYT, 7/18/1954

The Kuomintang is *for* Prohibition. Today we still arm the KMT, Burmese, Thai and Indonesian warlords, the Sicilian and Chinese gangs still own the docks, and the *Lions Globe* just keeps on comin', like toothpaste out of a tube.

And what is the rationale for our support of Asia's fascist dope peddlers? *Pharmacophobia: the demonic image of heroin* - successful, meaningless, scary, institutionalized *propaganda*: "The conscious and intelligent manipulation of the organized habits and opinions of the masses," to quote the father of public relations.

In 1920 the army's former chief neuropsychiatrist, Pearce Bailey, revealed in April's *Mental Hygiene* that "It is in them [heroin users] that mental contagion which leads up to hysterical mass movements, spreads with the greatest rapidity, and in their minds sedition finds an easier route than realism.... Suggestible, they easily become the tools of designing propagandists in spreading seditious doctrines, or in the commission of acts in defiance of law and order."

Dr. Alexander Lambert, of the Towns-Lambert method, President of the AMA and head of their "Committee on the Narcotic Drug Situation in the United States," amplified Dr. Bailey's insights in the *Journal of the AMA*, May 8, 1920: "We know that the misfit can no longer be ignored. He is too numerous; he has learned the lesson of organization; and he had learned through association means of cheap satisfaction that deaden for a time his elemental cravings, even though they return him to society more of a menace and a care than before."

"If he had 'nerves,' someday he will get a nightmare vision of himself as a piece of social wastage, a victim of conditions far more far-reaching than his individual life. When he becomes organized and vocal, society may awaken to the fact that he is an I.W.W., a bolshevik, or what not. He is not wholly to blame."

NYT, 5/6/1952, and [VA] *Daily Sun*, 3/19/1955

"If he finds his environment impossible to manipulate through lack of training, he will seek forgetfulness in some form of self-gratification. And some form is usually found in the unwholesome environment of the ordinary city street. If he comes in contact with those using narcotic drugs, they will find him responsive to imitation-suggestion./The correctional cases should be committed to institutions with no age limit - from the cradle to senility, if necessary."

Here we have the basic elements of today's propaganda barrage: political treason associated with drug addiction, peer pressure, street gangs, and three strikes and you're out. This inquisitorial equation of all ecstatic *pharmakon* use with illness and subversive mania isn't camp; this quack wrote today's drug laws, now administered by an army of careerist quacks with a vested interest in having "a clientage furnished through governmental coercion."

In 1930, years before fen-phen, *The Literary Digest* reported that the fluid from blisters raised on the heroin user and injected was a promising new treatment of interest to the AMA.[34] In 1931 *Scientific American* reported that the standard rabies treatment worked well on these mad dogs.[35] In 1932 two Cornell researchers reported that "washing the brain" with sodium rhodanate would help "thin the thickened blood cells of the addict."[36] In 1933, the year of repeal, three anesthetists reported that intravenous injection of grain alcohol was useful.[37] In 1935 Drs. Klingmann and Everts revived the Towns-Lambert method, with an emphasis on the scopolamine.[38] In 1940 two geniuses reported "curing" addiction with "frozen sleep."[39] In 1957 the Naval Medical Field Research Laboratory at Camp Lejeune spared an addict "the distressing symptoms of withdrawal" by severing his frontal lobes from the rest of his brain.[40]

Rabies Treatment for Drug Addicts

FREQUENT dog-bite cases from an Egyptian village led to the discovery that the villagers, addicted to narcotics, were resorting to subterfuge to gain access to a rabies hospital in Cairo, where they believed the treatment would cure their craving for heroin, according to a report made public by the Department of State.

The doctor in charge of the Cairo Antirabic Institute noticed a curious frequency of dog-bite cases from a particular village in lower Egypt. Usually in a large propor-

Why Brain Surgery Relieves Drug Addicts

> WHEN drug addiction has its origin in intolerable pain, the synthetic drugs usually utilized to relieve the distressing withdrawal symptoms are ineffective. In this case, brain surgery has been found effective.

The operation known as lobotomy, cutting of the connections between the frontal lobes and other parts of the brain, relieves not only the withdrawal symptoms but also the intolerable pain.

Sci.Amer.,1/1931; Sci.News Ltr.,2/23/1957

Today's Quack Commander in Chief, promulgating today's update of this same pharmacopropaganda, is the "progressive" Joseph Califano, a key CIA operative both before and after Kennedy's assassination, Carter's Secretary of Health, Education and Welfare, and now founder and president of Columbia University's Center on Addiction and Substance Abuse. Califano helps to channel a torrent of public money into 1930's-style politicized research, and coercive, Lambert-style "treatment." Califano's CASA is one of McCaffrey's major tools for coordinating national propaganda.

For Califano *all* drug use is a "disease," an "epidemic," to use his words, which, not so coincidentally, are the same as those used by the Pope in 1484 in *The Malleus Maleficarum* about "witches' medicines." Like so many Roman lawyers before him, the man is a genuine anthropological ignoramus. Not once in the psuedo-scientific *Radical Surgery* (1994) does he mention the origins of human inebriative behavior, tribal culture, or a single significant pharmacologist, anthropologist, ethnobotanist or psychoanalyst, although he insists that "substance abuse and addiction...is - the most devastating health pandemic threatening our people."[41] Apparently it's uniquely contemporary, like computer fraud. There's not a single scholarly annotation in the whole book, which is written on a tenth-grade sound-bite level. In fact, he quotes prosecuting attorneys as anecdotal medical authorities.

According to Califano, the absurd artificial value Prohibition gives inebriants, and the criminalization of people for simply trying to medicate themselves, in the absence of any sympathetic *curanderismo*, isn't the cause of today's street war. It's the act of self-medication *per se*, despite the fact that the leading sociologists insist, and can prove, that safe herbal inebriants, in cultures which teach their traditional uses, cause no social problems whatever. Califano will wring his hands about collegiate "binge drinking" and never once mention an empirical expert on alcoholism. His idea of an expert is "the [unnamed] president of one of the nation's top Jesuit colleges."[42]

His discussion of "The Rodney King Story" never once mentions the ruthless police beating of a helpless man to within an inch of his life. It was their acquittal, of course, despite that incredible videotape, that set off the 1992 Los Angeles riots. But Califano never mentions the beating, which so many felt symbolized their own experience. Instead, he focuses on King's drinking, concluding that "Months later, after the policemen's acquittal, the riots began - not at the courthouse or at city hall - but at Pay-less Liquor and Deli in South Central L.A. There, around 4 P.M., five angry gang members stole some bottles of malt liquor, yelling 'This is for Rodney King!' Around 6 P.M., an angry mob, pelting passing motorists, chose its first target for looting: Tom's Liquor store, from which the mob took more than a hundred cases of forty-ounce malt liquor bottles and ninety cases of sixteen-ounce malt liquor cans."

"The focus of the crowd should not be a surprise. As *U.S. News &*

World Report noted, 728 licensed liquor outlets smothered South Central L.A.'s crumbling landscape - an opportunity to buy booze around just about every corner."[43]

"Why, day befo' yeste'day I had a count made an' theah were three thousand four hundred an' sixty-seven idle niggahs in the fifty-nine saloons o' the levee district! That was the end, Clif, an' the long an' the sho't of it is - we're goin' dry!"

Califano prescribes legal coercion to force all users trapped by the law, about 5% per year of the total of about 30 million,[44] into a huge brainwashing bureaucracy, attached to the court system, that will pummel them until they submit. He plausibly advocates treatment over incarceration, accurately pointing out that "$1 invested in treatment saves $7 in crime, health and welfare costs."[45] But his "progressive compassion" is just as vicious as Lambert's.

He says he knows that "Addiction is a chronic disease, more like diabetes and high blood pressure than like a broken arm or pneumonia, which can be fixed or cured in a single round of therapy."[46] But he then suggests that "Instead of across-the-board mandatory sentences, keep inmates with drug and alcohol problems in jails, boot camps or halfway houses until they experience a year of sobriety after treatment."[47] He adopts Dr. Leshner's mainstream disease model, as he must to be plausible, but then advocates precisely the opposite therapy advocated by Dr. Leshner. Do we keep diabetics in boot camps until the diabetes goes away? Cigarette addicts? White man speak with forked tongue. This nasty hypocrite tells us that addiction is a chronic condition, and then proposes punishment for its sufferers, as the mainstream of drug abuse experts most certainly do not.

For Califano, addiction is really a "turpitude" to be corrected, not a symptom of a real medical condition requiring continuing pharmacotherapy. His medical compassion is simply a necessary pose. He repeats, as if it were a medical prescription, the Bush-Bennett *National Drug Control Strategy*: "That doesn't mean we should soften up the toughness required to get them to quit, such as threat of dismissal from a job or incarceration upon repeated relapse or violation of drug laws."[48] Just what an addictive personality needs - the stress of unemployment and the threat of incarceration. That's sure to promote sobriety. However one defines "addiction," I know of no physician who thinks denial of pain killers to those in pain, or imprisoning diabetics and denying them insulin, is medically indicated.

"The grim reality, shrouded for too long in our self-denial, is that any effort to provide all Americans health care at affordable cost is doomed to fail unless we mount an all-fronts attack on abuse and addiction involving all substances - cigarettes, alcohol, marijuana, cocaine, crack, heroin, PCP, hallucinogens, sedatives, tranquilizers, stimulants, analgesics, inhalants, and steroids."[49]

So far as I can tell from his book, that's his idea of all substances. Califano neither distinguishes herbs from concentrates nor use from abuse, even in the vast majority of cases that involve no abuse. A positive test automatically means "addiction to witchcraft." It is precisely this indiscriminate idiocy that popularizes the street alkaloids and cigarettes. The Secretary tells us that his personal model for all drug use is his compulsive, 28-year tobacco addiction, up to 4 packs a day when he was busy telling Lyndon Johnson victory is just around the corner in Vietnam.[50] Why wasn't he thrown into a halfway house?

Califano is apparently, or conveniently, unaware that the average marijuana user smokes one cigarette for every pack consumed by a tobacco addict, and that addiction to marijuana is medically unknown. Dr. John Morgan: "Of course, a 'heavy' smoker of marijuana consumes 3 or 4 cigarettes per day, while a heavy tobacco smoker may consume 40 or more cigarettes per day. This probably explains the rarity of reported carcinoma in marijuana smokers."[51] Califano sophistically equates pot with tobacco, and then insists that pot escalates cancer costs.

He dreamily insists that all traditional inebriative herbs are equally dangerous, and that all herbs are, magically, so to speak, as dangerous as the most dangerous isolates and artificial compounds. All inebriants, therefore, deserve no policy distinctions. This is also the official position of the U.S. State Department. Califano makes no connection between the unavailability of safe traditional herbs like marijuana, coca leaf and opium sap, which he never once mentions, and the wild popularity of relatively dangerous, but profitable to smuggle, street alkaloids like cocaine and heroin. Nor does he associate the unavailability of safe herbs with the popularity of poisonous crap like glue and PCP. On the contrary, he equates the herbs with the poisons.

Califano therefore advocates making crack worth an artificial fortune, and is then outraged when poor ghetto kids gang up to make it. Prohibition has created a multi-billion-dollar street trade run by kids cutting concentrated, amateurishly-produced alkaloids with sugars, procaine, baking soda, quinine, even poisons, forcing Uncle Joe to conclude that health problems from this garbage are ultimately caused by marijuana leaves. Califano informs us that teenagers who smoke pot are "85 times more likely to use cocaine."[52]

The intentional sophistry of this "stepping stone" statistic is disgusting. NIDA, the outfit he founded as Carter's Secretary of HEW, derived the "85 times more likely" snow-statistic in 1991 by dividing the proportion of U.S. marijuana users who ever used cocaine, 17%, by the proportion of cocaine users who never used marijuana, almost none, 0.2%.[53] That is a sociological, not a pharmacological measurement. By that measure, tobacco, gin or sirloin steak could be shown to be causative cocaine-use factors.

83% of regular pot smokers never used cocaine, but that's something Califano won't advertise, since that would demonstrate that marijuana is a "terminus" rather than a "gateway" drug. NIDA's own 1991 survey concluded that 68 million Americans had tried marijuana, but that there were only about 6 million drug addicts or abusers in the whole country, most abusing inebriants other than marijuana. In other words, according to NIDA's own stats, marijuana leads to very little abuse.

NIDA says that 17% of U.S. marijuana users have used cocaine at least once. The Dutch figure is less than one-tenth that; it's so small it can't even be accurately measured, which proves, obviously, that the supposed pharmacological connection between pot and coke is pure fiction. The connection is *sociological* - related to *public policy*, and proves the *exact opposite* of what the sloppy-thinking Califano is so hysterically trying to prove.

Here is part of the official end-of-year report from the Dutch Ministry of Welfare, Health and Cultural Affairs, 1995, signed by the Ministers of Health, Justice and Interior: "Dutch policy on the use of cannabis is based on the assumption that people are more likely to make the transition from soft to hard drugs as a result of social factors than because of physiological ones. If young adults wish to use soft drugs - and experience has shown that many do - the Netherlands believes that it is better that they should do so in a setting in which they are not exposed to the criminal subculture surrounding hard drugs. Tolerating relatively easy access to quantities of soft drugs for personal use is intended to keep the consumer markets for soft and hard drugs separate, thus creating a social barrier to the transition from soft to hard drugs.... The decriminalization which took place in the 1970's did not lead to an increase in the use of soft drugs then either."

"The view held by some that the use of cannabis products alone causes a physiological or psychological need to use hard drugs as well - what is known as the stepping stone theory - has been belied by actual developments in the Netherlands. Dutch young people who use soft drugs are perfectly well aware of the greater dangers of using hard drugs such as heroin and have no desire to experiment with them. In the Netherlands the percentage of soft drugs users who also go on to use hard drugs is relatively low. In light of these findings the stepping stone theory should be regarded as one of the many myths in circulation about the use of drugs, though one which under certain circumstances could become a self-fulfilling prophesy: by treating the use of cannabis products and hard drugs such as heroin and cocaine in the same way may in fact make it more likely that cannabis-smokers will come into contact with hard drugs. Moreover, equating the one with the other undermines the credibility of the information provided about drugs to young people."

The average age of Dutch heroin addicts is over thirty, that is, this policy, which has been in place for more than twenty years, has succeeded in radically reducing the use of heroin among the young. Holland now has less than one-seventh our rate of alkaloid abuse, and crime. "The fact that there are virtually no young people under 20 using heroin or cocaine in the Netherlands is extremely gratifying..." By refusing to distinguish herbs from either natural or artificial concentrates, Califano is actually *engineering* widespread concentrate use. And that, like it or not, is an historical function of military fascism, which has always been financed by the *Yakuza*, the *Mafia*, as I will proceed to demonstrate.

Remember Califano's other domino theory, the one about Vietnam? We could have *bought* the Vietminh for a tenth of the price we paid to lose to them. Do we really want to take national policy cues from one of the engineers of the worst strategic disaster in American history?

The Dutch know what they're doing. With this evidence in hand, The European Parliamentary Commission on Civil Liberties and Internal Affairs recommended to the full European Parliament, 1/29/95, continent-wide marijuana decriminalization, insisting that the legal equation of soft and hard drugs *caused* hard drug use.[54] The U.S. pulled out all the stops to prevent this political humiliation at the hands of the EP, which usually accepts the recommendations of its official commissions.

Califano is peddling his "devil-drug" for all it's worth, wringing his hands, crying in his beer for all those "crack babies." This talented propagandist, a master at hyping "new studies" designed to induce artificial hysteria, constantly repeats the phrase "pediatric pandemic," a great alliteration.[55] Fascism is always maudlin.

Califano: "Put the children of drug- or alcohol-addicted welfare mothers who refuse treatment into foster care or orphanages.... Subject inmates, parolees and welfare recipients with a history of substance abuse to random drugs tests, and fund the treatment they need. Liberals must recognize that getting off drugs is the only chance these individuals (and their babies) have to enjoy their civil rights."[56]

Dr. Wilder D. Bancroft, left, of Cornell University, and Dr. G. H. Richter, have discovered that drugs coagulate human nerve cells.
NYT, 1/16/1932

JAMA: "Media-generated hysteria over 'crack babies' has led to the imprisonment of women who use cocaine during pregnancy. Many health care workers believe that the fear of prosecution and imprisonment discourages many of the women who most need prenatal care from seeking it. Ironically, properly controlled scientific studies suggest maternal cocaine use may pose less danger to a fetus than maternal cigarette smoking."[57]

While cigarette-addict Califano does include some boilerplate about cigarettes and alcohol, he doesn't advocate criminalizing them, despite the fact that while only 2.5% of U.S. newborns may have some prenatal exposure to cocaine, 73% have some prenatal exposure to alcohol and 38% to cigarettes.[58] And while there's no medical doubt about the devastating effects alcohol has on a developing fetus, there's considerable doubt that cocaine is anywhere near as harmful. When the Yerkes Primate Research Center in Atlanta put pregnant rhesus monkeys on an intravenous cocaine drip for the entire duration of their pregnancies, all their babies were born perfectly normal.[59] The worst effect of prenatal cocaine use may be that users tend to smoke more cigarettes and drink more booze.

Califano: "Legalizing drug use would write off millions of minority Americans, especially children and drug-exposed babies, whose communities are most under siege by drugs."[60] That's funny, I thought they were under siege by the police. I can't remember the last time time I saw a pot plant smash a kid in the face with a nightstick, or shoot one in the back. Is that like Pope Gregory's "it's better to burn in this world than to burn in the next"?

The Idol of Both

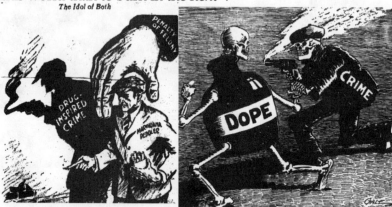

Times-Picayune, 6/5/1930; American Newspapers, Inc., 1938

All urban police departments, even if they won't mention the tension they bring to the situation, stress that it's the economics of Prohibition, the artificial underground economy, combined with the lack of opportunity, that is responsible for the gang warfare, not pharmacology *per se*.

Baltimore Mayor Schmoke, a former police officer: "Drug traffickers kill to protect or seize drug turf, and addicts commit crimes to get money for drugs. Almost half the murders in Baltimore in 1992 were drug related."[61] "When we say drug-related," explains Deputy Raymond Kelly of the New York City Police Department, "we're essentially talking about territorial disputes or disputes over possession.... We're not talking about where somebody is deranged because they're on a drug."[62]

Califano, and his clone McCaffrey, are careful to invert this, insisting, in classic reefer madness style, that by some demonic magic pharmacology is the reason kids are shooting each other over dealing territory. Collapse the price with legalization, and the violence will collapse instantly. By creating an underground economy and then demonizing the normal money-seeking and ecstatic behavior of the young, we instigate their murder. As Eddy Engelsman, the former Dutch Minister of Health, puts it, "The effects of heroin and cocaine use are too often confused with the effects of their illegality."

DENY FINDING OF GIRLS DRUGGED IN BASEMENT

Rector Street Merchants Call the Rumors Move to Hurt Trade of Lingerie Shops.

Rumors that from three to thirteen drugged and bound girls were found recently by the police in the basement of a Syrian lingerie shop in Rector Street, between Washington and Greenwich Streets, were strenuously denied yesterday by the Rector Street Merchants' Association, the police, a private detective and an official of a bank from which one of the girls was said to have been kidnapped. A desire to hurt the business of the lingerie shop owners on the block was given as a possible motive for the inception of the story by Abraham Lutfy of 21 Rector Street, who heads a committee of association members who are trying to track down the reports.

"In fact we have no basements," said Lutfy, "so how could any merchants hide girls in them? It's

Bert Longworth in "U. S. Camera"

"Have you ever seen that funny reefer man? He says he swam to China . . ." sings Cab Calloway

NYT, 3/6/1928

When I was 17, in 1962, a classmate of mine went down to north Harlem with a buddy to buy five dollars worth of pot and go to the movies. When they got busted, Steve's buddy panicked and made for the subway, where it's easy to hop one of the many trains flowing through the dense crowd. Just before the kid got to the stairwell the cop shot him in the back - dead. That is an absolutely typical Drug War story.

On February 21, 1995, the cops set up 16 year-old Lawrence Meyers at his Patterson, New Jersey housing project. The enraged kid panicked and ran, at which rookie housing cop Ronald Cohen shot him through the back of the head. According to Califano, Lawrence Meyers was more of "the debris of drug use on city streets."[63]

Country roads are also seeing their share of debris. In the middle of the night of April 28, 1995, in Wisconsin, four Dodge County troopers burst into Scott Bryant's trailer with no warning and shot him dead: "They rushed the door but they didn't holler anything. As soon as they kicked the door in, we heard the shot."[64] Bryant had offered no resistance, no firearms were found, and he was in possession of barely enough pot to make three joints. The idiots had simply worked themselves into a frenzy for the midnight raid and shot the terrified victim to death as he flinched. His stricken seven year old boy watched his Daddy die on the living room floor. "Liberals must recognize that getting off drugs is the only chance these individuals (and their babies) have to enjoy their civil rights."

If coca leaf preparations were legal, the mild, healthful coca leaf high, about as potent as coffee but far more delightful, would largely replace cocaine on the street. Until Decree 22095 of 1978 prohibited the possession and sale of coca leaves at altitudes below 1500 meters, cocaine use was virtually unknown in Lima.

Coca is the basic sacrament and medicine of Andean culture (see 'Leopards'). It is given to babies as a tonic and is used as a specific for altitude sickness, dysentery and various other complaints. When unavailable, it is not missed; there's no such thing as "addiction" to coca leaves. Califano handles this logical problem of his anti-legalization argument the same way NIDA chemists often do, by sophistically equating coca leaves with polluted street cocaine. He absolutely never mentions the leaves at all.

Like coffee, coca leaves are a work and concentration stimulant. They increase the efficiency with which the muscles use oxygen, as Freud demonstrated in 1884.[65] The Incas, working in the oxygen-thin high Andes, named their Goddess Mama Coca.[66] Coca leaves are the premier sacrament of Andean culture - and that's why they're illegal. Isolated cocaine has absolutely nothing to do with it. Coca leaves were immediately demonized by the Spanish on conquest, hundreds of years before the isolation of cocaine. *The Drug War is motivated by reflexive, unconscious cultural hostility.* That's why the pro-legalization rationalists are having such a hard time getting their point across, despite the empirical integrity of their case. Neurosis isn't susceptible to rationality - it is emotional compulsion.

Webster's Third New International Dictionary defines *neurosis* as "individual or group behavior that is characterized by rigid adherence to an idealized concept of the personal or social organism especially when that concept is significantly at variance with reality and that results in interpersonal, cultural or political conflict and the development of discomfiting intraorganismal tensions (the atmosphere of conformity, introduced by our present *neurosis*)." (Parenthesis theirs.) Califano has no more reason to demonize Mama Coca than Pizzaro had, or, rather, he has the same reasons.

The powerful *Confederación Sindical Unica de Trabajadores Campesinos de Bolivia*, the Indian union, insists on the distinction between "the sacred leaf," quite literally the Sacred Eucharist to them, and refined cocaine, as does the influential *Central Obrera Boliviana*, the largest trade union confederation. Native America is the majority down there, Euro-fascism or no. Has Joseph Califano ever sat down over a cup of coca leaf tea with an Incan shaman? Has he ever chewed a quid? He probably doesn't even think it's worth the effort; thinks he's got nothing to learn, or too much to lose.

Cocaine's or heroin's availability through physicians or licensed distributors, at 5% of street prices, would a) bankrupt all the smuggling organizations and therefore render concentrates unavailable on the street - and that is the only way to do that; b) economically force all concentrate users into the hands of medical professionals; c) leave those professionals free to prescribe as they saw fit; d) remove the milieu and incentive for armed robbery and turf wars instigated by the cost of illegal inebriants.

Herb legalization and controlled concentrate dispensation would also give the campesinos a legal market for, and partially collapse the price of, their most valuable crops. Crop substitution would then make some economic sense. End of Drug War. But does military intelligence really want the war to end?

Califano, a major military intelligence operative of the Vietnam War years, reveals his rank dishonesty when he asserts, in his 1994 book, that "Arguments for legalization are notoriously short on details. Would we legalize all drugs or only some? Could they be marketed like alcohol and tobacco? How old would you have to be to get legal drugs? Old enough to drive a car? Would you have to prove you are already addicted? Could drugs be sold in pharmacies? In every neighborhood?"[67]

Do you have to prove you're addicted to buy beer? Does any

sane person advocate drunk driving? Selling whiskey to eight-year-olds? Califano goes on with more inane staccato questions, prosecuting attorney style, always confusing traditional herbs with isolates and poisons, as if he were completely unaware of the large body of specific work, long on details, produced by so many.

These include Dr. Arnold Trebach and the dozens of reputable scholars contributing to the Drug Policy Foundation Press and the Drug Reform Coordination Network, which runs a definitive index at drcnet.org. Their index includes the National Organization for the Reform of Marijuana Laws, NORML, The Lindesmith Center, The Cato Institute and David Boaz' alcohol model of legalization,[68] and The National Drug Strategy Network, which runs a huge index of its own at ndsn.org. Amsterdam's Foundation For Drug Policy & Human Rights, at drugtext.org, also runs a vast network of easily accessible groups and information.

Professor Steven Duke and Albert Gross are the authors of the *America's Longest War: Rethinking Our Tragic Crusade Against Drugs*. These two brilliant lawyers and sociological thinkers presented their own detailed legalization plan in fifty pages of text. Am I to believe Califano never heard of this seminal best-seller on his subject, published the year before his own, or the work of so many others, long on details? This is intellectual dishonesty, overt lying.

Concludes Califano: "In his epic, *A Study of History*, Arnold Toynbee concluded that great civilizations are destroyed by self-inflicted wounds - not by enemies from outside, but from within. The threat from substance abuse is not the only internal threat our nation faces, but it is certainly as pernicious and costly as any other. Nowhere is this more evident than in the hospitals, emergency rooms, and doctors' offices crowded with its victims and in the trail of shattered lives and families in every part of our nation."[69]

Rep. Richmond P. Hobson of Alabama, 1911: "History is a record of a sad procession of world tragedies. Nations and empires in turn have risen to greatness only to fall. Before the death blow was struck from without the evidence shows in every case the ravages of a titanic destroyer within, under whose operations the vitality and strength of the nation were submerged in a general degeneracy."

"For centuries the world's philosophers and historians have looked on appalled, overwhelmed. Only in the last few years has science taken up the question. Following her patient, rigid methods, under which nature and life have slowly yielded up their secrets, science has at last cleared up the mystery and identified the great destroyer as alcoholic poisoning."

In 1925, Hobson, echoing virtually all of officialdom, including Califano, insisted that "Heroin changes a misdemeanant into a desperado of the most vicious type.... Narcotic addicts lose their soul-life. They sink to the level of the brute."[70] Hobson, like Califano, violently opposed maintenance clinics that simply prescribed the desired inebriant under medical supervision, that is, that were allowed to practice harm reduction or limited legalization.

Dr. S. Dana Hubbard, one of the chief clinicians at the New York City Heroin Clinic in 1920, pointed out that the huge numbers of addicts imagined by the alarmists "are mythical and untrue and...therefore the fear of a panic of these miserable unfortunates was negative."[71]

Even Lambert had to agree that strict enforcement turned up only about 7000 addicts in all of greater New York. Almost all of them were completely nonviolent, and, given a cheap supply of morphine or opium, law abiding. Despite the constant political hysteria, this has been the conclusion of every serious study of addiction and crime ever since.[72] As innumerable highly productive opiate users have demonstrated, given a cheap supply of opiates and a good work-study program, there is no heroin problem. Just as Vietnam, and we, would have been better off if we simply ignored it, so too would the "drug problem."

Dr. Arnold Trebach, after a learned consideration of historical policy and pharmacology, concluded that, ideally, a major part of *The Heroin Solution* would be precisely what Dr. Lester Volk said it was on the floor of Congress in 1922: the family physician and smoking opium - and an end to the artificial hysteria.[73]

Dr. Volk, the only physician in Congress, pointed out, on January 4, 1922, that the AMA's Lambert was a corrupt fraud, a co-proprietor of Towns' hospitals, studying "the different shades and colors, consistency, and solidity of the products of elimination by which the learned gentlemen administering the medication determine the exact status of the will power of the patient."

He noted that the two most famous American experts on addiction, Dr. George Pettey, who wrote *Narcotic Drug Disease and Allied Ailments* and Dr. Ernest Bishop, author of *The Narcotic Drug Problem*, were either completely ignored or under indictment by the USDA.

"As a substitute for open discussion of known medical facts there has been set up a propaganda for the incarceration of all drug users, their treatment by routine methods, and complete elimination of the family doctor. An undeniable effort is now being made whereby physicians are to be denied any discretion and power in the prescribing of narcotic drugs and to force all those addicted to the use of these drugs into hospitals exploiting questionable 'cures.'"[74]

ON THE HEELS OF "REFORM"

Chicago Herald and Examiner, 1926

In *The Medical Record*, Dec. 1921, Volk added: "For over two years the lay press has been pretty constantly portraying various spectacular, criminal, or morbid angles...of what is popularly called the 'drug

Drug War

evil.'.... The whole situation presents a picture of...strife, of influence, of power and of propaganda and publicity.... About the only undisputed fact...is the rapid extension of criminal and illicit 'underworld' smuggling and peddling, and the increase of addiction through its commercial extension..."

A million dollars worth of smuggled drugs seized in a single raid in Philadelphia

The price of heroin skyrocketed from $6.50 an ounce in 1913 to $100 an ounce in 1920, as Harrison enforcement began in earnest, according to police.[75] By forcing the physicians out, the USDA was enforcing an ironclad monopoly in favor of the hoods and their fascist military allies, handing them a completely artificial multimillion dollar trade they had every incentive to expand as rapidly as possible. Before the 1923 closing, on Narcotics Chief Levi Nutt's orders, of the prescribing Shreveport Clinic, the Shreveport *Journal* reported that the street trade in drugs was unknown, but that on the closing of the clinic, a lively underground trade had developed. This gave Arnold Rothstein, Meyer Lansky, Lucky Luciano, Frank Costello, Huey Long and their banana-republic allies one more game to run in Louisiana.[76] Do you think Levi Nutt, who had a business relationship with Rothstein, didn't know that?

The amount of California acreage devoted to wine grapes went from 97,000 in 1919 to 681,000 in 1926, at the height of Prohibition, because Prohibition had made grapes worth an artificial fortune.[77] In 1931 the presidential Wickersham Commission concluded that Prohibition had caused an *increase* in the consumption of alcohol.[78]

Marijuana, as everyone knows, is the number one cash crop in many states, despite the fact that it has to be grown surreptitiously. Can you imagine pot being the number one cash crop in $20 billion agribiz giant California? It is - simply because of the intense demand for it - people absolutely love it - and because of the artificial value given it by Prohibition. Pot is also the leading cash crop in Alabama, Colorado, Hawaii, Kentucky, Maine, Rhode Island, Tennessee, Virginia, and West Virginia. It ranks as one of the top five cash crops in 29 other states. The 1993 wholesale value, $16 billion, of the nation's top legal crop, corn, was rivalled only by soybeans, hay and the artificial Prohibition-value of pot.[79]

In their frustration, the Prohibitionists have responded with an inquisitorial lethality that should scare the hell out of everyone: "I think Montanans and indeed all Americans will be shocked to hear that a crop-killing fungus is being genetically engineered and tested in our communities," said Montana NORML Director John Masterson [8/12/99]. "What's particularly abhorrent about the cannabis-killing manufactured organism being created in a Montana laboratory is the fact that the Montana House of Representatives just passed a pro-industrial hemp resolution with a 95-4 vote."

Fusarium oxysporum is of the same strain that Florida state drug czar Jim McDonough wants to use to eradicate cannabis, despite claims that the fungus could easily become lethal to much of the rest of Florida agriculture. "This 'Jurassic Park' idea that the mutant fungus will simply go away after it has rid the United States of cannabis is contrary to all we know about biology and evolution," said Tom Dean, Esq., NORML Foundation Litigation Director. "What will prevent the fungus from spreading to other countries where industrial hemp is an essential part of their economy? How do we stop the fungus from evolving into a tomato or wheat killer?"

This lunacy has become institutionalized. The U.S. Defense Department has developed, it insists, a strain of *Fusarium oxysporum* that attacks only coca leaves. Agence France Presse reports, 3/8/2000, that the UN International Drug Control Program is now negotiating "field trials" with the Colombian government as a preliminary to massive "Agent Orange" type operations throughout Colombia.

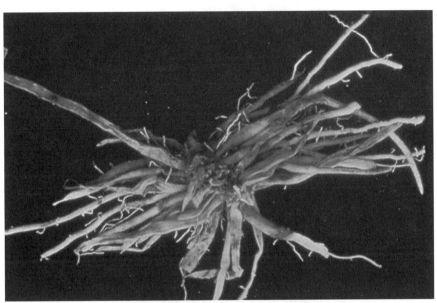
Asparagus killed by *Fusarium oxysporum*
Hypermedia en Protection des Plantes (section pathologie); Association de coordination technique agricole, Paris
www.inra.fr/USER/PRODUCTIONS/BDD/HYP3/pathogene/6fusoxa.htm

Free Burma!@http://metalab.unc.edu/freeburma

Drug War

Neocolonialism

Coffee prices multiply approximately 3-fold from producer's wholesale to retail. Heroin multiplies approximately 200-fold from its Prohibition-inflated wholesale price to retail.[1] Heroin now retails, by weight, for 10 times the price of gold.[2] That, of course, makes it the basis of military power in Burma.

Military power is built on money, and, thanks to Prohibition, drug trafficking is the most profitable business on the planet. As the State Department itself puts it, in its end-of-year 1996 Enforcement Affairs report, "In terms of weight and availability, there is currently no commodity more lucrative than drugs. They are relatively cheap to produce and offer enormous profit margins that allow the drug trade to generate criminal revenues on a scale without historical precedent."

As anyone who has grown it knows, pot is as cheap and easy to grow as corn or squash, and can be mass-produced for a few dollars a pound. A *legal* pound of primo pot would retail for about $300. An *illegal* pound of primo pot now retails for about $3000.

The U.N estimates the global drug trade in the early 1990's to be worth 400 billion untaxed dollars a year.[3] In 1994 Apolinar Biaz-Callejas of the Andean Commission of Jurists put it at $460 billion. That's about one-tenth of all global commerce. The legal value of that trade would be about a tenth of that.

The Guardian Weekly, 7/14/99: "The world's organised criminals have a greater economic output than Britain, according to a United Nations report. Their turnover is now greater than all but three of the world's economies."

"The UN's 1999 Human Development Report estimates that organised crime syndicates gross more than $1,500bn a year. The UK's economic output is just over $1,200bn. The report says the syndicates' economic power rivals that of multinational corporations."

"The biggest growth area is drugs, which is now a bigger global industry than motor manufacturing. Over the past 10 years, the production of opium has more than tripled and the production of coca leaves has doubled. The illegal drug trade - supplying 200m customers - is worth around $400bn, or 8% of world trade."

According to the research arm of the U.S. Department of Justice, "drug traffickers launder an estimated $100 billion per year in the United States."[4] Biaz-Callejas estimated "$260 billion, which is circulated through its [the U.S.] financial system, in contraband, and through other ways."[5]

Since military power is built on money, and since governments, or at least relations between governments, are built on military power, the structural effect of the artificial value has been to create, over the decades, an unbreakable symbiosis between drug-dealing and covert military intelligence. Each is the greatest strategic ally of the other. The political effect has been the institutionalization of global industrial fascism, death-squad genocide, wherever campesinos threaten to take control of their own land. I speak of Burma, Guatemala, the Philippines, Argentina, Mexico, Peru, Bolivia, Paraguay, Indonesia, Malaysia, Afghanistan, Pakistan, Uruguay, Congo, Liberia, Nigeria - the list is endless.

If they're lucky, these police states will evolve into propaganda-managed neofascist "democracies" that "reeducate" rather than assassinate. That's the preferred American model, like El Salvador after the U.S.-induced genocide. The fascist drug smugglers of ARENA are still in control, but with a "democratic" image, to use the appropriate Stalinist term.

Thanks to the peace accord signed on 12/29/96 by Guatemalan President Alvaro Arzu and leftist rebel leaders, Guatemala is now also a "democracy." The drug-dealing army that conducted the genocide is still in control of state machinery, but with a spruced-up image that will allow continued massive U.S. military assistance. That is, the peace accord will guarantee that the flow of drugs from the Guatemalan military will remain uninterrupted.

The Guatemalan National Police parade with anti-civilian riot gear, 1995

The image of the "democracies" will be reinforced through massive propaganda, legal coercion, imprisonment and *selective* assassination, rather than the clumsy, counterproductive genocide the Guatemalan or Salvadoran military had previously preferred. As in the

U.S., the propaganda barrage, backed by the threat of imprisonment, property confiscation and "reeducation," is said to reduce "demand." And, as in the U.S., "demand" is reduced selectively, politically, using a "profile."

According to the U.N. Drug Control Program, the biggest heroin and cocaine trading institutions in the world are the Burmese, Pakistani, Mexican, Peruvian and Colombian militaries - all armed and trained by U.S. military intelligence - in the name of the antidrug effort, of course. Funny how all that effort never has any strategic effect.

The centers of power controlling the trade in these demanded global commodities are the same centers of power disseminating the artificial hysteria necessary for their continued criminalization. That keeps the retail price a hundred times higher than the legal value and the trade exclusively in the hands of *the muscle.*

Another name for *the muscle* is *military intelligence.* The $500 billion dollar drug trade is run by allies we train and arm. The CIA, in its operational guidelines, actually emphasizes that its interest in the drug business is confined to the effect that business has on geopolitical power. Operationally, that has meant that the CIA's dope-dealing Batista was no more an aberration than Somoza, or Diem, or Ne Win, or Chiang, or the Shah, or Marcos, or Salazar, or Papadopoulos, or Stroessner, or Mobutu, or Amin, or Videla, or Noriega, or Cedras, or Samper, or Salinas, or Suharto, or Fujimori.

The Civil Police Administration (CPA), created in 1955, was headed by the CIA's Byron Engle. Engle had helped to bring the Japanese police up to snuff under MacArthur and thereafter trained numerous police and intelligence agencies. In Japan Engle worked with Maj. Gen. Charles Willoughby, MacArthur's G-2 chief, using the dope-peddling *Yakuza* gangs as goons against leftist unions.[6] This meant, of course, that, to that extent, the *Yakuza* were licensed to operate. In the 50's Engle coordinated CPA training at the Inter-American Police Academy in the Canal Zone with the International Association of Chiefs of Police.

Under Kennedy, Engle's outfit turned into the Office of Public Safety (OPS) within the Agency for International Development (AID), spending hundreds of millions training and supplying police in at least 50 countries. Engle's grad school was the International Police Academy in Georgetown. The great democrats of South Vietnam, Panama, Guatemala, Argentina, Paraguay, Bolivia, Chile, El Salvador, Haiti, Uruguay, Venezuela, Brazil, Mexico, Nicaragua, Greece,

Burma, Thailand, Malaysia, Liberia, Uganda, Zaire, etc. graduated from Engle's "school for torture."[7]

It was protested, as assistant secretary of state Elliot Abrams did in 1984 before a Congressional subcommittee investigating police torture, regularly practiced by all the above, that "if they learned a little bit more about modern professional police tactics, they would be more effective and more compassionate."

It is perfectly true that the CIA knows that structural fascism, with a velvet glove, is far more long lasting than dirty-war-style bloodletting. Computerization can save a lot of interrogational sweat. But two academic experts on the evolution of the OPS, Cottam and Marenin, reveal the intentions of the training: "State Department officials and OPS advisors tended to argue for a civil police force subject to law, public demands, and legally instituted political authority. Civil, democratic police forces are visible, dispersed, and accessible; their members live among the people and conduct their work in the open. They use arms and force sparingly and concentrate on maintaining order, controlling crime, and providing services."

"In contrast, U.S. officials working for secret and military agencies tended to argue for a paramilitary, intelligence-oriented counterinsurgency police force. Such forces tend to be concentrated for easy command: they are armed, secretly or openly repressive, concerned with gathering intelligence, and subject to direct political control."[8]

Professor Nadelmann adds, "Despite efforts to reconcile these two models, Cottam and Marenin observed, the paramilitary one ultimately prevailed.... Although often scorned by CIA agents abroad as just police trainers, OPS advisors in many countries developed close relationships with the CIA, provided occasional cover for intelligence operations, and pursued similar goals."[9]

Since "insurgency" usually meant the reluctant rebellion of tortured campesinos who had no other option, "counterinsurgency" meant the repression of tortured campesinos. That was the OPS paramilitary curriculum. The U.S. Army coordinated its counterinsurgency training with the OPS at its School of the Americas at Fort Benning, Georgia, founded in 1946 in Panama and moved to Georgia in 1984. Among its 60,000 Latin graduates it numbers Anastazio Somoza of Nicaragua, Manuel Noriega and Omar Torrijos of Panama, Leopoldo Galtieri and Roberto Viola of Argentina, Juan Velasco Alvarado of Peru, Guillermo Rodriguez of Ecuador, Hugo Banzer Suárez of Bolivia, Michel Francois of Haiti, Roberto D'Aubuisson of El Salvador and Julio Roberto Alpirez of Guatemala.

The politic Clinton administration, on June 28, 1996, released the report of its Intelligence Oversight Board: "The Army School of the Americas . . . used improper instruction materials . . . certain passages appeared to condone practices such as executions of guerrillas, extortion, physical abuse, coercion, and false imprisonment." As Clinton's continued support for the military fascists in Indonesia, Burma, Peru, Colombia, etc. proves, that understatement was just a "partial hangout," intelligence damage control, not a basic policy shift.

Guatemala is the archetypal CIA-OPS operation, a real pattern-setter. In October of 1944 a popular coup led by liberal young army officers finished the brutal 14-year dictatorship of General Jorge Úbico. In March of 1945, Dr. Juan Arévalo, an idealistic scholar, was elected president with 85% of the (literate male) vote.[10] Arévalo's political hero was Franklin Roosevelt, whose "four freedoms" - freedom of speech, freedom of religion, freedom from want and freedom from fear - became the basis of his political program.

The triumvirate that led the 1944 coup: Major Francisco Arana, Jorge Toriello and Captain Jacobo Arbenz; Rafael Morales

Arévalo aimed at land reform, unionization, education and permanent political democracy. In the 1951 elections Arévalo was replaced by his Defense Minister, 41 year old Jacobo Arbenz, one of the engineers of the 1944 October Revolution that brought electoral democracy to Guatemala. Arbenz was elected with the votes of 63% of an electorate that now included literate women.[11] The problem with the brilliantly competent Arbenz was that he proceeded to do everything Arévalo had so eloquently promised.

Following the plan outlined for him by no less a radical organization than the World Bank (The International Bank for Reconstruction and Development), Arbenz began the construction of a publicly-owned port on the Atlantic coast to compete with United Fruit's Puerto Barrios, until then the only Atlantic port in Guatemala. Likewise Arbenz began the construction of a national Pacific-to-Atlantic highway to compete with United Fruit's railroad monopoly, IRCA.

Arbenz nationalized *nothing* except some unused rural land. He left all businesses in place, but set out to break the most destructive monopolies, what he called "feudalism," by competing with them, creating a "a national and independent capitalism."

He began the construction of a government-run hydroelectric facility to compete with the Fruit-run monopoly and also initiated rural electrification and telephone service. These were, of course, the same infrastructure techniques that had been used to build the United States. Private enterprise built *none* of our highways, public schools or harbors, and almost all of our seminal railroads and hydroelectric facilities were publicly financed.

Arbenz then challenged United Fruit's rural slave-labor system, which dominated 90% of the country's 3 million people, 60% of them Indians, and most of the rest mestizos, known as *ladinos*.[12] The 1952 Agrarian Reform Law aimed mostly at plantations larger than 670 acres, although *fincas* of over 223 acres were vulnerable if more than a third of the land was unused. Arbenz confiscated only unused arable land, distributing 1.5 million acres to thousands of landless families, in 42 acre plots.[13] Arbenz himself, his extraordinary Salvadoran wife and his Foreign Minister, lost thousands of acres.

The key term here is "landless," since 1934 a Guatemalan legal definition that required "landless" peasants to work 150 days a year for private growers or the state whether they wanted to or not. This was a cosmetic "reform" urged on Úbico by the Rockefeller Foundation, which found the medieval debt bondage then in place too transparent. Úbico had come to power in 1931 with the help of the State Department and the Rockefeller Foundation, which preferred him to the nationalists that threatened to take over.[14]

Thus, by law under Úbico, landless peasants were forced to accept whatever wages were offered, such as room and board for the harvest season, which left them nothing to show for their work and nowhere to live afterwards. The Labor Department was part of Úbico's National Police, so that those breaking the "labor" laws found themselves facing Úbico's Nazi-loving killers.[15]

Arbenz at his inauguration; Rafael Morales

Arbenz used Arévalo's 1947 Labor Code, which was based on Roosevelt's Wagner Act. It insisted on the right of plantation workers to unionize, strike and bargain collectively. For the first time in Guatemalan history, the campesinos had military protection. Arbenz established rural cooperatives, public schools, public clinics, public buses and local cultural institutions.[16] Everything Arbenz did, in fact, conformed to John Kennedy's 1961 Alliance for Progress model.

One of the designers of the Alliance for Progress, Kennedy's Special Assistant Arthur Schlesinger, wrote in 1946: "All across Latin America the ancient oligarchies - landholders, Church, and Army - are losing their grip. There is a ground swell of inarticulate mass dissatisfaction on the part of peons, Indians, miners, plantation workers, factory hands, classes held down past all endurance and now approaching a state of revolt."[17]

Like Arbenz, Schlesinger understood that the key to political stability was economic, so he looked to the inclusive social democratic parties, which built from the ground up. Kennedy would have given Arbenz all the help he could, in order, as Schlesinger put it, "to check *Peronismo* and Communism." Dulles, quite literally, chose *Peronismo*. At the 1950 Inter-American Association for Democracy and Freedom, meeting in Havana, Arthur Schlesinger met Ròmulo Betancourt of Venezuela, Juan Bosch of the Dominican Republic and Salvador Allende of Chile.

Practicing sweat-equity free-enterprise, Arbenz immediately put the confiscated land into production by providing government-run support systems, as Roosevelt had done. He instituted no political repression of any kind in a mixed economy that was, for the first time, beginning to grow by leaps and bounds. United Fruit, Ike and the Dulles brothers insisted that this constituted "Communism in the Caribbean" and "a Russian toehold" in the hemisphere.[18]

Guatemala, of course, had virtually no relations at all with Russia. The Communist Party, in fact, had been the only party that remained illegal under the idealistic libertarian Arévalo, who insisted that communism was "contrary to human nature." Arbenz' Revolutionary Action Party legalized the Communist Party (PGT) in 1951, and it held 4 of 56 seats in Congress.

Since Arbenz was serious about land reform, he put committed Marxists, whom he trusted not to sell out, in charge of administering the Agrarian Reform program. But they were bound by the strictures of the law, and the basis of that law was sweat-equity free-enterprise. The market that the campesinos were encouraged to enter was just that, a free market. Arbenz' Agrarian Reform Program was his idea of a rural Small Business Administration. He was succeeding in rendering thousands of campesinos economically independent, creating a genuinely nationalist, capitalist alternative to corporate colonialism. What the U.S. proceeded to do, however, convinced the 25 year-old Argentine doctor Ché Guevara, who was part of this, and quite a few others, that militaristic communism was indeed the only alternative to United Fruit.

United Fruit, with 550,000 acres the country's largest landowner, and with 40,000 workers the largest employer, had become the leader of the old Spanish aristocracy, which owned most of the rest of the country, including the Church. The Papal Nuncio, Monsignor Gennaro Verrolino, became a key anti-Arbenz activist. Like the aristocracy, the Church was accustomed to ministering to Indians who were on their knees.

United Fruit was accustomed to government-guaranteed low wages, total exemption from sales taxes and regulation, and duty-free import of all supplies.[19] Arbenz, it was clear, intended to break both United Fruit's stranglehold on the nation's economy and its racist slave-labor system.

Arbenz seized nearly 400,000 of United Fruit's 550,000 acres, all unused, and all originally seized from the Indians. He compensated United Fruit in government bonds based on the company's own radically deflated 1952 book value, which the company had used to lower its already miniscule land taxes. The company was enraged, and the company was led by Sam "the Banana Man" Zemurray, one of the craftiest and most dangerous fighters ever to rise from the streets of New Orleans.[20]

Zemurray's team included not only his Mafia partners on the New Orleans docks, led by the deadly Carlos Marcello, but the Boston Brahmin Thomas Cabot, for a short while a president of United Fruit. Thomas Cabot was the brother of John Moors Cabot, the Assistant Secretary of State for Inter-American Affairs.[21] Another major Fruit stockholder was Senator Henry Cabot Lodge, who violently denounced Arévalo's unionism from the Senate floor in 1949.[22]

Both Secretary of State John Foster Dulles and his brother Allen Dulles, CIA Director since 1953, were major Fruit stockholders. Through their law firm, Sullivan and Cromwell, they had helped arrange, through Schroeder Banking, the 1936 United Fruit takeover of Guatemala's rail system, the International Railways of Central America, IRCA.[23]

Allen Dulles was a director of the British-based Schroeder Banking Ltd, which he had turned into a key conduit of CIA funds. United Fruit was, therefore, a *de facto* CIA proprietary. When the Dulles brothers engineered the destruction of the Mossadegh government in Iran in 1953, the largest corporate beneficiary was the denationalized Anglo-Iranian Oil Company, largely controlled by Schroeder Banking.[24] Like Arévalo, Mossadegh had in fact refused to legalize the Communist (Tudeh) Party.[25] Mossadegh's threat was economic nationalism, not the communism the Dulles brothers had falsely accused him of. Like Arbenz, Mossadegh was a liberal democrat replaced by a murderous fascist dope peddler. The results, as we have seen, have not been happy.

In 1939, as England and France were fighting for their lives, the Dulles brothers' law firm, Sullivan and Cromwell, refused to close their German offices. In 1940, John Foster Dulles, through Sullivan and Cromwell, arranged dummy Swedish ownership of the U.S. branch of the German Bosch engine-parts company. This enabled the Nazis to maintain actual ownership - and operatives in key U.S. defense installations.[26]

Allen Dulles was the Schroeder representative in Germany before the war. Since he had extensive contacts in the German business community, and the cover of actually working for them, he was tapped to establish the Office of Strategic Services base in neutral Switzerland in 1942, making it through the border literally on the last train before the Germans sealed it. He executed some spectacular German infiltrations, intelligence coups and surrenders, dealing with anonymous moles as well as the likes of Himmler, Canaris and Gehlen. He also executed the survival of significant parts of the Nazi machine.

The May 1945 tactical surrender of Hitler's best intelligence officer, 40 year-old Reinhard Gehlen, was regarded as a windfall by American military intelligence. Gehlen had not only microfilmed all his Eastern-front records, but preserved his entire operating intelligence organization, which was strongest where the OSS was weakest - in Russia. Gehlen ran a large cadre of in-place Russian monarchists and death squad butchers, called the Vlasov Army, who now went to work for Allen Dulles' U.S. Secret Intelligence Branch in Germany.

Gehlen also ran Ukranian, Latvian, Lithuanian, Byelorussian, Albanian, Estonian and other East European former Waffen-SS units, so-called "forces of national liberation." They weren't humanitarians, reasoned the U.S. high command, but they *were* anticommunist. Assisting Dulles were Frank Wisner and Richard Helms.[27] As former OSS Bucharest bureau chief, Wisner had contested control of Romania with Stalin, and was Gehlen's chief contact during his tactical surrender to the U.S.

Gehlen was personally escorted to the U.S. by Eisenhower's chief of staff., General Walter Bedell Smith, on Ike's own VIP aircraft.[28] Assisting Smith was Colonel William Quinn, future head of the Defense Intelligence Agency. Gehlen's U.S. headquarters, fittingly, were at Pullach, a former *Waffen-Schutz Staffel* ("Armed-Defense Forces") training center. Many of Gehlen's high command were famous war criminals, expert in torture and mass-murder.[29]

According to Victor Marchetti, the CIA's former chief analyst of Soviet military plans and capabilities, Gehlen's supposed Soviet expertise served as a screen behind which the Counterintelligence Corps and the CIA could exaggerate Soviet might and intentions, and thereby continually increase their budget, part of which always went to Gehlen.[30]

"In my opinion, the Gehlen Organization provided nothing worthwhile for understanding or estimating Soviet military or political capabilities in Eastern Europe or anywhere else.... The agency loved Gehlen because he fed us what we wanted to hear. We used his stuff constantly, and we fed it to everybody else: the Pentagon; the White House; the newspapers. They loved it, too. But it was hyped up Russian boogeyman junk, and it did a lot of damage to this country."[31]

That is, the CIA adopted the Nazi "Communist conspiracy" model of foreign affairs whole hog for covert institutional and political reasons which utterly corrupted the empirical value of its intelligence, much as the Nazis themselves had done. In 1946, when the bankrupt, exhausted and overextended Soviet Army was tearing up the East German rail system, essential to the Soviet military in Germany, and sending it back to Russia, Gehlen insisted that they were preparing to use East Germany to attack the West.[32]

By 1948, General Lucius Clay, America's European commander, was cabling Washington that war was imminent. Given that Stalin and Beria were also falling all over themselves to employ Nazis, perhaps it was. Then again, perhaps it was a measure of our institutional corruption that we valued the same Nazi bullshit that Stalin and Beria did.

In 1948, Operation Bloodstone, designed by the geniuses of "containment," placed 250 top Nazi administrators, their most dangerous people, in high positions in the U.S. State Department and in each of our military services. Those directly involved in Bloodstone included the entire ruling elite of the CIA and the State Department.

Gustav Hilger, a top aide to Nazi Foreign Minister Ribbentropp, had helped to negotiate the Hitler-Stalin Pact of 1939. Hilger reported directly to Hitler on the progress of the Holocaust in Eastern Europe. By 1950, thanks to Operation Bloodstone, Hilger was reporting directly to Truman, as a top aide to the State Department's George Kennan, the designer of the doctrine of containment. Kennan's idea of an ideal government was Salazar's Portugal, a fascist Catholic theocracy. He was bitterly opposed to the Nuremberg trials, insisting that the bulk of what was "strong, able and respected in Germany" was in the Nazi party.[33]

The U.S. actually used Gehlen's postwar SS commando structure to site Soviet targets for the coming nuclear war. The East European guerrilla army we were going to employ after we destroyed Soviet infrastructure was disguised as the U.S.-created "Labor Service Divisions" in Germany. They were created from, and led by, Gehlen's former Waffen-SS units. The 4000th Labor Service Company, the Albanians, were used by Dulles and Wisner in 1949 in an abortive "spontaneous uprising" in Albania. Since these units were thoroughly infiltrated by double agents, Uncle Joe was ready and waiting to greet his errant Albanians.[34]

Gehlen's own plans for these Labor Service Divisions, led by his League of Young Germans, that is former Wehrmacht professionals, were exposed in a famous 1952 scandal. They included the elimination of the entire leadership of the West German Social Democratic Party in a *coup d'etat*. These "Labor Service" and "Young German" troops were trained and financed by the U.S. Army Counterintelligence Corps. And the Nazis had not been reticent with their trainers about their political intentions.[35] The U.S. rationale for this reorganization of Wehrmacht killers was, of course, the need to counter Soviet activities. These non-American contract killers were, obviously, deniable, and gave the U.S. the ability to effect cross-border penetrations and assassinations. Latvians don't stand out in Latvia.

These contract killers were organized with the help of the very powerful fascist elements within the Vatican. Working closely with Gehlen and Allied military intelligence, they organized a vast "refugee relief" program for these Latvian, Croatian, Ukranian, Romanian, Byelorussian and Hungarian war criminals.

The majority of the German puppet governments in Europe during the war were led by Catholic fascist political parties. Nazi Slovakia was run by Monsignor Jozef Tiso. Admiral Nicholas Horthy's Hungary was ruled by the Church. It willingly cooperated in identifying and legally isolating the "Zionist/Bolshevik" elements of society, although Horthy himself, to the annoyance of Hitler, hesitated at actual mass-murder, as did Mussolini. Vichy France, Franco's Spain and Mussolini's Italy, of course, were all fascist Catholic states. The Polish genocide was very popular with the pro-Nazi elements of the Polish Catholic Church, which to this day has the gall to contest control of Aushwitz with the remnants of Polish Jewry. Croatia's Ante Pavelic, leader of the Ustashi, a mass-murderer, was received by the Pope.

After the war, the Allied secret services, working with the fascist elements within the Vatican, provided the well-organized East Europeans Nazis with false papers and passports, and smuggled them out through "rat lines" in Trieste and Genoa. Lithuanians went to Reverend Jatulevicius on the Via Lucullo, Hungarians to Padre Gallov on the Via dei Parione and so forth.[36]

These Western intelligence operations, working exclusively with former Nazi collaborators, functioned parasitically on the Vatican's generalized relief operations. The technique, perfected by Reinhard Gehlen, was to place operatives in key refugee assistance posts. Thus, Theodore Oberlander, the Nazi commander of the Ukranian genocide, served as West German minister for refugee affairs until 1960.

Intermarium ("Between the Seas"), the influential Catholic lay organization, became the single most important source of CIA East European assassins and "exile" political leaders. A U.S. Army Intelligence report defined Intermarium, established in the mid-30's, as "an instrument of the German intelligence [Abwehr]."[37]

Archbishop Ivan Buchko of the Ukraine, for instance, on Intermarium's ruling council, intervened with Pope Pius XII to win freedom for a Ukranian Waffen-SS legion. Virtually the entire original Intermarium ruling council were Nazi collaborators. As the Abwehr's senior officer in the East, Reinhard Gehlen had worked closely with Intermarium on behalf of Hitler. He performed the same function for U.S. military intelligence.

Intermarium became a mainstay of Radio Free Europe/Radio Liberty. The CIA umbrella organization for Radio Liberty, the American Committee for the Liberation of the Peoples of Russia, was originally created by Hitler's SS and the Nazi Foreign Office in 1944, as the German Committee, as were its member groups, the North Caucasian National Committee, the Georgian Government in Exile and so forth. All the CIA groups, which kept their original Nazi names, were led by the original Nazi leaders.[38] Some Nazi war criminals, such as Viorel Trifa and Vilis Hazners, actually became well-known personalities on Radio Free Europe.

Monsignor Don Giuseppe Bicchierai of Milan, who helped Allen Dulles negotiate the surrender of German troops in Italy, also helped Walter Rauff of the SS to escape retribution. Rauff was the inventor of the gas truck extermination program, which killed, by suffocation, at least 250,000 women and children. Rauff, as he later testified, was hidden "in the convents of the Holy See."[39] During the 1948 Italian elections, Bicchierai lead a CIA-financed goon squad of 300 men. Dulles worked with Bicchierai for years.

The Croatian Ustashi part of the Vatican "refugee" operation, run by Monsignor Draganovic and Father Levasic, was run out of the *Instituto di Santa Jeronimus* at 132 Tomaselli Street in Rome.[40] During the war, in Croatia, Krunoslav Draganovic had helped Ante Pavelic "relocate" at least 400,000 Serbs and Jews.[41] With the help of Draganovic and Abwehr officer Kurt Merk, who was running his spy network for U.S. Army Counterintelligence, Lyon Gestapo chief Klaus Barbie, the most hated Nazi officer in France, made it to Bolivia in 1951. With bases in La Paz, Buenos Aires, Chicago, Madrid, Asunción, Melbourne and throughout Europe, Ustashi functioned as contract killers for Stroessner, Trujillo and the CIA (in the Congo, for one).

The Republican Party's 1952 "ethnic" effort was headed by Arthur Bliss Lane, former ambassador to Poland. His Russian and Ukranian specialist was Vladimir Petrov, who ran the Nazis' publicity campaign for Gehlen's Vlasov Army and administered the city of Krasnodar during the gas truck extermination program. The 1984 Republican Party "Guide to Nationality Observances" listed April 10, 1941, the day the Nazis invaded Yugoslavia and the Ustashi ("Insurrection") joined the SS, as "Croatian Independence Day."[42]

Civil engineer John Kosiak, leader of the Byelorussian Liberation Movement, active in the Chicago Republican Party, built the Minsk ghetto for the SS. He is wanted for war crimes in Russia. The Daugava Hawks, led by officers of the Latvian Waffen-SS death squads, became, under CIA sponsorship, the Latvian-American Republican National Federation and the Committee for a Free Latvia.[43]

Between 1945 and 55, the CIA spent at least $200 million on the Gehlen Organization, which became the West German BND. The pragmatic Nazis themselves, as CIA analyst Marchetti says, were "sucking off both tits," that is, functioning as double agents for the Russians whenever convenient. Gehlen's own agenda entailed using his most dangerous agents, like Otto Skorzeny and Klaus Barbie, to build an operating chain of fascist terror groups - in Spain, Paraguay, Greece, Argentina, Brazil, Turkey - all working as contractors for the secret services of those countries and all financing themselves with drugs and arms.

Papadopoulos' Greece, Peron's Argentina and Stroessner's Paraguay became major drug entrepôts thanks to cooperating German, British, French and American secret services. During the 1947 civil war in Greece between the popular leftist coalition that had defeated the Nazis and the British-backed Royalists, the U.S., using Gehlen's agents, backed IDEA, the Holy Bond of Greek Officers. These were the fascist elements in the professional army that had fought with the Nazis during the war. With enough American matériel for 15,000 men, Colonel George Papadopoulos, a Nazi war criminal, was able to take control of Greek intelligence, the KYP, and thereby control the Greek military. In 1967, Papadopoulos took direct control of Greece in a bloody coup that initiated a period of death squad assassinations for which Greek democrats have yet to forgive the U.S. Stroessner and Peron also had strong CIA/Nazi ties.

Aside from the "Peronist" Dulles brothers and the high command in the State Department, Zemurray's United Fruit team included "Tommy the Cork" Corcoran, one of Roosevelt's original brain trusters. Corcoran represented the Teamster insurance company, U. S. Life, Chiang Kai-shek's brother-in-law, and the CIA's proprietary airline, Civil Air Transport.

CAT had been founded in 1946 as an OSS-Kuomintang operation by Claire Chennault and Paul Helliwell. Chennault, from 1937 to 1945, was Chiang Kai-shek's senior air force advisor. Helliwell was OSS chief of special intelligence in China.[44] CAT was the peacetime version of Chennault's Flying Tigers, also cofounded with Helliwell. That grew into the CIA proprietary Air America, also a Helliwell operation.[45]

During the war, the Flying Tigers and the OSS functioned in China through the Sino-American Cooperative Organization, SACO, under the directorship of General Tai Li. Tai Li headed Chiang's vast secret police, which ran as many as 300,000 operatives from China to San Francisco. It was this organization that was the inspiration for the KMT's World Anti-Communist League (WACL).

Chiang's Kuomintang used the Shanghai Green Gang, their Mafia, to organize its vast opium-for-arms trade. Green Gang death squads had helped Chiang and Tai Li put down the 1927 Communist uprising in Shanghai, and had been a key factor in Chiang's power structure ever since. Tu Yueh-sheng, the Green Gang leader, had been invested with the rank of major general by Chiang.

Wherever the Japanese conquered in north China after 1930, they immediately encouraged the planting of opium. Tu Yueh-sheng, on behalf of Chiang, worked out a plan whereby Japanese gunboats would ferry his and their Yangtze opium to his 24 heroin labs in Japanese-controlled north China. The heroin was then sold throughout all of China, in the north by the Japanese Army through its new chain of 6,9000 pharmacies, and in the south by Chiang's KMT.[46] In return, Tu, Chiang and Tai-Li were left in control of the Yangtze River opium trade and the export market for their surplus heroin. One of their more famous distributors was Lanksy-Luciano partner Lepke Buchalter.

The OSS expected Chiang's opium traders to function as intelligence agents behind Japanese lines. Tai-Li and Tu, for instance, controlled all the dives and opium dens in Japanese-controlled Shanghai, as well as most of the labor unions and police. Thanks to Tai-Li, when the retreating Japanese decided to demolish the port, the OSS had the street muscle to prevent it.[47] The inverse, of course, was also operative. Many of SACO's street fighters were Japanese agents, since the vast opium/heroin trade was sanctioned by both sides across the battle lines.

The OSS Far Eastern chief, Capt. Milton Miles, was Tai-Li's first Deputy Director of SACO. Miles launched OSS operations throughout the opium-producing Golden Triangle of Burma, Laos and Thailand, closely coordinating his efforts with Tai-Li. Tai-Li's elite officer corps was trained by American agents on loan to the OSS from Hoover's FBI and Anslinger's FBN.[48] At this time Tai-Li was the biggest opium and heroin smuggler in the world.[49]

Col. Fletcher Prouty:"I was with the Air Transport Command in Cairo then. We sent a transport plane every month with the Finance Officers to Burma so they could physically pay the troops with cash. These men had 'foot-lockers' full of cash: American for the Americans, British for the British and foot-lockers packed with small white envelopes of heroin to pay the Chinese. That was the customary Chinese 'pay.'"[50]

Stilwell with "the little peanut" and his famous dragon lady

General 'Vinegar Joe' Stilwell, commander of American forces in the China-Burma-India theater, protested that the alliance with "the

Drug War

little peanut" Chiang was a de facto alliance with the Japanese, since Tai-Li, whom he called "the Chinese Himmler," was trading dope and arms on a massive scale with the enemy. The practical effect of this was to turn Chennault's vaunted Flying Tigers into Flying Dope Peddlers who, under orders, assiduously avoided doing what they had proven they could do very well - shoot down Jap planes.

OSS agents who moved independently against SACO's pro-Japanese dope smugglers were murdered. Mao's Yenan-based force, which had to face SACO's KMT dope smugglers as well as the Japanese, was implacably hostile to all aspects of the opium trade, perceiving it as a security threat on all levels. Mao's troops, if they valued their lives, did not smoke opium. Stilwell, a great field general, insisted that Mao's force was "battle-hardened, disciplined, well trained in guerrilla war and fired by a bitter hatred of the Japanese."[51] This from the commander of one of the greatest fighting units in the history of American arms, Merrill's Marauders.

Generals Frank D. Merrill and Joseph W. Stilwell planning the mission to capture the all-weather airstrip at Myitkyina. Capturing the airstrip was the key component in the North Burma campaign, as it would allow supply planes flying over the Hump to refuel en route. Hoover Institution

Stilwell strongly advocated an all-out alliance with Mao, and Mao wanted a U.S. alliance as a counterweight to both the Kuomintang and the Russians. Although many OSS officers agreed that Mao's was the far superior anti-Japanese force, Chiang was able to prevent the Stilwell-Yenan alliance through his direct contact with the likes of Tommy Corcoran, thus giving the Russians a leverage with Mao they otherwise never would have had.

Merrill's Marauders crossing a river in the Burma monsoon. The Myitkyina attack was the climax to four months of unrelenting combat that saw 5 major and 30 minor engagements. The 2400 Marauders suffered 80% casualties, most from disease. Every single member of the unit won the Bronze Star. Hoover Institution

Chiang demanded and got Stilwell's recall in October of 1944. Stilwell became chief of Army Ground Forces and commanded the U.S. 10th Army on Okinawa in the final months of the war, but lost his influence on China policy. Like Castro and Ho, Mao started out as strongly pro-American. Stilwell's pro-Yenan OSS officers, our most effective fighters, and their allies in the State Department, became a target of the Hoover-McCarthy witch hunters in the 1950's.

One of the OSS's violently anti-Japanese, pro-Yenan intelligence officers was 27 year-old Capt. John Birch, a Baptist missionary attached to Chennault's Fourteenth Air Force. While on a mission from Sian, Birch's team was stopped by a group of Chinese teenagers operating with Mao's troops. Birch yelled irritably at the nervous young pistoleros to get the hell out of the way and was shot dead.

John Birch is a good symbol of the Cold War precisely because he did *not* share the neofascist sympathies of the John Birch Society that was named after him (the JBS has matured responsibly). Birch regularly fought *with* Mao's troops against the KMT's Japanese-allied irregulars.[52] Birch was a fascist-killer, a good one. Had it not been for the U.S. Marines operating with the KMT, Mao's wildly popular army would have taken Beijing in 1945, and, had he not been killed by a crazy kid, John Birch would have helped Mao do it.

In 1947, two years before his final military defeat on the mainland, Chiang moved the KMT base to Formosa. The native Formosans were reluctant to give up their autonomy, so, in March of 1947, 12,000 KMT regulars slaughtered 20,000 Formosans, the leading lights of the society. Thereafter Formosa became "Taiwan," with a million Chinese nationalists ruling 15 million Formosans in a death-squad police state that made Mao's China look like Paradise on a clear day.[53]

American Military Intelligence, led by MacArthur, then decided that Chiang's Taiwan was the perfect base from which to pursue the Korean War. The American Military Assistance Advisory Group showered this fascist killer with a torrent of arms and money. John Singlaub of Iran-Contra fame was CIA deputy chief in South Korea at this time.

In 1954, Chiang founded the Asian People's Anti-Communist League. Chiang's partners were the CIA's partners. There was Park Chung Hee, founder of the Korean Central Intelligence Agency, who became President of Korea in 1961. Park was a fascist who fought with the Japanese in China and then broke the Korean Communist Party as a double agent for Synghman Rhee.

Then there was the absolutely incredible Reverend Sun Myung Moon, who is the Son of Jesus Christ. Sun is also the Son of the KCIA. The Unification Church was run by Colonel Bo Hi Pak, who used to be the KCIA military attaché in Washington. Richard Nixon Himself acknowledged that Reverend Moon's message resonated with God Almighty Himself. When Moon's International Federation for the Extermination of Communism, financed by the Tong-il Armaments Company, opened up its American branch, the name was wisely changed to the Freedom Leadership Foundation - so much more, *como se dice*, Republican.

Joining Chiang, Park and Moon in founding the Asian People's Anti-Communist League were Japan's Ryoichi Sasakawa and Yoshio Kodama. Just after the war American occupation forces had arrested Sasakawa and Kodama as Class A war criminals. However, thanks to their wholesale rape of China, they were fabulously wealthy Class A war criminals - and their *Yakuza* street gangs were needed to break the so-called communist unions. American Military Intelligence, if that's the right word, then decided, in 1948, to rehabilitate these misunderstood patriots by allowing them to form the Japanese Liberal Democratic Party, which has ruled Japan as a "liberal" one-party police state ever since. Thus, the old fascist *Yakuza*-industrialist coalition that had started World War II came back into power, resurrected as "democrats" - with a 99% criminal conviction rate and violently enforced social conformity.

These Asian "anticommunists" were represented in Washington by "Tommy the Cork" Corcoran. Corcoran was the mid-50's diplomatic escort of Claire Chennault's widow, Anna Chen Chennault, head of the KMT China Lobby. The China Lobby was very worried about a Commie takeover of the opium-producing Golden Triangle, now partly controlled by the hard-core remnants of the mainland KMT. That army was serviced as a CIA Special Operation by Corcoran's client airline CAT/SEA Supply operating from Taiwan and Bangkok.[54]

In 1950, Gen. Chennault, under the guidance of the influential CIA agent Paul Helliwell, had sold CAT, the nucleus of Air America, to the CIA. Helliwell worked with Frank Wisner in the CIA's action-oriented alter ego, the Office of Policy Coordination, which was merged with the CIA's Office of Special Operations in 1952. Wisner, former OSS Romania chief, was the officer who shepherded Reinhard Gehlen into the Allied fold. Under his guidance the OPC grew from 300 to more than 6000 contract employees, many of them active guerrillas. Wisner was given enormous independent power as the first director of the CIA's new covert operations division, the Directorate of Plans.

Helliwell founded SEA Supply of Bangkok in 1950 specifically to transport cargo, such as arms from Okinawa, to his Civil Air Transport for the Burma KMT operation. The 1950 idea was to use the Kuomintang troops in Burma to threaten "China's soft underbelly." But, since the underbelly didn't turn out to be so soft, the entrepreneurial KMT settled into the opium business instead, sending CAT's arms supply planes back to Bangkok and Taiwan loaded with opium or morphine from Burma's Shan states of Kokang, Wa and Kengtung.[55]

In fact, with military control of the richest opium-producing area in the world, the KMT was no longer dependent on even the pretense of political legitimacy, since it now had the tactical support of the Thai and Taiwanese armies. The CIA's KMT operation, therefore, became self-sustaining, an enlightening object lesson for all intelligence professionals in achieving complete independence from civilian policy control. As DCI William Casey, who worked under Helliwell, later put it, "a completely self-funding, off-the-shelf operation."

Even Gen. Bill Donovan, the wartime head of the OSS and 1953 ambassador to Thailand, had lost political control of the CIA's covert operations. Burma had protested in the U.N. that the Kuomintang was conquering northeastern Burma with CIA help. But Donovan found that his strong demands for a complete KMT withdrawal were met with a transparent charade that left the situation unchanged.

The KMT's main Bangkok connection, Gen. Phao, the commander of the Thai police who coordinated CAT air traffic with Gen. Li Mi's 5,000 Shan State KMT, was also the commander of the Thai government's relationship with the CIA. Explained KMT Gen. Tuan Shi-wen, "To fight you must have an army, and an army must have guns, and to buy guns you must have money. In these mountains, the only money is opium."[56] So the KMT went into the business of enslaving the Karen hill tribes of the Shan States as opium sharecroppers.

According to Professor McCoy, the first snow-white #4 heroin lab was opened by KMT-affiliated Hong Kong chemists on the Thai-Burma border in the late 60's.[57] The KMT are also known, fittingly, as the "White Chinese."

The KMT's lawyer, "Tommy the Cork" Corcoran, was also United Fruit's lawyer. Corcoran was intimate with the entire leadership of the CIA, which he had helped to organize, and which was, in any case, extremely sympathetic to United Fruit.[58] Walter Bedell Smith, Gen. Eisenhower's wartime chief of staff and Truman's CIA director, was now John Foster Dulles' Undersecretary of State. In 1953 he had asked Corcoran for the presidency of United Fruit, and in 1955 was named to its board of directors. Gen. Robert Cutler, chairman of the National Security Council, already sat on the United Fruit board.[59] Robert Hill, ambassador to Costa Rica, got to the UF board in 1960. Hill was connected to Grace Shipping, another CIA friend heavily invested in Guatemala.

Sam "the Banana Man" Zemurray's team also included Edward Bernays, the formidable "father of public relations," who filled the American media with phony reportage about "communism in Guatemala."[60] The right-wing John Clements, a Hearst vice-president with his own major magazines and PR firm, did the same. Once the "demographics" had been taken care of, Eisenhower and the Dulles brothers had the support of every Democrat in Congress. With Nicaragua's Somoza, the Dominican Republic's Trujillo and Cuba's Batista champing at the bit, Operation Success began in early June of 1954.

With control of the air, the sea and all the neighboring countries, Allen Dulles' CIA had no trouble overwhelming Jacobo Arbenz with a military and propaganda campaign coordinated from both inside and outside the country. Aerial bombardment of the presidential palace was combined with a mercenary ground force of about 180 men, led by Guatemalan Col. Carlos Castillo Armas, the size and popularity of which was wildly exaggerated by well placed Radio Liberty transmitters.

The propaganda campaign was run by David Phillips, who would play a prominent role in the war on Castro and the assassination of JFK. The propaganda was scripted by OSS China veteran Howard Hunt, the Political Action Officer who went on to become one of the most notorious figures in American history. The invasion was timed to coincide with Henry Cabot Lodge's tenure as head of the U.N. Security Council, so Lodge was in a position to prevent Guatemala's complaints of international aggression from being considered by the U.N.

The American contingency plan, "Hard Rock Baker," had U.S. fighter planes at the ready and a Marine landing force loaded onto 14 cargo planes, but Plan A worked so well that Plan B wasn't needed.[61] When the phony war achieved a high level of hysteria in Guatemala City, agents were sent in to buy off key army officers. Arbenz, disheartened by the prospect of civil war with his own army, resigned on June 27.

The young doctor Ché Guevara, who had come to Guatemala filled with hope, vainly tried to organize guerrilla units to retreat into the mountains to continue the fight. Guevara realized that it was Arbenz' failure to inflame and arm the populace that made his defeat inevitable. Intelligence professionals, it was obvious, could always rent mercenary troops and manipulate the media. The enraged Guevara made his way to Mexico City, where he met a like-minded Fidel Castro, himself a miraculous survivor of bold attempts to overthrow both Trujillo and Batista. Back in Guatemala City, David Phillips, pouring over Arbenz' captured documents, opened a file on Ché Guevara.

One of the first things Guevara told Castro on their accession to power in January of 1959 was that "We cannot guarantee the Revolution before cleansing the armed forces. It is necessary to remove everyone who might be a danger. But it is necessary to do it rapidly, right now!"[62] By taking that advice, Castro became as ruthless a streetfighter as Allen Dulles himself - three hundred executed *Batistianos* by March of 1959. Castro did that because he knew he was under CIA military attack, and those officers were key CIA cadres.

The Cuban Communist Party, both because it was close to Batista and because it had orders from Moscow, had opposed Castro when he was in the hills. In 1959, before he was driven into Russian arms as a matter of survival, the CIA agent who interviewed the cooperative Castro concluded that: "Castro is not only not a Communist, he is a strong anti-Communist fighter."[63] The only thing intractable about

Castro, concluded Agent Bender, was his social idealism and his nationalism. Although the military and political pressure inherent in his situation forced Castro to embrace the radical left, he always preferred his *Fidelismo*, what he called "utopian socialism," to Guevara's *Communismo*.

Castro met with Vice-President Richard Nixon in April. Despite Castro's willingness to compromise, and before he had expropriated anything, Nixon, Eisenhower's point man on Cuba, decided that all-out war was the only answer. Nixon recommended using the newly-exiled *Batistianos* as the spearpoint. This was, of course, a CIA Special Operations Group plan that had already been designed before Castro's visit.[64] For Castro, talking to Nixon was like talking to a wall. The political signals from the Eisenhower administration, which had immediately recognized Castro, were far more positive, but the wary Castro always kept his eye on the military signals.

Col. J. C. King, chief of the CIA's Western Hemisphere Division, the man who had been the CIA's chief liaison to United Fruit during the Guatemala coup, had advised Eisenhower, in his Cuba "action plan," that "Thorough consideration be given to the elimination of Fidel Castro."[65] Eisenhower signed off on the plan on March 17, 1960, after Allen Dulles' formal presentation of "Operation Pluto" to the National Security Council. But, however sympathetic he may have been to the elimination of Fidel, Eisenhower had approved only a small 300-man force of small-team infiltrators, not the massive 3000-man over-the-beach invasion presented to Kennedy. In the transition from Ike to Kennedy, January '61, diplomatic relations were broken with Cuba. Brigade 2506 was set to invade.

Castro, who had plenty of double agents among the *Batistianos*, realizing he was under attack, opened diplomatic relations with Moscow on May 7, 1960. In October he began the process of nationalizing every significant U.S. business in Cuba. Dulles' protégé, Richard Bissell, who had replaced Wisner as Deputy Director for Plans, was in charge of the "covert" Operation Pluto.

The model for all the Cuba planners was their Guatemala operation of 1954. The Cuba plan included not only assassination, but sabotage and an expert operation, that almost succeeded, aimed at destabilizing Cuba's currency.[66] This, ultimately, was no more than Castro expected. "Imperialism" was not an empty word to Fidel and Ché. They never forgot Jacobo Arbenz and the destruction of democracy in Guatemala, and they knew, right from the start, that they would be treated the same way. It was Arbenz' fate that convinced Ché that the

Communist military model - a model developed in reaction to the death-squad fascism of the Czar and the 1919 invasion of Russia by the colonial powers - was the only survivable alternative to CIA-United Fruit "democracy."

All the intelligence services were aware of the Dulles thesis, that revolt in Eastern Europe had proven impossible to foment under Stalin, but possible under Krushchev, whose relative liberalism gave intelligence operatives wiggling room.[67] "We should also like to extend a special greeting to Jacobo Arbenz," said Ché in 1960, "president of the first Latin American country which fearlessly raised its voice against colonialism; a country which, in a far-reaching and courageous agrarian reform, gave expression to the hopes of the peasant masses. We should also like to express our gratitude to him, and to the democracy that gave way, for the example they gave us and for the accurate estimate they enabled us to make of the weaknesses which that government was unable to overcome."[68]

The essential militarism of communism, of course, enraged Castro's democratic supporters, like Manolo Ray, Huber Matos, Manuel Arrutia, David Salvador and Amador Odio, all heroes of the revolution who broke with Castro, but those that didn't end up behind bars in Cuba found little comfort among the CIA's *Batistianos*. Ché knew that real political democracy presented an opportunity for the CIA to destabilize the revolution from the inside, as it had done with Arbenz.

The then-current CIA destabilization of the neutralist government of Souvanna Phouma in Laos was a case in point. Souvanna Phouma was driven into an alliance with the Pathet Lao and the Vietminh, both of which had vast popular support, by a corrupt gang of fascist dope peddlers who had no popular support whatever, just a mountain of CIA money and arms. The "Royal Laotian Army" and the "Royal Lao Air Force" were created out of whole cloth by the CIA - they literally didn't exist before the Dulles brothers invented them, and had no funding, including Laotian, other than American.

In 1958 the Pathet Lao, through legal elections, became an important element in Souvanna Phouma's neutralist coalition. The Dulles brothers immediately cut off all aid and engineered the military collapse of the coalition, using the CIA's strongman, the former French-serving Gen. Phoumi Nosavan.

Nationalist paratroop captain Kong Le, in an attempt to return Souvanna's coalition to power, took Vientiane away from Phoumi in August of 1960. But Kong Le couldn't hold it in the face of the combined CIA forces of Phoumi and Vang Pao, operating in the Plain of Jars. So, in December 1960, Kong Le led a substantial portion of the Royal Laotian Army, in American trucks loaded with American equipment, into the Plain of Jars to join up with the Pathet Lao and challenge Vang Pao. The sum total of the Eisenhower-Dulles policy in Laos was to radicalize the Pathet Lao, vastly increase its strength, and badly weaken the democratic center.

The whole mess was then handed to John Kennedy, who found the CIA's Laotian strongman Phoumi completely intractable. Kennedy cut off Phoumi's American funding, at least that part of the funding he was aware of. But, as Kennedy aide Arthur Schlesinger recalled, of both the Eisenhower and Kennedy administrations, "The CIA station chief refused to follow the State Department policy or even to tell the Ambassador his plans and intentions."[69]

Rather than accede to the State Department's demands for another coalition government, Gen. Phoumi, who continued to receive covert CIA funding, sent Gen. Ouane Rattikone into Burma to arrange independent funding for the Royal Laotian Army. Using his vast stores of CIA arms as barter, Ouane was enabled to build up enough regular trade with the Shan state opium armies to become the first Chairman of the secret Laotian Opium Administration, in 1962.[70]

The CIA, meanwhile, as the French had done, had been organizing the Hmong army of Vang Pao in the Laotian highlands, the only possible military counterweight to the Pathet Lao in northern Laos. The only cash crop of the Hmong was opium, and there was no way 30,000 Hmong troops would fight for any outfit that didn't support their economy. It was largely the Pathet Lao hostility to the opium trade, a traditional tool of the colonialists, that turned the scattered Hmong highlanders, who had been French allies, into American allies. Phoumi and Ouane shipped their Laotian opium, as their Burmese, to Ngo Dinh Nhu in Saigon via the CIA-run Royal Lao Air Force.

Ché knew that the CIA *modus operandi* in Guatemala and Cuba was no different than in Laos. It not only originated with the same policy makers, it employed the same CIA agents and military trainers, the same individuals.

As Ché looked on from Mexico City, Secretary of State Dulles instructed the U.S. ambassador to Guatemala to instruct Col. Castillo that all unionists were to be labeled "communist" and that all "communists" were to be charged with high treason and either shot or summarily exiled. The obedient Castillo immediately outlawed all political parties, labor unions, peasant and Indian organizations and restored the old dictator Úbico's death-squad chief to his old post, as head of the secret police. That is, Dulles insisted on the revitalization of the old political death-squads. At least 8,000 people, many of them political and union leaders, were murdered in the first two months of the Castillo regime, and another 10,000 imprisoned.[71] Every political leader who could, left the country.

The secret police imposed press censorship and even burned all "unauthorized" books, including not only the writings of Arévalo, but Dostoyevsky and Victor Hugo. Castillo's party was called the National Democratic Movement. His personal secretary, a man who had proven very handy with a gun, was Mario Sandoval Alarcón, the man who, funded by the CIA, went on to become "the godfather of Latin America's death squads."

Castillo drove all the peasants off the land Arbenz had given them and gave it back to the old landlords, returning the country to the monocrop coffee and banana slave-labor economy, virtually bankrupting it. Vice-President Nixon, after his 1955 visit, declared that "President Castillo Armas' objective, 'to do more for the people in two years than the Communists were able to do in ten years,' is important. This is the first instance in history where a Communist government has been replaced by a free one."[72] Fascist double-speak, all his life.

In 1957 the intrepid Mafia point-man and Batista operative, Johnny Rosselli, made another trip to Guatemala City, as he had done many times throughout 1956. This time the trip was in reaction to Castillo's jailing of his partner, casino operator Ted Lewin.[73] Castillo was promptly gunned down, and Col. Enrique Trinidad Oliva, Johnny Rosselli's gambling and narcotics partner, became the new head of Guatemala's secret police.[74]

Col. Trinidad Oliva was also the key CIA contact in the Guatemalan government, working under his half-brother, the defense minister. Trinidad Oliva coordinated all "foreign aid" coming through the CIA conduit ICA, the International Cooperation Administration, the forerunner of the Agency for International Development, AID.

Rosselli and Trinidad then helped the murderous old Gen. Miguel Ydígoras Fuentes, one of Úbico's assassins with close ties to mob partner Trujillo, to become head of state. Mario Sandoval Alarcón organized the right-wing of Castillo's party into the National Liberation Movement (MLN) and hired himself out to Trinidad and Rosselli.

The same year that Johnny Rosselli helped the CIA engineer the change in the Guatemalan government, he was asked by his Syndicate associates to put together Giancana in Chicago, Costello in New

York, Lansky in Miami, and Marcello in New Orleans for the huge $50 million Tropicana construction project in Las Vegas. According to Fred Black, a political fixer who was close to Rosselli, Bobby Baker and Lyndon Johnson, Rosselli's influence was such that he gave orders to the Dorfmans, who controlled the Teamsters' huge Central States Pension Fund.[75] During the 50's and 60's, it was Johnny Rosselli who "set up protection" in Las Vegas.[76]

Throughout 1956 and 57 Rosselli travelled back and forth from Mexico City, the planning center for all CIA operations in Latin America, and Guatemala City. An experienced ICA operative noted that "John had access to everyone and everything that was going on there. He had an open door at the embassy in Guatemala, and in Costa Rica. He was in there plenty of times. I know because I saw him. He supplied information to the government, and had a hand in a lot of the intrigues that were going on."[77]

This means, operationally, that Johnny Rosselli's interests became the CIA's interests. "Throughout Latin America," notes Frank McNeil, a junior political officer in the Guatemalan Embassy in 1960, "there were two American governments - one intelligence and one official."[78] McNeil's boss, Ambassador John Muccio, learned of the Bay of Pigs invasion force being trained in Guatemala only after the story broke in *The New York Times*. As John Kennedy found out to his chagrin, Rosselli, his Syndicate and *Batistiano* allies, had more operational clout than the State Department.

But Gen. Ydígoras' death-squad rule was not popular, even with the Guatemalan military, nor was his gift of a military base in Retalhuleu to the Americans, for the training of their *Batistiano* invasion force. Castro's macho nationalism was deeply admired by Latin military men, and Ydígoras was bitterly resented for turning Guatemala into another "USS *Honduras*." In November of 1960, a month before Kong Le joined up with the Pathet Lao, more than half the Guatemalan army rose against Ydígoras. The U.S., fearing harm to the Bay of Pigs operation, squelched the revolt as a training exercise for its fascist Cuban force, which now had the run of Guatemala.[79]

This created an alliance in Guatemala, as it had in Laos, of the nationalist military and the revolutionary left. In Guatemala, the left was led by the PGT and its Revolutionary Movement of November 13th (MR-13). Both nationalist military rebels who led their regular troops into the hills to join up with the PGT, Luis Turcios Lima and Marco Antonio Yon Sosa, had U.S. counterinsurgency training. Master-spy Rosselli, following traditional intelligence practice, maintained relations with both sides in this guerrilla war, supplying arms and selected information as necessary.

Rosselli had important ties to Standard Fruit, the smaller of the two fruit giants, through Seymour Weiss and Carlos Marcello in New Orleans, fruit importing mafioso Jack Dragna on the West Coast and the Genoveses in New York. Using Col. Trinidad Oliva and some of Dragna's best hitters from the Coast, as well as guerrilla hit teams from MR-13, Rosselli convinced United Fruit that it would be cheaper to allow Standard Fruit to use United's rail and port facilities than to fight with Rosselli.[80] This was also the position of the U.S. Justice Department, which supported "free enterprise" in Guatemala.

The popular Guatemalan guerrilla war was a convenient "crisis" for the intelligence services, providing a willing John Kennedy an excuse to approve the sending of Office of Public Safety trainers to organize a "pacification" program in Zacapa and Izabal provinces. U.S. Special Forces were flown in from Laos, and Ydígoras' best killers were matriculated from the CIA's counterinsurgency college in the Canal Zone. The ensuing mass murder made even the arch-conservative churchmen puke in public, and they were a constituency John Kennedy heeded. In January of 1963 Kennedy engineered the departure of Ydígoras in favor of a hopefully more politic murderer, who disappointed expectations.

Over the next few years, under the OPS-Military Assistance Program, Guatemala's "counterinsurgency" force was modernized with tens of millions of dollars. The Zacapa-Izabal campaign turned into a political mass-assassination program, run by the same OPS-Green Beret operatives who ran Operation Phoenix in Vietnam.[81] This became the most horrible genocide in Guatemalan history. Amnesty International said that in 1966 alone, 30,000 Guatemalan civilians were assassinated by the OPS death squads.[82]

Leading those death-squads was Mario Sandoval Alarcón, who, with CIA-KMT help, had organized his MLN into a politico-military unit that not only fielded troops, but local *jefes politicos* capable of regimenting the campesinos and identifying death-squad targets.[83] When a village wouldn't submit to an MLN political chief, U.S. Special Forces jets, operating out of the U.S. Southern Command in Panama, bombed it with napalm. Hundreds of Guatemalan children were burned to death by flaming jelly.[84]

This is what earned the Guatemalan army commander, Col. Carlos Arana Osorio, Sandoval's commanding officer, the sobriquet "Butcher of Zacapa," which he took as a compliment. The CIA/OPS, working with Sandoval, founded and funded numerous free-lance assassination teams, with cute acronyms like OJO, "Eye for an Eye" and MANO, "National Organized Anticommunist Movement." By 1970 over 30,000 Guatemalan police had received Office of Public Safety training, many going directly into the free-lance death-squads, all of which supplemented their income by running drugs for their employers, the Syndicate and the Guatemalan secret police.[85]

The Salvadoran equivalent of the MLN, ORDEN ("Order"), the Democratic Nationalist Organization, was created by the OPS in El Salvador between 1960 and 1965. Taiwan's Col. Chu was instrumental in organizing ORDEN on the populist KMT model, with 80,000 cadres.[86] As in Guatemala, rural ORDEN informants turned over subversive names to the Salvadoran National Security Agency, ANSESAL, headquartered in the Presidential Palace, which dispatched a death squad to deal with the "traitor." The infamous Roberto D'Aubuisson was strongman Blondie Medrano's protégé in ANSESAL.

Brazil went through the same process, with some 100,000 police receiving OPS training. This resulted directly in General Branco's 1964 overthrow of President Goulart's parliamentary government, and the resurgence of Brazil's death-squads.

The *Confederación Anticomunista Latina*, CAL, was part of the CIA-KMT's World Anti-Communist League, WACL, an extension of their Asian People's Anti-Communist League.[87] The first meeting of the CAL was organized by the CIA's Howard Hunt in 1958, to celebrate the 1954 Guatemalan coup, in which he played a major role.[88] Old OSS hand Hunt had direct ties to Taiwan's KMT.

Ray Cline, CIA station chief in Taiwan from 1958-1962, later Deputy Director, founded the WACL along with Chiang Ching-kuo, Chiang Kai-shek's son. Ching-kuo headed the Kuomintang's secret police under Chiang and rose to become President of Taiwan. He was overall military commander of the KMT's Shan states opium armies.[89] The WACL's finishing school was the Political Warfare Cadres Academy in Peitou. Roberto D'Aubuisson, "Major Blowtorch," graduated from both this school and the International Police Academy in D.C., as did many of South America's finest. When appropriate, courses at Peitou, Taiwan, were taught in Spanish.

"Political warfare" is a combination of sheer terror and unrelenting propaganda aimed at the merciless domination of the bulk of the population by the ruling industrial elite - what the KMT calls "total war." The cadres are schooled in the arts of interrogation, propaganda, militarily-based social organization and terror. Major Blowtorch got straight A's. D'Aubuisson's party, ARENA, the Nationalist Republican Alliance, is structured exactly like the Kuomintang. It "has a politico-military organization which embraces not only a civilian party structure but also a military arm obedient to the party," to quote President Carter's ambassador to El Salvador, Robert White.[90]

White is a good example of the deep divisions that exist within the structural U.S. government between many of the democratically-minded professionals of the State Department and the pro-fascist elements of military intelligence. By 1961, the American military was providing 75% of Taiwan's budget. Kuomintang heroin, from the American-armed Burmese fascists, as well as cocaine from the American-armed Bolivian and Peruvian fascists, still finds its way into the U.S. through the American-armed, Kuomintang-trained fascists of ARENA, who are still in control of "democratic" El Salvador. That's why you won't see any reduction in the flow of heroin any time soon.

The 1958 Mexico City CAL meeting was chaired by Antonio Valladores, Carlos Marcello's lawyer. He was the partner of one of Guatemala's prime ministers, Eduardo Rodriguez-Génis. These men arranged Marcello's phony Guatemalan birth certificate, and so became indicted coconspirators in Marcello's 1963 deportation case engineered by Robert Kennedy.[91]

Also attending the 1958 CAL meeting was Yaroslav Stetsko, a leader of the Galician (Western) branch of the Organization of Ukrainian Nationalists (OUN), a Waffen-SS death squad that specialized in machine-gunning Ukranian Jewish children. When the Nazis arrived in Lvov in June of 1941, they were spearheaded by the Ukrainian Nightingales, commanded by Yaroslav Stetsko. Stetsko proceeded to slaughter more than 7000 civilians in one week, mostly Jews, but also intellectuals, Russians and Party members. The Nazis, who were always impressed with efficiency, named Stetsko Ukrainian Premier. All told, the OUN helped the Nazis kill more than a million Jews in the Ukraine.

Stetsko's commanding officer in the OUN was Stefan Bandera, put out of action by the KGB in Munich in 1959. Stetsko went on to hear Ronald Reagan tell him, on July 13, 1983, in the White House as leader of the Anti-Bolshevik Bloc of Nations, that "Your dream is our dream. Your hope is our hope."[92]

Theodore Oberlander, the Nazi commander of the Ukranian genocide, who served as West German minister for refugee affairs until 1960, led the "European Freedom Council" to the WACL conferences. The "Freedom Council" included delegations from Dutch, Swedish,

Slovak, Albanian, Latvian and Italian Nazi groups. *Sint Martinsfonds*, for instance, claimed the membership of 400 former Dutch SS officers.

Another World Anti-Communist League and Anti-Bolshevik Bloc of Nations activist was Stejpan Hefer of the Croatian Liberation Movement, with chapters throughout Europe, the USA and Australia. Working under Ante Pavelic, their Ustashi did the same work for the Nazis in Croatia that the OUN did in the Ukraine. "A good Ustashe," Pavelic told his troops in Zagreb, "is one who can use a knife to cut a child from the womb of its mother."[93] This horror became their trademark.

The Romanian Orthodox Church also organized a Nazi-run smuggling effort.[94] Viorel Trifa, who ran *Waffen-SS* Iron Guard death squads in Romania, became a bishop of the Romanian Orthodox Episcopate in America in 1952. It was great cover. In 1955, at the invitation of Vice-President Nixon, he led the opening prayer for the U.S. Senate. This is a man who literally skinned "kike" children alive.

In 1952, the CIA uncovered proof of a $100,000 bribe to Nixon from an Iron Guard operative, Nicolae Malaxa, who had been in business with Hermann Goring's brother during the war.[95] Viorel Trifa was stripped of his U.S. citizenship in 1984 and deported to Portugal, where he proceeded to go to work for Horia Sima, the Iron Guard's man in Madrid, and for Chirila Ciuntu, who, like Sima, did SS dirty work on the Russian front. Ciuntu was another Iron Guard delegate to the WACL conferences, the business of which was to turn the WACL into an efficient global trade organization that financed political assassinations and arms transfers with dope.

One of the WACL's superstars, Col. Arana, the Butcher of Zacapa, was handed the presidency of Guatemala in 1970. He named his death-squad organizer, Sandoval, president of the National Congress. "People ask if the death squads are controlled by the Army. They are the Army."[96] From 1974 through 1978, Sandoval was Vice President of Guatemala, under the unelected Col. Kjell Laugerud Schell. Christian Democrats who protested, who were themselves right-wing conservatives, were shot. Until December of 1996, only right-wing and centrist parties were legal in Guatemala, and, since 1954, only the right-wing, composed of the Christian Democrats, the Army's Institutional Revolutionary Party, or Sandoval's MLN, has come to power.

Throughout the 80's the Guatemalan economy relied on exports which included marijuana, coca, opium,[97] coffee, tea, bananas, cotton, cardamom, meat and sugar. The legal crops were grown mostly in large-scale operations originally financed by AID and setup by a consortium of U.S. agribusiness companies organized by the Bank of America, sort of cooperating United Fruits. All were possessed of a deep interest in cheap labor and all were vulnerable to fluctuating world commodity prices.[98] Also important were the new *maquiladora* ("final-touch") manufacturing plants, so dear to Reaganauts, which simply reassembled imported components for export. These plants too were mostly controlled by foreign capital.

The result of this top-down investment was that basic commodities such as wheat, and even the ancient Mayan staple corn, had to be imported, as peasant smallholdings, the most productive land in the country, continued to be expropriated by the Army. As late as 1976, 50% of peasant income came from the cultivation of smallholdings; by 1988 that had dropped to 25%. The campesinos were forced into the cash economy - as wages remained at subsistence level and unemployment soared.[99] Only one-third of the work force was fully employed year-round. By 1979, urban workers were earning 74% of their 1970 real wages, and rural workers were earning 54%.[100]

85% of Guatemalans were living below the poverty line.[101] Since children continued to go hungry and without medical care, the economic pressure for unionization and land reform remained, as did the rationale for the death squads. The scorched earth policy of the 1980's saw the destruction of 440 highland villages, many by napalm bombing, and the killing of over 100,000 civilians.[102] Thousands of Indians took up arms.

Since 1954 the U.S.-financed and trained Guatemalan military has killed more than 200,000 of its own people.[103] That part of the national budget that doesn't go to finance the huge military debt goes to pay for Army "reinvestment." Over the past 30 years, Army-connected entrepreneurs, working with Syndicate-CIA operatives like Howard Hughes, Robert Vesco, the *Batistiano* Cubans and Sunbelt S&L owners, have acquired much of the country's best land. They have also opened the first munitions plant in Central America, established the Bank of the Army, and taken control of the national airline AVIATECA, the public telephone system GUATEL, and the major ports.[104]

This, of course, is precisely the disaster Jacobo Arbenz had been working to prevent. Arbenz died in Mexico City in 1971 and was buried in El Salvador, his wife's home. His reburial in Guatemala City, October 20, 1995, was the most heavily attended funeral in Guatemalan history.

Guatemalan Guerrilla; Richard Lord

Guatemalan soldiers face off with Native protesters, 1996

Neocolonialism

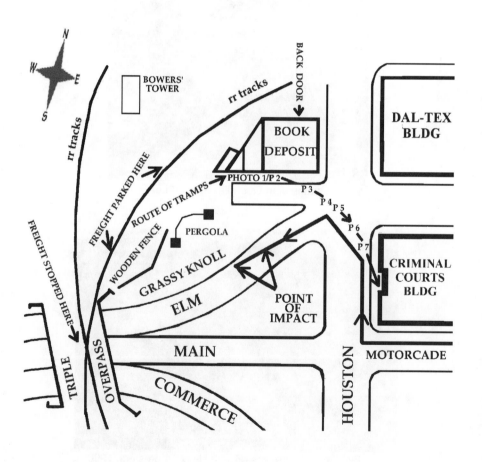

Drug War

Assassination

During the war the Office of Naval Intelligence had to use Mafia chief Lucky Luciano to secure New York's docks. Too much information was getting through to the deadly U-boats. The U.S. and its allies lost 120 merchant ships to German U-boats off the American coast in the first three months after Pearl Harbor. Freight specifics and sailing routes were insecure on the New York docks.

The docks weren't run by Luciano, but by Luciano's *amici*. The *capo mafioso* wasn't really *capo di tutti capi* because 'organized crime' wasn't really that organized. It wasn't a corporation with a rigid hierarchy. Luciano could defend his turf where he could, and others could do the same. Many of those others weren't Italian and many chose to remain quite anonymous. But many were Italian or Sicilian, and the old Sicilian structure, the *Mafia*, provided methods whereby an underground economy could be managed. The mafiosi, for all their bloody reputation, were actually quite good at cooperating with one another, and few could touch them for guts, street smarts and organization.

Socks Lanza ran the Fulton Fish Market with an iron hand, but his Brooklyn distribution depended on the trucks of other *amici*. Cockeye Dunn's Longshoremen helped run Luciano's bookmaking on the docks and fix his smuggling. Luciano and his allies reciprocated by distributing Dunn's hot cargoes and helping out with 'labor problems.' There was no way Cmdr. Charles Haffenden's naval intelligence unit was going to penetrate the docks without these bosses.

Haffenden went to Tom Dewey's experts, D.A. Frank Hogan and his top aide, Murray Gurfein. They knew enough to contact Lanza, head of Local 16975 of the United Seafood Workers. Lanza, after trying to go it alone for a while, admitted that the only one with juice enough was Luciano, then languishing upstate, thanks to Dewey, in frigid Dannemora on the Canadian border. Luciano's lawyer, Moe Polakoff, told the Feds that the only person who could successfully broach this subject with Luciano was his trusted partner Meyer Lansky. Lansky, who hated the Nazis guts, was glad to help. He was assigned his own code number as a naval intelligence contact, as was Luciano, who got transferred downstate to the more pleasant confines of Comstock.[1]

The Mafia was needed not just for protection and intelligence on the docks, but to organize Sicily behind Patton. With street-level Mafia cooperation, recent Sicilian immigrants, many professional fishermen, were funneled into the New York office of Naval Intelligence. They helped to refine very accurate maps of the Sicilian coast and hinterland, providing the invasion force with tide tables and the location of docks, key roads, mountain passes and guerrilla groups. They also provided regular communication with the Mafia powers behind German lines in Western Sicily.

Don Calogero Vizzini and Don Giuseppe Genco Russo, although flexible enough to survive, had been badly weakened by Mussolini's serious attempt to replace their coercive power structures with his own. Knowing that the Americans were unstoppable anyway, they provided a ready-made guerrilla army to roll out the red carpet for the invaders.

When Lt. Paul Alfieri landed on Licata Beach, his Sicilian contacts were able to give him safe passage to the secret HQ of the Italian Naval Command. Inside, Alfieri found maps of the disposition of all German and Italian naval forces in the Mediterranean. The Mafia put out the word that Italian troops who resisted the Americans would be marked for reprisal, but those that deserted would be given civilian clothes and protection. Italian troops deserted by the truckload. Mafiosi guided Patton's Seventh Army through the labyrinthine San Vito mountains, enabling Patton to split the 400,000 fascist troops in two. These Sicilians were directly responsible for saving thousands of American lives during the 1943 invasion.

Unfortunately, this was turned into a political tragedy for Sicily. Sicily's economy was almost entirely agricultural. But, until the Land Reform Act of 1950, land wasn't generally passed on in small family plots, but in large *latifundia*, plantations. Small plots were rented out for shares. The great Dons were landlords who violently opposed the efforts of the sharecroppers at land reform.

The Allied Military Government made Don Calogero Vizzini, his successor, Genco Russo, and many other mafiosi, mayors of important towns. Coordinating the AMGOT effort was the former lieutenant governor of New York, Col. Charles Poletti, whom Luciano described as "one of our good friends," that is, a made mafioso.[2]

Col. Poletti, military governor of Sicily, made New York's most powerful expatriate Mafia capo, Vito Genovese, his official interpreter, thus putting New York organized crime at the very heart of Allied intelligence in Italy.

Genovese, who fled New York in 1937 to avoid indictment by Dewey, spent the war in Naples helping to finance Mussolini, with whom he was personally close. Genovese and his Corsican ally

Antoine d'Agostino played the fascist side of the fence, while Luciano's mafiosi worked the Allied side. Their operational connections with each other made them indispensable to both sides.[3]

By 1944, under AMGOT auspices, Genovese's hoods controlled major Italian ports, most of the black market in diverted American and Sicilian goods, and numerous "anticommunist" goon squads on call for U.S. military intelligence. Not only the black market, but much of the legal and political structure fell into their hands as well.

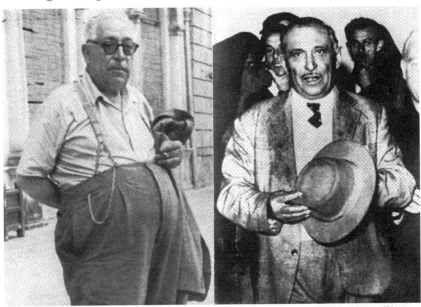

Don Calogero Vizzini, left, and Don Giuseppe Genco Russo; Italy's News Photos; Keystone

Politically active peasants had their crops burned and their cattle slaughtered. When, in 1944, their leaders, Michele Pantaleone and Girolamo Li Causi, challenged Don Caló in his home town of Villalba by holding a political rally there, 19 demonstrators were left wounded.

On May 1st, 1947, hundreds of peasants drove their gaily painted donkey carts to Portella delle Genestre to celebrate Labor Day. As the speeches began, submachine guns opened up on the crowd from the surrounding hills. Eleven people were left dead and 56 wounded.

Because they insisted on breaking up Sicily's plantations, the Socialists and Communists were so popular that the Mafia found it necessary to assassinate 500 of them from 1944 to 1949.[4] This gave the Mafia, and their Christian Democrat allies, absolute control of the island. The Land Reform Act of 1950, which prohibited estates of larger than 500 acres, was largely vitiated by Mafia control of the Land Reform Boards.

Although Sicilian socialists were just poor farmers, they were identified by AMGOT as 'potential Soviet agents.' The very first major operation of the newly-formed CIA was the fixing of the 1948 Italian elections in favor of the Christian Democrats, the Mafia's ally throughout Sicily and Italy. James Angleton, running the Strategic Services Unit in Rome, had no problem with Mafia control of Palermo's port. He engineered it by allowing Mafia control of AMGOT's Palermo structure. The only alternative was leftist control of the port.

Angleton worked with Harry Anslinger's top international agents, George White and Charles Siragusa.[5] Their rationale, the one they were willing to talk about, at least, had something to do with the Russians, but they gave the Sicily-based mafiosi a protected worldwide reach.

Luciano himself was deported to Sicily in 1946, there to better manage his end of the vast Turkey or Indochina to Lebanon to Sicily to Marseille to Cuba to U.S. heroin run. He was joined by Joe Adonis, Sam Carolla, Sal Vitale and at least four hundred others. In 1948, another deported Sicilian, Joe Pici, got caught sending 35# of pure heroin to his boys in Kansas City.

In 1950, a Sicilian reporter snuck into the Hotel Sole in the center of old Palermo, then the residence of Don Caló Vizzini - and Lucky Luciano. He snapped a picture of Luciano schmoozing with Don Caló's bodyguards. This so infuriated Luciano that the reporter was flogged to within an inch of his life.

Luciano roughing it in Naples, 1949

Luciano and Don Caló, the previous year, had set up a candy factory in Palermo, which exported its produce throughout Europe and the USA. They also shared a hospital supply company and a fruit export operation - all ideal smuggling covers. In 1952, Luciano's close childhood friend, Frank Coppola, had twelve pounds of heroin seized by Italian police on its way from Coppola in Anzio to a well-known smuggler in Alcamo.

In 1956, Joe Profaci, in Brooklyn, was recorded talking about the export of Sicilian oranges with Nino Cottone, in Sicily. Cottone lost his life that year in the battle for Palermo with rival mafiosi, but Profaci's oranges kept on coming. The Brooklyn number rung by Cottone was the same number rung by Luciano from Naples and Coppola from Anzio. All were recorded by the Palermo Questura talking ecstatically about high grade Sicilian oranges. In 1959, Customs intercepted one of those orange crates. Hollow wax oranges, 90 to a crate, were filled with heroin until they weighed as much as real oranges. Each crate carried 110 pounds of pure heroin.[6]

At all points, in exchange for their "anticommunist" political violence, the hoods had the protection of the local military intelligence, though, as the busts indicate, not always of the local police. But enough support was provided so that the mafiosi were enabled, for years, to feed their network of heroin labs in Italy and Marseille with morphine base supplied by a Lebanese network run by the chief of the antisubversive section of the Lebanese police.[7]

The CIA used the Mafia's allies, the *Union Corse*, to take Marseille away from the independent and communist unions, leaving the Corsican hoods in control of the most important port in France. The geopolitical rationale for this, from both the French and the American perspective, wasn't only the threat the leftists posed to control of France, but to the Indochina war. The Vietminh had considerable support among French leftists in 1947.

In an attempt to force the French government to negotiate with the Vietminh, the communist dock worker unions, which were full of former Maquis fighters, refused to load American arms destined for Vietnam. The only outfits with enough muscle to challenge the communist unions for control of the docks, and the Marseille city council, were the union-busting Corsican hoods and their puppet-union goon squads. The 1947-48 street war for control of Marseille's docks, financed and coordinated by American military intelligence, was nasty, brutish and short.[7a]

The French secret services, also financed by American military intelligence, had been using Corsican opium dealers throughout Indochina to finance their operation against the Vietminh. Thus they had a system in place for the collection and distribution of opium and morphine base from all over the Golden Triangle of Laos, Burma and Thailand.

Morphine base is easily manufactured in makeshift jungle labs. Opium's major alkaloid is precipitated out of the raw sap by boiling it in water with lime. The white morphine floats to the top. That is drawn off and boiled with ammonia, filtered, boiled again, and then sun-dried. The resultant clay-like brown paste is morphine base.

That's where the Corsicans came in. Heroin is diacetylmorphine, morphine in combination with acetic acid, the naturally-occurring acid found in vinegar. Heroin is preferred by users because the acetic acid renders it highly soluble in blood, therefore quicker acting and more potent than unrefined morphine.

The combination process requires, firstly, the skillful use of acetic anhydride, chloroform, sodium carbonate and alcohol. Then the last step, purification in the fourth stage, requires heating with ether and hydrochloric acid. Since the volatile ether has a habit of exploding, the *Union Corse* had to advertise for a few good chemists.

With huge protected surpluses of morphine base available, the Corsicans built a network of labs to refine not only the Indochinese, but also the Persian and Turkish product, shipping the finished snow white #4 heroin out of a Marseille they now controlled. The *Union Corse* heroin was often shipped on the order of their Mafia partners, who controlled the great American retail market.

With that much leverage, the Corsican hoods became major CIA "assets" throughout the fifties. Anslinger's star international agents in the 50's, George White, Charles Siragusa and Sal Vizzini, actually brag in their memoirs about their operational CIA/*Deuxieme Bureau* connections. That is, as they themselves obliquely admit, their mission was essentially political, with the occasional cosmetic bust thrown in for credibility, or to destroy a competing "asset." White is the man who pretended that Burmese-KMT heroin came from the Reds. Siragusa is the man who caught Luciano with a half-ton of heroin being readied for shipment to Trafficante in Havanna - and, pursuant to Anslinger's orders, just let him go.[8]

The U.S. had initially supported the Vietminh in Vietnam, and then shifted its support to the French, who proceeded to lose anyway. In 1954, as the French were collapsing, President Eisenhower addressed these remarkable words to the National Security Council: "The key to winning this war is to get the Vietnamese to fight. There is just no sense in even talking about United States forces replacing the French in Indochina. If we did so, the Vietnamese could be expected to transfer their hatred of the French to us. I cannot tell you how bitterly opposed I am to such a course of action. This war in Indochina would absorb our troops by divisions!"[9] That from the organizer of D-Day.

The Dulles brothers ignored Eisenhower, sending their most dangerous operative, the CIA's Col. Edward Lansdale. Lansdale had just finished stomping the Filippine campesinos into submission. In the process, he replaced President Quirino with our chosen commercial puppet, Ramón Magsaysay. This was done using the old Reichstag Fire trick. The threat posed by the largely mythical HUK rebels was wildly exaggerated by staged incidents which were splashed all over the media. Then Magsaysay, the young Lone Ranger Congressman, rode to the rescue, in the media.

Lansdale, a former advertising executive, was the lead unconventional warfare officer attached to the Saigon Military Mission. His 12-man team was in place by July 1954, less than 2 months after the French defeat at Dienbienphu. They found that the well-organized Binh Xuyen street gang, which was in effect an arm of the *Deuxieme Bureau*, directly controlled Saigon's police force. Lansdale used the mountain of American money and matériel at his disposal to buy the defeated French Vietnamese army, the ARVN. When it was ready, in April of 1955, the ARVN, in a savage 6-day battle that left 500 dead, took Saigon back from the Binh Xuyen.[10]

Lansdale worked in tandem with Lucien Conein, who, during the war, led OSS paramilitary operations in North Vietnam, fighting in the Tonkin jungle with French guerrillas. He was instrumental in rescuing the French population in Hanoi from Vietminh retribution on their 1945 takeover. In this effort he worked with Gen. Phillip Gallagher and Maj. Archimedes Patti, OSS liaison to the Vietminh. Having worked with the French throughout their Indochina war, Conein knew North Vietnam well enough to operate there for Lansdale in 1955. His intimate knowledge of French forces, and his skillful use of troops, helped Lansdale take Saigon.[11]

After all that effort, of course, it would have been a shame to lose "South Vietnam," an American fiction, to Ho Chi Minh in the 1956 all-Vietnam elections guaranteed by the Geneva Accords of 1954. The Accords had simply divided Vietnam into French- or Vietminh-controlled electoral districts. But France lost control of its district. "South Vietnam," with its American-controlled ARVN, refused to participate, despite French insistence that the Accords, formally recognized by the U.S., were internationally binding.

Instead, Lansdale rigged a fake election, installing our puppet, Ngo Dinh Diem, as President of the previously nonexistent South Vietnam in October of 1955. There is no doubt that Ho's victory in a southern election would have been a landslide, though, unlike the North, other parties had strength. France was set to formally recognize one Vietnam under the Vietminh.

Diem was a French-trained lawyer with the psychology of his mandarin ancestors. He worked alternately with and against the French throughout the 30's, 40's and 50's, hoping to inherit their structure. He spent most of the French Indochina War in Catholic institutions in the U.S. In 1953 he was introduced to the American power elite by New York's Francis Cardinal Spellman.

The mission of the Saigon Military Mission was the destabilization of southern Vietnam. By artificially creating anarchy, banditry and guerrilla war, where none existed before, the situation was militarized. The Red Menace would then require Diem's military police state. The puppet regime would then become a reliable source of huge defense contracts. *That's* advertising.

The Geneva Accords had split the country into two roughly equal electoral districts at the 17th parallel. They also provided that Vietnamese were free to move from one district to another. The Saigon Military Mission used this loophole to foment hysteria among Catholics in the North. This terror was entirely the work of Lansdale's northern "psy-ops" teams, led by Conein. It had nothing to do with, and was not the policy of the Vietminh. But when Catholic peasants are machine-gunned by people who *say* they are Vietminh, and who *look* like them, well, psy-ops really do work.

The departing French helped to herd the terrorized Catholic peasants into Haiphong harbor, where they were loaded onto U.S. Navy transports. The CIA's Civil Air Transport also pitched in, and many just walked across the border.

By 1956, more than one million Vietnamese, mostly impoverished Catholic Tonkinese, were dropped, with no social support, among the traditional villages of the southern Cochinese in the Mekong Delta. These populations had never mixed before and despised one another. The homeless Tonkinese Catholics were outnumbered by the native Cochinese Buddhists 12:1.

Diem then did his job. He proceeded to confiscate traditional village lands and hand them to homeless northern Catholic bandit groups. Since "South Vietnam" had never existed before, it had no governmental structure - no tax system, military, police, legislature, civil service - nothing. Diem filled these slots with his pet Catholics. He then abolished all municipal elections and filled those slots with Catholics as well. Diem was creating a mirror of the French administration. His army commander, Gen. Tran Van Don, had been born and educated in France, and fought both WW II and the French Indochina War with the French.

Diem then did something truly diabolical. He destroyed the traditional Mekong Delta barter economy by expelling all ethnic French and Chinese. The rural economy - the grain and commodity markets run for centuries by the mercantile Chinese, collapsed. Commodities as basic as dry-season drinking water became unavailable as the harvests rotted for lack of buyers. Dung-soaked rice-paddy water is undrinkable. The situation did indeed militarize.

Lansdale, Diem and a Catholic prelate; Lansdale Collection, Hoover Institution

Until Lansdale and Conein's psy-ops, one of which was Diem himself, southern Vietnam had been introverted, tribal, peaceful and wealthy - and for the most part completely unaware of the Vietminh. But in the face of starvation, uncontrolled banditry by homeless northern invaders, the systematic destruction of their economy and property rights, and enslavement at gunpoint in "strategic hamlets" - most southern Vietnamese accepted the discipline of the only Vietnamese-led army in Vietnam, the Vietminh.

Since the urbane, Catholic, French-speaking Diem lacked the popular support of the Vietminh, in rural, Buddhist, Vietnamese-speaking Vietnam, he was forced to rely for his financing on his brother, Ngo Dinh Nhu, a world-class opium and heroin dealer tied to the Corsicans.[12]

Lansdale pitched in with a coordinated effort to repeat the French Operation X, which organized the Hmong of highland Laos to operate against the popular Pathet Lao and Vietminh.[13] Lucien Conein had helped the French run Operation X, and so had a relationship with Nhu's Corsicans. Since the only cash crop of the Hmong was opium, that put CAT-Air America, which tied together their disparate mountain villages, firmly in the opium-for-arms business.[14] The proceeds were used to finance both the Hmong army, led by the former French-serving Vang Pao, and Diem's nepotistic regime.

All of Diem's five surviving brothers had important government functions. Ngo Dinh Nhu's weird Personalist Labor Party, composed mostly of former French-serving Vietnamese Catholics, staffed the bureaucracy, while he supervised the CIA-trained secret police. Nhu's man at the head of the secret police, Dr. Tran Kim Tuyen, managed the large-scale dope dealing, feeding the profits to the family patriarch, oldest brother Ngo Dinh Thuc, the Archbishop of Hué, who managed the family's expanding financial empire. Government contracts were invariably let to the Ngo Dinh's army of relatives.

Ngo Dinh Can controlled central Vietnam as a traditional warlord. There was no government spending on rural infrastructure, schools, housing or medical care. Rural spending was confined, á la Lansdale, to the forced resettlement of the peasants into "strategic hamlets." The peasants placed their hopes with the Vietminh, which had always been wise enough to strengthen their rural economy. For the Vietminh, a healthy, traditional village, militarily strong enough to defend itself, was a "strategic hamlet." Such hamlets were incinerated with napalm, bombed, or strafed by high-speed gatling guns. Between 1956 and 1963, Diem and his American allies killed about 100,000 Vietnamese men, women and children.

Diem, acting under brother Archbishop Thuc's advice, was actually stupid enough to criminalize some Buddhist religious celebrations, in favor of his officially sanctioned Catholicism. He thus alienated right-wing Buddhists who otherwise might have supported him. Thuc was eventually excommunicated by the Vatican for religious extremism.

In the summer of 1963, in mindless defense of their kleptocracy, the Ngo Dinh brothers initiated a completely unnecessary series of bitter street confrontations with their only potential Vietnamese support. These demonstrations, which completely destroyed any vestige of legitimacy Diem may have had, included the shooting of unarmed protesters and the mass arrest of the revered monks. This led to the spectacular self-immolation of holy men. The unforgettable fashion plate Madame Nhu earned the undying hatred of many Vietnamese when she ridiculed the monk's "barbeque."

Her husband, Ngo Dinh Nhu, continued to funnel his American-supplied Laotian opium to the world market through Saigon, Bangkok and Hong Kong. The Golden Triangle opium/heroin trade remained the financial mainstay of the Saigon regime long after the November 1, 1963, CIA-engineered demise of the transparent, and increasingly independent, Ngo Dinh brothers.[15]

"Indeed, the long and sordid history of CIA involvement with the Sicilian Mafia, the French Corsican underworld, the heroin producers of Southeast Asia's Golden Triangle, the marijuana- and cocaine-trafficking Cuban exiles of Miami, and the opium smuggling *mujaheddin* of Afghanistan simply reinforces the lesson of the Contra period: far from considering drug networks their enemy, U.S. intelligence organizations have made them an essential ally in the covert expansion of American influence abroad."[16] Scott and Marshall then go on to document the Contra period in horrifying detail in their masterful *Cocaine Politics.*

Prohibition artificially inflates the value of the prohibited commodity 20 to 100 fold. Only genuine agricultural "commodities" are subject to such inflation. That is, the demand is an evolutionarily structural, a permanent, feature of the global economy. You can *pretend* that it's possible to outlaw wine or pot, but it's not. Prohibition of a commodity simply creates a hood monopoly. The kind of power Prohibition put in Lucky Luciano's hands left every New York cop, and Mayor, quacking in his boots. There is no way around the geopolitical power that Prohibition creates. As Luciano put it, "There wasn't a chance for Roosevelt to get the delegates from the city without makin a deal with Tammany, and in 1932 the guys who ran Tammany was run by me and Frank Costello."[17]

It was Frank Costello's muscle that helped Joe Kennedy run his imported Irish rum in the 20's. Joe Kennedy was also close to Owney Madden, a New York powerhouse during Prohibition. After repeal, Costello's Alliance Distributors, with its House of Lords Scotch and King's Ransom, competed with Kennedy's Somerset Liquors, which owned the Haig and Haig, Dewar's and Gordon's Gin franchises.

"The Strong Man"; McKay in the *New York American*, 1930

Joe Kennedy, a brilliant corporate predator, had the deep respect of many Syndicate leaders. As the owner of Chicago's huge Merchandise Mart, he himself was a Chicago power. He used his connections to deliver the awesome Chicago mob in 1960, despite the objections of Jimmy Hoffa.[18]

Giancana, Accardo and Humphreys

Sam "Momo" Giancana, who shot his way to the chairmanship of the Chicago Commission, convinced his fellow commissioners, Anthony Accardo, Paul Ricca and Frank Ferraro, that Joe Kennedy's deal was worth taking. The hoods used their powerful labor fixer, Murray "the Camel" Humphreys, to deliver hundreds of key unions and Teamster locals in primary fights throughout the country.

When it came time to deliver Illinois for Kennedy in the general election, it was the murderous Momo who helped Mayor Daley deliver Chicago. Kennedy won Illinois by about 9,000 votes, and without such mob strongholds as Illinois, Missouri, Nevada, Texas and New Jersey, Nixon would have won in 1960.[19] The popular vote was almost a dead heat - Kennedy got a 112,000-vote margin out of a popular vote of more than 68,000,000. It was the closest election since 1884.

Giancana, of course, was expecting the fix he paid for. The younger Kennedys had laid a lot of heat on the mob during the McClellan hearings, and old Joe's deal was that the heat was off. The Syndicate took JFK's continuing war on them as a mortal betrayal - as a fear-stricken Joe Kennedy, who still played golf with Sam Giancana and Johnny Rosselli, repeatedly warned his reckless sons.

Once Prohibition makes marijuana, coca and opium worth as much as tin, silver and gold, either you deal with the dealers or you get your brains blown out on the street. In 1960 Giancana's Chicago outfit was said to gross $2 billion a year - that's something like $12 billion in today's money. Marcello's 1963 Southeastern U.S. operations were estimated by the conservative New Orleans Crime Commission at $1.2 billion a year.[20] Others estimated $1.6 billion.[21] By 1966 the figure was $2 billion.[22] Marcello's dope, gambling, prostitution, extortion and theft empire was the largest conglomerate in Louisiana. As the beleaguered Crime Commission repeatedly complained, Marcello owned Louisiana - its police, judges, mayors, state senators and governors.[23] And who Marcello couldn't buy, he killed.

Marcello was one of the key distributors of Luciano's Sicilian and Rosselli's Guatemalan dope. Through the Guatemalan prime minister, his lawyer, Marcello was a financier of the CIA's heroic effort to reclaim Cuba for Batista. The Bay of Pigs operation took off from Guatemala on April 17, 1961, within the first 90 days of Kennedy's presidency. Like Nixon, JFK thoroughly enjoyed the mob's hospitality in his father's old stomping ground. He too was deeply offended by the loss of Cuba, and he beat poor Richard to a pulp on the issue.

The Cuba invasion was presented to JFK, both as a candidate and as the President-elect, as an urgent necessity to avoid the impending introduction of Soviet MIGs, after which no small-scale invasion could hope to succeed. But no one at the Cuba desk in the State Department was asked to comment on the plan, or even knew of its existence, so that only those who devised the invasion judged its chances for success.[24] Was Castro really so unpopular that a pinprick invasion would set off a general uprising? Was there really an intact underground ready to strike? Did a 1500-man force have a snowball's chance in hell on the beach? Or was Kennedy being maneuvered into a situation that would force him to use American troops?

Kennedy, after all, was heading for a June summit in Vienna with Krushchev. He had to consider that if he took Cuba by undeniable American force, he might, since the KGB was at least as crazy as the CIA, force Krushchev to take Berlin, something he knew was well within Krushchev's power. The consequences of that were literally too horrible to contemplate.

The highly classified *CIA Inspector General's Survey of the Cuba Operation* was dated October of 1961. It has since been declassified and posted on the net. It concluded that "it is essential to avoid grasping immediately, as many persons have done, at the explanation that the President's order cancelling the D-Day air strikes was the chief cause of failure.... that...would merely raise this underlying question: If the project had been better conceived, better organized, better staffed and better managed, would that precise issue ever have had to be presented for Presidential decision at all? And would it have been presented under the same ill-prepared, inadequately-briefed circumstances?"

"Furthermore, it is essential to keep in mind the possibility that the invasion was doomed in advance, that an initially successful landing by 1,500 men would eventually have been crushed by Castro's combined military resources."

"The fundamental cause of the disaster was the Agency's failure to give the project...appropriate organization, staffing throughout by highly qualified personnel, and full-time direction and control of the highest quality."

"Thus, the project lacked a single, high-level full-time commander possessing stated broad powers and abilities sufficient for carrying out this large, enormously difficult mission. In fact, authority was fragmented among the project chief, the military chief of the project's Paramilitary Staff, and several high-level officials, whose wide responsibilities elsewhere in the Agency prevented them from giving the project the attention it required."

The requisite command-and-control, of course, would have made it an *overt* U.S. operation, at least to the extent that it was subject to the CIA's own formal internal review process. That process, since the CIA operates under the orders of the President's National Security Council, gave the new President a veto over the whole operation.

"In mid-January 1961 various major policy questions were, at CIA's request, under discussion by the Special Group. These included: (a) use of American contract pilots for tactical and logistical air operations over Cuba; (b) use of a U.S. air base for logistical flights to Cuba;

(c) commencement of air strikes not later than dawn of the day before the amphibious assault and without curtailment of the number of aircraft to be employed from those available; (d) use of Puerto Cabezas, Nicaragua, as an air-strike base and maritime staging area."

"In the end, only one of these policy questions was resolved in the affirmative, that with regard to the use of Puerto Cabezas. It should be especially noted that the project's paramilitary chief had strongly recommended that the operation be abandoned if policy should not allow adequate tactical air support."

"...the revised concept...was apparently acceptable to the President although he indicated he might order a diversion. Before that he had authorized the Agency to proceed with mounting the operation, but had reserved the right to cancel at any time."

"...the plan had been swiftly and successively altered to incorporate four characteristics which had been deemed essential in order to ensure that the operation would look like an infiltration of guerrillas in support of an internal revolution and would therefore be politically acceptable."

"The four characteristics were: a. an unspectacular night landing; b. possibility of conducting air operations from a base on seized territory; c. a buildup period, after the initial landing, to precede offensive action against Castro's forces, and d. terrain suitable for guerrilla warfare in the event the invasion force could not hold a lodgement."

But, as the Inspector-General indicated, the DCI under fire, Allen Dulles, had reason to believe that even a successful invasion force wouldn't be able to hold Cuban territory without U.S. help. The CIA's report made Dulles uncomfortable, because it revealed very uncharacteristic, perhaps intentional, mismanagement of the planning. It was Dulles who divided authority so disastrously, an amateur's mistake this CIA grey eminence was unlikely to have made unintentionally.

In a 2/15/62 memorandum to the new DCI John McCone, Dulles protested that "the Inspector General's report suffers from the fact that his investigation was limited to the activities of one segment of one agency, namely, the C.I.A.... Judgements could not properly be rendered in this matter without a full analysis, as was made by the Taylor Committee, of actions of all the participating elements...particularly...the Department of State, the Department of Defense, the Joint Chiefs of Staff and to certain elements of the Executive Department of the Government."

The Taylor Study Group, Kennedy's executive postmortem, was chaired by Gen. Maxwell Taylor, Eisenhower's former army chief of staff. It included Bobby Kennedy, Allen Dulles and Adm. Arleigh Burke. They found that Castro's remaining three jet fighters, T-33 trainers, were powerful enough to destroy any chance the Brigade had to set up a perimeter and take the local airstrip. Those T-33's knocked out 16 of the Brigade's lumbering B-26's, raked the beach with heavy machine gun fire, and sank the supply ships. As the Brigade started to lose, it was Adm. Burke who strongly advocated a direct U.S. naval attack. Burke's seemingly extemporaneous plan was vetoed, for policy reasons, by Kennedy.

Burke wanted the postmortem to focus on the operational failure of the political leadership, Kennedy's supposed cancellation of the second airstrike. Dulles, in the memo to McCone, strongly agreed with Burke. But the Taylor "report," actually a less formal "letter," didn't say Kennedy cancelled the airstrike - it said: "At about 9:30 p.m. on April 16, Mr. McGeorge Bundy, Special Assistant to the President, telephoned General C.P. Cabell of CIA to inform him that the dawn air strikes the following morning should not be launched until they could be conducted from a strip within the beachhead."[25]

Bundy later claimed to have "a very wrong estimate of the consequences" of that decision. That is, he admitted that the decision was his. DDCI Cabell, who could not possibly have misunderstood the consequences, did nothing to reverse them. He didn't even bother to take the issue to the President, despite the fact that the entire operation hung in the balance - and despite the fact that the President's own order of 1:45 the previous afternoon had *approved* the airstrike.

RFK was also interested in the revelation that other overt presidential orders, such as the strong injunction not to use any Americans in the invading force, were ignored.[26]

It was also interesting to RFK that the CIA had lied through its teeth when it assured Kennedy that the small invasion would spark a popular uprising. It had the report of the Office of Naval Intelligence in Guantanamo, which insisted that Castro was profoundly popular, the keeper of the economic hopes of most ordinary Cubans. This inconvenient intelligence was never presented to the Bay of Pigs planning group.[27] The CIA leadership knew precisely how popular Castro was, and how unpopular their *Batistianos* were. The Inspector General's report stressed that the CIA knew that no organized underground existed. The hawks were trying to engineer a *fait accompli*, a military situation in which Kennedy would feel compelled to use U.S. troops.

Castro, in fact, was militarily well-organized, competent and popular, all the things Kennedy had been told he was not. Since the CIA had failed to keep its promise to kill *El Commandante* on the eve of the invasion, Cuban troops continued to have very effective leadership.

Allen Dulles, the architect of the invasion, contrary to all established procedure, was vacationing in Puerto Rico on D-Day. The invasion was managed by Deputy Director Gen. Charles Cabell and Richard Bissell, the Deputy Director for Plans. McGeorge Bundy, the President's Special Assistant for National Security Affairs, who actually called off the D-Day air strike, was their chief White House operative. And Bundy was in a position to intercept appeals to the President.

At 1 a.m. on April 17, the day of the landing, the CIA commander at Puerto Cabezas airstrip in Nicaragua called Col. Fletcher Prouty, chief of the Office of Special Operations, the key military supply officer of the invasion force. He frantically begged his old friend to intercede with the Joint Chiefs to override the grounding of the airstrike. A launch later than 2 a.m. from Nicaragua couldn't get to Cuba before dawn. That second strike needed darkness because the old WW II workhorses being used - plausibly not current U.S. military aircraft - were too slow to avoid Castro's antiaircraft fire. But under cover of darkness, they could easily take out those last three jets on the ground, just as they had the first seven the day before. This would give Brigade 2506 enough time to establish a beachhead, take the local airstrip and receive reinforcements. But the last-minute cancellation, and Cabell's refusal to do anything about it, assured that there would be no time to reverse it.[28] Prouty's attempts to reverse the order were met by the brick wall of Bundy, Cabell and Bissell.

Since the CIA knew that no internal Cuban resistance could succeed against the wildly popular Fidel, it engineered an immediate U.S. invasion by crippling the Cuban invasion from the start. A successful *Batistiano* invasion would have seen a vast outpouring of volunteers for Fidel - it would have revealed Fidel's political strength. Dulles' uncharacteristic poor planning, and the rejection of key support and backup plans, were intentional, as, obviously, was his D-Day absence.

After cancelling the air strike from Puerto Cabezas, Bundy could plausibly tell Kennedy that they had to consider that the American contract pilots flying the second strike might end up in shackles, or coffins, on Cuban television - *prima facie* proof of direct U.S. aggression. Rather than risk the consequent confrontation with the Soviet Union, Bundy cancelled the second air strike. Kennedy, rather than publicly admit his own lack of operational control, chose to take responsibility for Bundy's action.

Kennedy was maneuvered into a situation that would force him to order a U.S. invasion. But he refused. The CIA's own internal Survey concluded Kennedy had been buffaloed behind "poor planning." So Kennedy fired the planners - the DCI, Allen Dulles, his top aide, the Deputy Director Gen. Charles Cabell, and the next ranker, Richard Bissell, the Deputy Director for Plans. But, since Kennedy had taken public responsibility for cancelling the predawn airstrike, the CIA could plausibly insist that its leadership were being used as scapegoats for Kennedy's own operational incompetence. Kennedy's real failure, of course, was simply not to have followed the script.

Having viscerally enraged the most dangerous men in the military, the Kennedy brothers then moved for direct operational control of the CIA. In June of 1961 they issued three National Security Action Memoranda designed to force executive control of CIA covert operations, NSAM's 55-57. These were the operational fixes designed by the Cuban Study Group. Col. Prouty, as the briefing officer for the Chairman of the Joint Chiefs of Staff, was charged with delivering and explaining these NSAM's to the key elements in the high command. "Nothing I had ever been involved with in my entire career had created such an uproar. NSAM 55 stripped the CIA of its cherished covert operations role, except for small actions. It was an explosive document. The military-industrial complex was not pleased."[29]

The CIA had defined intervention in Katanga on behalf of Moise Tshombe as a "covert" operation, although it was a full-scale war. The killing of Patrice Lumumba, the legally elected Prime Minister, was justified in Cold War industrial terms. Lumumba's popular nationalism might see all those militarily valuable rare metals in Commie hands. Belgian, French and American mining companies had rights too. The nazi Mobutu regime we put in Lumumba's place, which held power for thirty years, completely destabilized the Congo and ruined its economy. Vietnam, another full-scale war, was also a CIA "Cold War" or "covert" operation.

As the fix suggested by the Bay of Pigs disaster, NSAM 55 attempted to take those operations out of the hands of the CIA and put them squarely in the hands of the Joint Chiefs of Staff, that is, under direct, overt Presidential control. "I wish to inform the Joint Chiefs of Staff as follows with regard to my views of their relations to me in Cold War [covert] Operations:... The Joint Chiefs of Staff have a responsibility for the defense of the nation in the Cold War similar to that which they have in conventional hostilities."[30]

Gen. Maxwell Taylor won Kennedy's trust by conceiving and writing this mechanism for him. He worked in this effort with Adm. Burke and Allen Dulles in the Cuban Study Group. As later events proved, this was a measure of Dulles' subtlety. Dulles, a master at issuing "clarifications" and "cover letters," knew that the current head of the Joint Chiefs, Gen. Lemnitzer, had no interest in running covert operations, that is, undeclared wars. Most CIA wars started out as "small," that is properly CIA, operations. Dulles also assumed that the next Chairman of the JCS would be his man. He was right.

The Berlin Wall started going up in June. In late October the tank standoff at Berlin's Checkpoint Charlie, initiated by our own ambassador's idiotic desire to see the opera in East Berlin, almost turned into The Match. Kennedy's personal backchannel diplomacy prevented the fuse from being lit, but the confrontation left him in no doubt that he was playing global nuclear chicken.[31] Cuba, therefore, ceased to be Cuba. It became a pawn in the global confrontation - impossible to consider independently of Russia's power in eastern Germany.

And Vietnam, therefore, ceased to be Vietnam. It became strategic position and resources to be denied the enemy. Throughout his administration Kennedy gave full support to the CIA's effort to beat the Vietminh in Vietnam. He rubber-stamped the CIA's every authorization, including the 1962 introduction of napalm, defoliants, offensive airpower and indiscriminate shelling of "free-fire zones." But he hesitated at putting American combat troops on the ground in Southeast Asia, despite the rosy walk in the park predicted by Maxwell Taylor.[32]

Like his pet hawks, Kennedy thought to reverse the political damage suffered at the Bay of Pigs by actually taking Cuba. He asked Air Force Maj. Gen. Edward Lansdale, the CIA point man who had just handed the Binh Xuyen to Diem, to devise the attack.

Operation Mongoose, outlined under National Security Action Memorandum 100 on October 5, 1961, was approved by Kennedy on November 30, the same month Allen Dulles departed. Dulles left the CIA in his command car, an armor-plated limousine replete with all the latest communications equipment. That is, Allen Dulles was out, but not out of touch. Lansdale was instructed "to use all available assets...to help Cuba overthrow the communist regime."[33]

Mongoose was run out of Miami's CIA station JM/WAVE, with covert funding in the hundreds of millions. Under the command of

Ted Shackley, it became the largest in the world, with 600 agents, at least 4,000 operatives, and enough matériel to conquer most small countries. Diversified hit and run, sabotage, surveillance, propaganda and assassination teams were systematically thrown at Cuban targets, to "build gradually toward an internal revolt," as Lansdale put it.[34]

The fact that these actions, executed by *Batistianos*, left Castro stronger and more popular than ever did not go unnoticed at the CIA.[35] Complained Samuel Halpern, the executive officer of Task Force W, the CIA's coordination component with Mongoose, "The Kennedys were sold a bill of goods by Lansdale. We would refer to Lansdale on the telephone as the FM - for field marshal."[36]

Dulles, Lansdale and Cabell: www.astridmm.com/prouty

1962 saw many National Security Action Memoranda flow from the same font, many aimed at Vietnam. The Vietnam strategy was the reverse of the Cuban, in that military violence was being used to prop up a hated regime. That Diem became weaker with every assassination we engineered only forced the strategic geniuses of counterinsurgency to conclude that more violence was called for.[37]

Lansdale's White House liaison, with whom he was in almost daily contact, was Robert Kennedy, who subscribed to this hook, line and sinker. Although Kennedy removed Dulles and a few of his top aides, he didn't disassemble the CIA control apparatus that Dulles had built. Lansdale's immediate superior was the CIA's number two man, Richard Helms, the new Deputy Director for Plans, a trusted Dulles operative since their days together in Germany.[38] Dulles' longtime main man, James Angleton, was left in charge of Counterintelligence, that is political assassination and dirty tricks, also known as the "alternative CIA."[39] Both used J. Edgar Hoover's domestic Counter Intelligence Programs (COINTELPROS) to function within the United States.

January 1957 saw the start of the McClellan labor racketeering hearings. October saw Albert Anastasia, one of New York's most murderous bosses, filled full of holes in the barbershop of the Park Sheraton Hotel. This happened immediately after Anastasia's two business meetings - with the Cuban contractors building Havana's new Hilton Casino, and with Cuba boss Santos Trafficante. Trafficante, immediately before the shooting, hurriedly checked out of the neighboring Warwick Hotel. The next month saw the spectacular detention of 58 mafiosi, including Santos Trafficante, Vito Genovese, Carlo Gambino and Joe Profaci, as they left the Apalachin, New York estate of bootlegger and dope dealer Joe Barbara.

Trafficante toasts Carlos Marcello, left, and Frank Ragano, right,1966; AP/WW

The time had come, the Justice Department reasoned, to set up a Special Group on Organized Crime.[40] To Sam Giancana's consternation, Senator McClellan's man, Attorney General RFK, expanded this group from 15 to 60 legal eagles, most recruited from tough big-city DA's. RFK also forced Hoover, technically his subordinate, to create an FBI Organized Crime (Special Investigative) Division, run by a trusted Kennedy ally from the McClellan days, Courtney Evans, a 25-year FBI veteran who would likely have been the brothers' choice to replace Hoover.[41]

The Kennedys needed Hoover's silence about their remarkable sex lives and hood associations, but, pursuant to their usual ballsy brinksmanship, enraged him, by criticizing his ridiculous assignment of 400 agents to investigate communism in New York City and only 4 to investigate the Mafia.[42] The Kennedys knew Hoover was an anachronism - and Hoover knew the Kennedys were horny pinko nigger lovers.

The problem with Evans' Organized Crime Division, from both Hoover's and the CIA's perspective, was that it targeted the street allies of Hoover's other divisions, the Espionage Section and the Domestic Intelligence Division (Division Five), running the COINTELPROS. Dangerous foreign agents, masquerading as American citizens, were challenging Mafia control of many labor unions, so the patriotic mafiosi did all they could to help the Counter Intelligence Programs, going so far as to stick ice picks into subversive hearts.

New York Syndicate operatives Max and Louis Block, for instance, worked hand-in-glove with Hoover and his tool Joe McCarthy to "decommunize" the Fur and Leather Workers Union.[43] This "decommunization" drove committed activists, who opposed union-management sweetheart fixes, out of the union, and forced its merger with the Amalgamated Meat Cutters, already controlled by the Blocks. The result was enormous Mafia power over the grocery companies dependent on union labor - and the disappearance of the defunct union's huge pension fund.[44]

The mafiosi ran their sweetheart unions and security firms for the red-baiting propagandists in the American Security Council. The ASC was financed by major defense contractors such as General Electric, Lockheed, Motorola, Rockwell, Honeywell and General Dynamics. They and their myriad subcontractors grossed more than $600 billion from the Vietnam War.[45]

The defense contractors were inspired by the Christian Crusade of Billy James Hargis, which advised religious patriots to "Kill a Commie for Christ." This was the uplifting message General Edwin Walker delivered to his troops, prompting the Kennedys to sack him.[46] Billy Graham, Nixon's high priest, also repeatedly insisted during the fifties and sixties that "Asia can be won!"[47] This became a basic theme of Secretary of State John Foster Dulles, a spokesman for the World Council of Churches. This was also a favorite theme of Cardinal Spellman, who had strong secret society ties to European Catholic fascists.

An anticommunist holy war, such as could be organized in Vietnam, would be a windfall for the defense contractors and their CIA and oil company allies. Aside from the huge military contracts they could engineer, they would, upon victory, come into possession of Indochina's vast natural resources, including the huge opium crop, traditionally used by Asian war lords to buy weaponry from said

Christian defense contractors.

APRIL 6, 1956

I.S News World Report

WHERE THE BOOM IS HEADING

EXCLUSIVE INTERVIEW

Billy Graham

Says –

"ASIA CAN BE WON"

His Holiness, 4/6/1956

Kennedy's low-intensity warfare aimed at Cuba, aptly named Mongoose, gave both Fidel and Krushchev the same idea - nuclear missiles, both land and sea based, for either bargaining or Armageddon.

At the height of the Cuban missile crisis of October, 1962, the Joint Chiefs, on Kennedy's orders, fielded a full-scale invasion force of 225,000 men plus Navy and Air Force to take Cuba. The force was under the operational control of the joint Army-Air Force U.S. Strike Command based in Florida, led by Gen. William Rosson, who had been part of Lansdale's Vietnam team.[48] The Joint Chiefs, led by the new Chairman Gen. Maxwell Taylor, recommended an immediate massive airstrike followed by full-scale invasion - despite the possibility that this could trigger use of the Cuban nukes on American cities.

General Issa Pliyev had 42,000 troops in Cuba and control of more than a hundred short and medium range nuclear missiles. He was a key commander during the battles for Stalingrad and Moscow, and could be counted on to go down fighting. Aside from incinerating the East Coast, the Ruskies could also start a full-scale European land war.[49] Berlin, after all, was an island in Russian territory. But the Ruskies kept their cool, confining the confrontation to Cuba. They did not go on global high alert, although the American military did.

Kennedy led his emergency Executive Committee to recommend naval blockade, which lasted from October 22nd to the 28th. Krushchev was pushed to agree to remove the missiles in return for free access to Cuba and a vague guarantee that the island would be left in peace. Kennedy acknowledged Krushchev's point by covertly accepting his initial proposal, the removal of U. S. missiles from Turkey. Krushchev pondered Kennedy's, about free access to West Berlin.

The leaders then went on to use the opening to engineer the first atmospheric nuclear test-ban treaty, signed in July 1963. The Joint Chiefs, led by the Navy's Arleigh Burke and the Air Force's Curtis LeMay, were not pleased with any limits on their testing. Terry Southern was moved to write *Dr. Strangelove*.

Kennedy Special Assistant Arthur Schlesinger likes to say that "He was a prudent executive, not inclined to heavy investments in lost causes. His whole presidency was marked precisely by his capacity to *refuse* escalation - as in Laos, the Bay of Pigs, the Berlin Wall, the missile crisis."[50] Well, *ultimately* prudent, anyway. Kennedy was a gunslinger who consistently used confrontation to spark diplomatic results, especially when they were militarily convenient. Given that we had already developed underground nuclear testing, the atmospheric test ban treaty simply froze our strategic advantage in place.

But it was precisely this insider's savvy that made Kennedy so dangerous to the radical hawks - he threatened to actually take command. "Let us reexamine our attitude toward the Cold War," said Kennedy at American University in June of 1963, as he installed a direct "hot line" to the Kremlin.[51] That, combined with Secretary of Defense Robert S. McNamara's warnings that defense spending might be continued "at a lower level" made the defense contractors very unhappy.

When McNamara's team successfully stood up to the combined forces of Boeing, the Air Force and the Navy in awarding the huge $6.5 billion TFX fighter-bomber contract to General Dynamics, the contractors knew that their Cold War spigot was in danger of being throttled. Former Ford CEO McNamara flatly declared that the day had past when the services would be allowed to develop their own weapons systems.

On April 9th, 1963, McNamara's Deputy Secretary of Defense, Roswell Gilpatric, addressed a powerful group of bankers on "The Impact of the Changing Defense Program on the United States Economy." He assured them that "I have not the slightest doubt that our economy could adjust to a decline in defense spending."[52]

From 1955 through 1964, Col. Fletcher Prouty was the Joint Chiefs' "focal point" officer for the military support of CIA military operations. As an Air Transport Command VIP pilot during WW II, he flew the Chinese delegation to the 1943 Tehran Conference. He was on duty for both the Cairo and Tehran Conferences of November, 1943. He also flew deep penetration missions through the Urals to the Russians, and into Japan, before the surrender, to set it up. Through the Kennedy years he was the head of the Office of Special Operations - the main military disbursement and intelligence officer of the Joint Chiefs for CIA covert military operations.

In 1956 he set up the Air Force's Office of Special Operations to coordinate Air Force work for the CIA. As founding Chief of the OSO he literally wrote the Air Force manual for this work, and set up its worldwide system of offices and communications. Prouty's unique interservice coordinating office was moved from the Air Force to the Office of the Secretary of Defense and then, during the Kennedy years, to the Office of the Joint Chiefs of Staff.

To facilitate CIA-Defense Department coordination, Allen Dulles sent Prouty on a worldwide tour of CIA stations.[53] "If the Agency needed an Air Force plane I'd give them one, but I'd try and put somebody on it or at least, if it was a totally clandestine mission, have somebody out there who would just fuel the plane. He could note the time the plane took off, the time it came back, and who went on board. In other words I'd run a counter-Agency operation, and I had the best system for monitoring the Agency that ever existed."[54] Prouty worked for the Joint Chiefs, not the CIA.

Prouty also helped set up the Presidential Protection system that coordinated the Secret Service with specially trained military units, "flying wedges." As President Kennedy's security advisor, he had hoped to help the President reverse the creeping CIA takeover of the regular Army that he had been observing with increasing alarm through the Eisenhower years - an alarm he shared with Eisenhower himself.

Enraged by Kennedy's assassination, and by the consequent CIA-engineered Vietnam War, which many in the Army high command had bitterly opposed,[55] Prouty wrote *The Secret Team: The CIA and Its Allies in Control of the United States and the World*, and *JFK: The CIA, Vietnam, And The Plot to Assassinate John F. Kennedy*. Prouty was Oliver Stone's technical advisor for his carefully researched JFK. He was the officer, played by Donald Southerland in the film, who contacted Jim Garrison.

Prouty reported on a 1961 Joint Chiefs briefing: "Finally, the briefings on atomic energy matters, missiles and space, and other highly classified matters took place. Then the Chiefs began to hear some of the more closely held intelligence matters. The last item was the one that pertained to the CIA operational information. As I was ushered into the room I noted that everyone was leaving [for security reasons] except the chairman and the commandant of the Marine Corps. The chairman was General Lyman L. Lemnitzer, and the commandant was General David M. Shoup."

"When the primary subject of the briefing had ended General Lemnitzer asked me about the army cover unit that was involved in the operation. I explained what its role was and more or less added that this was a rather routine matter. Then he said, 'Prouty, if this is routine, yet General Shoup and I have never heard of it before, can you tell me how many Army units there are that exist as "cover" for the CIA?' I replied that to my knowledge at that time there were about 605 such units, some real, some mixed, and some that were simply telephone drops. When he heard that he turned to General Shoup and said, 'You know, I realized that we provided cover for the Agency from time to time, but I never knew that we had anywhere near so many permanent cover units and that they existed all over the world.'"[56]

That started an informal conversation between the three men that revealed to them the depth of penetration the CIA had achieved in an Army they thought they controlled. With control of strategic requisitions and contracting units, air bases, naval bases and customs units, using Army, Air Force, Navy or Marine resources, the CIA was able, without funding, to mount truly covert and unauthorized operations anywhere in the world. With CIA control of the oversight apparatus, oversight ceased to exist. *Ex post facto* approval was always granted. With the ability to move hundreds of millions covertly, the CIA was able to build Air America into the largest contract carrier in the world.

Arthur Schlesinger: "It had almost as many people under official cover overseas as State; in a number of embassies CIA officers out-numbered those from State in the political sections. Often the CIA station chief had been in the country longer than the ambassador, had more money at his disposal and exerted more influence. The CIA had its own political desks and military staffs; it had in effect its own for-eign service, its own air force, even, on occasion, its own combat forces. Moreover, the CIA declined to clear its clandestine intelligence opera-tions either with the State Department in Washington or with the ambassador in the field; and while covert political operations were cleared with State, this was sometimes done, not at the start, but after the operation had almost reached the point beyond which it could not easily be recalled."[57] At this time, CIA's listed budget was 50% higher than State's.

Prouty: "At that top echelon the Office of Special Operations acted as the liaison between the CIA and the DOD. What most people in Defense were totally unaware of was that in the very office that was supposed to serve the military departments and shield them from promiscuous requests, there were concealed and harbored some of the most effective agents the CIA has ever had. Their approval of CIA requests was assured. The amazing fact was that their cover was so good that they could then turn right around and write orders direct-ing the service concerned to comply with the request."

"This is a clear example of how far the Agency has gone in getting around the law and in creating its own inertial drift, which puts it into things almost by an intelligence-input-induced automation sys-tem, without the knowledge of its own leaders and certainly without the knowledge of most higher-level authorities.... what secrecy there was - what real deep and deceptive secrecy existed - existed within the U.S. Government itself. More effort had been made by the Secret Team to shield, deceive, and confuse people inside Government than took place on the outside."[58]

Prouty's melodramatic phrase "Secret Team" lends itself to deri-sion as another "conspiracy theory," but what this brilliant military intelligence officer is saying is that policy ceased to be driven by an empirical analysis of the strategic facts, as honestly presented to the political leadership, and instead became driven by covert centers of economic power, intentionally presenting false intelligence to the po-litical leadership. Eisenhower, hardly a "conspiracy theorist," recog-nized this as operational fascism. He truly feared this loss of political control at the top.

Eisenhower had wanted to leave the Presidency as a great peacemaker. To this end he launched his Crusade For Peace, arranging a May, 1960 Summit in Paris with Nikita Krushchev. The two old WW II allies were planning a profound de-escalation of the Cold War - and the consequent diversion of national resources to the civilian sector. As part of normal preparations, Eisenhower ordered that all U.S. troops, overt and covert, were to avoid all combat. He also ordered all U-2 spy flights over Soviet territory grounded. These were unambiguous conventional orders from the Commander in Chief. Tragically, even our heavy air support of the Khamba resistance in Tibet, run by Col. Prouty, was halted.

Prouty received his orders to ground the Tibetan operation from the CIA's Deputy Director for Plans, Richard Bissell, the same officer who ran the U-2 operation. It is, therefore, not possible that Bissell missed Eisenhower's order. But on May 1, Bissell ordered Capt. Francis Gary Powers to overfly the Soviet Union with his high-altitude cameras. According to Allen Dulles' own closed testimony before the Senate Foreign Relations Committee, Powers' U-2 was forced to land at Sverdlovsk because of engine trouble.[59]

The spy plane had been launched directly contrary to Eisenhower's emphatic order, and had been fixed to fail halfway through its long flight, specifically to ruin Eisenhower's Summit. Prouty says the plane can be easily fixed by draining the required amount of auxiliary hydrogen fuel. The spectacular landing of the state-of-the-art spy plane at Sverdlovsk, of course, did force cancellation of the Summit.

It was Col. Prouty, the Air Force's senior intelligence officer, that Eisenhower called to decipher the mess. It was Prouty who briefed Dulles before his Senate testimony. These tough soldiers had witnessed the CIA use its mole tactics to infiltrate all the U.S. command and control mechanisms to which it was legally responsible, concentrating on the "enemy" only as an adjunct to control of U.S. policy and power. The evolving covert government-by-defense-contractor scared the hell out of them.

This was the impetus for Eisenhower's January 17, 1961 televised speech, a speech he knew to be his most historic, his last presidential address. The old soldier solemnly warned that "The conjunction of an immense military establishment and a large arms industry is new in the American experience. The total influence - economic, political, even spiritual - is felt in every city, every State house, every office of the Federal government.... In the councils of government, we must guard against the acquisition of unwarranted influence, whether sought or unsought, by the military-industrial complex. The potential for the disastrous rise of misplaced power exists and will persist."

Prouty: "In the case of the FAA, the actual CIA slotted men are in places where they can assist the ST with its many requirements in the field of commercial aviation, both transport and aircraft maintenance and supply companies." The CIA slots in FAA, granted years before by other administrations, gradually expanded until they controlled basic FAA policy. Administrations change, bureaucrats just acquire seniority. "Turnover being what it is in bureaucratic Washington, it would not be too long before everyone around that position would have forgotten that it was still there as a special slot. It would be a normal FAA-assigned job with a CIA man in it."

"This same procedure works for slots in the Departments of State, Defense, and even in the White House.... This is intricate and long-range work but it pays off, and the ST is adept at the use of these tactics. Of course, there are many variations of the ways in which this can be done."[60]

Lt. Col. William Corson, Special Assistant to the Secretary of Defense and advisor to the Church Intelligence Committee, points out that CIA and DIA operatives have so thoroughly infiltrated the OMB that internal criticism of CIA's budgetary requests is all but eliminated.[61]

Prouty: "Thus the CIA has been able to evolve a change in the meaning of and the use of the control word 'direct' and then to get its own people into key positions so that when they do present operations for approval they are often presenting these critical clandestine schemes to their own people."[62]

"This was the plan and the wisdom of the Dulles idea from the beginning. On the basis of national security he would place people in all areas of government, and then he would move them up and deeper into their cover jobs, until they began to take a very active part in the role of their own cover organizations. This is how the ST was born. Today, the role of the CIA is performed by an *ad hoc* organization that is much greater in size, strength, and resources than the CIA has ever been visualized to be."[63]

"Allen Dulles was able to get Maxwell Taylor into the White House as personal military advisor to President Kennedy.... Maxwell Taylor was not the White House military advisor in the regular sense; he was the CIA's man at the White House, and he was the 'paramilitary advisor.' ....During the last days of the Dulles era, Maxwell Taylor served as the Focal Point man between Dulles and his Agency and the White House."[64]

Taylor never challenged Kennedy politically, never opposed his policy. For that matter, Kennedy never opposed Taylor's policy. The two had no policy differences. That's why Kennedy made Taylor Chairman of the Joint Chiefs. Kennedy agreed when Taylor wrote into NSAM 57: "A paramilitary operation...may be undertaken in support of an existing government friendly to the United States or in support of a rebel group seeking to overthrow a government hostile to us."[65] Kennedy instinctively accepted the idea that Vietnam ought to be a Catholic-led American colony, and Taylor fully supported the "Vietnamization" idea, which left most of the fighting to the rented gooks.

Even if he didn't, he would have had no other choice in the face of Kennedy's Commandant of Marines, Gen. David Shoup: "in every case...every senior officer that I knew...said we should never send ground combat forces into Southeast Asia."[66] Shoup's 1964 successor, Wallace Green, said much the same thing. "Vietnamization" was the only policy wedge left, a wedge that Cold Warrior JFK was more than happy to see driven home.

Kennedy, who talked constantly of "communist aggression" and "assault from the inside," subscribed wholeheartedly to the "limited counterinsurgency" doctrine espoused by Taylor. He saw Vietnam as the place to "stop the hungry Chinese" from dropping "the Bamboo Curtain." That U.S imperialism was the only thing Vietnam and China agreed on never seems to have occurred to him. So all Taylor had to do was feed Kennedy enough strategic bullshit to make escalating military involvement seem plausible.

Shoup, Lemnitzer, MacArthur, Mountbatten, Ridgway, Bradley, Gavin, Prouty and many others were horrified. They saw us heading for a repeat of the Korean nightmare. They predicted, before it ever happened, 60,000 American dead and a loss. They did not regard that as an option. It is not policy, but its predecessor, intelligence, dishonest intelligence, that Prouty refers to. That was the problem at the Bay of Pigs, and so it remained.

Taylor's 1961 cables to Kennedy are a good example of the kind of policy-convenient bullshit he and his CIA cohorts practiced right through the Johnson years. "[South Vietnam is] not an excessively difficult or unpleasant place to operate...comparable to parts of Korea where U.S. troops learned to live and work without too much effort...North Vietnam is extremely vulnerable to conventional bombing....There is no case for fearing a mass onslaught of Communist manpower into South Vietnam and its neighboring states, particularly if our air power is allowed a free hand against logistical targets."[67]

Our Korean War commanders, MacArthur and Ridgway, who suffered the painful failure of air power in Korea, knew that was idiotic, dishonest. U.S. troops learned to live and work in Korea only after nearly being driven into the East China Sea by the Chinese army. The 1951 winter retreat from the Chinese-North Korea border back to the Pusan Perimeter, below Seoul, was one of the most nightmarish in U.S. history. We had a far higher casualty rate in Korea than in Vietnam - 34,000 dead, another 120,000 wounded, in three years. At that rate, we would have lost more than 100,000 dead in Vietnam.

Taylor's bullshit was good for Air Force appropriations, not the grunts at Ia Drang and Khe Sanh. At Ia Drang American troops were awestruck, and badly bloodied, by an unrelenting hail of machine gun fire, despite heavy air support. We dropped more high explosive on little Vietnam than all sides dropped in all of World War II, and we still found ourselves facing "a mass onslaught of Communist manpower." What's a logistical target in North Vietnam? A mountain range? A forest? A thatched hut? A bicycle on a jungle trail? Five million widely dispersed cadres with shovels and Chinese machine guns?

Misperceiving this manipulative liar as an old school straight talker, Kennedy installed Taylor as Chairman of the Joint Chiefs when he moved Lemnitzer up to NATO. In so doing, he lost all hope of controlling the CIA, since the explicit National Security Action Memoranda he issued necessarily relied on the power of the Joint Chiefs for CIA oversight. Taylor fed Kennedy a steady stream of policy-convenient bullshit masquerading as military intelligence, bullshit designed by Dulles, Helms, Angleton, Lansdale, LeMay, Lodge and the other committed "counterinsurgents."

Taylor, as Chairman of the Joint Chiefs, wrote to Kennedy on September 2, 1963: "Finally, progress continues with the strategic hamlet program. The latest Government of Vietnam figures indicate that 8,227 of the planned 10,592 hamlets had been completed; 76 percent, or 9,563,370 of the rural population, are now in these hamlets."[68] This bore no relation to reality.

Douglas MacArthur himself, a military genius and a savage anticommunist, had warned Kennedy in the White House in 1961 that a Vietnam war was military suicide, predicting in detail everything that happened after Kennedy's death.[69] MacArthur, who nearly lost his entire army to the Chinese in Korea, pointed out that China was still allied with neighboring Vietnam. As he went for the kill against the North Koreans on China's northeast border, the Yalu River, MacArthur was suddenly overwhelmed by a tidal wave of Chinese troops.

When Gen. Creighton Abrams, Patton's superb European point brigade commander, inevitably asked President Johnson for permission to take Hanoi, the High Command had to refuse. It knew Abrams could easily do it, but it also knew that would force China into the war. And you can't actually *use* nuclear weapons. MacArthur laid this all out before it ever happened. He knew that any American commander would face protracted guerrilla war in Vietnam against overwhelming numbers without the possibility of military victory.

Gen. Matthew Ridgway, who replaced MacArthur in Korea, also bitterly opposed American troops on the ground in Vietnam, and used all his influence to prevent it. Gen. Omar Bradley did the same. Eisenhower's Chief of Plans for the Army, Gen. James Gavin, was also horrified at the thought of an Asian land war. Noted the prescient Gavin, "What appears to be intense interservice rivalry [in favor of intervention] in most cases...is fundamentally industrial rivalry." Eisenhower, Lemnitzer, Shoup and Prouty understood the meaning of that all too well.

In 1959, Gen. J. Lawton Collins insisted that he did not "know of a single senior commander that was in favor of fighting on the land mass of Asia." In 1952, Secretary of Defense Robert Lovett told NATO Commander Eisenhower that the Joint Chiefs were "unanimously opposed to the commitment of any troops" in Vietnam.[70] In 1950, U.S. military intelligence told Douglas MacArthur, then in charge of our troops in Korea, that 80% of the Vietnamese people supported Ho Chi Minh, and that for the overwhelming majority this support had nothing to do with Ho's politics, but his nationalism.[71]

This, of course, was not news to MacArthur. He told Kennedy that Viet Nam's only Vietnamese-led army was synonymous with nationalism. He emphasized that the Vietminh was a genuine national liberation front so popular that, if put under attack, it could mobilize virtually the entire population, giving it a numerical superiority that would enable it to absorb high losses indefinitely and still inflict unacceptable damage on any invader.

In 1954 the French had placed 16,000 men at Dienbienphu on the North Vietnam-Laos border. This large "hedgehog" garrison had been placed in supposedly inaccessible mountain terrain to serve as a base for offensive operations to protect French assets, including their Hmong opium army in Laos. 80,000 Vietminh porters, aided by the local hill tribes, then proceeded to do what the French high command had assumed was impossible. They hauled 200 heavy cannon and ample ammunition, disassembled piece by piece, through the vast rugged mountain range and up the heavily forested peaks surrounding the French garrison - and flattened it. The French air force and the CIA's contract airline CAT were able to fly only 28 heavy guns through the flak to the French pancakes.[72]

On the French collapse, the Vietminh, which had been heavily armed by the U.S. in 1945, inherited all the U.S. weaponry the French had to leave behind. Mass produced Vietminh land mines turned jungle roads into death traps. Even neighboring China feared the Vietminh. No Western invader, said MacArthur, could match Vietminh manpower in Vietnam. This was, of course, the same thing that Earl Mountbatten, the Allied commander in Indochina, and Vo Nguyen Giap, the OSS' man at the head of the anti-Japanese guerrilla army known as the Vietminh, had to say. MacArthur was talking about the army that he and Mountbatten helped to build.

Ho Chi Minh, then known as Nguyen Ai Quoc, addresses the French Socialist congress in 1920. This remarkable man was fluent in Vietnamese, French, English, Russian and Chinese. The refusal of the powers at Versailles to hear him 2 years earlier led him to begin organizing armed rebellion. The only military support he could find was in Moscow; Black Star

Complained OSS Indochina intelligence chief Paul Helliwell in 1943, "The French were infinitely more concerned with keeping the

Americans out of Indochina than they were in defeating the Japanese or in doing anything to bring the war to a successful conclusion in that area."[73] Most of France's colonial forces collaborated with the Japanese, managing Vietnam for their war machine. French forces were riddled with Japanese agents, so that the minority that wanted to resist failed. Poor French intelligence repeatedly got OSS sabotage teams bushwhacked. The only reliable help we had in northern Vietnam came from the Vietminh.

Roosevelt, at the Cairo and Teheran conferences of December, 1943, got Stalin and Chiang to agree that Vietnam should be placed under an international trusteeship after the war, as a preliminary to complete independence. Churchill, protesting his ancestral love of colonialism, squelched the deal, to the great relief of the Gaullists. But by 1944 the Vietminh had taken complete control of the northern Tonkin provinces. They were a military reality. They were feeding the OSS South China command at Kunming genuine intelligence, supporting its raiding parties and rescuing its fliers. So we sent them rifles, machine guns, mortars, bazookas and grenades as they took Vietnam from the Japanese.

The OSS Deer Team trains the Vietminh, Tonkin, 1944; Patti Collection

Ho based the Vietnamese Declaration of Independence, September 2, 1945, on the American. "All men are created equal. They are endowed by their Creator with certain inalienable rights, among them Life, Liberty, and the Pursuit of Happiness." Ho was flanked by his American military mission when he read those words to the vast crowd gathered in front of the Hanoi Municipal Theatre. The American military plane that flew overhead was wildly cheered.

That was also the day Japan formally surrendered to the U.S. At this time Ho repeatedly sent formal offers to the American government, through the OSS team attached to him, inviting massive American investment and lucrative government-to-industry partnerships.[74] The Pentagon responded by sending half of the unused Japan-invasion stockpile on Okinawa to Vo Nguyen Giap in Hanoi - enough weaponry, including heavy artillery, for 150,000 troops.

America could have had anything it wanted from Ho Chi Minh in 1945. Virtually all our intelligence officers who interacted with the Vietminh, 1944-46, insisted on their common sense, legitimacy, and grass-roots support. These officers recognized that Australian journalist Wilfred Burchett's reporting from the Mekong Delta in the early 1960's was accurate.

Burchett was one of the nerviest frontline correspondents to come out of World War II. Seven days after we incinerated Hiroshima, Burchett, unaccompanied, rode a Japanese train, loaded with angry Japanese troops, to ground zero. As the first Allied journalist on site, his graphic reports mesmerized the world. On the eve of the final battle for Dienbienphu, Burchett shared meals with Ho Chi Minh and Vo Nguyen Giap, listening to them explain their strategy. Because he loved these freedom fighters, his accurate reporting was dismissed as "communist propaganda." Only too late did the French realize that Burchett hadn't exaggerated Vietminh popularity, or the effectiveness of their tactics, at all.

So too the Americans. The intrepid Burchett spent the better part of 1960-1964 living with the Vietminh, under attack, in the Mekong Delta. But his dispatches were dismissed as propaganda by those for whom they were inconvenient. The CIA, by this time, had degenerated to the point where it was quoting its own political line as if that were military intelligence.

An early-60's CIA directive flatly asserted that there was no need to count the population at large as part of the "Viet Cong" because their support had been coerced. Burchett pointed out that mothers don't have to be coerced into supporting their sons. Captured enemy documents, since they revealed the incredible depth of the Vietminh "liberation associations" in rural South Vietnam, were actually systematically ignored in the CIA's reports to policy makers.

When an astute CIA analyst, Sam Adams, who naively thought his job was to objectively analyze the intelligence, insisted that NLF numbers were so overwhelming that we needed to reconsider our basic strategy, his information was intentionally withheld by Helms & Co. from policy makers. In fact, the stubborn analyst was hounded out of the service. Helms lied through his teeth to Congress about Vietminh strength, and most of the apple pie pansies swallowed it whole hog.[74a]

Most of those few Vietnamese who didn't actively support the Vietminh were neutral. Our side had the active support, at most, of 2% of the population. *We* were the externally-supported minority trying to shoot our way into power. That meant that we were sending our boys into a meat grinder.

It might have been convenient for imperialists to blur it, but the Vietnamese sense of nationhood was intense. "Nam Viet" first became a nation in 208 BC. The first time anyone ever heard of "South Vietnam" was in 1955. Ngo Dinh Diem knew that. Ho Chi Minh means "He Who Liberates." The "Vietminh" was the *Viet Nam Doc Lap Dong Minh Hoi*, the "Vietnamese Independence League," "Vietnamese Liberation." It was a jungle tiger.

Burchett's 1965 paperback *"Vietnam: Inside Story of the Guerrilla War,"* became the bible of the anti-war movement. The proof that it accurately depicted the political situation is that it accurately predicted the military outcome. I no longer have the copy I read then, but, as I recall, the last words in the book were something like "They can be killed, but they can't be conquered."

Kennedy chose to attempt both, as he encouraged Taylor's "counterinsurgency" double-speak. He had, after all, just nosed out Nixon in an election that was, to a great extent, a competition in red-baiting. Both Kennedy and Taylor talked of the Vietminh as if they came from Mars, or China. The U.S., Taylor told an approving Kennedy, was "protecting" Vietnamese peasants from the Vietminh. This was done by destroying their villages and herding the survivors at gunpoint into barbed-wire-enclosed "strategic hamlets," where they were "free" to "choose" "democracy." This double-speak was necessitated, of course, by the obvious facts, as outlined by American military intelligence throughout the fifties.

Marine Commandant David Shoup, a veteran of an awful lot of combat, refused to play this defense-contractor boondoggle game. He was livid at the venality that drove this Nazi-like corruption of our military intelligence. He did not forgive the reckless waste of his troopers', or Vietnamese, lives. He told a 1966 convocation, "I believe that if we... would keep our dirty, bloody, dollar-crooked fingers out of the business of these nations so full of depressed, exploited people, they will arrive at a solution of their own."[75]

Ambassador Lodge did not share these hippie sentiments. In a classified October 1963 communication to President Kennedy, he complained that "[South] Viet-Nam is not a thoroughly strong police state...because, unlike Hitler's Germany, it is not efficient."[76] This is the man who called Jacobo Arbenz a communist in the United Nations as Arbenz protested the American invasion of Guatemala. Lodge also complained of the pragmatic willingness of Diem, in the face of military defeat, to talk truce with the Vietminh. Again, so disappointingly unlike Adolf. Kennedy agreed with Lodge. If Diem wouldn't "focus on winning the war," then we would find someone who would.

Like MacArthur, General DeGaulle had also warned Kennedy that Vietnam was "a bottomless military and political swamp." Kennedy's trusted Senate majority leader, Mike Mansfield, told him the same thing after his late 1962 fact-finding trip.[77] The powerful and respected Senator Fulbright was also protesting that we were "bogged down" in a hopeless morass. After nearly three years of frustration, the pugnacious Kennedy was finally ready to accept this wisdom. He ordered Fletcher Prouty to organize the high profile, high-level Vietnam intelligence-gathering trip on which Kennedy's NSAM 263, his last, was ostensibly based.

Mark Lane: "'Kennedy dictated the rich parts of 263,' Prouty told me. 'He was not satisfied with the withdrawal of all U.S. military personnel, he wanted all Americans out of there.' He meant, Prouty continued, 'all CIA officers and agents.' Prouty said that at the CIA there was despair. 'They had been there since 1945. They were furious.... The Pentagon was outraged. JFK was a curse word in the corridors.... When Kennedy signed it, he signed an order for the almost immediate withdrawal of one thousand men, for all Americans to leave not long after the next presidential election, for the political kickoff for his 1964 campaign and, of course, not known to him, his own death warrant.'"[78]

NSAM 263 was actually hammered out and elaborated by Kennedy himself in 26 high-level meetings with the Joint Chiefs of Staff between August 28 and November 13, 1963. Prouty's immediate superior officer, Maj. Gen. Victor Krulak, was at 23 of those meetings as the President's Special Assistant for Counterinsurgency and Special Activities. Prouty, as chief of the Special Operations Office of the Joint Chiefs, was the lead officer on the receiving end of Krulak's orders pursuant to those meetings.

It was Krulak and his SACSA staff, not McNamara and Taylor, who wrote the McNamara-Taylor Trip Report of October 2 that became NSAM 263 a few days later. Krulak's trip to Vietnam the previous month provided most of the current data, and calls to McNamara in Vietnam provided the rest. Prouty was one of the officers who actually wrote NSAM 263, using Kennedy's own personal comments and notes. The completed report was then flown to McNamara and Taylor as they arrived in Hawaii from Vietnam. They presented Kennedy's own report to him as their "trip report." Such was the policy discipline demanded by Kennedy from McNamara and Taylor.[79]

NSAM 263, October 11, 1963, is very terse, and doesn't necessarily commit the U.S. to unconditional withdrawal, only withdrawal "without impairment of the war effort." It orders "an increase in the military tempo," so as to enable "the Vietnamese" to assume the "essential functions now performed by U.S. military personnel" by the end of 1965. "It should be possible to withdraw the bulk of U.S. personnel by that time....the Defense Department should....withdraw 1000 U.S. military personnel by the end of 1963. This action should be explained in low key as an initial step in a long-term program to replace U.S. personnel with trained Vietnamese without impairment of the war effort."

The report went on to explain that "any significant slowing in the rate of progress [of the war effort] would surely have a serious effect on U.S. popular support for the U.S. effort." But it insisted that "No further reductions should be made until the requirements of the 1964 [military] campaign become firm."[80]

White House Report

U.S. TROOPS SEEN OUT OF VIET BY '65

AN AUTHORIZED PUBLICATION OF THE ARMED FORCES IN THE FAR EAST

FIVE-STAR EDITION 10¢ DAILY 15¢ WITH SUPPLEMENTS

Vol. 19, No. 276 Friday, Oct. 4, 1963

Koufax, L.A. Top N.Y. 5-2

Compiled From AP and UPI

NEW YORK—Lefthander Sandy Koufax set a World Series strikeout record Wednesday as he pitched the Los Angeles Dodgers to a 5-2 victory over the New York Yankees in the first game of the fall classic.

President Kennedy gets a firsthand report on the situation in the Republic of Vietnam from General Maxwell D. Taylor (left), chairman of the Joint Chiefs of Staff, and Defense Secretary Robert McNamara. (AP Photo)

NSAM 263 still aimed at military victory, but it was to be the victory of surrogates - if they could pull it off. The CIA knew they could not. Kennedy, of course, realized that too, but nonetheless laid out the specific plan by which American troops were to be extricated from Vietnam. He did this before their numbers reached 20,000.

Right in the middle of that intense series of meetings with the Joint Chiefs in which he actually hammered out this policy, on September 2, 1963, Kennedy told Walter Cronkite, on the air, "In the final analysis, it is their war. They are the ones who have to win it or lose it. We can help them, we can give them equipment, we can send our men out there as advisers, but they have to win it, the people of Vietnam, against the Communists."

Kennedy based his withdrawal order on the Agency's own absurdly rosy projections of a "manageable" situation evolving within the next year - Taylor's bullshit. He always talked the Agency's language, which, of course, gave him a shot at actually taking control of Agency policy. It wasn't just the policy specifics in NSAM 263 that enraged the hawks, although that rage was expressed mostly in policy terms. It was the immediate threat of real executive policy control. *Stars and Stripes* ran the headline "U.S TROOPS SEEN OUT OF VIET BY '65." That was the looming disaster. There were hundreds of billions in military contracts, tens of thousands of jobs at stake. The Vietnam War was *mandatory*.

Prouty, a key operational officer, was surprised, in September, 1963, to learn that his November assignment was to escort a group of VIP's on an extended trip through Antarctica and our South Pole facilities. But these were elected officials and important defense contractors, and he did know a lot about those facilities. He looked forward to the trip as a paid vacation.

In early November, Gen. Lansdale made a point of telling Prouty to enjoy his trip. Prouty was dispatched on November 10, 1963. When he lunched with Mark Lane on Capitol Hill in June of 1991, he showed him a photo taken in Dallas on the day of the assassination, part of which is opposite, showing a man striding away from the camera, providing a side-back view.

"There is no doubt in my mind," Prouty told Lane, "that it's Ed Lansdale."[81] Prouty had known Lansdale intimately for years. They were both attached to Gen. Krulak's SACSA unit. When Prouty showed the photo to Krulak, the instantaneous reaction, which Prouty has angrily advertised on his website, was: "The haircut, the stoop, the twisted left hand, the large class ring - it's Lansdale."

Prouty learned of the assassination from the public address announcer of the Hermitage Chalet at the foot of Mount Cook in rural New Zealand. Later he called his contact in the 316th Field Detachment of the 112th Military Intelligence Group at Ft. Sam Houston in San Antonio, the unit that normally would have been used to provide a flying wedge of protection for the motorcade. Prouty was one of the inventors of that system and so was acquainted with the unit's commander.

"The commander of that unit, Lt. Col. Rudolph M. Reich, had offered his unit's services for the entire Texas trip, but 'they were point blank refused.' He was 'categorically refused by the Secret Service.' Hot words were exchanged between the agencies.... The president had almost no experienced protection that day."[82]

One of the things Presidential protection units were trained to do is shut all windows overlooking the parade route. Any photo will show that many windows overlooking Dealey Plaza were left open.

George Smith: Fort Worth Star Telegram in National Archives

If the 316th flying wedge had been on duty, it wouldn't have been possible for a 6th floor window in the Texas School Book Depository, or any other window in the Depository or the Dal-Tex Building, to house a shooter, because the closed window, once opened, would immediately have been targeted by an Army sharpshooter.

In the absence of a military flying wedge, the Secret Service was to provide one. This was clear, established Secret Service procedure - and it was not followed. Breaks in established procedure require specific, emphatic orders.

On Monday the 18th, the Chief of the Secret Service unit in Dallas, Forrest Sorrels, inexplicably added two abrupt turns to the Presidential motorcade, from Main Street onto Houston Street and from Houston onto Elm, taking the President precisely to the point of the assassination.[83] This change was immediately announced to the Dallas *Morning News* and the *Times-Herald*, and printed by them on the 19th.

Who had the juice to order Sorrels, in contradiction of all established security procedures, to set up a sharp eleven-mile-an-hour turn directly below tall buildings? Speeds below 40 were officially defined as dangerous. But there were no Secret Service agents on the roofs of any of the buildings surrounding Dealy Plaza - no walkie-talkies, no sharpshooters, no window-closings. Who had the juice to tell the Secret Service to stand down?

Another indication of an internal setup, noticed by all, is the fact that when the shooting started, the Secret Service agent driving the President's limo *slowed down* for a crucial five seconds, time enough for the third shot to explode Kennedy's head. Who decelerates under fire? Secret Service agents? It actually takes incredible reflexes *not* to speed up.

That there were moles at the 112th seems likely, since it was Col. Robert Jones, operations officer of the 112th, that notified the FBI, within an hour of the shooting, that Oswald was carrying a false draft card with the cover name of "Hidell" on it. Although their Presidential Protection Unit was refused, there were a few agents of the 112th in Dallas. Jones said that as soon as one of them told him of Oswald's arrest with the phony "Hidell" draft card, he cross-referenced the name and found the Oswald-Hidell file, the contents of which he read to the Dallas FBI Agent-in-Charge, Gordon Shanklin.

The Oswald-Hidell file was opened, said Jones, when Oswald went to the Soviet Union in 1960, and also included information on his recent pro-Castro activities. The only problem with this testimony is that the name "Hidell" was first used publicly by Oswald in this country *when ordering the rifle*, in March of 1963, and, afterwards, in setting up the phony Fair Play for Cuba chapter in New Orleans. Oswald's use of the name "Aleksei Hidell" in Russia was a covert matter. Jones inadvertently admitted that Army Intelligence had been running, or was fully aware of, Oswald. This explains why the file Jones used was never seen by any investigator and was confirmed as destroyed by the House Assassinations Committee.[84]

Senator Richard Schweiker: "I think that by playing a pro-Castro role on the one hand and associating with anti-Castro Cubans on the other, Oswald was playing out an intelligence role. This gets back to him being an agent or double agent.... I personally believe that he had a special relationship with one of the intelligence agencies, which one I'm not certain. But all the fingerprints I found during my eighteen months on the Senate Select Committee on Intelligence point to Oswald as being a product of, and interacting with, the intelligence community."[85]

That was also the opinion of Gerry Hemming, the CIA assassin who admits meeting Oswald in January of 1959 at the Cuban consulate in Los Angeles: "At that point in time I felt that he was a threat to me and to those Castro people, that he was an informant or some type of agent working for somebody. He was rather young, but I felt that he was too knowledgeable in certain things not to be an agent of law enforcement or of Military Intelligence, or Naval Intelligence.... Somebody had briefed him; somebody told him to approach me."[86]

Oswald, a highly intelligent Marine, probably met Sergeant Gerry Hemming at the U-2 spy base in Atsugi, Japan in 1958, despite Hemming's assertion that they met a year later. Oswald was tapped for a course in Russian at the Monterey School of the Army (now the Defense Language Institute). After being trained by Naval Intelligence in Russian, Oswald "defected" to the Soviet Union, just as Hemming "defected" to Cuba, with visas and clearances promptly provided by a cooperative State Department.[87]

As a qualified radar operator, Oswald may have been carrying some disinformation about the U-2 or other technical bait to Russia. Oswald and his Russian wife Marina, who may herself have been the same sort of security plant that Oswald was, returned to the U.S. in June of 1962.

Far from being arrested for divulging what technical information he had to the Russians, in violation of his Security Termination Statement, Oswald was greeted in New York by Professor Spas T. Raiken, a CIA-connected Anti-Bolshevik Block of Nations activist who later became a member of Nixon's 1973 Fairness to the President Committee. Raiken ushered Oswald into the highest levels of the powerful Dallas White Russian emigré community.

Oswald's first Dallas-Ft. Worth handler was oilman and CIA agent George DeMohrenschildt.[88] When Oswald moved from Ft. Worth to

Dallas in October, 1962, it was DeMohrenschildt who arranged the job at Jaggars-Chiles-Stovall, a graphics arts company that contracted with the U.S. Army Map Service. DeMohrenschildt took an intense interest in Oswald's welfare, going so far as to chauffeur the family from time to time.

DeMohrenschildt's father was a White Russian nobleman, the chosen representative of the landed aristocracy to the throne. He had been a pre-revolutionary director of Nobel Oil. He was allowed to put his expertise to the service of the revolution as head of the Soviet Department of Agriculture - until he was caught operating with the Church in opposing the revolution's antireligious violence. His son George graduated from the Polish cavalry academy before coming to the U.S. on the eve of World War II. The elder DeMohrenschildt spent WW II helping the Germans with their oil problem. During the war young George was ejected from Mexico for spying with Douglas MacArthur's nephew.

By 1945 he was working for Warren Smith, president of Pantipec Oil, owned by the parents of William F. Buckley. Smith and DeMohrenschildt formed the Cuban-Venezuelan Oil Trust Company, which, until Castro nationalized it, held the oil rights to about half of Cuba. Throughout the fifties DeMohrenschildt worked on CIA-related intelligence projects, such as the assessment of Yugoslav military strength while ostensibly doing a geological oil survey for the U.S. Economic Cooperation Administration. DeMohrenschildt was in Guatemala when the Bay of Pigs operation was launched from there. His ECA "oil" itinerary was like that. Most of the various oil and land development companies he owned were CIA assets.

DeMohrenschildt knew Jackie Kennedy's parents, the Bouviers, well enough to play tennis with them. When DeMohrenschildt moved to Dallas in 1962, he joined the exclusive Dallas Petroleum Club.[89] DeMohrenschildt shared personal and business interests with banker Richmond Harper, a Nixon associate who helped Marcello handle his money. Harper often worked through Herman Beebe, a major player in the S&L debacle. Harper was indicted in 1972 in an arms-for-drugs operation along with Barry Seal and Murray Kessler, a Gambino operative.[90]

DeMohrenschildt also knew and worked with another key Marcello ally, oilman Clint Murchison Sr, who owned the Del Mar racetrack and the Hotel Del Charro resort.[91] A fifth of the Murchison Oil Lease Company was owned by Gerardo Catena of the enormously powerful Genovese family.[92] Lyndon Johnson was Clint Murchison's political protégé.

DeMohrenschildt partnered up with Haitian banker Clemard Charles, money launderer for André Labay, Mario Renda, Carlos Marcello, Herman Beebe and Frank Fiorini Sturgis. They put together a holding company for Haiti's oil reserves. In May of 1963, according to the House Select Committee on Assassinations, which forced the release of his CIA file, DeMohrenschildt and Charles took part in a Pentagon-CIA meeting that may have discussed the overthrow Haiti's aging lunatic Papa Doc Duvalier.[93] DeMohrenschildt's Army Intelligence contact, Col. Sam Kail, was also one of the agents who ran Antonio Veciana of Alpha 66, to which Oswald was connected through Guy Bannister.[94-95]

DeMohrenschildt, through Clint Murchison, knew J. Edgar Hoover. Clint Murchison entertained J. Edgar annually, for years, at his high society-hoodlum blowout at the Hotel Del Charro. In 1958, Murchison, through his publishing company Henry Holt, published Hoover's committee-written red-baiting classic *Masters of Deceit.*[96] At the Del Charro, Hoover rubbed shoulders with the Genoveses and their Las Vegas allies, as well as with Bing Crosby, Clark Gable, Greer Garson, Senator Joe McCarthy, Richard Nixon, W.R. Grace, Carlos Marcello and George DeMohrenschildt.[97]

Why would a powerhouse like DeMohrenschildt suddenly become so passionately concerned about the likes of Oswald - unless, of course, Oswald's presence at an upcoming high society-hoodlum blowout was absolutely necessary?

In March 1977, the night before investigators from the House Assassinations Committee could get to him, George DeMohrenschildt's head was blown off by a shotgun. His personal telephone book, dating to the early 60's, contained this entry: "Bush, George H.W. (Poppy) 1412 W Ohio also Zapata Petroleum Midland."[98] The next week, just before investigators could get to him, one of DeMohrenschildt's more interesting associates, former Cuban president Carlos Prio, was also shot to death.[99]

Oswald left Dallas for no apparent reason and arrived in New Orleans on April 24, 1963. While he looked for a job and a place of his own, his bunked with his uncle, "Dutz" Murret, one of Carlos Marcello's bookies. Growing up in New Orleans with his uncle Dutz and his mother, living in Exchange Alley in the French Quarter, Oswald knew any number of Marcello operatives and they knew him. Murret worked under Sam Saia, a New Orleans boss very close to Marcello.

Oswald found a job at the William Reily Coffee Company. Reily was an active supporter of the Cuban Revolutionary Council, the CIA's Cuban government in exile. The CRC had its New Orleans office around the corner from Reily's company, at 544 Camp Street.

It was in late May that Oswald began the *pro*-Castro posturing for the Fair Play For Cuba Committee, of which he was the only member in New Orleans. The address on Oswald's FPCC leaflets was 544 Camp Street, the offices shared by the CRC and the racist fascist Guy Bannister, who worked for Carlos Marcello and J. Edgar Hoover, in that order.

The House Assassinations Committee found that Marcello was probably the key mob assassination engineer, because it "identified the presence of one critical evidentiary element that was lacking with the other organized crime figures...credible associations relating both Lee Harvey Oswald and Jack Ruby..."[100]

Bannister was a slugger - former Agent-in-Charge of the FBI's Chicago office and ex-New Orleans Deputy Chief of Police. He had ties to pro-Batista, Trujillo and Somoza terrorist groups and to their financiers, the Marcello/Trafficante drug dealers.[101]

Bannister helped run the FBI's Fair Play for Cuba Committee COINTELPRO, which did indeed destroy the reputation of this peaceful group. The COINTELPRO was run with Ed Butler, an intelligence agent who ran Standard Fruit's Information Council of the Americas (INCA).

The COINTELPRO was also run with Carlos Bringuier, head of the *Directorio Revolucionario Estudiantil* (DRE), one of the CIA proprietaries that had penetrated Castro's revolution by working with it. Bringuier has been one of Batista's cops. His DRE, operating from its base in the Escambray Mountains, actually took Batista's palace for the revolution, but was left out of Castro's post-revolutionary power structure.[102]

A September 1963 liaison note from the CIA to the FBI, published by the Senate Intelligence Committee in 1976, states that "Also during May 1961, a field survey was completed wherein available public source data of adverse nature regarding officers and leaders of FPCC was compiled and furnished [Hoover's top aide] Mr. DeLoach for use in contacting his sources."[103]

As an integral part of this COINTELPRO, Oswald was under heavy FBI surveillance and control from the moment he arrived in New Orleans. When Hoover told the Warren Commission that it had affidavits from every FBI agent who had contact with Oswald, he left out the two most important, the agents running the FPCC

COINTELPRO.

Agents Milton Kaack and Warren deBrueys met with Oswald frequently, according to one of Bringuier's operatives, Orest Peña, who was involved in the phony debates and street confrontations designed to advertise the Fair Play for Cuba Committee, and Oswald. This was confirmed by FBI security clerk William Walter, who saw documents, before the assassination, indicating that Oswald was a Bureau informant.[104]

DeBrueys had served in various South American embassies as a "legal attaché," that is, a CIA counterinsurgency expert. Hoover, who was running deBrueys, wrote a 1961 memo discussing the use of Oswald's name to buy trucks for his agent Guy Bannister's network in New Orleans. Hoover was working with Marcello to run Guy Bannister, who was running Oswald.

When Oswald was arrested in August following one phony street fight with Bringuier, he was bailed out by Emile Bruneau. Bruneau worked for Nofio Pecora and Joe Poretto, Carlos Marcello's two key aides, the men who gave orders to Oswald's uncle Dutz.

Ben Tragle was the operator of a bar partly owned by Marcello, just down the road from Marcello's headquarters, the Town and Country Motel. Tragle had mentioned to his employee, FBI informant Eugene De Laparra, a conversation he had with "the professor" (probably Marcello operative David Ferrie) in March in which the professor asserted that a plot was afoot to kill Kennedy. De Laparra himself claims to have overheard Tony Marcello, one of Carlos' six brothers, tell Tregle that "The word is out to get the Kennedy family." De Laparra says that Oswald knew Tragle at this time, that is, that he was acting as a runner for his bookie uncle Dutz.[105] Another FBI informant reported seeing Joe Poretto hand Oswald money in the Town and Country restaurant, at the end of April, 1963.[106]

Attorney General Robert Kennedy had been ruthlessly hunting Carlos Marcello from the moment he took office. Just after he took office, on April 4, 1961, RFK had the INS virtually kidnap and deport Carlos Marcello to Guatemala. Marcello had listed Guatemala as his place of birth on a phony birth certificate because it was nearer his Louisiana base than Tunisia, where his migrating Sicilian mother had actually born him.[107-108] Since Marcello came to the U.S. in 1910 as a babe of seven months in his mother's arms, his case for citizenship, although he never formally applied for it, was actually quite good.

The head of the Cuban Revolutionary Council (CRC), Tony de Varona, who had been Cuba's Prime Minister under President Prio's kleptocracy, shared offices with Guy Bannister. With his Havanna connections, Varona was a key assassination team contact for the CIA's ZR/RIFLE hit team run by Johnny Rosselli.

Delphine Roberts, Bannister's personal secretary and lover, who had extensive personal memories of Oswald, told Anthony Summers, author of the superb *Conspiracy*, that the dapper Rosselli visited Bannister at 544 Camp Street. Rosselli, in any case, knew and worked with virtually every major operative Bannister did. Sergio Arcacha Smith, one of Batista's more diplomatic operatives, was New Orleans representative of the CRC. Arcacha said that 544 Camp Street was the "Cuban Grand Central Station."[109] Carlos Marcello was Arcacha's main New Orleans financier.[110]

The CIA's CRC coordinator was Howard Hunt, veteran of the Guatemala coup and organizer of the Latin American Anti-Communist Confederation's first 1958 convocation. Bannister was a key operative of the Anti-Communist League of the Caribbean, a Somoza project tied to the CAL, as such worked closely with Hunt.[111]

Many of the Latin CAL death squads were Trafficante/Marcello drug gangs. Explained a member of a Honduran death squad coordinated by the *Confederación Anticomunista Latina*, "CAL is also called The White Hand, The White Force, and The White Brigade. It got its name because it has the backing of powerful people who erase all evidence surrounding a murder."[112]

Bannister was also working with Carlos Marcello's lawyer, G. Wray Gill, and his aide, the extraordinarily strange David Ferrie, a former Eastern Airlines pilot who ran daring terrorist raids against Castro and, apparently, participated in the Bay of Pigs operation. Ferrie, a member of the CRC, took a leave from his pilot duties at the time of the Bay of Pigs and was fired by Eastern shortly thereafter. His wrongful dismissal suit against Eastern brought him into contact with Gill. Before that, Ferrie was part of the CIA-Syndicate smuggling operation that ran arms *to* Castro in the Sierra Maestra. Jack Ruby was also part of that operation.

In 1955, when Oswald was 16, Captain Ferrie, a predatory homosexual, taught him to fly as a member of the Civil Air Patrol, as he had Barry Seal, who ran Bush's Contra coke operation. According to CIA agent Victor Marchetti, who was a top aide to CIA Director Richard Helms, Ferrie was one of the contract agents Helms was running when he was Deputy Director for Plans in 1963.[113] Oswald and Ferrie were seen together in 1963 running a minor sting on a local voter registration drive organized by CORE, a COINTELPRO target.[114] At least ten different witnesses saw Ferrie and Oswald together at various places that summer, including one who heard Ferrie, a vociferous member of the CRC, talk of the desirability of killing Kennedy.[115]

When Oswald was arrested following the assassination, he was carrying a library card with Ferrie's name on it. Although the card itself immediately disappeared, Marcello's lawyer, Wray Gill, was immediately warned by someone in the Dallas police department. Gill went to Ferrie's apartment two days after the assassination, on November 24th, and told his roommate to warn Ferrie about the card as soon as he returned from his hysterical post-assassination trip to Texas. That information found its way into the November 28th FBI report. But when the FBI interviewed Gill, his transparent fabrications were accepted as gospel, and his claim that Ferrie's November telephone records were "unavailable" went unchallenged.[116]

Neither the FBI nor the Secret Service interviews of Ferrie, November 25 and 26, totaling more than 100 pages, were mentioned in the FBI reports or turned over to the Warren Commission. The investigation of Ferrie was immediately dropped. It is absurd to pretend that this was FBI "incompetence." Ferrie was one of Oswald's closest associates, and he tied Oswald to Marcello, one of Kennedy's most dangerous enemies. And Marcello, through Bannister and his associates, tied Oswald and Ferrie to the CIA and the FBI.

This FBI/CIA pattern, seen throughout the investigation, can only be an internal fix indicating collusion in the assassination, as well-placed CIA agent Victor Marchetti indicates. Helms, Marchetti's immediate superior, was running Ferrie, Marcello's dutiful subordinate. That, of course, means that Helms and Marcello were working together. That is a virtual certainty, since without Marcello there could have been no ZR/RIFLE hit teams aimed at Castro, most of whose members, especially its operational leader Rosselli, were Marcello operatives. Rosselli, it will be recalled, rearranged the Guatemalan government for the CIA in 1957.

The highly intelligent Ferrie met regularly that year with Marcello, supposedly planning legal strategy to block Robert Kennedy's ongoing effort to deport Marcello. But why would Marcello need Ferrie to plan legal strategy, when he had Wray Gill, Mike Maroun and the brilliant Washington lawyer Jack Wasserman? It was the possibly illegal tactic of judicial kidnapping employed by RFK that gave Marcello enough legal juice to hold Kennedy off in court as they tussled over Marcello's deportation. Wasserman was far more qualified to deal with this arcana than Ferrie, who was a pilot, not a lawyer. More likely

Marcello and Ferrie were planning the handling of Ferrie's good buddy Oswald.

When Marcello was violently dumped into Guatemala by RFK in April 1961, he was flown back to the U.S. two months later by a pilot who was identified by the Border Patrol, at the time, as David Ferrie.[117] Marcello spent the two weekends prior to Kennedy's arrival in Dallas, the 9th and 10th and the 16th and 17th, sequestered at Churchill Farms, his country estate, with David Ferrie. A few months later, Marcello bought Ferrie a lucrative gas station franchise.

Ferrie's other employer, Guy Bannister, twice took Oswald to Louisiana State University to engage in loud denunciations of Kennedy's pro-civil rights stand.[118] Oswald himself wasn't a racist, but was obviously willing to engage in any kind of theatrics his employers desired.

On Saturday, November 23, the day after the assassination, Bannister and his close associate, Jack Martin, both a little stewed, got into a nasty fight, during which Martin shouted, "What are you going to do - kill me like y'all did Kennedy?" At which Bannister pistol-whipped Martin, warning him, as Martin told the House Assassinations Committee, to "watch himself and be careful." The enraged Martin, who knew the working relationship of Bannister, Ferrie and Oswald, called a friend who was close to New Orleans Assistant DA Herman Kohlman. It was that call that set off the search for Ferrie.[119]

Immediately after the assassination, Ferrie travelled 350 miles to Houston, in an hysterical, nonstop, overnight trip to Marcello's Alamotel, from where he called Marcello collect. Ferrie then took a short sleep and went to the Winterland Skating Rink, where he spent two hours on the pay phone, making untraceable calls. At the same time, visitors to Jack Ruby's Carousel noticed Ruby become progressively more upset by the calls he was receiving. At 5:30, after taking calls for 2$^{1/2}$ hours, Ruby pocketed his revolver and went straight to Dallas Police Headquarters, stalking Oswald. Ferrie then went to another rink for another hour of calling, then drove to nearby Galveston, where he met Ruby operative Breck Wall. Ruby is confirmed to have called Galveston that night.[120]

On February 22, 1967, after months of interrogation by Jim Garrison, during which time Garrison gathered enough evidence for an arrest warrant, Ferrie was murdered. Within hours of that murder, Ferrie's close associate in the CRC, former *Batistiano* congressman Eladio del Valle, was shot through the heart at point-blank range. Three months later, Ferrie's closest female friend, in whom he confided, Dr.

Mary Stults Sherman, was murdered in her New Orleans apartment.

Bannister had frequent visits from Col. Orlando Piedra, the chief of Batista's secret police and a key element of the CIA's Operation 40, the control or point group of Brigade 2506.[121] Operation 40 was led by Joaquin Sanjenis and Felix Gutiérrez, veterans of both Batista's secret police, the hated SIM, and the Bay of Pigs. They moonlighted as leaders of the paramilitary arm of Trafficante's organization. Operation 40 included most of the CIA operatives, like Frank Sturgis and Bernard Barker, who penetrated Castro's movement prior to his victory.

Bannister was the Louisiana organizer of the CIA-run, Marcello-financed Minuteman hit teams. Ferrie and Oswald trained together at a Minuteman camp on Lake Pontchartrain, which was armed with Bannister's help. Louisiana's huge Lake Pontchartrain, which feeds the Gulf, was the locus of a complex of CIA bases and marinas. The Minuteman Lake Pontchartrain camp at which Ferrie and Oswald trained was seized by the Kennedy wing of the FBI on July 31, 1963.[122]

The camp, near Marcello's hunting lodge at Lacombe, on the north shore, was owned by a Trafficante operative, William McLaney, an old Havana gambling boss. It was set up by "Minuteman" Gerry Hemming, the CIA agent who was a sergeant at Atsugi, Japan in 1958 when Oswald was there.

Assisting was Frank Fiorini Sturgis, a Trafficante and Operation 40 agent who had worked with Hemming on the 1958-60 Castro penetration project.[123] As one who didn't hesitate to shoot *Bastistianos* dead, Sturgis rose to become Castro's Chief of Air Force Security.

The CIA coordinator of these operations was also the coordinator of the Watergate break-in, former Guatemala propaganda officer E. Howard Hunt. The hero of Hunt's 1949 dime novel, *Bimini Run*, is gambler/soldier-of-fortune Hank Sturgis. Frank Fiorini adopted the name 'Sturgis' in 1964.

Other Minuteman financiers included such CIA cutouts as the powerful oil barons, the Texas Hunt brothers, the media mogul Luces, and Senator Eastland, the Senator from Marcello's favorite social club, the KKK. Eastland, working through his Senate Internal Security Subcommittee, was using the likes of Bannister to pin the Red label on Martin Luther King. Bannister's *Louisiana Intelligence Digest* portrayed integration as a communist plot.[124] Bannister's former boss, J. Edgar Hoover, also made the connection between "Castro's Cuba and integration problems arising in the South." As J. Edgar told Supreme Court Justice Tom Clark, "I'm not going to send the FBI every time some nigger woman gets raped."[125]

Bannister had a convenient fatal "heart attack" before the Warren Commission could interview him. And Hoover made sure that the FBI didn't investigate his cutout seriously, by disguising the relationship to Oswald and changing the telltale address of 544 Camp Street, which would have flagged even the Warren Commission, to 531 Lafayette Street, which was the corner door. Most of Bannister's files were seized and destroyed.[126]

Frank Fiorini Sturgis' first hit team, a Vice-President Nixon-approved 1960 operation, was the International Anti-Communist Brigade, organized and paid for by Marcello's major ally, Santos Trafficante, for whom Sturgis had worked in Cuba.[127] Sturgis also had financial ties to former Cuban President Carlos Prio.

Prio won the Cuban presidency in a 1948 election and proceeded to rape the country as thoroughly as possible. Fulgencio Batista, every bit as much of a thief, was a far better tourism developer, so Trafficante, Lansky and Company backed Batista's 1952 anti-Prio coup. Prio spent the rest of the fifties using operatives like Fidel Castro and Frank Sturgis trying to take back Cuba from Batista. It was Prio who first financed Castro's move to the Sierra Maestra.

After Sturgis was caught actively supporting the Bay of Pigs invasion he worked openly against Castro with two key CIA-Syndicate operatives, John Martino and Johnny Rosselli. Martino used to spin Trafficante's roulette wheels in Cuba. He was planning to open a whorehouse next to Trafficante's Havana Deauville when the revolution struck. He was an old associate of Jack Ruby. Sturgis, Castro's 1959 Air Force Security chief and Minister of Gaming, used the Tropicana as a base. That was managed by Trafficante operative Lewis McWillie, a very close friend of Ruby's.

Pursuant to Operation Pluto, in October of 1960 at the Miami Fontainebleau, Rosselli, Trafficante, Giancana, Jim O'Connell and Robert Maheu had their first operational meeting to plan Castro's death. Maheu was a former FBI intelligence expert who transferred to the CIA. He worked under Guy Bannister in the FBI's Chicago office during WW II. Explained Jim O'Connell, CIA security operations chief, to Senator Church's 1975 Committee, Maheu handled "several sensitive covert operations in which he didn't want to have an agency or government person get caught."[128]

When Columbia University lecturer Jesús de Galindez, who had worked for Rafael Trujillo, started documenting Trujillo's CIA/Syndicate contacts and political murders in the Spring of 1956, it was a Robert A. Maheu associate, specifically New Jersey mob boss Joe

Zicarelli, who traded arms for dope with Trujillo, who handled the assassination.[129] Thirteen days after he started talking, Galindez disappeared.

Aside from the CIA and the Syndicate, Robert A. Maheu Associates represented the powerful defense contractor Howard Hughes, the Teamsters, and the Senate Banking and Currency Committee. Rosselli had refused to accept the Castro contract from Maheu until he met face-to-face with the CIA's Jim O'Connell, in Maheu's presence. Within a week of that meeting, O'Connell's superior, Col. Sheffield Edwards, met with his superior, Richard Bissell, as well as Deputy CIA Director Charles Cabell and Director Allen Dulles, at which time, Bissell recalled, in sworn testimony, "the plan would be put into effect."[130]

"The plan" was to be executed by the "Executive Action" unit, code-named ZR/RIFLE. Just before he handed the helm to Helms, in late 1961, Bissell ordered the "application of ZR/RIFLE program to Cuba."[131] Helms told Senator Church's 1975 Senate Intelligence Committee that he had approved the mob assassination operation without the knowledge or approval of Kennedy or his CIA director McCone.[132] Despite the proforma "deniability" for the superiors, Helms admitted, in sworn testimony, organizing the CIA/hood assassination teams.

As operational chief of Mongoose, Helms' subordinate Gen. Lansdale, Bobby Kennedy's top military aide, certainly knew and approved of ZR/RIFLE. RFK assumed virtual operational command of Mongoose, pressing all those around him for quick results and micromanaging the operation. Given the Kennedys' independent contacts among the *Batistianos*, and their relationship to Lansdale, it is certain that both Kennedys were fully aware of the attempts on Castro's life. Whether they had ordered those attempts, or were able to control them, is open to question.

ZR/RIFLE was under the formal command of the famous fat assassin William "The Pear" Harvey. Harvey had been CIA station chief in Berlin and Rome during the most dangerous early periods of the Cold War. He honed his assassination skills under the tutelage of Col. Boris Pash, who fought with the Czarists in 1917. Pash joined U.S. military intelligence in the 20's, and had been security chief at the Manhattan Project. As the war was ending, Pash was sent to Europe to rescue Hitler's best chemical and nuclear warfare experts.

Pash's Branch 7 unit was responsible for fomenting rebellion and dealing with inconvenient enemy agents behind the Iron Curtain.[133]

Harvey was one of the Pash agents who instigated the Hungarian revolt of 1956 - by lying through his teeth to those desperate people about the probability of U.S. intervention. It was Harvey's engineering of the tunnel under East Berlin that opened East German telephone traffic to Western ears. Harvey was an old ally of Counterintelligence chief Angleton, Pash's finger man.[134]

The mission of ZR/RIFLE wasn't merely the assassination of Castro, that was just one of its many tasks. The operational function of Harvey's unit was assassination in general, as tasked, globally. Harvey also headed Task Force W, which was the Agency's coordinating component with Operation Mongoose. In that capacity Harvey worked with Howard Hunt, also a Boris Pash protégé. In April of 1962, pursuant to orders, Harvey met once again with Jim O'Connell and Johnny Rosselli to plan a new round of Castro assassination attempts.

Between 1960 and 63, Rosselli's teams made eight serious attempts on Castro's life, closely coordinating their efforts with Trafficante, for mob liaison, as Trafficante himself confirmed before the Assassinations Committee in September of 1978.[135]

ZR/RIFLE also boasted the services of David Sanchez Morales, a famously savage murderer known as "El Indio." Morales had recently returned from a grotesque murder spree aimed at the Tupemaros in Uruguay. El Indio had a bloody hand in the Guatemalan coup of 1954 and had worked, as an attaché of the American consulate, with the Batista/Trafficante death squads during their final spasm of 1958-59.[136]

Trafficante's most dangerous assassin, Johnny Rosselli, provided with false papers and the rank of Colonel, had complete access to CIA station JM/WAVE in Coral Gables. It was from a motel near there that Rosselli and El Indio planned Fidel's assassination with snipers.[137] Capt. Bradley Ayers, a combat trainer for Operation Mongoose, insisted that "Any suggestion that Rosselli's activities were less than legitimized by the establishment is total bullshit....he had virtual carte blanche into the highest levels of the station."[138]

Rosselli and Hunt probably assassinated Rafael Trujillo in May of 1961, on Kennedy's orders, at least according to the Church Committee and Trujillo's 1960 security chief, Gonzalez-Mata, who identified Rosselli as "a friend of Batista."[139] This was a ZR/RIFLE operation, under the command of Bill Harvey. Their Dominican contact was Henry Dearborn, the deputy chief at the American Embassy. Rosselli and Hunt also worked together with Tony de Varona, leader of the Cuban Revolutionary Council.

Rosselli and John Martino also operated together in 1963, out of a Key Biscayne motel. Martino, a security systems expert and gambling technician, had been one of those jailed by Castro along with Trafficante and Jake Lansky. Unlike the others, Martino wasn't released until late 1962. Martino actually went on a June 1963 hit-and-run anti-Castro mission with the powerful Ambassador William Pawley himself, a trusted Dulles/Helms operative.

Pawley had been U.S. ambassador to Batista's Cuba and erstwhile owner of Havana's bus system and Cuban sugar refineries. He was close to Paul Helliwell, with whom he had worked in Asia and the Caribbean in the founding of the Flying Tigers, Civil Air Transport, SEA Supply of Bangkok and Air America. As Truman's ambassador to Panama, Pawley had been one of the engineers of the 1954 Guatemala coup. Pawley may have wanted to observe up close the combined team of CIA and Syndicate assassins - Hemming, Sturgis, Bayo, Hall, Martinez, Robertson - sharpshooters all - that Martino and Rosselli were running.[140] In 1977, just before he was to testify for the Assassinations Committee, Ambassador Pawley "committed suicide," a highly unlikely course of action for that tough old goat.

Like Pawley and Martino, Rosselli didn't hesitate to go out on raids himself, and actually had two boats shot out from under him, barely escaping with his life. Rosselli would later claim, in a sophisticated disinformation effort forced on him by legal pressure, that Castro turned one of his hit teams back on Kennedy, who was, after all, trying to kill Castro.[141] This also just happens to be the current CIA line, originated, according to ranking CIA staff officer Victor Marchetti, by CIA Director Richard Helms in 1967, when the progress of the Garrison investigation became a regular topic at the morning staff meetings at Langley.[142]

Although plausible to some who haven't done their homework, it doesn't wash, as both the Church Committee and the House Assassinations Committee concluded. Killing Kennedy was idiotic from Castro's perspective, since it would have doomed the détente Castro desperately wanted, which included an end to the crippling embargo, something Castro knew Kennedy was actively considering. It would also have provided grounds for a U.S. invasion of Cuba, which Castro could not have survived.[143]

Like most intelligence legends, the Helms-Rosselli assertion is, nonetheless, believable. Castro knew Trafficante, Sturgis and Hemmings well, since they were part of the Nixon-approved 1959 CIA operation that penetrated Castro's movement by selling arms to it.[144] The operation was led by Col. Jack Cannon, and used Syndicate operative Roughhouse Rothman to organize the smuggling. Rothman was a very close aide of Santos Trafficante, managing the Sans Souci Casino and the Tropicana slots for him. Jack Ruby also participated in this operation.[145]

Castro used Sturgis to conduct his initial bargaining for the continuation of mob operations in Cuba after he took power.[146] Castro's reaction to the April 1959 failure of his negotiations with Vice-President Nixon was to go back to Cuba and throw Santos Trafficante and Jake Lansky in jail. That was his idea of bargaining with Richard Nixon.

Although Trafficante and Lansky ultimately lost their casinos to Fidel, Trafficante's imprisonment was luxurious and temporary, probably because he found a medium of exchange other than plastic chips. Fidel, who had a personal appreciation of the utility of cocaine on the battlefield, had operational guerrilla groups throughout Latin America - enough leverage and territorial control to deliver a whole lot of coke and pot to Don Santos. On his release from Castro's country club detention, Trafficante stayed in Havana, and continued talking with Raoul Castro, the country's chief military officer.[147]

Lansky lost his extensive Cuban interests, including his beautiful new twenty-one story, 440-room Riviera Hotel and Casino, and so backed those intent on toppling Fidel. But Lansky was essentially a gambler, not a hitter, and proud of it. He had the muscle to maintain his interests, but his relationship to Batista had to do with his uncanny understanding of tourist development, something in which Batista was intensely interested. Rosselli and all his hitters, on the other hand, worked for Trafficante, the quietly brilliant, utterly ruthless organizer who helped run Batista's dope-dealing death squads.

Santos Trafficante Jr, who took over the family business when his old man died in 1954, grew into one of the most powerful drug-traffickers of the century. *Trafficante* actually means "trafficker" in both Italian and Spanish. I wonder if it's a *nom de guerre*.

Brigade 2506 itself, since it was composed of and organized by former Batista officers, was virtually Santos Trafficante's private army. Trafficante's dope-dealing *Batistianos* were indeed grateful for all the free bases, boats, arms and communications equipment provided by Mongoose. But somehow Rosselli's expert hitters always managed to miss Fidel. High-ranking CIA agent Scott Breckinridge, one of the authors of the CIA's *Inspector General's Report of 1967 on CIA Plots to Assassinate Fidel Castro*, was forced to the conclusion "that Trafficante had been providing Castro with details of the plot all along."[148]

Castro had warned Kennedy, in a very serious way, not to lie down with the dogs. On September 7, 1963, Rolando Cubela, a highly placed Cuban security officer and hero of the revolution, met with Desmond FitzGerald, former CIA Far East chief, and other CIA officers in Brazil. Cubela offered, for the second time, to pursue their ongoing plans to kill Castro. *At the exact same moment, at the Brazilian Embassy in Havana*, Castro walked up to reporter Daniel Harker and said: "United States leaders should think that if they are aiding terrorist plans to eliminate Cuban leaders, they themselves will not be safe. Let Kennedy and his brother Robert take care of themselves since they, too, can be the cause of an attempt which will cause their death."[149]

Castro remembers the interview but not his exact words. Castro told the House Assassinations Committee that he was simply fully aware of the boomerang potential inherent in dealing with Trafficante, Helms and Company.[150] Given the penetration of his intelligence and the political and military realities, that is almost certainly the truth, as the 1979 Assassinations Committee concluded. If Castro had been planning to kill Kennedy, he would hardly announce it to the press in advance. Castro was warning Kennedy, trying to change policy, not threatening him. Castro lost big on Kennedy's death, though his covert mob liaison, and the economic utility of the dope trade, remained.

In September of 1963 Martino, at this time Rosselli's close partner, went from Miami to Dallas to address a meeting of one of the *Batistiano* groups supporting the Cuban Revolutionary Council. At the meeting, Martino said he knew Amador Odio, the left-wing anti-Communist, a close ally of Manolo Ray, imprisoned by Castro. Amador Odio was the father of 26 year-old Silvia Odio. That same month, on September 26, when either the real or the fake Oswald was in Mexico City, the real or the fake Oswald was introduced to Silvia Odio by two CRC operatives who showed up with him at her Dallas apartment.

The visit came as a total surprise, because Odio's group, *Junta Revolucionaria*, was left-wing and pacifist, considered the embodiment of "Castroism without Castro." The two CRC operatives were complete strangers to Odio. Two days later one of them called her on the phone and told her, unprompted, that sharpshooter Oswald, who had said virtually nothing at their meeting, intended to shoot Kennedy. "The American says we Cubans don't have any guts, He says we should have shot President Kennedy after the Bay of Pigs." That is, word for word, the B-movie dialogue recounted by a Somoza operative to Ambassador Mann in Mexico City in yet another attempt to implicate Oswald, dialogue Odio herself could not have been aware of.

Since Odio was a Kennedy supporter who hated political violence, she immediately sensed an intelligence setup, an effort to use her in a legend. The worried Odio wrote of this in a letter to her imprisoned father in Cuba, weeks before the assassination. She also discussed it with another witness, and her teenage sister Annie, who was there, corroborates the story.[151] Odio, of course, realized the accuracy of her fears on November 22, and the immediacy of her reaction to the television pictures indicates that she was introduced to the real Oswald. Both Sylvia and her sister picked Oswald as the man who visited them from the FBI's set of photos.

Howard Hunt, the probable author of the Mexico City B-movie dialogue, was John Martino's CIA liaison. Said Martino, in a private conversation many years later, Oswald "didn't know who he was working for - he was just ignorant of who was really putting him together."[152] Incredibly, in October 1963, a month before the assassination, in two meetings observed by the FBI, Martino's close partner, Johnny Rosselli, met Jack Ruby in Miami.[153] Ruby's phone records at this time reveal a spate of calls to various Rosselli associates.

Marita Lorenz, who was travelling with Frank Sturgis in October and November of 1963, claims to have been at meetings with Sturgis, Howard Hunt, Gerry Hemming, Jack Ruby, Lee Harvey Oswald and the CRC's Orlando Bosch. She identified them, under oath in Mark Lane's 1985 Hunt libel suit, as the men who killed Kennedy.[154] There is a great deal of corroborating evidence that makes this possible. It was Sturgis, while still working for Castro, who turned 18 year-old Marita Lorenz, Castro's lover, who felt trapped and scared by the relationship, into a CIA agent, in exchange for help escaping.

The internal CIA memo leaked by Marine Col. William Corson, signed by Helms and Angleton, places Howard Hunt in Dallas on the day of the assassination, just as Marita Lorenz testified.[155] Mark Lane's 1985 Miami jury, in fact, found that Howard Hunt had not been libelled by *Spotlight* magazine, when the CIA's Victor Marchetti asserted in an article that Howard Hunt was part of the team that killed Kennedy, because the assertion was true.[156]

There is further incredible confirmation of this - photos of Hunt, Sturgis and a third man, dressed as tramps, being marched by Dallas police on Nov. 22 from a boxcar on the railroad tracks just behind the grassy knoll to the Criminal Courts Building, across the street from the Texas School Book Depository. The back door of the TSBD opens directly onto the railroad yard.

William Allen, *Dallas Times Herald*

Lee Bowers, the railroad towerman, was the reason the "tramps" didn't just ride out on their boxcar. He stopped the train on his own initiative and told the police that they needed to search it. That's how the tramps were found, 45 minutes after the assassination. As they were being paraded the three blocks, local newsmen snapped several pictures of them. Above is part of the sixth picture, P6 on the diagram.

The first thing one notices about the photos is that these men are playing dress-up. They are obviously in very good health, showing none of the effects of the hobo life, and they are all wearing new shoes. The police are also playing dress-up - their rifles and parts of their uniforms are not standard issue. Oddly, although records exist of almost all the other interviews, no record exists of the tramp interviews. In fact, unusually, these men were immediately turned over to the FBI, and the FBI just let them go.[157]

As Weberman and Canfield point out in detail in *Coup d'etat In America*, the older tramp, in back, is a dead-ringer for the CIA's Cuba point man, Nixon's Watergate organizer, Howard Hunt. Photo analysis proves that the older tramp is 5'8" tall, exactly Hunt's height. Above left, Nov. 22, 1963, right, Watergate, 1973. Acetate overlays, in the book, show them to be the same man.

Drug War

The tallest tramp, above, just happens to be the spitting image of Hunt's longtime operative, his fellow Watergate burglar Frank Sturgis. Photo analysis shows the tallest tramp to be 6'1", exactly Frank Sturgis' height. Left, in Dallas Nov. 22, with dyed hair and no mustache. Right, Cuba, 1959. Again, acetate overlays show them to be the same man. Marita Lorenz had told the truth.

Sturgis had penetrated the upper levels of Castro's revolution. He funneled ex-President Prio's money to Castro and organized some of Fidel's most dangerous hit teams. He was Castro's first post-revolution Chief of Air Force Security and Minister of Games of Chance - until Castro discovered the huge spy network he had built. Sturgis was exactly what Castro said he was, a very dangerous double agent.

The third tramp bears an uncanny resemblance to the first FBI sketch of Martin Luther King's killer. The FBI had this sketch, made by a Mexican artist from its own eyewitness descriptions, distributed as a lookout poster to Mexican border agents. When former FBI agent Bill Turner pointed to the uncanny similarity to the third tramp, the FBI disowned the sketch.[158] Weberman has shown, on www.weberman.com, that the photo of the third tramp is an exact match for a later photo of former CIA Technical Services Division Chief David Christ.

Christ, Hunt and Sturgis, of course, worked for ZR/RIFLE, Gen. Lansdale's assassination team run by Rosselli and Harvey. Look at the rest of that photo, below, that apparently caught Lansdale's back. It is a photo of Lansdale with these men.

Note the deference of the police, supposedly escorting possible suspects - how they hang back, how loosely they carry their weapons. Neither their weapons (shotguns), nor their uniforms (patches, hats) are standard Dallas police issue - these men are actors; George Smith: Ft. Worth Star Telegram in National Archives

The CIA actually intervened with American publishers to prevent the publication of Mark Lane's first book, the seminal *Rush To Judgement*, first put into print in Britain. I remember riding in a car with Lane in the Spring of 1964, after having helped to organize his lecture at the University of Buffalo, where I was a freshman. His cheerful enthusiasm gave me no idea of the risk he was running.

During a collegial 1977 debate with Lane at UCLA, former CIA Western Hemisphere chief David Phillips, the probable "Maurice Bishop" himself, in a perhaps too enthusiastic partial hangout, after admitting that the Mexico City Oswald evidence had been faked (!), said, "There are certainly a number of things I regret, and I regret the attempts to destroy Mr. Lane."[159] That's the repentant KGB talking, right?

Trafficante's Chicago partner, Sam Giancana, was helping to finance and organize the Rosselli-Hunt assassination teams. In July 1975, Giancana, just before he was to testify before the Senate Select Committee, was murdered. One of Rosselli's hitters, involved in the anti-Castro plots, who knew Giancana well, complained to Anthony Summers that "all Sam was going to say was 'I did a contract for Santos - period.'"[160] That was apparently way too much for Santos. Aside from the first fatal shot in the back of the head, Giancana was shot once through the mouth and stitched five times in a semicircle under the chin, a traditional Mafia warning to respect *omertá*, the code of absolute silence.

Rosselli, in the midst of repeated Congressional appearances in 1976, was also murdered, as was Charles Nicoletti, the Giancana enforcer who replaced Rosselli on the Castro project. Rosselli was last seen alive on a boat owned by an associate of Santos Trafficante. His decomposing body was found August 7, 1976 floating in a drum in Dumfoundling Bay.[161]

Joey Aiuppa, new boss of the Chicago Syndicate, was upset that Rosselli's body, which had been weighted with chains, was found. He screamed at hit-man Frank Bompensiero, "Trafficante had the job and he messed it up!"[162] That was also the conclusion of the Assassinations Committee, although they couldn't prove it. John Martino was also murdered in 1976, just before the Church Committee could get to him. His private papers revealed a decades-long relationship with Santos Trafficante.[163]

In 1979 the Congressional Assassinations Committee formally concluded that "the CIA-Mafia-Cuban plots had all the elements necessary for a successful assassination conspiracy - people, motive and means - and the evidence indicated that the participants might well have considered using the resources at their disposal to increase their power and alleviate their problems by assassinating the President."

Considering organized crime alone, the Committee said that "extensive investigation led it to conclude that the most likely family bosses of organized crime to have participated in such a unilateral assassination plan were Carlos Marcello and Santos Trafficante."[164] The chief counsel of the Assassinations Committee, Prof. Robert Blakey, named Rosselli and Giancana as the most likely engineers of the assassination, with Marcello, Trafficante and Hoffa functioning as their financiers.[165]

The chief CIA covert operative organizing all these elements, the designer of Operation Mongoose, was Maj. Gen. Edward Lansdale. Just as the Missile Crisis was developing, on October 16, 1962, six days before JFK announced it to the world by instituting the naval blockade, RFK called Lansdale up on the carpet. According to Richard Helms, who recorded the meeting in a same-day memo, RFK was furious that Castro was still alive.. He sacked Lansdale, who went to work, under cover of a Pentagon posting, for Helms.[166] Helm's depiction of RFK's position may be self-serving - the fight was more probably about political control of Mongoose.

Bill Harvey, the professional assassin who ran Task Force W, was also repeatedly upbraided by RFK during operational meetings. Samuel Halpern, Harvey's executive officer on Task Force W, witnessed Harvey's temper snap during a Missile Crisis meeting. Reacting to one more accusation of failure, Harvey angrily told both the President and RFK that "We wouldn't be in such trouble now if you guys had had some balls in the Bay of Pigs!"[167]

Harvey was sent to Rome, but Kennedy ordered much of the vast Mongoose/Task Force W structure to continue to operate under Harvey's replacement, Desmond FitzGerald, former CIA Far East chief. The Missile Crisis arrangement with Moscow, however, required that these groups be deniable. That led to a complete loss of executive control, as RFK and the CIA competed for influence with the craziest of the *Batistianos* and the mafiosi. FitzGerald's immediate superior was Richard Helms, director of covert operations.

Control of the Mongoose monster had been the problem from the beginning. Kennedy had not approved the killing of Russians in the Alpha 66 raid of October 1962, on the eve of the missile crisis.[168] That's probably what got Lansdale sacked by RFK. Lansdale, of course, wasn't sacked by Helms, simply "reassigned." It was this lack of political control at the top that sharpened Kennedy's appreciation of the need to take the CIA.

Significantly, the CIA refused to cooperate at all with the House Assassinations Committee, exercising a legal right it should not have. The House Assassinations Committee's refusal to subpoena even a single document from any intelligence agency may simply have been an unavoidable political function of the CIA's adamant refusal to cooperate.[169] The Committee, of course, did use documents already pried loose by other committees and court actions, and did subpoena witness, quite a few of whom were murdered before they could testify.

Trafficante had become a major Bobby Kennedy target. He told José Alemán Jr, son of a high-level Batista and Prio operative, in a Florida hotel in Sept. 1962, as he arranged a $1.5 million Teamster loan for him, that John Kennedy would not live to be reelected: "He is going to be hit."[170] Alemán, showing crazy courage, reported this to the FBI at the time, but was ignored. Trafficante's Louisiana ally, Marcello, also prophesied Kennedy's assassination in Sept. of 62 to an outsider who reported it before it happened, Ed Becker.[171]

Trafficante and Marcello counted among their allies two little fruit companies, United Fruit and Standard Fruit, which shipped their bananas, and dope, out of their "Banana Republics." United Fruit was born in the Northeast after the Civil War, and Standard was born on the New Orleans docks in the 1890's. It was there that both outfits found their street muscle, in the Machecas (United) and the Vaccaros

(Standard), who competed for control of the waterfront.[172] After all, if you can't unload the fruit, it rots.

Former New Orleans police chief Guy Molony, an engineer of the 1911 Honduran coup, was one of the inventors of the "Banana Republic." He helped the Fruits get through the Depression by pioneering the Honduras to New Orleans heroin run.[173] Depression-era Honduras was run by United Fruit's Tiburcio Carias Andino, one of the world's great heroin dealers. Carias remained in power from 1934 to 1963, when there was a brief flirtation with semi-representative democracy and the Alliance for Progress, soon corrected by the Fruits.

Sitting on Standard Fruit's Board of Directors was Seymour Weiss, Carlos Marcello's boss during their early days with Huey Long, Lucky Luciano, Meyer Lansky and Frank Costello. Standard Fruit, United Fruit, and the politician-hustlers that helped the mob run the docks were Huey Long's backers. Frank Costello, "the prime minister of the Mafia," ran the Louisiana operations that Lansky and Luciano had designed, using Meyer's good ol' boys, Dandy Phil Kastel and Seymour Weiss.

Weiss, like Costello an expert political fixer, performed these services for Huey Long. Long's convenient death in 1935 helped Weiss avoid an IRS investigation into the Win or Lose Corporation that he fronted for the Kingfish.[174] It also probably consolidated the Syndicate's hold on Louisiana's rackets. Seymour explained to the police, his employees, just how it happened.

In 1939, in return for his continued exemplary cooperation with law enforcement, J. Edgar Hoover arranged for his top aide to give Weiss and Louisiana Governor Leche a guided tour of FBI headquarters. The next year Seymour Weiss went to jail for fraud. That same year the entire New Orleans dock board were indicted for extortion and embezzlement, along with Lucca Vaccaro, a founder of Standard Fruit, and Earl Long, the Kingfish's brother and successor as governor.[175]

Weiss gave the Marcellos the West Bank franchise for Costello's Indian-headed "Chiefs." All the boys were profoundly impressed with the success of the Marcello brothers' Jefferson Music Company, which had its one-arm bandits, juke boxes and pinball machines in every joint on the West Bank. It was hard to say no to the seven Marcello brothers. The ruthlessly efficient Marcellos made Costello's one-arm bandits pay big. By 1944, at the age of 35, Carlos Marcello had become the biggest slot operator, gamer, loan shark, fence, extortionist, burglar, armed robber, pimp and dope peddler on the West Bank. As such he was invited by Lansky and Costello to take a piece of the plush new gambling house they were building in Jefferson Parish.

By this time Weiss had immersed himself in the Fruit and political fix business and left most of Costello's affairs to Frank Coppola. When Coppola was deported to Sicily in 1946, Marcello was tapped to run all of Costello's gambling operations in Louisiana. In 1947, Silver Dollar Sam Carolla, the biggest drug wholesaler in Louisiana, was also deported to the Mafia's protected free port. This left Carlos Marcello free to distribute all the heroin Coppola, Carolla and Sal Vitale, another Luciano ally, could ship out of Sicily.[176]

One of the most profitable hustles Marcello inherited was Costello's Southern News Company wire service, the racing wire monopoly without which no bookie in Louisiana could operate. The statewide influence the wire service alone gave Marcello was enormous. His personal combination of the politician's populist touch, generous graft and terror made him the most influential man in the state.

By 1950 Drew Pearson was calling him "the crime czar of New Orleans."[177] That was no exaggeration. "The Big Payoff" was a system that had Marcello paying off the New Orleans police department by rank: captains got $100 a week, while sergeants got $20. D.A. Aaron Kohn, when he became head of the New Orleans Crime Commission, revealed another perk-by-rank enjoyed by New Orleans cops - rape. Attractive women arrestees were regularly gang-raped - with captains going first and patrolmen getting sloppy sixths.[178] In January of 1951 Marcello took the Fifth 152 times before Senator Kefauver.

Marcello's enormous illegal profits were invested in a wide array of legal businesses. The largest account of his Pelican Tomato Company was the U.S. Navy. Seymour Weiss, sitting on Standard Fruit's Board of Directors, remained a lifelong ally of Marcello, an important bridge between the mob and the feds. J. Edgar Hoover himself met regularly with Marcello's old boss Frank Costello throughout the 40's and 50's, although Hoover continued to assure the public that the Syndicate didn't exist, and opposed Senator Kefauver's efforts to prove that it did. Hoover's relationship with Costello was confirmed by, among others, William G. Hundley, former head of RFK's Organized Crime and Racketeering Section.[179]

Standard Fruit's Seymour Weiss developed long-standing ties to J. Edgar Hoover's close friend Lewis Rosenstiel, the veteran anticommunist and ex-bootlegger who ran Schenley Distilleries. In 1957 Lewis Rosenstiel hired Hoover's trusted propaganda chief Louis Nichols to head Schenley's lobbying and PR efforts. Rosenstiel simultaneously endowed the J. Edgar Hoover Foundation, to the tune of one million dollars, to promote "Americanism."[180] Nichols had been the FBI's congressional liaison to Joe McCarthy and Richard Nixon, feeding them the bogus evidence they advertised to such good effect during their 1948-1953 HUAC hearings.[181]

Schenley Industries and Standard Fruit, Rosenstiel and Weiss, financed FBI and CIA contract groups, such the American Jewish League Against Communism and the Information Council of the Americas (INCA), which pumped out "information" as needed. INCA's president, Dr. Alton Ochsner, was an Air Force "consultant" who also sponsored *Latin America Report*, edited by United Fruit PR man, and admitted CIA agent, William Gaudet. INCA, based in New Orleans, was founded by Ed Butler, just after his "release" from a U.S. Army intelligence unit. INCA's staff included former FBI agent William Monaghan, who was Standard Fruit's security chief, and Eberhard Deutsch, Standard Fruit's general counsel.[182]

The Fruits were not pleased with Kennedy's refusal to recognize the September 1963 overthrow of Alliance for Progress ally Juan Bosch in the Dominican Republic, nor with his equally adamant refusal to recognize the October overthrow of Ramón Villeda Morales in Honduras, another important Alliance ally. Kennedy angrily broke relations with Santo Domingo and Tegucigalpa, insisting that coups are "self-defeating...not only because we are all committed under the Alliance for Progress to democratic government and progress but also because of course dictatorships are the seedbeds from which communism ultimately springs up."[183] Clearly, Kennedy wasn't running the CIA.

Thomas Mann, a bitter personal enemy of Robert Kennedy, was U.S. ambassador to Mexico at this time. Mexico City was the CIA station from which all Western hemisphere coups were run. Mann had been Assistant Secretary of State for Inter-American Affairs during the 1954 Guatemala coup, during which he worked with Howard Hunt. He later presided over Johnson's 1965 stomping of the Dominican Republic, once again keeping Juan Bosch, the legally elected leader and another Alliance ally, from power.[184]

Mann was at the center of the "second Oswald" charade. He was the vehicle for the release of the fairytale told by Gilberto Alvarado, a Somoza agent claiming to have seen Oswald in the Cuban consulate in September take money to kill Kennedy. In his ecstatic communiques to the FBI, State Department and the White House, Mann insisted that he had cracked the case, since he knew Castro to be "the Latin type of extremist who reacts violently rather than intellectually and apparently without much regard for risks."[185]

Under questioning by the Mexicans, which included lie detector tests, Alvarado admitted that he was reciting lies, scripted, apparently, by Mann's old ally Howard Hunt, CIA Station Chief in Mexico City at this time.[186] At any rate, Alvarado recounted Oswald's imaginary conversation with the Cubans in the same kind of B-movie argot - "guts," "man enough" - that Silvia Odio repeated and that Hunt wrote into his pop spy novels.

Castro and Kennedy had, in fact, been making peaceful overtures to one another in the fall of 1963. Castro had reacted to Kennedy's vicious trade embargo, which included the poisoning of Cuban food shipments and the sabotaging of machine parts, by distributing much of the American property he had expropriated to the poor. This brilliant political maneuver helped Kennedy understand that buying Castro might be the cheapest way to wean him from Mother Russia. So, while he still approved the occasional pinprick raid as a warning against hemispheric interference, the authorized raids dwindled to an insignificant trickle.

But unauthorized raids, such as the March 1963 raid of Antonio Veciana's Alpha 66, which shot up a Soviet army installation and freighter, proliferated. This caused a major diplomatic incident and threatened the progress of the nuclear test ban negotiations. That, apparently, was the CIA intention. Veciana insisted, before the Schweiker-Hart Senate Intelligence Committee in 1976, that it was his CIA case officer, "Maurice Bishop," who planned the attack. Bishop repeatedly told Veciana that the purpose of the raid was to destroy détente.

Apparently détente wasn't the only thing the CIA wanted to destroy. Veciana later testified, before the House Assassinations Committee, that in late August 1963, at his meeting with Bishop at the Southland Center in Dallas, Lee Harvey Oswald was present.[187] Assassinations Committee Chief Counsel Blakey concluded that "Veciana's allegations remain undiscredited..."[188]

Kennedy reacted to the March Alpha 66 raid by having Attorney General RFK announce, on March 30, that the FBI would be employed to stop unauthorized raids. On April 12 Kennedy categorically declared that "There will not, under any conditions, be an intervention in Cuba by United States armed forces..."[189] That, of course, had been precisely what Dulles, Helms & Company had been trying to engineer from the beginning.

Throughout the fall of 1963 the CIA continued to actively oppose the peaceful option. That's why operational control of the CIA became so important to the Kennedys. "I remember him saying that the CIA frequently did things he didn't know about, and he was unhappy about it. He complained that the CIA was almost autonomous," recalled JFK's close friend, Senator George Smathers.[190]

Seriously gunning for Castro would have cost Kennedy any hope of détente with Russia, a far more important matter. Stepping on Cuba would have forced Krushchev to step on Berlin, risking the total disaster that had just narrowly been averted during the Missile Crisis. Tensions were still quite high, and that, apparently, was where the militarists in the CIA wanted them.

It was during this contest for control of Agency operations, on July 31, that Marcello's Minuteman Lake Pontchartrain camp, run by Hemming and Sturgis, at which Ferrie and Oswald trained, was seized by RFK's FBI.[191] But, although the Kennedys could arrest a few operatives, they were unable to control the massive Mongoose monster they helped to create. Mongoose was discontinued, but Task Force W remained, renamed the Special Activities Staff. With independent covert CIA funding, much of it from Trafficante's and Marcello's huge dope profits, the rogue weasels born of Mother Mongoose went on an uncontrolled rampage.

On September 7, 1963, CIA officers were even finalizing plans with Castro insider Rolando Cubela to kill Castro. This was done without the approval of the President, the Attorney General or the Director of the CIA, according to the Senate Intelligence Committee testimony of the senior officer involved, Deputy CIA Director Richard Helms. Noted Kennedy's close Special Assistant Arthur Schlesinger, "The whole Cubela thing raises even deeper questions. The CIA [Helms' Directorate of Plans] was reviving the assassination plots at the very time President Kennedy was considering the possibility of normalization of relations with Cuba - an extraordinary action. If it was not total incompetence - which in the case of the CIA cannot be excluded - it was a studied attempt to subvert national policy."[193]

Important elements of the military and the CIA were strongly in favor of continuing the ecologically devastating, militarily destabilizing atmospheric nuclear tests banned by the Moscow Treaty. The U.S. lithium-deuteride "fission-fusion-fission" H-bomb set off in the deep Pacific in 1954 created not only massive immediate destruction, but a 20 mile wide radiation belt that was lethal as far as 140 miles downwind. Many Marshall Islanders, in harm's way, remained unwarned so as to create "a useful genetic study of the effects on these people."[193a]

On September 8, Moscow radio accurately, and ominously, pointed to Kennedy's inability to control the *Batistianos*: "Increasing provocations against Cuba are now being organized at a time when the United States Senate is discussing the Moscow Treaty banning nuclear tests.... This cannot be regarded as mere coincidence. The opponents of the Moscow Treaty wish, apparently, to take advantage of an aggravated situation in the Caribbean to prevent, if they can, its ratification."[194-195] Exactly.

Kennedy knew, partly because Castro told him, that the embrace of the Russian bear was stifling, and that the U.S. trade embargo gave him great leverage. Kennedy's Ambassador William Attwood, special advisor for African affairs at the U.N., had been told by the Guinean envoy to Cuba that Castro was looking for a political lever to get him out from under the international Communists, like Ché Guevara, in the Cuban leadership. Castro, always first and foremost a Cuban nationalist, was alarmed at the growing Russian control of the island.[196]

Attwood, foreign affairs advisor McGeorge Bundy and Undersecretary of State Averell Harriman, advised Kennedy to open secret talks with Carlos Lechuga, Castro's U.N. envoy. These talks began in late September, and were aimed at establishing direct negotiations. Finally, on November 19, in a deal worked out on the phone partly with a concerned and eager Castro himself, it was arranged for Attwood to go to Havana to "see what could be done to effect a normalization of relationship."[197] Such a normalization would have been Castro's greatest victory, and it would have politically defeated his own hard liners.

Castro, for his part, knew that Kennedy was a Somoza and Trujillo enemy, that he had in fact just organized the 1961 assassination of the elder Trujillo, and that his Alliance For Progress was, to some extent, at least, "subversive" by CIA standards. That is, Castro understood that he might be uniquely positioned to help Kennedy gain control of the CIA by defusing its Latin American military operations. Castro, for the first time since his disgusting confrontation with Richard Nixon in 1959, communicated his willingness to make major concessions in exchange for peace.[198]

In mid-November of 1963 Kennedy sent the distinguished French journalist Jean Daniel of *L'Express* from the White House with the message that he accepted responsibility for the "economic colonization, humiliation and exploitation" of Cuba. "The United States can coexist with a nation in the hemisphere that espouses a different economic system, the Monroe Doctrine notwithstanding. It is the subservient relationship with the Soviet Union that creates the problem."[199] If Castro would leave Kennedy free to pursue his Alliance For Progress without revolutionary interference, Kennedy was prepared to recognize Castro. The deal, which never got past this initial stage, probably would have entailed the lifting of the embargo in exchange for the return of American property, the expulsion of Soviet troops, and a guarantee of hemispheric nonintervention.

Daniel, who had just finished delivering Kennedy's message, was lunching with Castro when news of the assassination came over the radio. "*Es una mala noticia*," mumbled the stricken Castro, over and over again, utterly shocked. When Oswald was identified as a member of the Fair Play for Cuba Committee and an admirer of Castro, Fidel protested, very worried, "If they had proof, they would have said he was an agent, an accomplice, a hired killer. In saying simply that he was an admirer, this is just to try and make an association in people's minds between the name of Castro and the emotion awakened by the assassination. This is a publicity method, a propaganda device. This is terrible…"[200]

Castro and all those around him were in deep fear of a massive revenge strike by the U.S. military, something they knew full well they could not survive. When the conversation turned to Johnson, Castro asked Daniel, "What authority does he have over the CIA?"[201] As if in answer, Johnson immediately killed Attwood's peace mission and recognized United Fruit's General Oswaldo Lopez Arellano in Honduras. He then sent the Kennedy-hating Thomas Mann as his ambassador to Chiquita Banana, perhaps just to get Mann out of the spotlight in Mexico City.

Only cooperating command elements within the CIA, Army Intelligence, the National Security Agency and the FBI had the reach to coordinate what actually happened at Dallas and during the Warren Commission cover-up - *and protection of the geopolitical power financed by the international drug trade was at the very heart of it.*

At the very first meeting of the Warren Commission, Allen Dulles, *de facto* chair of the "Warren" Commission, handed out a book that insisted that American assassinations had traditionally been committed by loners. Kennedy's, said Dulles, clearly fit that pattern.[202] Since the investigation had yet to begin, it's not clear how Dulles could have known that. He could, however, have known the opposite.

Dulles' close political ally, J. Edgar Hoover, *five hours* after the arrest of Oswald, asserted that the assassination "very probably" was solved.[203] Three days later Hoover told presidential aide Walter Jenkins, "The thing I am most concerned about, and so is Mr. Katzenbach, is having something issued so we can convince the public that Oswald was the real assassin."[204]

Both Hoover and Dulles sent orders through their respective agencies, Dulles operating through Helms and Angleton, that proving the lone assassin theory was the *purpose* of the investigation. The ostensible reason given was the cover story created by Oswald's phony legend, that he was a Russian-Cuban agent, and that revealing that could lead to a disastrous war with Russia.

Dulles used Hoover to supervise the Commission's investigation, and, as every decent book on the assassination, as well as the 1979 Congressional Assassinations Committee, points out, both Hoover's FBI and Helms' CIA systematically destroyed, distorted and hid essential evidence - all toward the end originally outlined by Dulles and Hoover. It was Dulles and Hoover, working with Deputy Attorney General Katzenbach, in the absence of the distraught RFK, who squelched the idea of an independent investigative staff for the Warren Commission, leaving it wholly dependent on Hoover, Helms and Angleton. That alone points toward complicity in the assassination.

Katzenbach's memo to presidential assistant Bill Moyers, written three days after the assassination, states "1. The public must be satisfied that Oswald was the assassin; that he did not have confederates who are still at large; and that the evidence was such that he would have been convicted at trial. 2. Speculation about Oswald's motivation ought to be cut off, and we should have some basis for rebutting thought that this was a communist conspiracy or (as the iron curtain press is saying) a right-wing conspiracy to blame it on the communists."[205]

Consistent with these objectives, Allen Dulles, sitting on the Warren Commission, never once mentioned the mob assassination teams, deeply connected to Oswald, Ruby, Marcello and Trafficante, that he himself had set up. Immediately, that is, the investigation was turned into a CIA-FBI disinformation operation.

Democrat Johnson, a lifelong Hoover-Murchison-Marcello ally, appointed an awful lot of Nixon and Rockefeller-connected Republicans to the Commission. Aside from Dulles and Warren, there was Congressman Gerald Ford, whose chief aide, John Stiles, was field director of Nixon's first presidential campaign. John J. McCloy worked for the Rockefellers, did business with George de Mohrenschildt's father at Nobel Oil, engineered the merger of the Chase and Manhattan Banks - and David Rockefeller's chairmanship thereof, himself became Chairman of the Board of Chase-Manhattan, a director of the Rockefeller Foundation and a board member of United Fruit. Republican John Sherman Cooper of Kentucky became Nixon's Ambassador to India.

Democrats Richard Russell and Hale Boggs threatened to write a minority report. Senator Russell called the Warren Commission Report "a sorrily incompetent document." The confusing, unindexed 26-volume Report actually bears very little relationship to its own evidence and documents. The actual author of much of the Report, Air Force historian Arthur Goldberg, worked for Adm. Arleigh Burke at the CIA's Center for Strategic Studies at Georgetown University. The other author, Arthur Marmor, was also an Air Force historian. In 1971 Boggs complained, on the House floor, that the FBI had used Gestapo tactics on Commission witnesses and members, subjecting them to illegal surveillance and personal blackmail. The next year Boggs had a fatal plane crash.

The 1975 Senate Intelligence Committee and the 1979 House Assassinations Committee determined that Hoover, like Dulles, not only knew of the ZR/RIFLE hit teams and failed to tell the Warren Commission, but had taped the 1962 and 63 mob threats to Kennedy's life. Hoover, fully aware of the threats, failed to tell the Secret Service or the President at the time. That makes Hoover, at the very least, an accessory before the fact.[206]

That Hoover micromanaged this information is beyond question. As Courtney Evans, assistant director of the FBI at this time, put it, "Hoover saw everything that came in."[207] Hoover, according to all who knew him, was a bureaucratic genius. Evans himself, a staunch Kennedy ally, was systematically cut out of the investigative loop by Hoover.[208]

The agents Hoover put in charge of the investigation, from the Domestic Intelligence Division and the Espionage Section - Sullivan, Belmont, Branigan and their aides - were the same FBI-CIA liaison agents who had handled Oswald *before* the assassination. They were also the same agents who ran Hoover's COINTELPRO's against such subversives as the Fair Play for Cuba Committee, the Congress of Racial Equality, Martin Luther King, the ACLU, the CIO, the Maryknoll Sisters, Amnesty International, the Black Panther Party and the American Indian Movement.

Kennedy's refusal to continue gunning for Castro provoked rage in the Cuban Revolutionary Council. Miró Cardona, then president of the CRC, resigned in fury - death threats were heard. Captain Charles Sapp, Chief of Miami's Police Intelligence Bureau, put his unit on alert as the *Batistianos* handed out bills that insisted "Cuban patriots" could expect to return home quickly only "if an inspired Act of God should place in the White House within weeks a Texan known to be a friend of all Latin Americans."[209]

In October 1963 an audience member made a tape recording of a meeting of the John Birch Society held in a Dallas suburb. The tape was given to a senior Dallas cop, who held onto it until 1978, when he gave it to author Anthony Summers. Bay of Pigs veteran Nestor Castellanos was recorded raving that "Mr. Kennedy is kissing Mr. Krushchev! I wouldn't be surprised if he had kissed Castro, too! I wouldn't even call him *President* Kennedy. He stinks. We are waiting for Kennedy the 22nd, buddy. We are going to see him, in one way or the other. We're going to give him the works when he gets in Dallas."[210] If this loco weed knew that, so did the CIA.

On November 9 Sapp's Miami intelligence unit recorded a racist fascist with ties to Bannister, Joseph Milteer, specifically describing ongoing plans to take Kennedy out in Dallas "from an office building with a high-powered rifle…"[211] Captain Sapp was able to control Miami security, actually cancelling a Kennedy motorcade. He also warned the FBI and the Secret Service, in the strongest possible terms, but neither communicated the warning to their Dallas offices. The Secret Service didn't even question Milteer.

James Hosty, who headed up the FBI's Dallas investigation, was the same agent who investigated Oswald in Dallas *just before* the assassination. When Oswald left New Orleans in late September, supposedly for a short trip to Mexico City, he returned to Dallas, not New Orleans. Although Kennedy's Dallas trip wasn't publicly announced until early November, it had been planned in June. Oswald rented a room in Dallas from Earline Roberts, the sister of Bertha Cheeks, a friend of Jack Ruby's.

Hosty began his "routine surveillance" in early October, a surveillance he acknowledged under oath in 1975. Hosty's name, address and telephone number were found in Oswald's address book, although the FBI's typed transcript of the book given to the Warren Commission omitted only this information. Why, if the surveillance was so routine, was Hosty's name omitted?

On November 1, Hosty, looking for Oswald, visited Oswald's wife Marina, staying with her friend Ruth Paine on the outskirts of Dallas.

Michael and Ruth Paine were introduced to the Oswalds by George DeMohrenschildt. Michael Paine had security clearance at Bell Helicopter, and Ruth Paine's father worked for the CIA's Agency for International Development. Four days later, Hosty called again, looking for the address of Oswald's rented room in Dallas. The women gave him neither the address nor the telephone number, only Oswald's workplace, the Texas School Book Depository. Oswald, angered by the surveillance, went directly to the Dallas FBI office, where, according to both the receptionist and Hosty, he left a threatening note. Why did Hosty's attention upset Oswald? Was Hosty manipulating Oswald under pressure?

Two days after the assassination, just after Oswald was killed, according to the senior FBI investigator, Counterintelligence chief William Sullivan, Hosty destroyed Oswald's note.[212] This felony was confirmed under oath by Hosty himself, who said that Agent-in-Charge Gordon Shanklin ordered him to do it. This was confirmed by Agent Howe. Hosty claims that Oswald wrote that "If you have anything you want to learn from me, come talk to me directly. If you don't cease bothering my wife, I will take appropriate action and report this to the proper authorities."[213]

What might explain the "angry note," whatever it actually said, is the repeated appearance in Dallas at this time of "the Second Oswald." This obnoxious loudmouth often advertised the name "Lee Harvey Oswald" when Oswald was at work at the book depository. He bought rifle ammo at a gunshop, had a rifle firing pin repaired and had a telescopic sight mounted on a Mannlicher-Carcano - with one more drilled hole than the Carcano found. The imposter also bought Western Union money orders, cashed checks, shopped for an expensive car because he was coming into "a lot of money" and applied for a job in a building that overlooked Dealey Plaza - and made a point of mentioning that. The imposter also got himself remembered at a rifle range for being a crack shot and for intentionally shooting up his neighbor's target, a gross breach of etiquette for which he was not apologetic.[214]

Both Hosty and Sullivan were of the opinion that the order to destroy Oswald's note came directly from Hoover. And Hosty, pondering his possible appearance before the House Assassinations Committee in 1978, said "I am the one they are afraid is going to drop bombs - if they are going to try to contain this like the Senate Intelligence Committee and the Warren Commission, they don't want me there."[215] That is all but an overt admission that Hoover's spy agency was helping to run Oswald. In 1978, former FBI Counterintelligence chief William Sullivan, the COINTELPRO expert, just before he was to testify for the House Assassinations Committee, was shot dead.

In New Orleans, Hoover assigned the same agent who handled Oswald *before* the assassination, Regis Kennedy, the Agent-in-Charge, to handle the assassination inquiry. As late as 1978, in front of the Assassinations Committee, Agent Kennedy was still insisting that Carlos Marcello was just a misunderstood "tomato salesman and real estate investor." He "did not believe Marcello was a significant organized crime figure." It was Regis Kennedy, in 1962, whom Hoover assigned to investigate Marcello's mortal threats against the President, about which the President was not informed. It was also Regis Kennedy who colluded with Carlos Marcello, Wray Gill and David Ferrie to provide Ferrie with his phony alibi at the time of the assassination.[216]

Hoover's FBI also didn't tell the Warren Commission that it knew that Jack Ruby was a mob hit man, drug dealer, pimp and political fixer with lifelong ties to the Chicago mob and to Dallas mob boss Joseph Civello, Carlos Marcello's lieutenant. Nor did it mention Ruby's 1959 visit to Santos Trafficante, while Trafficante was in Castro's detention. The 1979 House Select Committee on Assassinations concluded that "the Bureau's own organized crime and Mafia specialists [the most pro-Kennedy people in the Bureau] were not consulted or asked to participate to any significant degree....The committee also determined that the Bureau's lack of interest in organized crime extended to its investigation of Oswald."[217]

The CIA's nominal head, John McCone, was a businessman with no military experience, an amateur guided by his number two, the deadly Richard Helms, chief of covert operations, who had operational control of the Agency. Under this guidance, McCone did exactly what Hoover did, picking the same Counterintelligence team that created the phony Oswald legend in Mexico City *before* the assassination, led by longtime Dulles subordinate James Angleton. One of Angleton's specialties, for years, was assassination.

On September 17, 1963, Oswald walked into the Mexican consulate in New Orleans and applied for the tourist card that would enable him to enter Mexico. He was given card number 824085. With the help of Mexican authorities, the FBI was able to present to the Warren Commission a complete list of all the other people who applied for entry into Mexico on September 17. Only one name was missing, the holder of card number 824084, immediately preceding

Oswald. Said the Hoovers, "No record of FM 824084 located."

That was an intentional lie. In 1975 the cardholder was revealed to be none other than William Gaudet, CIA agent and United Fruit PR man, editor of *Latin America Report*. Gaudet, whose office was just around the corner from 544 Camp Street, admitted seeing Oswald with Bannister, Ferrie and Arcacha. Gaudet also admitted working for the CIA. He explained to the FBI that he couldn't talk to them until he had been briefed by his CIA case officer in New Orleans, who told him to shut up.[218]

On September 26, the day the papers confirmed Kennedy's Dallas visit, someone calling himself Oswald left for Mexico City from Texas on a Trailways bus. He did some acting on the bus, establishing himself as an unforgettable left-wing loudmouth. He was in the company of John Bowen, also known as Albert Osborne, a fanatical Nazi.[219]

On September 27, a fake "Oswald," much shorter, ten to fifteen years older and fifty pounds heavier, showed up at the Cuban consul's office in Mexico City and insisted on an in-transit visa to Cuba and Russia, which was impossible without prior clearance from the Russians for travel there. "Oswald" also lacked the necessary personal photos. Returning a few hours later with the photos, "Oswald" raised hell when his visa was still refused. He reacted with protestations of allegiance to Russia and a loud display of his phony left-wing credentials, which Sylvia Duran, the Mexican processing clerk, didn't buy. "Oswald" created an unforgettable scene for Duran and Cuban Consul Eusebio Azcue, who talked at length to "Oswald" twice, once a few days later. Both are sure the man bore no resemblance to the real Oswald, and that the purpose of the encounter was the scene, not the visa.[220]

That was also the testimony of journalist Oscar Contreras, then a politically active law student at the National University. While talking to two other young left-wingers, he was interrupted by the same short, pudgy guy who introduced himself as Lee Harvey Oswald, slowly spelling the entire name, and then complaining that the Cuban consulate was giving him a hard time with his visa. Could Contreras and his friends help him with their contacts at the Cuban Embassy? How, thought Contreras, out of all the thousands of students in Mexico City, could this guy pick three who actually did have contacts at the Cuban Embassy?

The CIA's "corroboration" of "Oswald" in Mexico City was surveillance photos, purportedly taken at the Cuban Embassy, apparently with a Brownie operated by the visually impaired.[221] All that can be seen is a blurry fat guy, below left, who don't look like Lee, right.

If the Cuban Embassy really was under CIA surveillance - and it was - why didn't the Warren Commission get a whole roll of crystal clear photos of Oswald taken by CIA pros? That's exactly what Assassinations Committee investigator Edwin Lopez found when he got one of the real CIA files in 1978. Of the dozen photos taken at the Embassy, only one was of the real Oswald, the other eleven were the imposter. Lopez concluded that the real Oswald never was in Mexico City.

Anthony Summers, who was shown some of the classified information in this file, says that the twelve photos weren't released because eleven are obviously not Oswald and the twelfth, which was of Oswald, was later destroyed because it also showed some of his CIA handlers.[222] That twelfth photo, however, could indicate that Oswald may have been in Mexico City sometime during the summer or fall of 1963 - providing cover for his double.

The CIA, of course, is a huge bureaucracy composed of factions which are more than willing to step on each other's toes. During the Missile Crisis, one CIA agent, Richard Nagell, was assigned to keep tabs on the *Batistianos* in Mexico City. He was to do that by hiring himself out to Soviet military intelligence as a double agent, thereby penetrating their awareness of former "defector" Oswald and the CIA Cubans. The Soviets were perfectly well aware of the *Batistiano* plans to smear Castro as a presidential assassin, and Nagell was part of their effort to avert that disaster. In that complex role, during the late summer of 1963, Nagell apparently ran into the real Oswald in the company of his *Batistiano* handlers. Oswald bragged to Nagell that they were going to kill Kennedy.

Since Nagell knew the *Batistianos* to be very serious CIA operatives, he went to his Mexico City KGB case officer, who ordered him to eliminate the plotters, something Nagell couldn't bring himself to do. Instead, on September 13, he sent a registered letter to J. Edgar Hoover, detailing the plot to kill Kennedy. In the absence of any response from Hoover, on September 20, Richard Nagell walked into an El Paso bank and put two rounds from his .45 through the ceiling. He then walked outside and sat down on the curb, waiting to be arrested. He told the arresting officers of the plot to kill Kennedy, explaining that he wanted protective custody and to advertise the plot before it became fact.

But after his arrest in El Paso, Nagell was held incommunicado for nine months in a county jail. Although his only visitors were FBI and Secret Service agents, and although the six names of CIA agents found in Nagell's notebook in September of 1963, before the assassination, were repeated in Lee Harvey Oswald's notebook, no mention whatever was made of Nagell in the Warren Commission's 26 volumes. Instead Nagell was imprisoned for five years on trumped up bank robbery charges, because of the shots he put through the bank ceiling. Nagell had never mentioned the bank's money, and, in fact, didn't even wait for a reaction before walking outside and sitting down on the curb.

Ignored and marginalized as a psycho, Nagell went to Europe on his 1968 release from prison. But future investigators couldn't ignore the fact that Nagell, an acknowledged CIA agent who had penetrated the Mexico City KGB, had proven that he knew of the plot to kill Kennedy beforehand and had tried to stop it. In late October of 1995, the Congressional Assassination Records Review Board, mandated by the JFK Records Act of 1992, summoned Nagell to reveal the "smoking guns" he claimed to have in a bank vault in Zurich. These were said to include a copy of the letter he sent to Hoover, and Mexico City photos and recordings of Oswald and the *Batistianos* surreptitiously made by Nagell *before* the assassination. On November 1, 1995, immediately after the Congressional decision to summon Nagell had been made, he was found dead in his Los Angeles apartment.[223]

Oswald obviously was involved with Marcello and his Louisiana Cubans, and with the Mexico City *Batistianos* as well. The other corroboration of Oswald's Mexico City presence from September 27-October 3 tends to indicate that his real presence was used to cover the activities of an imposter.

The day of the assassination the CIA sent the Dallas FBI tapes of eight wiretapped telephone calls placed by "Oswald" to the Soviet Embassy in Mexico City, some from the Cuban consulate. One of the tapes mentioned Valery Kostikov, chief of the KGB's Western Hemisphere terrorist operations.

The very next day, while Oswald was still alive in custody, J. Edgar Hoover himself, in this overhasty top secret report to the head of the U.S. Secret Service, James Rowley, wrote that: "Special Agents of this Bureau, who have conversed with Oswald in Dallas, Texas, have observed photographs of the individual referred to above and have listened to a recording of his voice. These Special Agents are of the opinion that the above-referred-to individual was not Lee Harvey Oswald."[224]

After listening to the CIA tapes and examining the photos, the seven FBI interrogators, who had just finished talking at length with the real Oswald, *officially concluded* that the Mexico City "Oswald" was an intelligence setup, a fake. That is, these hardboiled pros concluded that key command elements within the CIA conspired to lie to the Dallas FBI by using a false Oswald legend created *before* the assassination.[225]

Realizing that he had let the cat out of the bag, Hoover immediately made his hasty preliminary report unavailable to the Warren Commission.[226] Hoover's preliminary report was pried loose in court by Mark Lane post-Watergate, in 1977, under the Freedom of Information Act. Hoover also ordered the Dallas Special Agent-in-Charge, Gordon Shanklin, to destroy the CIA tapes. This is the same agent who ordered Hosty to destroy Oswald's note.

The CIA's description of the tapes, given to the FBI *eight weeks before the assassination* but never turned over to the Warren Commission, says "The American spoke in very poor Russian to the Soviet representative…"[227] Oswald's Russian was so good he could pass for a native. He had studied Russian intensively, had lived in the country for more than two years and had a Russian wife.

Prominently offering bogus excuses for the CIA's Mexico City evidence was David Phillips, former CIA Chief of the Western Hemisphere Division. When Phillips was stationed in Mexico City in the fall of 1963 he was a Chief of Covert Operations, in charge of all Cuban operations. He was working with station chief Win Scott, and took orders directly from Desmond FitzGerald and Richard Helms. That is, Phillips was the man who issued the *Batistianos* their marching orders. Before that, in 1960, Phillips was a covert operative in the Directorate of Operations, stationed in Havana. It was most likely he, along with banker, and terrorist, Tony Veciana of Alpha 66, who engineered the sabotage of Cuba's currency in 1960. Before that, in 1954, Phillips had run, along with Howard Hunt, the Guatemala coup propaganda operation. Phillips was propaganda chief of the Bay of Pigs operation, and Hunt was his chief subordinate.

Because of Veciana's description, the circumstantial evidence, and the positive identification of a CIA case officer stationed at JM/WAVE, who was given anonymity, Phillips is the House Assassinations Committee's top candidate for the role of "Maurice Bishop." Although Veciana has refused to make a positive identification, he did say that he saw "Bishop" in the presence of Oswald a month before the assassination, in late August, just before the Mexico City adventure started. Veciana's Army Intelligence contact was Colonel Sam Kail, who was also the contact of George DeMohrenschildt, Oswald's Dallas handler.

Immediately after the assassination, before the Mexico City "Oswald" fell apart, "Bishop" asked Veciana, who had a cousin by marriage named Guillermo Ruiz in the Cuban Embassy in Mexico City, "to see if Ruiz would, for money, make statements stating that Lee Harvey Oswald had been at the Embassy for a few weeks before the assassination."[228]

The 1979 House Select Committee on Assassinations determined that immediately on the 1971 death of former Mexico City CIA station chief Win Scott, Counterintelligence chief Angleton, although retired for years, flew down to Scott's house and, in front of his wife, rifled the family safe, retrieving only documents related to the CIA's Mexico City handling of "Oswald."[229]

Facing the scepticism of the Warren Commission's independent-minded Senator Richard Russell, the CIA "found" the bus tickets Oswald was alleged to have used to leave Mexico City, 6 months after the investigation began. The person who found them, in Marina Oswald's magazines, was Priscilla Johnson, who somehow became the only journalist allowed to interview the CIA-kidnapped Marina Oswald.[230] Priscilla Johnson, whose name was found in Oswald's personal notebook, also just happened to be the CIA agent who kept tabs on Lee Harvey Oswald in Moscow, when he was on assignment in 1960-61 to pose as a defector.[231]

Priscilla Johnson's parents were the first hosts of Svetlana Aliluyeva, Stalin's daughter, when she defected in 1967. Johnson is a graduate of the Russian Research Center at Harvard, part of the CIA-funded Center for International Affairs. She played the same game with Marina Oswald that Luce played with the Zapruder film. She bought the rights to Marina's story, held onto it for years and contractually prohibited Marina from talking to anyone else. When *Marina and Lee* was finally released, in 1977, it proved to be, according to Marina, a tissue of overt lies that bore no relation to the story she told Johnson.

Priscilla Johnson's husband, George McMillan, just happened to be the author of the FBI's major disinformation effort advertising James Earl Ray as a lone nut, just like Oswald.[232] (This role has now been assumed by the Dan Rather-advertised Gerald Posner.) Jerry Ray, McMillan's major "source," insists that McMillan also made up his testimony out of whole cloth. James Earl Ray, in fact, had connections to some of the same Marcello operatives, and FBI agents, that Oswald did. It appears that the violently racist - and pro-Vietnam War - Carlos Marcello organized King's assassination as well, using Ray as the patsy of an elaborate plot, and that Marcello, again, was protected by Hoover's FBI during the subsequent investigation.[233] King was shot dead when he threatened to bring his enormous muscle into the anti-war movement.

It is way beyond the scope of this general history to delve into the King assassination, but it is worth pointing out that the disinformation on both assassinations flowed from the same font. Hoover, who ran the King investigation as another disinformation operation, with words like "nigger," "coon," and "tomcat" constantly spewing from his lips, prompted the House Select Committee on Assassinations to characterize the FBI's treatment of Dr. King as "morally reprehensible, illegal, felonious, and unconstitutional."[234]

There is little doubt among the experts that President Kennedy's body was surgically altered in transit from Parkland Hospital in Dallas to Bethesda Naval Hospital near Washington, to make small entrance wounds seems like large exit wounds, that is, to change the apparent direction of the shots.[235] Obviously, that could have been done only by those with "security clearance." What threat could have made Dr. James Humes, the autopsy surgeon at Parkland, burn all his original notes?

Consistent with his miserable record of deception, J. Edgar Hoover, in the official Warren Commission report, printed the two Zapruder frames following the head shot in reverse order, thereby falsifying the evidence to change the apparent trajectory of the bullet.[236]

The Zapruder film, a piece of evidence that screwed up the whole scenario, clearly shows what many, including the very sophisticated surgeons at Parkland saw - that the fatal head shot came from the front.[237] The red-hot bullet's trajectory can actually be seen on the film, and Kennedy's head is jerked violently backwards on impact, as all physicists tell us must be the case.

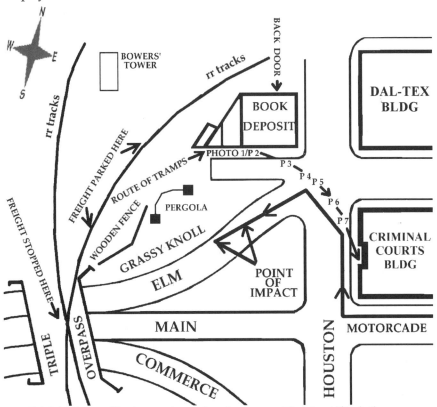

Of 266 formally interviewed witnesses, 51 identified the grassy knoll *in front* of the President as the source of the shots, 32 claimed the Book Depository or the Dal-Tex building, which were *behind* the President, and the rest, 183 eyewitnesses, claimed both.[238]

The grassy knoll, *in front* of the President, was also instantaneously identified by numerous expert eyewitnesses, including Secret Service Agent Paul Landis and Dallas County Sheriff Bill Decker, both very close to the shooting, who immediately directed their troops to it.[239] The House Assassinations Committee concluded that the third shot was "fired from a point along the east-west line of the wooden stockade fence on the grassy knoll..."[240]

On November 20th, two Dallas police officers noticed several men on the grassy knoll engaged in mock target practice, aiming rifles over the wooden fence at the point of the assassination. Their report, given to the FBI on November 26, was never shown to the Warren Commission, and remained buried until 1978.[241]

Thanks to the Zapruder film, there is no doubt about the exact location of the President's car when he was shot. Aiming at that spot from the sixth floor of the Book Depository, a shooter would have had to fire through the heavy foliage of a large tree. No trained Marine would attempt such firing. Cameras and gun sights can see past obstructions by focusing past them, but red-hot bullets, which have to go through them, get knocked helter-skelter. You would simply miss.

Bystander James Tague, on Main Street, was photographed just after he had been slightly wounded by the same burst of gunfire that killed Kennnedy. The next day, the curbstone with the impact mark of the bullet that wounded Tague was dug up and replaced. Tague was in a line with Kennedy, but the line leads back to the second floor of Dal-Tex Building, not the sixth floor of the Book Depository.

Within a minute or two of the shooting, the elevator man in the Dal-Tex building noticed a passenger "acting suspiciously" and ran to get a policeman, who detained "Jim Braden," a recent name change adopted by Eugene Brading. Braden's associate was also detained, a young man wearing a black leather jacket and black gloves. Braden claimed to have walked into the building after the shooting looking for a phone, but a Dal-Tex employee sighted Braden in the building at the time of the shooting. Unlike almost everyone else detained that day, Braden was released without fingerprinting or a serious security check. His leather-clad associate was released without even the recording of his name.

Braden had arrived in Dallas only the previous morning, and had booked into the Cabana Motel. On the afternoon of the 21st, Braden met Jack Ruby in the offices of H L. Hunt, the racist oil tycoon who was financing the hit teams, as a CIA cutout. Braden was a thief, dope dealer and assassin who worked for Carlos Marcello and Santos Trafficante. Earlier that year, Braden, who had a rap sheet of 35 arrests, told his parole officer that his New Orleans address was the 17th floor of the Pere Marquette Building. That was the address of Marcello operative David Ferrie.

Ferrie, 8 weeks before the assassination, had called Jean West in Chicago. The night of the assassination, Jean West was staying in the same Cabana Motel in Dallas with another Ruby associate, Lawrence Meyers, whom Ruby visited the night before the assassination. Jim Garrison's check of the motel records revealed that Meyers' son Ralph was also at the Cabana that night. Ralph Meyers was an Army Intelligence agent with top-level crypto-clearance. Late that night, at 2:30 a.m., Ruby called one of his employees from the Cabana.[242] So why did the Dallas police think Jim Braden wasn't worth investigating?

Ruby, of course, knew virtually every cop in the Dallas PD. Before he died of "cancer" in 1967, on the eve of being called to testify for Jim Garrison, he told a reporter that the assassination was a "complete conspiracy….If you knew the truth you would be amazed." It was also someone in the Dallas Police Department who put out a description of "an unknown white male, approximately 30. Slender build, height 5'10", weight 165 pounds, reportedly armed with a .30-caliber rifle," *fifteen minutes* after the shooting. Oswald wasn't nailed for an hour and a half.[243-244]

Oswald was seen by numerous coworkers who knew him, just before the shooting, calmly eating his lunch in the depository's second-floor cafeteria. When police officer Marrion Baker and the head of the depository, Roy Truly, walked into Oswald in the second floor cafeteria, 90 seconds after the shooting, Oswald, completely relaxed and not out of breath, was calmly sipping a coke.[245]

Kennedy was scheduled to pass Dealey Plaza at 12:25, but the motorcade was five minutes late. If Oswald had been the shooter, he would have been on the sixth floor awaiting his target when numerous people spotted him eating lunch on the second. Understanding this, the FBI altered the testimony of Carolyn Arnold, secretary to the vice president of the depository, who specifically remembered Oswald eating lunch at 12:15. The FBI changed the time to 12:35. Bonnie Ray Williams, who ate his lunch on the sixth floor at 12:15, saw no one else on the whole floor.[246]

Realizing he was the patsy, Oswald slipped out of the TSBD before it was sealed. He apparently went back to his room to get his pistol. The officer who stopped Oswald, J.D. Tippit, a John Birch Society activist, was also a known mob-contact and an acquaintance of Jack Ruby. Tippit was apparently hunting Oswald in the vicinity of his room. That is, he was aware of Oswald's identity before that identity had been established. And Tippit was out of his patrol district. Oswald, a competent pistolero, got Tippit before Tippit could get Oswald.[247] Oswald then forced the police to take him alive by going to a movie theatre full of witnesses.

The Dallas Police paraffin tests established that Oswald had fired a hand gun. They also proved that both of Oswald's cheeks showed no powder deposits.[248] Oswald hadn't sighted and fired any rifle, let alone the sloppy antique he was alleged to have used, which would have sprayed his right cheek with powder. The rifle was an Italian WW II-era mass-produced piece of garbage that sometimes sold wholesale for as little as $2 to mail order houses. The Mannlicher-Carcano found, furthermore, had a very sticky bolt. It was proven, by expert marksmen, to be incapable of the speed or accuracy demonstrated.[249]

Oswald was shifted from job to job by his handlers with the story that he was to investigate the illegal mail order sale of junk firearms.[250] Oswald worked moving books while he tried to get next to yet another FBI or ATF target, the credit manager, Guy Molina, a veteran who had joined the politically unkosher American G.I. Forum.

Oswald's right-wing sympathies made it just that much easier for his handlers to manipulate him, but he was no right-wing crackpot. His views on Kennedy, according to his own statements after capture as well as all who knew him before, were quite positive. Oswald strongly disapproved of racial segregation and agreed with Kennedy's handling of it. Oswald *liked* Kennedy. No one has ever been able to provide Oswald with a *personal motive* for the killing. This, of course, doesn't mean that he wasn't a willing part of the plot. He obviously thought of himself as an intelligence operative and certainly was a willing part of the plot. But did he bring the rifle to the TSBD parking lot to blow Kennedy away, or to set someone else up?

Jack Ruby told his last psychiatrist, Dr. Werner Teuter, that he should "read Buchanan's book" to get an accurate idea of what really happened. Buchanan contends that Oswald thought that it was his job to bring the rifle.[251]

On November 21st, Oswald had asked his fellow TSBD employee, Buell Frazier, who lived near the Paines' house where his wife was staying, to give him a lift that evening out to his wife. As Frazier recalled, Oswald mentioned something about getting "some curtain rods...to put in an apartment." Oswald stayed the night with his wife, and then drove back to work the next day with Frazier. He brought with him a large heavy brown bag, apparently the curtain rods.

Oswald walked far ahead of Frazier once they got to the TSBD parking lot, and the only person to see Oswald enter the building that morning testified that Oswald carried nothing into the building. But the brown bag was found on the sixth floor of the Texas School Book Depository, with Oswald's prints on it. Both Frazier and his mother, however, the only people who saw Oswald carrying the big bag, insisted that it was shorter than the disassembled Carcano, which had, in fact, been stolen from the Paine garage.

Oswald sent away for the famous mail-order rifle in March of 1963, paying the princely sum of $21.45, including postage. He was obviously acting on orders from his handlers, and the false name he was told to use, A.J. Hidell, was connected, by them, to the left-wing Fair Play for Cuba Committee. Oswald carried this phony ID the day of the assassination.[252]

The only reason Oswald would have laid a careful paper trail from "Hidell" to the rifle is that his handlers had told him he was gathering evidence for illegal sales by mail order companies and/or illegal purchases by Hidell of the Fair Play for Cuba Committee - that is, that he was setting someone up. Senator Dodd's committee, in fact, actually logged in identical mail order evidence from Klein's, whence came the Mannlicher-Carcano, and from Seaport Traders, the other company Oswald ordered from.[253] If Oswald had intended to shoot the President with a rifle, and live, he would have bought it anonymously over the counter in rural Texas - and this trained Marine would have bought a considerably finer weapon.

The photo showing Oswald jauntily brandishing the rifle can be shown to be a fake, and Oswald's prints weren't found on the rifle.[254] The three shell casings planted with the rifle in the depository and the round in the chamber were the *only* ammo found anywhere for the Carcano, either on Oswald's person, at his home or in his post office box. Nor was any gun-cleaning equipment found.[255]

The Warren Commission insisted that one bullet entered Kennedy's back below the right shoulder blade on a sharp downward trajectory from six floors above, then turned upward to exit his neck. This remarkable bullet then paused midair for 1.6 seconds, hit Governor Connally in the front seat in the right-rear armpit, then changed trajectory inside Connally's chest to shatter his right wrist. Then the *same bullet* took another radical u-turn and lodged in Connally's left thigh. Later, this magic bullet was found on a stretcher at Parkland Hospital, where both Kennedy and Connally had been taken. Despite the fact that some of the bullet was still in Connally's thigh, the bullet found was in pristine condition.

Two live recordings of the assassination exist. One is the Zapruder film. The other is the police dictabelt recording made by a motorcycle escort's open microphone. The distinguished acoustics expert hired by the House Assassinations Committee concluded from the dictabelt that four shots had been fired in 7.91 seconds. The expert also concluded, confirming most of the witnesses and the Zapruder film, that the third shot came from the front.[256] The splattering of Kennedy's brains to the left and rear of the limo also proves that the devastating third shot came from the right front of the limo - and from ground level - the grassy knoll.

The House Committee's chief counsel concluded "That there were two shooters, and thus a conspiracy, is a scientifically based fact."[257] Three shots, in any case, can't be matched up to the eight nonlinear holes made - there had to have been at least two more, one of which slightly wounded Tague a block away.

The shocked Oswald, who consistently denied having done the shooting, was exactly what he said he was, "the patsy," and his handlers were sophisticated as all hell. Eisenhower's special assistant for psychological warfare, the CIA's C D. Jackson, "Henry Luce's personal emissary to the CIA," who became the owner of *Life* magazine, rushed to Dallas to buy, and bury, the Zapruder film. He published carefully selected stills from it once and then made it unavailable until March 1975, when pressure from the Church Committee forced its showing on television.[258] The selected stills were published in reverse order, making it appear that the ferocious head shot came from the rear, not the front.

The CIA-kidnapped Marina Oswald's story was also published in *Life*, ghostwritten by veteran CIA propagandist Isaac Don Levine. Allen Dulles had used the Jackson-Levine team to coordinate the psyops reaction to Stalin's death. C.D. Jackson was the propaganda planner, along with the elder Anastazio Somoza, of the 1954 Guatemala coup. Levine was instrumental in convincing Whittaker Chambers to frame the State Department's Alger Hiss, thus handing Richard Nixon his first great anticommunist publicity.

Allen Dulles and Frank Wisner, working with *Time's* Henry Luce and Jackson and Levine, set up "Operation Mockingbird," which actually went into the media acquisition business. That's how C.D Jackson came to own *Life* and *Fortune*. Working with Dulles in this effort were his political soul-mates, Phil Graham of *The Washington Post*, a graduate of the Army Intelligence School in Harrisburg, PA; William Paley of CBS; Arthur Hays Sulzberger of *The New York Times*; Barry Bingham Sr. of *The Louisville Courier-Journal*; and James Copley of the Copley News Services. Other organizations which cooperated more peripherally included ABC, NBC, the Associated Press, United Press International, Reuters, Hearst Newspapers, Scripps-Howard, *Newsweek*, the Mutual Broadcasting System, *The Miami Herald*, the old *Saturday Evening Post* and *The New York Herald-Tribune*.

Journalist Ben Bagdikian: "The power of a few corporations to control a larger reach of the standard, mass media continues to grow. In the early 1980s, when I started out on this project, about 50 companies had most of the business in newspapers, magazines, radio, television, movies, and books. And in each edition of *Media Monopoly*, the number of companies has grown smaller and their reach has grown larger. The latest edition - 1992 - reported that 23 companies now control the media."[259] Defense contractors GE and Westinghouse, of course, now own NBC and CBS. This has a profound influence on the course of the public dialogue, simply by virtue of the corporate culture, the hiring practices, evolved at the networks.

Carl Bernstein wrote a famous 1977 *Rolling Stone* article that named over 400 journalists uncovered by the Church Commission working for the CIA.[260] You can bet Senator Church's electoral competition was very well financed after that. By Bernstein's time, the polished CIA apparatus had evolved the ability to form public opinion simply by leading the debate with stories it could plant at will all over the mass media.

Like the one about the lone assassin. Immediately after the assassination, newspapers all around the world were publishing detailed biographies, with photos, of Lee Harvey Oswald - his late 1959 defection to the Russians, his Russian wife, his pro-Cuba activities. This made media professionals all over the world deeply suspicious. Oswald's name wasn't made public until his arrest, an hour and a half after the shooting. Yet, within an hour of the assassination, news bureaus all over the world were inundated with detailed information about this previously unknown young man, information no reporter had time to dig up. This was a prearranged scenario, an intelligence operation. The *Life* photo is a paste of Oswald's face on another body.

The Mayor of Dallas, in control of the parade route, the police force and all the initial evidence, was Earle Cabell, the brother of General Charles Cabell, Dulles' second-in-command, the Deputy Director of the CIA fired by Kennedy in the wake of the Bay of Pigs. Since a trial would have given Oswald's defense attorney the right to subpoena evidence and witnesses, it was essential that be avoided. That was the official conclusion of the 1979 House Select Committee: "the murder of Oswald by Jack Ruby had all the earmarks of an organized crime hit, an action to silence the assassin, so he could not reveal the conspiracy."[261]

The Assassinations Committee established that Ruby had the help of Cabell's Dallas police in getting to Oswald. Dallas police sergeant Patrick Dean was in charge of security when Oswald was hit. Dean actually bragged, within earshot of Peter Dale Scott, whose *Deep Politics* is such an expert analysis, of his good relations with Mafia boss Civello. Dean said Civello had helped him in the "many, many dope cases I made."

After Civello returned to Dallas from his unhappy 1957 visit to Apalachin, New York, where he functioned as Carlos Marcello's representative, he had dinner with Sergeant Dean. Dean always insisted that Dallas "had no trouble with the Italian families."[262] He certainly didn't, anyway. The Dallas County sheriff into whose hands Oswald was being transferred, Bill Decker, was Civello's character witness in his pardon application after Civello served six of the fifteen years he was sentenced to in 1937 for dealing dope.

A former Civello employee, outraged to hear on TV that Ruby had no organized crime connections, went to the FBI and outlined his detailed knowledge of Civello's and Ruby's long relationship. Bobby Gene Moore's testimony, which included considerable proof, was deliberately hidden by the FBI from the Warren Commission.[263] Civello's top lieutenants, the Campisi brothers, were among Ruby's closest friends and associates. A 1956 FBI file links Ruby to a "large narcotics setup operating between Mexico, Texas, and the East," explaining that one "got the okay to operate through Jack Ruby of Dallas."[264] Ruby was the influential fixer who transmitted Civello's OK and picked up the vig.

During the original FBI investigation, Atlanta FBI Agent Daniel Doyle uncovered the fact that Ruby had run guns to Castro with Eddie Browder, an operative of Trafficante lieutenant Roughhouse Rothman. When these facts were "washed out" of the Atlanta FBI report finally sent to Washington, Doyle resigned in protest.[265] Browder's FBI file, more than a thousand pages, was never shown to the Warren Commission. When suspicious Warren Commission lawyers Griffin and Hubert asked the CIA for information on this, they got none.

Ruby himself had admitted to the Warren Commission that he

had sold jeeps to Castro in 1959, but, despite that admission, the Commission adamantly insisted that "no substantiation has been found for rumors linking Ruby with pro- or anti-Castro Cuban activities."[266] Despite the fact that Hoover and Dulles knew, the Commission was never told that Ruby visited Trafficante in Cuba in 1959.

Ruby warned his first lawyer that the name "Davis" would mean trouble. Ruby had met bank robber and assassin Thomas Davis in one of his clubs shortly before the assassination. Davis was one of Rosselli's hitters in ZR/RIFLE, run by CIA agent Bill Harvey. When Davis was arrested in Tangier a month after the assassination, he was sprung by CIA agent QJ/WIN, possibly Rosselli. This again raises the distinct possibility that the Kennedy hit was a ZR/RIFLE operation, as Rosselli himself obliquely asserted - just before his own assassination. Correspondence at the time shows Hoover to have been personally aware of Davis' Moroccan detention, but he never mentioned any of this to the Warren Commission, despite the fact that Davis had a relationship with Ruby.[267] In 1976, just as Congress was about to hear what he had to say, ZR/RIFLE's Bill Harvey had a fatal "heart attack."

By not investigating Ruby's CIA/Syndicate links, the FBI avoided having to investigate itself. It officially interviewed Ruby, as a paid Potential Criminal Informant, nine times in 1959 alone. This certainly related to Ruby's hood/CIA work, the penetration of Castro's movement.[268] Ruby was in and out of Cuba a lot in 1959, bringing an awful lot of electronic eavesdropping equipment with him.

In 1950 Jack Ruby actually appeared before the staff of the Kefauver Senate Rackets Committee. The quid for Ruby's testimony, according to his lawyer Luis Kutner, who was at that time a staff lawyer for Kefauver, was that Kefauver stay away from Dallas, which he did.[269] Kutner, a practicing expert in these matters, said that "Ruby was a syndicate lieutenant who had been sent to Dallas to serve as liaison for Chicago mobsters."[270]

Before moving to Dallas in 1947, Ruby had been arrested by Chicago police in connection with the 1939 murder of Leon Cooke, founder of the Scrap Handlers Union local in which Ruby was secretary. The shooting happened in Ruby's presence, and resulted in the installation of Paul "Red" Dorfman, Allen Dorfman's stepfather. Dorfman proceeded to bring the Scrap Handlers into the Teamsters, and then to help engineer Jimmy Hoffa's takeover.

Red Dorfman was a Capone operative close to Anthony Accardo, one of Capone's more powerful successors. The Dorfmans ended up in control of the entire Teamsters' Central States, Southeast, and South-west Areas Pension Fund, "the Mafia's private bank," from which hundreds of millions have been skimmed.[271] Ruby's associate John Martin had been acquitted in the Scrap Handler's murder on grounds of self-defense.

But the murder attracted the attention of Attorney General Kennedy in his war on Hoffa, which, ultimately, was a war for control of the Democratic Party. Kennedy had Hoffa indicted twice in 1963, once, in May, for jury tampering and once in June for fraud. Although Chicago police transmitted Ruby's 1939 arrest sheet for the Scrap Handlers murder to the Texas Attorney General, who gave it to the FBI, it never reached the Warren Commission. Coincidence? As the growling villain in *Dollars* put it, "I don't believe in coincidence."

RFK started the war as counsel to Senator McClellan's Rackets Committee in 1957, on which sat Senator John Kennedy. As chief counsel to the Senate Select Committee on Improper Activities in the Labor or Management Field from 1957-59, the savagely brilliant RFK amassed an encyclopedic knowledge of the Syndicate, with which he often tripped up astonished witnesses.[272] It was Kennedy's relentless police work that uncovered Joe Valachi, the first made mafioso to spill his guts, in detail, before Senator McClellan, in September, 1963.

By 1963 Kennedy was getting nearly 400 organized crime convictions a year and had forced the FBI, which was becoming Kennedy's FBI, into an aggressive war on the hoods - extensive wiretaps, stings, audits - the works. This was not the fix Sam Giancana had authorized. Buffalo boss Stefano Magaddino fumed, over a wiretap, "They know everything under the sun. They know who's back of it, they know *amichi* [made mafiosi], they know *capodecina* [family captains], they know there is a commission. We got to watch right now, this thing, where it goes and stay as quiet as possible."[273]

In an effort to avoid deportation, Marcello had contributed $500,000 to Nixon's 1960 campaign, funneling the money to Nixon's lawyer, the versatile Irving Davidson, through Jimmy Hoffa.[274] Marcello also had the help of the Kingfish's son, Senator Russell Long, working the Democratic side of the fence, but to no avail.

RFK's Organized Crime Section had also targeted virtually all of Marcello's most powerful underworld allies - not only Hoffa, but incredibly, Santos Trafficante, Meyer Lansky, Mickey Cohen, Frankie Carbo, Tony Corallo, Angelo Bruno and even Sam Giancana.[275] Kennedy actually succeeded in making it a federal crime to transmit gambling information across state lines electronically, thereby effectively criminalizing the mob's most profitable hustle.

When Bobby Kennedy deported Carlos Marcello to Guatemala in 1961, he enraged some of the most dangerous men in the world. In September, 1962, Marcello told his longtime associate Carlo Roppolo, in the presence of Ed Becker, a private investigator then working with Roppolo, that the way to handle Bobby, the "tail" of the dog, was to kill John, "the head" that wags the tail. The idea, said Marcello, was to set up "a nut, like they do in Sicily."[276]

It was that same month that Marcello's closest and most powerful ally, Santos Trafficante, told José Aleman that Kennedy was "going to be hit."[277] Trafficante's assertion was made as he arranged a huge Teamster loan to Aleman on behalf of Jimmy Hoffa, who worked, essentially, for Sam Giancana. That same month Hoffa described his plans to Louisiana Teamster leader Ed Partin, an FBI informant, to use a sniper to blow John Kennedy's head off. Jimmy wasn't just whistlin Dixie. After Ruby murdered Oswald, Ruby's brother Earl approached one of Hoffa's lawyers to represent his brother.[278]

During the late 50's Santos Trafficante operated out of Havana, Tampa and Miami's Teamster Local 320, built especially for him by his partners Hoffa and Giancana. Hoffa was an important CIA conduit to Sicilians like Frank Coppola, a close Luciano-Marcello ally who was a key player in taking Sicily, by assassination, from the leftists in 1947.[279] Coppola, Lucky Luciano's close childhood friend, was family to Hoffa, his foster son's Godfather.

Hoffa was also a key conduit to Trafficante, the real employer of many of the CIA Cubans. Trafficante used Hoffa's Teamster trucking system for dope distribution throughout the U.S., whence his enormous economic power. As Robert Kennedy put it in 1958, "It shows once again the close relationship of not only gangsters but the lowest type of gangsters, those dealing in narcotics, being interested in certain elements in the Teamsters Union, namely in this case, [Pennsylvania boss] Mr. Bufalino."[280]

On September 22, 1966, New York City police interrupted Santos Trafficante having lunch at the La Stella restaurant with Carlos Marcello, Carlo Gambino, Thomas Eboli of the Genoveses, and Joseph Colombo, each with a vast professional army and tens of millions at his disposal, each a mortal enemy of the Kennedys.[281]

The Kennedys were going for the very heart of CIA-Syndicate power, in a serious attempt to control both. Roughhouse Rothman, Sam and Kelly Mannarino and Giuseppe Cotroni were partners in two major Cuban casinos, the Sans Souci and the Tropicana, fronting for the Lanskys, Trafficante and ex-Cuban president Prio. They were also major drug importers. In 1960 they were caught running guns to *Batistiano* Cubans using $8.5 million in stolen securities, what the FBI called "the biggest burglary in the world."[282] Rothman insisted that it was a "protected" operation and that, despite conviction, he and his codefendants would avoid imprisonment. They did. Their lawyer was Ruby's lawyer, Luis Kutner.

In 1971, when Nixon was President, Sam Mannarino was in trouble again, indicted along with two other mafiosi for stealing millions from the Teamsters Pension Fund. Mannarino had helped Vice-President Nixon, the CIA's O'Connell, Rosselli and Giancana put together the first ZR/RIFLE hit teams in 1960. In 1971, Mario Brod, the chief Mafia case officer of James Angleton's CIA Counterintelligence unit, walked into court and got Sam Mannarino and the other two mafiosi acquitted on grounds of national security.[283]

The FBI also knew that the FBN had questioned Ruby in 1947 in an opium smuggling case. That case tied Ruby to Cuban mafiosi and the fledgling DFS, the Mexican CIA, which had always worked with Syndicate operatives. But Hoover didn't give the Ruby investigation to Evans' pro-Kennedy Special Investigative Division, which would have explored the staples of organized crime - drugs, labor racketeering, gambling and prostitution. He gave it to Domestic Intelligence, Counterintelligence and Espionage, run by his political allies, Belmont, Branigan, Sullivan, Sizoo, Moore, and the others, the COINTELPRO experts.[284]

Jack Revill, a former commander of the Dallas narcotics unit, admitted to the House Assassinations Committee under oath that he had known Ruby since 1953. It was Revill, second in command of Dallas' Special Service (Criminal Intelligence) Bureau, who organized the search of the Texas School Book Depository that found the old Mannlicher-Carcano Oswald was alleged to have used. Revill was also present in the basement of the Police and Courts Building when Ruby shot Oswald.

In fact there was hardly a cop in the basement who didn't know Ruby, who protected his position by becoming the unofficial mob liaison, easy loan shark and pimp for the Dallas Police Department. It was common knowledge in the Dallas mob that when access to the cops was needed, the man to see was Jack Ruby.

Barney Baker, Jimmy Hoffa's muscle man, was telephoned by Ruby just before the assassination, as were other old hood associates, in a flurry of calls both just before and just after the assassination.

The powerful Teamster fixer Irwin Weiner was also called. Weiner, who reinvested the huge Vegas skim, worked with Las Vegas' Johnny Rosselli for years. Ruby, of course, knew assassination-engineer Rosselli and met with him a month before the assassination. At the time of the assassination, Weiner told the Warren Commission that he was in Miami meeting with Santos Trafficante.[285]

Ruby also called Dusty Miller, another key Hoffa operative, head of the Southern Conference of Teamsters. Ruby both received a call from and made a call to Marcello's top aide, Nofio Pecora.[286] Ruby was close to Harold Tannenbaum, who lived on Pecora's property, helping to manage the many strip joints run by Marcello's brother Pete and others. Ruby spoke to any number of Hoffa, Trafficante and Marcello intermediaries during this period. A series of ten calls went to Lewis McWillie, the Trafficante operative who worked with Giancana and Rosselli.

Mob infiltration of the Dallas police department, as mob infiltration under Rosselli of the Los Angeles police department, had the practical effect of targeting liberal outfits like the American Civil Liberties Union and the mayor's political opposition, and protecting the KKK and the vice rackets. As Lt. George Butler put it, "half the police force in Dallas were members of the KKK."[287] He oughta know, he organized them. Butler worked with the Special Service Bureau, which handled intelligence, vice and narcotics, and so worked closely with Jack Ruby for years. Butler was in the basement just before Ruby shot Oswald, and film shows him to be uncharacteristically nervous, literally trembling in anticipation.[288] Just after the shooting, Butler insisted that Ruby had nothing to do with the Mafia.

Two Dallas cops, Senkel and Turner, not only managed to be at every important evidentiary discovery relating Oswald to the assassination, but were also in the pilot car of Kennedy's motorcade. They arranged, ten minutes before the motorcade passed, for a phony ambulance call that slowed down the motorcade just as it passed Dealey Plaza.[289] Jack Ruby just happened to be in the Dallas Morning News Building, overlooking Dealey Plaza, when the assassination happened.

Oswald was questioned by Dallas Homicide chief Capt. Will Fritz, the FBI's James Hosty and Jim Bookhout, the Secret Service's Thomas Kelly and Forest Sorrels, U.S. Marshall Robert Nash and Postal Inspector Holmes. None called in a stenographer or even transcribed their long interviews, a gross unprofessionalism that had to have been ordered.[290] It is impossible not to see the hand of J. Edgar Hoover, Dallas Police Chief Jesse Curry and his boss, Mayor Earle Cabell, brother of Dulles' second-in-command, Gen. Charles Cabell, in all this.

While Oswald was alive in custody, on November 23, J. Edgar Hoover revealed, in a memorandum dated November 29, that his Special Agent Forsyth and Captain Edwards of the Defense Intelligence Agency correctly briefed "Mr. George Bush of the Central Intelligence Agency" about potential problems relating to the assassination.[291] The problems related to possible unauthorized military actions against Cuba, and George Bush was understood to be the CIA contact for such matters. That is, Bush knew what was and was not authorized.

Bush operated the CIA-front Zapata Petroleum Corp. and the Houston-based Zapata Off Shore Co. Col. Prouty was responsible for providing the ordinance and transport for the Bay of Pigs invasion, which he tells us was code-named "Operation Zapata." The disguised Navy ships Prouty provided for the invasion were named, after Prouty delivered them, "Barbara" and "Houston."[292] Isn't George romantic about Barb? What a nice guy, so civil.

At the height of the Cold War, Kennedy introduced himself to the CIA by firing its chief officers and attempting to take policy control of the Agency. Although Kennedy used "counterinsurgency" extensively to bolster his top-down, export-oriented Alliance for Progress in Central America, he insisted on supporting genuine centrists as well as rightists, often directly opposing specific CIA operations. He used Cuba, contrary to the *consensus ecclesiae*, to engage Russia in a *de-escalation* of the hysteria. His brinksmanship contained enough real statesmanship to produce the 1963 limited test ban treaty, a monumental psychological breakthrough - but a breakthrough that presaged civilian control of CIA covert operations.

Kennedy the insider was also Kennedy the visionary. The Peace Corps was a brilliant achievement. So was the June 1963 Comprehensive Civil Rights Bill, anathema to the Dulles brothers, Hoover, Eastland, the Hunts, Marcello and many others running the CIA's Cuba hit teams. Kennedy always threatened a charismatic policy shift. He was actively engaged in negotiating an accommodation with Cuba while at the same time supporting democrats Juan Bosch in the Dominican Republic and Ramón Villeda Morales in Honduras, both overthrown by the CIA just prior to the assassination. In both cases, Kennedy broke relations rather than recognize the unauthorized CIA coups.

There was a nasty fight brewing for control of the CIA, and the

CIA knew it. Kennedy repeatedly told his intimates that "When I am reelected, I am going to break that agency into a thousand pieces." Helms was perfectly well aware that Kennedy reserved unto himself the right to fire Helms.

RFK, also working from within military intelligence, with his own Justice Department and FBI strike forces, ran a coordinated attack on the very drug dealers being used by the CIA to finance and run the worst aspects of the Cuba and Vietnam operations. The fight wasn't about policy, stated policy. Kennedy, for the most part, didn't disagree with stated CIA policy. The fight was about the power to lead policy. No policy advisor ever talked about "our dope dealers." The subject never came up, except when forced by RFK. Obviously, RFK's FBI knew exactly who Carlos Marcello was financing. They busted one of his CIA Minuteman camps just prior to the assassination. From the moment he took office, RFK used all his muscle to get Marcello.

But, operationally, Helms, Lansdale and their army of agents were working for Marcello, Trafficante and Rosselli. Kennedy supported Juan Bosch, but Johnson overthrew him, when he again threatened to take power in 1965. Bosch, a genuine populist, was not dope-dealer-friendly, but Johnson was a Marcello-Murchison-Hoover man to the bone. RFK had a thick file on the Johnson-Marcello link, detailing heavy, regular payoffs, at least $50,000 a year, for years, from Marcello to Johnson. These went through Marcello's Texas political fixer Jack Halfen. In return, Johnson regularly killed all antiracketeering legislation in committee that might have been a threat to Uncle Carlos.[293] It was Johnson, of course, who insisted on a controllable Commission rather than an uncontrollable Congressional investigation.

Kennedy insisted that coups are "self-defeating...not only because we are all committed under the Alliance for Progress to democratic government and progress but also because of course dictatorships are the seedbeds from which communism ultimately springs up."[294]

The perspective of Fletcher Prouty is incredible, because he was simultaneously one of JFK's key military intelligence operatives and the chief Focal Point officer of the Joint Chiefs for CIA covert operations. The import of Kennedy's NSAM's, as Prouty is able to document in firsthand operational detail, was *political control* of policy. That is, operational command-and-control. *That* is something that fascist military intelligence reserves for itself. Prouty calls it "corporate socialism" or "communism," the worst insults he can think of.

As the overwhelming evidence proves, this is no "conspiracy theory." This is Dwight Eisenhower's dark prophesy come true.

Prouty was one of Eisenhower's senior technical advisors on CIA covert operations when Eisenhower invented the "National Security Action Memorandum" method of delivering "major directives" to the CIA - that is, when Eisenhower tried to create a structural solution to control of CIA covert operations.

After the CIA sabotage of his own summit, Eisenhower insisted, in an address that he knew to be his most historic, that "The conjunction of an immense military establishment and a large arms industry is new in the American experience....we must guard against the acquisition of unwarranted influence, whether sought or unsought, by the military-industrial complex. The potential for the disastrous rise of misplaced power exists and will persist."

A month after Kennedy's assassination, December 21, a heartbroken Harry Truman wrote in the *Washington Post* that "For some time I have been disturbed by the way the CIA has been diverted from its original assignment. It has become an operational and at times a policy-making arm of the government....I never had any thought that when I set up the CIA it would be injected into peacetime cloak-and-dagger operations."

Covert government by defense contractor means corrupt wars of conquest, government by dope dealer. When the world's traditional inebriative herbs become illegal commodities, they become worth as much as precious metal, precious metal that can be *farmed*. That makes them, by definition, the preferred medium of exchange for armaments. Illegal drugs, solely because of the artificial value given them by Prohibition, have become the basis of military power anywhere they can be grown and delivered in quantity. That's why Paul Helliwell, OSS chief of special intelligence in China during the war, helped run SACO's KMT opium and heroin. He was arming the KMT. To this day American defense contractors are the biggest drug-money launderers in the world.

In the early 50's Helliwell organized Civil Air Transport, SEA Supply of Bangkok and Air America, which kept our opium-producing Golden Triangle armies supplied. He then organized the Bahamas' Castle Bank of Nassau, the CIA-Syndicate money laundry through which the Bay of Pigs and the Cuban hit teams, serviced by SEA Supply, were funded.[295] Helliwell's law firm represented Trafficante-Teamster partners in Resorts International, as they developed Bahamas gambling, with the help of Johnson's bag man Bobby Baker.[296] They distributed the Indochinese heroin ferried by Air America, which was not subject to customs inspection, throughout the U.S. All as a covert

CIA operation designed to finance our defense of South Vietnam's dope dealers. *That's* fascism.

Morality, like patriotism, is often the last refuge of a scoundrel. Illegal prostitution isn't dangerous because lonely grown-ups are getting laid, or because poor women are making a buck. It's dangerous because it's illegal, an unreachable source of criminal financial power and AIDS transmission, the latter a perfect metaphor for the former. Illegal gambling isn't dangerous because grown-ups are doing what they please with their own money, it's dangerous because it's illegal. Illegal drugs aren't dangerous because people are getting inebriated, they're dangerous because they're illegal. Drugs, gambling and prostitution were the basis of the vast power of Carlos Marcello and Santos Trafficante, two of the most powerful operatives the CIA ever had.

What's interesting about the Kennedy assassination is the picture it paints of fascism today. There was nothing aberrant about the hood participation in covert military operations. The names will change, the bureaucratic alphabet soup will continue to be reshuffled, but the artificial value of demanded commodities and services will continue to be the basis of covert geopolitical power.

As the most charismatic liberal since Roosevelt, Kennedy threatened to strengthen the global social democracy that was anathema to the Peronist military establishment built by the Dulles brothers. The ideals, and actions, expressed by the Alliance for Progress clearly made room for the likes of Jacobo Arbenz, Juan Bosch and Salvador Allende.

Kennedy had the guts to pick real policy fights with the military-industrial-hood complex - in Cuba, Laos, the Dominican Republic, Honduras, Russia - and on defense spending and civil rights. The Kennedy brothers, possessed of their old man's savvy and nerve, were very dangerous in the halls of power. But if you lie down with Johnny Rosselli, sometimes you don't get up. As Richard Nixon put it, "You don't fuck with Dick Helms."

Richard Helms and James Angleton

Drug War

LSD

A CIA covert operation, MK-ULTRA, designed by Richard Helms under the direction of Allen Dulles, was directly responsible for the wide availability of LSD in the 60's. MK-ULTRA was also responsible for the massive distribution of improperly prepared street poison masquerading as LSD. The CIA also introduced PCP, STP and other artificial poisons as an intentional COINTELPRO.

Looking for a truth serum in 1942, the OSS' General William Donovan enlisted Harry Anslinger, no doubt for access to the FBN's operational capacity, along with a few prominent physicians and pychiatrists. They experimented with a potent cannabis extract, THC acetate, finding that it induced "great loquacity and hilarity," and even, in cases where the subject didn't feel physically threatened, some usable reefer madness. Mescaline and scopolamine were simply too much of a fantasy trip.[1]

Donovan, and his successors Walter Bedell Smith and Allen Dulles, had always regarded Beria and Canaris as teachers as much as adversaries, so the Nazi experiments with mescaline at Dachau aroused great interest. So great, in fact, that when the CIA imported 800 Nazi scientists in Operation Paperclip and others between 1945 and 55, it made sure to include Dr. Hubertus Strughold, who became "the father of aviation medicine." Strughold's high-altitude-pressure, low-temperature experiments at Dachau, for which his subordinates were tried as war criminals, involved unspeakable torture. He did, however, learn a lot about human endurance, and the cactus alkaloid mescaline. Dr. Kurt Plotner, running the mescaline part of Strughold's program, suggested new ways of approaching the "truth drug" problem to our early experimenters.[2]

This was the mind-set that the CIA took to its drug work. The Nazis weren't just evil, they were *good*. This amoral pragmatism led, of course, to the MK/ULTRA experiments in which Americans were dosed with very potent drugs without their knowledge or consent.[3]

Dr. Albert Hofmann, the Sandoz chemist who made ergonovine basic to obstetrics, synthesized LSD in the same series of experiments. He used the naturally occurring lysergic acid radical, the common nucleus of all ergot alkaloids, as the major component of the molecule. As Hofmann was fully aware, the grain fungus ergot (the microscopic mushroom *Claviceps purpurea*) had a long cultural history as both medicine and poison. These experiments, conducted over a period of years in the 1940's, also yielded hydergine, essential today in the improvement of cerebral circulation in geriatric patients, and dihydroergotamine, an important blood pressure stabilizer.

Naturally occurring lysergic acid derivatives include the human neurotransmitter serotonin and the mushroom alkaloid psilocybin, also first synthesized by this seminal chemist. The human neurotransmitter and the plant alkaloids are closely related. That is, exactly as ancient Greek midwives used to say when they administered their ergot-based "mixture," "the mother of your mother will help you to become a mother."

It was such ancient cultural hints that led the erudite Hofmann, above, to the isolation of ergonovine, one of the most important tools of modern obstetrics. The "mixture" (*kykeon*) used by the ancient Greek midwives was the same brew that was drunk at Eleusis, the central sacrament of Classical Greece.[4] Sacramental Mayan morning glories, beautifully depicted at the ancient Mayan temple-palace complex at Teotihuacán, dating to about 500 CE, also contain ergot-based entheogens.[5]

But, aware of the artificial potency of his synthetic ergot concentration, Dr. Hofmann was against the general use of d-lysergic acid diethylamide tartrate-25: "...the very deep effects of LSD are not at all just pleasurable. There is always a confrontation with our deepest ego....It turns out that my fear was well-founded because so many people were not conscious enough to use it well. They did not have the respect which the Indians in Mexico had. The Indians believe you should only take the mushrooms if you have prepared by praying and fasting and so forth, because the mushrooms bring you in contact with the Gods. And if you are not prepared they believe it can make you crazy and even kill you. That's their belief based on thousands of years of experience..."[6]

In a culture that is careful to raise pharmacological ignoramuses, shamanic incompetence came as no surprise to Dr. Hofmann. LSD, invaluable for many psychiatric purposes, is thousands of times more potent than the traditional herbal mixtures. In fact, it is thousands of times more potent than the milder of the entheogenic isolates. It is effective at doses of as little as ten-millionths of a gram, which makes it 5000 times more potent than mescaline. It should not be taken without training or supervision.

Early CIA experiments with LSD, in 1951, were impressive because the stuff was a cinch to slip into a drink and often induced not only real psychological nudity and revelation, but such an intense trip that the subject couldn't later remember what information had been revealed.

Of course, since mind-set and setting are so important, an anxious intelligence operative could simply be thrown into an introverted paranoia. More robust souls became rebellious and aggressive, or mystical and transcendental. This, of course, suggested the possibility that leftist politicians could be dosed just prior to a big speech, during which they would babble incoherently. This may in fact have actually been done by Howard Hunt to Senator Edmund Muskie the morning of the cry baby speech that ended his presidential hopes.[7]

Propaganda, in its simplest form, is accusing the other guy of doing what you are doing. Allen Dulles, at Princeton, on April 10, 1953, warned that the human mind was a "malleable tool," and the the "brain perversion techniques" of the Reds were "so subtle and so abhorrent" that "the brain…becomes a phonograph playing a disc put on its spindle by an outside genius over which it has no control."[8] Dulles, of course, was that genius. Three days after warning of these techniques he approved Richard Helms' Operation MK/ULTRA to perfect them.

Dr. Sidney Gottlieb, the CIA's expert on lethal poisons, headed up the operation as chief of the Chemical Division of the Technical Services Staff.[9] Former U.S. Army Special Forces Capt. John McCarthy, who ran the CIA's Saigon-based Operation Cherry, aimed at assassinating Prince Sihanouk, says that MK-ULTRA stands for "Manufacturing Killers Utilizing Lethal Tradecraft Requiring Assassination."

By late 1953 the CIA was funding just about every qualified LSD researcher it could find, through such contractors as the Society for the Study of Human Ecology, the Josiah Macy, Jr. Foundation, and the Geschickter Fund for Medical Research. John Marks, in *The Search for the Manchurian Candidate*, identifies the CIA's LSD pioneers as Robert Hyde's group at Boston Psychopathic, Harold Abramson at Mt. Sinai Hospital and Columbia University in New York, Carl Pfeiffer at the University of Illinois Medical School, Harris Isbell of the NIMH-sponsored Addiction Research Center in Lexington, Kentucky, Louis Jolyon

West at the University of Oklahoma, and Harold Hodge's group at the University of Rochester.[10]

The psychiatric interest in LSD, of course, was genuine, and, except in a few cases, the CIA rarely dictated the direction of the research - it simply soaked up the results. Drs. Max Rinkel and Robert Hyde began their experiments in 1949, and Dr. Paul Hoch followed shortly thereafter. These early LSD experiments led to the "model psychosis" or "psychotomimetic" model of LSD inebriation, which was an important step toward understanding the biochemical basis of much schizophrenia and depression.[11]

The CIA, of course, wasn't interested in curing schizophrenia, it was interested in causing it. It was distressed to be told, by Dr. Nick Bercel in the early fifties, that a central water supply *couldn't* be poisoned with LSD, because the chlorine neutralized the LSD.[12] This drawback was immediately overcome. The CIA had visions of a battleship rendered useless by a stoned crew, chlorine or no chlorine. In 1959 the CIA-Army researchers discovered BZ, a toxic synthetic that literally short-circuits the brain, producing real schizophrenia for about three days, ten times longer than LSD. BZ came to be considered militarily superior to the far less incapacitating LSD.

Throughout the fifties, at the U.S. Public Health Service Hospital in Lexington, Kentucky, Dr. Harris Isbell used his captive drug users to test over 800 new drugs for drug companies and the CIA, including LSD. Isbell rewarded his human guinea pigs with heroin or morphine, the stuff he was supposed to be weaning them from.

"I have had seven patients who have now been taking the drug for more than 42 days," Isbell wrote in the middle of a test which kept his captives on LSD for *77 days straight*. He called their reactions "the most amazing demonstration of drug tolerance I have ever seen."[13] Trying to "break through this tolerance," Herr Doktor administered triple and quadruple doses of LSD to his unwitting subjects. Isbell, a member of the FDA's Advisory Committee on the Abuse of Depressant and Stimulant Drugs, was the voice of paternalistic sobriety in the fifties, a perfect example of the compulsive hypocrisy induced by pharmacological monopoly.[14]

Dr. Paul Hoch, the developer of the "model psychosis" model of LSD inebriation, performed even more Nazi-like experiments for the CIA at his New York State Psychiatric Institute. He gave uninformed patients large intraspinal doses of LSD and mescaline, simply to observe the "immediate, massive, and almost shocklike" effects.

In 1953 Hoch and Dr. James Cattell gave massive forced injections of a mescaline derivative to tennis pro Harold Blauer, causing his death. Cattell later told Army investigators that "We didn't know whether it was dog piss or what it was we were giving him."[15] Hoch actually gave LSD to mental patients without their knowledge and then *lobotomized* them to compare the effects of LSD before and after "psychosurgery." "It is possible that a certain amount of brain damage is of therapeutic value."[16] This gorilla became New York State Commissioner for Mental Hygiene.

Dr. Robert Heath, at Tulane, under CIA contract, in an effort to discover just how manipulable his captive mental patients were under LSD, used implanted electrodes to stimulate their brains while they were under the influence. His control group, presumably, wasn't stoned. These Nazi-like horror stories, involving very prestigious MK-ULTRA-funded psychiatrists, are actually quite numerous.

Pursuant to MK-ULTRA, Helms' Clandestine Services asked Harry Anslinger for one of his toughest narks, George White. White was involved in 1943 OSS experiments with THC, using it as a "Truth Drug" on unsuspecting mafiosi cooperating in the Sicilian invasion. It was White who pretended that the Burmese Kuomintang heroin he busted in 1959 was really Red Chinese heroin, thus leaving the KMT free to continue dealing.

Consistent with his moral imperative, Agent White proceeded to open up a whorehouse in San Francisco. Sitting behind a two-way mirror, the alcoholic White, who had no scientific training, observed, pen in hand, the dosed Johns engage in psychedelic sex. White sat behind his two-way mirror from 1955 to 1963, often taking time out in the evenings to commit random acts of violence against San Francisco's pot-smoking beatnics.[17]

The flamboyant Captain Al Hubbard, also an OSS and CIA agent, was famous for his flair and enormous good humor. He himself continually took LSD and shared it with as many people as possible. If Hubbard, who displayed complete freedom of action, had an assignment from the Agency, it was to turn on as many people as possible. Of course, there is no one "Agency"; that's just a general term for an alphabet soup of cooperating or competing centers of power, any number of which Hubbard was associated with.

In 1956 Hubbard interested Dr. Humphrey Osmond in giving LSD to the alcoholics he was treating at Weyburn Hospital in Saskatchewan. Of 1000 confirmed alcoholics treated, the recovery rate was an incredible 50%, the highest ever recorded for any therapy. Osmond's team continued these controlled experiments for thirteen years, formally publishing their findings, which confirmed the initial results.[18] That LSD contained the same *kykeon* entheogens Hippokrates used to induce his curative incubation in ancient Greece was not lost on Osmond.

It was Osmond who first pointed out the structural similarity between human neurochemicals and the isolates of the traditional sacred plants. It was also he who coined the word *psychedelic*, which means "mind-manifesting," sort of the opposite of "psychosis-inducing."

It wasn't about LSD, but about mescaline, supplied by Dr. Osmond, that Aldous Huxley wrote his seminal 1954 *The Doors of Perception*. Mescaline is the predominant alkaloid of peyote.

Dr. Osmond, right, reported on his peyote experiences as a guest of the Native American Church in 1961.[19]
Saskatoon Star-Phoenix in *Psychedelic Review* #9, 1967

Huxley was a shaman with an intensely personal vision of history: "I continued to look at the flowers, and in their living light I seemed to detect the qualitative equivalent of breathing - but of a breathing without returns to a starting point, with no recurrent ebbs but only a repeated flow from beauty to heightened beauty, from deeper to ever deeper meaning. Words like 'grace' and 'transfiguration' came to my mind..."[20] Obviously, this ain't the CIA talking, and, given Huxley's incredible intellectual power, vision and compassion, we're not talking about a "model psychosis" either.

Giving someone mescaline while they're being tortured to death at Dachau, or lobotomized, or electrified, is going to tell you more about torture than mescaline. Noted Huxley, "Those idiots want to be Pavlovians; Pavlov never saw an animal in its natural state, only under duress. The 'scientific' LSD boys do the same with their subjects. No wonder they report psychotics."[21] The CIA didn't want to bomb its enemies with beatitude, but that's exactly what occurred to Huxley and his children, the "sixties generation." Jim Morrison led *The Doors [of Perception]*.

Timothy Leary grew up in this CIA-funded research milieu. From 1954 to 59 he was the director of clinical research and psychology at the Kaiser Foundation Hospital in Oakland. The personality test that made him famous, "The Leary," was actually used by the CIA to test prospective employees.

Leary's graduate school classmate, CIA-contractor Frank Barron, worked at the Berkeley Institute for Personality Assessment and Research, which Leary knew to be "funded and staffed by OSS-CIA psychologists." In 1960 Barron, with the Agency's funding, founded the Harvard Psychedelic Drug Research Center. Leary followed Barron to Harvard, becoming a lecturer in psychology. Leary's Harvard associates included former OSS chief psychologist Harry Murray, who had monitored the early "Truth Drug" experiments, and numerous other witting CIA contractors.

Intelligence analyst Mark Riebling, through extensive digging and interviews with Leary and many others involved, has verified most of the following extraordinary story:

In the Spring of 1962, Mary Pinchot Meyer, recently divorced wife of old Kennedy friend and ranking CIA agent Cord Meyer, visited Leary at Harvard. She asked Leary for some LSD for "a friend who's a very important man, who wants to try LSD for himself." The aristocratic and sexy Mary Meyer was John Kennedy's lover. Her more than thirty visits to the White House have been confirmed by Kennedy's close friend and secretary Kenneth O'Donnell. In late July of 62, as Mary recalled to her close friend James Truitt of the *Washington Post*, she and JFK, alone in the White House, shared two joints as a preliminary to imbibing Leary's LSD.

Leary met Mary again in the Spring of 63 at Boston's Ritz Hotel. She was upset that her affair with Kennedy had been exposed. "I don't trust the phones or the mail." She told Leary not to make contact with her until further notice.

In May of 63 Mary warned Leary, by phone, that he was attracting "too much publicity," thereby violating the implicit contract he had with his implicit funders. Leary, of course, fascinated by the automatic creativity he was unlocking, and heavily influenced by his friend Aldous Huxley, had just told his funders, implicit and explicit, to go to hell.

By September of 63 Leary was ensconced at the large private estate in Milbrook, New York that he made so famous. The well-connected Mary presented Leary with an appropriate housewarming present - a large bottle of "the best LSD in the world," from the National Institute of Mental Health. She was, however, nervously taking countersurveillance measures, complaining that "We had eight intelligent women turning on the most powerful men in Washington. And then we got found out.... I made a mistake in recruitment. A wife snitched on us... I've gotten mixed up in some dangerous matters."

Just after JFK's assassination, on December 1, Mary told Leary by phone that "They couldn't control him [JFK] anymore. He was changing too fast. They've covered everything up.... I'm afraid. Be careful."

On October 12, 1964, Mary Meyer was shot to death, execution-style, at 12:45 p.m., in a park by the Georgetown Canal in Washington, D.C. Her body was identified by Ben Bradlee, Cord Meyer's brother-in-law, editor of the *Washington Post*. CIA counterintelligence chief James Angleton immediately, personally, confiscated Mary Meyer's diary, which was never seen again.[22]

The point about the sixties is, in a sense, embodied in Leary's rebellious rejection of his institutional funders. He remembered the divinatory shamanism, the ecstatic creativity, of his tribal ancestors, and said so. But traditional shamanic herbalism was herbalism, not alkaloidism. Overenthusiastic revolutionaries like Leary and Ginsberg failed to stress that, although the technically competent Leary clearly understood the concentrated potency of LSD, carefully stressing mind-set, setting and dosage in the wonderful book he wrote with Ralph Metzner and Richard Alpert, *The Psychedelic Experience*.

But *The Psychedelic Experience* was based on an ancient shamanic manual, *The Tibetan Book of the Dead*, that referred to an herbal brew that was far less concentrated than LSD, and insisted on yogic discipline as an inherent part of the process. Incan shamanism, for instance, an invaluable source of knowledge and power, uses whole herbs like ayahuasca and coca leaf, not their refined alkaloids, and spiritual technique is taught as an inherent part of the process. Lower alkaloid doses - and that's what herbal concentrations deliver - require a yoga to utilize the weaker dose.

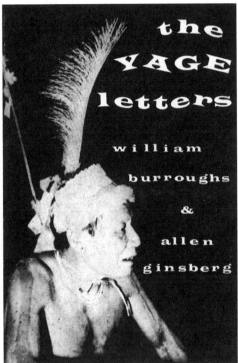

For young adults who are surrounded by friends and lovers, small doses of LSD are quite safe. Dosage, however, is a learned art, and LSD was the most highly concentrated psychoactive substance known. Overdoses produce very bad trips, something young people tolerate very poorly.

The inquisitors, using their fascist violence in concert with the rank ignorance and emotional instability of many LSD users, had found their "devil drug," replete with tragic horror stories of bone-lonely young people quite unprepared for such an artificially powerful entheogen. It was also well within Company rules to sell LSD laced with strychnine so as to create usable horror stories. Dr. Hofmann himself chemically confirmed the presence of pure strychnine in street samples of "LSD."[23] That could only have come from the Department of Dirty Tricks.

That jive phrase "the drug culture" was born, as if the sixties had been a uniquely contemporary mania and not, in large part, a remarkable exercise in genuine *mnemosyne*. "Flower power" had seen a creative explosion that included the politically potent insertion of true poetry into pop music, the transformation of visual art, and the birth of the ecology and women's liberation movements. The powerful flower was the ancient shamanic herb marijuana, not the refined concentrate LSD. As Arthur Koestler told Leary the day after his first trip, "This is wonderful, no doubt, but it's fake, ersatz, instant mysticism….There's no wisdom there. I solved the secret of the universe last night, but this morning I forgot what it was."[24]

LSD gave me a lot, but Soma, the ancient sacred mushroom, far less potent and more difficult to reach, gave me much more. In order to reach Soma I needed music and discipline, both of which continue to induce creative *ekstasis*, even without the Soma. As William Burroughs put it, "Remember, anything that can be done chemically can be done in other ways. You don't need drugs to get high, but drugs do serve as a useful shortcut at certain stages of training."[25]

Leary testifies; Leary laughs with John and Yoko

What was exciting about refined LSD, psilocybin and mescaline, of course, was that they revived, instantly, the ancient *mnemosyne* that the inquisitors had worked so many centuries to crush. Instinctive vision and versification came automatically alive. The cultural contrast to the conformist fifties couldn't have been more profound, or more shocking to the power structure, which was fixated on manipulation and conquest, not the exact opposite, automatic creativity. The ecstatic Leary was most dangerous to the power structure when he waxed poetic about using proprioceptive creativity to break free of the manipulative fascist imagery. The eloquent Ginsberg, probably the most influential public speaker of the 60's, was not only iconoclastic, but brilliantly and ruthlessly empirical.

The first time I heard the word "proprioception," "self-sensing," was as a sophomore at the University of Buffalo in 1964, when Charles Olson was teaching there. The poet and mythologist was first turned on to psilocybin, apparently both the refined alkaloid and the mushrooms, by Leary. As his first trip was wearing off, he turned to Leary and said, "When they come after you, you can hide at my house."[26]

Allen Ginsberg, a friend, Timothy Leary, and the influential poet and publisher Lawrence Ferlinghetti, San Francisco, 1963

The whole point about hippie dress was that it was Native American, a conscious rebirth of tribal shamanism. As Olsen instantly understood, Col. Custer was still running the constabulary, which still violently disapproved of all pharmacoshamanism. Each generation must be conquered anew - industrial indoctrination as the destruction of the archaic techniques of *proprioception*.

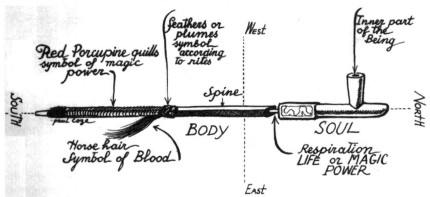

Marijuana continues to be sacramental to millions of Americans. The pipe is a portable altar: to smoke is to commune with the Holy Spirit, as so many of our greatest healers, scientists, musicians, artists, writers and filmmakers continue to insist.

Consistent with its policy of confusing the ancient shamanic herbs with extremely dangerous artificial compounds, thereby destroying real *mnemosyne* in the culture, military intelligence pumped numerous chemical poisons, masquerading as "psychedelics," into the market. The formula for STP, originally developed as an incapacitating agent for the Army in 1964 at Dow (the maker of napalm), was published by Dow in 1967.[27] It was then immediately pumped into the market by the Department of Dirty Tricks, using its Mafia dealers. This potent synthetic put many unsuspecting kids on a three-day trip, and sent many, hysterical with anxiety, to the emergency room. That, of course, was the purpose of its distribution.

The Army tested Angel Dust (PCP) on GIs in the late fifties at Edgewood Arsenal. It was also tested by Operation MK/ULTRA at McGill University's Allain Memorial Institute in Montreal. The Army then stockpiled PCP as a "nonlethal incapacitant." Higher doses, however, according to the CIA, could "lead to convulsion and death."[28] PCP was soon flooding the streets. This was, and is, a COINTELPRO - this is how the distribution of mild, pharmaceutical-grade psychedelics can be demonized. Teach the kids that there is no difference between safe whole herbs and artificial poisons, make the best of the traditional herbs and the milder of the pharmaceutical-grade natural isolates unavailable, and then flood the streets with artificial poisons. Angel Dust continues to be a great Prohibitionist argument.

These fascist tactics were learned from the Nazis, and were, I guess, appropriate for use against them. But the COINTELPROS were aimed by the CIA/FBI against its own people. Every American Indian Movement or Black Panther community event or political demonstration was turned into an armed confrontation by the simple device of physically attacking it. A good example of a typical FBI COINTELPRO was Sullivan's rigging of the 1974 elections for Oglala tribal president at Pine Ridge. Although the Commission on Civil Rights concluded that the election had been fixed and that AIM leader Russell Means was the real winner, FBI goon Dick Wilson was installed, literally at the point of a gun. Wilson's FBI-run death-squads then proceeded to murder more than 60 AIM activists. Means himself was shot repeatedly, surviving at least three separate assassination attempts.[29]

It is extremely strange that when the manufacture and distribution of LSD fell apart in 1969, as the California Brotherhood of Eternal Love - CIA-connected bikers - disintegrated, due to the lack of ergotamine tartrate and internal and external pressures, a CIA agent put it back together again. That agent was the amazing Ronald Stark, who could speak Arabic, German, Chinese, French and Italian as fluently as English. Stark had unlimited funds, contacts in business and intelligence throughout the world, and a French manufacturer of LSD.

When Stark was arrested for drug trafficking in Bologna in 1975,

Italian magistrate Giorgio Floridia ordered his release on the grounds that he had been a CIA agent since 1960. Floridia documented this with a list of Stark's intelligence contacts. Using the CIA's Castle Bank of the Bahamas, Stark refinanced and reorganized the Brotherhood and so continued the massive production and distribution of a very toxic batch of LSD known as "Orange Sunshine," which was about as mellow as a sledgehammer in the hands of a biker.[30]

Worse, the streets began to be flooded with LSD spiked with strychnine, or was it strychnine spiked with LSD. I was actually lucky enough to ingest this or a similar poison in the winter of 66, although I have no way of knowing what it actually was. It could simply have been poorly prepared LSD, which can be quite toxic, or it could have been intentional poison. If strychnine were involved, it would have to have been LSD-tainted strychnine, not strychnine-tainted LSD, since LSD is active in micrograms, and the much less potent strychnine in milligrams. In any case, the reports, from Dr. Hofmann and many other labs operating at the time indicate that many types of poison, some intentional and some not, were out there. Hofmann, one of the greatest chemists in the world, confirmed LSD-tainted strychnine, real poison. Pharmaceutically pure LSD itself, since it is built around a naturally-occuring mushroom alkaloid with a very long cultural history, isn't poisonous - in the right dose.

My poisonous 1966 "LSD" was nothing like the mellow Sandoz and Owsley stuff I had previously used. It immediately attacked my spinal cord, giving me eight excruciating hours of chemical electrocution. I couldn't talk normally for weeks, and was shaken for months. Youngsters really were driven to suicide, or to the mental ward. God knows what Art Linkletter's famous lonely daughter actually took before she jumped to her death.

Warned the prescient William Burroughs, at the beginning of *Nova Express* in 1964: "Throw back their ersatz immortality.... Flush their drug kicks down the drain - *They are poisoning and monopolizing the hallucinogenic drugs - learn to make it without any chemical corn.*"

"Since the use of marijuana and other narcotics is widespread among members of the New Left, you should be on the alert to opportunities to have them arrested on drug charges," Hoover informed his agents.[31] The list of political drug arrests is, of course, endless.

Joining Hoover in this effort was one of Helms' senior operatives, Mary Meyer's ex-husband Cord Meyer, whose 1967 Operation CHAOS specifically targeted the New Left for infiltration and assassination. In 1972 Meyer led the CIA's effort to stop Harper & Row from publishing Alfred W. McCoy's blockbuster exposé of *The Politics of Heroin in Southeast Asia*. This effort, recorded by McCoy in his 1990 update, included threatening Harper's owner with a National Security lawsuit, tapping McCoy's phones, auditing his taxes, attempting to cut off his federal education grant - and threatening to assassinate his international interpreters.

It is quite strange that Janis Joplin, Jimmy Hendrix and Jim Morrison, embodiments of poetic ecstacy, all under close scrutiny by the FBI, all died of "overdoses." I grew up on the streets of New York. That's how pigs off heads. While it can't be denied that youthful excess is a possibility, it also can't be denied that the propaganda value of those deaths wasn't lost on the COINTELPRO experts.

POISONED BY DRUGS, DIES.

Newark Man, Called Most Active Narcotic Peddler, Succumbs at 25.

Death ended yesterday the career of Philip Broman of 394 Badger Avenue, Newark, said by the police to have been one of the most active drug peddlers in the metropolitan district. Broman, who was 25, died in the Newark City Hospital from narcotic poisoning.

Broman was arrested by the Newark police last Saturday. The following day he was taken ill and sent to the hospital. According to the police,

NYT, 1959

CIA/Syndicate

Col. Fletcher Prouty: "Maxwell Taylor...by the time he had returned to the Pentagon as chairman of the JCS, was actually more of a Judas goat, as far as the military was concerned, than the leader of the herd, as he had been when he left three years before. Few great armies have been so vastly demoralized and stricken by an integral campaign as had the U.S. Army since those dark days of 1964 and 1965, when Maxwell Taylor and his ST counterparts led them into Vietnam under the banner of counterinsurgency."

"With McGeorge Bundy in Taylor's old job in the White House, responsible for all clandestine activity; with Bill Bundy as the principle conduit from the CIA to McNamara (later in State), and with Taylor on top of the military establishment, the ST had emerged from its nadir on the beaches of Cuba and was ready for whatever might develop in Vietnam. "[1]

The CIA had the legal authority to command Johnson's attention every single day, and it told him exactly what it wanted him to hear. Johnson was only two cars behind JFK in Dallas. He literally heard the bullets whiz by his head. He also knew that, contrary to all established procedure, Kennedy's entire cabinet was directed to be out of Washington on November 22. They were all at a conference in Hawaii. This prevented the formation of a Cabinet quorum on the day of the assassination. The subject of that conference, conducted by the CIA, was the need to escalate the Vietnam War.

We can now understand Johnson's deep reluctance to accept the 1964 Presidential nomination, despite the fact that he knew he'd win in a landslide. He also knew, as he told Lady Bird on the day of the nomination on those tapes she gave to Michael Beschloss, that he had no chance of controlling basic policy.

Johnson's first National Security Action Memorandum, 273, stated that "The objectives of the United States with respect to the withdrawal of U.S. military personnel remain as stated in the White House statement of October 2, 1963," that is, in Kennedy's last NSAM, 263. But 263 predicated withdrawal on military progress, consonant with the successful "Vietnamization" of the war.

Immediately after Kennedy's death, the CIA decided that no military progress had been made, that complete "Vietnamization" was not possible. As NSAM 273 put it, "It remains the central objective of the United States in South Vietnam to assist the people and Government of that country to win their contest against the externally directed and supported communist conspiracy."

Less than a month after the assassination, Chairman of the JCS Maxwell Taylor was ordering Vietnam commander Westmoreland to "fight the war right, the way we did in France. It's a big war and we'll fight it like one. We must bring enough firepower and bombs down on the Vietcong to make them realize they're finished; only then will they toss in the sponge."[2] When Taylor said that, we had only 16,000 troops in Vietnam, most technical support personnel, not fighters. Unless he were planning it, how could he know it was going to be "a big war"?

As Prouty puts it, "In the hands of Lemnitzer, NSAM #55 [for whom it was originally intended] meant no more clandestine operations, or at least no more unless there were most compelling reasons. In the hands of Maxwell Taylor, this meant ....the new military force of response, of reaction, and of undercover activity - all summed up in the newly-coined word 'counterinsurgency.'"[3]

Taylor's rosy projections of easy victory, on which Kennedy's plans for withdrawal were based, were withdrawn at that strange Hawaii conference - 2 days before Kennedy's death. Johnson was fed a steady stream of grim reality. After many months of unrelenting VC progress, Johnson, despite his best political instincts, was willing to accept that without American troops, South Vietnam would collapse. Withdrawal, if it had ever been, was no longer an option.

Maj. Gen. Victor Krulak's Special Assistant for Counterinsurgency and Special Activities staff was charged with coordinating the inexorable escalation within the Department of Defense. Col. Prouty was Krulak's lead officer on the SACSA staff: "His contacts in this select circle in the Office of the Secretary of Defense, were such men as Major General Edward D. Lansdale, who was McNamara's special assistant for all matters involving the CIA and special operations; William Bundy, who appears throughout the Pentagon Papers as one of the key men of the Secret Team and was at that time a recent alumnus of the CIA, with ten years in that agency behind him; John T. McNaughton, another member of the ST and a McNamara favorite; Joseph Califano, who moved from the Office of the Secretary of Defense to the White House...and others."[4]

Johnson terminated the counterproductive Cuba operation in April of 1964. This interrupted the efforts of Joe Califano. Califano was in charge of overall Defense Department liaison with the Cuban exiles, 1963-64, both before and after the assassination. Lt. Col. Alexander Haig worked under Califano.

Joe Trento, in the *Wilmington News-Journal*, 1/10/81: "Califano and Haig worked hand in hand in keeping the nationalists from the Cuban Brigade happy. They even checked out potential members for the hit teams with older members of the Cuban Brigade." This was confirmed by both Ricardo Canette, a leading member of the hit teams, and a top official of the Defense Intelligence Agency who was Haig's Marine liaison in 1963-64.

Califano reported directly to Secretary of the Army Cyrus Vance. The "older members of the Cuban Brigade" Califano and Haig were so concerned to keep happy included the hard core of Santos Trafficante's *Batistiano* assassins, the former leaders of Batista's secret police.[5] When the Cuba operation was discontinued, military intelligence sent Califano to the White House as Johnson's advisor.

Califano is a key to understanding the drug propaganda not only by virtue of an analysis of his intentional sophistry, but by virtue of his covert relationships. Is it a coincidence that a high-level CIA agent who helped run Santos Trafficante's dope-dealing assassins became the country's leading antidrug propagandist? I don't think so. *The centers of power responsible for dealing the drugs are the same centers of power disseminating the artificial hysteria necessary for their continued criminalization.* That keeps the retail a hundred times higher than the natural value and the trade exclusively in the hands of *the muscle.* Another name for *the muscle* is *military intelligence.*

For American military intelligence, the Vietnam War was, to a very large extent, a drug war, and, just as in Cuba, *we* were the dealers. Oil and other mineral wealth, of course, played a major role, as did the great defense contractor boondoggle. The Vietnam War was worth $240 billion to defense contractors in overt appropriations, and at least another $300 billion in covert and indirect appropriations. The artificial Prohibition-created value of the opium from Laos, Burma and Thailand became, therefore, a major factor in the Indochinese military equation - the means by which our clients could pay for our arms. Drug Prohibition has made the illegal drug trade the economic basis of military power throughout much of the world.

Califano's propaganda tactics for today's Drug War are identical to those he used to promote the Vietnam War. He pulls the emotional trigger with a staccato barrage of snow-statistics, weeping for the babies that will die if we don't ESCALATE THE WAR RIGHT NOW! As Prouty puts it, "...alumni of the intelligence community - a service from which there are no unconditional resignations. All true members of the Team remain in the power center whether in office with the incumbent administration or out of office with the hard core set. They simply rotate to and from official jobs and the business world or the pleasant haven of academe."[6]

By late August, 1964, the Joint Chiefs were realistically insisting that "accelerated and forceful action with respect to North Vietnam is essential to prevent a complete collapse of the US position in Southeast Asia."[7] The planted axiom, of course, was that continued incremental escalation could be effective.

Prouty: "McGeorge Bundy, Mike Forrestal, Joe Califano, Maxwell Taylor, and the others always looked good when they could sit down, calm and composed, with the President and with Rusk and McNamara, already knowing what was in the reports these men were poring over page by page. McNamara would give one of his classic 'fully charted' briefings...and have the President and other Cabinet officers hanging on his every word - words he had been learning and rehearsing while he sped by jet from Honolulu. At the same time, the Secret Team members were secure in their knowledge that they already knew every word that McNamara was going to say and that they had staff studies and Presidential messages already drafted to send to the Ambassador and the commanders in Indochina."[8]

As the deep rage of Prouty, Shoup, Ridgway, MacArthur and many other ranking intelligence officers indicates, they equated lying through your teeth to the Commander-in-Chief with treason. Strategically speaking, withdrawal was the only option. The Vietminh had made that point long ago. They were the overwhelming majority, therefore there was no military option but to treat them as such. That had always been perfectly clear to American military intelligence. Dwight Eisenhower, Douglas MacArthur, Matthew Ridgway and David Shoup did not consider 60,000 American dead, or genocide, an option.

Support for Saigon's dope dealers was rationalized by the same Nazi-like counterinsurgency double-speak that rationalized support for Trafficante's sluggers. I remember hearing Secretary of State Dean Rusk rationalize Johnson's Vietnam escalation as a necessity to prevent the whole region from going communist. That was the official rationalization contained in NSAM 288, March 17, 1964. That speech became an antiwar poster when someone noticed that it was, virtually word for word, the 1940 speech given by Joseph Goebbels in defense of the Nazi invasion of Russia, with "Vietnam" substituted for "Russia." The Nazis were very concerned about the domino effect of "Bolshevism." They were also, like the Japanese, and U.S. military intelligence, great dope dealers.

Califano's Vietnam era playmates, William Colby, Edward Lansdale, Ted Shackley, Thomas Clines, Edmund Wilson, Lucien Conein, Richard Secord, Richard Armitage, John Singlaub, Felix Rodriguez, Barry McCaffrey and Oliver North, engineers of the Vang Pao-Laotian Opium connection, went on to engineer Reagan's Trafficante-supported Contra-Cocaine connection.

Shackley and Colby

Ted Shackley, "the Blond Ghost," functioned as Santos Trafficante's chief requisitions officer as head of the CIA's huge Miami station during Operation Mongoose. He then transferred to Vientiane, Laos, where he served as CIA station chief from 1966-68. There he directed operations for the CIA's Hmong opium army, working with such heroes as Michael Hand, a CIA Green Beret who later founded the notorious dope-dealing Nugan Hand Bank. Thomas Clines was Shackley's second in command in Vientiane, with special responsibility for Hmong relations at Long Tieng. Edwin Wilson, who became famous for supplying plastic explosives to Khaddafi, who used them, was also an integral part of this team.

General Richard Secord conducted their Air America operations, without which there was no Hmong opium army. Serving under Secord in Laos was Oliver North. One of Secord's "cargo-kickers" in Laos was Eugene Hasenfus, whose downed plane in Nicaragua, eighteen years later, revealed a virtual address book of CIA-Contra connections.[11]

Mainstream critics of the war, ever fearful of media blacklist, obsequiously called our ruthless mass-murder "an excess of righteousness and disinterested benevolence," and "defending the South" (John

King Fairbank) or "blundering efforts to do good." (Anthony Lewis).[12]

Only hippie crackpots like Allen Ginsberg, a practicing shaman, insisted that we were doing good by financing mass murder with dope. *Time*, Feb. 9, 1959, derided Ginsberg for making that claim, but in 1972 the intrepid Alfred W. McCoy proved it was true with the publication of his seminal *The Politics of Heroin in Southeast Asia*.

Gregory Corso, Allen Ginsberg and Peter Orlovsky in *Time*, 2/9/1959. *Time* captioned this "Don't shoot the wart hog."

Wrote McCoy, "It was not only General Belleux who convinced me that the Vietnam drug problem needed investigation. At a street demonstration in New Haven for Black Panther leader Bobby Seale, I met the beat poet Allen Ginsberg, who insisted that the CIA was deeply involved in the Southeast Asian opium trade. To back his claims and aid my research, he mailed me a carton containing years' worth of unpublished dispatches from Time-Life correspondents that documented the involvement of America's Asian allies in the opium traffic."[13] That Ginsberg was an enthusiastic pharmacoshaman and McCoy rather pharmacophobic is beside the point. Both were antifascist.

On June 21, 1970, the Bureau of Narcotics announced the dénouement of Operation Eagle,[14] "the largest roundup of major drug traffickers in the history of federal law enforcement." 105 of the 150 dealers arrested were Cuban veterans of the Bay of Pigs. They were defended by Frank Ragano, Santos Trafficante's lawyer. Attorney General Mitchell said that this was "a nationwide ring of wholesalers handling about 30 percent of all heroin and 75 to 80 percent of all cocaine sales in the United States."[15]

Operation Eagle is yet another example of "poor communications" between the Feds and the CIA. Nixon's CIA proceeded to sabotage most of the Eagle indictments, and nearly all the heroes of Brigade 2506, who had originally been recruited under Vice-President Nixon, went right back to work for Don Santos.

Nixon's much-touted "war on drugs" took the media focus off his escalation of the Vietnam War. This included the genocidal B-52 carpet-bombing of much of Vietnam and Cambodia, and the simultaneous invasion and overthrow of the neutralist Cambodian government. Nixon's incredible brutality was an attempt to outrun the visceral rage the obvious genocide was producing back home.[16] The Drug War was also a way of turning the police loose on the antiwar demonstrators, many of whom considered pot sacramental.

"If we cannot destroy the drug menace, then it will destroy us. I am not prepared to accept this alternative," intoned President Nixon in June of 1971.[17] That same year, 8 kilos of General Ouane Rattikone's Double U-O Globe Laotian heroin was seized by Customs in New Jersey from the U.S. military postal system. A Filipino diplomat was arrested with 15 kilos of Double U-O Globe heroin. Another with forty kilos. The son of Panama's ambassador to Taiwan was arrested with fifty kilos. And a Laotian prince, the Royal Laotian ambassador to France, was arrested with sixty kilos of Double U-O Globe heroin he had attempted to bring into Paris under his diplomatic pouch. These were all anticommunist allies *financed* by Richard Nixon.

The Laotian prince, Sopsaisana, was the head of the Asian Peoples Anti-Communist League, the chief political advisor of Vang Pao, military commander of the CIA's Laotian Hmong army. The heroin itself was refined from Hmong opium at Long Tieng, the CIA's headquarters in northern Laos, and given to Sopsaisana on consignment by

Vang Pao. The consignment made its way from Vang Pao in Long Tieng to Sopsaisana in Vientiane via Vang Pao's division of General Secord's Air America.[18] That, apparently, was an alternative Richard Nixon *was* willing to accept.

Vang Pao points out a target

Professor McCoy: "The importance of these CIA clients in the subsequent growth of the Golden Triangle's heroin trade was revealed, inadvertently, by the agency itself when it leaked a classified report on the Southeast Asian opium traffic to *The New York Times* [6/6/ 1971]....'the most important [heroin refineries] are located in the areas around Tachilek, Burma; Ban Houei Sai and Nam Keung in Laos; and Mae Salong in Thailand.'"

The trouble with leaks and partial hangouts, of course, is that they're likely to be picked up by analysts capable of using them. The *Times* didn't bother to explain, but McCoy, who had spent some time asking rude questions and dodging bullets in that neighborhood, knew that Tachilek was run by Shan rebels formerly allied with the CIA. Ban Houei Sai was owned by the CIA's very own General Ouane Rattikone, former commander of the Royal Laotian Army. Nam Keung was a CIA Yao base and Mae Salong was a CIA-supplied KMT base.[19]

The only traditional cash crop of the scattered highland Hmong villages was opium. It was only Vang Pao's status as the premier opium broker that enabled him to organize the CIA's 30,000-man Hmong army. That status was entirely dependent on Vang Pao's CIA-supplied weaponry, air power and commercial transport. Vang Pao's opium was transported via CAT/Air America and Nguyen Cao Ky's South Vietnam Air Force to international hubs throughout Southeast Asia.

Vang Pao receives the press

In 1961, when the CIA organized 32 C-47's into the First Transport Group to trade Hmong Laotian opium for CIA arms via Ngo Dinh Nhu's distribution apparatus, Col. Nguyen Cao Ky was its commander.[20] Six weeks after Ngo Dinh Diem's 1963 overthrow, the French-trained Ky was in command of the entire South Vietnamese air force. In June of 1965, Ky, who had no political base whatever, became Prime Minister of South Vietnam.

In September, 1972, Nixon very publicly ordered all U.S. embassies to cooperate with the CIA in the global antidrug effort. He called staff from 54 embassies back to DC to hear him formally order the CIA to engage "the slave traders of our time."[21] The practical effect of that, of course, as Nixon well understood, was to give the CIA *carte blanche* in U.S. embassies throughout the world.

The CIA's Lucien Conein had helped Ky's security chief, Gen. Nguyen Ngoc Loan, revive the old Saigon-Corsican-Binh Xuyen alliance. Loan became world-famous when he was photographed executing a Vietminh guerrilla during the Tet offensive. He did that in defense of his vast vice network. Vice-financed street-gang rule was the only way to prevent NLF control of Saigon's streets. This extra legal structure included the entire South Vietnamese air force and security apparatus, the Cholon Chinese gangs and Gen. Ouane Rattikone's Royal Laotian Army, which included Vang Pao. It fed heroin or morphine base, largely through the Hong Kong gangs and Taiwan, to

Santos Trafficante's vast refinement and distribution system.

As Gen. Edward Lansdale pithily put it, in his May 1968 report to Ambassador Bunker describing the relative strengths of the Ky and Thieu factions, "Loan has access to substantial funds through extra legal money-collecting systems of the police/intelligence apparatus."[22] Lansdale and Conein, of course, had helped Loan and Ky build that extra legal apparatus. As both *Ramparts* and Senator Ernest Gruening put it, in May of 1971, "Marshal Ky: The Biggest Pusher in the World."

The French-born Conein with some of the Vietnamese military team he used to overthrow Diem. Conein's old friend, the French-born Gen. Tran Van Don, center, organized the team. Both helped France and the U.S. finance their Indochina wars with Corsican heroin; Black Star

When Lansdale returned to Saigon in 1965 as Ambassador Henry Cabot Lodge's security chief, he worked out a truce with Saigon's Corsican underworld. Lansdale's key contact with the Corsicans, Lucien Conein, fought with them against both the Germans and the Vietminh as a French-speaking OSS agent. He had been on intimate terms with the Paris, Marseille, Saigon, Bangkok, Vientiane and Phnom Penh Corsican hoods for years. The Corsicans fed vast amounts of Indochinese morphine base to their chemically sophisticated brethren in Marseille, who could handle the tricky fourth step in the manufacture of white heroin.

The *Union Corse* was an important element of the Ky and succeeding Thieu power structures, and so was assiduously cultivated by U.S. military intelligence, despite the fact they were largely responsible for the easy availability of high-grade heroin to U.S. troops. When Ky was Prime Minister, 1965-67, Lansdale was his senior CIA liaison officer and prime U.S. defender. When Prime Minister Ky met with President Johnson in Honolulu in February of 1966, the fluent "Great Society" speech he gave was written for him by Lansdale's CIA team.[23] The brilliantly manipulative Lansdale had been an advertising executive before he joined the military.

In 1968, Santos Trafficante, after visiting his Chiu chau associates in Hong Kong, stopped in Saigon to meet with Corsican syndicate leaders. In the absence of the possibility of legal redress, these personal meetings of Syndicate leaders connoted the most solemn contractual undertakings. On Conein's departure from Saigon, the same Corsican syndicate leaders presented him with a heavy gold medallion embossed with the Napoleonic eagle and the Corsican crest, a traditional symbol of Corsican syndicate leadership. The medallion was engraved *Per Tu Amicu Conein*, "For Your Friendship, Conein."[24]

Although Conein himself was an important part of Nixon's DEA intelligence apparatus, Nixon's BNDD/DEA hardly ever mentioned Southeast Asian heroin, preferring instead to live in the clichés of the fifties. Nixon aimed almost exclusively at breaking the Corsican-Turkish "French Connection," about which we heard so much, leaving Asian heroin production almost completely untouched.

The "French Connection" was convenient not only as Nixon snow, but as security to France's pro-American President Georges Pompidou, who needed to break the power of France's far-right secret services. These were led by the SDECE, the *Service de Documentation Extérieure et du Contre-Espionage*. Its street fighting arm was SAC, the *Service d'Action Civique*.[25] The *Deuxieme Bureau*, the Second Bureau, is the military intelligence branch of the French Expeditionary Corps.

When the U.S. took Indochina from France, the Corsicans kept their Marseille labs humming by aligning themselves with the new powers and adding Turkey as a major supplier of morphine base. This enabled them to keep their vast distribution apparatus supplied with Marseille's famous snow-white #4 heroin.

Most of Marseille's heroin was turned into cash via the French distribution apparatus in South America. France's ambassador to Uruguay in the late 60's was Colonel Roger Barberot, a very dangerous top-level SDECE agent, as was France's ambassador to Bolivia. Both were mortal political enemies of Pompidou. These men functioned as politico-military liaison to the huge South American dope-arms-terror network of Auguste Ricord, which supplied most of the snow-white Marseille heroin on American streets.

Ricord, a former Gestapo agent, was particularly powerful in Argentina, Peru, Paraguay and Bolivia, strongholds of his old Nazi-Gehlen allies. These included arms dealer Klaus Barbie, who boasted the Bolivian Army's Chief of Staff, Alfredo Ovando Candia, on the board of his shipping company Transmaritima. Ovando became Bolivian president on Gen. Barrientos' convenient death in a 1969 helicopter crash.

Ricord could also count on Frederich Schwend in Peru, who had been involved in Operation Bernhard, the SS attempt to forge enough Bank of England notes to turn itself into an independent economic power. Like Barbie, Schwend was a postwar beneficiary of the U.S. Army Counterintelligence Corps.

Schwend and Barbie teamed up to keep South America's right-wing death squads well-supplied with high quality German arms - from Merex and Gemetex. Merex was controlled by Hitler's favorite commando, Col. Otto Skorzeny.[26] These were first-line NATO heavy arms - tanks, rocket launchers, air cannon - the works. That this was an American, French and German-driven effort, or at least an effort of their cooperating secret services, is demonstrated by the fact that the Israelis worked right alongside the Nazis. Ovando of Bolivia, Laugerud of Guatemala, D'Aubuisson of El Salvador and countless others had Israeli training and were loyal customers of the Israelis as well as the Germans.

There was also Hans Ulrich Rudel in Paraguay, the former Luftwaffe air ace. Rudel was personally close to Stroessner in Paraguay, and became a good buddy of Chile's Pinochet as well.[27] The host governments of these Nazi agents usually suffered, since they traded the secrets to which they were privy as easily as any other commodity. What didn't suffer was the trade in their favorite commodities - arms and dope.

With the help of Otto Skorzeny in Spain and Portugal and Reinhard Gehlen in Germany, these Nazis helped Ricord coordinate the South American secret services with the young European fascist death squads. Ricord's Germans and his entrenched Corsicans had Trafficante and his Syndicate allies by the economic and military throat in Latin America, and so were regarded as a security problem by the Syndicate's global partner, CIA covert operations.

Unfortunately for Ricord, when Pompidou decided to use the CIA to gain control of French intelligence, the French Connection was doomed. Nixon's ally pulled the political protection out from under the Marseille labs and Ricord's SDECE distribution network. According to the U.S. Bureau of Narcotics, Pompidou's police busted at least ten major SAC heroin distributors in France in 1970-71.

On April 5, 1971, an SDECE agent named Roger de Louette was intercepted on the Elizabeth, New Jersey dock with 45 kilos of Marseille heroin. De Louette led investigators to Col. Paul Fournier, one of the SDECE's commanding officers, who was formally indicted in November, 1971.[28] Major bust followed major bust as the joint BNDD-CIA-French intelligence operation unraveled the Corsican-SDECE structure. Between 1971 and 1973 virtually the entire Ricord network was destroyed.[29] It made great publicity for Nixon, of course, but it actually *increased* the volume of heroin coming into the U.S., since it destroyed the American Syndicate's only competition.

Nixon bought off Turkish opium production for a pittance in foreign aid, but that only strengthened the KMT-connected Chinese gangs running Southeast Asian dope. Efforts were made by a DEA team in Bangkok to stem heroin exports from there, but these amounted to little more than public relations for Thailand's dope-dealing military. Besides, Mexican heroin production was ready to pick up any slack let drop by the Asians. By 1975, Mexico was supplying 90% of U.S. heroin.[30]

Afghanistan and Pakistan, responding both to American pressure on the Golden Triangle and a 2-year drought in Southeast Asia, soon captured the European heroin market. Then Nixon's ally, the Shah, announced that Iran would resume opium production, putting 50% more land under poppies than Nixon had just bought off in Turkey. This move was wildly popular in Iran - hailed as a defense of traditional Iranian culture.

Scoring the opium seed capsules, Shiraz, Persia, c.1920. An elegant Teherani lady enjoys the results; *Asia*, c.1925

By the early 80's Southeast Asian production had recovered, so that the sum total of Nixon's pressure on Turkey and the "French Connection" was to vastly strengthen the world's heroin production capacity. And Nixon left the geographically flexible American Syndicate distribution apparatus, controlled largely by Teamster partner Santos Trafficante, a longtime Nixon financier, almost completely untouched. These were the conclusions of the 1977 House Select Committee on Narcotics Abuse, as well as virtually every other expert.[31]

Paraguay simply became a German-American rather than a German-French operation. Ricord himself was extradited to the U.S. in 1973, but his Paraguayan partner, Pastor Coronel, the chief of Stroessner's secret police, was left stronger than ever, the recipient of a mountain of Nixon's "antidrug" and "antiterrorism" aid. Pastor Coronel was very "antidrug" and "anticommunist." He attended all the Latin American Anti-Communist Confederation meetings, along with most of the CIA's Latin American station chiefs.

Nixon's most dangerous drug enforcement unit, Lucien Conein's Special Operations (Assassination) Group within the newly-created DEA, was a collection of Latin CIA killers, many Trafficante operatives, calling themselves Deacon 1. The CIA suggested that "With 150 key assassinations the entire heroin-refining industry can be thrown into chaos." But the attached hit list omitted all the key CIA players, including Trafficante's Cubans, Conein's Corsicans and Vietnamese, and their related Thai, Laotian and Burmese powerhouses, all clients of U.S. military intelligence. Small independents who competed with Don Santos found Conein's Deacon 1 unit hell on wheels, but Trafficante's operation, the largest and most visible dope distribution network, went almost completely untouched.[32]

Is it a coincidence that some of Conein's agents were also Orlando Bosch (later CORU) agents, and that Conein, Trafficante, Bosch, WerBell and Vesco took meetings together in Costa Rica at this time (74-75)?[33] Conein associates charged with major drug trafficking during his tenure at DEA include Robert Vesco, Trafficante operative Frank Sturgis, assassination expert and manufacturer of the Ingram M-10 machine pistol Mitch WerBell, and former Costa Rican President Pepe Figueres, to name a few.[34]

When the CIA's very own Shah announced the resumption of Iranian opium production, putting 20,000 hectares under cultivation, we heard nothing at all.[35] Lucien and Don Santos had no problem with the Shah's "Eagle-Earth" opium - they knew exactly what to do with it.

Nixon's relationship with Santos Trafficante's *Batistiano* assassins, of course, started when he was Eisenhower's point man on Cuba. Nixon's chief of staff, H. R. Haldeman, in *The Ends of Power*, described Nixon's search for a way to silence Howard Hunt and the Watergate burglars he ran - Sturgis, Barker, Martinez and Gonzalez. All were involved at the Bay of Pigs and probably at Dallas. Nixon, a close friend of "Mr. George Bush of the Central Intelligence Agency," was also in Dallas the day of the assassination.[36]

Eagle-Earth opium, the Shah's brand

On June 23, 1972, Nixon gave Haldeman the following message for Richard Helms at the CIA: "If it gets out that this is all involved, the Cuba thing would be a fiasco. It would make the CIA look bad, it's going to make Hunt look bad, and it is likely to blow the whole Bay of Pigs thing, which we think would be very unfortunate - both for the CIA, and the country, at this time, and for American foreign policy. Just tell him to lay off."

Helms' rage at being threatened with "the Bay of Pigs thing" forced Haldeman to conclude that "It seems that in all of those Nixon references to the Bay of Pigs he was actually referring to the Kennedy assassination." Haldeman noted that "After Kennedy was killed, the CIA launched a fantastic coverup."[37] When the Watergate scandal broke, in January 1973, Nixon's immediate cover-up effort included no fewer than *eleven* former staffers and members of the Warren Commission.[38]

George Bush was Nixon's man at the head of the Republican National Committee at this time, simultaneously Kissinger's Ambassador at the U.N. In 1974, Ambassador Bush became Kissinger's man in Beijing. His immediate predecessor was David K. E. Bruce, chief of OSS European operations during the war, Allen Dulles' wartime boss, a true CIA grey eminence.

It is strange that Ellis Rubin, the lawyer who defended Watergate's Miami Four, also defended Arthur Bremer, who shot George Wallace in 1968. If Wallace hadn't been shot, if the White Southern vote had been split, Nixon probably couldn't have gotten to the White House. An hour after Bremer shot Wallace, Nixon's attorney, Charles Colson, ordered Howard Hunt to burglarize Bremer's Milwaukee apartment.[39] What needed cleaning?

Bremer had mob ties *and* ties to Sirhan Sirhan.[40] Carlos Marcello's ally, Mickey Cohen, controlled the Santa Anita racetrack where Sirhan, and Thomas Bremer, Arthur's brother, worked. The apolitical Palestinian hustler actually had no problem with Robert Kennedy's politics or anyone else's. But he owed the hoods a lot of money. Sirhan was the patsy, apparently drugged or hypnotized, and firing loud blanks, standing in front of RFK, who took most eyes away from the lethal shooter, RFK's mob-hired bodyguard, Lockheed security man Thane Cesar, who fired from behind.[41]

Mickey Cohen

The autopsy evidence, provided by coroner Dr. Thomas Noguchi, proved that RFK was shot at "point blank" range from behind, at a distance of no more than three inches. Sirhan never got closer than three feet, and was never behind Kennedy. This evidence was kept out of court by Sirhan's chief defense lawyer, Grant Cooper, who also just happened to be Johnny Rosselli's lawyer. Most of the other useful evidence was immediately destroyed by the LAPD.

Former LAPD narcotics detective Mike Ruppert penetrated the upper echelons of the LAPD's intelligence divisions in the late 70's, working closely with all the original RFK assassination investigators. "After all I had been through in what was then fifteen years of exposing CIA's deep role in the drug trade I had no knowledge how closely my life was tied in with Bobby's death. It was not until Jonn Christian, coauthor of *The Assassination of Robert F. Kennedy* with former FBI Agent Bill Turner sought me out that I began to discover what has been, for me, the most haunting of truths about my own experience."

"Jonn found me shortly after *People* Magazine ran a story about me and my years of struggle against CIA.... He revealed to me that he had in his possession all thirteen volumes of LAPD's RFK investigation, unredacted, and we started talking. He began mentioning names from LAPD, which jarred me because they were people I knew quite well. Some had been involved with CIA's protection of drug dealers and the CIA."

"In 1993 I went to Montana with Jonn and a retired LAPD Sergeant named Paul Sharaga who had been the first LAPD supervisor to respond to the shooting call at the Ambassador Hotel. Paul was never supposed to be there and he had paid the price by having his report rewritten (forged) to delete information about a second suspect when Bobby was shot. But Paul had kept a carbon copy of his original. Like I, he did not know for many years how CIA had touched his life. It was Christian who had found Sharaga, showed him the rewritten report and watched as Sharaga grasped that Lt. Manny Pena, the Officer-in-Charge of Special Unit Senator [SUS] had not only committed a crime, but a cover-up which kept getting uglier and uglier. Manny Pena had left LAPD a year or so before the shooting and gone to work for the Agency for International Development only to 'change his mind' and return just in time to handle the cover-up of Bobby's murder by CIA, in conjunction with the LAPD."

"A Venice Division Watch Commander had been Lt. Tackaberry of METRO Division, on duty and in the field on the night of June 5. He directed METRO personnel to the Ambassador as Rampart Division officers tried to broadcast descriptions of suspects other than Sirhan. Tackaberry authorized my first ride-along as a civilian [trainee] with LAPD field units."

"One afternoon, as I was working at the Accident Investigation Division out of LAPD's Parker Center the phone rang and I was immediately assigned for a special project in Chief Ed Davis' office under the supervision of [Sgt. Dave] Brath. Dave wrote me a lengthy commendation which 'drew' me to the attention of Commander Carroll Kirby. Dave Brath had been one of the three principal authors of the SUS report and had handled or reported about every key piece of evidence in Sirhan's frame up."

"Shortly after receiving the commendation from Brath Commander Kirby reported reading a survey response I had written. I was immediately transferred into the Inspection and Control Section of the Office of the Chief of Police. Among other members of Kirby's staff was a Senior Administrative Assistant who had worked in SUS. On the night of June 5th, 1968 Kirby had been the Captain Commanding LAPD's Communications Division. He had shown up at the Ambassador Hotel, unexpectedly a few minutes after Bobby was shot and just as a nine-minute unexplained radio blackout had prevented officers from broadcasting descriptions of the girl in the polka dot dress and others who had been involved in Kennedy's murder. In 1993 I got to listen to those tapes and I saw how evidence had been destroyed, time lines altered and a conspiracy concealed."

"There were 76 witnesses in the pantry the night Bobby was killed. Not one of them gave a statement which agreed with LAPD's final report.... I could spend hours telling you about what I learned going through LAPD's terrible investigation and lousy subsequent cover-up. I could tell you that key LAP people were moving into place before Bobby was shot. I could take LAPD's own documents and prove them to be guilty of conspiracy to commit murder.... To this day Sirhan Sirhan has absolutely no recollection of the events that night. He was hypnotized and he was a patsy, firing loud blanks to distract the witnesses from the real assassin, Thane Eugene Cesar. Please, somebody sue me! Let's go to court."

"It was [Sgt.] Carl Thompson who supervised my first loan into Wilshire Division Narcotics as a policeman. Carl had taught me about the Narcotics Intelligence Network (which was, I later found out, the system CIA used to protect their own drug operations). Carl also knew my fiancée Teddy who directly exposed me to CIA drug trafficking and tried to recruit me to work for CIA while I was a police officer. [The beautiful American-educated Teddy was, incredibly, the niece of the Shah of Iran, an intelligence operative.] Because I was promoting so rapidly, the chances were that I would promote right in to a spot where I could directly assist CIA. When I found out that drugs were involved I categorically refused and Teddy left me. Carl Thompson had been a detective in SUS and he had joined LAPD after leaving the highly secret Army Security Agency."

"Teddy had frequently talked of [Detective III] Lee [Goforth] as she talked about CIA operations. Lee was a powerful man in LAPD and the Department's assigned rep to the Law Enforcement Intelligence Unit (LEIU). Lee was also a Brigadier General in the California National Guard. It was Lee Goforth I was assigned to work with after Teddy left me and it was Lee Goforth who suggested, along with his partner Norman Bonneau that I was likely having mental problems after I came back from New Orleans and reported that I had seen CIA dealing drugs. On the night of June 5th, 1968 Lee Goforth had been Ethel Kennedy's bodyguard."[42]

The FBI rushed to confirm the LAPD's considered judgement that Sirhan was a lone nut. Sirhan's other lawyer, Russell Parsons, was actually investigated by RFK himself during the McClellan hearings. Obviously, if the glamorous and brilliant RFK hadn't been shot, Nixon certainly couldn't have made it to the White House. Said RFK, two days before his murder, "I now fully realize that only the powers of the Presidency will reveal the secrets of my brother's death."[43] With bone-tough RFK in the White House, "the whole Bay of Pigs thing" would certainly have hit the fan. Assassination had a funny way of being useful to Richard Nixon, and the CIA.

Nixon used Gerry Hemmings' CIA assassination team, virtually the same team of Trafficante hitters put together by Rosselli and Hunt in 1963, to make another three tries on Castro's life in 1971, when Castro was visiting Allende.[44] Nixon got the legally elected Allende, using David Phillips, chief of the CIA's Chile Task Force, otherwise known as "Maurice Bishop." But it's funny how Trafficante's CIA-hit teams kept missing Fidel. I think maybe the Don thought his health was dependent on that of the Commandante.

In 1974, as Nixon crumbled, the Army's Criminal Investigation Command, put into action by the likelihood of impeachment proceedings, found "strong indications of a history of Nixon connections with money from organized crime."[45] Only Nixon's July resignation prevented the pros in the CIC from laying out all the details, the most obvious of which was Nixon's longtime relationship with Murray Chotiner.

One of Chotiner's oldest and closest associates was D'Alton Smith, a trusted Marcello operative. Marcello's two top aides, Nofio Pecora and Joe Poretto, were D'Alton Smith's brothers-in-law. Chotiner numbered hundreds of organized crime figures as his clients.[46] RFK had called Chotiner to testify before the McClellan Committee about his extraordinary client list. Chotiner was not only Richard Nixon's first campaign manager, in 1946, but Earl Warren's as well.[47]

As soon as Nixon took office in 1968, he named Chotiner as Special Assistant and gave him his own office in the White House. While Marcello was apparently planning Kennedy's assassination with a CIA hit squad containing some of the same people used by Nixon in Chile, Nixon, through Chotiner, had a direct line to Marcello. Oddly enough, the only time Nixon was in Dallas in 1963 was the day before and the day of Kennedy's assassination.[48]

The mob makeup of Nixon's assassination teams was corroborated by CIA contract agent Robert Maheu's sworn testimony during his bitter 1974 court fight with Howard Hughes, for whom he had arranged multi-billion dollar defense contracts. In 1967 Rosselli and Hoffa arranged, through Maheu, for Hughes to buy the Desert Inn in Las Vegas from Moe Dalitz and company.[49] This was a typical deal for Rosselli, the mob's "ambassador-at-large," although, as it turned out, the mob could trust Rosselli a whole lot more than Hughes could.[50] Maheu ran all of Hughes' vast Las Vegas operations, until he got caught splitting the skim with Rosselli.

The maniacal Hughes actually commissioned Maheu, working through Chotiner, to see what could be done "to keep the Vietnam war going."[51] The result, apparently, was the "Nixon strategy." In return for such plums as the half-billion dollar *Glomar Explorer* contract, Hughes Aircraft, Hughes Tool and TWA became worldwide CIA conduits. In 1968, when Hughes needed Nixon's help to buy Air West and to squelch antitrust pressure against his acquiring yet more of Las Vegas, Hughes gave Bebe Rebozo a hundred grand in cash; he got what he paid for.[52]

Rebozo, a lifelong Syndicate operative, helped Rolando Martinez, Frank Sturgis and Bernard Barker loot America's banking system. This team of *Batistianos*, through Miami's Ameritas Realty, paid for Watergate. Nixon's banking ties to Syndicate/CIA money were so extensive that they comprised virtually his entire financial web. Keyes Realty, for instance, through which he bought the Florida White House, was a major money laundry for hundreds of millions of Trafficante, Lansky, Batista and Prio dollars.

When the CIA's Castle Bank & Trust of Nassau came under IRS scrutiny in 1972, Nixon, or at least Nixon's CIA, pulled the plug on the investigation.[53] Castle Bank was founded by legendary CIA agent Paul Helliwell, founder of SEA Supply of Bangkok and Air America. According to *The Wall Street Journal*, "pressure from the Central Intelligence Agency...caused the Justice Department to drop what could have been the biggest tax evasion case of all time." In making its case for dismissal to the Justice Department, the CIA admitted that it was using Castle Bank "for the funding of clandestine operations..."[54]

When the U.S. Attorney for New York City, the deadly Robert Morgenthau, working with Wright Patman of the House Banking Committee, began to unravel the massive Vegas to Miami to Bahama to Switzerland Syndicate money wash, which included Castle Bank, Nixon fired Morgenthau, despite his widespread Republican support. He also made a point of destroying Patman's tough international banking legislation, thereby laying the foundation for the mob's trillion dollar rape of the FDIC.[55]

As Castle Bank became too hot, Nugan Hand Bank was on hand to take over. Green Beret Michael Hand served as a CIA contract agent in Laos in the mid-60's, working with the Laotian Hmong opium army. He was close to Vientiane CIA station chief Ted Shackley, and to Shackley's deputy, Thomas Clines. Hand moved to Sydney in late 1967, where he met Maurice Bernard Houghton, an older and very well-connected CIA agent. Houghton entertained the political, intelligence and criminal elite at his Bourbon and Beefsteak restaurant in Sydney. In 1973, Houghton helped Hand and Australian lawyer Frank Nugan found the Nugan Hand Bank.

Their Hong Kong branch, founded in 1974, was their first breakthrough into the big-time of illegal money transfers in support of clandestine arms and drug deals. In support of apartheid in South Africa, Hand's Pretoria trading company ran CIA arms to UNITA in Angola and to the heroes of White Rhodesia. Houghton, in Washington DC, arranged arms shipments to Hand in Pretoria through Office of Naval Intelligence agent Edwin Wilson. Wilson had the help of Hand's old Vientiane buddies, ranking CIA agents Ted Shackley and Thomas Clines, who had moved up Langley's corporate ladder since their opium-dealing days in Vientiane.

Wilson, who was dismissed from the ONI in 1976, was convicted in 1982 of illegally arming Muammar Khaddafi with 21 tons of C-4, the most powerful nonnuclear explosive known. It was Shackley and Clines' cover for Wilson's operations that crippled their CIA careers, thanks to Carter's CIA chief Adm. Stansfield Turner. Wilson and Houghton also arranged the illegal transfer of a state-of-the-art spy ship to the Shah.

The Australian Government's Joint Task Force officially concluded that the Nugan Hand Bank used its branches in Chiangmai, Thailand and Hong Kong to facilitate large scale heroin transfers from the Golden Triangle through Hong Kong to the U.S. At this time, Chiangmai was the major trading center for the Burmese heroin run by Khun Sa's Shan United Army, General Li Wen-huan's KMT Third Army, and the Thai Army.

Hong Kong is a power-center of China's Swatow-born Chiu chau hoodlum elite, their mafiosi. Swatow is, in effect, the Chinese Sicily. The Chiu chau helped Nugan Hand build a network of twelve offices reaching from Thailand to the Cayman Islands. In the Cayman Islands, according to the testimony of a former CIA agent in the Wilson case, Nugan Hand took over for Helliwell's recently defunct Castle Bank of Nassau "for shifting money for various covert operations around the globe."[56]

Nugan Hand's managing staff were almost all CIA/DIA operatives. Adm. Earl Yates, President of Nugan Hand Bank, had been Chief of Staff for Plans and Policy of the U.S. Pacific command. Gen. LeRoy Manor, manager of the Manila branch, another "counterinsurgency expert," had been chief of staff of the U.S. Pacific Command and U.S. liaison to Ferdinand Marcos. Gen. Edwin Black, president of the Hawaii branch, commanded U.S. forces in Thailand and was close to Allen Dulles and Richard Helms. Gen. Erle Cocke Jr. ran the Washington office. Walter McDonald, former CIA deputy director for economic research, was a key executive. The manager of the Taiwan branch, Dale Holmgren, was former chairman of the CIA's Civil Air Transport. Nugan Hand's chief legal counsel was William Colby, former head of the CIA.

When Nugan Hand collapsed in 1980, all the uninsured desposits that American expatriate workers had made into Nugan Hand's Saudi office, some $5 million, simply vanished. Insolvency, illegality and alcoholism probably contributed to the apparent suicide of Frank Nugan on January 27, 1980. The bank's relative anonymity was blown on April 11, 1980 by a reporter for *Target*, a Hong Kong financial newsletter. Shortly thereafter, Michael Hand disappeared.

After Nugan Hand's cover was blown the CIA looted its resources and redirected many of its operations to a front in Hawaii, BBRDW, Bishop, Baldwin, Rewald, Dillingham and Wong. By the end of 1980, BBRDW started setting up offices in Hong Kong, Taiwan, Indonesia, Singapore, and Australia, all former Nugan Hand locations, staffing its offices with Nugan Hand personnel.

A meeting of the National Security Council, May 1, 1972. From left to right are Alexander Haig, Henry Kissinger, Admiral Thomas Moorer, an unidentified man, CIA Director Richard Helms, an unidentified man, Secretary of State William Rogers, President Richard Nixon and Secretary of Defense Melvin Laird; official White House photo

Reader's Digest, 2/1955

Propaganda Due

Nixon's 1970 Controlled Substances Act criminalized any herb or concentrate with a "potential for abuse." That "potential" is defined by the general consensus of industrialized nations that drugs are worth far more illegal than legal, and that without the international Inquisition their own internal fascism would be harder to justify, and finance. "It was ironic," reported a secret 1977 House Government Operations subcommittee, "that the CIA should be given the responsibility of narcotics intelligence, particularly since they are supporting the prime movers."[1] It is also ironic that although Congress can put its finger on it, it can't do a damn thing about it.

In 1974, at about the same time that Nixon was collapsing, the Office of Public Safety (OPS) within the Agency for International Development (AID), the CIA's major international police trainer, was spending hundreds of millions training and supplying police in at least 50 countries. But the OPS had been publicly associated with Vietnam's mass-murdering Operation Phoenix, which it ran, and with Costa Gavras' 1973 film *State of Siege*, about the OPS torture-murder operation against the Tupemaro guerrillas in Uruguay.

Congress, in its righteous indignation, reacted by outlawing the use of foreign assistance money for police training - *except for drug enforcement programs.*[2] OPS agents simply became DEA agents and went right on with their work. The OPS became the DEA. Instead of being paid through AID, they were now paid through DEA from the State Department's Narcotics Assistance program.[3]

Since the CIA is charged with international counterintelligence, and the FBI with domestic counterintelligence, the two agencies, by charter, have always functioned together through shared offices (the State Department's Counterterrorism Office) and liaison officers (the FBI's international Legal Attachés).[4] That is, the FBI always was the CIA-FBI. The CIA-FBI merged with the DEA in 1982 and is now the largest overt foreign intelligence and police training operation of the U.S. government. Congress, in other words, in 1974, aside from teaching the CIA a good lesson in political subtlety, did *nothing*.

The Bolivian military was built up by massive CIA/OPS assistance after its collapse in the 1950's in the face of a leftist uprising led by Victor Paz Estenssoro, a populist Peronist. Paz, leader of the National Revolutionary Movement, nationalized the mines, instituted universal suffrage and land reform, and permitted the foundation of COB (*Central Obrera Boliviana*), the trade union organization, and CSUTCB (*Confederación Sindical Unica de Trabajadores Campesinos de Bolivia*), the peasants (Indian) national union. By giving the Quechuan and Aymara majority the vote and securing their hold on the land, the revolution of 1952 changed Bolivian politics forever.

But Paz was no Jacobo Arbenz. He had totalitarian tendencies and connections, which dated to WW II, to the Nazi-infested secret services. His administration drifted steadily rightward. His 1960's vice-president was air force General René Barrientos, who overthrew him with CIA help in 1964.[5]

Nazi assassin Klaus Barbie went to work for Barrientos, identifying "enemies of the state" from his perch in military intelligence. Ché Guevara died trying to reverse this coup. It was under a 1967 AID contract, ostensibly for a Bolivian road survey, that overflights, using new infrared film, were able to pinpoint Ché's nighttime heat signature through the jungle canopy. Ché, against Moscow's orders, had gone up against a full-scale CIA Special Operations Group.[6]

One of the CIA's shooters on that Special Operations Group was *Batistiano* assassin and Operation 40 vet Felix Rodriguez. Rodriguez was a close associate of George Bush, according to Bush's own admission, and the numerous smiling photos of the two published in Rodriguez' self-adulatory 1989 biography *Shadow Warrior*. Rodriguez also published his photo of him marching Ché to his death, 10/9/1967. Rodriguez wore Ché's watch when he went to Vietnam to help out in Operation Phoenix. Rodriguez lifted the watch just after the captive Guevara had been machine gunned to death.[7] Rodriguez' boss in Nam was Donald Gregg, Bush's White House assistant for national security affairs. Gregg kept an autographed picture of Rodriguez on his White House desk.

Rodriguez' deputy, Luis Posada Carriles, another member of Batista's secret police and an Operation 40/Brigade 2506 vet, had provided cover jobs, through DISIP, the Venezuelan secret police, for Nixon's 1973 assassination teams in Chile. Posada worked closely with Orlando Bosch, another *Batistiano* assassin and Operation 40 vet, who founded the Cuban Action terrorist group. Pinochet put Bosch up in style immediately after the CIA's 1973 murder of Allende, financing his terror campaign.[8]

When Ford-appointee George Bush and Nixon-appointee Vernon Walters were running the CIA, in 1976, they asked another CIA-trained Bay of Pigs veteran, Frank Castro, to help Orlando Bosch put together an umbrella organization for Bosch's Cuban Action, Brigade 2506, the Cuban Nationalist Movement and the other Cuban splinter groups. CORU, the Command of United Revolutionary Organizations, ran contract terrorist warfare for the CIA and Chile's DINA, not only against Cuba, but throughout the world.[9]

In Rome, on October 6, 1975, former Chilean Vice President Bernardo Leighton, and his wife, were shot in the head and back with a 9-mm Beretta. Both lived, crippled for life. It was a DINA contract job, paid for by Augusto Pinochet, who was put in power by Richard Nixon, Henry Kissinger and David Phillips. They were shot by Pier Luigi Concutelli, Stefano delle Chiaie's *Ordine Nuovo* hit man.

Italian magistrate Vittorio Occorsio, during his investigation of the August 1974 bombing of a commuter train that killed twelve people, uncovered evidence connecting the assassins of the Italian fascist group *Ordine Nuovo* to *Fuerza Nueva* in Spain, *Forces Nouvelles* in France and other European terrorist groups linked under the *Eurodestra* fascist umbrella. Thirteen bullets from an Ingram M-10 were found in Vittorio Occorsio's body on July 14, 1976.

The Ingram M-10, CIA contract killer Mitch WerBell's silenced machine pistol, was manufactured at WerBell's Marietta, Georgia plant under supervision and sold only to intelligence agencies. WerBell had served in the OSS in China with Helms, Cline, Singlaub and Hunt, and so was a trusted Company player.

In the late seventies WerBell's deadly silent pistol turned up in the hands of contracting fascist terror groups throughout Europe.[10] Stefano delle Chiaie of *Ordine Nuovo*, a major target of Occorsio, was the protégé and partner of Count Borghese, head of Mussolini's murderous intelligence apparatus. He was provided with the Ingrams by Spain's *Brigada Central de Informacion*, in exchange for his considerable help in running anti-ETA death squads throughout the Pyrenees.[11] When delle Chiaie's favorite hit man, Pierluigi Concutelli, was trapped by police in January of 1977, he was found with the Ingram M-10 that had killed Occorsio, traceable from WerBell's Georgia plant to the Spanish secret service.

Junio Valerio Borghese, Stefano delle Chiaie, Pierluigi Concutelli

Ordine Nuovo's second-in-command, Elio Massagrande, was nailed by Italian police for masterminding that crime, as well as a 1976 bank robbery that netted *Ordine Nuovo* $25 million. But the SID, the *Servizio Informazione Difesa*, Italy's major secret service, had been working since the late sixties with Stefano delle Chiaie and *Ordine Nuovo* to pin the terrorist label on the Italian left. They used the old Reichstag Fire trick - framing innocent leftists for their own vicious attacks on civilians. Massagrande, who knew way too much, was therefore allowed to escape to Paraguay, where he helped the aging General Stroessner with his dope-dealing duties.

Hitler's favorite commando, Col. Otto Skorzeny, working with the Portuguese secret service and French OAS veteran Yves Guérin-Serac, had set up Aginterpress, an espionage bureau masquerading as a news bureau. This was a Gehlen-BND-CIA operation to coordinate the various European fascist groups. Thus the Italian delle Chiaie, who had worked for Aginterpress, was in ready contact with Spain's *Fuerza Nueva* and the secret service behind it. In 1977 *Fuerza Nueva* terrorists burst into a conference of nine liberal lawyers and machine-gunned them all to death. One *Fuerza Nueva* maniac actually walked up to a politically active high school girl and shot her in the head. Elio Massagrande attended the CIA-funded 1979 meeting of the World Anti-Communist League.[12]

When CORU's Orlando Bosch needed to arrange a contract in Europe, he knew who to call. In the first ten months of its operations

CORU took credit for more than 50 bombings and assassinations, including the murder of Pinochet's most dangerous critic, Orlando Letelier, Allende's ambassador to the U.S.[13] One of Letelier's indicted assassins was Michael Townley, David Phillips' CIA assistant in Chile. Phillips' good work in establishing Pinochet won him the directorship of CIA Western Hemisphere operations. Townley went to work for the DINA, coordinating it with CORU.

In July of 1976, the U.S. Ambassador to Chile, George Landau, sent a cable to the State Department asking that two DINA agents - one likely Townley - be allowed to enter the U.S. with Paraguayan passports. The cable specifically requested a meeting with Gen. Vernon Walters, Bush's outgoing Deputy Director. The July-August cable traffic with Walters and Bush was revealed in Townley's trial, but was then immediately expunged from the record. When CORU operatives, and fall guys, Ross and Novo were arrested, along with Townley, for the murder of Letelier, they were in possession of more than a pound of uncut cocaine.

In 1976 CORU's Bosch arranged the assassination of Miami Cuban liberal Luciano Nieves. Nieves had the effrontery to challenge Castro to an open election, something Castro was apparently willing to consider. Treating Castro as if he too were a Cuban was not tolerated in Little Havana, which saw more than a hundred of these murders between 1976 and 77.[14] CORU also took credit for the midair destruction of a Cubana passenger jet which snuffed 73 lives.

Responding to Castro's specific charges, Venezuelan police raided the offices of Luis Posada's detective agency. They found evidence of connections to Orlando Bosch, the Letelier assassination and the Cubana bombing.[15] Posada, a close associate of Bush operative Felix Rodriguez, was formally charged with planting the Cubana bomb, but "security considerations" forced dismissal of the case. In 1977 Orlando Bosch's daughter and son in law were arrested on cocaine smuggling charges.[16]

But that was small potatoes compared to Bill Tyree's CIA/Special Forces operation:

"Affidavit of William M. Tyree, Jr., signed under the pains and penalties of perjury on this date, September 6, 1990:

"1. That, during December 1975, while assigned to the 1st/17th Air Cavalry, 82d Airborne Division, Fort Bragg, N.C., I was active in a military operation, code named "WATCHTOWER". Operation Watchtower was a classified mission which operated from Albrook Air Station in Panama and fielded within Columbia. The mission project was to insert three SPECIAL ACTION TEAMS (SATs) inside Columbia. Once the SATs were in place they would activate electronic beacons which aircraft would follow through a specific corridor out of Columbia and into Panama where the aircraft, which were loaded with cocaine, would land at Albrook Air Station."

"2. That, the December 1975 mission lasted 24 days and approximately 37 aircraft of various descriptions flew out of Columbia and into Panama, all following the SATs electronic beacons."

"3. That, the Commanding Officer during the 1975 mission was Colonel James Baker. (a.k.a. Bo Baker)"

"4. That, to my knowledge, there were no incidents during the 1975 mission. Each SAT was comprised of 6 to 7 men. Some of the men were identified to me as being members of the 7th Special Forces Group, Airborne...other(s)...as...82d Airborne Division."

"5. That, in February 1976 a second WATCHTOWER mission was undertaken and I was active in it also. The mission objectives were identical to the 1975 mission. The Commanding Officer of the February 1976 mission was Colonel Edward Cutolo. This February 1976 mission lasted 19 days and 29 aircraft flew out of Columbia into Panama, again following SATs electronic beacons."

"7. That in March 1976, a third WATCHTOWER mission was fielded. This mission lasted 29 days and 40 aircraft flew from Columbia into Panama and landed at Albrook Air Station. I was a crew chief assigned to a sterile UH-1B helicopter. The mission of the helicopters was to transport the SATs to the borders of Columbia and Panama and drop them off...."

"10. That, following the conclusion of the December, February and March WATCHTOWER missions, I personally witnessed members of the Panamanian Defense Force (PDF) help unload the bails of cocaine from the aircraft onto the tarmac of Albrook Air Station. Among the PDF officers were Colonel Manuel Noriega, Major Roberto Diaz-Hererra, Major Luis del Cid, and Major Ramirez. These men were always in the company of an American civilian identified to me by other personnel involved in the operation as Edwin Wilson, of the CIA [George Bush, DCI]. Another civilian in the company of Wilson, I have since learned was Israeli Mossad Agent Michael Harari. I personally saw a man involved in Operation Watchtower that I later learned [from a photo] fit the description of Michael Harari."

"21. That, following my [October 1977] arrival at Fort Devens....Colonel Cutolo took command of the 10th SFG(A) and began to field a surveillance operation instituted under Army Regulation AR 340-18-5, file number 503-05. I was involved in ten separate surveillance missions in the New England area, all under this same operation. This operation was satirically referred to as Operation Orwell."

"27. That, I was told by Sergeant John Newby, that he had been involved in the surveillance of several prominent citizens in the New England area. Amongst those he stated by name were U.S. Senators John Kerry and Ted Kennedy. Sgt. Newby also stated to me just prior to his death in October 1978, that he had been involved in surveillance of 'some judges' in the new England area...."

"28. That, the same Sgt. John Newby also gave me the name of Major Arnett. Arnett was assigned to Fort Bragg, N.C., at that time in 1978. Arnett had commanded a team that allegedly maintained surveillance on U.S. Senator Jessie Helms. According to Colonel Edward Cutolo, the connection between Helms, Kennedy and Kerry, was that all three were critical of the U.S. involvement in Latin America. He stated that they were among the last people in a position of authority that should learn of Operation Watchtower, as they would undoubtedly use that information to pull the U.S. out of Latin America, which in turn might affect the 'security' of that area and eventually the U.S."

"29. That, in October 1978, my wife, Elaine Tyree, and I began to receive threatening phone calls, as well as short notes left on our parked vehicle. The notes basically said 'Tell your wife to stop doing what she is doing'. The threats made no sense to me but were reported to my Chain of Command at Fort Devens.... I also spoke directly to Colonel Edward Cutolo concerning the threats.... My parents also contacted U.S. Senator E.J. 'Jake' Garn (R-Utah). Senator Garn was told by the U.S. Army and Fort Devens that the threats would be investigated. The threats were never investigated prior to the murder of my wife, Elaine.

"30. That, on January 30, 1979, after we had received numerous threats, my wife of 13 months was murdered at our off post residence.... Within two weeks I would be arrested for her murder."

"31. That, just prior to my arrest on the evening of February 13, 1979, I had confronted Earl Michael Peters concerning his part in my wife's murder. Peters drew a .45 caliber pistol...and pointed it at my chest. ....once he drew the pistol, he admitted that he had in fact killed my wife. He told me how he committed the murder and what his motive was. His motive pertained to a set of diaries my wife kept which contained certain matters that related to his criminal activities in and around Fort Devens. The sole reason I confronted him was because Colonel Edward Cutolo had shown me photographs taken by U.S. Army Personnel which had my apartment under surveillance. The photographs basically depicted Earl Michael Peters entering and leaving my apartment building. Peters entered through the front door of the building and left through a bedroom window in my apartment. The photographs proved that Peters had been in my apartment on the date of the murder."

"37. That, either in late 1986, or early 1987, Colonel Rowe told me by telephone that the surveillance instituted under AR 340-18-5 was ongoing...."

"38. That, this same Colonel Rowe also told me that he had substantial evidence to support his belief that Colonel Edward Cutolo, Colonel James Baker, and Colonel Robert Bayard were all victims of foul play due to their knowledge or association with certain Israeli individuals involved in Operation Watchtower."

"40. That, the last message I received from Colonel Rowe was prior to his departure overseas. In April 1989, Colonel Rowe was assassinated in Manila. He was allegedly the victim of Muslim backed communist forces."

Odd combination that, religious fundamentalist communists, hmm. And why would the Israelis murder every American officer whose cover was blown by Elaine Tyree's voluminous diaries if Operation Watchtower were an American operation? Israelis burn their American bridges very reluctantly. And why were the diaries of the overly perceptive Elaine, herself also in the Army and cooperating with the Criminal Investigation Division, seized by none other than Edwin Wilson, the coordinating CIA agent Tyree had witnessed offloading coke with Manuel Noriega?

Tyree was railroaded because an open trial would completely blow Operations Watchtower and Orwell. Hence his sworn 1990 deposition, seeking a new trial. Tyree can prove everything he is saying. Because of the incredible political content, Tyree was helped by William McCoy, the respected investigator who helped the Cristic Institute try to nail the CIA for the La Penca bombing, aimed at Eden Pastora, that killed and wounded so many reporters. Bill McCoy died under suspicious circumstances in the fall of 1997. McCoy's close friend, ace investigator, and webmaster, Mike Ruppert, is now helping, and has made all of Tyree's court-filed documentation available online at his site, www.copvcia.com.

Tyree's 1999 lawsuit, with the work of these investigators included, contains eyewitness affidavits showing that Elaine Tyree's diaries ended up in the hands of Syndicate/CIA courier Col. Albert Carone. Carone's daughter Dee filed supporting affidavits with the court confirming that her father knew Tyree and possessed the diaries. "Big Al," recalled Dee Carone, "delivered the diaries to Langley." Big Al Carone can be tied to George Bush, the DCI during Operation Watchtower. The evidence shows that Bush directly ordered Carone to Massachusetts to seize Elaine Tyree's diaries. Carone was working hand in glove with Edwin Wilson, a Shackley operative Bush had worked with since the Bay of Pigs, when Shackley was Miami CIA station chief.

Ruppert, of course, is the former LAPD narcotics detective who became enraged at the massive CIA drugs-for-arms trade he discovered in the mid-70's, a trade that later proved to have connections to the assassination of RFK. Tyree's extraordinary perspective is further proof that this trade has been a structural feature of U.S. intelligence operations for decades before anyone ever heard of the Contras - in this case, for the better part of one decade.

In July of 1983 George Bush's 1976 CIA contractor, CORU chief Frank Castro, was named as an unindicted coconspirator in the smuggling of more than 1.5 million pounds of pot into the U.S. "Unindicted" because he helped to supply arms to the Contras, in exchange for license to deal. He and his partners, Hernandez-Cartaya (Trafficante) and Tony Fernandez, were allowed to buy federally insured banks with their drug money.[17]

The CIA-trained Bay of Pigs veteran Guillermo Hernandez-Cartaya funneled money to CORU through the World Finance Corporation, WFC, which functioned as Trafficante's money laundry. In the late 70's, WFC came under state and federal scrutiny for drug smuggling, money laundering, gun running, extortion and terrorism. At least 12 WFC board members or employees had CIA ties.[18] One, founding director Walter Sterling Surrey, was an old OSS/State Department hand. Another WFC director, Juan Romanach, was identified by Interpol as a Trafficante operative. Sharing offices with and borrowing from WFC was Dominion Mortgage Corp., which supplied drugs to Las Vegas and attempted to buy Caesar's Palace.

The CIA pulled the plug on the WFC investigation.[19] Hernandez-Cartaya, convicted of bank fraud in 1982, had a long-term relationship with Oliver North's ally Adnan Khashoggi and the Bank of Credit and Commerce International, BCCI, the CIA's tool in Pakistan. BCCI was convicted of money-laundering and banned from the U.S.[20]

This recurring structural corruption, financed by Prohibition, has caused many in the world's police agencies to question basic Drug War policy. The FBI's Bud Mullen, who himself ended up questioning policy, took over the DEA in 1982, when it became a subdivision of the FBI. The FBI's home Office of Liaison and International Affairs, created in 1987, coordinates their various international Legal Attachés with the CIA, DEA, State, Interpol, and special and temporary operations. Interpol's U.S. office, the National Central Bureau, saw its staff go from 6 to 110 between 1979 and 1990, vastly increasing the intelligence interchange between U.S. police agencies and Interpol headquarters in Lyon, France. U.S. influence on Interpol policy also increased.[21]

That made Raymond Kendall, Secretary General of Interpol since 1985, the world's top cop, very uncomfortable. On June 8, 1994, Kendall called for the international decriminalization of drug possession.[22] The former Scotland Yard detective told BBC radio that "I am in favor of decriminalization but not in favor of legalization.... If someone is caught with drugs they should be treated, not convicted." Kendall timed his remarks to coincide with the annual drug conference of Britain's Association of Chief Police Officers, which also called for coordinated international decriminalization.

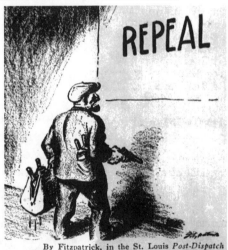

By Fitzpatrick, in the St. Louis *Post-Dispatch*
BAD NEWS FOR THE UNDERWORLD

Kendall expanded on his reasoning at the annual congress of his 176-nation International Criminal Police Organization meeting in Beijing in October of 1995. "If you look at the real threat to our societies today, what you have is a combination of organized crime and drug trafficking." Decriminalization, since it would collapse the commodities' value, would bankrupt the traffickers. This tactic is necessary because "we're pretty overwhelmed." Traffickers "have the ability to corrupt our institutions at the highest level. If they can do that, then it means our democracies are in real danger."[23]

The Scotsman(UK):4/21/99:"'The illegal trade in narcotics is increasingly interwoven with the regular economy, at a national as well as international level,' says Raymond Kendall...now head of Interpol. 'This interweaving makes the combating of the drug trade on the financial front all the more difficult. Countries now face the increasing globalisation of crime and criminal organisations.'"

"It seemed that whenever the CIA had an 'interest' in a doper, the doper never appeared in the DEA computer."[24] Frontline DEA agent Michael Levine, a 25-year veteran of the force, knows whereof he speaks. In 1980, as the DEA's Country Attaché to Argentina and Uruguay, he was working dangerous undercover operations to set up the biggest coke dealers in neighboring Bolivia. The famous dealers he was hunting not only failed to appear in the DEA computer, but, with CIA and Argentine help, overthrew the centrist, anti-dealing Bolivian government Levine had been cooperating with:

"The only ruling government of Bolivia - a nation that produces the raw material for as much as 90 percent of the cocaine entering the United States - that ever wanted to help DEA defeat their drug barons was paid for its faith in our sincerity with torture and death at the hands of CIA-sponsored paramilitary terrorists under the command of fugitive Nazi war criminal (also protected by the CIA) Klaus Barbie."[25] (Levine's parenthesis)

The nazi killers Levine was hunting literally tortured to death the Bolivian ministers he was working with, with the help of his own agency. That's how the enraged Michael Levine, a fierce agent who believed in his work, fell out of love with the DEA. There was, of course, nothing at all he could do about it except pick up a pen. When Levine sank his teeth too deeply into the real dealing structure, he found himself in trouble with his own command structure.[26] That, of course, was precisely Raymond Kendall's point.

The DEA is actually run by its internal security, the Office of Professional Responsibility, which has the authority to bring recalcitrant agents up on charges based on its 1300-page Manual: "A collateral - and frequent - use of the Manual was as a terror tool to keep street agents in line. Its rules and regulations made all street agents vulnerable to termination at the whim of the suits.... When the suits 'throw the Manual' at a street agent, it means they are after his job, and there's usually not much the agent can do about it."[27] DEA agents call the

OPR "the Gestapo," which, in Levine's case, has very special irony indeed.

His 25 years as a frontline DEA agent led Levine to the inescapable conclusion that the CIA is running the drug trade. He calls his book *The Big White Lie: The CIA and the Cocaine/Crack Epidemic*. That's also what the best student of the Asian heroin trade has to say. Professor McCoy, who, like Levine, has been immersed in this study for the past 30 years, calls his 1991 masterwork *The Politics of Heroin: CIA Complicity in the Global Drug Trade*. McCoy's single most valuable recommendation is the one he got from John Kennedy: eliminate the CIA's legal ability to conduct any covert operations without direct executive control.

The Bolivian excuse, once again, was "communism," meaning, in this case as in so many others, a coalition of moderate liberal nationalists who believed in a mixed economy. Today, the bogeyman, in the absence of "the scourge of communism," is "the scourge of drugs," supporting precisely the same fascist dynamics. I can't say it better than former Green Beret General Barry McCaffrey, an original defender of the Hmong opium connection. McCaffrey took over in March of 96 as Clinton's Drug Czar: "The new problems are obvious - they're counterterrorism, they're counterdrugs, they're illegal movements of peoples, they're arms smuggling, they're transnational Marxist movements that have now become international criminal conspiracies, narco-guerrilla forces."[28] That is, in this masterpiece of fascist doublespeak, the new problems are the old problems.

And to combat these horrible leftists, McCaffrey is going to ship all the arms he can to the Bolivian, Argentinian, Mexican, Honduran, Guatemalan, Peruvian, Salvadoran, Colombian, Pakistani, Philippine, Taiwanese and Burmese military. With McCaffrey in charge, the fascists have nothing to worry about. "Every government in the Western Hemisphere is a democracy but Cuba," Clinton told Dole in the Presidential debate of 10/6/96. Dole agreed. This is a given. "And Cuba," added Dole, "is infested with drug dealers."

If, by McCaffrey-Clinton-Dole-IMF standards, "democratic" Brazil has the world's 8th largest economy, why does it rank 80th by measures of social welfare? Most of Latin America has a higher hunger, infant mortality, illiteracy, poverty and disease rate than most of the rest of the third world. The U.N. Food and Agriculture Organization declared in 1990 that hundreds of thousands of Brazilian children die of hunger every year. It said that 40% of Brazilians, more than 50 million people, go to bed hungry every night.[29] Most of them, of course, are completely disenfranchised. Populist political leaders are regularly assassinated by the "democratic" "anti-drug" death squads armed and trained by McCaffrey and Company.

It is no coincidence that the Italian fascist conspiracy that helped the CIA finance the Bolivian Cocaine Coup that so enraged Agent Levine, as well as financing Argentina's dirty war, as well as attempting to take over Italy itself, was called *Propaganda Due*, P-2. You know - like *Reichstag Zwei*, R-2 - Play it again, Adolph.

A major planner of the Bolivian Cocaine Coup was General Carlos Guillermo Suárez Mason of Argentina's First Army Corps. He was inducted into P-2 through José Lopez Rega, Juan Peron's Minister of Social Welfare, the country's top police officer.[30] Lopez Rega was an ally of the fascist Paladin terrorist group in Spain, founded by Gehlen operative Otto Skorzeny. Lopez Rega used the Argentine Anti-Communist Alliance (AAA) that he founded, based on the Paladin death-squad model, to take over Argentina's massive cocaine business.

In May 1974 Lopez Rega and the U.S. ambassador signed a much-publicized agreement to fight drug trafficking in Argentina. Lopez Rega declared absolutely that "Guerrillas are the main users of drugs in Argentina. Therefore, the antidrug campaign will automatically be an antiguerrilla campaign as well."[31] Gen. Barry McCaffrey, word for word. As a U.S. Southern Command counterinsurgency expert, McCaffrey was, in fact, personally involved in supplying Lopez Rega's troops with their military equipment and training.

The next year a confidential report from Argentine military intelligence declared that Lopez Rega himself, with his death-squad army of AAA irregulars, was one of the largest cocaine traffickers in the world.[32] Although the report caused the political sacrifice of Lopez Rega, who went back to Spain, it had no effect whatever on American policy, which continued to finance, through the DEA and McCaffrey's Southern Command, Lopez Rega's dirty war on the Argentine left, now led by his protégé, Gen. Carlos Guillermo Suárez Mason.

Suárez Mason was made head of army intelligence and eventually rose to command the entire Argentine military. In 1980, under the direction of the CIA, he coordinated the overthrow of the socialist coalition that had taken over in neighboring Bolivia from Gen. Hugo Banzer in 1978/79. This was the interim parliamentary government of President Lidia Gueiler that had worked so well with Agent Levine. Gueiler had the support of Air Force Gen. Juan Pereda. Suárez Mason used 200 Argentine agents working with Bolivia's "Fiancés of

Death," the predecessors of today's Bolivian Leopards.[33]

Los Novios de la Muerte were originally the private army of the Bolivian cocaine cartel, which was headed by Roberto Suárez, financier of both Hugo Banzer and Suárez Mason. Roberto Suárez, the King of Cocaine, was the primary supplier of coca paste, from his vast coca fields in Alto Beni, to Colombia's Medellín cartel. He was the grandnephew of Nicolás Suárez, the late-nineteenth century rubber baron who controlled an incredible 16 million acres of tropical forest, an area the size of Ireland. For Roberto Suárez, then, coca paste was just another traditional agricultural product.[34]

Los Novios, more than 600 of them, were organized and trained by Nazi war criminal and CIA cutout Klaus Barbie, the Gestapo's "Butcher of Lyon." Before Lyon, Barbie had headed up one of the SS *einsatzgruppen* extermination squads on the Eastern Front.

French and immigrant Jewish children in hiding at the Children's Welfare Organization refuge in Izieu, near Lyon, 1943. Gestapo Oberssturmfüher Barbie went out of his way to hunt them down and have them all gassed at Auschwitz; *The Children of Izieu*

Barbie, who had helped the CIA kill Ché as an operative of Gen. Barrientos, had been *de facto* head of secret police under Gen. Banzer, another drug-dealing "anticommunist" brought to power by the CIA, in a very bloody 1971 coup. Banzer is a 1950's graduate of the U.S. Army School of the Americas and recipient of the Pentagon's Order of Military Merit.

Barbie helped run Banzer's 1970's Ministry of the Interior, organizing *Los Novios*, setting up political terror operations and concentration camps, and refining the torture-interrogation methods of Ministry police. At the same time, the CIA, the DEA and the U.S. Southern Command provided Banzer's Ministry with its equipment and international police coordination.[35] Barbie's 1980 Bolivian performance was, therefore, an encore.[36]

Klaus Barbie's Bolivian Secret Police ID Card. He took the name of a rabbi he had murdered; *The Children of Izieu*

In 1977, at the height of his power under Banzer, Barbie personally organized a high level meeting between the CIA and the Chilean and Bolivian intelligence services, held in the Yungas region of Bolivia.[37] The purpose of the meeting was the promotion of Condor, the CIA-designed system of death-squad cooperation and target-sharing between U.S.-supported fascist regimes throughout Latin America.

Thus, Chile's murderous secret service, DINA, introduced Barbie to Stefano delle Chiaie of *Ordine Nuovo*, who was to become his top aide. The accomplished Italian terrorist came to Bolivia as part of Chile's contribution to the Argentinian delegation of secret police trainers for the Bolivian coup operation.

Delle Chiaie and the cadre around him, Pierluigi Pagliai, Joachim Fiebelkorn, Maurizio Giorgio and Olivier Danet, the core group of the 1980 Fiancés of Death, were formally charged in September, 1982, in Bologna, with the August, 1980 bombing of the Bologna railway station that killed 84 people and wounded another 200. This was more of McCaffrey's "leftist terrorism." They had travelled to Bologna from Bolivia.

The Bolivian elections of June 29, 1980 threatened to bring none other than Hernán Siles-Zuazo back into power, the leftist Peronist who, along with Víctor Paz Estenssoro, led the 1952 social revolution.

On July 17, just after Siles-Zuazo's parliamentary majority was assured, Barbie and delle Chiaie executed a carefully planned orgy of killing, including the torture-murder of much of the Gueiler government and its leading supporters. Women were gang-raped and then beaten to death, men were castrated.[38] Lidia Gueiler herself survived.

After a couple of days of both indiscriminate and political murder, General Luis García Meza was in unchallenged control of the Bolivian government. His *Novios de la Muerte*, commanded by cocaine baron Roberto Suárez' cousin, Col. Luis Arce-Gómez, Klaus Barbie's boss, herded thousands of populist leaders into the La Paz soccer stadium and machine gunned them all to death.

That left García's patron, the Argentine military, still busy with its own dirty war, in direct control of one of the world's greatest cocaine producers. It also, obviously, left the Bolivian diplomatic pouch, which is not subject to customs inspection, open for large-scale export of cocaine.[39]

The very first official act of the new government was the freeing of all imprisoned major drug dealers, who immediately went back to work for their government monopoly. Monopoly, in this case, is not too strong a word. García Meza set up the National Coca Agency (*Acopio de Coca*), which appropriated the sole legal right to purchase coca throughout Bolivia. Uncompetitive prices were paid to the small growers, and those who wouldn't accept these miserable wages had their coca leaves confiscated - for processing into cocaine by the Agency.

Scores of independent small processors and dealers were very publicly killed or jailed to satisfy the demands of public relations, and to eliminate the competition. Barbie's boss, Arce-Gómez, the Minister of the Interior, became universally known as the Minister of Cocaine.[40]

Exactly one month *before* the coup, on June 17, 1980, six of Bolivia's biggest traffickers, led by Suárez and Arce-Gómez, the ones who didn't appear in Levine's DEA computer, met with the Argentinians and the Bolivian military to firm up their post-coup arrangements. One of the Argentines present dutifully sent a tape of this meeting to his CIA employers.[41]

The fascist grip on power was so secure that a newspaper in La Paz, three weeks before the coup, reported that "A leading businessman in La Paz has suggested that the possible army takeover next month should be called the Cocaine Coup."[42] The name stuck. Reported *Newsweek*, 11/23/81: "At least 40 Bolivian officers have traveled to Argentina to study 'antisubversive techniques,' and Argentinians practiced in torture [are serving as] interrogators."[43] All trained, armed and financed by McCaffrey's U.S. Southern Command, often under DEA cover.

USS John C. Stennis patrols the northern Mexico coast; U.S. Navy photo

Augusto Sandino of Nicaragua and Emiliano Zapata of Mexico

Generals Jorge Videla and Roberto Viola of Argentina

SETCO

Reagan was as tied to the Syndicate as Nixon. During his Hollywood years as head of the Screen Actors Guild, he enthusiastically worked with Johnny Rosselli, who started his career as a Capone hit man. Ronald Reagan's longtime producer, Bryan Foy, who began his career as a pioneer of sound technology at Warner Brothers, was Johnny Rosselli's partner in Eagle Lion Productions, his lifelong best friend.[1]

In 1927, because he couldn't take the Chicago winters, Rosselli, at the age of 23, moved to LA, there to captain a street war, as Jack Dragna's right-hand man, for control of LA's booming rackets. The mafiosi pushed out the old crowd, which had been headed by Guy McAfee, former chief of the LAPD vice squad. McAfee had used that position, as so many before and since, to take control of the rackets.

Rosselli was Dragna's key contact with the enormously powerful Capone organization, which didn't even flinch at the loss of Capone himself.[2] Rosselli had been one of Capone's favorite button-men, sworn into the Mafia by Capone himself, and he knew all the top lieutenants. With California's rackets as their economic foundation, the Syndicate set its sights on the film industry, which had combined assets throughout the country, including theatres and production facilities, that made it the fourth largest industry in the U.S.[3]

Old New York street fighter Harry Cohn, head of Columbia Studios, became fast friends throughout the 30's and 40's with Rosselli. Their friendship was based not only on their mutual love of horse racing and gambling, but on Rosselli's access to huge amounts of mob cash and his clout with the unions that Cohn had to contend with. Another Rosselli friend, Joe Schenck, was head of United Artists. Schenk was originally bankrolled by Arnold Rothstein. Like MGM's Louis B. Meyer and Jack Warner, Schenck was a lover of high-stakes gambling and even higher stakes union-busting.

In 1933 the studios used Rosselli's goons to break a production strike by the International Alliance of Theatrical Stage Employees, IATSE, which represented Hollywood production technicians and projectionists nationwide. In 1934 Rosselli's Chicago allies took control of IATSE, using Rosselli's intimate knowledge of the Hollywood profit structure to organize the wholesale extortion of the film industry. A beefy gunsel named Willie Bioff became IATSE's nominal head in Hollywood, literally at the point of a gun, but Bioff took orders from Rosselli, and Rosselli took them from Frank Rio, Frank Nitti, Nick

Circella, Lou Campagna, Rocco Fischetti and Paul Ricca.

Willie Bioff, Frank Nitti and Rocco Fischetti

In 1935, during negotiations with the producers, IATSE demonstrated its power by closing down more than 500 Paramount theatres from Chicago to St. Louis.[4] Those theatres were the only distribution apparatus Paramount had. For years thereafter, Hollywood became a virtual IATSE closed shop, leaving both the moguls and the 12,000 studio technicians paying their regular dues to the Syndicate.

From the studios' perspective, this actually made sense. IATSE had the muscle to enforce its sweetheart contracts with the studios, to the great cost of its members, who had to accept nickel-and-dime pay raises when they could have had dollars. Projectionists actually suffered severe pay cuts: between 1933 and 1938, average weekly wages in Philadelphia dropped from $120 to $68.[5] Rival start-up unions never survived the combination of street-muscle and red-baiting that IATSE and the studios were able to bring to bear.

The mob-connected studio power structure, the mob-built-and-run production and distribution giant MCA, and the mob-led unions, IATSE and SAG, actively encouraged the House Un-American Activities Committee, HUAC, to come to town. Ronald Reagan, President of the Screen Actors Guild, was a star "friendly witness" in the late forties and early fifties.

Reagan helped to draw up enormous blacklists, some 2,000 names, who were then prevented from organizing independent unions or infecting the airwaves with their idealism.[6] Historian C. Vann Woodward documented this in a 1987 *New York Times* piece. Reagan "fed the names of suspect people in his organization to the FBI secretly and regularly enough to be assigned an informer's code number, T-

10."

As President of the Screen Actors Guild, it had been Reagan's job to negotiate with MCA, which he did by acceding to its every demand and red-baiting his critics. In return for helping to engineer MCA's virtual monopoly in early television production, Reagan was made part owner of MCA. When the Kennedys went after MCA as a price-fixing monopoly, Reagan went after the Kennedys, attacking "government bureaucracy." His reward was the statehouse.

On assuming the Presidency, Reagan appointed Walter Annenberg's wife Leonore as White House chief of protocol. Walter Annenberg, publisher of *TV Guide*, was the son of racing wire kingpin Moe Annenberg, a very major mob figure. Moe was convicted of tax evasion and racketeering in 1939 and died in the Lewisburg Penn. Leonore was the ex-wife of Lewis Rosenstiel of Schenley Distilleries, the anticommunist ex-bootlegger close to J. Edgar Hoover. Like their friend Edgar, Rosenstiel, Annenberg and Reagan were early-50's operatives of CIA Operation Mockingbird's "Crusade for Freedom," which raised money to help East European Nazis relocate in the U.S. The Annenbergs were close lifelong friends of Sidney Korshak, Johnny Rosselli's lawyer.[7]

Korshak was "often delegated to represent the Chicago mob, usually in some secret capacity," as a 1942 IRS report put it. Just as Rosselli was the Chicago mob's most trusted street operator in Los Angeles, so Korshak was its most trusted legal eagle. Korshak, who began his career in Chicago as Big Al's lawyer, was an early, and major, stockholder in Red Dorfman's Union Casualty Company.[8] This is the Chicago company that became the awesome Teamsters' Central States, Southeast, and Southwest Areas Pension Fund.

Korshak was pursued by Bobby Kennedy on the McClellan Rackets Committee in 1957. The New Jersey Casino Control Commission called Korshak "a key actor in organized crime's unholy alliances with corrupt union officials and its pernicious efforts to frustrate the rights of working men and women by infecting legitimate unions, to rob their members' future by stealing the benefits they have earned in the past from honest labor."[9]

The very first official stop in Washington of the Reagan-Bush administration, immediately following their victory, was the headquarters of the Teamsters Union, where they met with Jackie Presser, Roy Williams, Frank Fitzsimmons and Sidney Korshak's very own Andy Anderson of Los Angeles Teamster Local 986.[10] Reagan asked the Teamster high command to pick his Secretary of Labor and other top administration officials.[11]

They picked Ray Donovan of Schiavone Construction Company of Secaucus, NJ, accused at his confirmation hearings of being close to "Tony Pro" Provenzano and "Sally Bugs" Briguglio of the Union City Teamsters, top Genovese operatives. Both were indicted for the 1961 killing of Anthony Castellito, which resulted in the Provenzano reign in Union City.

This is the pair, according to *Time*, that quickly chipped in $500,000 in cash to cover Nixon's January 1973 covert Watergate expenses. Allen Dorfman, on Frank Fitzsimmons' orders, matched the Union City Teamsters with another half million in cash.[12] Provenzano and Briguglio were also accused, in 1978, by Family member Little Ralph Picardo, of killing Jimmy Hoffa.[13] Sally Bugs did not live out the year.

Donovan was also accused of being close to New York mafioso William Masselli, then under indictment for manufacturing synthetic cocaine and hijacking trucks. Schiavone Construction was accused of being Masselli's money laundry. Assistant Director of the FBI Bud Mullen successfully prevented the confirmation committee from finding out what the FBI knew about Donovan, and so Donovan was confirmed as Secretary of Labor.[14] Mullen was then rewarded with the leadership of the Drug Enforcement Administration. Donovan was finally forced out of government, in late 1984, after being indicted, along with 9 top New York mafiosi, for murder, grand larceny, fraud, extortion and labor racketeering.

The phrase "labor racketeering" conjures up images of hoods bullying workmen for a piece of their wages, but as with IATSE, the scam is much more monumental than that. If 20% of all the meat sold in the U.S. has to pass through the New York City market, and if you control the powerful New York locals of the Amalgamated Meat Cutters and Butcher Workmen of North America, AFL-CIO, with more than half a million members nationwide, then you also control access to every supermarket chain in New York. Since no packer can live without the New York market, you are in a position to demand that every packer in the country give you a regular piece of its action or face bankruptcy.

Iowa Beef Processors, the largest meat packer in the country, was brought to its knees in the late 60's by Syndicate control of the New York market. By the mid-70's Iowa Beef had Syndicate operatives on its Board of Directors, its employees were represented by the Teamsters, its trucks were Syndicate-run and both the price and quality of its product suffered, though certainly not its distribution.[15] Major commercial shippers throughout the country discovered that a few well-placed millions to key members of the Teamster high command could save their outfit tens of millions with a sweetheart exemption from the National Master Freight Agreement.[16]

The Teamsters' Jackie Presser was the son of convicted labor racketeer William Presser, Cleveland associate of Moe Dalitz, Jimmy Licavoli, Allen Dorfman and Sidney Korshak. The Pressers ran the Ohio Teamsters, as well as numerous other Cleveland-based rackets.[17] Reagan made Jackie Presser "senior economic advisor" to his transition team. Asked Senator Sam Nunn: "Is it a violation of fundamental principles of government ethics for Mr. Presser to help organize the very department that has brought suit against him?"[18] You bet.

In the first Reagan budget, for fiscal 1982, he imposed a 33% cutback of the FBI's ongoing investigations of organized drug-dealing, contract murder, contract arson, organized prostitution and gambling, and eliminated all new undercover investigations of organized and white collar crime. He stressed instead "violent" crime, that is, crime committed by poor kids. He also unsuccessfully went after the Justice Department's Strike Force Against Organized Crime and the equally effective ATF effort, and succeeded in cutting the DEA budget by 18%. In 1984 Reagan cut the Customs Service funding by 50%, thereby getting the government off the smugglers' backs. As the mob was taking over toxic-waste dumping, Reagan put Las Vegas mob-lawyer James Watt[19] in charge of environmental policy.

As cover for these law enforcement cuts, Vice-President George Bush was put in charge of the noisy South Florida Drug Task Force. Bush's chief of staff was Admiral Dan Murphy, former Sixth Fleet commander and Deputy Director of the CIA. A Coast Guard lieutenant commander in south Florida called the Bush-Murphy effort "an intellectual fraud," and Florida's Claude Pepper said "I can't see a single thing [Bush] has accomplished. The lack of coordination…is disgraceful."[20] Bush simply rushed down to Florida every time the Coast Guard made a bust to pose for pictures. And it worked! Bush got the image he wanted - and Florida got the dope it wanted.

Immediately on taking office, Reagan began the "deregulation" of the savings and loan industry, allowing S&L's to offer any interest rate they wanted and do anything with the money. Reagan's administration regularly approved unqualified hoods for federally-insured bank ownership.[21]

Hood banks often looted their entire cash reserves, lending them to their own front companies, washing the money out the front companies through various transfer tactics, and then declaring the front companies bankrupt, which in turn forced the bank's collapse. The money was gone into hood hands, and the FDIC/FSLIC was liable to reimburse depositors, to the tune of *hundreds* of *billions* of taxpayer money - some estimates go as high as *one trillion dollars* - that's one-seventh the entire annual GNP.[22]

These cooperating hoods and businessmen, Marcello, Beebe, Renda, Mischer, Lyon, Khashoggi, Murchison, Helliwell, Hernandez-Cartaya, Charles, Rebozo, the Bushes, etc. were indistinguishable from the intelligence community and from the Republican establishment, although there are certainly plenty of Democrats on the list as well.[23]

President Bush's Federal Housing Administration Commissioner, Catherine Austin Fitts, Assistant Secretary of Housing under HUD Secretary Jack Kemp, got a close-up look at the *modus operandi* of this establishment. During the Reagan years, Fitts was a Managing Director and Board member of the prestigious Wall Street investment bank Dillon Read & Co. As manager of their huge municipal and government portfolios, she oversaw the financing of multi-billion dollar urban transportation and renewal projects, including the renovation of the NYC subway system. Nicholas Brady, George Bush's Treasury Secretary, was her partner and boss at Dillon Read.

Unlike many of her fellow Reaganauts, Fitts was a religiously-motivated idealist, not a money-motivated hustler. As Bush's manager of the FHA's gigantic $300 billion mortgage and properties portfolio, she set out to revamp the system from the bottom up, whoever's ox got gored. Secretary Kemp, fearing for his oxen, fired Commissioner Fitts.

After leaving at loggerheads with the corrupt bureaucracy she found at HUD, Catherine Austin Fitts did something really remarkable. She showed new HUD Secretary Cisneros, in 1993, how to save taxpayers billions by empowering the very people in danger of defaulting on their HUD mortgages or living in HUD-supported housing.

Using a bottom-up rather than top-down model, Fitts' new Hamilton Securities Group developed a pilot project at a HUD housing project, Edgewood Terrace. Hamilton taught the local women how to use computers to build data bases that tracked the money flowing through their own neighborhood. Since their neighborhood wasn't particularly different than the other 63,000 neighborhoods in HUD's database, what Edgewood Technology Services did was help Hamilton

Securities create software and money management tools applicable to the whole country.

The women of Edgewood Terrace proved that they could be as computer literate as anyone else, given the sweat-equity subsidy, and were rewarded with stock in their company and a decent income doing highly productive work. The real value of Edgewood Terrace property, of course, rose as its pain level dropped. Edgewood Terrace could no longer be bought for pennies on the dollar for condo conversion. Fitts' practical tools for dealing with "How the $ Works and How to Reengineer How the $ Works" can be found at her site, www.solarivillage.com.

One of the obvious things Fitts was able to demonstrate was that HUD was often paying its pet contractors $200,000 per housing unit when perfectly good units were available in the neighborhood for $40,000. But, of course, the cheaper local units weren't owned by HUD-connected contractors.

The politically insubordinate Fitts was viciously, and falsely, attacked by the politicized HUD legal bureaucracy. Her ally, Secretary Cisneros, found that his sex life somehow became more important than his ideas about structural poverty. The painfully expensive legal infighting, however, didn't stifle Fitts' remarkable creativity.

With her 'geo-coded' data base she was able to demonstrate that defaulted HUD mortgages were concentrated in areas of structural poverty, and that those were precisely the "drug areas" the Prohibitionists were most up in arms about. "Freeway" Ricky Ross' Harbor Freeway, running right through the center of South Central L.A., was a concentrated mass of defaulted HUD/FHA single family loans. Fitts' map of defaults looks quite like a pollution-induced disease cluster centered around the Harbor Freeway.

Failure to address neighborhood structural poverty results in a pain-filled neighborhood dependent on the default painkiller economy. The resultant anarchic poverty and violence collapses neighborhood property values. Why pay off an apparently worthless mortgage when it makes more sense to move? Prime urban real estate can then be bought for pennies on the dollar.

And who was buying this prime real estate? The HUD contractors -indistinguishable from the intelligence community and the Republican establishment. The same "liquidators" that had made the neighborhood ripe for a "drug epidemic" in the first place, the same military intelligence operatives dealing the drugs, were using their drug money to buy the now devalued neighborhoods for a pittance -

for cheap conversion into condos, malls and industrial parks. These were the very same radical Prohibitionists demonizing those using the pain killers and then vying for the resultant prison contracts.

Fitts: "Let's look at how the Section 8 owners, managers and tax partnership beneficiaries worked alongside the drug traffickers. Let's look for patterns of loan brokering, money laundering, cleansing and other relationships between real estate, land, prison growth and privatization and the kind of investors who control CIA and intelligence networks. Then let's look how this ties in to campaign fundraising.... Support all this by a national media owned by defense contractors and other corporate interests. That way the nightly news has lots of moneymaking incentives to cover HUD OIG sponsored drug raids in black communities rather than doing a story on CIA drug trafficking."[24]

This was precisely the point made by Malcolm X and Fred Hampton years ago. "Crack" is a fascist red herring, a way of demonizing the symptom rather than the disease. The problem is structural poverty, not too few incarcerated poor. Crack is nothing but a symptom of massive systemic pain. Given the criminalization of the safe herbal painkillers and euphoriants, and the Prohibition-created default economy, crack may have become the euphoriant/painkiller of choice, but the problem is the pain, not the painkiller.

The Bloods, the Crips, the Cobra Stones, and especially the Gangster Disciples, repeatedly stress that they have the inalienable right to participate in the only economy open to them, rather than rotting in abject poverty in the concrete jungle. The Disciples call themselves "Brothers of the Struggle," but their political message is uniformly ignored, even by those supposedly sympathetic to their plight. They're just "drug dealers." These pistoleros are perfectly well aware that "drug dealer" is just another word for "nigger," just as the assassinated Fred Hampton said, and just as it was in the old yellow press. The most important point about the Drug War, for me, is the point that never gets mentioned - it is an *armed rebellion*. Most prisoners of the Drug War are *political* prisoners.

Pointing out that the GAO estimates a total annual cost per prison bed of $154,000, Fitts stressed the insanity of not financing business incubation projects that would leave vulnerable people with an alternative other than the underground economy. But such projects are directly contrary to the interests of the powerful "liquidators" Commissioner Fitts found driving HUD policy.

"But if we assume that taxpayers were paying for 1MM in prison

Drug War

and 4MM in the criminal justice pipeline and then 9MM in public, assisted housing or on welfare, we had a total warehousing population that are 'managed' by a professional bureaucracy of public and private organizations of approximately 15 MM people."

"It would appear that the Crime Bill of 1994 and related politics coming into the 1996 election had the potential to replace most of the drop off from welfare reform and assisted and public housing. The switch to prisons would be very attractive for the 'slug' portion of the business community. We could keep the same 15MM folks out of the market economy in a way that a portion of the business community makes far more dollars. Here is why:

-prisons would mean big construction....

-prisons may mean short term cash benefits to budgets. To the extent that private prison growth occurs through acquisition of state and federal prisons, budget makers may benefit from up front cash proceeds where they do not recognize the cost to the taxpayers of the service contract obligation on a sale-leaseback type of arrangement....

-prisons would mean rural economic development....

-prisons would mean the ability to lock in long term government contracts that could be financed long-term with municipal bonds and the stock market.... Prisons are the one place where the political will exists to do large long-term deals with the private markets, as long as you can keep the media image and the market spin supporting increased sentencing and keep the taxpayers in the dark. Given the ability to do all this off balance sheet, a 1/2 - 1 trillion dollar commitment can be made by the public sector to the private sector and the capital brought in with no public conversation on the overall direction, simply approvals on individual sites once the steamroller is well underway."

"There are several things the Prison Bed Model would need to be ascendant:

-no place-based financial statements or reengineering....

-the 15MM are hopeless. It is critical that black people, minorities, and even women are considered hopeless in terms of being able to provide productive products and services....

-no on line access to education and job opportunity. This game requires that the poor are left behind as much as possible and as long as possible - black and white and city and rural.... This is how we have welfare reform but tremendous opposition to learning centers and business incubation....

-the drug business.... on line education and private community investment does not leave lots of folks available to provide a low cost work force and distribution locations for the drug business, who can then provide the population to feed the prisons in a manner that will produce the headlines necessary to prove that the politicians ...are doing something about drugs.

-get tough on the young and Afro-American, minority and older women. To make the numbers work, the American people have to support the young - men and women - heading into prison while the elderly women die off in assisted and public housing....

-prison industries...."

"The various people we talk with about on line businesses and venture capital in communities reject our notions that low-income minority urban and white rural populations can be productive in a variety of functions. However, the a-similar group seem to believe that this population can be quite productive when they are working in prisons and their salaries are going to pay for the prison or the state. What is so frightening is that the implications to the taxpayers of not offering education and employment alternatives to drug dealing and criminal activities, means that the whole country will go bankrupt from the drug business twice. Once, from losing potential taxpayers to the criminal justice system. Second, to paying to warehouse them in it. Taxpayers make much more money with folks working from home rather than prison. No one has illuminated the numbers. The political spin is very much based [on the idea] that the promotion of prisons is good for taxpayers."[25]

And the conformist Black leaders, "role models" who stupidly blame the symptoms for the disease, just like they're supposed to, support the massive arrest and imprisonment of their own people. They buy into the fascist line that "values" have to be enforced by law. Whose values? General Dynamics'?

Jesse Jackson commiserated with General McCaffrey on CNN, 1/25/98: "Somehow it seems that our own appetite, maybe our society is so wealthy or so egregious, some kind of values crisis here is driving the demand. But what about the supply? It seems that in a couple of countries that there is some slowing down of the drug supply. But Mexico, it seems to be 70 percent of the drug flow. How can we stop it coming from the greatest source?" This was McCaffrey's cue to explain that victory is just around the corner if we'll just keep beefing up the Mexican army and expanding the police function of the military.

Charming Charlie Rangel, the D.A., made a career of throwing "my people" into prison before he became the Black Richmond P. Hobson. Jackson, at least, consistently uses the word "fascist" to describe the dope dealers, but, since he is an unempirical theocrat, has absolutely nothing original to offer in the way of policy. He quite rightly calls for "an urban policy" while, at the same time, in the same sentence, calling for "a real War on Drugs."[26] If he were a baseball player, his nickname would be "Clueless."

Garvey, center; Jake Homiak, Smithsonian Institution

Jackson consistently portrays African-American culture as if it were composed entirely of middle-class Baptists. I never hear the Rastafarians I smoked with in the back of so many subway cars mentioned. The largest mass-movement in African -American history was overtly shamanic, overtly tribal African. Marcus Garvey's Universal

Negro Improvement Association was an awesome force throughout the Caribbean, North and South America in the 1920's. Those Africans revered their ancient tribal sacramentalism.

The criminalization of African sacraments was a basic part of the of the cultural genocide necessary for enslavement. The Rastafarian memory of history is simply photographic. This memory is very much alive on the Mau Mau streets. Thanks to the ruthless cultural genocide directed at them, many young African-American shamans would rather go down fighting with their local posse.

But, since Jackson and Rangel are adamantly amnesiac about their own tribal roots, they can only peck around the edges of policy. By not fighting the militarization of American culture, the conformist Black politicos collaborate in the diversion of billions that should be going into structural sweat-equity antipoverty programs, to which they pay only lip service. Instead, they help the fascists demonize their own young. This has not only confused the Black community, but split it right down the middle, completely destroying the unity that made it such a formidable force during the days of the civil rights struggle.

"Taking drugs is a sin," says Jesse, a Dope with Hope. "Since the flow of drugs into the U.S. is an act of terrorism, antiterrorist policies must be applied."[27] That's just what the KKK's Hobson said, and that's just what L.A. police chief Daryl Gates did, telling the Senate that "casual drug users" should "be taken out and shot."[28] Well, beaten to a pulp with nightsticks, anyway.

Has this brutality made the situation better or worse?

William Moffitt of The National Association of Criminal Defense Lawyers, agreeing with the defendants in a case before the Supreme Court that the statistical evidence proves racially biased enforcement, was rebutted on the *Today* show, 2/26/96, by Attorney General Janet Reno. Reno, determined to out-Republican the Republicans, insisted that "crack is a tremendously violence-inciting drug," and that therefore the Republican hicks have it right. How is that a defense against selective enforcement? Niggers are violent?

It is true, of course, that if you smash Snoop Doggy Dogg in the face with a nightstick while he's smoking some crack he's liable to get violent, but that's the nightstick working, not the crack. Crack is just cocaine stretched and rendered smokable by heating it with baking soda and water. The resultant crystals "crack" when smoked. This simple cutting technique makes it much cheaper than powder, since it is not only diluted in an edible base, but smoked. The lungs absorb vapor far more efficiently than the nose absorbs powder, delivering an immediate, ecstatic painkilling flush.

In December of 1990 Judge Pamela Alexander in Minnesota's Hennepin County Court threw out the crack possession convictions of five Black defendants as racist. Minnesota's Office of Drug Policy had officially concluded that *there was no pharmacological difference between crack and powder*, and therefore, concluded Judge Alexander, the Draconian sentence for miniscule quantities of crack was culturally, or economically, prejudicial.[29]

A 1989 government study of all 193 "cocaine-related" murders in New York City concluded that 87% grew out of fights over money or dealing territory, and almost all the others were also alcohol-related. In only one case was the perpetrator actually high on coke. Professor Goldstein's study of New York's 218 "drug-related" murders during 8 months of 1988 came to exactly the same conclusion. In only one case could cocaine be shown to have actually been a possible pharmacological contributant to a homicidal mania.[30] If cross-examined, Attorney General Janet "violence-inciting drug" Reno will no doubt proudly admit that she knows nothing at all about pharmacology.[31]

George Bush's favorite Nark was LAPD Chief Daryl Gates, so tolerant of police racism that he sparked the 1992 L. A. riots. Asked to account for the high number of police nightstick choke-hold deaths inflicted during his tenure, Gates explained that "We may be finding that in some Blacks, when [the choke-hold] is applied, the veins or arteries do not open as fast as they do on normal people."[32]

Between 1978 and 1988, virtually the entire job base of South Central Los Angeles collapsed as manufacturers and warehouses fled to more stable locations. Unemployment in South Central soared to 60% or more. Reagan cut CETA, Comprehensive Employment and Training Act funds, and eliminated the Job Corps. Los Angeles itself allocated virtually no funds to South Central's parks or libraries, and actually eliminated the municipal Summer Job Program. There was almost no legal way for many young people in South Central to make a living. LAPD Chief Gates, in April 1988, then announced that the problem was crack cocaine.

Gates institutionalized Operation Hammer, massively funded by the Bush administration. Gates rousted the young Black men of South Central for virtually anything at all - dress, hairstyle, curfew. The LAPD, between 1988 and 1992, arrested 75% of all the young Black men in LA. 90% of those arrested were released without charges, but their names went into the counterinsurgency database. I can't remember being more enraged as a kid in the Bronx than when I was rousted for nothing at all on my own home grounds. It was a denial of my right to be there. Daryl Gates was the best recruiter the Crip guerrillas ever had.[33]

As of early 1994, 1500 Black Americans per 100,000 were behind bars. The figure for Whites was 210 per 100,000.[34] As of 1997, the U.S. had an incredible 645 people per 100,000 behind bars, while rates in countries such as Canada, France, Germany, Finland, Sweden and Australia varied from 40 to 125 per 100,000. Our imprisonment rate is higher than the world's worst police states, literally the highest in the world. 60% of all federal, and 25% of all state prisoners are there on drug charges.

In 1993, 2.3 million Black men were sent to the slammer while 23,000 received a college degree - that's a hundred to one. *That's* what's fascistic about all that "role model" propaganda - the 1% are "role models" - the 99% are "dealers," "niggers." By mid-1997 there were 100,000 federal prison inmates, 1,060,000 state prisoners and 600,000 in municipal lockups - and 51% of them were Black.[35]

Blacks comprise about 15% of the U.S. population. We leave millions of ghetto kids unemployed, without neighborhood social centers, to fend for themselves amidst Prohibition-created violence and economics, throw their parents in the slammer for medicating their own pain, hunt them like wolves - and then act surprised when they turn into wolf packs. Some Republican from Kansas, working for the contractor lobby, then gets righteously indignant on the floor of Congress and decides that day-care money would be better spent on more new prisons.

Gary Webb, in his seminal *Dark Alliance*: "The CIA's secret warriors [militarily led by Gen. McCaffrey] were not only killing the citizens of Nicaragua, Honduras, and Costa Rica, but ...were using L.A.'s inner city as an addict base from which to draw money to buy their guns. At the same time the Contras was being sold to American citizens as their great, shining hope for freedom and democracy in Latin America, they were providing the demons for the Reagan Administration's hyperbolic War on Drugs at home. The Contras [as Webb documents in detail] were largely to blame for the birth of the L.A. crack market. They were part of why the L.A. gangs had gotten so powerful and fearsome. And those developments were part of the reason for the Draconian anti-crack laws that came out of Washington that summer, a product of the Congressional stampede whipped up by all the lurid anti-crack propaganda the media was carrying. It was a self-perpetuating cycle, nice and neat, with obvious benefits for both foreign and domestic policy initiatives."[36]

That is, from the perspective of the "liquidators," there is no difference between Angelinos and Campesinos. Economic fascism, corporate colonialism, is indeed threatened by prosperous, empowered campesinos because they represent an economic model that could easily spread throughout the third world, quite like Fitts' bottom-up American model. The little domino that finally snuffed the drug-dealing, U.S.-run maniac Anastasio Somoza Debayle, whose family virtually owned Nicaragua from 1934 to 1979, was therefore viewed as a serious threat by the Reagan/Bush administration. It could become a model for the entire region.

Immediately on assuming office, Reagan's CIA Director William Casey, OSS veteran, mob partner and mob lawyer,[37] Nixon's SEC chairman, went into action against the Sandinistas. He arranged with his Cocaine Coup partners, Argentine President-designate Gen. Roberto Viola and Chief of Staff General Alvaro Martínez, Gen. Suárez Mason's boss, to use veteran trainers from their dirty war to remold the remnants of Somoza's National Guard. They called themselves the Nicaraguan Democratic Force, the FDN, but the Sandinistas' derisive nickname, "the Contras," was the one that stuck. This effort was begun by CIA cutouts Videla of Argentina and Stroessner of Paraguay immediately on the fall of Somoza, a year before Reagan took office in 1980, under Carter's orders.

Anastasio Somoza García and Augusto Sandino, just prior to Somoza's assassnation of Sandino; Nicaraguan National Archives

In 1934, the elder Somoza, at the head of the U.S.-trained National Guard, secured his power by assassinating the dashing Augusto Sandino, a charismatic poet and mystical socialist revolutionary. Sandino had fought the U.S. Marines and the puppet Nicaraguan government to a standstill in a spectacular 7-year guerrilla war. He was assassinated under a flag of truce, while peacefully negotiating a coalition government.

U.S. Marines operating against Sandino, 1929; Butler, left, on maneuvers with his troops, 1924. Only his collar stars distinguish him from a rank-and-file leatherneck.

Gen. Smedley Butler, 1881-1940, the legendary Marine sent to track down Sandino's predecessors, was so disgusted by the cruelty and slave-labor he encountered that he concluded Sandino was right.

The Capture of Fort Riviere, Haiti, 1915; Major Butler, Sergeant Iams and Private Gross are pictured in the action that won them the Congressional Medal of Honor; by Colonel D.J. Neary, USMCR; Marine Corps Art Collection, Washington, DC

To say that Butler is a Marine legend is an understatement. He is *the* Marine legend, one of the few to win the Congressional Medal of Honor twice. He was a frontline hero of every major conflict the U.S.

participated in during the first quarter of this century, including the Boxer Rebellion, the Spanish-American War and the Great War.

In 1935, after vocally supporting his fellow WW I veterans in their Bonus Army March - to the consternation of his own former high command - Butler reflected, "I spent thirty-three years and four months in active service as a member of our country's most agile military force-the Marine corps. I served in all commissioned ranks from a second lieutenant to major general. And during the period I spent most of my time being a high-class muscle man for Big Business, for Wall Street and, for the bankers. In short, I was a racketeer for capitalism."

José de Paredes, Augusto Sandino and Augustín Farabundo Martí

"Thus I helped make Mexico...safe for American oil interests in 1914. I helped make Haiti and Cuba a decent place for the National City Bank to collect revenues in... I helped purify Nicaragua for the international banking house of Brown Brothers in 1909-1912. I brought light to the Dominican Republic for American sugar interests in 1916. I helped make Honduras "right" for American fruit companies in

1903."

Sandino, 1928; Butler on his Chinese show-the-flag mission, 1928

Butler was disgusted by the stealthy assassination of Sandino, a legitimately elected populist democrat. He felt humiliated to have been an indirect part of it. After that, Butler repeatedly insisted that the interests of the corporations weren't worth the life of a single one of his boys. *"War is a Racket,"* wrote this marvelous old warrior. "Only a small 'inside' group knows what it is about. It is conducted for the benefit of the very few, at the expense of the very many. Out of war a few people make huge fortunes.... How many of these war millionaires shouldered a rifle?"[38] His small book then goes on to excoriate, by name, the multinational corporations then running Central American politics for their own advantage.

Like Emiliano Zapata and Joe Hill, of course, Augusto Sandino never really died. After they took power in July of 1979, the Sandinista National Liberation Front won an award from the World Health Organization for the radical drop in the infant mortality rate they engineered. Their budget stressed health care and education, and they instituted an effective land reform program which enabled their rural campesinos to become self-sufficient.

The Sandinistas turned the huge absentee-owned coffee, cotton and banana plantations, export monocrop slave-labor factories, into diversified family farms or community-owned cooperatives. Women with key roles in rural health and vaccination programs were also encouraged to lead the rural literacy programs. These were often organized around church Bible study groups.[39]

It was these programs that President Carter wisely backed with $125 million in aid. Carter's *quid pro quo*, which the Sandinistas were perfectly happy to live with, was that they not ship arms to the rebels in El Salvador. Of course, when the Reagan administration blocked Carter's funds and started attacking Nicaraguan campesinos with an army of *Somocista* murderers, the deal was off.

In 1985, Daniel Ortega, in response to questions put to him by Peruvian writer Mario Vargas Llosa on behalf of Venezuelan President Jaime Lusinchi, repeated what had always been the Sandinista position: "We're willing to send home the Cubans, the Russians, the rest of the advisors. We're willing to stop the movement of military aid, or any other kind of aid, through Nicaragua to El Salvador, and we're willing to accept international verification. In return, we're asking for only one thing: that they don't attack us, that the United States stop arming and financing the gangs that kill our people, burn our crops and force us to divert enormous human and economic resources into war when we desperately need them for development."[40]

But stopping Sandinista development was precisely the point. The Sandinistas weren't building from a top down, IMF-defined production-for-export model, they were building from the bottom up. It's the difference between a Nicaragua that is an agricultural giant able to grow all its own food, and a nation of serfs dependent on absentee-owned factories and plantations producing for export. It's the difference between campesino-owned family farms, and sweatshop slums peopled by ex-campesinos, who must trade their miserable wages for cupfuls of imported U.S. grain. This is not a question of capitalism vs. socialism, because independent family farms are capitalist institutions. It's a question of a "national and independent capitalism vs. feudalism," as Jacobo Arbenz put it - owners vs. sharecroppers.

Prosperous family farms, of course, generate buying power. But that buying power isn't consumerist, it's tribal - spent on local goods and services. In 1983, the Inter-American Development Bank declared that the Sandinistas' "noteworthy progress in the social sector" was "laying a solid foundation for long-term socioeconomic development." The World Bank called Nicaragua's development under the Sandinistas "remarkable.... better than anywhere in the world."[41] That, of course, was before the massive U.S. warfare and economic sanctions took their toll.

If Sandinista economic nationalism spread to neighboring countries, what would become of the absentee landlords? As Nixon's Secretary of State Henry Kissinger succinctly put it, "I don't see why we need to stand by and watch a country go communist due to the irresponsibility of its own people."[42]

The Contra staging areas, originally set up under Carter, were in Guatemala and Honduras. Mario Sandoval Alarcón's MLN played the role of host in Guatemala.[43] In 1978 the President of Guatemala was the unelected General Romeo Lucas García, former president Laugerud's defense minister. Lucas and Sandoval were particular favorites of Reagan's constituency.

In December of 1979 a delegation from the American Security Council, led by "retired" Generals John Singlaub and Daniel Graham - the one a very high ranking CIA agent and the other, Graham, a former Director of the Defense Intelligence Agency - visited Lucas in Guatemala City. They denounced Carter for calling this mass-murderer a mass-murderer and cutting off military aid. Lucas was promised that Reagan would resume military aid as soon as he took office.

Singlaub and Graham were followed by the Young Americans for Freedom, the Heritage Foundation, the Moral Majority and the Center for Strategic and International Studies. Pat Robertson and Jerry Falwell prayed for "mercy helicopters" for Lucas. The Guatemalan leader of this publicity campaign was none other than Roberto Alejos Arzu, whose *finca* in Retalhuleu had been the staging area for the Bay of Pigs invasion.[44] The CIA's very own Vernon Walters, who represented the interests of an oil company, Basic Resources, in Guatemala, also made a point of stroking Lucas.

Reagan, of course, did resume both overt and covert military aid, from Taiwan, Israel and Argentina, which was immediately put to use by Lucas in a "pacification" plan designed by U.S. military experts.[45] In May of 1982 the Guatemalan Conference of Bishops, a very conservative group, declared that "never in our history have such extremes been reached, with the assassinations now falling into the category of genocide."[46] These same Church officials estimated that Lucas killed as many as 150,000 Guatemalans.

Obviously, the guerrillas gained many new adherents as Lucas resorted to burning their highland forests, causing, like Saddam Hussein, massive, irreversible environmental destruction.[47] A destruction, oddly enough, almost never mentioned in the American mass media, which prefers to fixate on celebrity sexuality, plane crashes and wacko loners.

On Feb. 11, 1982, three months after President Reagan first formally authorized covert CIA operations against the Sandinistas in National Security Decision Directive 17, Attorney General William French

Smith, at DCI Casey's request, released the CIA from its legal responsibility to report the narcotics law violations of its own contractors.

Smith's letter to Casey was published as part of CIA Inspector General Frederick Hitz' 1/29/98 report to Congress on Contra-CIA drug connections. The letter was read into the Congressional Record on 5/7/98 by L.A.'s enraged Rep. Maxine Waters, despite the CIA's insistence that the entire report was "classified." It is interesting that Smith didn't release the CIA from any of its other responsibilities under federal law - the requirement to report murder, Neutrality Act violations, espionage, arson, etc. - but only the requirement to report narcotics law violations.

A series of concomitant Executive Orders and National Security Decision Directives, many of which have been declassified, reveal that Vice-President Bush, the former DCI, had formal executive control of all Reagan administration intelligence operations, and was, in fact, DCI Casey's commanding officer.

The set up for Casey's ability to dictate law enforcement to the Attorney General was Reagan's Executive Order #12333, also dating to Nov., 1981, the week he formally sicked the CIA on the Sandinistas. The new rules required the CIA to sign off on the Justice Department's crimes reporting procedures. Casey's request for the narcotics reporting exemption, then, was more of a demand.

The AG complied, 2/11/82: "Dear Bill:.... In light of these provisions, and in view of the fine cooperation the Drug Enforcement Administration has received from CIA, no formal requirement regarding the reporting of narcotics violations has been included in these procedures."[48]

This legal exemption was an organic part of the initial administration planning for Contra operations, indicating a premeditated conspiracy to do what the Reagan administration actually did - operate a massive, illegal, international drugs-for-arms network.

May 14, 1982: "National Security Decision Directive 3, Crisis Management, establishes the Special Situation Group (SSG), chaired by the Vice President. The SSG is charged...with formulating plans in anticipation of crises.... [Relevant agencies are to] provide the name of their CPPG [Crisis Pre-Planning Group] representative to Oliver North, NSC staff...." The memo was signed "for the President" by Reagan's national security adviser, William Clark, and declassified during the Iran-Contra hearings.

Later spin-offs of this structure, which cut "non-operational" State Department people out of the loop, included the Vice President's Task

Force on Combatting Terrorism, and the Operations Sub-Group, composed of the same people - Bush, Gregg, Clarridge, North, Poindexter, Allen, Oakley, Koch, Moellering, Revell and others.

Their first crisis was not long in coming. On December 21, 1982, Congress passed the Boland amendment to the Defense Appropriations Act: "None of the funds provided in this Act may be used by the Central Intelligence Agency or the Department of Defense to furnish military equipment, military training or advice, or other support for military activities, to any group or individual ... for the purpose of overthrowing the government of Nicaragua."

Mass murder in Guatemala, apparently, was not proscribed. The transparent Lucas was replaced as President in late 1982 by Gen. Efraín Ríos Montt, a graduate of just about every counterinsurgency course offered by the U.S. military. Although Ríos Montt's "Plan Victoria" was simply a repeat of Lucas' highland scorched earth policy, his line was smoother. This enabled the January 1984 Kissinger Commission to certify the great human rights improvement wrought by this more subtle lunatic, so massive overt military aid was resumed.

This resulted in the Constitution of 1985, which redefined Guatemala as a CIA-KMT militarized state, replete with pacified model villages, into which the survivors of the genocide were herded. They were required to participate in "civil defense" units that were subject to strangely sadistic military discipline. The courts handed down such sentences as "death by pummeling." Those chosen campesinos who refused to pummel their own neighbors to death were themselves subject to the same punishment. "Development projects" on all levels of government were planned by the military, thereby effectively turning the captive campesinos into military slave labor.[49]

At this time Roberto D'Aubuisson was deputy chief of the CIA-created and funded Salvadoran National Security Agency, ANSESAL. Working with Guatemala's Sandoval, Nicaragua's Somoza and his Salvadoran allies Cuellar and Santivañez, D'Aubuisson used ANSESAL to form the Armed Forces of National Liberation - War of Extermination, the FALANGE. D'Aubuisson's FALANGE spawned the White Warriors Union, the Secret Anticommunist Army and other contract death squads. Pursuant to his CIA-KMT training, D'Aubuisson gave his death squads a political base by forming the party of the Army, the Nationalist Republican Alliance, ARENA.

D'Aubuisson reacted to the October 1979 Salvadoran coup engineered by reformist junior officers by activating his death squads. First he killed the attorney general of the new pluralist government, Mario

Zamora, brother of FMLN leader Rubén Zamora. Then, in March 1980, D'Aubuisson went after his next most dangerous critic, the Archbishop, who was shot through the heart while giving mass.[50] Archbishop Oscar Romero had insisted that the neighboring Sandinistas were preoccupied with their own development and therefore were no military threat to El Salvador.

In a famous letter sent just before his death, the Archbishop begged President Carter not to aid ARENA's military. He said such aid would be used to "sharpen injustice and repression against the people's organizations" which were struggling "for respect for their most basic human rights." Nicaragua's Sandinistas, said the Archbishop, seemed to be acting more like Christians than Communists. The morality inherent in their economic model reflected the true message of Christ, and therefore was a good economic model for El Salvador. Salvadorans, added the Archbishop, were right to insist on absolute freedom of speech and regular democratic elections.

"You can be a Communist," explained Roberto D'Aubuisson, "even if you personally don't believe you are a Communist."[51] Ten days after the murder of the Archbishop, Roberto D'Aubuisson explained to his American Republican supporters, in a meeting room of the U.S. House of Representatives, that "In order to define the State Department policy, we could use this axiom: who is a communist? Those who consciously or unconsciously collaborate with the Soviet cause. We can ascertain that present [Carter] State Department policy toward Central America has candidly favored communist infiltration."[52] That was, word for word, the line peddled at the 1980 Buenos Aires meeting of the CIA's *Confederación Anticomunista Latina*, CAL, that D'Aubuisson would attend in September, in celebration of the Bolivian Cocaine Coup.

Also attending the September 1980 CIA/CAL celebration was John Carbaugh, an aide to Republican Senator Jesse Helms. Helms, a rabid red-baiting segregationist in the 1950's, was an enthusiastic supporter of the fascists.[53] As a ranking member of the Senate Foreign Relations Committee, of course, Helms knew all there was to know about the death squads, but that didn't stop him from solemnly taking testimony from ARENA's distinguished killers. Between 1980 and 1992 Helms helped funnel $6 billion into the Salvadoran military.

Hobnobbing with Carbaugh at the CAL confab was Stefano delle Chiaie, Barbie's top aide. Carbaugh had extensive personal contact with D'Aubuisson, and was instrumental in packaging the ARENA publicity campaign in Washington. Also attending the 1980 CAL meeting was Margo Carlisle, legislative aide to Senator James McClure (R-ID) and staff director of the Republican Conference of the U.S. Senate. Carbaugh and Carlisle hired Mackenzie-McCheyne to handle ARENA's advertising, while Paul Weyrich taught ARENA operatives effective campaign tactics.

In 1980 ARENA killed at least 10,000 Salvadorans, including quite a few members of the new progressive junta, which collapsed under the terror. In July of 1980 D'Aubuisson was fêted in Washington by the Heritage Foundation, the Council for Inter-American Security, the American Security Council and the American Legion. ARENA became, under Reagan, the very symbol of democratic liberalism and the recipient of all the military hardware it could absorb. When the going got too tough for the freedom fighters of ARENA, of course, they could always count on American jets to drop high explosives and napalm on El Salvador's desperate campesinos. The ranks of the FMLN, the Marti Front for National Liberation, swelled, as whole villages were incinerated.

The Contras were led by the CIA's Enrique Bermúdez, who had been Somoza's military liaison in Washington. *Somocista* National Guard Maj. Ricardo Lau, Bermúdez' counterintelligence chief, worked with D'Aubuisson to set up the Contra supply system operating out of Ilopango in El Salvador, headquarters of the U.S. Military Group.[54] Lau was accused by former Salvadoran intelligence chief Col. Roberto Santivañez of accepting $120,000 from D'Aubuisson to use his Contra death squad to assassinate Archbishop Romero. Three days after Romero's murder, D'Aubuisson travelled to Guatemala to personally give the Contras that amount. Lau's name and telephone number were on the checks.[55]

The CIA's chief of Latin American operations, Dewey Clarridge, oversaw the distribution to Contra troops of the CIA training manual, *Psychological Operations in Guerrilla Warfare*.[56] The manual suggests "Selective Violence for Propagandistic Effects" and "Implicit and Explicit Terror." *Psychological Operations in Guerilla Warfare* was based on the 1968 lesson plans of the Army Special Warfare School at Fort Bragg.[57] It is quite sophisticated and well written, borrowing as much from Ho Chi Minh, Mao Zedong and the Huks as from the Third Reich.

American "counterinsurgency" or "pacification" doctrine has taught, since Sherman's Civil War and the brutal turn of the century massacre of tens of thousands of Filipinos, the most ruthless terror in "Indian territory." As refined by Generals Sherman, Sheridan, Bell and Lansdale, "benevolence" in the pacified or protected areas has been the traditional carrot to the stick of "free fire zones" and the ostentatious massacres of civilians "for propagandistic effect."

Contra troops specialized in the blowing up of school buses full of little children, the rape, mutilation and murder of young girls, and the use of children's heads spitted on stakes as warnings not to attend government schools. The women rural literacy volunteers were also special targets for rape and mutilation. The regular bayonetting of infants is also well documented.[58] Clinton's Drug Czar, Gen. Barry McCaffrey, was the Green Beret coordinator with these operations. Reagan, in a famous phrase that has come to epitomize his hypocrisy, called the Contras "the moral equal of our Founding Fathers."[59] Pat Robertson's Christian Broadcasting Network raised millions for these moral avatars, most of which ended up in secret bank accounts in the Cayman Islands.

Clarridge's predecessor as head of the CIA's Latin American Division, Nestor Sanchez, had been moved up to the Pentagon's Bureau of International Security Affairs, from which he was able to support Clarridge in the field. Sanchez had been the CIA's deputy chief of station in Guatemala in 1954. Clarridge's assistant, Vincent Canistraro, was transferred to the White House National Security Staff office of Oliver North, the Vietnam vet who was the NSC's counterterrorism director. Even most of the State Department people dealing with Latin America were veterans of Operation Phoenix and other "rural pacification" programs - many, like Clarridge, unable even to speak Spanish. Green Beret Barry McCaffrey, his hands drenched with Vietnamese blood, arrived at the U.S. Southern Command in 1969 as a "counterinsurgency expert." Commented the *Washington Post*, 11/28/82, "The Gang That Blew Vietnam Goes Latin."

That gang had plenty of Latin charter members. Bay of Pigs and Operation Phoenix vet Felix Rodriguez coordinated Contra supply flights out of Ilopango in El Salvador. According to Bush aide Gregg, his boss in Vietnam's mass-murdering Operation Phoenix, Rodriguez was a genius with napalm. He pioneered its use on the campesinos of El Salvador. From 1979 to 1981 these maniacs killed 30,000 Salvadorans, most innocent campesinos, and their children, in SS-style death-squad massacres, their theory being, quite literally, the Nazi theory of rule by terror.

In May, 1980, at the Sumpul River crossing, more than 600 unarmed men, women and children were machine gunned to death by cooperating Salvadoran and Honduran troops on either bank as they tried to flee Salvadoran territory into Honduras. Little children, caught in the middle of the river, were cut to ribbons.

In December of 1981, at the villages surrounding El Mozote in El Salvador, more than 800 defenseless people were massacred, according to the Salvadoran Catholic Church.[60] In 1992, *Tutela Legal*, the legal arm of the Salvadoran Church, hired the distinguished international experts of the Argentine Forensic Anthropology Team to conduct excavations at El Mozote. In the ruins of a single-room building attached to the village church, the team found 143 human skeletons, 131 of which were children under the age of 12. They had all been machine-gunned to death by standard U.S. Army issue M-16 ammunition manufactured at the Lake City Plant in Independence, Missouri. That was the ammo used by the Atlacatl Batallion, which had been formed by experts from the U.S. Army School of Special Forces in March of 1981, Barry McCaffrey's outfit.

Aside from massacre by rifle fire, the Atlacatl Batallion and its clones practiced rape, decapitation and disembowelment on a massive scale. By 1982, 600,000 Salvadorans were left homeless - and terrified enough to stop demanding any political rights at all.[61]

The CIA-Contra military plan run by Gen. McCaffrey and Col. Steele out of Milgroup at Ilopango was based on the same idea as the Bay of Pigs. The idea was to seize a patch of Nicaraguan territory, 1500 square miles of uninhabited mountains in fact, and force overt U.S. military intervention in support of "Free Nicaragua." But even the CIA couldn't sell that one to the Joint Chiefs. They knew that an overt U.S. invasion of Nicaragua would be a bloody nightmare. The Pentagon's Rand Corporation estimated that the popular Sandinistas could bog down 100,000 U.S. troops almost indefinitely.[62] That, of course, would completely enrage all our Latin friends. Colombia, Mexico, Panama and Venezuela - the Contadora group - were in fact quite sympathetic to the Sandinistas, traded with them extensively, and violently opposed military intervention.

The *Somocistas*, at any rate, had so little popular support they couldn't hold a mountaintop long enough to dig a deep latrine.[63] They could hit, and they could run. The CIA, and certainly the State Department, did what it could to patch together a centrist coalition of Nicaraguans who weren't *Somocistas*, but their coalition had no operational control of "their" military. 46 of the 48 top Contra leaders were CIA *Somocistas*, that is, former officers of Somoza's National Guard.[64] The other two, apparently, just liked killing. An August 1985 incident is typical. When the Contras couldn't hold the town of La Trinidad for more than five hours, the time it took Sandinista troops to reach them, they beheaded quite a few townspeople by way of farewell.[65]

The mountaintop fortress of Ilopango; Castillo

The frustrated CIA then hit on the bright idea of blowing up international shipping in Nicaragua's harbors with mines, a transparently illegal act of international terrorism. In fact if Nicaragua had done that to the United States, it would have constituted legal grounds for a declaration of war. Hundreds of mines were placed in January and February of 1984. The small mines, designed to be nonlethal, sank a few fishing boats and punched holes in a few freighters, but had no effect whatever on Nicaragua's trade. The U.S., however, found itself facing a losing case in the World Court. And the Soviet Union was provided with the pretext it needed to begin delivering Mi-25 Hind helicopter gunships, the "flying tanks" Daniel Ortega was now convinced he needed.

A humiliated Congress, facing the outrage of all our allies, led by the chairman of the Senate Select Intelligence Committee, Barry Goldwater, whose advance consent was supposedly required for such an operation, ended the entire Contra aid program. "The second Boland amendment" banned any further consideration of Contra aid until March of 1985. Contra aid continued unabated, however, since Congress couldn't find a way to end the illegal cocaine, heroin, pot or arms trade.

The Honduran airline SETCO, according to the Kerry Subcommittee, "was the principal company used by the Contras in Honduras to transport supplies and personnel for the FDN...from 1983 through 1985....SETCO received funds for Contra supply operations from the Contra accounts established by Oliver North."[66]

Choppers returning Contra troops to Ilopango from Nicaragua; Castillo

SETCO was run by Juan Ramón Matta Ballesteros, an agent of the Mexican DFS who had worked with the legendary Mexican-based CIA Cuban Alberto Sicilia Falcón. Matta, a Honduran chemist, had helped Sicilia set up his Andean cocaine connections.[67]

Matta was hunted as a major drug kingpin by the DEA throughout the 70's. The DEA first arrested him in 1970 at Dulles Airport with 54 pounds of cocaine, but that was in his small-time early days.[68] When Sicilia fell in 1976, Matta inherited much of his network, including a heroin franchise from Guadalajara's great opium grower and heroin manufacturer Miguel Angel Felix Gallardo and a cocaine distribution franchise from the Medellín cartel.

Matta, and his Guadalajara cartel partners, ran the "Mexican trampoline" that bounced cocaine from Colombia into the U.S. They became the business partners of Gen. Policarpo Paz García, and in 1978 financed the *Honduran* "Cocaine Coup" that brought Paz into power.

Both worked with Col. Gustavo Álvarez Martínez, head of the Public Security Forces (FUSEP), the secret police. Both also worked with Norwin Meneses, brother of three of Somoza's leading officers and the chief contact of the dying Somoza regime with the great cocaine cartels of Bolivia and Colombia. Webb quotes a recently declassified 1986 CIA cable describing Meneses as "the kingpin of narcotics traffickers in Nicaragua prior to the fall of Somoza." Meneses went on, of course, to finance the Contras the same way, contributing mightily to the smog in L.A. A 1990 DEA report describes Meneses and his key California distributor, *Somocista* Danilo Blandón, as heading "a criminal organization that operates internationally from Colombia and Bolivia, through Bahamas, Costa Rica, or Nicaragua to the United States."[69]

Matta and Paz also worked with Álvarez' CIA-DIA contact, Maj. Gen. Robert Schweitzer, a director of strategy for the Army's deputy chief of staff for operations. Schweitzer had been engineering the use of Honduras as a *Somocista* base since early 1980, a year before Reagan took office. Much of the financing for this effort came, either directly or through the likes of Meneses, from Bolivian cocaine baron Roberto Suárez. Since Schweitzer promised these ballsy entrepreneurs an avalanche of largesse from the U.S. military, they volunteered to help him supply the Contras. Bush/Casey made Schweitzer an advisor to the National Security Council.[70]

The CIA's chief of Latin American operations, Dewey Clarridge, visited Paz, Álvarez and Torres-Arias, chief of Honduran military intelligence, in Honduras in August of 1981. He brought with him Col. Mario Davico, the vice chief of Argentine military intelligence, one of the engineers of the ongoing dirty war and the recent Bolivian Cocaine Coup, also financed by Bolivian cocaine baron Roberto Suárez.[71]

As soon as new President Roberto Suazo Córdova took power in January 1982, he elevated Álvarez, who had studied terror in Argentina under Videla and Davico, to total command of the Honduran military. Enrique Bermúdez solidified the Contra position in Honduras in December of 82 by appointing Álvarez' classmate in Argentina, *Somocista Guardia* officer Emilio Echaverry, as his chief of staff. Col. Leonidas Torres-Arias, the chief of military intelligence, succeeded Álvarez as head of FUSEP.

Col. Torres-Arias had been running the Mexican trampoline with Matta for years. Álvarez understood that the power this conferred on Torres-Arias could prove to be a threat to his own position, since Torres-Arias, like Álvarez, was functioning from within Honduran military intelligence. That is, for instance, cocaine either seized or imported by Honduran military intelligence was funneled to the likes of Norwin Meneses in California, for distribution there, or to the Florida Cubans, Colombians and Jamaicans, for distribution throughout the Southeast. Meneses was not a competitor of the CIA Cubans, rather a financier and close associate of several members of Brigade 2506.[72] Webb's detailed documentation of Meneses' L.A. distribution is a microcosm of a multi-billion dollar system that supplied cocaine to urban centers worldwide. These days, L.A. isn't that different than To-kyo.

One of the most interesting revelations in Webb's seminal *Dark Alliance* is his documentation of the role of drug importer and arms manufacturer Ronald Lister, who contracted with the CIA to set up covert Contra arms factories in El Salvador. Lister worked closely with Roberto D'Aubuisson and the Barry McCaffrey-trained Atlacatl Batallion, perpetrators of the El Mozote massacre, on this project. The L.A.-based Lister was an important Meneses operative, making formal arms presentations to the Contra leadership, selling Meneses' great L.A. distributor Freeway Ricky Ross' Crips much of their considerable arsenal, and overseeing the delivery of the occasional boatload of cocaine.

When an LAPD narcotics squad raided Lister's house in 1986, they seized a ten-page note handwritten by Lister, detailing weapons deals. The list included the names of the CIA-financed Ray Prendes, former head of the Salvadoran Christian Democrats; ARENA assassin Roberto D'Aubuisson; and Bill Nelson, from 1973 to 1976 the CIA's chief of covert operations.[73] It was Nelson who ran the 1973 Chile operation that overthrew Allende.

Lister's other notes included repeated references to the Contras and the Defense Intelligence Agency, then currently illegally supplying arms to the Contras using contractors dispersed throughout South America. SM-90 machine guns, for instance, were manufactured at two separate Bolivian facilities, and sold not only to the Contras, but to the FARC guerrillas in Colombia as well. This effort, happily supported by the Bolivian high command, reinforced the value of two of Bolivia's chief exports, arms, and the cocaine used to finance them.

Contra purchases of Lister's covert CIA/DIA/NSA arms were largely financed by the cocaine Meneses bought from, or with, Honduran military intelligence. By removing Torres-Arias as head of the Honduran secret police, Honduran army chief Álvarez became Matta's new senior partner in the Mexican trampoline.

Torres-Arias' reaction to this betrayal was to spill the beans in Mexico City, in August of 1982, about the Honduran-based *Somocista* invasion force aimed at Nicaragua and the Honduran death squads Álvarez had set up.[74] But, since Álvarez was also engineering the American-financed modernization of the Honduran military, the charges had no effect whatever on Álvarez' position. In fact the Honduran Congress itself was reduced to an Álvarez-CIA rubber stamp.

Although this proved to be politically disastrous for Álvarez in the long-term, the only short-term threat was the DEA station chief in Tegucigalpa, Tomás Zepeda, who simply refused to go along. Zepeda went after Álvarez, Torres-Arias, Matta and most of the Contra leadership for drug trafficking.[75]

The CIA, which had already asked the DEA to define "the level of drug trafficking permissible for an asset,"[76] proceeded to pull the rug out from under Zepeda. In June of 1983, as the CIA station was doubled in size, the DEA shut down Zepeda's office completely, claiming lack of funds, thus giving the big green light to the key cocaine transshipment center in Latin America. Zepeda, in the *L.A. Times*, 2/13/88, insisted that the CIA intentionally sabotaged his investigation.

Zepeda, and Cele Castillo, and innumerable other pros in a position to know, suspect that the DEA's chief of Latin American operations, Ed Heath, based in Mexico City, was CIA. Michael Levine: "[Heath was] a man so mistrusted by the street agents working for him in Mexico that they conducted enforcement operations without informing him."[77] While Reagan starved the DEA for funds, between 1982 and 1987, he pumped $1.2 billion into the hands of the Honduran military.

A 1983 Customs Investigative Report stated that "SETCO stands for *Servicios Ejecutivos Turistas Commander* and is headed by Juan Ramón Matta Ballesteros, a class I DEA violator.... SETCO aviation is a corporation formed by American businessmen who are dealing with Ballesteros and are smuggling narcotics into the United States."

Juan Ramón Matta Ballesteros

So, armed with this intelligence, Lt. Col. Oliver North, under specific orders, proceeded to set up the bank accounts through which SETCO would be paid for services to the U.S. military.[78]

The July 9, 1984 entry in North's diary, obligingly published by Senator Kerry, states, in Ollie's own hand, "wanted aircraft to go to Bolivia to pick up paste, want aircraft to pick up 1,500 kilos." The July 12, 1985 entry reads, "$14 million to finance [arms] Supermarket came from drugs."[79] August 9, 1985: "Honduran DC-9 which is being used for runs out of New Orleans is probably being used for drug runs into U.S." All told, Ollie referred to CIA drug dealing in more than 250 entries.

When thinking about the credibility of people like Oliver North, it's always a good rule to ponder how much human blood they have on their hands. Lotsa blood, little credibility. Killing campesinos requires a deeply ingrained moral dishonesty.

Contra troops return to San Miguel in El Salvador after a mission in Honduras; Castillo

It is interesting that the diagram found in North's White House safe, outlining the Contra "private aid" network, shows many of the same banks and foundations involved in the savings and loan debacle and also indicted as drug money laundries. All were close political allies of North's commanding officer, Vice-President George Bush.[80]

Álvarez' escalating insistence on starting an overt war with neighboring Nicaragua alarmed Honduran centrists, who realized that virtual direct CIA control of the Honduran military, and the *Somocista* crazies, had become a clear and present danger to Honduras. President Súazo therefore replaced Álvarez at the head of the Honduran military with the more nationalistic Gen. Walter López Reyes, a man closer to the Honduran center.

On November 1, 1984, one of Álvarez' most important allies, Gen. José Bueso Rosa, and his Cuban and Honduran henchmen, were arrested by the FBI in south Florida with 763 pounds of cocaine, about 10 million dollars-worth, wholesale.[81] Bueso, who was then Honduran military attaché to Pinochet in Chile, had been trying to finance the assassination of Súazo and the reinstallation of Álvarez. This was apparently a Pinochet-CIA plot foiled by the FBI. As the ever-patriotic Oliver North put it, "The problem with the Bueso case is that Bueso was the man whom Negroponte, Gorman, Clarridge and I worked out arrangements [censored]."

Gen. Robert Schweitzer, the NSC contact of Honduran Cocaine Coup engineers Matta and Paz, begged the court to understand that "General Bueso Rosa has always been a valuable ally to the United States." The court understood. Despite conviction for conspiring to murder a head of state and arrest for possession of nearly a half-ton of cocaine, Bueso served only three years at the Eglin Air Force Base country club in Florida, keeping his silence throughout. But years later, in 1995, Bueso revealed to the *Baltimore Sun* some of what he participated in: he described the CIA setup, equipping and training of the Honduran army's official death squad, Battalion 316, under Álvarez. Hundreds of innocent Hondurans were murdered.[82]

One of Bueso's indicted coconspirators was Jerome Latchinian, Bush operative Felix Rodriguez' business partner in the CIA's gunrunning Giro Aviation Group. Latchinian had been Álvarez' right-hand man during the CIA's buildup of the Honduran military. In his defense, Latchinian insisted that it was CIA coke, from the chief of the Honduran secret police, not private enterprise coke. This was likely true, since the other indicted coconspirators were CIA Cubans.[83]

On October 5, 1986, a nineteen year-old Sandinista trooper got lucky with a shoulder-launched SAM-7 ground-to-air missile, bringing down a C-123 loaded with Contra arms. This disaster was immediately reported to the office of the Vice President by the flight's Ilopango coordinator, Felix Rodriguez.

The C-123's only survivor, cargo-kicker, Eugene Hasenfus, obligingly told his Sandinista captors about the Ilopango operation, naming Felix Rodriguez, aka Max Gomez, and Luis Posada, aka Ramón Medina, as his CIA handlers and flight coordinators. Hasenfus' notebook contained George Bush's office telephone number.

Hasenfus' copilot, one of the three killed in the crash, was Buzz Sawyer. When Wanda Palacios, the wife of a Colombian trafficker, saw Sawyer's picture on the tube, she rushed to tell Senator Kerry, for whom she was testifying. Sawyer had been one of the Southern Air pilots she saw loading cocaine in Barranquilla, Colombia, in early October 1985. She had ridden to the transfer with Pablo Escobar, and had discussed the Southern Air Transport arrangement with Jorge Ochoa as well. Sawyer's CIA plane would come in loaded with U.S. arms, and exit loaded with Colombian coke.

When the Associated Press sent Robert Parry to Managua to cover the story, he was greeted by Sandinista military intelligence chief Ricardo Wheelock, who showed him Sawyer's flight logs, recovered from the downed plane. Three entries - for October 2, 4 and 6, 1985 - listed Sawyer flying a Southern Air Transport L382 from Miami to Barranquilla, and Palacios' passport established that she was in Colombia at the time. The FBI polygraph also indicated that Palacios was telling the truth.[84]

Hasenfus' Southern Air Transport C-123K, which saw duty in Laos in the late 60's, was the very plane NSA agent and drug smuggler Barry Seal had used to entrap Federico Vaughn, supposedly a Sandinista operative, loading coke with Pablo Escobar near Managua for the CIA's cameras. "This picture," intoned the Great Communicator, lobbying for his $100 million Contra aid package, "secretly taken at a military airfield outside Managua, shows Federico Vaughn, a top aide to one of the nine commandantes who rule Nicaragua, loading an aircraft with illegal narcotics, bound for the United States. No, there seems to be no crime to which the Sandinistas will not stoop - this is an outlaw regime!"

But the photos were hopelessly blurred, and Vaughn was actually a CIA operative. In fact, a recently declassified CIA cable identified Vaughn as "an associate of Nicaraguan narcotics trafficker Norwing [sic] Meneses Cantarero," the Contra cocaine financier.

And that one transparent sting, the one that got Seal shot dead by the Medellín coke dealers he betrayed, was politically uncharacteristic of both Escobar and Seal, who usually financed American military allies. The CIA, in 1984, and the Justice Department, in 1986, officially told the Senate Select Committee on Intelligence that no evidence of Sandinista drug dealing could be found. The DEA later confirmed this, saying that Seal's one CIA setup was the only drug flight involving the Sandinistas it was aware of.[85]

The high flying Barry Seal in 1972, the world's youngest Boeing 747 pilot. Seal got his first pilot's lesson in 1955, as a 16 year old summer camp trainee of the Louisiana Civil Air Patrol at Barksdale Air Force Base in Alexandria, La. His teacher was CIA agent David Ferrie. His fellow student was Lee Harvey Oswald. See Daniel Hopsicker's definitive work at www.madcowprod.com

In 1986, the Louisiana attorney general wrote to U.S. attorney general Ed Meese that, between 1981 and 85, Seal "smuggled between $3 billion and $5 billion of drugs into the U.S." That same year the commander and deputy commander of narcotics for the Louisiana State Police, in a letter to the DEA, insisted that Seal "was being given apparent free rein to import drugs in conjunction with D.E.A. investigations with so little restraint and control on his actions as to allow him the opportunity to import drugs for himself should he have been so disposed."[86] He was so disposed. He was, in fact, the chief importer of Medellín cocaine into the southeastern U.S., the chief supplier of their cocaine to the New York, Miami and New Orleans distribution hubs. This operation was run out of Mena, Arkansas, using the CIA's contract fleet of about 30 C-130 transports.

Seal in 1963

Seal's C-123K, "the Fat Lady," acquired through insider paper transfers, was sold by Gen. Secord to the CIA's Southern Air Transport for a nice profit. Eugene Hasenfus then rode this plane to worldwide notoriety, obligingly telling his Sandinista captors, on camera, that he was hired by the CIA to deliver arms to Contra rebels in Nicaragua.[87] These were the usual recipients of Seal's largesse.

Investigative journalists Sally Denton and Roger Morris were able to corroborate Hasenfus' confession through U.S. Customs sources. They insisted that Seal's operations at Mena and other bases were involved in the regular export of guns to the Contras, as well as to CIA clients in Bolivia, Argentina, Peru, and Brazil. Those exports were financed, they said, by the massive importation of drugs on the return trip.

The cocaine cartel connections of the three Colombians convicted of murdering Seal in Feb. 1986 were widely advertised. What wasn't so widely advertised was that they were armed by CIA asset José Coutin, whose Miami gun shop was used by Oliver North to arm the Contras.

Sam Dalton was the New Orleans attorney who represented the Colombian hit men in the penalty phase of their trial. After a long legal fight with the CIA and FBI, Dalton gained access to some of the contents of the trunk of the Cadillac Seal was driving on the night he was killed. "Some of the things that had been in it we didn't get back. But they had missed a few things that indicated just how valuable that trunk was. Because that's where that phone number was. That's where we found George Bush's private phone number. They were regularly talking to each other very seriously over what was probably a secure phone. Barry Seal was in direct contact with George Bush."[89]

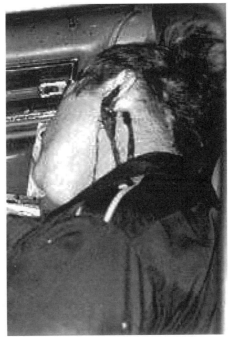

Barry's last ride; Daniel Hopsicker: www.madcowprod.com

In 1986, Lewis Unglesby, at the age of 36, was Barry Seal's lawyer. Today he's one of Louisiana's most famous and powerful attorneys. Unglesby chafed under Seal's "need-to-know" restrictions. "I sat him down one time," Unglesby told investigative journalist Daniel Hopsicker, "and said: I cannot represent you effectively unless I know what is going on. Barry smiled, and gave me a number, and told me to call it, and identify myself as him (Seal.) I dialed the number, a little dubiously, and a pleasant female voice answered: 'Office of the Vice President.'" "This is Barry Seal," Unglesby said into the phone. "Just a moment, sir," the secretary replied. "Then a man's voice came on the line, identifying himself as Admiral somebody, and said to me, 'Barry, where have you been?'" "Excuse me, Sir," Unglesby replied, "but my name is Lewis Unglesby and I'm Barry Seal's attorney." There was a click. The phone went dead. "Seal just smiled when I looked over at him in shock, and then went back to treating me on a need-to-know basis." Hopsicker's most highly-placed intelligence source adds, "Barry's been a spook since 1971. In fact, Barry goes all the way back to the Bay of Pigs."[90]

Adds Hopsicker, in parenthesis, "(The Admiral in question might well have been Admiral Daniel Murphy, assigned to work in the Office of the Vice President, from which numerous reports state Contra operations were masterminded.)" Murphy's subordinate, Oliver North, acknowledged his relationship with Seal in his memoirs.

North put Seal in touch with Thailand Air America vet Terry Reed, who trained Contra troops in the smuggler's arts - night landings, precision paradrops - at Nella, ten miles north of Mena in the Ouachita National Forest. Reed claimed, in his fascinating book *Compromised*, that he assumed the purpose of the training to be the military resupply of Contras operating behind enemy lines in Nicaragua, not the related drug smuggling that financed the operation. But Reed, as he himself proves, was in this far too deeply, and is far too intelligent, for this to be believed. His disingenuous protestation of shock at the drug smuggling is obviously a legal ploy.

But valuable information is often revelaed by rats seeking a way off a sinking ship. "Disinformation to work," Peter Dale Scott warned me, "has to be 80 percent correct. Single bits of it might be 100 percent correct." Reed can prove his 80%.

He was indeed a Spanish-speaking machine-tool expert as well as an experienced flight instructor, and did indeed set up a covert arms manufacturing operation for the Enterprise in northern Mexico, as Ronald Lister had done in El Salvador. Reed claims that his Guadalajara CIA contact, the infamous Felix Rodriguez, was using Reed's under-construction Guadalajara arms manufacturing facility to import huge amounts of cocaine into the U.S., via, among others, Barry Seal at Mena. Rodriguez used General Secord's huge Southern Air Transport C-130's operating under CIA flight cover.

I asked professional CIA investigator Mike Ruppert, no innocent fan of this slippery opportunist, what he thought of the following Reed description of the cross-border smuggling system: "From probably fifteen different sources I know that his description of how the air routes were handled and clearances obtained is on-the-money accurate. Whether the CIA, through the military or DEA or Treasury or Coast Guard went through EPIC and told them to allow planes or whether someone told someone to turn radars off or whether someone gave aircraft secret transponder codes which allowed them to pass, the mechanism is accurate."

Reed: "Specifically, Cathey [Oliver North] wanted to know, 'Now are you sure that if one of Southern Air Transport's planes delivers a load of guns to Terry's facility that Fierro can fix the international air traffic control system so that there is no permanent record of that flight? Either from its origination as it penetrates Mexican air space or to its destination at Guadalajara?'

"'Señor Fierro said to tell you he has a brother who provides this same service in the Bermuda Triangle,' Gomez joked. 'What flies in never flies out, or at least not from ATC point of view.' That took care of Mexican air space. With everyone still laughing, another problem occurred to Johnson ['Robert Johnson,' the CIA agent in charge of the meeting, was the *nom de guerre* of William P. Barr, later to become George Bush's U.S. Attorney General]."

"'What about our own satellite reconnaissance?'"

"Cathey had the answer to that. 'The same procedures as we used for Dodger sorties. We will have them blinded just as we did for Seal's departures and penetrations. The military's satellite coverage is from the equator north all the way into the U.S.'"

"'But I'm curious,' Johnson said. 'I've never understood how Seal got back in. Taking care of the defense system is one thing, but what about American ATC [Air Traffic Control]? Don't these two systems overlap?'"

"'Sea Spray is the coordinator,' Cathey replied."

"'For the purpose of my report, remind me what Sea Spray is,' Johnson requested."

"Cathey explained the technical details of Sea Spray, itself a black, joint Army-CIA unit that provided 'cover' for covert ops flights to enter and exit American air space undetected [confirmed by Seymour Hersh in the *NYT* in 1987], and added, 'Terry knows how it works. He went on a Sea Spray flight with Seal down to Panama. Remember, Max?'"

"Gomez[Rodriguez] nodded."

"'Beautiful,' Johnson said. 'The flights just never happen.'"

"Satellites in orbit provide the primary defense network that protects American coastal air space. By 'blinding' those satellites, Cathey was referring to the Defense Department's ability to selectively turn off their detection capability. This had to be done in order to prevent a triggered response from the military, whose mission is to intercept unauthorized incursions into U.S. air space."

"Southern Air Transport's aircraft, which would be carrying the weapons to Guadalajara, would be exiting and entering United States air space without flight plans. For such black flights to come and go, avoiding detection and interception by the military, certain select air corridors would momentarily be 'established,' allowing penetration without detection."

"Electronically, a 'hole' is temporarily created in the defense network. This is how Barry Seal was able to fly weapons south from Arkansas for so long, seemingly without interference. The same was true for return flights, when Seal and other were hauling drugs."[91]

The overlapping civil ATC system, controlled by the FAA, must also be blinded. We can now understand Fletcher Prouty's desperate military concern over the loss of civilian control of the FAA.

"Terry began to notice that when he was conducting Boomerang flight training sorties within the [covert] military operation areas (MOAs) and monitoring air traffic control (ATC) communications, he could hear the controllers intentionally divert other air traffic away from the area. He knew that ATC was fully aware of his presence in the area since the transponder lights in the training aircraft gave indications that they were being 'painted' or observed. Red Hall, Seal's Agency avionics expert, made sure their collision avoidance equipment was fully operational and it showed continuous 'interrogation' activity by ATC when flying above 4,000 feet MSL [median sea level] within the MOAs. It seemed obvious that the FAA was providing cover for Jade Bridge by attempting to keep unwanted aircraft out of the area."[92]

Much of Seal's drug money was being directly laundered at Mena by proprietary CIA small arms manufacturers, whose arms Seal delivered to the Contras on his return trips. The launderers included much of the financial structure closest to Governor Bill Clinton. Little Rock's Lasater & Company, an investment bank controlled by Clinton confidant Dan Lasater, was shown in court to have washed more than $300 million in untraceable Enterprise funds, only a percentage of which went to pay for arms. Like Mexico's great 'liberal' Cuauhtémoc Cardenas, who may have engineered Reed's CIA arms manufacturing operation in Morelia, the 'liberal' Bill Clinton engineered the use of his Arkansas Development and Finance Authority as the money wash for all the CIA manufacturing jobs he attracted to Arkansas.

The wash was managed by operatives, like Webb Hubbell and Seth Ward, who worked very closely with both Clintons, often through Hillary Clinton's prestigious Rose law firm, where Hubbell was a partner.

When Governor Clinton's security chief, Buddy Young, and his aide, former Arkansas State Trooper Tommy Baker, tried to discredit Reed with false evidence, and hide Reed's real evidence, federal judge Frank Theis, in the 1988 *United States v. Reed*, concluded that Young and Baker had acted "with reckless disregard for the truth."[93] But a reckless disregard that employed very sophisticated "stolen plane" evidence falsely generated by a whole team of intelligence experts on secure government FAA computers.

Just as the internal logic of Reed's description of the air smuggling system holds up, so too does the internal logic of Reed's analysis of the Air Hasenfus disaster. Reed puts this analysis into the mouth of Amiram Nir, the key Mossad operative in Central America who had coordinated the Israeli end of all the Contra-Iran business.

Reed says that Nir sought him out in an effort to avoid seeing them both go down as the dope-dealing Iran-Contra fall guys. Nir believed that Ilopango flight director Felix Rodriguez was a double agent who had, for both monetary and covert politico-economic reasons, set up the C-123 Contra supply plane for shootdown in concert with Sandinista military intelligence.

The facts of the shootdown didn't add up to Nir. ".... Nir expressed his belief that Rodriguez was a double agent.... 'Number one, you knew Bill Cooper much better than I. I've been told he was an excellent flyer. You don't live to be a 60-year-old pilot by acting reckless! What was he doing flying many miles off his flight plan and directly over a Sandinista stronghold...a military training camp no less?'"

"'Number two, why did the aircraft have unnecessary and classified documents aboard? Documents from prior missions reflecting the dates of the flights, the crew members' names, the tonnage and descriptions of the munitions and the coordinates of the drop zones.'"

"'Number three, why was the crew not sanitized as the orders always called for? My God, Bill Cooper even had his Southern Air Transport identification card with him. That we cannot accept as an accident. My God, a direct link to the CIA. Cooper knew better!'"

"'Number four, this guy Hasenfus...the dumb-ass survivor...what kind of a story is this? No one was to have a parachute. The intention is to always go down with the craft in case of an incident like this. You know from your training that is the procedure: no one is to live. No loose ends. Instead, this guy claims his brother bought him a parachute in Wisconsin. My God, if it wasn't so serious, it would be funny.'"

"Number five, how does he know the plane was hit by a surface-to-air missile? If he was blown out of the plane by the explosion, as he claims, he wouldn't even have seen it coming, let alone recognized the type of weapon.'"

"'No sir, it's all too convenient. Daniel Ortega "accidentally" captures an American flyer who immediately spills his guts and starts babbling "CIA, the White House, guns, Southern Air Transport," and then to top it off, he's put on trial as a war criminal, convicted for his crimes and released as a humanitarian gesture! Shot down in October and home by Christmas. I'll bet your Vietnam POW flyers would have liked such an opportunity. Just think of it all.'"

"'But I've saved the best morsel for last.... We warned Seal back in early 1986. Just before his murder, we warned him that your side had a leak, which could bring about a political thunderclap. And that's exactly what happened when the C-123 crashed and exposed to the world the deviousness of the Reagan administration.'"

"'.... Oh, Medina [Luis Posada Carriles]. That's another example of your CIA stooping to use terrorists to do agents' jobs. What did Medina ever do besides blow up civilians in airliners? These damn Cuban rebels, they're just not professionals.'"

"'.... An agent of ours in El Salvador reports that Rodriguez boasted that he was responsible for the killing of both Seal and Camp. You know Rodriguez. He must continually brag of his exploits.... My God, it's just so apparent to us that he is a double-dipper. He must be eliminated one way or the other." Nir offered to help Reed physically bust Rodriguez' CIA drug network.

Whether the drugs-for-arms business was the actual bone of contention or not, or whether Reed was involved by Nir as a key player, as Reed claims, it is a fact that this time period saw the start of a street war that ended with Nir's death. Reed says that this conversation with Amiram Nir took place in July of 1987 in Terry Reed's airplane while flying over his CIA weapons facility at Michoacán's Morelia Airport. In November of 1988, at almost exactly the same spot, Nir would plunge to his death in a single engine commuter aircraft. Rodriguez was still operating in the area.

Nir insisted that the autopsy performed by the Nicaraguans, the results of which had been forwarded to the CIA, proved that Cooper and Sawyer, the C-123 pilot and copilot, were dead before the plane took off. Israeli agents confirmed on the ground that the plane had exploded outward, from an internal explosion. Hasenfus, the talkative survivor, was perfectly able to fly the airplane by himself. And the third dead crew member also didn't die from the crash - his throat had been slit! The plane was personally sent on its way from Ilopango by none other than Felix Rodriguez and Luis Posada, the CORU terrorist convicted of blowing up the Cubana airliner, known, for years, as Nir indicated, as "The Bomber."[95]

Felix Rodriguez' boss, Gen. Richard Secord, ran Southern Air Transport for Bush, Casey, Murphy and Gregg. He was the original 1960's Laotian Air Opium employer of most of the operatives Barry Seal worked with. When Leslie and Andrew Cockburn were sued by Secord for defamation of character for the revelations contained in their indispensable 1987 *Out of Control*, the court found the Cockburns not guilty because their allegations of Secord's complicity in the drug trade were true.[96]

Ex-CIA officer David MacMichael ran across another covert operative Secord, Rodriguez and Company worked with, and his story confirms much of the CIA/Syndicate structure Reed described. MacMichael is the founder of the Association of National Security Alumni. Like many 'alumni,' MacMichael felt deeply betrayed by the vicious fascism he found on the front line, and so dedicated his ANSA to ending CIA covert operations.

To that end, MacMichael turned to his trusted friend, former professional detective Mike Ruppert, to investigate the allegations of Dee Carone, daughter of ranking CIA agent Col. Albert Carone. Ruppert found that Dee Carone could prove most of what she was saying. That proof, from whence comes most of the following Dee Carone quotes, is available from Mike at www.copvcia.com.

The first flag couldn't have been more obvious. Albert Carone died on 1/7/90 of "a chemical toxicity of unknown etiology." On his death every single record of Albert Carone vanished - his driver's license, work history, insurance records, bank accounts - even those accounts he held in partnership with others.

And then there was Dee Carone: "Dad was very good friends with Richard Stillwell. Dad called him 'the General." He used to pick him up at the airport a lot. He also talked about Paul Helliwell whenever he talked about Stillwell. He knew them both."

Col. Stillwell (no relation to the great Vinegar Joe Stilwell), in the late forties, was chief of covert operations for the CIA's Far Eastern Division. He worked closely with Paul Helliwell, William Willauer and Desmond Fitzgerald in the 1950 conversion of Chennault's Flying Tigers/Civil Air Transport to Air America. It was they who set up the opium/heroin financing of the Burma-based KMT. This team went on to institutionalize this *modus operandi* in CIA covert operations. They were, literally, Bill Casey's teachers.

Continued Dee Carone Ferdinand: "I knew Santos Trafficante as 'Uncle Sonny,' Joe Percilia as 'Joe Pickles.' I grew up with them around all the time. My father knew Joe Black, Vito Genovese, Carlo Gambino, Benny Eggs, Matty 'the Horse' Aienello, Jimmy Bruno, Joey Lugosa and Pauly Castellano. Most of them were at my wedding. My father was an NYPD detective so we had two rooms full of people at my wedding and no one from one room ever talked to the people in the other.... When he retired [from the NYPD, 1966] and went on active duty he said he was crossing over from Army Intelligence, CIC, into the CIA."

Albert Carone grew up in Brooklyn, literally running errands for Vito Genovese as a boy. He functioned as a loyal "son of the heart" for this mafioso, and his heirs, all his life. Carone's personal phone book lists Gambino chief Pauly Castellano's number right next to Bill Casey's. Both were real hard to get numbers. Casey, a powerful Wall Street broker before becoming Nixon's Chairman of the Securities and Exchange Commission, used Carone to communicate inside information to Castellano, with whom he was very close. Casey was also close enough to Albert Carone to attended the christening of Dee

Carone Ferdinand's son Vincent. As Dee puts it, "A lot of money was made by a lot of people thanks to Bill Casey."[97] It was Pauly's streetwise people who turned Casey's Contra coke into cash. One of these magicians was John Gotti, a close friend of Albert Carone.

Both Albert Carone and his brother Pasquale, former chief psychiatrist of the NYC Police Dept. and former CIA LSD researcher, had ties to the Masonic P-2 Lodge, through the neofascist Catholic secret society Opus Dei, political home of Vietnam War engineer Cardinal Spellman. Casey was a member of the P-2-connected Knights of Malta.

During the early 80's, using an official USG passport (maroon), a diplomatic passport (black) and a conventional passport, the last two in his own name, Carone made numerous trips around the world and was witnessed handing off suitcases to known money launderers.

In the summer of 85 Carone returned from a four week mission in Mexico. He was functioning as Ollie North's bagman to, and from, the Guadalajara cartel, converting their protected narco-dollars into Contra arms. This was the Felix Rodriguez drug transport operation Reed fell into. Carone complained bitterly to his daughter Dee and her husband that the unintended result of the mission, code name Amadeus, was "the murder of many innocent women and children and the death of two DEA agents," one of which was the famous "martyr" Kiki Camarena. "My father was very good friends with Kiki Camarena," Dee told me, "he talked about him all the time."

According to Carone, who was a key agent in this operation, Camarena was threatening the boys from Guadalajara with the revocation of their license to deal unless he got a bigger cut of the vig. What he got cut was his throat. According to Dee, "He was taken out by the Agency and he was as crooked as the day is long."

Another unintended consequence of this operation was the massacre of an entire Mexican village. This was deemed necessary to hide a Guadalajara Cartel-run Contra training base near Veracruz. The victims were all buried in one unmarked mass grave. Albert Carone, a witness to this massacre, was seized with uncontrollable revulsion.[97] He realized that this meant that he was "not long for this world."

Enraged that her father was buried with a headstone identifying him as a staff sergeant, Dee Carone proved her intelligence contacts by locating Robert Maheu, the famous CIA contractor and Hughes operative involved, many believe, in the Kennedy assassination. Per Mike Ruppert's advice, she asked Maheu to help her contact none other than Ted Shackley, former Miami, Vientiane and Saigon CIA station chief. Less than ten days after contacting Shackley, Albert Carone's headstone was changed to full Colonel. If Maheu hadn't known who Albert Carone was, he never would have led his daughter to Shackley, and if Shackley, the former Deputy Director of the CIA, still working undercover, hadn't known Carone, he never would have had the headstone changed.

"Dad mentioned two men he worked very closely with. One was a man by the name of Jim Strauss. The other was a man by the name of John Caffey. After three years of trying to contact both men, Mr. Strauss called my home to state that we should be very careful of who we should speak to and where we go. He also told me and my husband that we could not watch our children all the time. He came to see us on November 29, 1992, and admitted to my husband, my mother-in-law and myself that my dad was eliminated, and that it was only business. He asked if 'I could bit e the bullet and go on' and if so he would personally try to help retrieve all bank accounts and insurance monies.... I was never able to find, and until recently did not know that John Caffey and Lt. Col. Oliver North are one and the same."

Here is the table of contents of the 1989 *Senate Committee Report on Drugs, Law Enforcement and Foreign Policy*, chaired by Senator John F. Kerry:

"DIACSA's president, Alfredo Caballero, was under DEA investigation for cocaine trafficking and money laundering when the State Department chose the company to be an NHAO [Nicaraguan Humanitarian Assistance Organization] supplier. Caballero was at that time a business associate of Floyd Carlton - the pilot who flew cocaine for Panama's General Noriega....The indictments of Carlton, Caballero and five other defendants, including Alfredo Caballero's son Luis, were handed down on January 23, 1985. The indictment charged the defendants with bringing into the United States on or about September 23, 1985, 900 pounds of cocaine. In addition, the indictment charged the defendants with laundering $2.6 million between March 25, 1985 and January 13, 1986. Despite the indictments, the State Department made payments...to DIACSA to provide services to the Contras."

D. VORTEX

"In each case, prior to the time that the State Department entered into contracts with the company, federal law enforcement had received information that the individuals controlling these companies were involved in narcotics."

VII. THE CASE OF GEORGE MORALES AND FRS/ARDE
VIII. JOHN HULL
IX. THE SAN FRANCISCO FROGMAN CASE, UND-FARN AND PCNE
X. THE CUBAN-AMERICAN CONNECTION
XI. RAMÓN MILIAN RODRIGUEZ AND FELIX RODRIGUEZ
FOOTNOTES

In 1987 U.S agents confiscated two loads of Honduran cocaine totalling 6.7 tons, "the largest such seizure ever made in the United States."[98] The chief counsel for the House Subcommittee on Crime, Hayden Gregory, concluded that the coke went "right to the doorstep of the Honduran military."[99] It was Colombian coke, purchased directly by CIA "asset" Juan Ramón Matta Ballesteros, owner of SETCO. When Gregory flew to Honduras to investigate, the U.S. Embassy wouldn't let him.

Ex-DEA agent Michael Levine: "The DEA documented fifty tons of Contra coke that was being routed to the U.S. by a Honduran connection. An agent bought two kilos in Lubbock, Texas, and made the arrest. The CIA comes quickly to the rescue. A closed hearing is held. Case dismissed."[100] The rescued trafficker was Eugenio Molina Osorio, brother of Matta's partner in SETCO.

When the DEA nailed a drug-carrying DC-4 in March, 1987, the owner, pilot Frank Moss, wasn't arrested because he was contracting with the CIA to supply the Contras. His partner in the company that owned the plane, Hondu Carib, was Mario Calero, chief supply officer of the Contras. Mario was the brother of the Contra political front, CIA agent Adolfo Calero.[101] Moss' notes, found on the plane, contained the names and numbers of two CIA agents and Col. North's Contra liaison, Robert Owen.

By 1987 Honduras accounted for at least a third (Levine says half) of all the cocaine smuggled into the U.S.[102] By 1988 the U.S. embassy in Honduras had grown to more than 300 people, one of the largest in the world. The whole thing, from start to finish, was a CIA operation.

Joe Fernandez, CIA Costa Rican station chief, told the Tower Commission that Ambassador Lewis Tambs told him, in his first organizational meeting in 1985, that "he had really only one mission in Costa Rica, and that was to form a Nicaraguan resistance southern front."[103] Tambs, a Helms operative who had just come from a stint in Colombia, was taking orders directly from Bush operative Oliver North. Both Tambs and Fernandez worked closely with the CIA's John Hull, whose 30-mile long "ranch" supported six airstrips, arms depots and the Radio Free America broadcasting tower.

What Tambs actually meant was that he was to help Hull wrest control of the southern front from the recalcitrant Eden Pastora, the former Sandinista hero who refused to place his ARDE troops under the command of the *Somocista* FDN.[104] This reduced itself to a cocaine turf war and included a famous attempt to blow Pastora to kingdom come. Coincidentally, on the same day the bomb at Pastora's border camp at La Penca went off, May 30, 1984, U.S. aid to ARDE was cut off.

Kerry went after a Brigade 2506 outfit called Ocean Hunter/ *Frigorificos de Puntarenas*, which used shrimp boats to trade U.S. Navy arms from Florida for Colombian coke via Hull's ranch. Ocean Hunter was created by convicted Medellín cartel drug-money launderer and CIA bagman Ramón Milian-Rodriguez. The "humanitarian" bank accounts were controlled by one of Ocean Hunter's owners, a CIA Cuban named Luis Rodriguez. According to Massachusetts law enforcement, Rodriguez ran the largest marijuana smuggling ring in the history of the state. Rodriguez was indicted on drug trafficking charges by the federal government on September 30, 1987, and on tax evasion in connection with the laundering of drug money through Ocean Hunter on April 5, 1988.

The Ocean Hunter "humanitarian" accounts were managed by Oliver North's senior field liaison, Robert Owen. Ocean Hunter financed the purchase and delivery of weapons, according to an Owen memo to North. All its officers, Moises Nuñez, Francisco Chanes, Carlos Soto and Ubaldo Fernandez, were not only known or convicted drug traffickers, but partners of CIA contractor Frank Castro, co-founder of CORU and himself a legendary drug dealer.

Brian Barger, UPI, Feb. 12, 1988: Moises Nuñez, *Frigorificos* Costa Rican manager, was "identified as an Agency [CIA] officer by two senior Costa Rican government officials, a U.S. intelligence source, and American law enforcement authorities.."[105] In January, 1986, the DEA took 414 pounds of cocaine off a *Frigorificos* shipment of yucca to Miami.

The FBI identified Frank Castro as a regular associate of Hull. John Hull himself was identified by a very experienced military intelligence operative, Robert Hayes, in a sworn affidavit in Florida, 1/8/88, as a CIA black ops specialist with whom he had worked throughout the 70's:

"After working for a Brazilian engineering company, I eventually formed Hayes-Bosworth, a Brazilian company engaged in heavy engineering and construction projects for Brazilian and foreign clients. Between 1972 and 1976, the company's success provided me with the funds, contacts and time to indulge my lifelong interest in Latin American politics."

".... After Ryan left the room, Sibley informed me that his 'real' name was John Joseph Michaels and produced corroborating identification that I recognized from previous experience as genuine CIA credentials. He then recited in great detail and accuracy my previous connections with and service for various U.S. intelligence organizations, including the agency. He also recited details of my work for Israeli and West German intelligence."

"Michaels then requested my assistance in illegal clandestine operations....[that] ranged from routine intelligence gathering to kidnapping, interrogation and assassination."

".... My relationship with Michaels ended abruptly in 1976 after Michaels proposed an operation that I considered not only absurd, but also contrary to the best interests of the U.S. government."

"In the Spring of 1976, Michaels proposed that I arrange to 'simulate terrorism.' I responded that there was no way to 'simulate' terrorism. I insisted that an act is either terrorist or not, and anyone knowingly engaging in a violent act against civilians is in fact a terrorist and beyond sanction."

".... When I asked what the target of this 'simulated' act was to be, he proposed three: A large Catholic cathedral in Sao Paulo, a twin theatre complex near the U.S. consulate in Sao Paulo and the U.S. consulate itself."

"Although I refused the operation in unmistakable terms, Michaels insisted that I reconsider and said two of his agents would contact me for further discussion."

"In late June or early July of 1976, I was approached at my office by two Americans I knew to be subordinates of Michaels. They once again proposed a bombing attack of one of three targets originally proposed by Michaels."

"The meeting resulted in two other meetings. The third and final meeting ended in an angry exchange in which I rejected both the operation and the concept and told Michaels' subordinates that I never wanted to see him or them again."

"The following week, the two Americans were found dead in a downtown Sao Paulo park with their hands and feet bound by wire. Each had been shot in the back of the head. No arrests were made in connection with their deaths."

"Reliable contacts in the Brazilian government and military and contacts in other circles warned me that my own death was imminent if I did not flee Brazil."

".... I was met at Miami airport by agents from the local CIA office. Although they denied any specific knowledge of me or my activities, they asked me what my plans were. Upon telling them that I planned to fly to Albuquerque, New Mexico to join my wife, who was staying there with her parents, they asked me to call the Denver CIA office after my arrival."

".... I eventually returned to Lakeland in 1981 and buried the Brazilian incident and my other intelligence activities in my past. But Michaels returned to haunt me late last year when I read a November 16, 1987 *Time* magazine article titled 'The Misadventures of El Patron.' The article detailed the activities of John Hull, an American expatriate operating a farm on Costa Rica's northern border with Nicaragua. Hull was identified in the article...as a CIA agent whose farm was used to transship weapons and other supplies to the Contra rebels opposing the Sandinista government in Nicaragua."

".... The article was accompanied by a color photograph of Hull, which I immediately identified as John Joseph Michaels. After subsequent research and further examination of the photograph, I remain convinced that John Joseph Michaels and John Hull are the same individual, and that Michaels' activities in Brazil are part of a continuing pattern of operations that led to the plot to bomb the U.S. embassy in Costa Rica, as he had asked me to bomb the U.S. consulate in Sao Paulo."

Also working in John Hull's Costa Rica operation were Rene Corvo, Ramón Sanchez, Frank Castro and other CIA Cubans suspected in innumerable bank robberies, drug deals and terrorist acts, as FBI Agent Currier pointed out to the Iran-Contra Committee. Frank Castro was indicted twice on drug charges in the early 80's, in Operation Tick-Talks and Operation Grouper, but both prosecutions were sabotaged by the CIA. Grouper, a Vice-President Bush Task Force on Drugs operation, was sabotaged from the inside, by a Bush operative who himself was indicted for smuggling, and promptly vanished.[106]

According to the U.S. Customs Service 1987 investigation, the owners of Ocean Hunter/*Frigorificos* included Danny Vasquez, another Brigade 2506 vet, who also just happened to own Florida Air Transport, which regularly traded multiton loads of arms for coke on Hull's airstrips. Five qualified witnesses confirmed that to Senator Kerry.

As Senator Kerry's report puts it: "Yet another guns for drugs flight was made two weeks later. On this trip, Betzner said he flew a Panther to an airstrip called 'Los Llanos,' about ten miles from Hull's properties and not far from the Voice of America transmitter in northern Costa Rica. Betzner testified that Hull met him again and the two watched while the weapons were unloaded and approximately 500 kilos of cocaine in 17 duffel bags were loaded for the return flight to Florida."

That is, as a CIA covert ops flight, Gary Betzner's plane wasn't subject to customs inspection. The coke was literally offloaded for Syndicate distribution at a CIA-controlled U.S. military base. Another Betzner trip traded mines picked up from the U.S. Milgroup at Ilopango in El Salvador for three tons of Colombian pot.[107]

One mutual associate of Tambs, North and Hull, former Sandinista fighter turned Contra leader Blackie Chamorro, was intercepted by Costa Rican police with 421 pounds of pure cocaine.[108] In 1990, Hull himself was charged with drug trafficking by Costa Rica.[109]

In July of 1989, Costa Rica officially declared that Lewis Tambs, Joe Fernandez, Oliver North, Richard Secord and John Poindexter were barred from the country because they were part of "an organization made up of Panamanians, Colombians, Costa Ricans and citizens of other nationalities who dedicated themselves to international cocaine trafficking..."[110] All took orders from George Bush.

George Bush explains the Ilopango Anti-Drug Mission at the Guatemalan Embassy, January 14, 1986. Cuban-American operative Ambassador Piedra looks admiringly on; Castillo

Left: Ilopango, 1986: Felix Rodriguez, General Juan Bustillo, Rep. Claude Pepper and Colonel James Steele, commander of the U.S. Milgroup in El Salvador

Bush with Celerino Castillo, the lead DEA agent in El Salvador and Guatemala, at the Guatemala City embassy reception, January 14, 1986. Castillo humiliated Bush by developing hard evidence that the Contras were trading cocaine for arms out of Ilopango; Castillo

Castillo

Cele Castillo on patrol in Vietnam, 1971

Felix Rodriguez' deputy at the U.S. Milgroup in Ilopango, CORU assassin Luis Posada Carriles, was the terminal chief that sent Eugene Hasenfus off on his ill-fated October 1986 flight. Gustavo Villoldo, who was with Rodriguez at the Bay of Pigs and hunting Ché in Bolivia, functioned as a "combat advisor" to the Contras under written orders from Bush aide Gregg. He helped Rodriguez and Posada turn Ilopango into a major drug port, according to Celerino Castillo, the DEA's Lead Agent in Guatemala and El Salvador from 1985 to 1990.[1] It was Castillo who had developed much of the DEA evidence used by Senator Kerry.

Castillo was a heavily decorated Vietnam combat veteran who had recently commanded very dangerous DEA operations in New York, Peru and Guatemala. In New York, in the early 80's, the bilingual street wise Tex-Mex demonstrated the nerve and talent to go after major dealers, producing bust after major bust. Castillo's biggest bust, of an extensive Sicilian heroin importing and distribution operation, actually depended on his ability to translate the Spanish Pig-Latin of the ring's warehouse manager.[2]

This caused Castillo to find himself, in 1984, as the only Spanish-speaking DEA agent in Peru. That, of course, is an indication of the suicidal racism endemic in law enforcement culture, as Castillo was painfully aware.

His continuing record of major busts found Castillo in tactical charge of Operation Condor, coordinating DEA, CIA and Peruvian military elements. He made the largest coke bust in Peruvian history, a cocaine manufacturing and distribution compound that housed more than 600 people:

"The South American newspapers published multi-page articles on the raid, repeating the numbers: Four tons of coca paste seized from a lab capable of churning out 500 kilos of pure cocaine every day. The Peruvian government estimated the compound's value at $500 million. It was the biggest cocaine lab capture in South American history.... We later discovered that the lab belonged to Arcesio and Omar Ricco, members of the Cali cartel."

Castillo, Guatemala, 1986; Castillo

The undiplomatic Castillo insisted on pointing the finger directly at the covert elements within the Peruvian command structure responsible for protecting this and other jungle refineries.

"When I wandered into the Lima office a week after the raid, I picked up a local paper left on my desk and almost choked on my coffee. My photo, snapped by a Reuters photographer with a telephoto lens, took up a quarter of the page."

Peter Rieff, Castillo's station chief, using Castillo's blown cover as the excuse, decided that the war on drugs would be better prosecuted with Castillo in Guatemala.

Cover Blown: "Celerino Castillo, mexicano, agente especial de la DEA y el general G.C. Walter Andrade, jefe de la *Policíe de Drogas*"

"The real reason my boss wanted me out of the country, I thought, was my relationship with the Guardia and UMOPAR. Instead of consulting with Rieff, the generals and colonels came straight to me for advice about anti-narcotics tactics. They knew I spent most of my time in coca country. They trusted my instincts. Rieff resented that."[3] That, and Castillo's consequent ability to put himself between the DEA and Peru's dope-dealing high command, using Peru's own reformist military officers. Despite the most spectacular record of any DEA agent who ever served in Peru, Castillo was transferred to Guatemala without the promotion, and the consequent authority, he had earned.

"In October of 1985, upon my arrival in Guatemala, I was fore-warned by Guatemala DEA, Country Attaché, Robert J. Stia and the CIA's Chief of Station, Jack McCavett, that the DEA had received intelligence that the Contras out of Salvador, were involved in drug trafficking. For the first time, I had come face to face with the contradictions of my assignment. The reason that I had been forewarned was because I would be DEA's Lead Agent in El Salvador."

Col. James Steele, commander of the U. S. Military Group at Ilopango, arranged for Castillo to co-train elite drug squads for Salvadoran military intelligence. Their Salvadoran Fire Arms Instructor was Dr. Hector Antonio Regalado, D'Aubuisson's top aide. "Regalado's prestige among the right wing stemmed from his ability to extract teeth - and information - without anesthesia. I wanted no part of *El Doctor*. I asked [U.S. Lt. Col. Alberto] Adame if the embassy had approved Regalado as an adviser. He said Col. James Steele, the U.S. Military Group commander in El Salvador, gave Regalado his blessing. The military obviously wanted this man aboard, human rights abuses and all. Regalado was hired, and we began spending a lot of time together."[4] Regalado combined his training at the School of the Americas in Ft. Benning with his expertise as a dentist to inflict excruciating pain during "interrogation." It was these Nazi skills that he taught to Castillo's "drug" squads.

"August 03, 1986, Ramiro Guerra, Lt. Col. A. Adame, Dr. Hector Regalado (Dr. Death, who claimed to have shot Archbishop Romero) and myself went out on patrol in El Salvador."

The situation was the same in neighboring Guatemala: "I participated in numerous joint operations with the CIA and Guatemalan security forces, principally the G-2 (Guatemalan military intelligence...).... The level of CIA and DEA involvement in operations that included torture and murder in Guatemala is much higher than the [6/28/96 Intelligence Oversight Board] report indicates. With US anti-narcotics funding still being funneled to the Guatemalan Military, this situation continues."

"The CIA, with knowledge of ambassadors and the State Department and National Security Council officials, as well as Congress, continued this aid after the termination of overt military assistance in 1990.... Several contract pilots for the DEA and CIA worked out of [the Guatemala] Piper [Company in Guatemala City] and most were documented narcotic traffickers."[5]

Castillo realized that he couldn't control the situation at all. He was simply being used for his logistical clout. The Salvadoran and

Guatemalan militaries controlled the actual busts, which were politicized, and from which the coke almost always found its way into the hands of military intelligence, which resold it, by the ton. These butchers were, in fact, the dealers. Castillo's stomach turned.

"I realized how hopelessly tangled DEA, the CIA, and every other U.S. entity had become with the criminals..... I began running the names of [Guatemalan President] Cerezo's top lieutenants through our computer, and almost every name came back with a black mark. The list read like a flowchart of the Guatemalan power structure. Among the Guatemalan high command documented as traffickers were the president's brother, Milton Cerezo-García; Claudia Arenas, a top aide; and two members of the Guatemalan congress: former interior minister Alfonso Cabrera-Hidalgo and Carlos Ramiro García de Paz."

"I leaned back in my chair, trying to absorb the enormity of what I stumbled upon. Our government had leaned on the Guatemalan military for elections and trumpeted the birth of a government whose top officials were involved in narcotrafficking.... Winning our narcotics war in Guatemala would mean taking down a good portion of their government, and that would never fly in Washington."

"On January 14, Vice President George Bush visited Guatemala City to put the U.S. stamp of approval on Cerezo's inauguration. I met Bush at the obligatory cocktail party at the ambassador's residence.... As he shook my hand, someone snapped a photo. I told him I was a DEA agent assigned to Guatemala. He said, 'Well, what do you do?' .... I just blurted it out 'There's some funny things going on with the Contras in El Salvador.' Bush didn't reply. He simply smiled and walked away, seeking another hand to shake. After that exchange, I knew that he knew."[6]

"In 1986, I placed an informant (Mario Murga) at the Ilopango airport in El Salvador. He was initiated and wrote the flight plans for most Contra pilots. After their names were submitted into NADDIS, it was revealed that most pilots had already been documented in DEA files as traffickers. (See DEA memo by me date 2-14-89.)" Castillo proceeded to develop hard evidence of "hundreds of flights carrying cash, drugs, and weapons through Ilopango. All of which was sanctioned by the US government."

"Early part of 1986, I received a telex/cable from DEA Costa Rica. SA Sandy Gonzales requested for me to investigate hangers 4 and 5 at Ilopango. DEA Costa Rica had received reliable intelligence that the Contras were flying cocaine into the hangars. Both hangars were owned and operated by the CIA and the National Security Agency. Operators of those two hangars were, Lt. Col. Oliver North and CIA contract agent, Felix Rodriguez, 'a.k.a.' Max Gomez."

Sandinista police were able to prove that Felix Rodriguez was running Salvadoran air force officer Marcos Aguado out of Ilopango. Former Somoza intelligence officer Enrique Miranda, the chief contact of *Somosista* cocaine financier Norwin Meneses to the Colombian cocaine cartel, testified in Nicaragua in 1992 that Rodriguez and Meneses sent Aguado to Colombia to pick up cocaine, which was then traded for U.S. arms on U.S. air force bases in Texas. Felix Rodriguez oversaw the distribution of those Texas arms on their arrival at Ilopango. Meneses, who made the mistake of trying to resume his life in Nicaragua after the 1988 end of the Contra war, was sentenced to thirty years in prison.[7]

But the cocaine-for-arms operation run by CIA agent Rodriguez was much more massive than that, as Cele Castillo, from within the belly of the beast, began to demonstrate:

"Feb. 05, 1986, I had seized $800,000.00 in cash, 35 kilos of cocaine, and an airplane at Ilopango. DEA # TG-86-0001;... March 24, 1986, I wrote a DEA report on the Contra operation. (GFTG-86-4003, Frigorificos de Puntarenas, S.A), US registration aircraft N-68435 (Cessna 402)."

"April of 1986, The Consul General of the U.S Embassy in El Salvador (Robert J. Chavez), warned me that CIA agent George Witters was requesting a U.S visa for a Nicaraguan drug trafficker and Contra pilot by the name of Carlos Alberto Amador. (mentioned in 6 DEA files)." Castillo asked Chavez to block the visa request.

"May 26, 1986, Mario Rodolfo Martinez-Murga became an official DEA informant (STG-86-0006). Before that, he had been a sub-source for Ramiro Guerra and Robert Chavez. Under Chavez, Murga's intelligence resulted in the seizure of several hundred kilos of cocaine, (from Ilopango to Florida) making Murga a reliable source of information."

"May 14, 1986, I spoke to Jack O'Conner DEA HQS Re: Matta-Ballesteros. (NOTE: Juan Ramón Matta-Ballesteros was perhaps the single largest drug trafficker in the region. Operating from Honduras he owned several companies which were openly sponsored and subsidized by C.I.A.)" (All Parentheses Castillo's)

"June 18, 1986, Salvadoran Contra pilot, Francisco "Chico" Guirrola-Beeche (DEA NADDIS # 1585334 and 1744448) had been documented as a drug trafficker. On this date, at 7:30 a.m., he departed Ilopango to the Bahamas to air drop monies. On his return trip (June 21) Guirrola arrived with his passengers Alejandro Urbizu & Patricia Bernal. In 1988 Urbizu was arrested in the US in a cocaine conspiracy case. In 1985 Guirrola was arrested in South Texas (Kleberg County) with 5 and 1/2 million dollars cash, which he had picked up in Los Angeles, California. (U.S. Customs in Dallas/ Ft. Worth had case on him.)"

At the time of his Texas arrest, Guirrola was carrying Salvadoran diplomatic credentials signed by his boss, Roberto D'Aubuisson. So well-known was Guirrola to CIA, that he accompanied D'Aubuisson to his May 1984 meeting with former CIA deputy director Vernon Walters. The $5.9 million in small bills seized in Texas was probably LA street drug profits, since the flight originated in Orange County, California. The Justice Department, despite the largest cash seizure in Texas history and ties to major drug dealers, let Guirrola off with simple forfeiture of the cash, and no prison time. A year later, Castillo watched in amazement as this documented perpetrator, flashing Salvadoran Air Force credentials, hauled cocaine and cash in and out of Ilopango by the planeload.

"In Aug. 1986, The Kerry Committee requested information on the Contra pilots from the DEA. The Department of Justice flatly refused to give up any information."

By now Castillo had been barred from direct access to the remote air base by none other than Edwin Corr, U.S. Ambassador to El Salvador, who had arranged Castillo's exclusion by his own DEA command. So he concentrated on related off-base operations.

"On September 01, 1986, Walter Grasheim (a civilian) residence in El Salvador was searched by the DEA Task Force. Found at the residence was an arsenal of US military munitions, (allegedly for a Contra military shipment). Found were cases of C-4 explosives, grenades, ammunition, sniper rifles, M-16's, helicopter helmets and knives. Also found were files of payment to Salvadoran Military Officials (trips to New York City). Found at his residence were radios and license plates belonging to the US Embassy. We also found an M16 weapon belonging to the US Mil-Group Commander, Col. Steele. Prior to the search, I went to every department of the U.S. Embassy and asked if this individual worked in any way shape or form with the embassy. Every head of the departments denied that he worked for them."

"The CIA had already briefed the ambassador about the raid. I briefed him again, studying his face when I came to the part about embassy license plates gracing Grasheim's Jeeps. Corr stared at me,

Castillo   439

the muscles in his jaw flexing."

"'You just hit the Contra operation,' he said flatly."

"'I told you I was going to hit Grasheim,' I shot back. 'Explain to me what the hell a U.S. civilian in El Salvador is doing with this stuff. I told you this guy's a documented trafficker. He could be arrested as a terrorist.'"

"Corr paused. The jaw flexed again."

"'Cele, it's a *covert* operation,' he said, holding his palms out."[7]

"<u>Sept. 26, 1986</u>, Meeting with Col. Steele Re: Mr. Grasheim (Col. Steele admitted that he had given an M-16 to Grasheim) and CIA George W. Also talked to Don Richardson (CIA) re: Ramiro Guerra. Talked to Col. Adame Re: CIA George.... <u>October 03, 1986</u>, Spoke to DEA Panama re: Mr. Grasheim. Was advised to be careful...."

Fiers/North operative Grasheim was the Salvadoran sales rep for the Litton Corp and other U.S. arms makers. He was also a sanctioned CIA adviser to the Salvadoran military. He was also documented in seven DEA files as a major drug smuggler, as Castillo demonstrated to any official who would listen. Grasheim was running the safe house used by Rodriguez, Posada, Villoldo and other Contra pilots and ground operatives, but Castillo had been barred by his own command from direct access to these perpetrators. Frustrated, he started talking to Senator Kerry and Joel Brinkley of *The New York Times*, open files or no open files.

Some of Grasheim's high explosives and communications gear; Castillo

What this nervy detective had to say proved profoundly discomfiting to the Reagan administration. The Salvadoran phone records of the Grasheim safe house revealed regular daily and weekly calls to Oliver North's and George Bush's offices in the White House.[8] The Bush office had to confirm, since it couldn't hide, that Rodriguez had been a frequent visitor of both Gregg and Bush at the White House for high-level confabs with Steele, North and others.[9] Castillo's prostitute informants at the safe house described many all-nighters "doing cocaine, having sex, and shooting rifles" with Contra pilots, government officials - and Oliver North.

Tim Ross, the BBC's correspondent in Colombia for twenty years, revealed that "In late 84, early 85, North brought five Afghani military advisers to Colombia on a speaking tour, three left, two stayed. The two that stayed were chemists who introduced heroin manufacturing to Colombia. He also brought in an Israeli agronomist who helped to cultivate opium poppies." Ross was summoned to the US Embassy in Bogotá and told, "You're going to lay off this story or you are going to die" by an "ex-marine, the type of guy who used to cut

Vietcong throats with his thumbnail." Ross, who knew he had BBC clout, ran the story anyway.

"October 23, 1986, HK-1960P Honduras. 1,000 kilos of cocaine. DEA-6 was written on this case."

"April 01, 1987, Bob Stia, Walter (pilot) Morales and myself flew to El Salvador. Met with two CIA agents who advised us that we could no longer utilize Murga because he was now working with them."

"Sept. 27, 1987, Central American CIA agent Randy Capister, the Guatemalan military (G-2) and myself, seized over 2,404 kilos of cocaine from a Guatemalan Congressman, Carlos Ramiro García de Paz and the Medellin cartel (biggest cocaine seizure in Central America and top five ever). However, several individuals were murdered and raped on said operation. CIA agent and myself saw individual being interrogated. The Congressman was never arrested or charged."

Castillo later found that much of the cocaine had been resold by Guatemalan G-2. This apparently necessitated the elimination of all the witnesses.

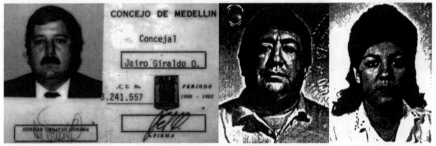

The murdered Jairo Gilardo-Ocampo, José Ramón and Maria Parra-Iniguez

"In one case (DEA file #TG-86-0005) several Colombians and Mexicans were raped, tortured and murdered by CIA and DEA assets, with the approval of the CIA. Among those victims identified was José Ramón Parra-Iniguez, Mexican passport A-GUC-043 and his two daughters Maria and Leticia Olivier-Dominguez, Mexican passport A-GM-8381. Also included among the dead were several Colombian nationals: Adolfo Leon Morales-Arcilia "a.k.a." Adolfo Morales-Orestes, Carlos Alberto Ramirez, and Jairo Gilardo-Ocampo. Both a DEA and a CIA agent were present, when these individuals were being interrogated (tortured)." The CIA agent, Randy Capister, Castillo tells me, was accompanied by none other than the documented drug trafficker El Negro Alvarado.

"The main target of that case was a Guatemalan Congressman, (Carlos Ramiro García de Paz) who took delivery of 2,404 kilos of cocaine in Guatemala just before the interrogation. This case directly implicated the Guatemalan Government in drug trafficking (The Guatemalan Congressman still has his US visa and continues to travel at his pleasure into the US). To add salt to the wound, in 1989 these murders were investigated by the U.S Department of Justice, Office of Professional Responsibility. DEA S/I Tony Recevuto determined that the Guatemalan Military Intelligence, G-2 (the worst human rights violators in the Western Hemisphere) was responsible for these murders. Yet, the U.S. government continued to order U.S. agents to work hand-in-hand with the Guatemalan Military. This information was never turned over to the I.O.B. investigation." (All parentheses Castillo's)

"October 22, 1987, I received a call from DEA HQS Everett Johnson, not to close Contra files because some committee was requesting file. If you have an open file, you do not have access to the files under Freedom of Information Act."

Castillo's evidence photo and note

"Dec. 03, 1988, DEA seized 356 kilos of cocaine in Tiquisate, Guatemala (DEA #TG-89-0002; Hector Sanchez). Several Colombians were murdered on said operation and condoned by the DEA and CIA. I have pictures of individuals that were murdered in said case. The target was on Gregorio Valdez (CIA asset) of the Guatemalan Piper Co. At that time, all air operations for the CIA and DEA flew out of Piper."

"With every killing, G2 took stacks of cash and bags of cocaine. In a faint nod to the law, they usually turned over a portion of the confiscated dope to beef up the country's drug war numbers. They sold the rest, or saved it to frame future victims."

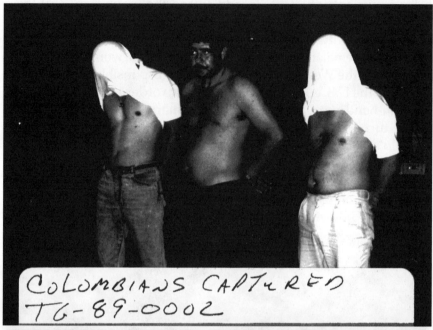

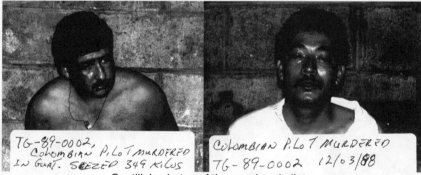

Castillo's photos of the murdered pilots

Castillo stepped up the pressure on the Company, filing detailed reports with DEA Station Chief Bob Stia in Guatemala. DEA internal affairs, the Justice Department's Office of Professional Responsibility, reacted by stepping up the pressure on Castillo and Stia. By 1990 Castillo was not only in bureaucratic but physical danger.

"<u>Aug. 24, 1989</u>, Because of my information, the U.S. Embassy canceled Guatemalan Military, Lt. Col. Hugo Francisco Moran-Carranza, (Head of Interpol and Corruption) U.S. visa. He was documented as a drug trafficker and as a corrupt Guatemalan Official. He was on his way to a U.S. War College for one year, invited by the CIA." (Parentheses Castillo's)

One of the dead pilots, drowned in a bucket of water; Castillo's note

"In a <u>Sept. 20-26, 1989</u>, series of debriefings and in subsequent debriefing on <u>Feb. 13, 1990</u>, by DEA agents in Los Angeles, Lawrence Victor Harrison, an American-born electronics specialist who had worked in Mexico and had been involved with the leading figures in the Mexican drug cartel, was interviewed. He testified that he had been present when two of the partners of Matta-Ballesteros and Rafael Caro-Quintero, met with American pilots working out of Ilopango air base in El Salvador, providing arms to the Contras. The purpose of the meeting was to work out drug deals."

"<u>Feb. 21, 1990</u>, I sent a telex-cable to DEA HQS Re: Moran's plan to assassinate me. Between Aug. 1989 and March 06, 1990, Col. Moran had initiated the plan to assassinate me in El Salvador and blame it on the guerrillas. On March 06, 1990, I traveled to Houston to deliver an undercover audio tape on my assassination. The Houston DEA S.A Mark Murtha (DEA File M3-90-0053) had an informant into Lt. Col. Moran."

The informant gave Castillo a tape of his meeting with Col. Moran of Guatemalan military intelligence: "Instead of talking about the bust the informant was setting up, Colonel Moran kept going on about how he was going to blame the rebels for my assassination. A hit squad was going to wait in the bushes and ambush me when I drove past on

Highway 8 in El Salvador."

Castillo played the tape for his DEA supervisors in Guatemala City, pointing out that Col. Moran was making huge deposits at the Panama City branch of the BCCI. Castillo's supervisors reacted by finding a pretext to order him to drive down Highway 8 in El Salvador. "I felt as if someone had painted a bullseye on the back of my head."

That's when Castillo turned to DEA HQ for protection. HQ wasn't all that quick to react: "March 15, 1990, After 6 months knowing about the assassination plan, DEA transferred me out to San Diego, California for 6 months."

"April 05, 1990, an illegal search was conducted at my residence in Guatemala by Guatemala DEA agents Tuffy Von Briesen, Larry Hollifield and Guatemalan Foreign Service National, Marco Gonzales (No search warrant). DEA HQS agreed that it had been an illegal search requested by OPR [Office of Professional Responsibility] S/I Tony Recevuto. (OPR file PR-TG-90-0068) On Sept. 16, 1991, a questionaire was faxed to me in regards to the illegal search."

"May 10, 1990, DEA HQS OPR S/I Tony Recevuto returned to Guatemala and requested from the U.S. ambassador, to please grant Lt. Col. Hugo Moran-Carranza a US Visa, so that he could testify before the BCCI investigation in Miami. The ambassador could not understand why anyone, for any reason, would request a US Visa for an individual who had planned the assassination of a US drug agent."

Although Iran-Contra Special Prosecutor Lawrence Walsh's FBI investigator Mike Foster interviewed Castillo extensively, not one word of his verifiable, professional testimony, backed up by DEA case file and NADDIS numbers, could be found in Walsh's voluminous 1993 *Final Report of the Independent Counsel for Iran/Contra Matters*. Walsh had no choice - Castillo's testimony had been "classified." Likewise the remarkable testimony of CIA agent Brenneke, elicited by Congressman Alexander.

Explained Walsh, "In addition to the unclassified Volumes I and II of this report, a brief classified report, Volume III, has been filed with the Special Division. The classified report contains references to material gathered in the investigation of Iran/contra that could not be declassified and could not be concealed by some substitute form of discussion."[10]

Senator Kerry, whose seminal 1986-9 investigation sparked Walsh's, also couldn't break the bureaucratic barrier. Despite the fact that much of his investigation was based on Castillo's hard-earned evidence, he either couldn't or wouldn't call on Castillo himself or any other active regional DEA agent. Referring to dope-dealing CIA Costa Rica station chief Joe Fernandez, who shared tactical control of the Contra air supply operation with Col. Steele, Walsh, in his final report, complained that "We've created a class of intelligence officer who cannot be prosecuted."

Castillo: "I have obtained a letter, dated May 28, 1996, from the DEA administrator, to U.S. Congressman Lloyd Doggett (D), Texas. In this letter, the administrator flatly lies, stating that DEA agents 'have never engaged in any joint narcotics programs with the Guatemalan Military.' I was there. I was the leading Agent in Guatemala. 99.9% of DEA operations were conducted with the Guatemalan military."[11]

"The CIA and Guatemalan army also label as communist sympathizers anyone who opposes the traditional oppressive role of the Guatemalan military. Therefore, they label as communists or communist sympathizers, priests and nuns who work to elevate the position of the poor in society, union organizers...indigenous leaders (the Indians are kept down so that they can be used as cheap laborers by the rich, who are supported by the military) and student activists.... The CIA supports the intimidation, kidnapping and torture, surveillance and murder of these people."[12]

DEA agents Von Briesen and Castillo with a machine gun toting Guatemalan G-2 agent in the background; Castillo's note

"As an example, look at the case of Dianna Ortiz, the American nun who was working with poor children and was kidnapped, raped and tortured by Guatemalan soldiers.... I was present at the US Embassy in Guatemala, when, just after the incident, several members of the DEA, State Department and CIA jokingly asked me if Dianna Ortiz had been good at sex. The reason they were teasing me was that she had said that an American Hispanic with possible ties to the US Embassy had been present during her torture and rape. Since everyone at the Embassy knew that I worked with the Guatemalan Military's D-2, and Sister Ortiz reported that soldiers had captured her, the people at the Embassy assumed that I was the American involved. (She was later shown photos of me and stated that I was not the person she had seen there, referred to by the soldiers as their boss.) I believe the reason that these DEA, State Department and CIA personnel would joke about such a thing is that they label Dianna Ortiz as a communist sympathizer. People with that mind set do not believe that she should be protected."

Castillo investigated Col. Julio Alpirez, who ordered the 1993 murder of captured guerrilla leader Efraín Bámaca, Jennifer Harbury's husband. Michael Devine, an American innkeeper, was also murdered by Alpirez. "He was killed in June 1990, murdered by Guatemalan soldiers, according to the IOB report. What the report does not mention, however, is that Colonel Alpirez was the director of the notorious Archivos while he was also a CIA asset and that he had previously been reported to the DEA for drug trafficking. This is documented in DEA General file number GFTG-88-9077 with filename "Corrupt Official" dated June 09, 1988. I was the agent who initiated the file."

"Colonel Alpirez is also documented as a narcotics trafficker in DEA case file number TG-88-0009 entitled "Moreno-Campos, Aparicio", dated August 25, 1988 and submitted by me. In both case files, Alpirez is named along with his subordinate, Carlos Rene Perez-Alvarez, who was known as Won Ton of La Mano Blanca (the White Hand of the death squads). Carlos Rene Perez-Alvarez operated "la panel blanca" (the White Van) that has patrolled the streets of Guatemala for so many years, kidnapping and murdering people for the death squads."

"On page A-3, the report refers to a personality profile on DeVine that was 'generally positive, but noted a somewhat aggressive manner and a readiness to denounce people involved in narcotics trafficking.' The latter comment is, in my view, a key to the reason that he was killed. The connections of DeVine to Alpirez, Alpirez to the CIA, the CIA to the D-2 [another name for G-2, Guatemalan military intelligence] and the D-2 to the murder of DeVine can all be found in the IOB report, supporting what I was told about the case."

Jennifer Harbury on hunger strike in front of the Guatemalan National Palace, 10/ 1994, with a picture of her murdered husband, Efraín Bámaca Velasquez

"Here is what I believe to be the truth about the DeVine case, according to my sources. 1. Colonel Alpirez was trafficking drugs. (see DEA case file number GFTG-88-9077 and number TG-88-0009). 2. Colonel Alpirez was a CIA asset (according to the IOB report and numerous other sources). 3. DeVine gained knowledge of Alpirez's drug trafficking activities while Alpirez was training Kaibil forces in the Peten close to his farm. 4. DeVine reported Alpirez's drug trafficking activities to the US Embassy in Guatemala. 5. After DeVine reported Alpirez to the US Embassy, Randy Capister, a CIA agent operating out of the embassy, contacted Colonel Francis (Paco) Ortega, former head of the D-2, and a CIA and DEA asset. He told Ortega that DeVine had reported Colonel Alpirez (another CIA asset) for drug trafficking. (per phone conversation between myself and Randy Capister after the death of DeVine in 1990). 6. Colonel Ortega contacted the new head of the D-2, Colonel Cesar Cabrera, who had been under Ortega's command earlier (When Colonel Ortega was head of the D-2, Cabrera was a lieutenant colonel and Ortega's second in command). 7. Cabrera, chief of the D-2 ordered the so-called "interrogation" of DeVine and was therefore 'indirectly responsible for DeVine's death' (See IOB report page A-3). (This "interrogation" included a machete blow that almost completely severed DeVine's head from his body.)" (All parentheses Castillo's)

It was this dealing structure, two years after the murder of DeVine, that Efraín Bámaca, Commandante Everardo, threatened to expose. Although Castillo could shed professional DEA light on CIA complicity in the drug dealing of its ally, Guatemalan G-2, Walsh couldn't "declassify" Castillo's testimony, or save his career.[13] Castillo's book, *Powderburns*, is essential reading for anyone after a realistic assessment of the Drug War.

The Office of Professional Responsibility actually used false testimony from Castillo's would-be Guatemalan assassin, Col. Moran, to force Castillo's premature retirement. Felix Rodriguez, on the other hand, was full of medals from Salvadoran generals and Col. James Steele.

Castillo: "In 1997, I joined DEA SA Richard Horn in a federal class action suit against the CIA. The suit is against the CIA and other federal agencies for spying on several DEA agents and other unnamed DEA employees and their families. United States District Court for the District of Columbia; Richard Horn vs. Warren Christopher, ...January 30, 1994."

In late 1990, CIA agent Mark McFarlin, who had worked with Col. Steele against El Salvador's FMLN, and Gen. Ramón Guillén Davila of the Venezuelan National Guard, arranged a huge shipment of cocaine to Florida. This shipment was intercepted by the U.S. Customs Service at Miami's International Airport.

Guillén was Venezuela's former antidrug chief. He was charged by the U.S. Justice Department, 11/22/96, with organizing the importation of more than 22 tons of Colombian cocaine into the U.S. Speaking from his safe haven in Caracas, Guillén insisted that this was a joint CIA-Venezuelan operation aimed at the Cali cartel. Given that Guillén was a longtime CIA employee, and that the drugs were stored in a Venezuelan warehouse owned by the CIA, the 'joint' part of Guillén's statement is almost certainly true, although the 'aimed at' part is almost certainly false.

The DEA officially concluded that the CIA intentionally withheld "vital information" on the Cali cartel, its business partner in this extended operation, from onsite DEA investigators. The Cali cartel, it should be noted, as the Samper investigation revealed, was financing CIA and Venezuelan-supported elements of Colombian military intelligence.[14]

The CIA was forced to officially admit its role in this affair after it was told that "60 Minutes" was planning to broadcast the results of its own investigation on CBS on 11/21/93. Attempting to control the damage, the CIA admitted, 11/19/93, that it had shipped one ton of pure cocaine from Venezuela in what it called "a most regrettable incident." The CIA's revelations came out in *The New York Times* on 11/20. The spin the CIA gave the *Times* was that it was trying to sting Haiti's National Intelligence Service (SIN) - which the CIA itself had created.

*New York Times:*11/14/93: "1980's CIA Unit in Haiti Tied to Drug Trade - Political Terrorism committed against Aristide supporters: The Central Intelligence Agency created an intelligence service in Haiti in the mid-1980's to fight the cocaine trade, but the unit evolved into an instrument of political terror whose officers sometimes engaged in drug trafficking, American and Haitian officials say. Senior members of the CIA unit committed acts of political terror against Aristide supporters, including interrogations and torture, and in 1992 threatened to kill the local chief of the U.S. Drug Enforcement Administration. According to one American official, who spoke on condition of anonymity, 'it was an organization that distributed drugs in Haiti and never produced drug intelligence.'"

How shocking to the innocents at CIA, who certainly had expected Haiti's policemen to be above venality. That is, the SIN dealers, led by Brig. Gen. Raoul Cedras and Michel Francois, who overthrew the legally elected populist Jean-Bertrand Aristide in September of 1991, were armed and trained by Bush's CIA. In fact, Bush's CIA Director, Casey's assistant Robert Gates, was actually stupid enough to call Cedras one of the most promising "Haitian leaders to emerge since the Duvalier family dictatorship was overthrown in 1986."[15]

When the DEA's Tony Greco tried to stop a massive cocaine shipment in May, 1991, four months before the coup, his family received death threats on their private number from "the boss of the man arrested." The only people in Haiti who had that number were the coup leaders, army commander Raoul Cedras and his partner, Port-au-Prince police chief Michel Francois, "the boss of the man arrested."

A 1993 U.S. GAO report insisted that Cedras and Francois were running one of the largest cocaine export rings in the world. In 1994, after this PR disaster, the U.S. militarily reinstalled Aristide. This was done on Clinton's condition that Aristide relinquish power almost as soon as he got it.

Clinton insisted that Aristide's three years in exile be counted as part of his 5-year term. The only American officer tried for "insubordination" during the reinstallation process was the one who insisted on looking into Cedras' prisons. Within 4 months of Aristide's 1994 reinstallation, U.S. troops turned Haiti over to the U.S.-trained National Police, recruited from Cedras' SIN security structure, *Tontons Macoutes* in uniform.

Human Rights Watch/Americas reports that the National Police regularly murdered political activists as well as rival drug dealers. After the January, 1995 parliamentary elections, Senator Turneb Delpe, head of Aristide's former coalition, the National Front for Change and Democracy, complained that "People may have voted freely, but then our political party observers were chased away, and ballot boxes confiscated. Is this democratic?"[16]

Aristide's 1996 replacement as president, his pre-coup prime minister René Préval, proved so powerless as to be unable to keep his own prime minister much of the time. The April 1997 parliamentary election was perceived as so corrupt that only 5% of the population voted.[17] *Los Angeles Times*, 3/8/97: "Lt. Col. Michel Francois, one of the CIA's reported Haitian agents, a former Army officer and a key leader in the military regime that ran Haiti between 1991 and 1994, was indicted in Miami for smuggling 33 tons of cocaine into the USA." Added the livid Rep. Maxine Waters, who quoted this story on the floor of the House, 3/18/97, "Members of this House literally had wrapped their arms around drug dealers. Members of this House not only swore by them and protected them, while they were protecting them, Francois was building an airstrip where he could receive the drugs..."

As of April, 1998, the U.S. government continues to refuse to return 160,000 pages of documents seized in 1994 from the Haitian military and its paramilitary arm, the *Front pour l'Avancement et Progrés d'Haïti*, FRAPH. Founded with CIA assistance, FRAPH was Cedras' death squad. The U.S. openly admits that it will return the documents only after it has finished excising the names of U.S. agents involved with the FRAPH.

Also being withheld from the Haitian Justice Ministry are documents and reports on the FRAPH's two most famous massacres, the December 1993 massacre of at least thirty residents of Cité Soleil and the 1994 massacre of at least fifteen people in Raboteau.

In August 1997, the State Department once again prevented the deportation of FRAPH leader Emmanuel Constant, who had received regular CIA payments throughout his tenure under Cedras. The Five Families that had financed Duvalier and Cedras are still in absolute control. But Haiti, the charmingly maudlin Clinton will tell you, is a democracy.

Both Cedras and Francois are graduates of the U.S. Army's School of the Americas. Both got their training during the Contra years in Haiti's CIA-founded National Intelligence Service structure led by Noriega allies Lt.Cols. Jean Paul and Prosper Avril, both indicted dopers. Like Noriega, they helped Maj. Gen. John Singlaub finance the Contras. It is here, at the highest structural levels of U.S. military intelligence, at the level that is able to consciously subvert the political will of the State Department, that 'Contra' turns into 'Iran-Contra.'

Wrote a seething Secretary of State George Shultz, "The CIA and the NSC staff, with the apparent support from the ...Vice President, were still proceeding as though nothing had happened. Congress was being misled now, a month and a half after the revelation [of Air Hasenfus] first appeared. What was worse, [Deputy Secretary of State] John Whitehead said, 'the CIA has told the Iranians that the State Department is just a temporary impediment, and that after it calms down, [ranking CIA agents] Cave and Secord will be back in action. The president is being ripped to pieces, and the CIA is reassuring the Iranians."[18] Funny how the conservative Reaganaut Schultz ended up with the same analysis of CIA/State relations as the liberal Kennedyite Schlesinger.

Cave and Secord's boss was John Singlaub, chairman of the World Anti-Communist League (WACL) in the mid-80's. He presided over Reagan's sophisticated campaign to spruce up its Nazi-tainted image. If there was one thing that actor understood, it was public relations.

Singlaub, from 1966-68, headed the Joint Unconventional Warfare Task Force, Operation Phoenix, the Special Operations Group organized by William Colby. Singlaub coordinated the murder of upwards of 60,000 Vietnamese, most while helpless in detention or by stealthy assassination. Special targets were village leaders, elder statesmen and leaders of women's groups.

In 1981 Singlaub, financed by Taiwan, founded the United States Council for World Freedom (USCWF), a vehicle for the cooperation of "distinguished" American conservatives with the WACL. Singlaub was assisted in his efforts by Gen. "Heine" Aderholt, the Special Forces commander who helped run Operation Phoenix. Serving under Aderholt in Vietnam was the moral avatar Barry McCaffrey. Aderholt was the unconventional warfare editor of *Soldier of Fortune* magazine, which actively supported Ian Smith's glorious defense of Cecil's Rhodesia.

Singlaub ran WACL and USCWF seminars conducted by expert old hands from AID, OPS, the U.S. Police Academy, the Rand Corporation and the CIA/DIA. Thus, at the 1984 World Anti-Communist League resistance movement seminars in San Diego, the Nicaraguan Contras could present their armaments shopping list to well-connected CIA cutouts who could deliver the goods, as could Savimbi's UNITA from Angola, South Africa's Renamo from Mozambique, Eritrean and Tigrean forces from Ethiopia, Royalists from Laos, "non-Communist" Khmer Rouge from Cambodia (seen by Kissinger and his successors - and their Chinese allies - as a counterbalance to Vietnamese power), and the opium-growing *mujaheddin* of Afghanistan.[19]

Another Operation Phoenix vet assisting Singlaub was Richard Secord, who had been Singlaub's Laotian air wing commander, he who delivered the Hmong opium. Secord established the dummy bank account in Geneva, "Lake Resources," through which Taiwan funneled money to the Contras. Secord also handled arms sales to Iran, Pakistan and Afghanistan - at inflated prices that left cash free for personal profit and the Contras.[20]

This operation, managed through Israeli military intelligence, received cash payment for hundreds of millions of dollars worth of arms *twice*. First, the U.S. Congress authorized payment for delivery to Afghan rebels, and then the arms, stockpiled in Pakistan, were actually delivered to the Iranians, who also paid for them.[21]

The Israeli motive was the defeat of Iraq, at that time far more dangerous to Israel than Iran. That American motives and Israeli were different is demonstrated by the fact that while Israel was playing the Iran card, America was also playing the Iraq card. Through the Banco Nazionale del Lavoro, between 1985 and 1989, the CIA/DIA illegally funneled at least $5 billion worth of arms, including cluster bombs and napalm, to Saddam Hussein. The calculation apparently had been made that America's strategic position would be improved if both sides incinerated one another. Then again, maybe the sheer value of these transactions drove them.

The American guarantors of these "agricultural loans" were the Export-Import Bank and the Commodities Credit Corporation. The Department of Justice, refusing to follow up on the Arms Export Control Act violations, which would have involved the Reagan/Bush administration and the CIA, simply indicted 6 BNL executives for bank fraud.[22]

Was this a factor in Bush's bizarre insistence that Saddam Hussein's army be allowed to survive Operation Desert Storm? I have yet to meet an American who doesn't feel betrayed by that. We could have snuffed that mass murderer in less than a week and organized U.N.-supervised general elections.

The Pakistani-based Afghan arms deliveries, of course, depended on the Pakistani Inter-Services Intelligence (ISI), which the CIA transformed from a bit player into a powerful asset. The ISI functioned in neighboring Afghanistan through its client armies, the greatest poppy growers and heroin dealers in West Asia.

The murderous Gulbuddin Hekmatyar of *Hezb-i-Islami* functioned as a contract killer for ISI for years before the Afghan war. *Hezb-i-Islami* actually advocated throwing acid in the faces of women who wouldn't wear the medieval *chador* over their faces. Hekmatyar spoke for God, doncha know.

He not only made war on the Russians, but on vulnerable Afghan rebel groups that wouldn't fight under his - that is, the ISI's - banner, committing repeated massacres of his own best fighters, many of them every bit as fundamentalist as he. The motive seems to have been territorial control of the substantial opium/heroin/arms trade.

In 1989, as the provisional post-Soviet Afghan government was taking shape, Hekmatyar attacked his chief rival for leadership of the *mujaheddin*, Mullah Nassim, who controlled so much of the fertile Helmand Valley that he could produce 260 tons of opium per year. Although the initial attack failed, Hekmatyar engineered Nassim's assassination a few months later, giving him control of the entire Helmand Valley.[23]

In 1985, when the ISI chief told the French ambassador that in future all French aid to the *mujaheddin* must go through the ISI, the French ambassador told him to go to hell. France continued to supply arms directly to the extraordinary Masoud, then an enemy of

Hekmatyar. Once, when a large Russian tank column pushed onto the floor of the Panjshir Valley, Masoud, using explosives placed high in the mountains overlooking the valley floor, buried the entire column in a huge avalanche of boulders.

An Afridi warrior prepares *charas*, often a potent mix of hashish and opium; *Asia*, 4/1925

Early in 1986, Pakistani Army Maj. Zahooruddin Afridi was arrested driving to Karachi from Peshawar with 220 kilos of pure snow-white #4 heroin. Two months later, Air Force Flt. Lt. Khalilur Rehman was intercepted with exactly the same load. He said it was his "fifth mission."

The heroin was converted Afghan opium delivered to Pakistani refineries by Hekmatyar's collection system. As *The Washington Post* reported in 1990, "Hekmatyar commanders close to ISI run laboratories in southwest Pakistan."[24] The retail value of the two intercepted loads alone, at least $600 million, was equivalent to a full year's worth of U.S. foreign aid to Pakistan.[25]

McCoy, drawing from Pakistani sources, estimates that by 1988 there were as many as 200 ISI-connected heroin refineries in the Khyber district alone. ISI arms trucks, from their National Logistics Cell, delivered CIA arms from Karachi to all points on the Afghan border. Those trucks, protected from police search by their ISI papers, often returned loaded with heroin from Hekmatyar's rural refineries. Of 40 major heroin syndicates identified by DEA agents operating out of Pakistan and Afghanistan during the 1980's, not one was busted by Pakistani enforcement.[26]

Hekmatyar's most famous victim, according to Asia Watch, was professor Sayd Majrooh, Director of the Afghan Information Center in Peshawar, a famous professor of philosophy at Kabul University before the war. He objected to the identification of independent *mujaheddin* like Masoud of the Panjshir Valley with the heroin trade, and so made the mistake of going public with what he knew about the ISI-Hekmatyar connection. He was assassinated in February of 1988.[27]

Afridi warriors on Pakistan's Northwest Frontier enjoy their traditional smoke, *Asia*,1925

In July of 1989, the newly-elected Benazir Bhutto went after the ISI. She arrested General Fazle Huq, the former governor of the Northwest Frontier, in effect Hekmatyar's commanding officer. His personal fortune was estimated at several *billion* dollars.

"But it's funny," an Afridi chief told a reporter from the *Financial Times* in 1989, "that the CIA are using the very people that the State Department are trying to stop. All these Western aid projects have helped opium poppy production in Afghanistan and the Americans have produced a new incentive - offering bribes to those who destroy their crops. They don't learn. They tried that in Pakistan and production went up."[28]

The Afridi chief himself ran numerous heroin refineries. The civil war now raging throughout Afghanistan and Tajikistan, which has devastated the local economies, has left traditional opium as one of the few commodities farmers can rely on to feed their families.

By September, 1996, the ISI's "fundamentalists" achieved control of 90% of Afghanistan. Although women haven't fared so well - literally losing their rights to education, employment, access public hospitals and bathrooms and dress themselves - opium has thrived. Since opium had been basic to their power, the Taliban encouraged its planting everywhere. By 1994, according to the UNDCP, Afghanistan surpassed Burma as the world's leading source of raw opium.

Iranian "bafouri"; *Asia*, c.1925

This was not considered a scandal in Afghanistan, however. In this part of the world it is alcohol that is viewed with opprobrium, not opium or hashish, the raw ingredients of primo *charas*. Former CIA Director Richard Helms was Ambassador to Iran in 1975, arranging alternative funding for the region's military fascists. He worked with the great dope-dealing team of Gen. Richard Secord, the Shah's Senior Air Advisor, Richard Armitage, Ted Shackley, Tom Clines and the ubiquitous Felix Rodriguez in this effort. Helms accurately reported that "In some educated, high society circles, it [opium] is smoked socially after dinner."[29]

When the Ayatollah took Iran, he declared that drug dealers were "first class traitors and a danger to society." But the drug he was talking about was alcohol. Opium, if not completely legal, remained, as it had been under the Shah, "decriminalized" - culturally tolerated and freely available, and in fact, a favorite among the Ayatollah's Revolutionary Guards. It is the height of cultural conceit to think that such ingrained attitudes can ever be overcome.

"Using the Ayatollah's money to support the Nicaraguan resistance is a neat idea," chirped Ollie.[30] Except if you get caught. On March 16, 1988, North, his immediate superior Poindexter, Poindexter's predecessor Robert McFarlane, Richard Secord, and Secord's business partner Albert Hakim were indicted for violating the Congressional ban on arming the Contras (the Boland Amendment), illegal arms sales, conspiracy, fraud and theft.

Of course, these were operations executed by intelligence professionals. All we get to see, thanks to the painstaking and dangerous digging of reporters like Lawrence Lifschultz, is the tip of the iceberg. In 1987, the *Far Eastern Economic Review* reported serious allegations that $700 million of the $1.09 billion appropriated by Congress between 1980 and 1986 to the CIA Directorate of Operations for the *mujaheddin* never reached them.[31]

In February of 1996, the director and the deputy director of the spy satellite program, the National Reconnaissance Office, were sacked by John Deutch, the political appointee ostensibly in charge of the CIA, for "losing track" of over $2 *billion* in "classified" funds.[32] Deutch is now gone, but the operatives who engineered that, except for the two he nailed, are still in place.

"Classified" funds now total nearly 40 *billion* of the Defense Department's annual outlay. When Senator Church's Select Committee on Intelligence asked, in 1975, what percent of its budget the CIA dedicated to covert operations, it was told 3%. Upon investigation, the Committee concluded that the figure was more like 80%. That - in the absence of effective oversight - makes the CIA a policy-making institution.

As reported in the *Washington Post*, 5/28/89, DEA officials have consistently complained of the poor antidrug intelligence they get from the CIA. On June 28, 1996, the President's Intelligence Oversight Board, responding to the firestorm of publicity unleashed by Jennifer Harbury and Sister Dianna Ortiz, once again pointed to a politically corrupt intelligence apparatus, as if discovering that for the very first time:

"We found...two areas in which CIA's performance was unacceptable. First, until late 1994, insufficient attention was given to allegations of serious human rights abuse made against several station assets or liaison contacts. Second, the CIA failed to provide enough information on this subject to policy-makers and the Congress to permit proper policy and Congressional oversight."

"In the course of our review, we found that several CIA assets were credibly alleged to have ordered, planned, or participated in serious human rights violations such as assassination, extrajudicial execution, torture, or kidnapping while they were assets — and that the CIA's Directorate of Operations (DO) headquarters was aware at the time of the allegations."

Former CIA agent Ralph McGehee comments: "Since the earliest days of the CIA, it recruited people...who are psychologically-tested to be team-playing extroverts with rigid mentalities - sounding the death knell for controversial or accurate intelligence..... It should be clear why the CIA has such a terrible intelligence record. The politicized/bureaucratized structure ensures that managers, who owe their supervisory positions to political accommodations, can alter, negate or cancel unwanted information. The current CIA leadership is replete with those who have documented records of politicizing intelligence..."[33]

Just west of the Golden Crescent of Afghanistan, Pakistan and Iran is the enormous U.S. military strength in Turkey. On January 21, 1997, a judge in Frankfurt, presiding over the sentencing of three convicted heroin smugglers, concluded that, on the basis of the evidence before him, there were close ties between the Turkish government and Europe's major organized heroin traffickers.

Judge Rolf Schwalbe concluded that two Kurdish clans known to be heavily involved in heroin trafficking had "excellent relations with the Turkish government" and "personal contacts with a woman minister in the government."[34]

The Turkish publicity hit the fan on November 3, 1996, when a Mercedes Benz crashed in the Susurluk neighborhood of Ankara. The driver was Huseyin Kocadag, former Istanbul deputy police chief and CIA organizer of special counterinsurgency teams aimed at the PKK. The popular rebellion of Turkey's 15 million Kurds, led by the Partiya Karkeran Kurdistan, the Kurdish Workers Party, has drawn the CIA into yet another dirty war.

The death of the glamorous Gonca Us, the hood-connected beauty queen, in the Susurluk crash only served to advertise it further. Seriously injured was the Kurdish turncoat Sedat Bucak, Village Guard chieftain and True Path Party (DYP) parliamentarian. But it was the presence of Abdullah Catli in the Mercedes that made the heroin connection. Catli was a founder of the Grey Wolves, the street fighting arm of the fascist National Action Party (MHP). Since 1978 he has been wanted for mass murder and international drug smuggling. What was this famous international terrorist doing riding in a car with the most powerful police officials in Turkey?

And why was Catli holding a license to carry arms and a Green Passport reserved for senior Ministry officials, both signed by Interior Minister Mehmet Agar? Agar was the most powerful security official in Turkey, head of the 120,000-strong police and counterinsurgency force financed and trained by the CIA.

When Abdullah Catli entered Miami in 1982 under a previous Green Passport, he was accompanied by none other than Stefano delle Chiaie, one of Klaus Barbie's key CIA Cocaine Coup engineers, a Gehlen operative. The great heroin and cocaine smuggler Abdullah Catli had been taking orders from the most powerful security official in Turkey, as had Catli's senior Gray Wolf henchmen, also issued documents signed by Agar.

Deputy Prime Minister Tansu Ciller, the DYP "woman minister" Judge Schwalbe referred to, was forced to accept Agar's resignation. But she insisted that "those who have fired bullets as well as those who have been shot in the name of the state are honest."

Judge Schwalbe's investigation, however, confirmed the opposite. The CIA-founded and financed Turkish security apparatus had used Turkey's fascist hoods in a no-holds-barred street fight for control of the vast Golden Crescent heroin trade, a financial key, as Richard Helms and his experienced dope-dealing team well understood, to military power in Turkey.

The Gray Wolves, founded in the late 70's with the help of that team, the Shah's team, were a covert part of Turkey's security apparatus. Immediately on their founding they joined the CIA's Anti-Bolshevik Bloc of Nations and World Anti-Communist League, targeting not only the nascent PKK, but liberal journalists and politicians throughout Turkey. When this coalition overthrew Suleyman Demirel's conservative parliamentary government in 1980, the CIA's Ankara Station Chief Paul Henze cabled HQ in Washington, "Our boys have done it!"[35]

Free Burma!@http://metalab.unc.edu/freeburma

Drug War

Burma:8/8/88

New York Times:2/12/95: "Administration narcotics experts say heroin production in Myanmar, formerly known as Burma, has doubled since 1988 and now accounts for 60 to 70 percent of the American supply."

"Those experts are urging President Clinton to step-up anti-drug cooperation with the Burmese military junta. But human rights officials argue against cooperating with a government judged to be a serious abuser of human rights...."

"'There's been a fairly dramatic increase in heroin since the military came to power,' said Robert S. Gelbard, Assistant Secretary of State for International Narcotics Matters. 'There is a lot of concern about narcotics-related corruption, particularly in the mid-levels of the Burmese Army.'"

"Backing up Mr. Brown's call for increased cooperation are Thomas A. Constantine, director of the Drug Enforcement Administration; Timothy E. Wirth, the Under Secretary of State for Global Affairs, and Assistant Secretary of State Gelbard."

"The stepped-up cooperation under consideration would include sharing intelligence with Myanmar officials, training the country's police and providing equipment to them like police radios, drug-detection kits and trucks."

Brilliant. Supply the Burmese military, which we know is dealing the heroin, which just murdered thousands of its own people in an overt *coup d'etat*, with military intelligence telling them what we know, and with crowd-control equipment to help them murder more of their own people.

The incredibly courageous Daw Aung San Suu Kyi of Burma's National League for Democracy will be named Prime Minister if Burma's legally elected National Assembly is ever allowed to convene. She is the daughter of the legendary General Bogyoke Aung San, postwar leader of the Burman nationalists.

Burma was, in many ways, an artificial conflation of the British, combining ethnic groups that had not traditionally shared a government. General Aung San is, in effect, the George Washington of Burma, the political author of the federal constitution of 1947 that created post-colonial Burma. Just as he was set to assume the Prime Ministership, in July 1947, Aung San was assassinated, leaving Burma's strong territorial minorities facing a death squad central army, the probable author of the assassination, and a weak central government. The result was precisely the civil war that Aung San's new constitution had been designed to prevent.

General Aung San

All the armies were financed by the artificial Prohibition value of opium except the Kachins, who had their jade, ruby and sapphire mines. Unlike opium, which, if allowed to float in a legal market would be worth little more than extra fine produce, the value of sapphires isn't artificial.

Lahu hunters in the Shan hills, *Asia*, 1/1929

Complicating the situation further were the 12,000 CIA-financed

Kuomintang troops in the Shan states, the eastern mountains bordering Thailand and China. They were originally placed there to draw Chinese strength during the Korean War. Mao's reaction to the CIA-KMT alliance was to turn the Communist Party of Burma (CPB) into the same kind of well-armed client army as the KMT. Thus Burma degenerated into civil war.

A Karen woman enjoys a *thukeeta*, a banana-leaf pipe

Ne Win, in control of the Burma Army in the early sixties, brought many of the Shan state opium armies under his umbrella by legalizing the opium trade for those who would fight under his KKY (*Ka Kwe Ye*), local self defense, banner. Khun Sa, who eventually rose to control most of these Shan state opium armies, began his career as a

CIA student in his father's outfit, the Kuomintang's Shan operation.[1]

After the Burma Army drove the KMT into Thailand, Khun Sa heeded Ne Win's call to become a KKY leader. As such, Khun Sa was armed by Ne Win, and held the right to use all government controlled roads for opium transport. He also had the right to run morphine and heroin refineries. Thus heroin for export became the official mainstay of the Burma Army's war against the Karens, the Shans, the Kachins, the Wa, the Lahu, the Communists, the KMT and the other territorially or politically-based rebels.

A Lahu father and child, and a Kaw woman, the Shan States, *Asia*, 1/1929.
Criminalize the traditional contents of the pipe, criminalize the culture.

Since the American-led global Prohibition of opium sap popularized heroin, artificially making it valuable enough to trade for arms, many KKY leaders were enabled to co-opt the local ethnic or political movement. The Burma Army settled into the role of central wholesaler, issuing franchises to all the major players in control of opium-growing territory, using its KKY militia as trucking convoys for its franchisees. Thus did all sides in the civil war settle into a relatively peaceful marriage of convenience, a marriage that had the militarized heroin trade as its glue.

That is, when China's Deng Xiaoping turned Burma into a trading partner, the Communist Party of Burma made peace with the

Burma Army and went into business with it, as did the Kuomintang, Khun Sa's Shans and most, but not all, of the other guerrilla groups. Notably absent were the Karens, who did not choose to enroll as SLORC slaves.

Karen farmer-soldiers are inspired; metalab.unc.edu/freeburma

James "Bo" Gritz, as most Americans know, is a famous Vietnam War commando. He went on to command U.S. Special Forces in the Panama Canal Zone. After his 1979 retirement he functioned as a deep penetration expert for the DIA's Intelligence Support Activity. In 1986 Col. Harvey of the National Security Council asked Gritz' ISA team to check out reports received by Vice President Bush, that Khun Sa had possession of some missing U.S. servicemen. Upon reaching the jungle redoubt of this commander of 40,000 guerrilla troops, Gritz was absolutely astonished by what the warlord offered. This is what Gritz, under oath, told the Senate Select Committee on POW Affairs, 11/23/92:

"We established good rapport and determined that the reports of his having American POWs were false. I used both video and a CIA provided portable polygraph to produce proof that Khun Sa had no knowledge of U.S. POWs.... He promised to either secure any Americans found or give me 2,500 of his best troops to recover them. I was told to return in March for the results. I asked Khun Sa about trafficking in Heroin. He told me to take an offer back to President Reagan. Khun Sa was willing to eliminate all the Golden Triangle opiates and disclose the U.S. government officials who were his best customers for more than 20 years! In return Khun Sa wanted a trade agreement which would allow free world exploitation of the Shan State natural resources. VP Bush was leading the war on drugs and it sounded like an offer we couldn't refuse."

".... Harvey telephoned with congratulations on successfully resolving the POW report, Khun Sa's sweep of western Laos and offer to help in any rescue operation. When I inquired about the drug offer, Harvey said there was no interest. Such a negative response was surprising, but staff assistants in DC tend to develop tunnel-vision and see no importance outside of their own narrow focus. I returned to Burma and found reason why there was "no interest!"

".... 'After you left with my Reagan message in December, I thought maybe I'd see B-52 bombers overhead. Instead both the Thai and Burmese came to me and said they had to make it look like they were doing something or they could lose millions of U.S. drug suppression dollars. I told them to do anything they wanted as long as it included a road from Mae Hong Son Air Port.' Ten-ton trucks had replaced the horses and mules as the drug tonnage quickly indicated. A news article showing the U.S. Ambassador presenting the Thais with a $1.8 million check for all their hard work cooled political concerns."

"Khun Sa said he understood the problem. He sadly reported that after an exhaustive search his agents had turned up no evidence of U.S. prisoners alive in Western Laos, but he was willing to reveal some of the U.S. officials he had dealt with since winning the Burma-Laos Opium War in 1967! My ears pricked up when [Assistant Secretary of Defense] Richard Armitage was named as the person who handled the money with the banks in Australia! I was familiar with Michael Hand's Nugan-Hand Bank chain that laundered CIA drug money worldwide. The Chiang Mai branch telephone was answered by the DEA secretary. Mike Hand had been a Special Forces operative. Nugan was found shot to death after the bank examiners revealed their nefarious dealings. Hand disappeared. If Armitage was the bagman, then he wouldn't want live POWs coming home. Follow-on investigations would involve him as the responsible bureaucrat. Armitage and Harvey were close associates who lifted weights together at the Pentagon Officers Athletic Club. If Armitage was involved and saw Khun Sa's offer to name names, it could have sparked the "newspaper drug war" — something certainly did!"

"Immediately upon arrival at the Bangkok safehouse on 19 May

Chemicals and equipments used to produce heroin
Seized by Tamadaw (Armed Forces) & Law Enforcement Agencies on
July 24, 1997, from a used refineries, Mene Point,
near map reference: N-013114 and N-012115

Myanmar advertises its cosmetic anti-heroin effort

Ammonium Chloride 300 kilos in (12) bags, Lime 2,350 kilo in
(47) bags and other accessories to produce narcotic drugs.
Seized by Tamadaw (Armed Forces) & Law Enforcement Agencies on
October 24, 1997, at Mong Koo to Mong Kang road, Myanmar.

1987, I was called by Joseph Felter who informed me that U.S. Government authorities, had come to him so that I might be advised to erase and forget everything I had just learned from Khun Sa and return IMMEDIATELY with all documentation to be turned over to Harvey upon arrival. My failure to properly respond would 'hurt the U.S. Government!'.... I chose instead to present the information and was called to testify before Larry Smith's House Sub-Committee on Narcotics Oversight. It was a mistake. Smith did not allow the members to view the Khun Sa video record and questioned the "heroin highway" as being a road to attack Khun Sa. He said the charges against Armitage were old, investigated, and unfounded."

"The DEA finally admitted to a new road from Mae Hong Son to Khun Sa's HQ, but they said it was a "graduation road." Khun Sa wanted Thai officials to attend a special ceremony and didn't want them riding mules for miles so he had a highway built that they could drive along. Official heroin statistics record that in 1986 Khun Sa shipped 600 tons of opiates out of his Golden Triangle. The amount went up to 900 in 1987 (per highway), then 1,200 tons in 1988 and 3,050 tons in 1989! The road became so visible that Khun Sa had to alter the direction of flow and means of transportation, but not the volume. As Khun Sa said to me, "How do you think I can move so much opium product out of the jungle if it is not with badges?" Attorney General Richard Thornburgh indicted Khun Sa calling him the world's blackest criminal. Khun Sa had offered President George Bush one metric ton of #4 pure Asian Heroin that sells for over $1 million per pound on the metropolitan streets of America. It was to be a show of good faith that he would eliminate every one while divulging his best customers. There was no interest!"[2]

By 1988, Mandalay, in northern Burma, with dozens of refineries converting the vast highland opium crop into white #4 heroin, had become the heroin capitol of Asia.[3] This freed the Burma Army to stomp all over elected representatives in all parts of Burma, creating a spontaneous, countrywide uprising that began on 8/8/88, the uprising of the four 8's.

The automatic reaction of the Burma Army was massacre. At least 10,000 people died (see the superb film *Beyond Rangoon*). It was Singapore, which is so proud of its fascist antidrug laws, whose state arms company rescued the Burma Army's heroin traders as they were running out of ammunition during the Rangoon Massacre.

The diplomatic pressure created by the 1988 massacre forced the May 1990 elections, which the Burma Army was confident it had fixed by prohibiting opposition electioneering. Despite the repression, the National League for Democracy, led by Tin Oo and Aung San Suu

Kyi, won in a landslide - 82% of the popular vote, 392 of parliament's 485 seats.

This government has never been allowed to convene and Burma is now a dope-dealing death squad police state run by the Army's State Law and Order Council (SLORC), which has jailed or assassinated many NLD parliamentarians and thousands of Aung San Suu Kyi's supporters. The SLORC now calls itself the State Peace and Development Council, SPDC, but "Myanmar" is still Burma and the SPDC is still the SLORC.

To quote the February 1996 UN Commission on Human Rights report: "Torture, summary and arbitrary executions, forced labor, abuse of women, politically motivated arrests and detention, forced displacement, important restrictions on the freedoms of expression and association and oppression of ethnic and religious minorities..."

The forced labor is massive, with huge mining complexes literally serviced by slaves under the whip - and paid, literally, in heroin. They are *encouraged* to share needles and, since they are in so much pain, they do. Burma is the leading source of AIDS transmission in Asia.[4]

14 year-old Mon girls kidnapped to work as slave porters for SLORC platoons. Right, Mon women and children working under guard as forced labor to build the Ye Tavoy Railroad, May, 1995; metalab.unc.edu/freeburma

Many SLORC mining and road building operations use little children and women in advanced pregnancy as forced heavy labor. Those peasants who resist "volunteering" are charged with sedition, the punishment for which is the same as for handing out pro-democracy leaflets - five years or more at hard labor on a chain gang.

Burma's billion-dollar gas pipeline, for instance, is being built with slave labor. This a joint U.S.-French-SLORC venture. The U.S. company is Unocal, the French is Total, and SLORC supplies the road gangs. Once the gas starts flowing, the pipeline will be worth about $400 million a year to the Rangoon generals.

Unocal and Total have their contracts with the Myanmar Oil and Gas Enterprise, MOGE. Intelligence analyst Francois Casanier, with the Geopolitical Drug Watch in Paris, has shown that, despite its lack of income and assets, MOGE's Singapore bank accounts have seen the transfer of hundreds of millions of dollars. MOGE's only legitimate income is the relatively small monthly payments it gets from Unocal and Total. Much of MOGE's money can be shown to have come from Burma's most powerful drug lords, including Khun Sa.[5]

Since 1990, SLORC has gotten about two-thirds of its overt financing from foreign oil companies, including Britain's Premier Oil and America's Texaco and ARCO. Even the 1993 U.S. State Department Human Rights report said that the SLORC "routinely uses slave labor." Nonetheless, the EU, Japan, Singapore and China are all competing for a piece of the Burmese action.[6]

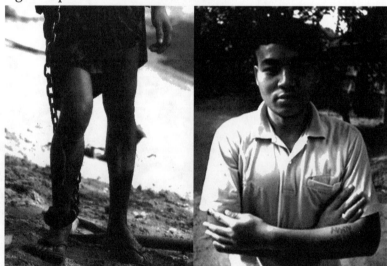

Leg irons on a SLORC chain gang, and a 17 year-old Karen student-soldier; metalab.unc.edu/freeburma

As of 1996, more than 3 *million* Burmese have been evicted from their confiscated homes, either for their value or to create "tourist meccas." For participation in "party politics" Aung San Suu Kyi's supporters have had their businesses confiscated. Effective NLD organizers are regularly assassinated or sent to slave labor camps for holding "illegal meetings" or "illegally using electrical power" or "adversely affecting the national interest." As of September 1997, 29 Members of Parliament elected in 1990 remain in death-camp prisons.

For celebrating Independence Day with Aung San Suu Kyi, two of Burma's most famous comedians, U Pa Pa Lay and Lu Zaw, were sentenced to seven years at hard labor. They probably won't live through it. Although Aung San Suu Kyi is the winner of the 1991 Nobel Peace Prize, she can't leave the country and expect to be able to return. Thanks to goon squad threats on her life, she is under virtual house arrest.

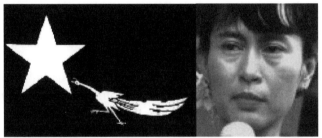

The NLD's fighting peacock Daw Aung San Suu Kyi

Under the brutal repression, which has thrown many Burmese into shock, Aung San Suu Kyi has become as mystically revered as Joan of Arc. Unfortunately, she faces similar dangers. But the Clinton administration refused to break relations to force the seating of the duly elected government, despite the fact that this was strongly advocated not only by the NLD, but by many members of the U.S. Congress on both sides of the aisle. Instead, in the name of Nancy and Apple Pie, Clinton chose to engage these killers in a "dialogue."

Clinton followed the lead of such antidrug pioneers as Rep. Charles Rangel. In February of 1990, Rangel, Chairman of the House Committee on Narcotics, actually conducted a meeting with a Burmese delegation that included Brigadier-General Tin Hla of the 22nd Light Infantry Division, the butcher who carried out the August 1988 Rangoon massacre. Tin Hla came to tell the Congressman and the gathered eminences of the DEA how deeply he deplored the drug trade, and how fervently he implored more "antidrug" assistance for the Burma Army.

In November of 1990 Burma's intelligence chief flew up to Kokang with some DEA and U.N. officials to stage an "opium burning." They heard Pheung Kya-shin, the CPB military commander (Burma Army franchisee) ask for support for his "program for the destruction and suppression of narcotic drugs."[7] Pheung failed to mention that he was running at least a dozen heroin refineries himself. Pheung was honest, however, in his sincere desire for more American money and police equipment.

The disgusted Senator Daniel Patrick Moynihan growled: "The Burmese regime has done nothing more than change business partners, turn on Khun Sa and get the public relations advantage that the DEA is giving them; use the former CPB, and turn them into a willing drug-trafficking partner."[8] Moynihan's "End of the Cold War Act of 1991," had it passed, would have transferred all CIA functions except intelligence to the State Department. Moynihan would have ended "Cold War/Covert" operations, those run by Armitage and Company.

As Gritz said, in December of 1989, a U.S. federal court indicted Khun Sa (Chan Shi-fu) on charges of smuggling more than $350 million worth of heroin into the U. S. between 1986 and 1988. This forced the SLORC to appear to turn on Khun Sa. But French and U.S. satellite photos, displayed at a U.N. Drug Control Program regional conference in November 1993, showed an explosion of poppy growth in Khun Sa's "surrendered" territory.

In January of 1996, in an elaborate public ceremony, the SLORC formally welcomed Khun Sa and his associates into their exclusive Rangoon circle as "our own blood brethren." This marriage was negotiated in December of 1995 by Khun Sa's uncle in Rangoon and the SLORC's Defense Commander Gen. Maung Aye. Maung Aye's dowry for the blushing Khun Sa was the bus concession from Rangoon to his Shan state opium empire.

On August 21, 1996, *The Bangkok Post* reported that "Rangoon has officially allowed former Mong Tai Army soldiers [Khun Sa's army] and Shan People at Ho Mong [Khun Sa's former headquarters] to grow opium poppies to ease poverty in the area."

The State Department, in its end-of-year 1996 Narcotics Control Strategy Report, deceitfully characterized this marriage as a victory in the Drug War, insisting that Khun Sa's "surrender...[was] ending an era in southeast Asia heroin trafficking history."

That's a very odd conclusion, given that in the Spring of 96 the SLORC signed a cooperative deal with Asia World Company Ltd. to operate a major new wharf at Yangon Port, which handles 90% of Burma's exports. Asia World is owned by Khun Sa's military ally Lo Hsing Han, who controls the most heavily armed drug trafficking organization in Southeast Asia.[9] 1996 saw him acquire control of Burma's biggest port.

"CHIANG MAI, Thailand, July 22, 1999 (Reuters) - Khun Sa, the Golden Triangle drug baron who retired after surrendering to Myanmar authorities four years ago, is back in business, Thai narcotics officials said on Thursday."

"There were signs the former commander of the separatist Mong Tai Army (MTA) in Myanmar's northeastern Shan state has become involved again with his son [Charm Herng] in the opium-growing Golden Triangle, they told reporters."

"Charm Herng is now playing an active role in drug trafficking. There are signs Khun Sa is also getting involved," said Pinyo Chaithong, the head of Thailand's Office of Narcotics Control Board (ONCB) based in northern Chiang Mai."

Thanks to the cease-fire agreements it now has with fifteen ethnic minorities, the Burma Army now controls every border checkpoint in the country. The SLORC-sanctioned leaders of those ethnic minorities, of course, are the most powerful heroin dealers in the world.

When Gen. Maung Aye headed the Burma Army's Eastern Command, which included Khun Sa's territory, the jungle warlord was allowed to operate unimpeded. Maung Aye is now Vice Chairman of the SLORC, the second most powerful man in Burma and successor apparent to SLORC Chairman Gen. Than Shwe. Than Shwe is the chosen successor of elderly dictator Ne Win, who gave up official power on the 1988 accession of SLORC. Both work closely with Lt. Gen. Khin Nyunt, head of Ne Win's CIA-trained secret police and intelligence structure. Secretary Gelbard called this is "the mid-levels of the Burmese Army."

In January, 1992, DEA agents in Rangoon were contacted by U Saw Lu, a Wa prince from the mountainous poppy-growing Shan state, Chairman of the United Wa State Anti-Narcotics and Development Organization. Lu was trying to get his people out from under the heel of the Burma Army, which had enslaved them as opium share-croppers. Lu documented the coercion of Wa farmers into growing opium by the imposition of arbitrary taxes, failure of which to pay resulted in land confiscation and imprisonment.

Lu presented detailed evidence of cooperation between the regional Burma Army intelligence chief, Major Than Aye, and Wei Hsueh-kang, a Wa commander with 7,000 troops protecting a very lucrative heroin and methamphetamine operation. Prince Lu was immediately arrested by the Burma Army and mercilessly tortured, to the point of death, for 56 days, by Major Than Aye himself. Lu's torture, however, provoked Wa leaders to personally threaten Khin Nyunt with a general uprising, so he was allowed to live through it.

Half a year later, the unreconstructed Lu presented the sympathetic new Rangoon DEA chief, Richard Horn, his evidence and his political program, entitled "The Bondage of Opium - the Agony of the Wa People, a Proposal and Plea." The enthusiastic Horn, who was delighted to have found a grass-roots democratic ally, forwarded Lu's plans and evidence to the DEA, by way of the American Embassy in Rangoon.[10]

Horn's reports were intercepted by Embassy Chargé d'Affaires Franklin Huddle, who insisted that Horn change the report's conclusions. Horn had insisted, as had Prince Lu, that political protection combined with subsidized crop substitution, rather than coercion, was the way to wean the Wa from opium. This, of course, threatened SLORC control of Wa territory. Huddle and his CIA operatives also bugged Horn's phone. Huddle quoted Horn's private phone conversations with his DEA superiors back in Washington verbatim in his State Department communications. The Rangoon CIA station chief, Arthur Brown, turned a copy of Lu's report over to his allies in Burmese military intelligence, who again threatened Lu's life.

Horn was able to prevent Lu's murder, but at the cost of his job. In September 1993 he was forced out of the country by Huddle's State Department under pressure from the CIA. Horn, who became a DEA group supervisor in New Orleans, filed a class action lawsuit, 9/12/96, in DC's Federal District Court, alleging that the CIA, the National Security Agency and the State Department illegally surveilled him and the numerous other DEA agents who joined him in the suit.

Obviously political control of the DEA, to some extent, is at stake in this groundbreaking lawsuit. Horn's response to my request for more information underscores that:

"I would like to help you... However, I have been put under threat of prosecution if I reveal classified information. My attorney and I take that threat seriously. The concerned agencies have interpreted 'classified information' in the broadest possible sense. Moreover, the CIA has lobbed 'scud missiles' filled with accusations about me to DEA. This, in turn, has resulted in an OPR (Office of Professional Responsibility) investigation that has lasted for nearly four years. And finally, all information that I distribute concerning this matter is now routed through the Court Security Officer (under the Department of Justice) before I circulate it. The Court Security Officer then arranges for the other agencies, ie., the CIA, NSA and DOS to 'suggest' changes."

"The changes that I have made concern only classification matters, not facts or substance. Beyond all of this, DEA must approve my public comments and all my contacts with the media."

I just didn't think I was the kind of media DEA would approve. Nor could I see submitting my work for CIA review prior to publication. Until he quits the Agency, Horn is muzzled. He has received no legal or practical help from Administrator Constantine, who has refused to increase the budget for anti-intrusion equipment in DEA offices.

Needless to say, Prince Lu's plans for crop substitution, which would have included economic and political protection for the poor dirt farmers he represents, went out the window. Wa farmers grow opium *or else.*[11]

This incident was part of a larger State Department/CIA-DEA turf war in which the State Department actually expelled three heads of the U.S. DEA from Burma, for working too closely with Burmese military intelligence. As of 1998, the State Department *says* it has engineered the suspension of economic aid to Burma, implemented an international arms embargo, blocked assistance from international financial institutions, downgraded our representation from Ambassador to Chargé, imposed visa restrictions on senior regime leaders and their families, and implemented a ban on new investment by Americans or overseas American firms.

But the arms embargo, the lynch-pin of the effort, is completely vitiated by the "anti-narcotics" loophole - aid given to Burmese military intelligence by the CIA-DEA. Reports the State Department, "With support from DEA and US embassies in Rangoon and Bangkok, the Burmese and Thai governments agreed to undertake joint operations against drug trafficking along Thailand's northern border with Burma. To this end, they agreed in principle to establish a joint antidrug task force in Tachilek, Burma, and Mae Sai, Thailand. This approach, which has been under consideration for several years, has the potential to permit coordinated enforcement operations in one of the most active trafficking areas in Southeast Asia."

"Formally, the Burmese government's drug enforcement effort is led by the office of the Central Committee for Drug Abuse Control (CCDAC), which is comprised of personnel from various security services, including the police, customs, military intelligence, and the army. CCDAC now has 18 drug enforcement task forces around the country, most located in major cities and along key transit routes near Burma's borders with China, India and Thailand. The CCDAC, which is under the control of the Directorate of Defense Services Intelligence (DDSI) and relies, in part, on military personnel to execute law enforcement duties, continues to suffer from a lack of adequate resources to support its law enforcement mission."[12] That is, to translate the McCaffrese, in order to fight drugs we have to arm Burmese military intelligence.

Burmese troops whack a few poppies for the camera

Light is thrown on the function of Burmese military intelligence by an International Monetary Fund study which pointed out that Burma's foreign exchange reserves for 1991 through 1993 were only about $300 million, but that the Burma Army purchased arms valued at $1.2 billion during the period.[13]

Karen soldiers wounded by SLORC phosphorus,2/95; metalab.unc.edu/freeburma

Overt military assistance to the SLORC is dependent on its continued paper cooperation with the DEA. Covert assistance, through the ASEAN members we arm, is dependent on nothing but Burma's ability to pay. Indonesia and Thailand attach no strings to their Burmese arms sales. Those ASEAN arms end up protecting Wa heroin refineries.

Drug War

In November of 1996, the United Nations Drug Control Program reported that the Asian heroin trade was worth $63 *billion* in profits annually. Burma, said the UNDCP, supplies more than 50% of that.[14] Karen land, then, assumes a value as artificially inflated as the opium it can produce.

Secretary Gelbard and his military intelligence allies were active supporters of the July, 1997 enrollment of Myanmar into ASEAN, the Association of Southeast Asian Nations, thus conferring diplomatic legitimacy on the SLORC. This is called "constructive engagement," as if little Burma had the geopolitical clout of China.

China, of course, is another major Burmese money laundry. As the State department puts it, "Chinese officials note that more than 90 percent of the heroin that flows through China comes from Burma. The 2000-kilometer border that China shares with Burma is considered China's friendliest."

ASEAN - Burma, Indonesia, Malaysia, the Philippines, Singapore, Thailand, Vietnam, Laos and Brunei - is often led by Thailand, the prime ministership of which was recently purchased by Gen. Chavalit Yongchaiyudh, former Supreme Commander of the Army, Minister of Defense, Interior Minister and Deputy Prime Minister. Chavalit is a graduate of the U.S. Command and Staff College at Fort Leavenworth. Prior to his accession to the prime ministership, the DEA, which has a thick file on Chavalit, and the American Embassy in Bangkok, referred to him as "Mr. White Powder."

Chavalit was part a long line of generals who have dominated Thai politics and business: Gen. Phao Siyanan, 1947-57, F. M. Sarit Thanarat, 1957-63, Gen. Krit Siwara, 1957-76, Gen. Thanom Kittikachorn, 1958-73, Gen. Kriangsak Chamanan, 1976-80, Gen. Prem Tinsulanan, 1980-88, Gen. Chatichai Choonhavan, 1988-91, Gen. Sundhorn Kongsompong, Gen. Wimol Wongwanich and Gen. Chavalit Yongchaiyudh.

Pro-democracy demonstrations in Bangkok were violently suppressed in March of 1992, and succeeding "civilian" governments have invariably been corrupt military-business fronts. The distinction between the military and big business is blurred in Thailand, to say the least. This of course, holds true throughout ASEAN, as the massive economic crisis that started in 11/97 demonstrated. That's the real Asian flu. Ecocide is the most dangerous virus the global economy faces.

During the Korean War era, Thailand's Gen. Phao was essential not only to the CIA supply of the Shan states Kuomintang armies, but to the original Burma to Bangkok to Sicily to Marseille opium/heroin run. The trade-off, of course, was that this American-armed fascist, who ran Shan states opium for the Japanese during the war, was allowed to exterminate democracy in Thailand without any American opposition. In fact, Phao's Thailand was hailed as "the free world's strongest bastion in southeast Asia" by Gen. William Donovan, wartime commander of the OSS and U.S. ambassador to Phao.[15]

A Karen shaman musically mourns the Thai clearcutting of the Karen-Thai border, 1996; metalab.unc.edu/freeburma

ASEAN's Indonesia, with 200 million people the world's fourth most populous nation, has been ruled since 1965 by our client army, the dope-dealing fascists of General Suharto. Suharto fought with the Japanese during WW II. In 1965, the populist, and, until attacked, parliamentary Communist Party of Indonesia, with 20 million members, was threatening legal electoral victory, so Suharto and his CIA advisors engineered the worst genocide in Indonesian history. Joked Australian Prime Minister Harold Holt, "With 500,000 to 1,000,000 Communist sympathizers knocked off, I think it is safe to assume that a reorientation has taken place."[16]

After the massive bloodletting, Suharto permitted only three official parties - his ruling Golkar Party, the minority UDP and the Indonesian Democratic Party. When the IDP got too uppity, it too was banned for a time. Other parties and mass associations exist, but they have no electoral standing. The legal parties compete for 425 seats in the 500-seat lower house of parliament, the People's Representative Council. The other 75 seats go to Golkar's military appointees. These are then joined by another 500 "presidential" appointees to form the People's Consultative Assembly, the body that "elects" the President - again and again and again.

The huge Indonesian archipelago, 17,500 islands stretching more than 3,000 miles, with the world's second largest rain forest, is a gold mine of natural resources. Also a silver mine, a copper mine, nickel, palm oil, coal and oil. Indonesia is the world's largest producer of natural gas. The economic crisis of 11/97 began when Suharto's massive slash-and-burn/clear-cut logging precipitated huge, out of control drought-fed forest fires, causing the most devastating ecological disaster in Indonesia's history. The choking smog killed thousands.

Suharto's illegal confiscation of Native lands for logging, mining, gas and oil operations has sparked numerous uprisings. "This sort of massacre happens on a routine basis here. Tens of thousands of Papuans have been killed by the Indonesian army since they took over the island 34 years ago."[17]

U.S. copper- and gold-mining giant Freeport McMoRan, based in Louisiana, is one of the archipelago's biggest employers. A very well-paid Henry Kissinger sits on Freeport's board of directors. Freeport happily shares its trucks, tractors and choppers with Indonesia's army.

Our Green Berets train that army - in the name of Nancy and Apple Pie, of course - the ongoing genocide in East Timor to the contrary notwithstanding. Between 1975, when Indonesia first occupied the former Portuguese colony, and 1998, the Indonesian army has killed about 200,000 Timorese, a third of the entire population.

A Catholic missionary described a 1981 search-and-destroy mission: "We saw with our own eyes the massacre of the people who were surrendering: all dead, even women and children, even the littlest ones. ... Not even pregnant women were spared: they were cut open. .... They did what they had done to small children the previous year, grabbing them by the legs and smashing their heads against rocks." "We did the same thing [in 1965] in Java, in Borneo, in the Celebes, in Irian Jaya," gloated one Indonesian officer, "and it worked."[18-19]

Indonesia's Timor troops were led by Suharto's son-in-law, Maj. Gen. Prabowo Subianto, promoted from leadership of the Army Special Forces to commander of the Strategic Reserve, the army's most elite unit, during the economic crisis.

When the ancient Suharto was finally replaced, on 5/21/98, it was by his handpicked vice-president B. J. Habibie. As research and technology minister, Habibie was associated with numerous gigantic boondoggles. Coveting East Timor's natural resources for his clients,

Habibie reacted to the 8/30/99 Timor referendum, in which 80% voted for independence, with outright genocide. The U.S. was finally forced to suspend military aid - temporarily.

Another contender for Suharto's throne had been "Indonesia's leading economist," Sumitro Djojohadikusumo, another former minister, who just happened to be Gen. Prabowo Subianto's father, father-in-law to one of Suharto's daughters, Titiek Prabowo.

Another daughter, Tutut, leads the "I Love The Rupiah" campaign, the implication being that Indonesia's Chinese shopkeepers don't. Gen. Subianto feeds this scapegoating by constantly referring to "the conglomerate group," that is, a few very wealthy Chinese merchants. Tutut just happens to own the largest instant coffee manufacturing operation in East Timor, an operation that has just entered the American market. Suharto family interests in East Timor are varied and extensive, including sugar cane, mining, cement, oil, gas and transportation.

Although half the country is starving, Forbes Magazine lists the Suharto family's personal wealth at $30 billion. Suharto operative Mochtar Riady, one of the richest men in Indonesia, attracted more attention than was good for him during the 1996 U.S. campaign-fundraising spectacle.

Golkar's divide-and-conquer COINTELPRO's have pitted the Moslem poor, for whom the price of rice, flour, cooking oil, sugar, soybeans and eggs is a hot-button issue, against the commercially talented Chinese minority, effectively disenfranchising both and drenching the nation in blood. But rather than allow former President Sukarno's formidable daughter Megawati Sukarnoputri to seize power in the 10/99 parliamentary electoral process, Golkar backed Abdurrahman Wahid, the frail, near-blind Muslim intellectual who campaigned as a compromise candidate. On 10/20/99 he became Indonesia's first democratically-elected president in more than 40 years, thanks largely to Golkar's transparently corrupt Habibie.

The U.S. State Department: "While Indonesia is not a major producer of narcotics or a narcotics-derived money laundering center, it is increasingly used as a transit point for Southeast Asian heroin destined for Australia, the United States, and Europe.... Indonesia's criminal code does not include controls on money laundering. These factors, along with pervasive corruption and lack of professionalism among police and customs officials, impede law enforcement efforts.... There are many indications that police officials themselves are involved in drug trafficking in Indonesia...."

The State Department report then slips into McCaffrese: "Indonesian law enforcement authorities have a good working relationship with the United States Drug Enforcement Administration (DEA), the United States Customs Service and the State Department Bureau of Diplomatic Security's regional security officer."[20]

They're corrupt and unprofessional, and trafficking in drugs, but they have a good working relationship with the DEA? Does that mean that victory is just around the corner?

The same U.S. military-intelligence structure that supports Indonesia's military supports Thailand's. The U.S.-trained Chavalit Yongchaiyudh was an important officer in Prem's army, commander of the elite Thai Rangers who successfully wrested control of the border from Khun Sa's Shan United Army in 1982. This simply meant that Khun Sa's opium profits were redirected to Prem. Professor McCoy:

"'We are like a "foreign legion" for the Thai armed forces,' remarked the Karen rebel leader General Bo Mya. 'We guard the border and prevent links between the Burmese and Thai Communists.' For nearly forty years the Thai military provided sanctuary, arms, and an opium market for the many mini-armies it supported. Usually located in the mountains north of Chiangmai, the guerrilla camps were tightly controlled by the Thai military and housed the logistics of the Golden Triangle heroin trade - troops, mule caravans, and heroin refineries."[21]

In March of 1997, Gen. Chavalit answered the DEA's extradition request for Li Yung-chung, who had been caught with more than a half-ton of pure heroin. Chavalit thereby qualified for continued American "antidrug" military subsidies, which Thai army chief Chetta Thanajaro coordinated with SLORC army chief Maung Aye.[22] If SLORC can turn the Karens into opium sharecroppers, it will.

McCaffrey told PBS' "Frontline" in May of 1997, "In Thailand we see continued suppression of opium poppy cultivation and significantly effective law enforcement. Thai cooperation in the extradition of several key drug traffickers to the U.S. has been superb. Laos is cooperating now with the U.S. through crop eradication, substitution, and increased law enforcement measures. Cambodia and Vietnam are also seeing greater counter-narcotics cooperation with their regional neighbors."

But the State Department's Narcotics Control Strategy Report for 1997, released by its Bureau for International Narcotics and Law Enforcement Affairs in March of 1998, directly contradicted General

McCaffrey: "The Government of Laos' ability to control the flow of narcotics within and across its lengthy, porous borders is severely limited by lack of personnel, resources, expertise, and ready access to many isolated areas of the country. Effective control over borders with Thailand, Burma, China, Vietnam, and Cambodia exists only in the vicinity of major population areas, along principal land routes, and at established river crossings."

Karen refugees fleeing SLORC troops on the Thai border, 1995

The Reds went into the opium-for-arms business with the Whites. Hun Sen's Cambodian People's Party was installed by the Vietnamese in 1979 when they stopped Pol Pot's genocide. By this time Hun Sen's Laotian ally, the Pathet Lao, had taken control of Laos. By 1980, a Laotian covert operation, Rasita Imports, was a major supplier, through Thailand, of Burmese heroin.[23]

In July of 1996, Hun Sen drove his co-Prime Minister, Prince Norodom Ranariddh, into exile and massacred Ranariddh's leading supporters, among them Interior Secretary Ho Sok. Ho Sok made the mistake of going after construction magnate Mong Reththy, a major Hun Sen supporter. Mong Reththy had been using his Import-Export Ltd. to export high-grade Cambodian pot and Burmese heroin. Reththy very publicly underwrites school-construction projects in Burma.

Another leading supporter of Hun Sen's Cambodian People's Party, Theng Bunma, head of the national Chamber of Commerce, is Cambodia's richest citizen. According to the DEA, he is also Cambodia's leading drug-money launderer. In 1994 Bunma floated a $3 *billion* no-interest "loan" to the Cambodian army for weapons purchases.[24]

According to the State Department, the UNDCP, DEA International Intelligence and Interpol, the flow of Burmese heroin through ASEAN continues unabated. The Burma Army is the greatest heroin trading institution in the world. It is a foundation stone of the power of the ASEAN military elites, most of which are long-term clients of American military intelligence.

General McCaffrey's answer to Burma's intransigence, which he had no choice but to admit, was to coordinate their acquisition of *more* arms, in the name of all the venial virtues. McCaffrey is in the business of legitimizing these bastards, cheerleading for them. His military structure is the deadliest enemy Aung San Suu Kyi has.

Free Burma! @ http://metalab.unc.edu/freeburma

A highland *coquero* with gourd and stick for adding *lejía* to his cheek wad

Drug War

Leopards

The Bolivian Cocaine Coup of 1980 ("Propaganda Due") was not a lasting achievement. It was simply too transparent. Carter's State Department raised hell, as did Congress, the more politic elements of Carter's DEA, the OAS, the enormously powerful Catholic Church and the Bolivian labor confederations.

The U.S. withdrew all overt military and economic aid. This caused another three cosmetic coups, which were seen for the shams they were. So, in October 1982, Hernán Siles-Zuazo, whose June 1980 election had triggered the Cocaine Coup, was allowed to resume the presidency. Siles-Zuazo, president from 1956-1960, had been a leader of the 1952 social revolution.

García Meza's Cocaine Coup power structure had its last overt spasm just as Siles-Zuaso took office. The drug police, who turned all confiscated coca over to García Meza's new government monopoly for processing into cocaine, gang-raped the wife and daughter of a Sud Yungas coca farmer whose hard-earned crop they had just stolen. The enraged Sud Yungas campesinos invaded the police headquarters in Chulumani, the capitol of Sud Yungas, burned the police station to the ground, and then castrated the rapists and burned them alive. The office of García Meza's Coca Agency was also destroyed. García Meza's Bolivian attempt to imitate the traditional Peruvian state coca monopoly collapsed.

The more moderate Siles-Zuaso disbanded the transparent "Ministry of Cocaine" as peasant co-ops and free traders resumed their competition for the market. This enabled the Reagan administration to resume "anti-narcotics" aid to the Bolivian Army. Immediately after the installation of Siles-Zuaso, the DEA funded, armed and organized the Bolivian Leopards, UMOPAR, *Unidad Movil de Patrullaje Rural*, the Mobile Rural Patrol Unit, again, in imitation of the Peruvian UMOPAR structure. Bolivia's UMOPAR was administered by the Special Antinarcotics Force, the core group of CIA-funded military assassins that ran García Meza's Cocaine Coup with Klaus Barbie.

The first thing the UMOPAR "Leopards" tried, in 1984, was the overthrow of the government, but the more nationalistic elements of Bolivia's power-elite, and the CIA, decided that was not a good idea. The DEA then concentrated on building an efficient "democratic" police state. It sent the Green Berets to train the Leopards, and funded the creation of courts, police intelligence gathering facilities and an army of prosecutors.

With the booming underground cocaine economy as the nation's leading source of foreign capital, Siles-Zuazo had nothing to put into structural economic development, and so watched helplessly as consumer buying power collapsed in the face of the untaxable hyperinflation. The democratic parties united behind Víctor Paz Estenssoro, allowing him to resume the Presidency in 1985.

Paz, the pragmatic populist who led the 1952 revolution along with Siles-Zuaso, knew that efforts to legalize coca were strongly advocated by the vast majority of his own people. In fact, despite its dependence on international largesse, Bolivia registered a formal reserve to the 1988 Vienna Anti-Trafficking Convention, insisting that coca leaf itself is not a "narcotic" and is perfectly healthful when used traditionally.

Paz, however, had no choice but to cooperate with American efforts at eradication and substitution in an effort to garner as much foreign aid as possible. His IMF-designed "New Economic Politics" increased private international investment and economic assistance from such institutions as the Inter-American Development Bank. But foreign aid is no substitute for real market value. Although Paz kept the Bolivian state solvent, he was never able to offer the campesinos anything that was remotely as profitable as the artificial value that Prohibition gives coca. And the price of Bolivia's other great export, tin, collapsed in the face of fierce global competition.

Paz was forced to institute economic "shock therapy" to control the hyperinflation as the situation militarized. This, of course, only made coca leaves more valuable. Many of the 22,000 tin miners fired by the downsizing state mining operation migrated to the Chaparé to farm coca. In January of 1986, when 245 Leopards were sent to the Chaparé to destroy coca maceration pits, 17,000 farmers rose in protest.[1]

By threatening Bolivia's international credit and foreign aid, the DEA was able to force passage of the 1988 Coca and Controlled Substances Law, "Law 1008." For the first time in history, Bolivia's most sacred and profitable crop was criminalized - except in specified traditional areas in the Department of Cochabamba. All other areas, containing most of Bolivia's subsistence farmsteads, were defined as either "transitional"- subject to voluntary eradication; or "illegal" - subject to uncompensated forced eradication. At this time coca was earning 50% of Bolivia's foreign exchange.[2]

Law 1008 had the effect of increasing coca's value and therefore the acreage devoted to it. Between 1963 and 1987 Bolivian coca acreage increased 20-fold. Because Prohibition artificially inflates the price, a pound of Bolivian coca is literally worth twice what a pound of Bolivian tin is worth. Bolivian coca and cocaine exports consistently exceed the multi-billion dollar value of Bolivian tin exports.[3]

That is, solely because of the artificial illegal value, cocaine is Bolivia's number one industrial export, as it is Peru's. More people are employed in the illegal cocaine business in Bolivia and Peru - growing, processing, trucking, refining, protecting - than in all legal mining and manufacturing operations combined. *The Economist*, in 1991, estimated that 1 in every 3.4 economically active Bolivians is involved in the coca/cocaine economy.[4] That can hardly be called a criminal aberration. The artificial illegal value creates an export-oriented monoculture that otherwise wouldn't exist.

"Crop substitution" is a transparent sham to highland smallholders for whom coca is worth twenty times the value of any substitute ($9000 for coca to $500 for citrus per hectare in 1984[5]). Since coca leaf can be cultivated year-round, and is harvested three or four times a year, highland coca production means year-round access to food and a cash income independent of agribusiness technology and banking.

The DEA estimated that when it turned up the heat on coca production in the Tingo María area of Peru in 1972, the amount of acreage devoted to coca shot from 4,000 to 50,000 by 1978.[6] Effective enforcement, since it increases the commodity's value, is a *stimulus* to production.

Frontline DEA agent Celerino Castillo, Peru, 1984:

"The *poseros* [processors] needed more than a hundred pounds of the thumb-sized green leaves to make one kilo of paste, which they sold to Colombian runners in light planes."

A Cochabamba family coca plot; Cultural Survival

"The system allowed the [Huallaga] valley's poor to earn a decent living for the first time in their lives. The rural farmers must have shook their heads in amazement when they discovered the new cash crop. By converting their fields to coca, they could easily double, triple, even quadruple their annual income. The plants matured in a few years, yielded as many as six crops a year, repelled pests naturally, and grew in poor soil. They did not even have to take their crop to market: The Colombians and *poseros* went door-to-door, leaving stacks of dollars in their wake.... For every dollar they paid Peru's coca farmers and processors, the cartels earned more than twenty dollars from American buyers."

"The Colombians owned Tingo Maria. Its quiet farming traditions, its institutions, and its morals crumbled like dry clay as residents jumped onto the coca economy.... The cartels played both sides by shoveling cash into the jaws of prospective enemies. They purchased the loyalty of Tingo Maria's military officers, who declared a truce with the traffickers. On Sundays, I wandered past soccer fields and watched Peruvian soldiers playing *fútbol* with Colombians. Snubbing the government's periodic efforts to wage war on coca, the military insisted its sole responsibility in the valley was protecting the peasants from Marxist subversives. Cracking down on the local coca farmers and traffickers, they argued, would drive the peasants into the arms of *Sendero Luminoso*."[6a]

The increased value strengthened the neighboring Colombian coke and marijuana distribution apparatus, which runs vast jungle plantations and pays hundreds of thousands of campesinos ten times what they could make in equivalent legal work. Twenty years ago, Colombia grew almost no coca leaf; now, in 1999, it has overtaken both Peru and Bolivia as the world's largest grower.

Colombia is also now the world's fourth largest source of opium.[7] Because of its artificial value, global opium production shot from 1,000 metric tons in 1971 to 4,300 tons in 1996.[8] In 1988 the Colombian cocaine industry employed 300,000 Colombians, earning 20% of the country's foreign exchange, $1.5 billion, as much as the country's biggest legal export, coffee.[9] Just two years later, Colombian cocaine earned at least twice as much as Colombian coffee.[10] Good ol' Juan Valdez.

"Even if you eradicate every coca plant on Colombian soil, you will simply raise prices and push production deeper into Peru, Bolivia, and Ecuador," notes Colombian sociologist and author Alfredo Molano. "You will also bring misery and suffering to many thousands of people."[11]

Since *ipadú*, the alkaloid-poor lowland variety of coca grown in Colombia, can be cultivated anywhere on the Amazonian jungle floor, even if it were possible to destroy coca production in the Peruvian and Bolivian highlands, *ipadú* would fill the gap. The use of *ipadú* is ancient in Amazonia. In fact the word *ipadú* can refer to the lowland variety of coca itself or to the traditional toasted mixture of coca and yarumo leaves.[12] The rain forest is being sliced up everywhere - in Brazil, Ecuador, Bolivia - because of *ipadú's* new-found value.[13] That is solely an effect of Prohibition.

Highland coca leaf prices have fluctuated greatly since their zenith in the mid-80's, partly due to competition from massive *ipadú* cultivation. This fluctuation only confirmed the ancient highland wisdom that coca, almost always a small-scale cash crop, must be combined with diversified subsistence crops if the family farmstead is to survive.

Anthropologist Alison L. Spedding stresses that the traditional Bolivian coca field can only be understood as "a total social fact." It can't be separated from Andean culture. The traditional coca-growing areas, the Yungas regions of the Department of La Paz, derive their Spanish name from the Aymara word for "hot valley," *yunkas*. These are sheer forested hillsides 600 to 2,000 meters up the eastern Andes.

"A peasant couple begins to plant coca in the first years of their marriage. By the time the fields come into full production, their children...can help them, and the fields go on producing until the children are grown and married and have coca fields of their own. Coca is thus integrated into the life-cycle of the peasant household.... While planting coca is the quintessential masculine task in the Yungas, picking coca is the special skill of women."[13]

"After it has been pruned the coca is no longer known as 'child coca' but as *mit'ani*. This means 'owns a harvest' but is also the title of the woman in a ...[married] couple." Women have traditionally played a leading role in the economic life of these communities.

"The symbolic parallels between the coca and a woman are completed in the last stages of its existence, when almost all the plants in the field have died and only a few, perhaps fifty years old with thick, knotted stumps an inch or more in diameter, remain. The field may be dug over again for coca, in which case these old plants are left standing and the new *wachu* [terraces for the transplanted seedlings] are built up round them. They are known as *awicha* (grandmother)."

'Mama Coca' is one of the most common epithets of the ancient Aymara Great Goddess.

A typical Bolivian cocal; Loren McIntyre

All the words describing the various processes of coca cultivation are traditional Aymara words. In this part of Bolivia, Aymara is often spoken to the exclusion of Spanish. In fact, the elaborate pre-Colombian textile patterns of the ancient Aymara clans (Macha, Laymi, Jukumani, Chayantaka, Pukwata and Sakaka) are still a major visual signal of personal identification throughout highland Bolivia. These clan markers denote participation in common land ownership, a particular religious-festival cycle, a distinctive musical style as well as married and professional status.

It is certainly worth mentioning that my erudite source for this information, the English-born, Aymara-speaking University of La Paz anthropologist and historian Alison L. Spedding, was sentenced to ten years in one of Bolivia's brutal prisons on 5/7/99 on false charges of drug dealing. She was caught with a small amount of pot, which is to her, as to me, sacramental. Her simultaneous possession of foreign currency, in readiness for her next-day trip to the UK, was used as a pretext to charge her with international drug dealing, an absurdity in the case of this dedicated scholar.

She shares a 9x12' cell in La Paz Women's Prison with three other inmates and their children, and is fed one inadequate meal a day. This has threatened both her health and her sanity. And that can be used as an excuse to keep her locked up indefinitely. The Bolivian Embassy may or may not respond to your queries.

Alison Spedding; Highland coca leaf drying patio; Bulletin on Narcotics 4:2:1953

In order to receive the "eradication money," some $2,000, for taking a coca field out of production, the "owner" must sign a pledge to never again plant coca in that field. But according to Aymara concepts of ownership, the field belongs to the heirs of the current user - it is held in trust for them, thus the pledge is illegal. In any case, no sane dirt farmer willingly eradicates a coca field in good production - it is usually his, or her, only money tree. Dying fields are sold for the cash which, often as not, is used to finance fresh fields.

Coca is the central *sacrament* and social euphoriant of this culture. It is no more a drug than wine, which is, in fact, the Blood of Christ, just as the Sacred Leaf is the Milk of Mama Coca. Wine is not a drug, it is a sacred food. Industrial slavers, intent on the cultural genocide necessary for enslavement, have always been violently antisacramental.

Spedding: "A perfectly packed, bright green coca, which demonstrates that the harvest, the drying, and the packing have all been of the highest standard, reflects a household in which everyone works hard and all their social relations are exactly as they should be."

Coca leaf is the traditional chew and breakfast tea of this culture. It is a genuine health food. One hundred grams of coca leaves actually satisfy the RDA for calcium, iron, phosphorus, vitamin A and riboflavin, and are higher in calories, protein, carbohydrates and fiber than most foods. Coca leaves are generally sucked in a cheek wad, which has been built up one leaf at a time. *Lejía*, a calcium-rich paste of vegetable ash, is added to the quid to release the nutrients.

Throughout Incan culture coca leaf is present in every significant ritual from birth to death. Coca leaves are considered a specific for hunger, exhaustion, indigestion, cramps, dysentary, stomach ulcers, toothaches, rheumatism, hangover, internal and external pain.[14] They are considered the premier health food, are given to babies as a tonic, and are chewed daily throughout life. They help to produce some of the most long-lived people on earth, famous among gerontologists for regularly living past a vigorous 100.

It did not escape the notice of these subtle and tenacious Native Americans that their hold on their land was being undercut not only by the war on their most valuable and sacred crop, but by the subsidized cheap food imports of the "crop substitution" idiots. Why subsidize mass-produced North American and Brazilian corn, wheat, citrus, potatoes, soybeans, coffee and yams, when the highlanders have their own traditional strains of corn, wheat, citrus, potatoes, soybean, coffee, peanuts, cassava and manioc? These are some of the diverse crops traditionally grown alongside the coca. Although coca remains the single most valuable cash crop, there is actually more Yungas acreage devoted to coffee and citrus fruits, the next most valuable cash crops.[15]

Rather than strengthen the traditional economy, the import-export airheads undercut the local staples with cheap imports and then coercively encouraged the experimental planting of passion fruit, pineapple and macadamia nuts - for export. Any professional exporter could have told them that there was no way experimental small-scale production of luxury items could compete with established international shippers.

At the first two National Encounters of Coca Producers, in 1987 in Cochabamba and 1988 in La Paz, not only the coca associations but the powerful national peasants union CSUTCB and the equally powerful national workers union, COB, called for the immediate cancellation of the U.N crop substitution program Agroyungas. They insisted that Agroyungas has done nothing but leave a trail of bankrupt homesteads.

Agroyungas, driven by American supermarketheads, pushed high-yielding varieties of lowland Colombian and Brazilian coffee. These strains are short-lived compared to the native varieties, intolerant of the sometimes sparse highland rainfall, and high yielding only if drenched in costly fertilizers and insecticides. They are grown almost exclusively on vast, irrigated lowland agroindustrial units.

Agroyungas sucked thousands into their program with "soft credits" to pay for the fertilizers and other imported inputs - and then international coffee prices collapsed. The homesteaders were left with very heavy debts and coffee literally too worthless to harvest. Even worse, the imported seeds brought a devastating insect infestation that spread to the native crops.

This disrespect for the ecological wisdom of highland agriculture, which is 50 times older than the Bolivian state itself, filled the Incas with rage. After decades of manipulation and coercion, not one single "substitute crop" is a commercial success. The U.N. Drug Control Program, which administers Agroyungas, itself officially concluded in 1991 "that outside organizations come promising them benefits which rarely, if ever, emerge." Almost three years after the collapse of Agroyungas, in April of 1992, the Minister of Peasant Affairs formally announced that the government would not forgive campesino debts incurred under the coffee program.

Agroyungas also promoted passion fruit, but was only able to offer an international price per metric ton of frozen passion fruit that was one-third the cost of production. Then the pig-raising project had to be dropped when it was discovered that the cost of the required refrigeration facilities was prohibitive.[16]

What's left to feed the family? Coca, which thrives in the nutrient-poor acidic highland soil - and the underground cocaine economy. When alcohol Prohibition went into effect, my grandmother happily turned her kitchen into a brewery. The idiots had made it worth her while. *Nobody* was going to tell Grandma that her *shabbas* wine was a drug. She was damn proud of her sweet red home brew, made from her own fresh grape juice.

Most Prohibition hooch, of course, was nowhere near as fine as my Grandmother's sabbath wine. If coca leaf is the wine, then amateurishly produced cocaine is the rotgut. But poverty and corporate neoliberalism being what they are, Bolivian campesinos must take whatever employment the underground economy offers.

Most highland Bolivian coca is grown either in the Chaparé or the Yungas region. About 7500 maceration pits in the central highlands of the Chaparé turn the coca leaves into cocaine paste or base.

Paste is made simply by stomping the crushed leaves in a dilute solution of water and sulphuric acid. The liquid that rises to the top of the stomping pit is decanted into a smaller pit, where it is mixed with kerosene, diesel fuel and calcium oxide (cement) or calcium carbonate to neutralize it. The kerosene is then drawn off, and sodium carbonate is added, producing a gooey sulfate precipitate, cocaine paste. The grey goo is filtered out through toilet paper.

This paste, 40-50% alkaloid cocaine, can be turned into the more lucrative 85-90% cocaine base by dissolving it in a solution of water and potassium permanganate, then reprecipitating it with ammonia.[17]

Either the paste or the base is then transported by the "ants" to only about 35 major dealers located in the Santa Cruz and Beni departments, who either resell the base to the internationally fluent Colombians, or, increasingly, convert the base themselves, in a complex process involving acetone, ether and hydrochloric acid, to cocaine hydrochloride. These powerful dealers are never busted, though their jungle labs and airstrips sometimes become the focus of contention.[18]

Law 1008 is, in effect, the Leopard Bill of Rights. It gives these storm troopers the right to search anyone anytime, to charge them with unsubstantiated evidence, and to hold them in filthy concentration camps, real death camps, for *years*. San Sebastian, one of Cochabamba's prisons, was built to hold 60 people in its 10,000 square feet. As of 7/95, it held 520, who had to share 3 broken-down toilets. No food was served. If you ate, it was because family came to feed you.

Originally, no bail was permitted before trial, and, according to Human Rights Watch/Americas, 7/95, only 7% of the prison population of Cochabamba had been brought to trial. Law 1008 required the government to appeal on acquittal of a defendant, and the defendant was required to remain in prison, without the possibility of bail, while the appeals process was ongoing. On a second acquittal, the government was required to appeal yet again, while the innocent defendant, twice acquitted, was required to remain in jail. The whole process took as long as five years.

The semiliterate arresting officers, most professional blackmailers, were required to prepare all the indictment papers for their own collars. Law 1008 actually declares that these papers alone may be considered sufficient legal proof. Article 79 provides for five years in prison for *criticizing* Law 1008. The U.S. threatened to cut off all foreign aid and IMF loans to Bolivia if this law wasn't passed.

Needless to say, these heavily armed swat troops have the run of the countryside - money, sex, coke - *anything* but ten years in the slammer. Until recently, Leopard vehicles had no license plates, and Leopard troops were masked or painted. In the Chaparé it had become virtually illegal to carry cash. Leopard roadblocks were set up at whim, all traffic stopped and all cash confiscated. Anyone who protested was charged with drug law violations. Chaparé peasants uniformly report that all household cash is seized along with "illegal" coca leaves, and that the leaves are never destroyed by the Leopards, but always sold for processing into paste.[19]

Gustavo Blacutt, legal advisor to the Bolivian Congressional Commission on Drugs, estimated that 99.35% of detainees under Law 1008 are indigent peasants, who comprise 70% of Bolivia's 6.5 millions. Not one major trafficker has fallen to the Leopards, who are simply running a street fight for control of the crop.[20]

In Villa Tunari, on June 27, 1988, Leopard troops machine-gunned 12 protesters to death while DEA agents squawked orders from the helicopter overhead. DEA personnel, often present at Leopard torture sessions, openly admit they don't interfere with Leopard "methods." Why should they, they not only taught them, they equipped them with their electric prods and torture needles. Peasant union leaders have a way of ending up dead after "interrogation."

Nonetheless, the nationwide protests of 1988, against the impending passage of Law 1008, did force a campesino *quid pro quo* into article 13: effective alternative development assuring "sufficient income for the subsistence of the family unit" must accompany coca eradication in "zones of surplus cultivation." The failure to provide viable alternative cash crops has convinced most campesino organizations that they are no longer legally required to cooperate with eradication.

The Bolivian Chamber of Deputies report on "Police Actions and Deaths in the Chaparé," August 1995: "Bloodshed and deaths are part of an increasingly serious picture of violent confrontation in which the police act with an unnecessary display of power, abuse and indiscriminate attacks against the civilian population in the Chaparé. Police interdiction activities seem to be guided by the assumption that all Chaparé residents are drug trafficking suspects and that therefore the UMOPAR's activities are guided only by the criteria of efficiency without the slightest respect for legal and procedural norms. There are persistent and consistent complaints which indicate police actions are preceded by a sort of armed occupation of the area in question, in which the residents, by sole virtue of suspicions, are subjected to mistreatment, physical aggression, verbal violence, illegal searches of their homes, arbitrary confiscation and taking of their goods and money, not to mention the agitation, tension and fear to which children, women and the elderly are subjected."[21]

Clinton, McCaffrey and Company, realizing that the more grotesque rights violations were fuel for the legalization fires, encouraged the enactment of the Law of Judicial Bond, which eliminated some, but not all, of the anti-bail provisions of Law 1008. The law also engineered the beginnings of accountability for UMOPAR troops by forcing them to wear name tags, ending their anonymity. This, of course, will legitimize the Leopards internationally.

It will also tighten the military's grip on the coca trade, since it will streamline the chain of command, thereby rendering the export of Bolivian cocaine - and the Bolivian acquisition of American "anti-drug" armaments - that much more efficient.

In 1991, President Jaime Paz Zamora (1989-1993) appointed Col. Faustino Rico Toro, chief of a secret army intelligence unit during the Cocaine Coup of 1980, to head Bolivia's elite, U.S.-created and funded *Fuerza Especial de Lucha Contra el Narcotráfico*. The U.S. State Department made its *pro forma* protest, but the Inter-American Development Bank pumped $1 billion into Paz Zamora's hands during the same period. In September of 1995, long after the departure of the Cocaine Coup Colonel, four tons of cocaine seized at Lima's airport were traced directly to the FELCN, which was still an American-financed unit of Bolivian military intelligence.

That is, "supply side" militarization is *good* for the fascist dope peddlers - it has just the opposite effect of crushing the trade - it centralizes it. This was confirmed by Riley in a 1996 RAND study: he demonstrated that a mere $700 worth of raw coca leaves, at local Bolivian prices, can be turned into $150,000 worth of cocaine, at U.S. street retail. Small-scale eradication programs therefore have no effect on overall supply, since the bulk of the money goes to the final processors and exporters, who are few enough in number to fix their prices on both ends.

They can manipulate the basic leaf price they pay to the small growers, switch sources of supply at will, and then turn around and gouge their wholesale customers. "Eradication," therefore, simply serves to militarize the trade, to turn the remaining small-scale growers - and almost all highland coca cultivation is small-scale - into intimidated sharecroppers. The very few big processors and dealers remain not only unaffected, but strong enough to buy every whore in the army.[22]

Adds Riley: "Even if coca is somehow almost fully eradicated from Bolivia and Peru...Colombia, Venezuela, Brazil and Ecuador stand ready as potential alternate suppliers." That of course is a reference to lowland *ipadú*, the trade in which is controlled by the same militarized structure.

The June, 1991 peasants march for "dignity and sovereignty" was triggered by the disclosure of the secret Annex III to the Cartagena drug summit, which committed Bolivia to the militarization of the war on drugs. Peasant opposition found wide support throughout Bolivian society.

The local subdivisions of the national peasants union, the *Confederación Sindical Unica de Trabajadores Campesinos de Bolivia*, are, in effect, the local governments throughout rural Bolivia. The CSUTCB, 1992: "We won't accept countries like the United States who are the principle producers of marijuana and synthetic drugs dictating standards to us about coca. We won't tolerate foreign functionaries, many times implicated in drug trafficking themselves and participants in arms trafficking who try to require a suffering and exploited people to comply with rules that they themselves constantly break."[23]

In 1994, President Sánchez de Lozada, trying to pry development money from the World Bank, proposed his maniacal "zero option" for the Chaparé: he would turn the entire region into a huge industrial park by forcibly removing the entire farming population to areas that wouldn't support coca cultivation. Even the bankers thought the idea was insane; its only effect was to bring the campesinos one step closer to open rebellion. 1995 saw Bolivia wracked by protest marches, hunger strikes and riots as the Leopards continued their CIA/DEA-led depredations.

On April 18, 1995, in response to U.S. pressure to get tough on these damn narcoterrorists, Bolivia declared a "state of siege" and threw, not the dealers, but 500 peasant union leaders in jail without charges. Mountain roads were blocked and the forests of the Chaparé began to ring with *"ant"* sniper fire as the "ecological police" continued to eradicate "unauthorized" coca production.[24]

On June 1, 1997, the PR-savvy General Hugo Banzer, Klaus Barbie's former employer, reassumed the Bolivian presidency, this time through legal elections. Banzer's center-right National Democratic Action party remained a power throughout the 80's. In order to win in 97, it allied itself with two center-left parties tied to the dealers, the Revolutionary Movement of the Left and the Civic Solidarity Union. Of the 3.2 million eligible voters, in a population of 6.5 million, Banzer got less than 500,000 votes. But that was enough to win a plurality in an election split by five top parties. The 71 year-old Banzer, who now talks of compassion for the poor and social welfare, still supports the IMF's production-for-export model - and the arms purchases it finances.

In early March of 98, Gen. Barry McCaffrey joined Banzer's Vice President Jorge Quiroga at a news conference in which Quiroga pledged to rid Bolivia of all illicit coca by 2002. This realistic goal, insisted Gen. McCaffrey, with a straight face, justifies the $45 million for "anti-narcotics" armaments for Bolivia: "I am confident that we can make the case to both houses that that's the level of support that they need."[25]

The Leopards are now contesting ownership of the highland Chaparé coca basket in the Department of Cochabamba. The Tupac Katari Guerrilla Army favors legalization of the Chaparé's traditional crop, but, of course, that would remove Gen. Banzer's excuse for stealing Tupac Katari land.

Despite the bureaucratic elimination of much of the electorate, the 97 elections also saw a leader of the Tupac Katari Guerrilla Army elected to Cochabamba's seat in parliament, with 60% of the vote. Most of the rest of the Cochabamba vote went to other Indian groups. According to the U.S. State Department's *Patterns of Global Terrorism*, the Tupac Katari guerrillas number less than a hundred individuals - just a few corrupt, vicious crackpots. How on earth, then, did they manage to get 60% of the vote in a major city like Cochabamba?

An Amazonian coca grower

http://flag.blackened.net/revolt/mexico.html

Drug War

Viva Zapata

In 1978 the CIA's *Confederación Anticomunista Latina*, CAL, adopted "the Banzer Plan" for the coordinated death-squad tracking of "liberation theology" priests and nuns throughout Latin America. This was an extension of the CIA's Operation Condor.

The populist priests and nuns of Catholic Action, for instance, had become a formidable force in Guatemala, bordering southern Mexico. Catholic Action organized at least 150,000 peasants into rural co-ops that provided economic autonomy, the very last thing that the fascists wanted to see. Catholic Action's "Christian Base Communities" stressed education and consciousness-raising, and cooperated with one another throughout the highlands. They presented an alternative to both the guerrillas and the government, and, in many cases, peacefully supported the political goals of the guerrillas.

Catholic Action stood in opposition to a Latin Church too often ruled by the likes of Archbishop Casariego, who, in a famous photo, blessed U.S. military equipment for the Zacapa mass-murder campaign. During the 70's, throughout Latin America, the local Catholic hierarchy was pushed into active support of "the Church of the Poor" by the genuine Christian mysticism of its working class priests and nuns.

The most famous convert to social activism was El Salvador's Archbishop Oscar Romero, whose support for the poor was deep and genuine.[1] The Maryknoll Sisters have also proven to be particularly effective international freedom fighters who have indeed brought glory upon the Church. Many have been murdered by CAL death squads.

Overseeing the Banzer Plan in Mexico was the Bolivian CIA station chief who was Felix Rodriguez' boss when they hunted down Ché Guevara, Hugh Murray. In Mexico, Murray operated as a DEA agent.[2] He had been recruited into the DEA to work with his old CIA buddy Lucien Conein, then running Nixon's covert DEA operations. "The Federal Bureau of Narcotics provided cover for the Central Intelligence Agency since just about the day it was formed," writes criminologist Prof. Alan Block.

That's also what Gary Webb found when he looked into the DEA/CIA in Costa Rica.[3] CIA/DEA agent Murray's two chief Mexican contacts, DFS chief Miguel Nazar Haro and Mexico City Police Chief Arturo Durazo Moreno, both made a fortune in the drug trade, and both ran fascist death squads.[4]

The DFS, the Federal Security Directorate, Mexico's CIA-trained combined CIA and FBI, was created as a subdivision of the Interior Ministry in the 1940's. In the mid-70's it organized Mexico's competing dealers and growers, centralizing all Mexican-based dope distribution. This operation was based in Guadalajara, home of the "Owl" death squads and the CIA's Autonomous University of Guadalajara, the Owl base, from which emanated the DFS's "White Brigade" death squads. The centralization enabled the DFS to rake off 25% of the cartel's gross - billions - and to protect its income more efficiently.

The Owls were founded by Carlos Cuesta Gallardo, a Mexican Nazi who spent World War II in Germany. Hitler's plan was to use Cuesta as his Mexican Quisling. The cofounder of the Owls was Father Julio Meinveille, an Argentine Jesuit. Meinveille is the author of *The Jew, The Cabal of Progressivism, Among the Church and the Reich* and *Conspiracy Against the Church*. These are the Owls' bibles.

High, very high up on the Owls' enemies list was Pope John XXIII, certainly the greatest Pope of the 20th century. He was a Jew, doncha know. Makes us Hebes proud. Pope Paul VI was not only a Jew, but a drug addict! Makes us dopers proud. Every time I take a poke, I get the heavenly feeling that I'm tokin with the Pope. Meinveille was the main speaker at the 1972 CAL conference in Mexico City. The Owls' front man at Vatican Council II was Jesuit Father Saenz y Arriaga, who was excommunicated for forging the signatures of Catholic leaders on hate literature.[5]

Carlos Cuesta Gallardo founded the Autonomous University of Guadalajara in 1935. By 1960 Gallardo's University was just a few dilapidated buildings with an annual budget of $50,000. But CIA agent Oscar Wiegland, U.S. consul in Guadalajara, arranged AID funds for the struggling "university." By 1975 Cuesta's annual budget was $10 million. This is a CIA-financed hate-center, posing as a university, that runs classes in fascist "philosophy" and, literally, coordinates CAL death squad activities, and the dope-dealing that finances them, throughout Latin America.

When Manuel Buendia, a famous investigative journalist for Mexico City's daily *Excelsior* revealed these facts in 1984, he was shot dead.[6] First on the murder scene was the Mexican DFS, whose agents immediately cleaned out Buendia's files, which were said to contain a videotape of high government officials meeting with Mexico's most powerful drug dealers.[7] The engineer of the murder was the head of the DFS, Antonio Zorilla, whom Buendia had trusted as a source and confidant. Buendia was apparently unaware that the DFS shared operational control of the Owls. On his 1989 fall from grace, Zorilla was charged with the murder of Buendia.[8]

At this time the DFS ran a fleet of 600 tanker trucks, ostensibly for ferrying natural gas.[9] According to both objective DEA investigators and an informant DFS agent considered reliable by these hardboiled pros, "They ran ten to twelve trucks a day into Phoenix and Los Angeles. They had the whole border wired."[10] The wiring was done, obviously, using the DFS border zone commanders. The DEA and FBI are always chasing some DFS (federal) border zone commander for trafficking, usually with his paper money trail or gaudy spending.[11]

The first director of the DFS, Capt. Rafael Chavarri, after he left the agency, went to work for Mexico's leading drug trafficker, Jorge Moreno Chauvet. Through the 40's and 50's Chauvet was a major Syndicate heroin distributor and pot and coke supplier. The Mexican border is as porous today as it was then, although the contest for control has gotten more violent. Elaine Shannon: "Most DEA agents who worked in Mexico and on the border considered the DFS the private army of the drug traffickers. They called the DFS badge 'a license to traffic.'"[12]

Since the drug trade is worth billions, it should come as no surprise that the most powerful traffickers carry DFS (now DGSN) and Interior Ministry credentials, have the right to carry submachine guns, install wiretaps and interrogate anyone. The DFS/DGSN, of course, is the enforcement arm of the PRI, Mexico's ruling party. PRI stands for "Institutional Revolutionary Party" - how's that for an oxymoron? It has ruled Mexico uninterruptedly since 1921, using and discarding "kingpins" as needed. What remains is the DFS/DGSN - the Federal Security Directorate/General Directorate of Investigations and National Security; the IPS - the Bureau of Social and Political Investigations; and the PJF - the Federal Judicial Police.

The DFS/DGSN Interior Ministry is the CIA's main base in Mexico. As one disgusted DEA agent put it, none other than Dennis Dayle, 1978-82 chief of Centac, the DEA's international strike force: "In my 30-year history in the Drug Enforcement Administration and related agencies, the major targets of my investigations almost invariably turned out to be working for the CIA."[13] Dayle turned to novelist and reporter James Mills to advertise this. The result was Mills' *The Underground Empire: Where Crime and Governments Embrace*. Concludes Mills:

"The tracks are everywhere. The dapper, aristocratic Mr. Lung - 02 to his American government contacts - speaks laughingly of CIA-supported Thais helicoptering up the mountains to collect their 'goodies' from CIA client Chang Chi-fu [Khun Sa], the world's foremost opium dealer. Chang's heroin-dealing colleague, Chinese General Li Wen-huan, is known to be a CIA dependent. The CIA terminates Operation Durian, a DEA assault against [Chiu chau] Lu Hsu-shui, whose wife happens to be a cousin of Poonsiri Chanyasak, the Communist Lao government's 'minister of heroin,' and who himself turns out today to be associated with a representative of Communist Chinese intelligence. Assassin Michael Decker, suspected of CIA connections [SEAL, Operation Phoenix], describes a CIA weapons brochure found in the personal papers of Alberto Sicilia Falcón, a major marijuana-heroin-cocaine dealer also suspected of employment by the CIA. Sicilia Falcón and his influential bullfighter friend Gaston Santos join in a CIA-sanctioned Portuguese arms deal. Sicilia Falcón's friend and advisor, CIA-trained José Egozi, also involved in the Portuguese weapons deal, talks to Centac agents and ends up hanging from a bed sheet in his Mexican prison cell. Sicilia, under torture, is said to confess to CIA drugs and weapons operations intended to destabilize Latin nations. Rearrested after his escape, facing assassination or further torture, Sicilia is rescued by a high Mexican official the CIA later identifies as its 'most important source in Mexico and Central America.' [Miguel Nazar Haro] In Panama the CIA inhibits a DEA intelligence operation, and blocks a Washington meeting between Panama's drug-dealing leader and DEA bosses."[14]

Dennis Dayle spent years demonstrating these facts to Mills, while he was running the DEA's Central Tactical Unit, Centac. A key CORU [CIA Cuban] contact for DFS Sub-Director Miguel Nazar Haro in the early 70's was CIA - and probably Castro and Trafficante - agent Alberto Sicilia Falcón, trained as an 18 year-old recruit by the U.S. Army at South Carolina's Fort Jackson in 1963. By 1972 Sicilia, sporting a passport issued in Havana by Fidel, was buying Rolls-Royces.[15] He had become Mexico's most powerful drug dealer. His right-hand-man, José Egozi, was a CIA-trained veteran of the Bay of Pigs.[16] His favorite hit man was Mike Decker, a SEAL-trained Phoenix program CIA assassin.[17] Sicilia used his network to feed arms to rightist death squads *and* leftist guerrillas throughout Latin America.

In 1975, the PRI's minister of *Gobernación* (Secretariat of Government), Mario Moya Palencia, was caught jetting around Mexico with Sicilia. It was Moya who had given Sicilia his official *Gobernación* credentials, thus ruining his own chances for the presidency and causing Sicilia to fall (one of Dennis Dayle's DEA Centac operations).

Sicilia's fall seems to have weakened his associate, Chicago's Sam Giancana, but it had no effect at all on Nazar, who took control of the DFS in 1977.[18]

Working with Bosch's CORU and the CIA, Nazar organized the CAL-connected "White Brigade" death-squads to deal with Mexico's many populist groups.[19] The Mexico City arm of the White Brigade was the Jaguars, created by Mexico City Police chief Arturo Durazo Moreno. Durazo was accused by a Florida grand jury of being a major heroin trafficker in league with Trafficante's Cubans, one of whom, of course, was Sicilia.[20]

When a San Diego grand jury indicted Nazar Haro for running the largest stolen car ring in North America, the CIA, through Associate Attorney General Lowell Jensen, blocked the indictment, citing his "indispensability as a source of intelligence in Mexico and Central America."[21] All told, 13 DFS operatives, including the operational leadership, were implicated in this beautiful FBI sting, but only a few foot soldiers were actually nailed.

The prosecuting U.S. Attorney, William Kennedy, was so enraged by CIA interference in his case that he went public, and was promptly fired by Ronald Reagan.[22] Nazar himself was forced to resign, in January of 1982, but that had no effect at all on the DFS relationship with the CIA, or the Guadalajara cartel.[23] Nazar's successor, Antonio Zorilla, signed the DFS identification cards that Rafael Caro Quintero, DEA agent Camarena's probable assassin, and his partners, were carrying when they were arrested in response to the Camarena killing.[24] Nazar himself was resurrected in 1989 by new president Carlos Salinas as chief of the Police Intelligence Directorate. I guess that tells us what we need to know about Salinas.

In 1975, in response to American political pressure, Mexican President Luis Echeverría initiated Operation Condor, the CIA-run "anti-drug" campaign that filled Mexican jails, and morgues, with politically active campesinos and small family-plot growers.[25] This created the political tension that forced the sacrifice of Sicilia.

Echeverría contracted with a gun- and drug-running airline operated by CIA Southeast Asia veterans, Evergreen/Intermountain, maintained by E-Systems,[26] to drop herbicide in areas of his own choosing. This knocked out a few hapless competitors of the big growers, leaving the large-scale marijuana and opium plantations untouched. The small-fry were obligingly noisy about their plight, giving Echeverría the image he needed. Aside from herbicide, the DEA choppers and fixed-wing aircraft used rockets, small arms fire and napalm on campesinos targeted by well-connected landowners.

In 1978 the Mexican Bar Association documented 18 forms of torture used by Mexican Operation Condor agents.[27] Not one major drug trafficker or grower was landed by Operation Condor.[28] Independent DEA agents weren't even allowed to overfly "eradication areas." "We're perpetuating a fraud just by being there," one disgusted DEA agent told a reporter: *Propaganda Due.*[29]

Enough poisonous paraquat did get sprayed to shift a considerable portion of the massive marijuana business to the Colombians, since Mexico's small growers sold their sprayed pot to the wholesalers anyway. Since this hurt the large growers, paraquat was discontinued. Mexican President José López Portillo, who inherited Operation Condor in 1976, reportedly "amassed hundreds of millions in criminal profits" and left office with vast estates in Spain.[30]

In November of 1984 Mexican Federal Police, trapped by conservative American diplomatic pressure and aggressive DEA agents - flashing incriminating aerial photos - were forced to raid one of their own protected operations.[31] With DEA agents, including Camarena, in tow, they turned up 10,000 tons of marijuana being grown on 150 acres in Chihuahua.[32] That is more pot than the U.S. officially estimated was grown in all Mexico that year - in one bust.[33]

DEA agents estimated the retail value to be $2.5 billion. This is real geopolitical power we're talking about, a weed artificially made as valuable as a precious metal. You better damn well not try to collapse that price. This enormously valuable high-tech plantation grew labor-intensive primo *sinsemilla*, "without seeds," marijuana in which the flowers are pinched back, causing the potent resin to accumulate in the leaves.[34]

It was the peons like those on the Chihuahua plantation, who had been working for $6 a day, who recently joined their brethren in Chiapas and revolted, advocating their right to grow whatever the hell they wanted on an acre or two of their own.

As Subcommander Marcos put it, in the Lacandona Jungle Declaration of August 1992 that announced the Zapatista rebellion: "Fifty-four percent of the population of Chiapas suffer from malnutrition, and in the highlands and forest this percentage increases to 80%. A campesino's average diet consists of coffee, corn, tortillas, and beans. One million Indigenous people live in these lands and share a disorienting nightmare with mestizos and ladinos: their only option, 500 years after the "Meeting of Two Worlds," is to die of poverty or repression."

"Government agencies made some horrifying statistics known: in Chiapas 14,500 people die every year, the highest mortality rate in the country. The causes? Curable diseases such as respiratory infections, enteritis, parasites, amoebas, malaria, salmonella, scabies, dengue, pulmonary tuberculosis, trachoma, typhus, cholera and measles."

Emiliano Zapata; Subcommander Marcos Drawing the Analogy

"The oldest of the old in the Indigenous communities say that there once was a man named Zapata who rose up with his people and sang out, "Land and Freedom!" These old campesinos say that Zapata didn't die, that he must return. These old campesinos also say that the wind and the rain and the sun tell the campesinos when to cultivate the land, when to plant and when to harvest. They say that hope is also planted and harvested. They also say that the wind and the rain and the sun are now saying something different: that with so much poverty, the time has come to harvest rebellion instead of death. That is what the old campesinos say. The powerful don't hear; they can't hear, they are deafened by the brutality that the Empire shouts in their ears. 'Zapata,' insists the wind, the wind from below, our wind."

On New Year's Day, 1994, the day NAFTA went into effect, the Zapatistas took San Cristóbal de las Casas, the old colonial capitol of Chiapas, and five surrounding towns. Dozens of federal police were killed before the Zapatistas retreated into the rugged Cañadas. Since then many Chiapas towns have kicked out the PRI and told its *caciques* what to do with their demands for a share of the crop.

The marching song of the original Zapatistas, who fatalistically called themselves "cockroaches," went: *La cucaracha, la cucaracha, ya no puede viajar, porque no tiene, porque no tiene, marijuana que fumar.*

A firefight between Federales, foreground, and Zapatistas, Morelos, 1913

Today's Zapatista National Liberation Army, understanding that their ancient Mayan sacrament has been used as a pretext for their rape at the hands of the conquistador PRI, has banned all drugs and alcohol while at the same time calling for the "legalization of soft drugs throughout the planet."

Mexican troops in the Chiapas highlands,1997; flag.blackened.net/revolt/mexico

The Zapatista "International Encounter" statement of August, 1996 insisted that the Drug War "has converted narcotrafficking into one of the most successful clandestine means of obtaining extraordinary profits" and called for "channelling the resources destined for combatting narcotrafficking into programs of development and social welfare."

The loss of the high-tech marijuana facility in Chihuahua, which had cost millions to set up, was one of the events that got DEA agent Camarena killed. The U.S. Justice Department investigation revealed that a few months before Camarena and his fellow agents maneuvered the DFS and PJF into raiding their own facility, in October of 1984 (apparently, according to the CIA's Col. Carone, for the worst, not the best, of reasons), the command structures of the Mexican cops and hoods held a high-level strategy summit.

The Guadalajara cartel was represented by Juan Ramón Matta Ballesteros, who ran SETCO for Oliver North; Rafael Caro Quintero, an old Richard Secord CIA ally; Ernesto Fonseca, Manuel Salcido Uzeta and Rubén Zuno Arce, President Echeverría's brother-in-law. Zuno was convicted in 1990, in Los Angeles, of complicity in the Camarena murder.

Four more top-level meetings followed, the idea being to protect both the trade and the traders from the American pressure. Fortunately for the Mexican police, the most dangerous American outfit, the one that actually knew what was happening, was with the DFS. All the cartel leaders carried DFS badges and operated with the active support of Federal Judicial Police chief Manuel Ibarra and his regional commanders. When Matta Ballesteros, staying in Mexico City, came under suspicion, Ibarra personally escorted him to his flight out of the country.[35]

DEA agent Celerino Castillo: "In a Sept. 20-26, 1989, series of debriefings and in subsequent debriefing on Feb. 13, 1990, by DEA agents in Los Angeles, Lawrence Victor Harrison, an American-born electronics specialist who had worked in Mexico and had been involved with the leading figures in the Mexican drug cartel, was interviewed. He testified that he had been present when two of the partners of Matta-Ballesteros and Rafael Caro-Quintero, met with American pilots working out of Ilopango air base in El Salvador, providing arms to the Contras. The purpose of the meeting was to work out drug deals."

"Several days earlier, on Feb. 09, 1990, Harrison had told DEA interrogators that Nicaraguan Contras were being trained at a ranch in Vera Cruz, owned by Rafael Caro-Quintero. It was at Quintero's Guadalajara ranch that DEA Agent Kiki Camarena, and his pilot were interrogated, tortured and buried alive."[36]

When Harrison's DEA overseer, Hector Berrellez, recommended that a federal grand jury be convened to investigate the CIA's knowledge of its Contra contractors, this highly decorated street agent was answered by transfer to a DC desk job until retirement.

Camarena was kidnapped on February 6, 1985. His body was found on March 5th, in Vista Hermosa, near Guadalajara. Killing an American agent, of course, was against the rules, and many Mexicans were sacrificed - lambs like Rafael Caro Quintero, Ernesto Fonseca and numerous PJF commanders. This caused the murder of at least thirteen material witnesses. The DFS even changed its name to the General Directorate of Investigations and National Security, the DGSN. But no structural political changes were effected - that would require a change in the value of money, something cops just don't know how to do.[37]

Reacting to the firestorm of publicity ignited by the murder, DEA Administrator Bud Mullen announced, in lieu of effective DEA action, that "Mexico hasn't arrested a major drug trafficker in eight years" - as if the strategic objective was a few key arrests.[38] Mullen got points from some reporters for making apparently honest noises, but when his isolated agents in Guadalajara, in immediate danger from the DFS and the PJF, urgently begged for reinforcements and/or diplomatic intervention, they were ignored.[39] Mullen never wrested control of his agency from the CIA, because it was bureaucratic suicide to try. He was no more able to protect his agents than Duarte was to stop the genocide in El Salvador.

As Subcommander Marcos, and the world's top cop, Raymond Kendall, the head of Interpol, says, the only way to stop the smugglers is to bankrupt them. The value of their commodity must be collapsed by decriminalization. Absent that, no high-level bureaucrat who doesn't go along will get along.

Mullen was, after all, first and foremost, a bureaucratic survivor. He got interestingly honest about Mexican corruption, to the great irritation of his own high command, only after his pension was secure, just as he was about to retire. DEA agent Michael Levine, who had to work under the FBI's Mullen, insisted that Mullen's chief contribution to narcotics enforcement was "more political bullshit" - like the new dress code he announced for DEA agents when he took over on the 1982 merger of the FBI and DEA.[40] Levine, who was not one of the suits, couldn't have been more disdainful.

It was Mullen who led Reagan's destruction of Dennis Dayle's Central Tactical Unit, Centac. Just prior to the FBI's acquisition of the DEA, Congress' investigative arm, the General Accounting Office, issued the results of its yearlong investigation of Centac. The GAO hatchetmen were amazed, issuing one of the few positive reports in their history. Centac was "an effective approach...that needs to be expanded....respond[ing] effectively to highly mobile national and international organizations." Under Dennis Dayle, Centac, in three years, racked up 731 indictments, 36% of which were "the highest-level violators."[41] The DEA average at the time was 12%. While comprising only 3% of all DEA agents, Centac accounted for 12% of arrests of major violators.

Needless to say, this made the DEA's regional and "drug-specific" commanders look inefficient, and caused innumerable political problems "in-country" - where the major violators were pillars of the establishment. The FBI's Mullen simply disbanded Centac. Clinton's DEA, under Janet Reno and Louis Freeh's appointee, Tom Constantine, has weeded out so many of the independent old streetfighters that they've taken to calling the DEA "Constantinople," after the original bureaucracy.

In June of 1985, the commander of the Yucatán eradication zone, Hugo Quintanilla, his chief of pilots, and the entire Federal Judicial Police unit from the state of Campeche were arrested for trafficking in cocaine with the Herrera family, the Mexican equivalent of the Genoveses.[42]

In July of 1990, the Mexican Secretary of the Navy, Adm. Mauricio Schleske, retired, to live part-time by his next-door neighbor in Houston, Adm. José Luís Cubria. Cubria was the recently retired Director General of the Mexican Merchant Marine. Between 1986 and 88, Schleske had military control of the Veracruz-Brownsville region, and Cubria controlled the access of commercial shipping to the same region. The Houston real estate each man bought during this period far exceeded in value anything their legal salaries could have afforded.[43]

On November 7th, 1991, 100 Mexican soldiers, helping to unload a planeload - tons - of Colombian cocaine near Veracruz, were interrupted by Mexican drug agents. Seven of the drug agents were shot through the head, execution style. The DEA plane that videotaped the incident was strafed. The Colombian plane escaped, the soldiers went unpunished, and the coke was distributed.[44]

It is this army that Clinton, McCaffrey, Gelbard and Company are now arming and training in the name of the antidrug effort. McCaffrey's "Hueys" and "Rapid Reaction Units," of course, are invariably aimed at the poor campesinos trying to maintain control of their own land. Shortly after the January 1994 onset of the Zapatista rebellion, in late April, Defense Secretary William Perry huddled with his Mexican counterpart, Gen. Enrique Cervantes Aguirre, to "explore ways in which our militaries could cooperate better."

In May, along with the first dozen of the 50 promised Hueys, combat helicopters, went Drug Czar Barry McCaffrey to oversee the formation of GAT, the Anti-Terrorist Group. GAT coordinates Mexico's secret service death squads with those of Guatemala, Spain and Argentina. Green Beret Gen. McCaffrey, who has operated as a "counterinsurgency expert" in the U.S. Southern Command since 1969, helped to coordinate the original Operation Condor death squads in the 1970's and 80's, which were also "antidrug" operations.

Just after the 1994 elections, Tabasco state governor, the PRI's Roberto Madrazo, officially reported spending $1 million on his election campaign. In June of 1995, through a mole in the Madrazo camp, the leftist opposition was able to produce documents, officially confirmed by the *Fiscalia*, that proved that Madrazo had actually spent $40 million to obtain control of Tabasco. Most of the money, it turned out, had come from the Banco Cremi, the Cali cartel's major Mexican money laundry.[45]

This is typical of the Salinas and succeeding Zedillo presidencies. Carlos Salinas retired from the Mexican presidency a billionaire, while half of Mexico's 90 millions live below the official poverty line. The Party of the Democratic Revolution (PRD), the principal leftist opposition, reported that between the beginning of the 1988 electoral campaign and 2/1/94, 263 of its people had been assassinated.

The seminal assassination, the one that gave all of Catholic Mexico a religious tableau of its tragedy, happened on May 24, 1993 at the Guadalajara airport. Tijuana cartel shooters killed the politically inconvenient Cardinal Juan Jesús Posadas Ocampo, one of Mexico's only two Cardinals.

At the front of the airport terminal, in a bulletproof Buick, sat Chapo Guzmán and three of his Sinaloa cartel bodyguards. At the Aeromexico terminal was Ramón and Javier Arellano and their Tijuana cartel hit team. Entering the terminal in his Mercury Grand Marquis was Cardinal Posadas of Guadalajara. The Tijuana Arellanos, supposedly stalking Guzmán, "accidentally" put 14 bullets into the Cardinal, while at the same time exchanging fierce fire with Guzmán and his Sinaloa crew. The Cardinal's driver, three bystanders and two shooters were also killed. Sinaloa kingpin Guzmán escaped unscathed.

Both Arellano brothers, and half their hit team, with weapons stashed in carry-on luggage, and without boarding passes, then quietly boarded a Tijuana-bound Aeromexico plane that had been held for them for 20 minutes. The Arellanos rode in first class, their young pistoleros in coach. The only other passenger in first class was reported to be Jorge Hank Rhon, owner of the Tijuana racetrack, the son of billionaire PRI "dinosaur" Carlos Hank González, former cabinet minister and Mexico City Mayor, a key power broker. The four state police officers who held the plane for the Arellanos were later accused of acting as their airport coordination team. A federal police commander, who just happened to be a boyhood friend of Javier Arellano, met with him just before the shootout. He testified that Javier told him that Guzmán was to be hit, so he honored Javier's request to guard the airport gate.

Not only the Cardinal, but his reputation, was shot to pieces. Immediately after the shooting, Tijuana's Father Gerardo Montaño arranged a face-to-face sitdown in Mexico City for Benjamín and Ramón Arellano with none other than the Papal Nuncio, Girolamo Prigione, the Vatican's ambassador to Mexico. The Arellanos protested their innocence, and the Papal Nuncio insisted that it was his duty to listen. Observers could only assume that this diplomatic recognition of the Tijuana cartel indicated that Cardinal Posadas had been engaged in relations or negotiations with either or both of the rival camps. Did this explain why both the Cardinal and the Sinaloa cartel leadership were at the airport at the same time, and how the Tijuana cartel knew about it? Had the Cardinal made a decision that Tijuana felt he couldn't live with? Was the murderous PRI dinosaur Hank Gonzalez sending a message to the PRI leadership? And how were the Arellanos, the most wanted drug kingpins in Mexico, able to have a public meeting in Mexico City with the Vatican's ambassador without being arrested?

Salinas' handpicked successor, Luis Donaldo Colosio, was gunned down at a Tijuana rally in March of 1994. Colosio, supposedly an anti-Gulf cartel reformist, had ties to the powerful Sinaloa cartel. As with the Cardinal, the Tijuana/Gulf cartel may have found that hard to swallow. But Colosio, for all his PRI and Sinaloa connections, had the respect of some of Mexico's proven reformers. A few weeks after the assassination, the reformist Tijuana federal police chief, Ernesto Ibarra Santes, on the trail of the State police who had cooperated in the assassination, was also gunned down. Ibarra's most important street ally, Tijuana antidrug chief García Vargas, was slowly tortured and then strangled to death.

On February 28, 1995, Raul Salinas, the former president's brother, was arrested on charges of having ordered the September 1994 assassination of the PRI's second in command, José Francisco Ruiz-Massieu, who had just decided to run for the presidency. Ruiz-Massieu had been married to Salinas' sister Adriana, and had been brought into the family business on that basis. The Salinas family then engineered Ruiz-Massieu's election to the governorship of the coastline port state of Guerrero.

Bagwoman Magdalena Ruiz Pelayo turned millions of dollars worth of real estate for the Salinas family - and for Mexico's major drug dealers. She formally told the FBI in July of 96 that hostility arose when Raul Salinas caught brother-in-law José Ruiz-Massieu in bed with a man, while still married to his sister. This has actually been turned into a soap opera on Mexican TV. José's brother Mario Ruiz-Massieu, who ended up in charge of Mexico's DEA, remained loyal to Salinas.

Ruiz Pelayo testified that she was at many meetings with the elder Raul Salinas, his children Carlos, Raul and Adriana, the Ruiz-Massieu brothers, the new governor of Guerrero - and Juan García Abrego, head of the Gulf cartel. García Abrego, an old associate of Papa Raul, knew the Salinas brothers well enough to party with them before Carlos became president in 1988.

That election was stolen for Salinas by PRI Interior Minister Manuel Bartlett Diaz. Seeing that the left-of-center forerunner of the Party of the Democratic Revolution (PRD), led by Cuauhtémoc Cardenas, was headed for victory, Diaz crashed the electoral computer, forcing a handcount. Ten days later Salinas was declared victorious with 52% of the vote, but an independent analysis revealed Cardenas over Salinas 42% to 36%.[46] Never mind.

Carlos' brother Raul, during the last year of the Salinas administration, 1994, transferred more than $120 million to Swiss banks. During this time, Deputy Attorney General Mario Ruiz-Massieu, the loyal brother, controlled Mexico's Federal Judicial Police and its entire counternarcotics program, including the INCD, Mexico DEA. On March 3, 1995, U.S. officials stopped Mario Ruiz-Massieu at Newark International Airport with a ticket to Madrid, more than $40,000 in cash, and $9 million more in the Houston Commerce Bank.

The forfeiture proceeding filed by the Houston Division of the U.S. District Court[47] alleges the systematic collusion of the Salinas administration with the country's top drug dealers. It specifically names the entire Salinas family - father Raul, his son Carlos, the president, and Carlos' brother and sister, Raul and Adriana. It then goes on to detail specific instances of cooperation with every major drug trafficker in Mexico, including Juan García Abrego, Miguel Angel Felix Gallardo, the four Arellano Felix brothers and Amado Carillo.

García's Gulf cartel owned the eastern coke routes. Amado Carillo of the Ciudad Juárez cartel owned Chihuahua, literally. Felix Gallardo's protégés and relatives, the Arellanos, fought a protracted war in Mexico's Northwest with Chapo (Shorty) Guzmán, Guero (Whitey) Palma and their Sinaloa cartel. At stake was control of the Pacific smuggling corridor and the California market. The war took the form of assassinating key police and army commanders loyal to either camp throughout Baja, Sonora, Sinaloa and Jalisco. As the 1995 U.S. indictment of Mario Ruiz-Massieu indicates, then, buying the Mexican Presidency was no small scam, it was troop deployment. One typical item, among dozens:

"May 1993, Massieu's home, Acapulco, $2 million: Mario Ruiz Massieu, Commandant Pizarro, Commandant Pizarro's brother (alias "El Flaco"), Commandant Pizarro's adjutant Raul Nava Arontes, Chief Commandant Cadena, Enrique Montano, the Chief of Police of Acapulco (General Acosta Chaparro), Ruben Figueroa Estrada. Payment to Massieu for the 'detouring' of part of approximately 22 tons of cocaine seized near Acapulco." You could actually ski on that much white powder.

Customs discovered Ruiz-Massieu's Texas bank accounts during their investigation of his role in the theft of over eight tons of cocaine from a jet seized in Sombrerete in August of 94. While stuffing millions from García's Gulf cartel into the bank, Mario Ruiz-Massieu was the CEO of Salinas' War on Drugs, using America's "antidrug" largesse, provided directly to his agency by the DEA, to buy protection for the Gulf cartel. Perfect.

To call this "corruption" or "narcocracy" is, in a sense, to miss the point. It's just economics. Thanks only to the artificial Prohibition-created value of drugs, Mexican drug gangs rake in $20-$30 billion a year in profits, according to a University of Guadalajara study.[48] That gives them billions to dedicate to buying key officials and police units. There simply is no other power in Mexico that can compete. The great drug gangs actually conduct turf wars in Mexico using whole police forces as proxies.

In May of 1994 Eduardo Valle Espinosa quit as Federal Deputy Attorney General. Valle, who had been waging frontline war against Juan García Abrego's Gulf cartel, insisted that "Nobody can outline a political project in which the heads of drug trafficking and their financiers are not included. Because if you do, you die."

The short career of National Action Party (PAN) reformist, Tijuana police chief Federico Benítez, 1992-1994, illustrates Valle's point. 1994 saw Benítez' Tijuana municipal police confiscate more drugs, and provide more drug intelligence to the U.S., than the antidrug unit of the Federal police. There were actually repeated gun battles between the Federal police and Benítez' municipal or state police when a key arrest or bust was made. Benítez was called to a sitdown with a powerful federal commander connected to the Sonora traffickers, Rodolfo García Gaxiola. Benítez told García to take his $100,000 a month and shove it. Benítez penned the details of that meeting into the notebook investigators were able to use to decipher these events.

The next meeting involved a Tijuana cartel field general, a hood known as El Mayel. Benítez told El Mayel the same thing he told García. He then stoically told his boss, Tijuana's Mayor Osuna, that he did not have long to live. On April 28, 1994, a well-coordinated Federal police hit squad, led by García Gaxiola, using multiple vehicles and radio control, emptied an AK-47 into Federico Benítez. Many U.S. cops North of the line were heartbroken, and left wondering why were were financing these *federales*. Benítez was the best they had ever seen.

Five days after the killing, Baja's deputy state attorney general, Sergio Ortiz, hot on the trail of the federal killers, was arrested at gunpoint by a federal agent. Tijuana's municipal Tactical Group and Baja state police rushed to rescue Attorney General Ortiz. They found themselves looking up at dozens of cocked shotguns on the steps of the federal police headquarters. The *federales* had acted on the orders of Rodolfo García Gaxiola. Attorney General Ortiz was falsely charged with corruption. Although the municipal Tactical Group eventually charged García Gaxiola with the murder of police chief Benítez, García Gaxiola, and his two brothers, who were also federal commanders, were transferred to other federal districts, where Baja state authorities couldn't touch them.[49]

In February, 1995, President Zedillo's newly appointed federal police chief, who had promised to oust corrupt police officials, was gassed in his sleep and left brain damaged. A month later, on March 15, 1995, just after Zedillo had appointed another PANista reformist, Antonio Lozano Gracia, to the post of Attorney General, police officers in Mexico City attempted to carjack Zedillo's eldest son in broad daylight. Zedillo's numerous bodyguards, traveling in separate cars, prevented the President from losing his son - to the Mexico City police.

Zedillo reacted, in June of 1996, by replacing Mexico City's police chief with Army Gen. Enrique Salgado Cordero, who explained that half of all Mexico City's crime originated from within the police force itself. Just before he quit, on March 12, 1994, Attorney General Valle officially informed the DEA that at least half of Mexico's federal police chiefs and attorneys general were on the *narcotraficante* payroll. Police chief posts are so lucrative, said Valle, that they sometimes go for as much as $2 million. Valle then fled to the U.S. for safety.

In July of 1995 conservative PANista businessman Ricardo Cordero Ontiveros was named head of the intelligence division in the Tijuana office of the Attorney General's National Institute for Combating Drugs, the INCD. By November 1995, Cordero was not only forced from his job, but had to leave under heavy military escort, for fear of assassination. The threat came not from the Tijuana pistoleros, but from the Federal Judicial Police. Cordero had outraged the federales by calling them a bunch of drunken slobs whose only work was the collection of graft from the Tijuana cartel. Since he could prove what he was saying, he had to leave Tijuana in a hurry.[50]

Barry McCaffrey was therefore relieved in December of 1996 at the appointment of a career army officer, Gen. José de Jesús Gutiérrez Rebollo, rather than another corrupt politician, to head the INCD. This coincided with the replacement of opposition party reformist Lozano as Attorney General, apparently for turning up way too much information on the PRI's family feud. Gen. Gutiérrez, said McCaffrey, "has a reputation of impeccable integrity, and he is known as an extremely forceful and focused commander."[51]

On February 19, 1997, after less than three months on the job, Gen. Gutiérrez was relieved of his INCD command and formally charged with being on the payroll of Amado Carillo Fuentes, Mexico's "Lord of the Skies." Carillo, a relative of the Medellín cartel's Jorge Ochoa, had pioneered the use of low-flying jetliners to transport multiton loads of cocaine from his Colombian partners to Mexico. A power for years under Salinas, Carillo did this from his position within Mexican military intelligence. He carried Mexican Federal Judicial Police Group Chief credentials for special investigations and an officer's gold card.

Lucindo Carillo, cousin of Amado, was also *un Jefe de Grupo de PJF*, in Agua Prieta, Sonora, a port. The PJF Commandant in Agua Prieta, Luis Manuel Palofax-Juarez, was also a documented associate of Amado Carillo. Gen. Gutiérrez, one of the most powerful men in Mexican military intelligence, and his two top military aides, were also formally charged with stacking the INCD with Carillo's agents.

Before he was relieved of command, Gutiérrez had been given repeated top-secret briefings on all Mexican-American antismuggling efforts and intelligence, including definitive lists of the INCD/DEA's paid Mexican informants. "The Lord of the Skies" might as well have been personally briefed by Barry McCaffrey himself. The head of the DEA, Thomas Constantine, said Gen. Gutiérrez probably would prove more damaging to the DEA than Aldrich Ames had been to the CIA.[52]

"Aw shucks," said Barry, "I didn't know." DEA spokesman James McGivney backed McCaffrey up: "It's not our job to vet these people. We don't go around spooking military and government officials; we've got enough to do with the crooks."[53] Pollyanna is running the DEA? Am I supposed to believe that the premier counterinsurgency expert of the vast U.S. Southern Command naval, air, radar and information system "just ain't too good at this intelligence stuff"?

Gen. Gutiérrez' narcotics trafficking was well-covered in the DEA's NADDIS (Narcotics and Dangerous Drugs Information System) database long before McCaffrey hailed him as Mexico's salvation at the head of the INCD.[54] On February 18, 1997, Mexican Defense Secretary Cervantes announced that Gutiérrez had systematically supported the Carillo cartel for 7 years.[55] As head of the U.S. Southern Command, Gen. McCaffrey worked with Gen. Gutiérrez for most of those years. It is interesting that while the DEA pegged Gutiérrez correctly, the CIA profile was solid McCaffrese.

Before he became Mexico's top nark, Gen. Gutiérrez was in charge of the coastline port state of Jalisco, the capitol of which is Guadalajara. Gutiérrez earned his reputation as a nark by helping the Guadalajara/ DGSN cartel deal with its competition, most notably with the June 1995 arrest of Hector "Whitey" Palma, a leader of the rival Sinaloa crew.

Since three-quarters of South America's cocaine must pass through Mexico on its way to the U.S., we are talking about a very high stakes power game - *tens of billions in regular trade* - $30 billion annually according to the U.S. Justice Department. That's fully 10% of Mexico's GDP. Mexican military intelligence is not about to let that kind of power slide. That's why Gutiérrez' two top military aides were also indicted - they were under *orders*. That kind of money buys armaments.

Gen. Gutiérrez blew his cover to both press and police when he moved into a posh Mexico City apartment owned by one of Amado Carillo's top lieutenants, with whom he was repeatedly seen. He was also sloppy enough to allow himself to be recorded talking money with Carillo himself on the phone. The General, whose INCD was directly financed by the DEA, must have felt very comfortable to have behaved so stupidly.

Gutiérrez was defended in court by Tomás Arturo Gonzalez Velazquez, a very tough 43 year-old former military colleague of Gutiérrez. Gonzalez repeatedly insisted that the general's arrest was part of a power struggle within Mexican military intelligence. Gonzalez got very specific about the collaboration of top commanders, including defense minister Gen. Enrique Cervantes Aguirre, with the chief smuggling organizations. He even asserted that President Zedillo's brother-in-law had ties to a major methamphetamine trafficker. In a classified report given to Attorney General Reno in February of 98, DEA officials confirmed many of Gonzalez' accusations. Tomás Gonzalez was shot dead on April 21, 1998.[56]

The Zapatistas march in Mexico City, 9/1997; flag.blackened.net/revolt/mexico.html

Although the July 1997 elections proved that the PRI's lock on power was vulnerable, the PRI still got 39% percent of the vote. Lozano's center-right National Action Party got 27% and Cardenas' center-left Party of the Democratic Revolution got 26%. Cardenas won the important mayoralty of the huge Mexico City metropolis. As of the 97 elections, PAN, the National Action Party, held 6 of Mexico's 31 governorships; the PRI still held the rest.

On July 9th, three days after the elections, the police chief in the coastal city of Pinotepa Nacional in the state of Oaxaca was found shot dead near his home. That is, power on the streets of Pinotepa Nacional has nothing to do with which party rules Oaxaca.

Although I heard "democratic progress" all over the media when the elections were held, the major centrist parties all spout the same line on the drug issue. Cardenas and Lozano have nothing to say about drug policy or corruption that Zedillo isn't saying. And any campesino party, such as the Zapatistas, that advocates herb legalization will find its candidates, or its children, murdered. The surviving Zapatistas will then be accused of preferring bullets to ballots.

On 12/22/97, 45 unarmed Tzotzil campesinos, including 15 children, were slaughtered in their highland Chiapas village of Acteal. "This is a situation that defies understanding, where there has been no official will to get the violence under control," protested Bishop Samuel Ruiz, the senior Catholic prelate in the Chiapas highlands.[57] Ruiz insisted that PRI death squads were behind the massacre, because the Tzotzils had been peacefully supporting Zapatista political demands. Enraged Tzotzil youngsters who march off into the highlands to join the guerrillas, after burying their little sisters, will then be accused of preferring bullets to ballots - and of being *narcotraficantes*.

Zapatista women prepare bread for the troops

In fact, Gen. Gomez, commander of the Chiapas military district, immediately accused Bishop Ruiz of San Cristobal de las Casas of being a guerrilla operative, as if that somehow mitigated the horror of the massacre. Gomez was apparently referring to the Bishop's protest against the NAFTA-engineered collapse of the price of Chiapas produce. The flood of cheap agricultural imports, which forced campesinos further into the slave-labor cash economy, was the major reason the Zapatistas rebelled in the first place.

Gen. Tito Valencia Ortiz replaced the busted Gen. Gutiérrez as Mexico's Drug Czar, and then the whole outfit was reshuffled, again. Barry didn't miss a beat, shoveling weaponry at Valencia just as fast as he shovelled it at Gutiérrez. Like his predecessor, Gen. Valencia uses Barry's bullets to chop up impoverished Mayans in the southern highlands, as if they were the ones who had been flying Carillo's coked-up 727's. If these poor campesinos are *narcotraficantes*, then I'm Nancy Reagan.

Burying the victims of the Acteal massacre. These people are afraid to reveal their identities even while burying their children; flag.blackened.net/revolt/mexico.html

Responding to repeated reports of vicious human rights abuses by his alumni, Marblemouth McCaffrey insisted that "It should not be my business how foreign countries organize for their counter-narcotics strategy." That's a very odd attitude for a financier to take toward the activity he is financing. McCaffrey did make it his business to enroll more Mexican officers in the Airmobile Special Forces school at Ft.Bragg, and to deliver another 50 HUEYS. Is McCaffrey saying, once again, that he doesn't give a damn how many gooks we kill?

In charge of those attack helicopters, rebel DEA agent Cele Castillo has revealed, is the same assassin who ran helicopter-based counterinsurgency programs in Vietnam and El Salvador, Felix Rodriguez, who ran Ilopango's dopers for Oliver North's NSC while Barry McCaffrey orchestrated the vicious Contra war. Coordinating this effort from Langley is none other than Ted Shackley, Santos Trafficante's chief requisitions officer at Miami's CIA station - later CIA manager of Secord's Air Opium in Laos.

When Mike Ruppert expanded on Castillo's information on a web page of the Crack The CIA Coalition (www.radio4all.org/crackcia), Castillo's contact in the U.S. Milgroup in Belize told Castillo to warn

Ruppert that Felix Rodriguez, an accomplished assassin, had threatened to kill him for publishing the information.

That Rodriguez' choppers have nothing whatever to do with their stated antidrug mission is further evidenced by their location - lowland Belize, directly east of Chiapas, where drug crops can't be grown. The old Hueys, furthermore, as the *L.A. Times* reported on 3/19/98, are useless at heights where drug crops can be grown.[58]

Despite the fact that not one single major *narcotraficante* had been extradited to the U.S. since the signing of a mutual extradition treaty in 1980, McCaffrey, on 2/26/98, called Mexican drug cooperation "absolutely superlative." He went on to trumpet the creation of new police units and more additions to the Mexican military's alphabet soup.

That same day, Thomas Constantine, the head of the DEA, in formal testimony before the Senate, adamantly disagreed with McCaffrey: "None of these changes have produced significant results.... None have resulted in the arrest of the leadership or the dismantlement of any of the well-known organized criminal groups operating out of Mexico.... Unfortunately, virtually every investigation DEA conducts against major traffickers in Mexico uncovers significant corruption of law-enforcement [military] officials."[59]

The Zapatistas advertised the real focus of American efforts in Aug. of 98 by kidnapping Thomas Gillen, the U.S. Embassy's Asst. Army Attaché, while he and his aide were on an intelligence mission in Chiapas.

Despite the obviously faked death of Gen. Gutiérrez' financier, the red-hot Amado Carillo, just before the 97 elections, his protected 727's are still flying high. Carillo, saying he was going into hospital for plastic surgery, supposedly died there. He then rigged a photo op in which his hambone mother wailed over an unrecognizably mutilated corpse - with no fingertips. Apparently they do plastic surgery in Mexico with a blowtorch and a meat cleaver. The coke trade, of course, hasn't been affected by this mummery at all. I got two words for these ghoulish bastards: *Viva Zapata.*

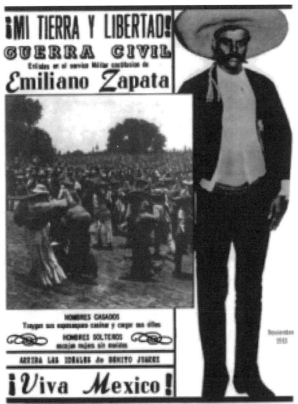

Zapatista recruitment poster, November, 1913: "My Land and Liberty!
CIVIL WAR: Enlist in the constitutional Military service of
Emiliano Zapata: Married Men: Bring your wife to cook and carry your rifles
Single Men: Can find unmarried women: Up with the Ideals of Benito Juarez
Long Live Mexico!" Below, Zapata's army in Morelos

Peruvian guerrillas on the Shining Path

Peruvian President Alberto Fujimori: www.blythe.org/peru-pcp/index.html

Drug War

S.I.N.

In Peru, McCaffrey's "narcoguerrillas" have many names, among them "The Shining Path," *Sendero Luminoso* and *Túpac Amaru*. The *Movimiento Revolucionario Túpac Amaru* is named after Túpac Amaru II, the last Inca king to rise against the Spanish, in 1780. 17 of Peru's 25 millions, most of Incan descent, live in extreme poverty. The most valuable cash crop in the vast, impoverished Huallaga River Valley is coca. It's the traditional basis of the economy.

Although the countryside is racked by epidemic cholera, the government puts nothing at all into medical care, sanitation or structural economic projects. Millions of people have virtually no access to medical care, and no political hope of ever getting any. If your 3-year-old daughter died of an easily preventable disease, and she was the last of your four children to die, would you pick up a gun?

During the 18 months prior to the seizure of the Japanese Embassy by *Túpac Amaru* in late December of 96, Peruvian President Fujimori imprisoned 500,000 poor campesinos on charges of terrorism or treason.[1] But when the Embassy was seized, Fujimori was quick to insist that this was an unpopular fringe group. Sure. Like the Vietminh. *Tupac Amaru* is allied with *Sendero Luminoso*, the Communist Party of Peru (PCP), which leads the Popular Army of Liberation (EPL). The EPL has the political allegiance of the overwhelming majority of Incan campesinos.

The guerrillas are Incan tribalists, committed to free medical care, education, and sweat-equity work for the poor. Incan tribal lands are traditionally held in common. "Communist," to an Incan campesino, means that the Incas once again have an army. That's why their leaders take the names of Incan kings. "The Shining Path" enforces a floor price for coca leaves, by far Peru's most valuable crop, and so serves as an armed force to prevent extortionate eradication. The guerrillas also provide a buffer between their people and the dealers.[2]

Brazil's Prof. Anthony Richard Henman, 1990: "...coca [is used] not only as an excellent physical stimulant, but also as a major element of traditional healing practices, and—through the support and stimulus given to myth recitation—the prime means of activating the collective memory. Thus, to attack coca chewing in the Amazon amounts to more than a minor act of behavioral retraining, on a par with making Indians cover their private parts. It involves a fundamental assault on the cohesion of a culture which has existed for millennia."

A family shares the power-giving coca during a fertility rite; Catherine J Allen

That is, coca leaf is the central religious sacrament of this culture. Quillabamba, peopled mostly by the highland Aymara of southern Peru, a *Sendero Luminoso* stronghold, is the ancient Incan capital of the department of Cuzco on the eastern Amazonian slopes of the Central Andes. It's a popular tourist stop on the way to the ancient mountaintop city of Macchu Piccu.

"By the mid-1960s, a process of land reform was under way, which has led in turn to the emergence of a strong peasant federation in the area—the *Federación de Productores Campesinos de La Convención y Lares* (FEPCACYL). Understandably, FEPCACYL is a strong and highly articulate defender of the legal market in coca leaves; probably for this reason, *La Convención* is the only major coca producing region in South America never to have suffered the effects of forcible eradication. With *Sendero Luminoso* guerrillas poised on the very hilltops surrounding Quillabamba, any attempt at armed intimidation of coca growers could only lead to widespread bloodshed."[3]

The government-connected dealers responded with paramilitary forces of their own, known as *rondas* or "blackheads." The *rondas* operate as irregulars for the Peruvian Army. Operation Aries, April, 1994, challenged *Sendero Luminoso* for control of the Huallaga River Valley. According to Peru's National Coordinator of Human Rights, the Peruvian Army's tactics consisted entirely of machine-gunning the mountain hamlets from the air, then landing in force to gang-rape, murder and loot. The Army didn't engage the guerrillas once. It hit their families. When the International Committee of the Red Cross came to investigate, it was denied access to the entire region.

As Peruvian Gen. Cisneros once explained, "It is necessary to kill ten peasants to kill one guerrilla." So how unpopular could they be? As of January, 1996, according to the Andean Commission of Jurists, official emergency zones included 50% of the Peruvian population and 28% of its national territory. Much of the territory in question is the most valuable land in the country, the coca basket.

President Fujimori's new laws define "provoking anxiety," "affecting international relations," or seeming to favor the guerrillas as treason. Those accused of treason are imprisoned without the possibility of bail until a final verdict is rendered. No evidence of guilt is required for imprisonment, and imprisonment often ends in extrajudicial murder, or a life sentence passed by anonymous, hooded military judges.[4] Fujimori's first year in office was characterized by "one of the world's most dismal human rights records."[5]

Alberto Fujimori, a grey academic aiming at a Senate seat, was elected president of Peru in an election rigged by the National Intelligence Service, SIN, Peru's CIA. Without the fraud, Peru's 1990 President would have been the great writer Mario Vargas Llosa. SIN's 1990 election liaison to Fujimori was Vladimiro Montesinos. The Madrid daily *La Vanguardia* called him "the second most powerful man in Peru, after the president."[6] That was an understatement.

In January 1973, Gen. Edgardo Mercado Jarrin became prime minister, minister of war, and commander-in-chief of the army. Mercado's Peruvian army was leftist and nationalist. It was led by Gen. Juan Velasco Alvarado, who had taken the government by force in 1968. According to Peruvian Army Maj. José Fernandez Slavatecci, in his autobiography *I Accuse*, artillery captain Vladimiro Montesinos was recruited into the CIA at the time of Velasco's leftist coup.

In 1973, Capt. Montesinos became one of Gen. Mercado's most

trusted aides. Col. Rafael Córdova, chief of army intelligence in 1990, charged that during this period Montesinos sold out the Peruvian military to the CIA and Pinochet, going so far as to peddle Mercado's specific plans for Peruvian defense in the event of war with Chile. This was confirmed by Col. Sinesio Jarama, another of Mercado's top aides.

The August 1975 coup of Gen. Francisco Morales Bermúdez saw the exile of the mistrusted Montesinos to a remote outpost near the Ecuadorian border. Montesinos immediately went AWOL - to the headquarters of American military intelligence in Washington, where he was spotted by Peruvian military operatives. On his return to Peru he was cashiered from the army, convicted of desertion and sent to prison for a year. The creative Montesinos used his prison time to earn a law degree.

Vladimiro Montesinos; www.blythe.org/peru-pcp/index.html

During the 80's, Montesinos built a reputation as the top drug lawyer in Peru. "Within a few years, Montesinos became a sought-after legal and administrative strategist for drug traffickers, providing services that went far beyond the practice of law. He rented homes for Colombian traffickers, advised accessories of traffickers when to go into hiding, managed the disappearance of files of fugitive Colombian traffickers to prevent extradition requests, and in at least one case, produced falsified documents to buttress his defense of a cocaine dealer.... For the drug mafia...Montesinos' handle on the system made him almost indispensable."[7]

According to Peru's most famous journalist, Gustavo Gorriti, quoted above, Montesinos had been investigated by the DEA for "his connection to the most important Peruvian drug cartel in the 1980s, the Rodriguez-Lopez organization, and also links to some Colombian traffickers."[8] In 1986, when Reynaldo Rodriguez-Lopez went on trial for running the largest cocaine smuggling organization in Peru, Vladimiro Montesinos ran his legal team.

Montesinos also represented the more important police generals indicted for being on Rodriguez-Lopez' payroll. In a brilliant series of covert moves among his police and military contacts, Montesinos used the case to take control of the Peruvian Attorney General's office, arranging the military replacement of the original prosecutor with his own puppet. Montesinos was back in power.

PCP fighters recruit in Uchiza, 1987; Victor Vargas

In 1990, this master-fixer, working under orders from the National Intelligence Service, arranged the quashing of tax evasion charges against presidential candidate Fujimori, who was SIN's only hope of beating the conservative and incorruptible Vargas. Immediately upon election, Fujimori chose to live and work in the Military Circle, an exclusive Army officer's club. This kept him unavailable to the press between the election and his inauguration. Montesinos remained Fujimori's SIN handler. His title was "national security advisor."

Fujimori's first move was to sack army intelligence chief Córdova and most of the rest of Peru's best prosecutors and antidrug police, whom drug lawyer Montesinos knew all too well. The Interior and Justice ministries were then stacked with Montesinos' own people. Montesinos then handpicked the Armed Forces Joint Command. He also chose Gen. José Valdivia for a senior post. Valdivia, who would become one of the Army's chiefs after the 1992 coup, was the butcher who had been accused of the Army's revenge massacre of 28 peasants at a wedding in the Ayacucho village of Cayara in 1988. Montesinos had been Valdivia's SIN lawyer, arranging such legal niceties as the disappearance of witnesses.

According to Human Rights Watch/Americas, "A death squad composed of members of the SIN and military agents and organized under Montesinos' direction has been responsible for some of the most serious rights violations attributed to the armed forces under Fujimori's administration, including disappearances, torture and illegal executions."[9]

On the night of November 3, 1991, a death squad armed with the army's assassination weapon of choice, silencer-equipped H&K submachine guns, burst into a Lima barrio chicken barbecue. The pro-*Sendero* sentiments of the locals had proven obnoxious, since Barrios Altos was less than 30 meters from the police intelligence directorate's headquarters and 50 meters from another police precinct.

Despite the presence of a troop transport filled with soldiers, or perhaps because of it, 16 people, including children, were left riddled with machine-gun bullets. A horrified witness jotted down the license plate numbers on the death-squad vehicles. One was assigned to the office of Santiago Fujimori, the president's brother, and the other to the office of David Mejía, the vice-minister of the interior.

The outraged Congress appointed a commission of inquiry, which revealed that the murders were the work of the officially-sanctioned death squad of the Army Intelligence Service, the "Colina Group." The Colina was led by Gen. Julio Salazar, a subordinate of Vladimiro Montesinos. Just as prosecutor Pablo Livia was preparing to do ballistic tests on weapons belonging to army intelligence, he was taken off the case. To prevent the Congress from taking corrective action, Montesinos' Army suspended it, the constitution, civil liberties, the vice-presidency and the supreme court - at gunpoint, April 5, 1992.

According to Gorriti, in one of the first actions taken after the April coup, "army intelligence officers had ransacked archives in the judiciary and in the prosecutor's offices mainly to get hold of all the cases in which Vladimiro Montesinos, Fujimori's closest advisor, was involved as a lawyer for drug traffickers and perhaps other documents that Fujimori does not want the public to know."

La Vanguardia quotes Peruvian Senator César Barrera as saying they were searching to "destroy evidence that Montesinos maintains close relations with the CIA despite the fact that the CIA knew he was protecting drug traffickers." More than 10,000 files were destroyed.

Gorriti says that "in late 1990, Montesinos also began close cooperation with the CIA, and in 1991 the National Intelligence Service he controlled began to organize a secret antidrug outfit with funding, training and equipment provided by the CIA."[10]

1998 protest at Lima's Presidential Palace; blythe.org/peru-pcp/index.html

This move enraged the DEA in Lima, because it switched Peruvian antidrug operations from DEA to CIA control. According to a 1991 DEA internal report quoted in the *Miami Herald*, "Montesinos has gained the president's unconditional confidence, and using that position, he arranges the appointment of ministers and advisors as well as transfers of Army officers . . . always with the aim of supporting narcotics trafficking." Remember, that's DEA intelligence experts talking.

But, adds Gorriti, "As far as I know, the secret intelligence unit never carried out antidrug operations. It was used for other things, such as my arrest." Gorriti, as the Peruvian correspondent for Spain's prestigious *El País*, had the juice to survive his arrest, but he had to leave the country immediately. The contents of his computer did not survive.

Former Vice President San Román declared that since the coup "the number of airplanes carrying drugs has been increasing steadily." Immediately after the 1992 coup the U.S. announced it was dismantling its antidrug night radars in northern Peru, without giving an explanation. According to San Román, this was done to facilitate the drug trade, which he says is now directly organized by Montesinos' National Intelligence Service.[12] "The CIA trains the SIN's intelligence units in everything from vetting witnesses to polygraph testing; it has even donated jeeps."[13] The CIA was the chief financier and trainer of the coup engineers.

1998 protest at Lima's Presidential Palace; blythe.org/peru-pcp/index.html

In late 1992, Fujimori's erstwhile Vice President, Máximo San Román, who had been proclaimed Peruvian President by the dissolved Congress, arranged the publication of loyalist intelligence reports on the Barrios Altos massacre. *Sí* magazine broke the story, identifying the SIN killers and tracing the chain of command all the way to Montesinos. Fujimori's reaction to the story was to specifically promote all the named killers.

"I fear that my country will fall into the hands of the Mafia," moaned San Román.[14] Mario Vargas Llosa has said the same thing, as has Peruvian-born economist Hernando de Soto, who negotiated the pact under which the Peruvian government was enlisted in Washington's war on drugs. All these critics are now in exile, fearing execution by Montesinos' secret police. But Peru, Clinton will tell you, as he shovels weapons at Montesinos, is a democracy.

U.S. Undersecretary of State for Latin American Affairs Bernard Aronson was present in Lima the day of the April 1992 coup. A few weeks earlier Aronson had urged all possible aid to Fujimori "to avoid a holocaust comparable to Hitler's gas chambers or Pol Pot's death camps." That is, the U.S. knew the coup was coming and publicly supported it. When it happened, President Bush not only prevented the OAS from taking any action, but had Vietnam vet Gen. Barry McCaffrey send Southern Command trainers down to teach Alberto and Vladimiro all about "strategic hamlets," which now dot the Peruvian countryside.

This was done in contravention of the post-coup U.S. Congressional ban on military aid to Peru - as an antidrug operation. Peru's main naval base in Puccallpa, in the department of Ucayali, was turned into the main U.S. base for regional antinarcotics operations. The entire department of Ucayali was then put under the martial law of the Peruvian Navy, as a combined U.S.-Peruvian antinarcotics operation. Peru's Navy was armed to the teeth during its "aid suspension."

This enabled the well-funded Navy to do double duty as the Peruvian Cocaine Transport Service. On July 3, 1996, police in Vancouver took 120 kilos of cocaine off a Peruvian Navy ship. On July 11, 62 kilos of coke were removed from the Peruvian Navy warship *Ilo*. This has been the uninterrupted pattern for years.

9/27/92, Decree Law 25,744, charges the antiterrorist branch of the police, the *Direccion Nacional Contra el Terrorismo*, DINCOTE, with the task of "preventing, investigating, denouncing and combatting" terrorism-related crimes. The decree requires DINCOTE to inform only the military of antiterrorist detentions, not the civil authorities. This has resulted in a dirty war as gruesome as Argentina's, with human rights activists, lawyers, professors and students tortured and murdered by the hundreds.

Those who aren't "disappeared" can be held from $2^{1/2}$ to 5 years without charges. Terrorism charges are heard not by civilian courts, but by a rigged Counsel of War Tribunal, which customarily issues 30-year and life sentences. All trials and appeals are heard in closed hearings, and the identity of all prosecutorial personnel is kept secret from the defense. These medieval bastards actually wear hoods. Lawyers are not permitted to represent more than one client at a time before the hooded judges. Fujimori's idea of a legal system is to charge the Association of Democratic Lawyers, which often represents members of the PCP, with being part of the PCP. This eliminates their ability to function.

Fujimori's rigged post-coup elections, 11/92, saw the creation of the Democratic Constituent Congress, the CCD. Since the two major opposition parties boycotted the polls, only 18% of the eligible electorate voted. Fujimori's "New Majority-Change 90" won almost absolute control of the new 80-member single chamber Congress. San Román's dissolved Congress had two chambers, and checks and balances.

On July 18, 1992, nine students and a professor were abducted from Lima's La Cantuta University, then under military control. On April 3, 1993, a group of active-duty army officers, calling themselves the Sleeping Lions, sent the new Congress an affidavit asserting that the La Cantuta "disappeared" had been killed by the Colina death squad. The Sleeping Lions named all the officers involved, proving their case with internal Army documents. The massive publicity put the CCD's Human Rights Commission into action. It also put Montesinos and Hermoza, who had ordered the hit, on the trail of the Sleeping Lions.

When the new Congress' Human Rights Commission threatened to indict virtually the entire Army high command, including Montesinos and Hermoza, Gen. Hermoza drove up to its gates with 50 tanks. This encouraged passage of the La Cantuta law, which placed such cases in secret military courts. The law was made retroactive. Since Fujimori had suspended the Tribunal of Constitutional Guarantees, the La Cantuta law was, by definition, constitutional.

Fearing for his family's safety, the leader of the Sleeping Lions, Gen. Rodolfo Robles, third in command of the Peruvian Army, asked for asylum at the American embassy on May 6, 1993. The respected commander of the Peruvian Army's academic centers denounced "the systematic violation of the human rights of the Peruvian population on the part of a group of thugs who, under the orders of the ex-army captain Vladimiro Montesinos Montesinos [sic] and the servile approval of EP General Nicolas de Bari Hermoza Rios, the unworthy commanding general of the EP, are committing crimes that are unjustly smearing all of the glorious Peruvian army.... an unscrupulous pair... in charge of a band of uniformed thugs,....[running] machinery for coercion, blackmail, and annihilation."

In a statement read by his wife and brother, the General then went on to catalog the many death-squad murders of pro-democracy Peruvians, including the Barrios Altos and La Cantuta massacres. "The crime of La Cantuta in which a professor and nine students were victimized, was committed by a 'Special Intelligence Detachment' that operates under the direct orders of presidential advisor and virtual chief of SIN Vladimiro Montesinos."

The General also catalogued dozens of Army field massacres and gang-rapes, all confirmed by Amnesty International and Peru's *Coordinadora Nacional de Derechos Humanos*.[15] Gen. Robles' 1996 book is called *Crime and Impunity: The 'Grupo Colina' and Power*. The bodies of the La Cantuta ten were found in July of 1993. The forensic evidence confirmed everything that General Robles said.

Three months later Fujimori announced that he was going to turn Peru's jungles into a "Little Vietnam." Thanks to all that "anti-narcotics" military equipment, he did. When the OAS came to investigate the mass-murder, Fujimori refused to allow it. That was the first time in its history that a member state refused to meet with an OAS human rights commission. By the end of 1995, the war had claimed more than 30,000 lives, caused $25 billion in damages, and forced 600,000 refugees to flee the countryside.

Warfare, of course, is big business. According to the Mexican paper *La Reforma*, the Fujimori cartel went into the business of buying black market Soviet heavy arms for resale to the Peruvian military. This is financed by 15 dummy corporations - Wotan International, Colinsa, Crousillat Brothers, Mobetek, Vifebrina, Debrett, Benavides, etc. - washing drug money.

A hint as to how this money is earned was provided by the May 10, 1996 discovery of 169 kilos of pure cocaine in Fujimori's own DC-8 heading to Paris. The pilot was Air Commander Alfredo Escarcena Ichikawa, Fujimori's military attaché and an old crony. The owners of the laundromat corporations are presidential brother Santiago Fujimori, nephew Isidro Kagami Fujimori, and cronies Augusto and Manuel Miyagusuku. Their surplus Nicaraguan Russian helicopter gunships are used to contest control of Peru's coca basket, the Upper Huallaga Valley.

The Huallaga River Valley is the stronghold of the wildly popular *Sendero Luminoso*, the Communist Party of Peru. The goals of the Peoples Army of Liberation, in its own angry words, are "to serve the people's...rights to education, culture, arts, science, philosophy, health care, adequate housing and recreation areas, and dignifying employment, with the proletarian application and development of technology to increase industrial production, thus reducing the required working hours and the number of working days; in synthesis, freedom from working one's skin off for greedy capitalists and landlords; which necessarily implies a society without exploitation nor repression."[16]

Utopian, yes, but certainly not maniacal. These people are caricatured as maniacal only because when shot at, they shoot back. The

PCP defines Peru's number one political problem as "feudalism," that is, the absentee ownership and sharecropping forced on the Native campesinos by the conquistador elite.

The Ashaninkas of lowland Amazonian Peru have joined *Sendero Luminoso* en masse. The PCP gave them a way to interrupt the systematic "rape, land theft, unpaid labor, and robbery through unequal trade." Socialist ideology is attractive to these people because tribal lands, and social responsibilities, are traditionally held in common. They associate "capitalist" with "conquistador."

Sendero Luminoso advocates land redistribution. This is to be combined with replacement of the ubiquitous coca leaf with diversified food crops. This would localize and diversify an internationalized monocrop economy. It would also remove the Army's excuse, and motive, for stealing campesino land. You can't buy weapons with corn.

Crop replacement is to be done not with coercion, however, but with economic incentive, by collapsing the price of coca leaf through controlled legalization. That is hardly the position of *narcotraficantes*. Any photo of *Sendero* support centers, as the one below, simply shows the local young women and men of fighting age. Decree 22095 of 1978 specifically criminalizes highland culture by prohibiting the possession and sale of coca leaves at altitudes below 1500 meters. It became illegal to be an Inca.

"The Maoists"; www.blythe.org/peru-pcp/index.html

For the time being, of course, in the absence of international legalization and agricultural infrastructure, the regional economy is dependent on Syndicate coca dealers. Since Fujimori's secret police are running the Syndicate, Fujimori's government has absolutely no intention of replacing the monocrop coca economy.

Fujimori, legally, runs the national coca monopoly he inherited from the Spanish, *Empresa Nacional de la Coca*, ENACO. ENACO legally converts some 5,000 metric tons of coca leaves into most of the world's medical cocaine. As things now stand, coca cultivation is the only way many campesinos can feed their families. Coca legalization, of course, would collapse ENACO's monopoly.

Fujimori *wants* a nation of sharecroppers. The sharecroppers want title to their land, a free market in coca, and Fujimori dead. Both the Huallaga River Valley of the Incas and the Ene River Basin of the Ashaninkas are now Fujimori free-fire zones. The typical Army tactic in the Ene River Basin is to massacre undefended campesino villages, and then publicize the murders as the work of "the Maoists."

Per their CIA training, military death squads and *rondas* dress up like *Senderistas*, then drop in on defenseless Indians who don't know them. The shocked survivors swear the guerrillas did it. The establishment media, peopled by reporters who have bravely ridden to the front in government helicopters, swallow this more often than not.

On November 26, 1996, the leader of the Sleeping Lions, the forcibly retired Gen. Rodolfo Robles, supposedly free on amnesty, was arrested by Montesinos. Robles had just revealed that the October 17 "Maoist" bombing of the television station in Puno was a Colina Group COINTELPRO. Robles was joined in military prison by Gen. Enrique Delgado, the commander who arrested the three army intelligence agents who planted the Puno bomb.

Labor leaders, who are potential PCP political allies, are also regularly assassinated in government COINTELPROS, which also frame the PCP. It's also easy to set off a "Marxist" car bomb. Undoubtedly, many car bombs and assassinations are the work of the guerrillas. Off-duty soldiers, for instance, aren't safe. This may give them pause when they're on-duty.

Another favorite CIA tactic is the use of Non-Governmental Organizations, NGO's, as military intelligence likes to call them. Women operatives head up 'Glass of Milk' and 'People's Cafeteria' campaigns. Milk-mother Gloria Helfer, of the Movement for Socialist Affirmation, was Fujimori's first minister of education.

Milk-mother Maria Elana Moyano, also of MAS, was hailed as a great feminist martyr by *Ms* magazine, 7/92, in "Peru: The Government, the Rebels, And the Women in Between." "As for Shining Path," wrote Ms. Schmidt, "its 'revolution' consists mostly of attacks on civilians." The PCP has killed "thousands of peasants." "Despite women's participation, Shining Path - with its emphasis on the infallibility of its leader, Guzmán - remains a patriarchal, indeed totalitarian, organization."

Ms. Schmidt sorta forgot to mention that the croaked Ms. Moyano was a key organizer of the Ronda death squads. "Yes, we are organizing neighborhood patrols. We are also acting in our other organizations -we know each other, we know who we are... If the people organize themselves and centralize their efforts, we can defeat Sendero." Those who wouldn't join her 'neighborhood patrols' had their names turned over to the Colina Group by Mother Moyano. The "thousands of peasants" Ms. Schmidt refers to are the Peruvian Army's Ronda hit-teams.

The police express their customary respect for Peruvian womanhood in front of the Presidential Palace in Lima, 1998; www.blythe.org/peru-pcp/index.html

Ms. Schmidt also forgot to mention that Mother Moyano's MAS and other United Left (IU) parties supported Fujimori from day one. All the IU parties supported the IMF's 'shock therapy,' which doubled the price of food for the vast majority of impoverished campesinos.

Tens of thousands of children go hungry while hundreds are fed by these "glimmering points of light."

The PCP has the highest ratio of frontline women commanders of any revolutionary group in the world. Incan culture is basically matriarchal. When the heroic young Edith Logos was murdered by the army in 1982, 20,000 people came to her funeral in Ayacucho, a town with a population of 70,000. Milk Mother Moyano's funeral in Villa El Salvador, with a population of 300,000, drew a grand total of 3,000 people, mostly soldiers, politicians, ministers, ex-officials and intelligence agents.

The Peruvian Army regularly strafes and bombs campesino villages with the help of the U.S. Southern Command. Drug Czar McCaffrey now coordinates the air forces of Peru, Colombia and Venezuela with the Southern Command via Operation Laser Strike, the PR for which has it "intercepting suspected drug-smuggling aircraft." This is done by incinerating campesino villages from the air. The hatred this engenders, of course, has made the badly outgunned *Sendero Luminoso* politically invulnerable throughout much of rural Peru, although not militarily so.

Explains *The Seattle Times*, 4/22/98, in its best Dudley-Do-Right McCaffrese: "As Seaman Walter Fitzgerald gunned his Boston Whaler boat out into the Amazon and gently pulled alongside a floating dock as if approaching another vessel, he kept up a steady stream of talk to his Peruvian counterparts, explaining each step in nearly flawless Spanish."

"Nearby, on land, Warrant Officer Marc Shifanelli crouched in the thick jungle underbrush, demonstrating to a group of Peruvian police how to conduct small-unit patrols, including how to carry their AK-47 assault rifles, with constant reminders not to 'aim at anything you don't want to destroy.'"

"Fitzgerald, a U.S. Navy SEAL, and Shifanelli, of the U.S. Army Special Forces, are part of a group of 30 specialized American military instructors implementing one of the most ambitious counterdrug programs the Pentagon has ever undertaken in Latin America. Special forces from the Army, Navy and Marines are training and equipping a specialized Peruvian counterdrug unit that would operate on water and land to cut off the growing flow of cocaine that makes its way from Peru to Colombia on the Amazon, and then on to the United States and Europe."

"Of the 30 trainers, 15 are Navy SEALs, 9 are with the Army's Special Forces, 4 are Marines and 2 are with the Coast Guard. All speak Spanish competently."

"The river training program, begun last month and estimated to cost $60 million over the next five years, underscores the growing U.S. role in Peru, a country that is scheduled to receive about $110 million in U.S. aid this year, one of the largest amounts in the hemisphere...."

"U.S. officials acknowledge that the trainers face some risk operating in this area, once a designated "red zone" where Marxist rebels operated. Now, however, the main threat is seen as coming from drug traffickers, so the trainers are not allowed to participate directly in counterdrug missions."

"A key reason the United States is willing to share drug intelligence with the Peruvian navy and air force, when it largely declines to do so in other countries, such as Colombia and Mexico, is the lack of corruption, U.S. officials said."

U.S. trainers confer in Peru's "Gringolandia," 1996

From 1990 to 1996, more than 300 Peruvian military personnel have been investigated on charges of drug dealing. The consistent allegation has been that regional commanders overseeing clandestine airstrips received a $10,000 kickback per planeload of cocaine.

In 1991, one of the most powerful Huallaga Valley drug lords was Demetrio Chavez Peñaherrera, known as *El Vaticano*, "The Soothsayer." When Montesinos demanded that *El Vaticano* double his $50,000-a-month protection payment to $100,000, Chavez went over to the Shining Path. This, of course, caused SIN to dub Chavez a *narcotraficante* and track him down in Colombia.

At his August 1996 trial, for subversion, Chavez insisted that his business relationship with Montesinos had included unhampered use of a clandestine military airstrip to export drugs to Colombia, and radio warnings of counternarcotics operations scheduled for the Huallaga Valley. Chavez's airstrip was just a few miles from a major counterinsurgency base.

In testimony before the Peruvian Congress, following Chavez' trial, Capt. Gilmar Valdivieso Rejas, a Sleeping Lion, asserted that the army commander of the Huallaga region, Gen. Eduardo Bellido, and his predecessor, provided cover for *El Vaticano* and other cocaine exporters. Valdivieso testified that in 1992, Lt. Col. Luis Aparicio Manrique had the engineers of the Upper Huallaga Special Project build a clandestine landing strip in Canuto, regularly used by Peruvian army helicopters to transport drugs.[17]

On January 19, 1995, in an apparent power struggle typical of real *narcotraficantes*, Gen. Bellido's predecessor, Gen. Jaime Araico, was found guilty of allowing cocaine to be transported to Colombia from Peruvian airstrips under his control. When the trial judge ordered his successor, Gen. Bellido, to testify, he not only refused, but had the Commander in Chief of the Peruvian Armed Forces, Gen. Nicolas de Bari Hermoza Rios, the U. S. anti-narcotics coordinator, back him up.[18]

On January 12, 1995, the largest shipment of cocaine in Peruvian history was intercepted. A diary belonging to one of the 38 arrestees, José Luís Mendiola, detailed meetings with Gen. Manuel Ortiz Lucero, a member of the ruling Armed Forces Internal Command Front. Ortiz was the Vice Minister of the Interior and commander of the National Police. Also named was Police Maj. Edwin Burgos, who worked in the Central Operations Department.

Evidence previously gathered, that led to the bust, linked the traffickers to the brother of Gen. Nicolas de Bari Hermoza Rios. Also named was Montesinos' law partner, Edgar Solis. When Judge Carmen Rojas, on January 10, 1996, issued a warrant for the arrest of Ortiz and Solis, he was summarily dismissed by Montesinos.

On October 2, 1996, Drug Czar Barry McCaffrey met personally with Vladimiro Montesinos in Peru. It was the first time that Montesinos, now official head of SIN, had been seen in public in six years. As head of the U.S. Southern Command in Panama, McCaffrey had worked with Montesinos for years. Montesinos, said McCaffrey, was "an honest advisor…and…an outstanding and knowledgeable strategist."[19] Given the *public* record, it is *impossible* that McCaffrey didn't know the drug-dealing assassin he was lauding.

That was also the conclusion of Senators Patrick Leahy and Christopher Dodd. In a public letter that immediately followed McCaffrey's meeting with Montesinos, to CIA Director John Deutch, these Senators demanded that the Agency cut its ties with Montesinos, because "We are aware of the links of Montesinos with violations of human rights, including massacres, torture, disappearances, and his links with drug cartels in Peru, whom he served before becoming an advisor to Fujimori."[20] Who's the liar, Gen. McCaffrey, or Senators Leahy and Dodd?

If Montesinos ever does get nailed, McCaffrey will no doubt do the same "aw shucks, I ain't too good at this intelligence stuff" routine he did when his Mexican Montesinos, Gen. Gutiérrez, got caught. Let us now recall the Oliver North rule of credibility when considering the word of military intelligence operatives: "Lotsa blood, little credibility." Barry McCaffrey has an ocean of campesino blood on his hands. But, like North, and Ríos Montt, he gives great pious.

Of 200 clandestine airstrips identified by DEA in 1995, SIN's Anti-Drug Police destroyed 3, which were immediately rebuilt. Of 650 tons of cocaine produced in Peru, SIN seized 7, which was later re-sold to wholesalers.[21] SIN's "antidrug" operation is simply selective commercial extortion. He who gets busted is either outside the loop or forgot to pay his taxes. Any small grower who complains is a "narcoterrorist." Any DEA agent who gets too close to this will be killed, set up by the SIN-CIA agents in his own command structure. In 1984, when the DEA's Cele Castillo busted a huge Cali cartel cocaine manufacturing and distribution compound that housed more than 600 people, he was immediately transferred out of the country. Similar busts did not follow.

The Peruvian Army that SIN controls is the recipient of virtually all the U.S. "antinarcotics" aid given to Peru. That's why that mountain of money has had absolutely no strategic effect whatever on the flow of cocaine. On the contrary, it has been used to turn the campesinos into coca sharecroppers.

Whether I succeed in updating this book regularly or not, the story will always be the same. Only the names will change. The fascist corruption, based on the artificial value Prohibition gives these demanded commodities, will remain the same - in Peru, Mexico, Colombia or Burma. Artificially inflated, cocaine accounts for more than 50% of Peru's foreign trade. In 1995, the United Nations Drug Control Program estimated that Peru produced more than 500,000 kilos of cocaine. That's more than 600 tons, with a wholesale value in New York of more than $30 billion. The *legal* value of that cocaine would be about $3 billion.

No one who doesn't support that trade, *and cocaine's continued illegality*, will rise to control of the Peruvian military, because without *illegal* cocaine the Peruvian Army couldn't pay for weapons. That would lead to widespread campesino control of the voting process, and, God forbid, a populist government in Lima. That's why *Sendero Luminoso* wants to collapse the price of cocaine with controlled legalization. It would end the fight for Indian land.

On July 2, 1996, the disgusted Vice-President of Peru's National Reserve Bank, Mario Tovar, complained that Fujimori's profligate weapons borrowing had ballooned the national debt to suicidal levels. Between 1990 and 1996, Fujimori increased Peru's debt from $22 billion to $33 billion, despite a billion-dollar-a-year repayment rate that robbed Peru of all the money needed for social programs and reinvestment. GNP growth plummeted.

Fujimori's austerity measures, which have slashed public spending, have indeed helped to control inflation. But they have done nothing for job creation in an economy with a spectacular 80% underemployment rate. The continued widespread poverty has contributed to renewed civil war, which will, of course, require more military borrowing. The only beneficiaries of that will be those companies selling equipment to the military.[22] That's what drives a "covert" operation.

Some of Fujimori's PCP prisoners celebrating International Women's Day: www.blythe.org/peru-pcp/index.html

Drug War

The Active Army

A shipload of *legal* marijuana would be worth a few million dollars. A shipload of *illegal* marijuana is worth in the neighborhood of one hundred million dollars, at master distributor discount. Does *less* pot pass through Panama now that "kingpin" Noriega is in jail? Has there been a crash in the pot market?

During the post-Contra confrontation with Noriega, the Reagan administration stressed the interception of his bulky, easy to smell marijuana, contributing to an explosion in the popularity of concentrated, profitable to smuggle cocaine, and the popularization of crack and concentrated heroin.

President Bush's replacement for Noriega, Guillermo Endara, was a director and secretary of Banco Interoceánico, targeted by both the FBI and DEA as a major money laundry for both the Cali and Medellín cocaine cartels. How is it possible that President Bush, the former Director of the CIA, didn't know that? It was George Bush who had authorized Noriega's substantial 1976 CIA paychecks, and it was he who insisted on putting Noriega back on the payroll in 1980, after Carter had the good sense to take him off.

From Bush's perspective, this made sense. Noriega and his Mossad advisor Mike Harrari, who worked closely with Bush aide Gregg, proved invaluable in arming the Contras. "Since the beginning of the supply of arms to the Contras, the same infrastructure that was used for arms was used for drugs. The same pilots, the same planes, the same airstrips, the same people," noted José Blandón, Noriega's former chief of political intelligence.[1]

Just before the December 1989 Panama invasion, in which Gen. Barry McCaffrey was in charge of barrio incineration, Endara's business partner, Carlos Eleta, was arrested in Georgia for conspiring to import a half-ton of cocaine per month. The charges were dropped as soon as Bush installed Endara as Panamanian president and Eleta became an "asset." Bush then insisted that "The answer to the problem of drugs lies more in solving the demand side of the equation than it does the supply side, than it does in interdiction or sealing the borders."[2] That'll keep the price up *and* justify turning the U.S. into a police state.

Bush's drug czar, Archbishop Bennett, therefore didn't get excited about the massive export of cocaine processing chemicals to Colombia, as Congress noticed. He was much more concerned with throwing American teenagers in jail, for their own good. Endara's attorney general, treasury minister and chief justice of the supreme court were all former directors of First Interamericas Bank, a wholly-owned subsidiary of Colombia's Cali cartel, one of its major money laundries, according to Panama's National Banking Commission.[3] "Take my word for it," intoned a determined George Bush at his inaugural, "this scourge will stop!"[4]

New York Times:1/10/95: "In a daunting new turn in the traffic of Colombian cocaine into the United States, smugglers are buying old passenger jets, taking out the seats and using the planes to fly huge amounts of the drug into Mexico, American and Mexican officials say. Travelling at night with their lights off, the Boeing 727's and French-made Caravelle jets are believed to be carrying as much as six tons or more of cocaine in a single flight. The cocaine is then transported overland into the United States, where the wholesale value of such a load is about $120 million."

That's enough to buy a new plane for each load, as the innovative Amado Carillo, and his partners in Colombian and Mexican military intelligence, well understood. The *legal* value of such a load would be 10% of the *illegal* value, or less.[5]

Inevitably, the economics of Prohibition has caused the fascist cancer to metastasize. "Leopards" are no longer just a Latin phenomenon. And the U.S. Leopards are a much more professional and well-financed lot. George Bush's Defense Authorization Act of 1989 ordered the Pentagon to a) integrate the various US command, control, communications and intelligence assets to monitor illegal drugs; b) enhance the National Guard's role in drug interdiction and enforcement operations; c) serve as the lead agency in detecting and monitoring drug smuggling.

This saw the formation of drug intelligence centers in most government enforcement bureaucracies. These included a CIA drug-intelligence clearing house and the El Paso-based Joint Task Force 6, set up in November 1989 at Biggs Army Airfield adjacent to Fort Bliss. JTF-6 coordinates regional narcotics enforcement with the DEA's El Paso Intelligence Center, also located at Biggs. JTF-6 fills thousands of missions yearly in "total integration" with border law enforcement, to quote its commander, Lt. Gen. Stotser.

One wonders, then, how come they're so damned ineffective. Has the strategic situation been misdefined to begin with? Is their Mexican border effort just cosmetic, given that the entire Pacific coast from Baja to Anchorage is equally porous? Are some of the strategic goals unstated, covert? Are we just playing the red-herring funding game?

Drug War

In May of 97 four Marines on a JTF-6 border patrol shot 18 year-old Ezekiel Hernandez Jr. to death while he was herding goats 400 yards from his Redford, Texas home. Hernandez was shot in the back by an M-16 at 230 yards, well outside the range of the old .22 he carried for rattlers.[6]

This murder was the inevitable result of the 1992 policy outlined in *Soldiers*, the official magazine of the U.S. Army: "The U.S. Military Police School at Fort McClellan, Alabama is providing free training in advanced police techniques and military aggression tactics to law enforcement personnel.... Subjects offered in this course include shotgun and submachine gun usage, night drug raids, and land navigation."

"Joint Task Force Six is one of three task forces organized to help fight the drug war.... The Active Army operates the National Interagency Counterdrug Institute at a camp at San Luis Obispo, California. It is staffed by soldiers who train civilian anti-drug law enforcement personnel in drug eradication and interdiction. They also teach civilian agencies how to make use of military assets in support of counterdrug operations. The Active Army can get under the Posse Comitatus Act [the 1876 law forbidding the U.S. Army to police Americans[7]] in operating this school by staffing it with California Guardsmen. Camp San Luis Obispo is also owned by the California National Guard."[8]

Do we really want to police Americans with "military aggression tactics"? Wasn't the political danger inherent in that the whole point of the Posse Comitatus Act? Although a federally paid adjunct of the Army, it has been legal, since 1988, for the National Guard to operate as state police.[9] Both the National Guard and the Department of Defense are lobbying for repeal of the Posse Comitatus Act.

On 1/4/95, Rep. Barbara Kennelly (D-CT) proposed the creation of a Rapid Deployment Force of 2500 troops within the FBI to function as on-call Storm Troopers for local jurisdictions. Once deployed the RDF would have the power of state police. 1996 Republican presidential hopeful Lamar Alexander, demonstrating his canny originality, proposed simply creating a new unit of the army with the specific mission of U.S. border drug and immigrant interdiction.

Bill Bennett and his congressional mouthpiece, the incredible Gerald Solomon (R-NY), Chairman of the House Rules Committee no less, went Lamar one better. They proposed that the mission of the U.S. military itself be changed to one of international drug interdiction, with all federal law enforcement agencies put under direct military command. That is, they proposed an overt military police state.[10] Senator Dole, running against Bill Clinton, supported a version of this, including a Defense Authorization amendment, wisely killed by the Pentagon itself, that would have authorized the U.S. military to seal the Mexico-U.S. border, that is, to repeat Nixon's economically disastrous 1969 Operation Intercept.

During Congressional hearings on March 29, 1995, a Dole-Helms ally, Rep. Dan Burton (R-IN), chairman of the House Western Hemisphere Subcommittee, proposed that the United States place an aircraft carrier off the coast of Peru and Bolivia and forcibly spray coca fields with herbicides despite the opposition of those governments. Needless to say, the reaction in Lima and La Paz was apoplectic. If these fools ever try it, they'll have the Peruvian Army joining *Sendero Luminoso*.

Unless the military knows a way to change the value of money, the rightwing proposals, if taken literally, would mean either partial or all-out war with all those countries officially threatened by the State Department with the cutoff of aid, or decertified, due to their noncooperation in the Drug War. Strategically successful drug-war models, like Holland, simply bankrupt the smugglers with controlled legalization. But Lott, Hastert, Solomon, Bennett, Helms, Faircloth, Gramm, Hatch, McCollum, Abraham, Inhofe, Gingrich, Souder, Mica and the rest of their airhead army actually proposed militarily attacking the drug-dealing infrastructures of Peru, Bolivia, Colombia, Burma, Mexico, Argentina, Laos, Afghanistan, Turkey, Taiwan, Ghana, Nigeria, India, Iran, Lebanon, Paraguay, Pakistan, Bahamas, Belize, Brazil, Cambodia, China, Dominican Republic, Ecuador, Guatemala, Haiti, Hong Kong, India, Jamaica, Malaysia, Panama, Taiwan, Thailand, Venezuela, Vietnam, Iran, and Syria.

But of course this is *covert* policy, it can't be taken literally. Those few real conservatives who do, find themselves at odds with their own power structure. The Republican defense contractors don't mean to attack *our* dopers, the ones buying *our* arms. This attack on "drugs" is defined by the Republican strategic geniuses as arming and financing the fascist military structures that are actually dealing the drugs: House leader Dennis Hastert (R-IL), in the Western Hemisphere Drug Elimination Act, passed as law by Congress 10/19/98:

"The drug crisis facing the United States is a top national security threat. The Department of Defense has been called upon to support counter-drug efforts of Federal law enforcement agencies that are carried out in source countries."

The Pentagon responded by upgrading the priority of "drug eradication and interdiction" in its Global Military Force Policy from the lowest, "4: non-hostile," to "2:military operations other than [declared] war." This means a huge "military operation" in Colombia, home of "narco-terrorists," but none at all in Brazil, Burma, Pakistan, Mexico or Bolivia, home of "strategic assets."

And, thanks to the ongoing incremental repeal of the Posse Comitatus Act, the Army's National Guard is Actively supporting the value of Mexican and Colombian pot by eradicating American pot. Actually, it's supporting the value of American pot also, vastly increasing the acreage these high-tech Keystone Cops have to worry about - thereby guaranteeing themselves employment and a steady expansion of their mission.

Drug War has been pursued with Draconian efficiency in the U.S. for years, with no effect whatever on availability and demand.[13] It has simply escalated the price, further strengthening the most violent of the dealers. This justifies the appropriations that enable military intelligence to run those dealers.

Ex-DEA Agent Michael Levine: "The drug war under President Clinton is bigger and healthier than ever. It seems like every department in the federal government has a part in it - DEA, FBI, CIA, NSA, IRS, DIA, ATF, State Department, Pentagon, Customs, Coast Guard, Army, Navy, Air Force, Marines - and each one is fighting for more turf and a bigger chunk of the drug war budget. When I started out in 1965 there were two federal agencies enforcing the drug laws, and the budget was less than $10 million. Today [1993] there are 54 agencies involved and the budget is $13 billion. Orchestrating the whole mess is a Drug Czar who is generally a political appointment with no special qualifications for the job."[14]

That is, McCaffrey is no psychiatrist or psychopharmacologist. But, of course, he *is* an expert at expanding the police mission of the military. A good short definition of a *fascist police state* would be *"a state in which publicly-funded military-police agencies drive policy."*

U.S. policy has been driven by the biggest publicly-funded police-agency propaganda barrage in history. The overt 1997 federal Drug War appropriation was $15.1 billion. The 1998 federal bill was $16 billion, the 1999 bill was $18 billion, with two-thirds of that simply being pumped into domestic law enforcement, that is, into filling the prisons with vulnerable kids.[15] Most of the rest goes into propaganda and "treatment," that is, "reeducation," in the Stalinist sense.

These budgetary figures don't include the tens of billions expended by the military, by the federal judicial and penal systems, or the state judicial and penal systems. In 1991, the RAND Corp. estimated the total outlay of public funds at $30 billion.[16] The 1999 figure must be many times that.

For fiscal 1998 Clinton and McCaffrey announced a billion-dollar ONDCP/Ad Council blitz: "There is every reason to believe that this absolutely will turn around drug abuse by youngsters," intoned Bombastic Barry.[17] I doubt there is a serious expert in the RAND Corp. or anywhere else anywhere who expects this blowhard to have any strategic effect whatever. But Barry McCaffrey knows that. McCaffrey's job is to keep the Drug War going, that's all. The Drug War is *designed* to be endless. At the same time he engineers artificial hysteria with the biggest propaganda barrage in history, he finances the military structures - Colombian, Peruvian, Mexican, Burmese, Thai, Pakistani, etc. - that are actually dealing the drugs. He finances, that is, the major customers of America's defense contractors, the biggest drug money launderers in the world.

That this fascist insanity turns many of its operatives into schizophrenic maniacs is inevitable. Did McCaffrey really see himself as a freedom fighter when he helped to engineer the drug-financed genocide in Guatemala and El Salvador? I don't know. I do know that he was just following orders.

What the fascist structure wants is the militarization of global industrial culture, a stranglehold on policy and wealth, absolute control of the industrial machinery. "Drug interdiction" is a necessary adjunct to this. It's a way of stealing tribal lands by criminalizing tribal sacraments - a way of criminalizing tribal culture itself, and a way of organizing the sports fans behind the patriotic campesino-stomping. And it's a way of attacking America's poor for being poor, a way of attacking the painkiller rather than the pain. It's a way of channeling all the cash needed to do something about structural poverty into the military-police complex.

This isn't radical political analysis on my part. It's conservative empirical analysis. President Johnson's Katzenbach Commission said the same thing in 1967: "The application of these laws often tends to discriminate against the poor and subcultural groups in the population, [so that] poverty itself becomes a crime."[18]

Nixon's conservative 1972 National Commission on Marihuana and Drug Abuse actually recommended decriminalizing pot, insisting that the effects of its criminalization are far worse than the effects of its pharmacology.[19] Presidential Commissions, pursuant to their mandate, tend to be empirical, which is why their recommendations are so often ignored.

In the absence of "communism," "drugs" have become the political engine of military-police appropriations. They are the *pharmakos*, the sanctioned sacrifice, the Fiend, the plausible target, the unconscious racist or cultural projection that enables corporate military imperialism. The droll Alfred Hitchcock, who knew a little something about psychology, called it the "McGuffin." I call it the "McCaffrey."

Drug Prohibition has made the illegal drug trade the economic, and political, basis of military power throughout much of the world. It is the most significant policy disaster in American history, as loss of control of CIA covert operations is the most significant structural disaster. Together they are the major tools of military fascism today. By artificially exploding street violence, Prohibition effectively diverts the culture's political eye, and wealth, from structural poverty, industrial ecocide, industrial oligarchy and confiscatory taxation. Prohibition is, as it has always been, a fascist protection racket.

On 2/15/96 Colombia's legislature indicted President Ernesto Samper for running his 1994 electoral campaign with Cali cartel money. That's like indicting Colonel Sanders for eating fried chicken. The crisis was initiated by Samper's political enemies, who got hold of a checkbook belonging to Gilberto Rodríguez Orejuela, a very powerful Cali-based employer of thousands. Rodríguez Orejuela owns a large chain of pharmacies with hundreds of outlets, a legal pharmaceutical lab, thousands of taxis, a soccer team, real estate and a bank or two. His checkbook implicated Fernando Botero, Samper's 1994 campaign manager and Defense Minister. That is, the Cali cartel is an organic part of the establishment that ended up in charge of the Colombian military.

Professor Nadelmann: "Since the early sixties the contraband traffic has replaced the public sector as the major source of finance for the purchase of equipment by the Paraguayan armed forces."[20] U.S. equipment, that is, for the Nazi murderer Alfredo Stroessner, our long-term ally against "narcoterrorism." The situation is the same in Burma, Mexico, Bolivia or Peru.

Professor Peter Lupsha of the University of New Mexico: "The United States is now facing a military elite in Latin America that is deeply involved in the narcotics business and has the resources - men, planes, ships, and communications. They have Americans on their payroll, sometimes former members of American special forces, who know how to tap telephones, do code encryptions, and who have the communications skills to put them on the level of a nation state."[21]

In Samper's Colombia, the MAS ("Death to Kidnappers") death squads were originally formed by the Medellín cartel as a tactical answer to the military pressure put on them by M-19 guerrillas. The death squads were staffed by CIA-trained Colombian officers, who already had a significant piece of the Medellín action. "The drug dealers' core military power lies in paramilitary groups they have organized with the support of large landowners and military officers," explained Alberto Galán, brother of assassinated 1994 presidential candidate Luis Carlos Galán.[22]

The Revolutionary Armed Forces of Colombia (FARC), protect not only their campesino constituents, but some of the most powerful dealers in Colombia. They are, in part, Fidel's contribution to Colombian politics.[23] Rather than target the hard-to-hit guerrillas, who hit back, and who in any case have fighters capable of protecting, or destroying, jungle labs, the death squads hit journalists, drug legalization advocates, labor leaders, human rights activists and other political threats to a drug-dealing military police state.[24]

After 50 years of guerrilla war, of course, since military power is built on money, the Colombian left has become as deeply dependent on the artificial Prohibition value of drugs as the right. That is, the artificially inflated value of drug crops has created powerful institutional support, on all political sides, for continued, endless Drug War.

New York Times:3/27/95: "In Guaviare - described as a 'sea of coca' by one police official - officials estimate that traffickers pay $5 million a year in protection money to the state's main guerrilla group, the Revolutionary Armed Forces of Colombia, or FARC.... To make peace, the Government promised to use aerial eradication only against plots larger than 7.5 acres....A week after the President's speech, guerrillas shot down a police helicopter in Putumayo, killing three police officers."

That chopper was worth $200,000 to the guerrillas that downed it - that was the Cali bounty. Between 1994 and 1997, FARC rebels downed twelve government planes. Because of cocaine's artificial value, the campesino-guerrillas working with the cocaine wholesalers to keep their family land are almost as well-armed as the government itself. They are as tough and angry as the Vietminh.

And they have the same political depth. The early summer 1996 aerial spraying of Ultra Glyphosate (Monsanto's "Round-Up") on 45,000 acres of Guaviare coca caused convulsive vomiting and hair loss among the children. The enraged mothers organized the August

1996 march of more than 150,000 campesinos in Guaviare, Putumayo and Caqueta provinces.[25] The Colombian *federales* diffused the protest with false compromises, then stealthily assassinated the march leaders. Many of the surviving campesinos turned, for the first time, to the guerrillas. The U.S. then insisted that Colombia allow it to switch to the far more poisonous tebuthiuron (Dow's "Spike"). That is, American policy has turned FARC into a major factor in Colombian politics and driven the nation into full-scale civil war.

The Turbo Thrush and armored Bronco OV-10 crop dusters are flown for Colombia's National Police by the CIA's DynCorp, under a State Department contract. DynCorp does not spray Army-protected coca fields. This is a street fight for control of the crop. As Randall Beers, acting Assistant Secretary of State for International Narcotics Matters, puts it in his fluent McCaffrese, crop dusting is "the most cost-effective way to reduce narcotic substances, particularly in areas not under control of the central government."[26]

On August 31, 1996, FARC guerrillas destroyed the Army base at Las Delicias in Putumayo, killing 27 troops and taking 60 as "prisoners of war." All told, FARC left 100 Colombian *federales* dead on August 31. In March of 1998 FARC completely annihilated the 3rd Mobile Brigade in Caqueta. The Miraflores "antidrug" base was overrun in the summer of 1998. El Billar and Mitu were also devastating defeats for the army. As with the Vietminh, all those American-supplied *federale* arms are now pointed at the *federales*.

FARC is already the only government in at least half of the Colombian countryside. That Colombian campesinos support FARC is revealed not only by its military success, but by the fact that the CIA crop-dusting in guerrilla areas is aimed not only at their drug crops, but at their food crops. The objective, as in Vietnam, is to turn them into docile sharecroppers.

On February 26, 1999, Colombian Gen. Fernando Tapias Stahelin told the gathered eminences at the Bogotá artillery school that the army would begin using heavy artillery against the rebels.[26a] This was necessary because FARC was now fielding units of 200-300 men.

The logistics of that escalation, of course, will make FARC more dependent than ever on the underground drug economy. McCaffrey is not lying when he says the guerrillas are dealing. He is lying when he says he is not. McCaffrey's Big Lie is the Stalinist lie that policy can dictate economic physics - that the economics of Prohibition can be managed by police state tactics. The Stalinist police state, the essence of which was Prohibition, collapsed - economically.

And if the campesino-guerrillas were the real "narcoterrorists," they would hardly be demanding the controlled legalization of all drugs, since that will collapse their value, making them useless as a source of military funding. As with the Zapatistas and Senderistas, the original FARC intention had been to empower the campesinos by eliminating the McCaffrey, that is, by eliminating the excuse for Colombian participation in the U.S. military-industrial complex.

But warfare often perverts good intentions. A veteran member of the foreign press corps, who has lived in Colombia for years, warns me not to lionize the left. "The FARC are not freedom fighters or defenders of the peasants. They might have been originally but they have degenerated into just another power block within this complex, brutal and absurd civil war we have now. So far as most intelligent observers can see, they really only have the Stalinist aim of keeping themselves in power, grabbing more territory and imposing their will by force.

"All of this power-grabbing is with the aim of eventually having the clout to get the government to make fundamental reforms in the system here, which is completely corrupt and unjust, but by now, after fifty years in the bush as guerrilla fighters, they have lost sight of political realities, are out of touch with the world as it is nowadays, don't really have the ability to administer a country well, have lost the support of intellectuals and technicians and in short, no longer really know what they want."

"For example, they talk about nationalizing oil, which is run by foreign companies. But at the same time they are living off pay-offs from these companies and would never in a million years be able to run the oil wells by themselves."

".... It was the guerrilla who killed the three US Indian rights people, two of them Native Americans, who came to Colombia to support a tribe in its fight against a multinational oil company who wants to exploit their natural resources. So what does that say to you!!!!"

"The peasants support them, in part, because the army is a traditional enemy and behaves even worse but more and more it is because the FARC have the guns and anyone who goes against them is bumped off. A lot of young guys and girls go into the FARC because there is no other economic alternative and because, for some half-literate, resentful 15 year-old kid, who never will have a chance to be anyone important, it's great to have a gun and be part of a group that pushes people about. Besides, this is no longer a country with a peasant majority, as it was before. It is more and more urban, which means that it is a much more complex economy and raises much more complex questions of who is guilty of exploitation. Is a middling guy who owns a shop or a truck a capitalist or not?"

And if he is, will the structural economy benefit by subsidizing his sweat? Is an Indian farmer, hoping to scratch a living from his produce, a sweat-equity capitalist deserving of state support? Jacobo Arbenz would have said so, but the IMF has a different idea. Juan Manuel Ospina, president of the Colombian Farmers' Society, points out that under IMF-US sponsored trade models, Indian grain, corn, rice, potato and onion farmers are undersold by cheap global imports - ADM's great humanitarian contribution to Colombia. Given the artificial Prohibition-value of the drug crops, starving Indians are forced into the drug-crop economy and into the civil war. Lowland Indians are growing *ipadú* coca, highlanders grow opium.

The 1998 Colombian senatorial campaign poster of Benjamín Jacanamijoy, son of a famous ayahuasquero shaman. His campaign slogan was "Preserva tu cultura, revive la tradición." He was narrowly defeated, and expects to win next time.

The solution, as Native Colombian politicians are well aware, is to collapse the value of drug crops with controlled legalization, thereby economically collapsing the militarization of the countryside. The money not spent on warfare could then be used to support sweat-equity production models.

A traditional Indian meeting place on the Río Mirití in south Amazonian Colombia
http://ocean.st.usm.edu/~nanzola/amazonas.html

As in the U.S., the herb legalization/alkaloid decriminalization movement has created an alliance of the centrist right and the centrist left. The Colombian right is keenly aware that the flow of narcodollars into the Colombian economy artificially inflates the value of the peso, badly hurting the viability of Colombia's legal exports on the world market. That is not an effect of pharmacology, it is an effect of Prohibition.

"LACE Financial Corporation: 6/29/99: In recent weeks, mounting concerns over Colombia's weakening economy and internal security problems have put renewed pressure on the nation's currency, the peso. Between last Thursday and Friday alone, the central bank spent approximately $284 million of its estimated $8.7 billion in international reserves to protect the band in which the peso is allowed to trade. To avoid a further drain on its reserves, the Colombian central bank decided to lower the peso's trading band by 9%, and increase the maximum allowable fluctuation in the currency from 14% to 20% per day."

"Colombia is currently in the midst of its worst recession since the 1930's and the news only seems to be getting worse. For the first quarter of 1999, the nation's gross domestic product (GPD) contracted 4.8% and unemployment rose to 19.5%. The nation is plagued by a ballooning budget deficit which could exceed 5% of GDP this year, and an increasing foreign debt load on which Colombia must pay $3 billion before year-end. There is also the national banking crisis for which the government will have to spend at least $4.5 billion to recapitalize beleaguered institutions. Furthermore, interest rates remain high following the rate hike which preceded the previous 9% currency devaluation on September 1, 1998, hampering economic growth."

"Additional factors which have intensified pressure on the peso include a rash of kidnappings and attacks by various paramilitary groups which have scared-off foreign investors, as well as the exchanging of large amounts of pesos to U.S. dollars by Colombian businesses...."

"LACE Financial is maintaining Colombia's country rating at "C/D" which means the country has a weak economy and possible problems in raising foreign exchange to meet trade agreements and foreign debt payments. We expect the condition of the Colombian banks to deteriorate significantly. LACE Financial recommends that all credits be placed on a secured basis."

So aside from the direct costs of the war - weaponry, property damage, terrorism, and a fall in agricultural production - there are the massive indirect costs, not just the artificial inflation of the peso, but the artificial inflation of property values and massive disincentives to investment. Saloman Kalmanovitz, a director of the Central Bank, and other Colombian equivalents of Paul Volcker, Milton Friedman and George Soros have joined Indian, campesino and urban centrists in calling for an end to the self-inflicted disaster of Prohibition.

An indication of the guerrillas' political sophistication is given by Juan Carlos Palou, the director of Plante, Colombia's crop-substitution program. Palou said no farmer has ever been killed by the guerrillas for giving up illicit crops, even though, under present conditions, those crops finance the guerrillas.[27] Indian family-plot growers tend to be treated as entrepreneurs by the guerrillas, deserving of a market-price.

But the long war has taken its toll on guerrilla idealism, seeing many descend into a Stalinist insanity that has alienated many who would otherwise be sympathetic. My journalist friend claims that the guerrillas now act no differently than the *federales*: "You should know that the guerrilla doesn't put dope smokers into jail, as the US govt. does, it shoots them. It does the same to gays, longhairs and other dissidents. They are extremely ignorant, intolerant and fanatic. And in a sense cowardly, because they spend more time killing off civilians than their armed opponents. They assault small towns to seize arms and money and make a political statement, and kill and blow up anything and anyone in their way, ruining the livelihoods of ordinary people who are certainly not exploiters or large scale capitalists."

FARC demonstrates a small part of its logistical clout; http://burn.ucsd.edu/~farc-ep

The civil war, that is, has degenerated, on all sides, into a duplicitous street fight for the crop, with both sides treating the hood dealers as kingpins, just as in Johnny Rosselli's Guatemala. My journalist friend writes to me, 10/99, ""A friend of mine, who works for national parks, just came back from the zone which the government handed over to the guerrilla to realize the peace negotiations. I have been reading a lot of newspaper reports about their terrorist rule there. What my friend tells me is that there is a kind of tense calm. What people are really worried about is that if the guerrilla withdraw, the place will be shot up by the paramilitaries, which happens all the time, just these random slaughters of civilians in zones controlled by the guerrilla (and vice versa) on the theory that if you are not with us, you are against us. But the interesting thing is this: just outside this zone is another town, only about fifteen miles away, where the paramilitaries are gathering and waiting to strike. But the paramilitaries rarely have groups of more than 200 armed men, where the guerrilla have thousands in this demilitarized zone. So what the hell is going on? Although the two are supposedly bitter enemies, you rarely hear of a combat between the paras and the guerrilla. This is just to give you some idea of how weird the situation is."

In government-held areas the drug economy is run by the large, paramilitary-connected landowners. On these large drug-crop plantations the campesinos tend to be treated as powerless sharecroppers. Since these plantations aren't in rebel territory, they are never targeted by the CIA crop-dusters. That's why all that "antidrug effort" has had no strategic effect on the flow of drugs. It is these growers who financed Samper's 1994 election campaign, and who continue to finance Colombia's generals.[28]

As it became obvious that Samper was willing to sacrifice Botero, who was forced from control of the army, Botero implicated Samper.[29] The evidence shows that the Attorney General, the President of the Chamber of Representatives, the Comptroller General and about half the Congress were on the Cali payroll. One quarter of the Colombian Congress was under formal investigation by the Supreme Court. The publicity forced the revocation of Samper's American travel visa, but it didn't stop the massive "anti-narcotics" aid from the CIA/DIA/ DEA to the Colombian military.

In late February, 1996, Clinton added Samper's Colombia to his list of "decertified" druggies, a grand total of 6, including Afghanistan, Burma, Iran, Nigeria and Syria. But that was just PR damage control, as well as a blow to the legal exports, which rely on our preferential tariffs and international lending. Most U.S. aid to Colombia is for drug eradication and seizure, and that money, hundreds of millions, is exempt from the ban on aid.

On 2/14/97, a year after "decertification," Robert S. Gelbard, Assistant Secretary of State for International Narcotics Matters, testifying before a unit of the House Government Reform and Oversight Committee, bragged that "anti-narcotics" assistance to the Colombian military had actually *doubled* since decertification. It amounted to nearly $150 million in overt military aid for fiscal 1996.[30]

In terms of military policy, decertification means absolutely nothing. It's just political leverage to enable the U.S. to gain policy control of the Colombian military. And it worked! Colombia's notoriously corrupt narks now have the right of property seizure and the U.S. Navy now has the right to patrol Colombian territorial waters. Gelbard was assisted in his testimony by two weeping uniformed Colombian generals, who insisted that decertification had reduced them to making their own loads.

The Samper investigation revealed that, while coordinating drug shipments, Cali traffickers racked up a $200,000 phone bill on a number assigned to Brig. Gen. Ismael Trujillo, then head of the Federal Judicial Police, the guy in charge of the U.S. Drug War in Colombia. And the Supreme Court of Colombia, in 1994, protecting both its GNP and its sovereignty, had already ruled that personal possession of inebriants is protected by the constitution.

In July of 1996, despite the overwhelming evidence, the Colombian Congress officially cleared Samper of corruption. That is, Clinton and McCaffrey were just backing one faction of dealers against another. The way out of the mess, of course, is to legalize the leaf and medicalize - license - the alkaloid, that is, to give the campesinos a legal market. But that would give them economic and political power - and that, as FARC - and the Colombian military - well understands, is the real issue.

Colombia's DEA-organized military police, the Special Anti-Narcotics Unit of the Federal Judicial Police, are now fighting the campesino-guerrillas of FARC and ELN (National Liberation Army) for control of the most lucrative coca fields, using the MAS death squads as an adjunct. Boilerplate Barry actually acknowledged this on his October 1997 visit to Colombia. McCaffrey told Samper, as if Samper didn't already know, that the "paramilitaries" are "no more than bands of criminals who profit from narco-trafficking and endanger Colombian democracy."[31]

Barry forgot to mention that it was he who set up the paramilitaries, using covert operatives from the U.S. Southern Command, then under his personal command. *The London Times*, 12/5/96:

"Vigilante squads terrorizing Colombia's rural areas were set up with assistance from the CIA, according to Human Rights Watch, an American organisation."

"In a report published this week, Assassination Squads in Colombia, the organisation says CIA agents went to Colombia in 1991 to help the military to train undercover agents in anti-subversive activity. CIA expertise was then used to set up a network of paramilitary groups to clamp down on.... suspected rebel sympathizers."

Yadira Ferrer, Bogotá, 2/13/98 (IPS): "The Colombian government said it would investigate incidents in the southern department of Putumayo in which at least 48 persons have reportedly been killed by right- wing paramilitary groups so far this year."

"Fourteen people have also been killed, meanwhile, over the past two weeks at mobile checkpoints installed by the army along highways in several regions to "keep public order.""

"The attorney-general's office, the office of the special prosecutor and the police are jointly investigating reports by the mayor of Puerto Asis in Putumayo, Nestor Hernandez, who blamed the 48 killings on right-wing paramilitary groups."

The massacre reports repeatedly stress the coordinated "para" use of regular army bases and aircraft. McCaffrey didn't threaten to cut off military aid to the regulars - he was just doing his customary "partial hangout" - necessitated by the repeated massacre reports.

The most powerful paramilitary leader, Carlos Castaño, leader of the militia alliance known as the United Self Defense Forces of Colombia, is a longtime CIA asset who can call on regular army support any time. *The Washington Post* reports, 12/30/98, that the DEA insists that Castaño is also a major Cali kingpin.

The Washington Post, 8/11/98: "Colombian Army's Third in Command Allegedly Led Two Lives; General Reportedly Served as Key CIA Informant While Maintaining Ties to Death Squads Financed By Drug Traffickers: For years Colombian Gen. Ivan Ramirez Quintero was a key intelligence source for the United States. After training in Washington he was the first head of a military intelligence organization designed by U.S. experts to fight Marxist guerrillas and drug traffickers, and served as a liaison and paid informant for the Central Intelligence Agency, according to U.S. and Colombian intelligence sources." That is, as the first head of the special counterinsurgency unit, it was Ramirez' job to coordinate military operations and weapons financing with Cali kingpin Carlos Castaño.

In fact, on Feb. 27, 1998, Secretary of State Madeleine Albright announced that Colombia, although still "decertified," would suffer no penalties for that decertification. This despite the fact that Colombia's new extradition law, passed in December of 97, formally protects Colombia's drug kingpins from extradition to the U.S. The Secretary explained that the waiver of penalties reflected support for the National Judicial Police and for efforts "to lay the groundwork for increased future cooperation."

Albright's acting Deputy Secretary for International Narcotics Matters, Randy Beers, insisted, in classic military-intelligence hyperbole, that Colombia was at "a critical turning point" because of the threats posed by increasingly aggressive leftist insurgents, still-powerful drug traffickers and a major increase in the country's cultivation of coca leaf, which he called "a narcotic substance."[32]

Mark Weisbrot, Research Director, The Preamble Center, Washington, D.C., in *The Miami Herald*, 7/24/99: "JUST SAY "NO" TO A BILLION DOLLARS FOR STATE-SPONSORED TERRORISM"

"The Clinton administration upped the ante last week with a proposal for a billion dollars of 'anti-drug aid' - widely acknowledged to be indistinguishable from other military assistance - to the government of Colombia over the next fiscal year. And now peace talks between the government and guerrillas that were supposed to resume this week have been postponed."

"A billion dollars is an enormous amount of money to fight an extraordinarily dirty war that most Americans know nothing about. Even at the height of President Reagan's war in El Salvador in the 1980s, US spending did not reach that amount."

"The Colombian war is very similar to the 1980s war in El Salvador (or Guatemala, for that matter). As in the Salvadoran war, most of the victims are innocent people - labor leaders, peasants, and even human rights workers. They are killed by the government or its allies, who often use hideous torture and mutilation in order to discourage opposition political activity. And most of the murders and atrocities are carried out by paramilitary groups with close links to the army and police. This allows the Colombian government to deny responsibility, and U.S. officials to pretend that they are aiding a democratic government...."

"Washington's problem in Colombia is that the guerrillas are much more entrenched, for various historical and geographical reasons. The two main guerrilla groups now control about half the national territory, and can blow up oil pipelines whenever they want."

FARC guerrillas relax; http://burn.ucsd.edu/~farc-ep

"These realities - as well as the overwhelming popular desire for an end to the war - have convinced Colombian President Andres Pastrana to pursue peace negotiations, which began in January. But Colombia's military, its drug-rich and commercial elite, and of course the paramilitary death squads want to pursue a "Salvadoran" solution: fight the rebels while killing and terrorizing their potential supporters among citizens' organizations that are seen as 'subversive.'"

"Yet we are about to give Colombia a billion dollars in military aid, plus $3 billion from the IMF and another $2 billion from other multilateral institutions like the Inter-American Development Bank.

Our military is now sharing intelligence with theirs, oblivious to the atrocities that may be committed with the help of this information."

Barry McCaffrey was the lead U.S. counterinsurgency officer in Ambassador Robert White's El Salvador. It was White's reaction to the crimes against humanity comitted by the Atlacatl Batallion and other McCaffrey-trained outfits that got him fired by the Reagan administration. White is now president of the Center for International Policy. He points out, in *The Washington Post*, 2/8/2000, that we can expect a repeat scenario:

"Has it truly escaped senior administration aides that the Colombian civil war is more about massacres of civilians and selective assassinations than armed confrontation? Does it really not matter that to declare war on the FARC puts us in league with a Colombian military that has longstanding ties to the drug-dealing, barbaric paramilitaries that commit more than 75 percent of the human rights violations afflicting that violence-torn country?"

"Nowhere in the official statements on Colombia will Congress find any discussion of risks vs. rewards or any measurement of objectives in relation to resources. Recall that in El Salvador, our bloody, divisive 12-year pursuit of military victory proved fruitless. We finally settled for a U.N.-brokered accord that granted the guerrillas many of their demands."

"The FARC-controlled territory that this program casually commits us to re-conquer is 20 times as large as El Salvador—roughly the size of California. The Colombian military has no experience in carrying the war to the insurgents. What will happen when FARC troops, at home in jungle and savanna, repel the army and shoot down our helicopters? Will we then swallow the bitter pill of political-military defeat? Not if Vietnam and Central America are any guide. Far more likely we will plunge deeper into the quagmire."

That quagmire, precisely because it is a quagmire, will be worth hundreds of billions in direct and indirect defense contract appropriations. *That* is Barry McCaffrey's job.

The Latin America Working Group, 7/23/98, reports that of 247 Colombian military personnel linked to serious human rights violations, 124 were graduates of the U.S. Army's School of the Americas in Fort Benning, GA.

The Village Voice: 8/5/99: "The wife of the Army commander leading the U.S. government's antidrug efforts in Colombia has been charged in connection with a cocaine smuggling ring that shipped that drug from an American military base in Bogotá to New York City, the *Voice* has learned."

"Laurie Hiett, the wife of Colonel James Hiett, was named in a criminal complaint filed in late June in Brooklyn federal court, according to records. She has been charged with conspiracy to distrubute cocaine."

Others named in the complaint reveal a vast, decentralized distribution system involving the entire structure around Col. Hiett, including many "embassy employees," direct military subordinates, their wives, chauffeurs and stateside contacts. The "embassy employees" were using the Army Postal Service (APO), which in Bogotá is a *de facto* part of the embassy's customs-free diplomatic pouch.

And whose coke was the antidrug Colonel exporting? Carlos Castaño's Cali coke. The Drug Inquisition has only served to *increase* the consumption of refined concentrates, since they are the only effective pain killers and ecstatics left available on the street, in the absence of the far safer traditional herbs. Can I get coca leaves? No. Can I get cocaine? Anytime. And who am I financing when I get cocaine? The Colombian or Argentine military, or, for that matter, the guerrillas, many of whom are tied to the very same dealers.

A thousand times more international effort goes into preventing poor people from medicating themselves than into getting medicine to poor people. The Pentagon spends more in one afternoon than the Peace Corps spends in a year. The thing that made Kennedy so politically charismatic, at the dawn of the 60's, was his vision of an equation of those ratios. How do you stop communism? "Stop fascism," replied Kennedy.

Most of FARC's constituents have never made a telephone call. 80% of the world's population still lacks basic telecommunications, let alone Internet access. 49 countries, 35 of which are in Africa, have fewer than one telephone per 100 people. There are more telephone lines in Manhattan than in all of sub-Saharan Africa. India has 8 million telephone lines for 900 million people, despite all the jive I see on TV about the cell-phone toting yuppies of Bombay.[33]

But the poor worldwide have shared in pollution-exacerbated epidemic disease. Cancer, heart and lung diseases kills hundreds of thousands of people each year in the U.S. alone, and are bankrupting our wealthy health care system, yet we spend thousands of times more building and selling weapons, police equipment, academies, prisons and global intelligence nets than solving the problems of disease and industrial ecocide.

In 1989, the World Health Organization estimated that 11 million children die annually of easily preventable diseases.[34] We have hundreds of millions of people around the world living like junk yard dogs, and yet the U.N. can't put together an Economic Relief Brigade from twenty of the world's richest nations. That energy goes instead into building military and intelligence structures, financed by the illegal drug trade, designed to dominate the internal affairs of those countries.

The Nation:7/19/99:"Almost three times as many people, most of them in tropical countries of the Third World, die of preventable, curable diseases as die of AIDS. Malaria, tuberculosis, acute lower-respiratory infections—in 1998, these claimed 6.1 million lives...."

"Total global expenditures for malaria research in 1993, including government programs, came to $84 million. That's paltry when you consider that one B-2 bomber costs $2 billion, the equivalent of what, at current levels, will be spent on all malaria research over twenty years. In that period, some 40 million Africans alone will die from the disease. In the United States, the Pentagon budgets $9 million per year for malaria programs, about one-fifth the amount it set aside this year to supply the troops with Viagra."

The dirty war in Argentina is over, but the Pentagon clients who engineered it are still in control of Argentina. The fascist effort has simply become more sophisticated, concerned as the military is to cooperate in the effort against "narcoterrorism."

When the World Health Organization insisted that coca leaves, central South America's most important medicine, and low-level cocaine products were safe, America threatened to withdraw funding unless the position were reversed.[35]

Poor little Bangladesh can't even approach its economic problems with objective sanity. Because cheap marijuana seeds grow almost anywhere and put down a one-foot taproot in 30 days, they break up compacted, dry soil and also help to bind wet soil subject to periodic flooding. They are therefore one of the best reforestation crops known, especially since they're not only ecologically but industrially valuable. Their use in "Bangladesh," however, would cost the "cannabis-land-people" their diplomatic legitimacy and all their foreign aid.[36] This, despite the fact that Prohibition is directly responsible for innumerable gigantic pot plantations around the world. In 1978, an aerial survey of Colombia's Guajira province, conducted at the request of the President, revealed 250,000 acres planted in marijuana.[37] Pot was the biggest employer in Guajira. That is solely an effect of Prohibition.

The E-3 Sentry Airborne Warning & Control System

Customs Radar Balloon

The California National Guard Inspects a Truck

The Customs Doggie at the Airport; www.customs.ustreas.gov

Drug War

Interdiction

If you ask the DEA what percentage of smuggled drugs they intercept, they'll give you exactly the same answer they gave in 1928 or 1948, "about 10%,"[1] which is both a wild exaggeration and a cover story. A busy port receives over 100,000 containers a week. They can't even search 1%, let alone nail 10%. A DEA official in "candid" mode will admit they really intercept only 5%, still an absurd exaggeration, although the confiscation laws do enable the narks to make money coming and going. They're just part of the system, on salary or on the take.

A wild peninsular coastline like Washington State-British Columbia is uncontrollable. *NYT*:1/31/95: "Canada has only a few Coast Guard cutters and Mountie patrol boats to watch 16,900 miles of [BC] coastline." The U.S. has almost 90,000 miles of coastline, 300 ports of entry.

As of early 1998, the U.S. had 7,000 agents patrolling the sexy 2,000-mile Mexican border, but only 300 covering the entire 5,500-mile Alaska-Canada-U.S. border. 99% of Canada's superb hydroponic pot gets through, making it a multi-billion dollar factor in the Canadian economy.[2]

Gene Kervan, customs director at the Blaine, Washington border crossing: "We have to learn how to do this smarter than we're doing it now. We can't back the traffic up to Alaska. We get 5 million cars a year at Blaine. Even if 99 percent of those people are OK, that's still 50,000 bad guys coming through."[3]

"You used to get a hundred kilos coming in on the East Coast docks, packed into a Citroen. Now you get maybe nine pounds a whack stuffed into the drive shaft or gas tank of a beat-up car driven across the border by a woman with a bunch of kids."[4] No sweat to slip something like that past an inspector doing 120 entrants an hour. "It's like trying to stop a piece of mercury with an ice pick. It just goes someplace else."[5]

And when Nixon, annoyed at Mexican haughtiness, tried Operation Intercept in September of 1969, seriously searching everything that came across the Mexican border for 20 days, virtually closing that busy crossing, the economic damage was so massive, on both sides of the border, with truckloads of Mexican produce rotting in the sun and Texas border towns going bankrupt, that it was never tried again.

Otay Mesa, next to Tijuana, is the main commercial truck entrance from Mexico's *maquiladora* TV, toy, plastic goods, clothing and auto factories into the U.S. It is overwhelmed with traffic, 24/7. "Spend a couple of hours at Otay Mesa, and you'll notice a lot of guys on either side of the border just hanging around, chatting a lot of the time on their cell phones. They're spotters for trucks on drugs runs. They tip off the driver about what time to come, which lane to use, what to say, and the DEA can't tap into their calls because they all have encryption or scrambler devices."[6]

That is, they're coordinating the drug run with their very own customs agents, who make as much as $50,000 in untraceable street cash simply for waving a hot truck through. That's a year's wages for ten minutes work.

U.S. Customs mapped 500 airstrips within a hundred miles of either side of the Mexican border.[7] Of nearly 7,000 suspicious flights detected by the Pentagon in 1990, 49 were caught.[8] In 1996, *The Christian Science Monitor* informs us, "AWACS provided information that led to four cocaine interdictions worth $945 million - about 35 percent of all cocaine intercepted coming into the US." That is, about ¼ of 1% of all the cocaine coming into the U.S.

CSM:"'Interdiction, although it is often bad-mouthed, has to be one of the principal components of the fight against drugs,' says a retired military officer who now serves in the president's Office of National Drug Control Policy. 'The capstone is the AWACS with their special "look down" radar. Nothing gets by them when they are up.' As it turns out, the green blip - signifying a small airplane flying low over the ocean, southeast of Florida - was not trafficking in illegal drugs."[9] That is, the celestial AWACS has no earthly way of distinguishing between the scores of small aircraft on its screen at any one time. That means that one scramble in 100 hits the mark.

Thanks to the political pressure, coke and pot seizures were up along the Mexican border in 1995. The Nogales Border patrol station seized a little more than a ton of coke in 95. But that's just a 1% tax to smugglers who can slip more than a hundred tons through Nogales each year.

But Mexican streetfighters don't take that Gringo crap nohow. Phil Jordan, 1995 DEA director of the El Paso Intelligence Center, had his brother shot dead in an El Paso street by a Mexican hit squad. And they're not above hitting his kids, either. This gives Jordan's subordinates serious pause when offered a piece of the action by a Mexican hit team.

"It's kind of like this," explains Robert Nieves, former DEA Chief of International Operations, "You're offered a bribe. If bribery doesn't work, you're offered violence. And that violence will be exacted against you or your family members."[10] *Plata o Plomo*, Silver or Lead, as the famous phrase goes.

Still, one still wonders why the border continues to be so porous, given the muscle the El Paso Intelligence Center, operating along with Army Joint Task Force 6 out of Biggs Army Airfield, can muster. Biggs employs some 300 people coordinating intelligence from all Pentagon, NSA, FBI, Treasury, DIA and CIA sources, and can mobilize military SWAT teams.

There are two answers. One is the example of the just-quoted DEA Chief of International Operations, Robert Nieves. Before rising to that exalted position, Nieves ran the DEA's Costa Rica office, running interference for the Contras and Manuel Noriega against the likes of reformist antidrug revolutionary Hugo Spadafora and reformist antidrug DEA agent Celerino Castillo. It was Nieves who ran Norwin Meneses for the CIA, protecting his huge Contra-cocaine supply operation, as Gary Webb has documented in such detail. Nieves then went on to head the DEA's cocaine task force in DC - with zero strategic effect, needless to say. After his 1995 retirement, Nieves went to work for body armor manufacturer Guardian Technologies - owned by Oliver North and Contra-era Costa Rica CIA station chief Joe Fernandez, both barred from Costa Rica for dealing in multiton loads of cocaine. With leadership like that, the pipeline is open.

Jorge Hank Rhon and Customs Port Director Jerry B. Martin

Senior Customs Inspector John Carman:"Millionaire-Smuggler-Crime Figure Jorge Hank-Rhon and Customs Port Director Jerry B. Martin. Both associated with former District Director Allan J.

Rappoport and John "Jack" Maryon, who were all under investigation, but Customs Internal Affairs, FBI, or the other Federal agencies investigating did nothing about these dangerous liaisons... I was 'ordered' not to put Jorge Hank Rhon's name into the Customs/Treasury look out system TECS (Treasury Enforcement Computer System) because of another Customs Supervisor named John "Jack" Maryon. Hank Rhon was later caught smuggling more currency at LAX international airport." (www.amerikanexpose.com/customs1.html)

The other answer to the porous border question is that their TECS, NADDIS and NIN (Narcotics Information Network) computer system is just another impotent eye in the sky. It don't tell them squat about the *cucarachas*. NADDIS can go after money-laundering "kingpins" all it wants. But it's the system - the bottom-up economics of street-dealing - that generates the "kingpin," not the other way around.

As Clinton deplaned in Mexico on 5/5/97, I heard reporters on all three major networks authoritatively declare that the Mexican drug problem was really "kingpin" Amado Carillo. That's just the fluff of the moment, the dehydrated, homogenized formula - just add air time and whip. The reportage on all three networks was virtually identical, word for word, as if these guys were reading press releases. Not one reporter mentioned the economics of Prohibition, although one did add some parenthetical mumbling about "corruption."

The DEA guesses that more than 500 tons of coke were successfully smuggled into the U.S. in 1996.[11] Their guess, and they admit it's a guess, is probably a gross underestimation, given that total coke seizures, including all maritime seizures, were close to 80 tons. But even according to the DEA's own figures, so much coke gets through that confiscations, however heavy, simply function to protect the value of the successfully smuggled imports.

To quote the State Department's own end-of-year 1996 Enforcement Affairs report, "in FY 1996 the total USG budget for international drug control operations was approximately $1.6 billion. That equates to 16 metric tons of cocaine; the drug trade has lost that much in two shipments and scarcely felt the loss."[12]

The General Accounting Office, in 1997, reported that all interdiction and seizure efforts made by the U.S. Government between 1988 and 1995 "made little impact on the availability of illegal drugs in the United States and on the amount needed to satisfy U.S. demand."[13]

That is, drug enforcement throughout the U.S. simply has the practical effect of protecting, indeed creating, the artificially inflated street value of illegal drugs, thereby financing the smugglers. That's the fascist game. That's why Santos Trafficante, a genius at smuggling contraband, worked for the CIA. Trafficante, of course, was also a genius at keeping himself relatively unknown.

We are constantly told that the death of a "kingpin" is a strategic victory, but it's the system that generates the dealer, not the dealer the system. I remember seeing roving U.S. ambassador Lewis Tambs, in a PBS *Frontline* documentary on Medellín "kingpin" Pablo Escobar, at pains to stress J. Edgar's old "public enemy" line. He said the drug business is "dealer-driven," and that if we'd only concentrate on these nasty people, we could ignore all that fussy economic stuff. Bullshit. Escobar's dead and Colombian coke is flying through the pipeline faster than ever. Cali "kingpins" are biting the dust too, but Colombian coke just keeps on flowing through *La Pipa*.

The State Department's end-of-year 1996 Narcotics Control Strategy Report also goes on and on, country by country, about the destruction of "kingpins," continually claiming completely imaginary strategic progress. It measures this progress not only by the death of this or that bad guy, literally counting bodies, but by its successful efforts to enhance "police-military cooperation" in-country with U.S. enforcement entities. "Progress," of course, justifies an ever-expanding budget. It also points to the real import of the Drug War - the enhancement of U.S. power "in-country."

On May 2, 1996, Attorney General Reno, flanked by a phalanx of heavies, treated us to her John Mitchell impersonation. She announced that the United States had smashed a major drug ring with "tentacles" extending into Colombia, Mexico and cities all across the U.S. The operation netted 130 arrests, $17 million in cash and 6 tons of cocaine. "The most sophisticated and the most well-coordinated effort that I've ever seen," beamed one DEA official, who surely must have known better. The bust was trumpeted, in a strangely homogenized way, all over the media as a tactical victory in the War. The fact that busts like this have been routine for the past 25 years, and that the Colombians replaced the coke and the street dealers within ten minutes, wasn't mentioned. All Reno actually did was reinforce the value of the mountain of coke that remained on the street, thus creating yet more incentive to produce more coke as rapidly as possible.

The Colombians distribute much of their coke through the Gangster Disciples, who are so powerful they can buy 300-kilo lots direct and manage the nationwide distribution themselves. That's not just a gang, that's a culture. "Gang violence has spread to every corner of America," intoned Janet Reno, as she announced the results of the

July, 1996 survey of gang activity, which showed an estimated 650,000 gang members in 25,000 gangs nationwide.[17] These figures demonstrate the need for yet more and better warfare aimed at the projects, insisted the AG.

Thanks to this logic, the Bloods, the Crips, the Vice Lords, the Cobra Stones and the Gangster Disciples have an ironclad monopoly on street dealing throughout the U.S. The power-hungry Disciples enforce their membership with savage rules of violence. You come to work on-time, and you come to work sober, *or else*. You *don't* screw up the brothers.

These guys are more disciplined than the Mafia ever was. These serious pistoleros won't be dignified in the media as freedom fighters, of course, but they sure as hell are fighters, and many see themselves as freedom fighters. The Gangster Disciples call themselves "Brothers of the Struggle." Try taking the night away from them in downtown Chicago.

Created in 1974 by an organizational genius named Larry "King" Hoover, from prison, the Disciples now have 30,000 members in 35 states - and an annual income of at least $100 million. You better believe they know how to defend their turf. So what if King Hoover gets another 200 years added to his life sentence. How's that going to affect his Midwest pistoleros, or the cops on their payroll? If you were offered $10,000 for one night's work, or a bullet in the head, which would you take?

House Speaker Newt Gingrich, as simplistic a demagogue as ever came down the pike, had an interesting variation on the "dealer-driven" theme. He introduced the Drug Importer Death Penalty Act of 1997. Newt proposed a mandatory death sentence for anyone twice convicted of smuggling more than 100 doses of any controlled substance. That would mean a death sentence for anyone twice convicted of smuggling more than two ounces of pot. "If the word gets back that we're serious and we're actually implementing it, then it will have a very chilling effect on people bringing drugs into the U.S."[18] He advocated mass murder - doing in "25-30 at a time." "If you deal drugs, we're going to kill you."

Is Gingrich really too stupid to know that he'd only be killing hungry mules? I think not. "There's a limitless supply of poor people in Mexico that these drug smugglers can prey upon. They offer these people what is to us a very small amount of money, perhaps $200, to drive a car carrying drugs across the border. These people are fungible," notes Frank Mangan, senior trial attorney for Federal Defenders of San Diego.[19]

Does Newt think he'd ever catch more than 1 or 2%? I think not. Does he know that, since 1975, Malaysia has been executing mules, driving the entire drug-using population so effectively underground that the drug economy expanded?[20] I think so.

KUHNE WOULD KILL ALL DRUG ADDICTS

New Yorker Tells Conference They Cannot Be Cured—Later Withdraws Lethal Expression.

Special to The New York Times.

PHILADELPHIA, July 5. — "Kill them off," Gerhard Kuhne, Chief of the Bureau of Criminal Identifications of New York City, said today, referring to drug users, in an address before the First World Conference on Narcotic Education. The expression was withdrawn later, when an auditor objected to its inclusion in the record.

NYT, 7/6/1926

Explained U.S. District Judge J. Lawrence Irving, a Reagan appointee in San Diego, as he quit the bench in disgust in 1990, "I can't continue to give out sentences I feel in some instances are unconscionable." When mules who drive a few kilos across the border for $500 are convicted, "you're talking ten, fifteen, twenty years in prison." Gingrich would have some single mother from Guadalajara, driving a few kilos across the border in her 76 Chevy in exchange for rent money, executed.

Of course thousands of *cucarachas*, each carrying a few keys, can transport tons. In 1989, 21 tons of cocaine, valued at $6.5 billion retail, was seized in a warehouse in Sylmar, California. Can you imagine the street muscle it took to organize that? Rafael Muñoz Talavera, the Ciudad Juarez slugger who organized that mountain of coke, had such good connections among Mexican police and prosecutors that he was able to sabotage the overwhelming case against him and is now once again a free *narcotraficante*.

U.S. Magistrate Judge Ronald Rose: "Instead of seizing pounds of cocaine, we now seize buildings full of the stuff. The drug lords in South America are laughing at us all the way to the bank. They know that for every mule or mid-level dealer we take out, there are fifty more waiting to take their place. There is just so much money to be made that the slim chance of being caught is always worth the risk. Believe me, after twenty years as a prosecutor and a judge, I can assure you that we only catch the stupid ones."[21]

Newt's proposal can best be understood in light of the subtle intellect of his electorate, and his fiscal priorities: the publicly-funded high-tech police and military contractors of his district, who finance his campaigns.

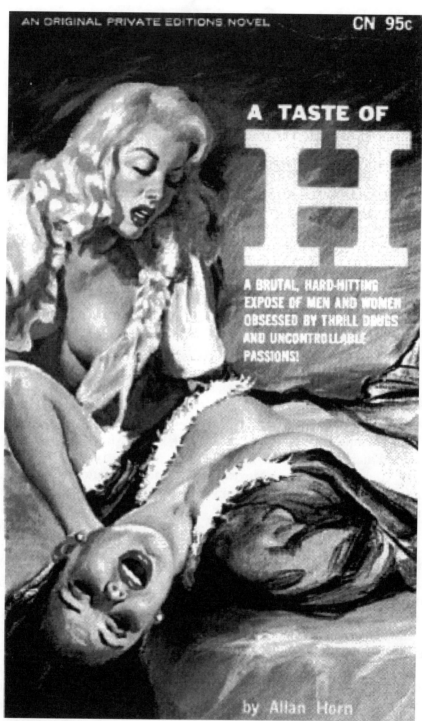

Doug Aanes

Drug War

Fake Science

After the November 1996 elections, when Californians and Arizonans voted to allow a medical defense for marijuana possession under state law, the Clinton administration's Drug Control Policy point man, Gen. Barry McCaffrey, was all over the tube repeating his two favorite lies. First, insisted the General, marijuana is a stepping stone to hard drugs.

When an expert team of medical scientists from the New York Academy of Medicine issued the 1944 "LaGuardia Report," which the mayor had commissioned six years earlier, they concluded that: "The use of marihuana does not lead to morphine or heroin or cocaine addiction. ...The instances are extremely rare where the habit of marihuana smoking is associated with addiction to these narcotics."[1]

That has been the conclusion of every single major study since then, including the greatest clinical trial ever done on pot decriminalization, known as Holland or The Netherlands. The Dutch Minister of Health, quoted above in "Propaganda," can be left to explain the official Dutch disrespect for McCaffrey's mythical "gateway theory." The Dutch have proven, and officially assert, that the *criminalization* of this mild herbal ecstatic and painkiller *causes* widespread use of the potent concentrates.

Secondly, insisted McCaffrey, over and over again in every interview, *no major national medical organization has endorsed marijuana for medical use.* This apparently excludes the American Public Health Association, the Physicians Association for AIDS Care and the Lymphoma Foundation, three of the most expert physician groups in the country.

The American Public Health Association officially endorsed medical marijuana in November of 1995. It is the oldest and largest organization of health care professionals in the world, with over 50,000 members, and has been a major force in public health policy since 1872. Their November, 1995 Resolution 9513, written exclusively by distinguished physicians, demands legal "Access to Therapeutic Marijuana/Cannabis."

The 1,000 physicians in PAAC, the greatest clinical experts we have, who treat 250,000 AIDS patients, recently joined the Lymphoma Foundation in yet another lawsuit to force the rescheduling of marijuana.

Both the American College of Physicians and the American Society for Clinical Oncology, in official position papers, have insisted on the re-categorization of medical marijuana, as has such prestigious journals as the *New England Journal of Medicine* and the *Annals of Internal Medicine.* And literally hundreds of *statewide* or *local* medical groups, such as the San Francisco Medical Society, representing 9,000 MDs, and the California Academy of Family Physicians, representing 7500 MD's, have officially endorsed pot as medicine.

The Federation of American Scientists, which numbers 47 Nobel laureates among its members, strongly endorsed medical marijuana in 1994. So did the National Academy of Sciences, in 1982, and the Australian Commonwealth Department of Human Services and Health, in 1994.

So have many of this country's most distinguished jurists. After careful judicial analyses of the evidence, medical marijuana was endorsed not only by the DEA's own chief administrative law judge, but, as long ago as June 25, 1983, by the National Association of Attorneys General. In fact, even NIDA's foremost marijuana expert, Dr. Mahmoud ElSohly of the Marijuana Project at the University of Mississippi, flatly asserted that "There is no question about the use of cannabis for certain conditions. It does have a history. It does have utility."[2]

In 1988, after two years of detailed testimony, the DEA's own chief administrative law judge, Francis Young, concluded that "marijuana is one of the safest therapeutic substances known to man....capable of relieving the distress of great numbers of very ill people....It would be unreasonable, arbitrary and capricious for the DEA to continue to stand between those sufferers and the benefits of this substance in light of the evidence."[3]

DEA Administrator John Lawn, that great physician, rejected this judicial recommendation, using the "no-license" catch-22: marijuana wasn't "widely prescribed" in the medical community [because illegal], therefore it had "no currently accepted medical use." This is the precise equivalent of allowing Anthony Comstock to decide what medicine is and is not legal for women. Since *the evidence is inadmissable,* there's no way the National Organization for the Reform of Marijuana Laws (NORML) or anyone else can force a binding jury trial of the evidence. Legally, all the administrative law judge can do is make recommendations, which the DEA is free to ignore.

This is the "purposeful ambiguity" precedent first written into Wiley's Food and Drug Act. The U.S. Court of Appeals told NORML in 1994 that there is no higher court on drug matters than the DEA, which alone has the legal right to "schedule" drugs. No binding jury trial of the evidence is available. Of course, since 95% of all illegal drug use in the U.S. is marijuana use, without illegal pot, this country's police structures would suffer severe budget cuts. Fascism, the militarization of culture, relies on the artificial production of stress and violence: simply criminalize the NORML.

Between 1978 and 1996, 36 state legislatures legally recognized marijuana's medical usefulness. These measures ranged from the establishment of state-sponsored therapeutic research programs to amending state law to allow physicians to prescribe marijuana for specific illnesses.

Marijuana, *official* from 1850 to 1942 in the *U.S. Pharmacopeia*, were it legal today, would be *official* for glaucoma, high blood pressure, migraine, anorexia, depression, sleep disorders, multiple sclerosis, spasticity disorders, chronic pain, AIDS wasting syndrome, asthma, motion sickness, depression, mood disorders, pruritis, menstrual cramps, the effects of cancer chemotherapy and epilepsy. This list, by the way, comes mostly from the official position paper of The American Public Health Association, written exclusively by experienced physicians.[4] Much of it, in 1999, has been legally adopted by The Netherlands.

Dr. Lester Grinspoon, associate professor of psychiatry at Harvard Medical School, began to write *Marihuana Reconsidered* after his 14 year-old boy started receiving chemotherapy for acute lymphoblastic leukemia. "Vomiting for 8 hours a day was so demoralizing for this beautiful child."[5] Grinspoon found that marijuana was the only thing that could control the violent nausea. "When I began to study marijuana in 1967, I had no doubt that it was a very harmful drug....as I reviewed the scientific, medical and lay literature....I came to understand that I, like so many other people in this country, had been brainwashed."[6]

"The greatest advantage of cannabis as a medicine is its unusual safety. The ratio of lethal dose to effective dose is estimated on the basis of extrapolation from animal data to be about 20,000:1 (compared to 350:1 for secobarbital and 4-10:1 for alcohol). Huge doses have been given to dogs without causing death, and there is no reliable evidence of death caused by cannabis in a human being. Cannabis also has the advantage of not disturbing any physiological functions or damaging any body organ when used in therapeutic doses. It produces little physical dependence or tolerance; there is no evidence that medical use of cannabis has ever led to its habitual use as an intoxicant."[7]

Reacting to the success of the 1996 medical marijuana initiatives,

Gen. McCaffrey, flanked by HHS's Donna Shalala and Attorney General Janet Reno, outlined his battle plan. The administration will try to strip doctors who recommend or prescribe marijuana, or any other Schedule 1 drug, of the federal registration they need to prescribe any drug. Rep. Solomon's "Medical Marijuana Prevention Act of 1997," and its senatorial equivalent, Sen. Faircloth's "Medical Marijuana Deterrence Act of 1997" were designed to effect this. McCaffrey also promised to try to strip those doctors of their inclusion in Medicare and Medicaid.

The Attorney General then declared that the Department of Justice will work "to limit the states' ability to rely on these and similar medical use provisions." That is, to disenfranchise the citizens. In 1998, the Justice Department succeeded. U.S. District Court Judge Charles Breyer closed California's medical marijuana clubs. He agreed with the Justice Department's argument that no claim of necessity could justify use of a drug federally classified as dangerous and having "no approved medical purpose." We literally have the spectacle of the Green Beret General who led the sickening Contra war and coordinated the Guatemalan and Salvadoran genocide, legally dictating medical practice to America's physicians, in contravention of the wishes of the electorate. Pass the pot, I'm gonna puke.

McCaffrey, of course, is a master of the "partial hangout." His visceral 1996 denunciations of "cruel hoaxes," "Trojan horses" and "Cheech and Chong" medicine - in which he cast the distinguished Dr. Tod Mikuriya as Chong - was followed by an admission that, well, yes, maybe we *should* get qualified physicians to look at this. So, in January of 1997, McCaffrey's Office of National Drug Control Policy commissioned the U.S. Institute of Medicine to write a report on medical marijuana.

This report was issued in March of 1999. Dr. Mikuriya, a world-class expert, was not invited to participate. It was essentially medical bullfighting, admitting that some of marijuana's synthesizable isolates have shown medical promise, but insisting that medicolegal issues, such as whether a physician should be allowed to prescribe pot, are "outside the scope of this report."

McCaffrey got his boilerplate. He's all for "science." The I.O.M. recommended further extensive research, but the National Institutes of Health continues to reject study proposals from qualified researchers, almost all of whom have found themselves facing a bureaucratic brick wall. And the feds have waged a vicious COINTELPRO war on California's medical marijuana groups, targeting leaders for life sentences as wholesale dealers.

But then, in September of 1999, the 9th U.S. Circuit Court of Appeals, which covers nine states, four of which have new medical marijuana laws, recognized the medical need to violate the federal anti-pot law in order to prevent more serious harm. That is, it recognized the basic legal premise of California's 1996 Prop 215. But the ruling was, in effect, a bureaucratic recommendation the feds continue to ignore. The legal situation continues to seesaw as chemotherapy patients continue to be forced outside the law to stop their convulsive vomiting and epileptics their agonizing seizures.

The dangerous teenage neurosis *anorexia nervosa* is sometimes treated with chlorpromazine,[8] which is synthesized from diphenylamine, used in dyes and explosives, and sulphur, used in explosives, insecticides, fungicides, metallurgy and gas refining. Although most current medical books stress that there is no "official" treatment for anorexia, the popular 1989 AMA Encyclopedia of Medicine calls chlorpromazine a useful "antipsychotic" in such cases, which is like calling calomel a "purgative," since the "untoward effects" include "drowsiness, lethargy, ...orthostatic hypotension, tachycardia... dizziness... edema, constipation, anuria, convulsions, nervousness, syncope, insomnia, nasal congestion, skin rash....dermatitis, parkinsonism, confusion or jaundice...erythema, localized nodular lesions, acneform lesions with stomatitis...pruritis."[9]

The actual list of poisonous effects takes up an entire page in the *U.S. Dispensatory*, leaving the poor patient, already emotionally exhausted, near suicide, which would, of course, be attributed to the anorexia. Any half-competent herbalist could do better prescribing relaxation, euphoria and a heavy case of the munchies, but "euphoria" is a form of "turpitude," and the patient might be needed on the assembly line any minute, so we wouldn't want to let her get too relaxed. Conventional "behavior modification" psychotherapy is based in legal institutionalism. It is to ancient psychotherapy as chlorpromazine is to marijuana.

But, as the "Drug Medicalization, Prevention and Control Act," Arizona's 1996 Prop 200, indicates, contemporary psychotherapy is becoming less and less conventional. It allows doctors to prescribe any Schedule 1 drug, not just marijuana, if they have a second physician's opinion and can show "documented scientific evidence" of potential benefit. Similar measures have passed in other states since 1996.

This will, hopefully, mean heroin for the terminally ill. Heroin, in

Britain, is the first choice of physicians dealing with the agony of terminal cancer. Physicians in this country have to go with second best, a real crime. Since physicians are computer-monitored by the DEA, which can lift their license to prescribe, "The undertreatment of pain in hospitals is absolutely medieval," according to Dr. Russell Portnoy of the Pain Service of Sloan Kettering Memorial Hospital.[10]

The sickening, deranging and relatively ineffective synthetic Demerol (meperidine), derived from a pepper alkaloid, is regularly given in U.S. hospitals instead of heroin, morphine or codeine. The famous Libby Zion case, which saw the meperidine-induced 1984 death of a healthy 18 year old, is a study in pharmacological politicization.

Libby showed up at New York Hospital's emergency room suffering from flu-like symptoms, complicated by her prescription for the monoamine oxidase inhibitor (MAOI) phenelzine sulfate, another "antidepressant" concocted from industrial solvents (phenethyl chloride and hydrazine hydrate). This contributed, as the *Physicians' Desk Reference* clearly warns, to a "hypertensive crisis."

To calm her, the inexperienced young intern prescribed "Demerol," meperidine, the morphine-substitute she had been taught to use. Demerol, unfortunately, is a political substitute, not a pharmacological substitute. As the PDR stresses, "circulatory collapse, coma, and death have been reported in patients receiving MAOI therapy who have been given a single dose of meperidine."[11] Libby Zion got her shot of meperidine and went into circulatory collapse, literally poisoned to death.

A New York jury found three of the four doctors involved negligent for prescribing the contraindicated Demerol. Rather than relaxing her with a traditional mood elevator, such as a single miniscule dose of morphine, which would have sent her off to a blissful nap, she was given a patented synthetic that actually increased her anxiety. How utterly incompetent, how unloving.

I've actually had my 93 year old father, in very frail health and considerable pain, and suffering from glaucoma, told that he can have neither pot nor morphine, because the doctor was worried about "habit formation." God forbid the old man should acquire a "habit" in the last few years of his life. The doctor is just reading from the DEA's canon.

All over the country cops are presented in high schools and town councils as empirical experts while the most distinguished physicians, psychopharmacologists, psychiatrists, ethnobotanists, anthropologists, archeologists, sociologists and economists are ignored. "I am reminded of Soviet party-line criticism of science which led to the phenomenon known as Lysenkoism," notes Prof. Grinspoon.[12]

Sanctioned frauds like Heath, Nahas, Kleber and Califano, engineers of today's disaster, are given far more political credence than the likes of Dr. Lester Grinspoon, Dr. Solomon Snyder, Dr. Marie Nyswander, Dr. Vincent Dole, Dr. John Morgan, Dr. Alfred Lindesmith, Dr. Richard Evans Schultes, Dr. Michael Harner, Dr. Peter Furst, Dr. Andrew Weil, Dr. Michael Taussig, Dr. Timothy Plowman, Dr. Anthony Richard Henman, Dr. Marija Gimbutas, Dr. Thomas Szasz, Dr. Arnold Trebach, Dr. Charles Snyder, Dr. Jerome Miller and Dr. Milton Friedman.

You can ignore Mountbatten, MacArthur, Ridgway, Shoup and Giap *on* Vietnam politically, but you can't ignore them *in* Vietnam militarily. The Hoover Institution Resolution of July, 1993 was signed by hundreds of the most experienced American experts in all relevant fields. Colombia's Nobel Prize-winning novelist Gabriel García Márquez, an ally of Colombia's mid-80's president Betancur, then published his *Manifesto* in Spain's *Cambio 16* magazine, which, like The Hoover Resolution, demanded controlled international legalization. Signed by 2000 leading intellectuals, it resonated throughout the Latin world. It was reprinted in *The New York Times*. The Drug Policy Foundation, 2/27/94, then published a list in the *Times* of 106 prominent experts opposed to the Drug War.

On 11/11/95, Britain's prestigious medical journal *The Lancet*, in a blunt editorial, insisted that "The smoking of cannabis, even long term, is not harmful to health. Yet this widely used substance is illegal just about everywhere…. Leaving politics aside, where is the harm in decriminalising cannabis? There is none to the health of the consumers, and the criminal fraternity who depend for their succour on prohibition would hate it. But decriminalisation of possession does not go far enough in our view. That has to be accompanied by controls on source, distribution, and advertising, much as happens with tobacco. A system, in fact, remarkably close to the existing one in Dutch coffee shops…. Sooner or later politicians will have to stop running scared and address the evidence: cannabis per se is not a hazard to society but driving it further underground may well be."[13]

On 6/8/98, the first day of the U.N. General Assembly's three-day Special Session on drug policy, *The New York Times* published the Lindesmith Center's open letter to Secretary General Kofi Annan. Hundreds of the world's most astute scientists, writers and political leaders insisted that "the global war on drugs is now causing more harm than drug abuse itself." The signers numbered among them Isabel Allende, Ariel Dorfman, Belisario Betancur, Oscar Arias, Gunter Grass, George Papandreou, Javier Perez de Cuellar, Alan Cranston, Milton Friedman, Stephen Jay Gould, Lester Grinspoon, Nicholas Katzenbach, George Schultz, George Soros and Paul Volcker.

The Vietnam War too provoked this kind of learned reaction, but it didn't end until the whole nation was vomiting in an ocean of blood, and then only because political defeat was combined with military defeat. In a 1989 *New York Times*-CBS poll, 64% of the American public named "drugs" as the most serious domestic problem. That was the highest percentage ever recorded by a single issue in any public opinion poll.[14] That is a measure of the psychological appeal of the propaganda.

The Vietnam analogy is apt. Since 1989, public support for the Drug War has shown a steady decrease. A nationwide survey in February 1995 by Peter Hart Research Associates for Drug Strategies found that 50% of the American people gave the Federal government a grade of F or D for dealing with drug use and addiction, and 59% gave those grades for dealing with drug-related crime. Although the planted axioms in the questions reveal, at best, profound ignorance, the answers show that, for most Americans, victory is obviously not just around the corner.

But the forces running the Drug War aren't susceptible to democratic pressure. Their reaction to pressure is to use their media clout to manipulate the "demographics." Peter Reuter, co-director of the Rand Corporation Drug Policy Research Center, is probably right when he says that "the legalization debate, for better or for worse" remains "largely a parlor sport for intellectuals, divorced from the policy-decision process."[15]

What chance does Milton Friedman or The Drug Policy Foundation or *The Lancet* have against the Clinton-McCaffrey billion-dollar ad blitz? What chance does rationality have against a grief-stricken Carol O'Connor, a genius in front of the camera, insisting that the lesson he learned from his son's tragic drug abuse is that he wasn't *tough enough*. What chance against a sobbing, charismatic Black actor, during the commercial break in the basketball game, begging his young compadres not to do drugs? "You got to understand," says Weeping Willie, "you're being locked up for your own good." This may not convince the Cobra Stones, but your average sports fan is sold on more Drug War.

Noam Chomsky: "If you want to learn something about the propaganda system, have a close look at the critics and their tacit assumptions. These typically constitute the doctrines of the state religion."[16]

In the wake of statewide legalization of medical marijuana in California and Arizona, the masseurs at *Newsweek*, 2/3/97, assured us that the stepping stone theory is established fact. The only issue, therefore, is federal policy regarding medical prescription. All the guest columnists invited to participate in the issue, who disagreed among themselves about prescription policy, accepted this basic assumption. "Legalization" was uniformly derided as a scientifically-established "stepping stone." Dr. Grinspoon, or the Dutch Minister of Health, was not invited to participate.

Those with their hands on the levers of power know that to buck "the demographics" is political suicide. Most, in any case, are either sold on the War or hopelessly snowed. Senator Moynihan, a truly compassionate man, insists that the choice between legalization or Prohibition is one of "An enormous public health problem on the one hand, an enormous crime problem on the other."[17]

As if he knows. Moynihan is another "authority" with no pharmacoshamanic experience whatsoever, and, apparently, no acquaintance with the work of the leading empirical experts. He demonstrates his absurd lack of sophistication, and his Orthodox Catholic value system, by dreamily praying for a "blocking or neutralizing agent" to move drug users "as near to abstinence as possible," as if "abstinence" was the highest ideal of the tough young street fighters he's going to "neutralize."

In 1974, Dr. Robert Heath of Tulane, who, during the fifties, had zapped LSD-stoned mental patients at the behest of the CIA, was further inspired by Nazi genius. He strapped two rhesus monkeys into gas masks and asphyxiated them for five minutes with enough marijuana smoke to make thirty joints, the equivalent of one hundred joints for human body weight. That's a year's intake for most users. He forced them to breathe not only the heavy concentration of smoke but all the carbon monoxide given off in burning as well as their own carbon dioxide. Five minutes of asphyxiation for a monkey is like fifteen for a human.

After 90 days of slow strangulation, incredibly, the monkeys started to get sick. Heath then took two healthy monkeys, killed them, and compared their brains to the ones he had slowly choked to death, publishing his monkey brain pictures as proof of marijuana-induced brain damage. Controlled studies done in the 1990's with 64 monkeys proved that marijuana does no such thing,[18] but Heath's scary dead monkey-brain pictures continue to show up on television, along with frying eggs: "any questions?"[19]

Disinformation is an interesting art. It is often best promulgated by a qualified technocrat. "Former" CIA agent Dr. Gabriel Nahas, an anesthesiologist, was a lecturer for the U.S. Information Agency and is an influential consultant to the U.N. Commission on Narcotics. Nahas claims to be an expert on the *Physiopathology of Illicit Drugs* (1991). Is "illicit" a medical word? Why "pathology" and not "physiology"?

Nahas "demonstrated" in the mid-70's that pot, contrary to canonical reefer madness, *hurt* the male sex drive, destroyed the immune system and, supposedly like LSD, caused chromosome damage. Luce ran lurid stories in *Life* of permanent brain and chromosome damage done by LSD, but when the Army Chemical Corps, no less, looked, it concluded that "Although human chromosome breaks have been reported by others, we found them much more frequently from caffeine and many other substances."[20] That from Dr. Van Sim, chief of clinical research at Edgewood Arsenal.

Nahas' 1973 classic, *Marihuana: Deceptive Weed*, was derided as scientific gibberish by the prestigious *New England Journal of Medicine.* As one scientific diplomat put it: "By no means have all studies of cell-mediated immunity in marijuana smokers or in vitro exposure of T-cells to cannabinoids - often conducted in exactly the same way - shown evidence of immunosuppression.... The responses of lymphocytes from the marijuana smokers were not significantly different [in many other controlled studies] from those who did not smoke the drug."[21] Nahas' studies, never repeated by another scientist, were so embarrassing that Columbia called a special press conference to disassociate itself from them and the NIH cut his funding, sending him to Europe.

Back in his native France, Nahas became an influential advisor to French conservatives, founding the "French National Alliance Against Toxicomania." "Toxicomania" is the Argentine fascist word for unauthorized inebriation, part of the name of their federal nark unit. The well-connected Nahas is now back at NYU, which is no doubt grateful for the NIDA funds he brings with him. Although the likes of Dr. John Morgan, professor of pharmacology at Mount Sinai School of Medicine, can dismiss Nahas' findings as "pseudo-scientific" and "undocumented,"[22] Nahas' political effect, his mission, is a complete success. The Attorney General, DEA, ONDCP, VISTA, DARE, The Partnership for a Drug-Free America and the rest quote him relentlessly. Worse, his gibberish is used to coordinate American and European policy.

A typical Nahas symposium, "For Health and Substance Abuse Professionals" was held in September of 95 at the University of Texas, sponsored by the "Houston Drug-Free Business Initiative." We were assured that all "drug taking is a behavioral problem."[23] Nahas' 1993 opus is *Cannabis, Physiopathology, Epidemiology, Detection*. It's strange to hear about the "epidemiology" of an herb many physicians would vote to reinstate in the *U.S. Pharmacopeia*. How does a medicinal herb get to be a germ? And why is a "physician" concerned with "detection"?

Nahas recently sued the French magazine *Maintenant* for libel for calling him a politicized fraud in an article by Michka, an ally of the *Mouvement de Légalisation Controlée*. Many of the most reputable scientists in Europe and America came to the magazine's defense.

Professors Christie and Chesher, of the Department of Pharmacology at the University of Sydney, published a review of a Nahas article entitled "The human toxicity of marijuana," which was published in 1992 in the *Medical Journal of Australia*: "We compared the claims of the authors [Nahas and Latour] with the information contained in the documents they cited and found that at least 28 of the 35 citations in this article were cited inaccurately.... All of these inaccuracies operate in the direction of finding an adverse effect of marijuana.... To fail to acknowledge the reported tobacco use and heavy alcohol intake gives the inaccurate implication that cannabis use was the sole risk factor in these cases....misrepresentation of...references."[24]

In just about the only honest bit of empiricism he has ever engaged in, Nahas publicly declared that "I am an enemy of cannabis and I will use all means possible to fight against cannabis."[25] In one of his "experiments," Nahas injected lab rats with the equivalent of 1200 joints worth of THC, adjusted for human body weight. Amazingly, the rats lived, which, it would seem, proves the exact opposite of Nahas' point.

Nahas was replaced as Columbia's "top drug expert" by the more credible Dr. Herbert Kleber, former deputy director of President Bush's Office of National Drug Control Policy. Kleber, an original promulgator of "zero tolerance," is now Califano's second-in-command at the Center on Addiction and Substance Abuse.

"Dr. Herbert D. Kleber, a top drug expert," writes Califano, "estimates that legalizing cocaine would give us at least 20 million addicts, more than 10 times the number today."[26] That's just what Califano said about Vietnam: if we recognize the Viet Cong, all Asia will go Communist! Well, we have recognized the Vietminh, and they're so grateful they're going capitalist. Califano clone Kleber is selling artificial hysteria, and is careful not to mention coca leaf products as an alternative to cocaine, they don't exist.

Kleber worked under Bill Bennett, the Orthodox Expert on the Meaning of Western Civilization. Bennett is another genius who understands all about drugs because he once was a nicotine addict. In fact, he couldn't assume the leadership of Bush's Office of National Drug Control Policy without first doing a few weeks at a therapeutic retreat to kick his heavy cigarette habit. He was forced to switch to the cigarette addict's equivalent of methadone, nicotine gum.

Bennett is now a chief spokesman for the Council on Crime in America, which is like making General Westmoreland a spokesman for the Council on Peace in Vietnam. This pious hypocrite, on *Larry King Live*, seriously suggested that the Saudis were a good model of the way to deal with drug dealers - by beheading them.[27] I can just imagine the reaction of the Gangster Disciples or the Cobra Stones to such a monstrosity perpetrated on one of their own.

Like Bennett and Califano, Herbert Kleber knows all about "drugs" because he used to be a tobacco addict. His hilarious title under Bennett was "deputy director for demand reduction." Rigid empiricist Kleber insists, *a priori*, that needle exchange programs don't work but that criminal punishment, *contra indicii*, would, "if applied swiftly and surely." Strict enforcement "is far preferable to proposals either to legalize drugs or to refrain from enforcing the laws prohibiting their use."[28] Next time I see Herbie light up, I'm gonna bash him in the face, cuff him and throw him in the slammer.

Kleber "argues that the current war on drugs has made substantial progress toward reducing drug use."[29] What's his idea of progress? Malaysia? Actually, yes. And conformist Japan with a 99% conviction rate, and even Communist China.

Kleber's Republican allies Gramm and Gingrich have actually proposed, in the National Drug and Crime Emergency Act of 1995, institutionalizing the Chinese system of penal slave labor. This system is already a fact in the U.S. Prison slave labor in California and Oregon manufactures textiles for export, and Boeing contracts for slave labor in Washington state's prisons. Dr. Jerome Miller: "In the 1930s, the Danish sociologist Svend Ranulf wrote about the German criminal-justice system. Everywhere he looked, he saw the need to punish. He excerpted a white paper written by the minister of justice for the Nazi Party in 1931 outlining their anticrime program - making prisons harsher, expanding the death penalty. It could have been written in Washington last week."[30]

Joe Califano's Center on Addiction and Substance Abuse at Columbia stokes this reefer madness with a steady stream of fake science. CASA is supported by the Carnegie Corporation, the Ford Foundation, the Kaiser Family Fund, the Robert Wood Johnson Foundation, the Commonwealth Fund, the superstar professional alcoholic Betty Ford and a host of national and international power brokers and agencies.[31]

CASA hosted the televised AIDS Awareness Day smarmfest on 12/1/95, "Tony Bennett: Here's To The Ladies," broadcast from the White House on CBS. Like many medicine shows, the entertainment was first-rate. Califano then pitched his snake-oil to President Clinton, who proudly accepted the "CASA Distinguished Service Award." In his acceptance speech, Bill Clinton assured us that "25% of AIDS cases are the result of drug abuse." That is political pandering, not empirical science. The fool actually helped to spread the epidemic by following CASA's insane advice and refusing to allow needle exchange programs. Compassionate outreach, Dutch-style, would "send the wrong message."

JAMA: "The news media continue to focus on the hundreds killed in drug wars but give little attention to the tens of thousands dying of diseases spread by IV drug use each year./According to the Centers for Disease Control and Prevention...from October 1992 through September 1993, 26,033 people...developed AIDS attributable to needles shared during IV drug use. Another 3576...developed AIDS though heterosexual contact with IV drug users. In addition, 397 children of IV drug-using mothers or fathers were diagnosed as having AIDS....Despite this great toll in death and the enormous strain on public health services, many political leaders still strongly oppose needle exchange programs, even though studies show that the programs are effective."[32]

Clinton's 25% figure is sheer fiction, a self-fulfilling prophesy. Even French conservatives support needle exchange. Needle exchange programs produce seroconversion rates near zero. Clinton knew that from the day he took office - that was the conclusion of the 1991 National Commission on AIDS, which criticized Bush's Office of National Drug Control Policy for "neglecting the real public health and treatment measures which could and must be taken to halt the spread."

Clinton's own 1997 AIDS Commission finally shamed his administration into allowing local needle exchange, if the locals were willing to pay for it. But Clinton still prefers to canonize a charter member of Bush's fascist team, Califano, and still continues to fund the ruthless police persecution of people suffering from chronic pain - medical users and neurotic abusers, as well as the vast majority of ecstatic users who are suffering from nothing more than ruthless police persecution. The result has been massive tragedy, an explosion not only in AIDS, but hepatitis, tuberculosis and other lethal infectious diseases. There isn't an epidemiologist in the country who wouldn't tell you that the best way to spread an epidemic is to drive it underground.

Oglala Shamans Call on Earth Grandmother, 1907

Drug War

The Cure

Today the fascist cancer, rationalized by the constant media pounding, has metastasized into massive arbitrary imprisonment and seizure of private property. Warned Fletcher Prouty: "We have been subjected to so many anti-American and pro-Communist notions all in the name of anti-Communism, that words and facts almost elude us."[1] For "communism" read "McGuffin," "McCaffrey," "drug."

"Imagine," Barry McCaffrey told the House Judiciary Committee's Subcommittee on Crime, 10/1/97, speaking of the medical marijuana initiatives, "a ballot initiative to change the rules by which the Federal Aeronautics and Aviation Air Traffic Control System manages commercial aircraft in California. It is disturbing to think that well-funded activists in one state could establish different procedures from the rest of the country on a matter that clearly affects the well-being of all of us."

McCaffrey literally equated, as do the laws, the intensely personal doctor-patient relationship with interstate commercial aviation, as if our own bodies were public carriers on which we must buy tickets. That, as Fletcher Prouty would say, is communist - the very essence of the bureaucratic rape of the individual. In fact, in February of 99, Al Gore and Barry McCaffrey literally announced another five year plan to cut drug use by 50% by 2005. A five year plan!

McCaffrey is answered by the lawyer who drafted much of the 1986 Anti-Drug Abuse Act for Congress, Eric Sterling, Counsel to the same House Judiciary Committee from 1979 to 89. Sterling saw the sharp distinction he drew between street-level quantities and dealer-level quantities destroyed in committee by grandstanding hardliners, so that kids caught on the street are now routinely facing mandatory sentences designed for big-time wholesalers. A $20 sale of cocaine on the street brings the same sentence as attempted murder. Sterling was so shocked by the cruelty that he has become one of the most effective legalization advocates in the country:

"The powers not delegated to the United States by the Constitution are reserved to the people. Where is the power in Article I, Section 8 of the Constitution that allows Congress to say, 'We declare that your brain is off limits to you. You cannot use those cells in your brain that opium can affect, or that marijuana stimulates. Your brain is not really yours to control. The space between your ears - that's not really yours to control. We're the Congress. That's our space. You are prohibited from using your brain in unapproved ways.' Is this a power that Congress has? If so, where did it get it and when?....is your brain interstate commerce? Is your bedroom interstate commerce?"

"Essentially the legal basis for the war on drugs depends on the assumption of total power by the Congress and the Federal government to regulate the most intimate aspects of our lives, the very dreams that we have. And the propaganda arm of the war on drugs has been successful in persuading us to unwittingly surrender this vital power over ourselves to the Federal government. Indeed the propaganda of the urgency of the war on drugs has been so successful, many of our fellow citizens consciously believe we must surrender ourselves for the good of the state."

"Seen in this light, the war on drugs is the corner stone of an as yet unbuilt edifice of totalitarianism./Challenging the war on drugs is the most important issue facing civil liberties and the preservation of the Bill of Rights."[2]

Through Interpol, the CIA-FBI-DEA has recently popularized, and legalized, property forfeiture, entrapment, informer payoffs and wiretapping among European police. Some of Europe's more charming traditions, such as warrantless searches, limitation of the exclusionary rule, limiting the right to counsel and lengthening uncharged detention time, have been legalized in the U.S. through DEA efforts.[3]

The mandatory minimums, of course, destroy yet another traditional bulwark of civil liberty, discretionary sentencing from the bench.[4] Although more than a hundred mandatory minimums exist on paper, four of them, applying only to drug and weapons offenses, account for 95% of all mandatory minimums handed down.

Since the Rehnquist court has severely limited the exclusion of illegally obtained evidence, cops have very little incentive to worry about the legality of their searches. It is the innocent, of course, against whom charges are never brought, who suffer most from illegal searches. Like so many others, former Kansas City and San José police chief Joseph McNamara sees us sinking into "incremental totalitarianism":

"...putting hundreds of thousands of people in jail using illegal police methods. In 1995, state and local police made roughly one million arrests for possession of drugs. Such arrests should require a search warrant, yet very few warrants were used. In hundreds of thousands of cases, otherwise honest police feel justified in illegally searching people and then lying about it under oath. They call it 'testilying' or 'white perjury.' In cities all across the country, thugs with badges have planted evidence, sold drugs, and committed other drug-related crimes that are often protected by a police code of silence... In the minds of many law-enforcement officers, the enemy is automatically guilty and must be destroyed."[5]

According to Buffalo police, only 10 people were charged with drug law violations in 1989 in over 600 stops at the airport. At Denver's Stapleton Airport it took 2000 stops to make 49 small-scale possession busts. Because of the "drug exception to the Bill of rights," many of those 2000 innocent people had to submit to strip searches and confiscation of their cash, and were devoid of any practical legal recourse.[6] The DEA's own records prove that only 17% of forfeitures involve big-ticket items over $50,000.[7]

Since 1984 property forfeiture requires virtually no evidence at all, only "probable cause," that is, the same vague suspicion that can be used to justify a search warrant. "Probable cause" can include hearsay, an anonymous tip or the opinion of a dog. By arbitrarily defining the matter as "civil," not "criminal," no legal proceedings whatever are required.[9] And in civil forfeiture cases, the burden of proof is on the property owner to prove that the property had *not* been used illegally. The inanimate property is legally guilty until proven innocent. The courts have even held that property illegally seized may be forfeited anyway if the police can show "probable cause" at the forfeiture hearing.[10]

Since many states don't allow the seizure of homes, police have taken to letting the local feds file charges in home seizures. The DEA gives them as much as 80% of the take. This innovation was enabled by Reagan's Comprehensive Crime Act of 1984, which empowered the feds to split the take with cooperating local agencies.

Rep. John Conyers: "A law designed to give cops the right to confiscate and keep the luxury possessions of major drug dealers mostly ensnares the modest homes, cars and hard-earned cash of ordinary, law-abiding people. This was not the way it was supposed to work." Rep. Henry Hyde: "Federal and state officials now have the power to seize your business, home, bank account, records and personal property - all without indictment, hearing or trial. Everything you have can be taken away at the whim of one or two federal or state officials."[11]

If that's not a working definition of fascism, I don't know what is. Neither does conservative Republican Henry Hyde. Neither does liberal Democrat John Conyers, who introduced a forfeiture reform even more wide-ranging than Hyde's. But, adds Hyde, "Criminal-asset forfeiture - following a criminal conviction - is an appropriate punishment of the guilty who have been accorded due process. Civil forfeiture even has a proper place in the prosecution of the war on drugs, but not as it's now being widely abused."

Although Hyde, Conyers and their numerous cosponsors seem fairly sensitive, I fear the practical effect of these reforms, if any ever become law, will simply be Drug War damage control, as Hyde's caveat indicates. Their incremental reforms will actually make forfeiture more plausible.

At present, even if you are acquitted after seizure, the DEA isn't automatically obliged to return your property. You must sue. You have only 15 days to file an appeal protesting illegal seizure, and in order to do so you must post a cash bond of 10% of the value of the seized property (except for real estate or property worth more than $100,000). Hyde would extend that to 30 days - what a libertarian.

Forfeiture nightmare stories number in the thousands - homesteaders who have lost the houses they built with their own hands, parents thrown into prison for life and their homeless, heartbroken children sent to orphanages, crippled old folks who have had their homestead stolen and were thrown into prison for a decade because of a few pot plants grown by their children. Check out Families Against Mandatory Minimums, www.famm.org.

Thousands of cars, boats and planes have been seized because they were the vehicle for unauthorized personal consumption. The Scripps Oceanographic Institute had a very expensive research vessel confiscated because a crew member left the remains of a single joint on board.[14] That is straight out of the *Codex Theodosianus*, 438 CE, the ancient Graeco-Roman inquisitorial code, which, apparently, is canonical to the U.S. Supreme Court. The *Codex*, via Justinian's Code, became the basic civil confiscation law of the medieval Inquisition.

Another classic inquisitorial device legally employed by today's narks is the seizure of all money needed to hire a lawyer before indictment.[15] Defense lawyers often have all their financial records subpoenaed, forcing them to become witnesses against their own clients and withdraw from the case. As of 1986, should a defense lawyer accept more than $10,000 from an accused drug dealer, specifically for the purpose of legal defense, the lawyer can be charged with money laundering and drug trafficking. These tactics has been used to keep the best lawyers out of court.[16]

Worse yet, in 80% of all "drug-related" seizures the owner is never charged with any crime![17] The "drug-relationship" is pure fiction! As former New York City Police Chief Patrick Murphy puts it, "The large monetary value of forfeitures…has created a great temptation for state and local police departments to target assets rather than criminal activity."[18]

Between 1985 and 1992, confiscations roughly doubled every year, reaching a total of almost $3 billion in cash and saleable assets, and $2 billion in unsold assets by the end of 1992.[19] Explained a high-ranking DEA official: "Increasingly, you're seeing supervisors of cases saying, 'Well, what can we seize?' when they're trying to decide what to investigate. They're paying more attention to the revenues they can get and it's skewing the cases they get involved in."[20]

Before the cops shot Donald Scott to death on his 200-acre Malibu ranch in their October 2, 1992 dawn raid, they had his valuable property appraised ($5 million). Scott had previously refused to sell his ranch to the National Park Service, which ran a large recreational area bordering Scott's ranch. This refusal was apparently a factor in the L. A. County Sheriff's Department's formation of an investigative team composed of agents from the LAPD, the Park Service, the DEA, the Forest Service, the California National Guard and the California Bureau of Narcotics Enforcement.

Had their SWAT troops found a few pot plants, they could have seized the whole ranch. But they found nothing. Scott didn't smoke pot. Ventura County DA Michael Bradbury concluded that the police lied to obtain the warrant, that there never had been any pot grown on the Scott ranch, and that the raid was motivated by the desire to seize the property. He called Scott's death a homicide, as did the death certificate. Scott's heartbroken widow got $5 million from the cops for wrongful death. This story is famous because it is typical of thousands. The only thing unusual is Scott's wealth, and the settlement.

70-year-old Byron Stamate's 44 acre ranch was confiscated when he was caught growing a small amount of medical marijuana for his longtime companion, Shirley Dorsey, who suffered from crippling back pain. Since they weren't legally married, Ms. Dorsey was compelled, under threat of imprisonment, to testify against her man. Under the relentless attack of an ambitious prosecutor, on April 1, 1991, Shirley Dorsey committed suicide. She left behind this note:

"They want to take our property, security and herbal medicine from us, even though we have not caused harm to anyone. It is not fair or in the best interest of the people of society. I will never testify against you or our right to our home. I will not live in the streets without security and a place to sleep. I am old, tired and ill, and I see no end to the harassment and pressures until they destroy us."

In a precedent-setting 1971 case, the Pearson Yacht Leasing Company had one of its yachts stolen by the police because a renter smoked a joint on board. The Supreme Court acknowledged that the owner couldn't have known, but insisted that "statutory forfeiture schemes are not rendered unconstitutional because of their applicability to the property interests of innocents."[21] Straight out of the *Codex Theodosianus*.

That is, the need of the police "to deter" takes precedence over the Fifth Amendment. That is precisely what the Founding Fathers were trying to avoid when they wrote the Fifth Amendment in the first place. Warned Thomas Jefferson: "A society that will trade a little liberty for a little order will lose both, and deserve neither."

An informant can plant some pot in a remote corner of a 300-acre farm, report it to the police, and receive as much as 25% of the value of the farm on its seizure. That's the same percentage that "denouncers" got under Theodosius. The farmer can't claim ignorance because the mere presence of the pot is presumptive evidence of "willful blindness" or "negligence." Although the 1988 Anti-Drug Abuse Act provides for an "innocent owner" defense, the courts have generally interpreted this to mean that the farmer can claim to be an "innocent owner" only if he regularly scoured his land and uprooted the pot before the police got to it, that is, if he did all that "reasonably could be expected to prevent the proscribed use of the property."[22] That catch-22 can first be found, no kidding, in the *Codex Theodosianus*.[23]

Eighty year-old Bradshaw Bowman had his scenic 160 acres in southern Utah, and his home, seized because a convicted drug-dealer showed police a few pot plants growing on a hiking trail well out of sight of the old man's house, plants the dealer himself could easily have planted. Solely on the word of small time hoods out for cash, police have repeatedly filed forfeiture proceedings against expensive real estate, because they too stand to profit.[24] What was done to that old man is unspeakable, and it is being done by police in this country all the time.

You can be stopped, cross-examined and dog-sniffed at the airport, and if you protest you can be strip-searched. Even if they find nothing, you have no remedy. Cops can fly a chopper over your house in the middle of the night with the search lights blaring. They can, without a warrant, burst into your barn and search it.[25] They can kick your door down in the middle of the night, hold a gun to your wife's head and trash your home because an anonymous informant, a year and a half ago, told them you smoked pot. Even if no pot is found, you have no easy remedy, although you do have a longshot at winning civil damages. Such damages will be paid by the police out of their property seizures.

These outrages are committed daily in the U.S., and, thanks to the Rehnquist court, they're all legal. Although Nixon failed to get Haynsworth and Carswell to the Supreme Court, he did live to see Rehnquist, his Assistant Attorney General under John Mitchell, get there. "First class mail may be opened without a warrant on less than probable cause….Automotive travelers may be stopped near the border without individualized suspicion even if the stop is based largely on ethnicity…and boats…may be hailed and boarded with no suspicion whatever." These measures are necessary, explains the deep-thinking Chief of Republican Justice, because there is a "veritable national crisis in law enforcement caused by the smuggling of illegal narcotics."[26] Rehnquist has consistently demonstrated the anthropological sophistication of Harry Anslinger.

But, not to overstate the case against Rehnquist, he, and his fellow Justices Stephen Breyer and Anthony Kennedy, have been so shocked by the practical consequences that they have recently come out against manadatory minimums. Kennedy called them "imprudent, unwise and often an unjust mechanism."[26a]

The Sentencing Project, 1/91, identified the Drug War as "the largest single factor behind the rise in prison population during the past decade."[27] That rise has seen the U.S. imprison a higher percentage of its people than any other nation in the world. As of mid-1997, women made up about 7% of the U.S. prison population, as compared to 5% in 1985.[28] One-third of those were in for drug crimes, as compared to one-eighth in 1985.[29] Two-thirds of those were mothers of underage children. Would all those women be in jail if they weren't in such intense pain that they needed to medicate it? Why is self-medication a crime? What's wrong with taking pain killers if you're in pain? Why aren't safe *pharmakons* available? Whose body is it, anyway?

Many of America's best law enforcement officials and public health workers are asking the same questions.[30] A Hoover Institute poll of over 500 law-enforcement leaders conducted at the 9th International Conference on Drug Policy Reform, Santa Monica, 10/19/95, by former Kansas City and San José police chief Joseph McNamara, found that 95% thought the war on drugs was lost and 98% thought drug use wasn't primarily a police problem.[31]

McNamara:"When you're telling cops that they're soldiers in a

Drug War, you're destroying the whole concept of the citizen peace officer, a peace officer whose fundamental duty is to protect life and be a community servant. General Colin Powell told us during the Persian Gulf War what a soldier's duty is. It's to kill the enemy. And when we allowed our politicians to push cops into a war that they'll never win, they can't win, and let them begin to think of themselves as soldiers, the mentality comes that anything goes."

Baltimore's chief nark told the Drug Abuse Council in 1975 that Baltimore police were using 800 active drug dealers as informants, in effect licensing them to deal and rat on the competition.[32] Of course, with that much close contact with the dealing, cops end up choosing, for a price, which dealers will survive and which won't. No big city police force can function any other way, and no big city police force has ever made a permanent dent in the availability of drugs on the street.

McNamara points out that there isn't a major urban police force in the country that isn't thoroughly infiltrated by drug money. Hundreds of narks are indicted for extortion, murder or drug-dealing every year.[33] And the newspaper stories of police brutality during drug raids could fill a 600-page book annually.

In 1989, Freeway Ricky Ross, the greatest crack dealer in history, had his sentence radically reduced because he was "a percipient witness in a case involving serious misconduct." That is, Ross could back up the evidence of the FBI's sting of L.A.'s premier narcotics squad, "the Majors," who had gone into the extortion and resale business. I mean those cops were driving Ferraris.[33a]

"Mayor Schmoke described a school visit during which children told him that most of the youngsters dropping out of school did so not because they were hooked on drugs, but because they were hooked on easy drug money."[34]

Great dealing structures, like the Gangster Disciples, can use their army of wholesalers to front ambitious 12-year-olds a "sixty-pack" of ten-dollar crack vials. An outgoing hustler can sell-out in half an hour. The kid keeps a hundred, turns $500 over to the wholesaler, and gets another sixty-pack. The kid can make $1000 in a day, a mind-bending fortune to a 12-year-old, and the wholesaler, running an army of little hustlers, makes many times that. The cops end up at war with the whole neighborhood.

It wasn't alcohol that drove the Prohibition gangs - they were hoods, not drunks. In 1918 Wayne Wheeler, the head of the Anti-Saloon League, insisted that the "contagious disease of alcoholism" would be stopped by a $5 million appropriation to the Prohibition Unit.[35] By 1927 the beleaguered sixth Commissioner of Prohibition told Congress $300 million couldn't do it. God knows how many hundreds of billions in today's money we incinerate every year. Prison spending alone was up to $40 billion in 1994, a 1000% increase in 20 years.[36-37]

60% of all federal prisoners are in jail for nonviolent drug offenses, and half of them are first-time offenders, kids.[38] 19 year-old Keith Edwards was asked by a nark to score a little crack on the street for him. The trusting kid made a few bucks and was asked to do it four more times. The nark accumulated enough weight to charge the kid with felony dealing, earning him a ten year sentence without the possibility of parole, ruining his life.[39] The nark got a commendation for a felony bust.

Nicole Richardson; www.famm.org

In 1990, 17 year-old Nicole Richardson, a high school senior in Mobile, Alabama, was called by a young dealer working with her boyfriend Jeff. The dealer had been entrapped by a DEA agent while selling Jeff's ever-popular LSD to his fellow psychonauts. Nicole, who knew Jeff needed the money the dealer owed him, told the dealer, in the tape-recorded conversation, where Jeff might be found.

Since Nicole, unlike Jeff, wasn't a dealer herself or even a user, she had no information of use to the DEA. She was therefore unable to trade information for a lesser charge. She is now completing her ten years without the possibility of parole for that one unsolicited telephone conversation she had with a friend of her boyfriend. Judge Alex Howard, who had no sentencing option, complained that "this case presents to me the top example of a miscarriage of justice..." That young woman was *tortured*.

28 year-old Tonya Drake, a mother of four with no criminal record, was offered $47 to mail a package by a casual old acquaintance. She didn't open the package, which contained 8 ounces of crack cocaine. She was sentenced to 10 years in prison, devastating her four little children.[40] These stories number in the thousands.

Tonya Drake and her children; www.famm.org

Half the 150 lifers in Michigan's prisons are first-time offenders sentenced for dealing over 650 grams of cocaine, about 1.4 pounds. Each would have gotten a more lenient sentence had he bludgeoned someone to death. In 1992 the average murderer doing time in state prison was released after serving 5.9 years, so as to make room for nonviolent drug offenders.

In 1985, before the 1986 advent of mandatory minimums, the average drug sentence was 1.9 years. By 1995 the average drug sentence was 6.9 years.[41] New York State's laws are typical: the peaceful sale of $10 worth of coke to an adult is a Class B felony, a more serious crime than nearly stomping someone to death in an attempt to rob them, a

Class C felony.[42] The Cato Institute confirmed that nonviolent drug offenders with no prior record are, on average, sentenced to one year longer in prison than violent offenders.

All over the country prominent judges are retiring from the bench in protest against this federally mandated savagery, and against the vast, overcrowded gulag it's creating. As of the end of 1996 more than 70 federal judges, who are tenured for life, have gone so far as to refuse to hear drug cases at all. That is an extraordinary protest, given that these are the most influential jurists in the country. These dissidents include as many right-wing Republicans as left-wing Democrats.

Judge Robert Sweet: "My contribution, if I have one, I think must come as a result of my experience as a trial judge, although some of my days as deputy mayor [of New York] might be relevant. The problem that was facing me in this present job [as U.S. district judge] is the sentencing of an eighteeen-year-old with no criminal record to a mandatory ten years because he sought to make $200 working as a security guard in a drugstore. Of course, it was the wrong kind of drugstore, and it was in the South Bronx, and there was a bust. That problem made me really focus on our present policy...."

"For me certain facts establish that the policy we have is a failure: An unregulated industry estimated to be at 150 billion dollars. Profit margins up to 5000 percent, federal expenditures of 11 billion dollars, an addict population of 5 to 6 million, and the greatest jail population in our history.[43] Looking at those facts persuaded me that money is the root of this particular evil and that the elimination of illegality would eliminate the money and the crime and that the money spent on balloons and interdiction would be better spent on treatment and education."[44]

Dr. Jerome Miller, author of *Search and Destroy: African-American Males and the Criminal Justice System*: "The war on drugs is causing far more destruction than the use of illicit drugs ever could. The widespread use of stiff sentences to force drug users and minor dealers to inform on others has helped escalate the violence. Gang-related murders have become the way young men are expected to establish membership in the group and convince fellow gang members that they're not snitches who will ever rat on them." The radical rise in the popularity of guns is directly attributable to the "search and destroy" behavior of the police. The reaction of a tough kid to police violence, and to the gang-up economics of Prohibition, is violence, not submission.

"Legalizing drugs would simultaneously reduce the amount of crime and improve law enforcement. It is hard to conceive of any other single measure that would accomplish so much to promote law and order."[45] Prof. Milton Friedman, a Nobel Prize-winning macroeconomic thinker, estimates that controlled drug legalization would free up 400,000 police officers, who could then get serious about serial, violent and organized crime. Of course, getting serious about organized crime has a political dimension that will appeal only to the truly antifascist.

According to the FBI, there were 1.35 million U.S. drug arrests in 1994. In the Netherlands there were 10,000, which translates to 170,000 for U.S. population. The 1995 U.S. figure is 1.5 million. Marijuana arrests throughout the U.S., 482,000 in 1994, nearly 600,000 in 1995, are more than double the arrests for rape, robbery and murder combined. "Legalize marijuana for everyone over 21," growled the *Oakland Tribune*. "That alone would take 450,000 arrests out of the system."[46]

By 1998 there was one marijuana arrest every 45 seconds around the clock, 1,900 a day, 700,000 a year. That, obviously, is simply cultural genocide, pure fascist violence - Jesse Helms' way of dealing with the sacrament of the 60's. This, despite the fact that there is no medical doubt that marijuana is safer and less "addictive" than cigarettes and alcohol. North Carolina's Helms, of course, is the Senator from Big Tobacco. He is often one of only two or three pro-tobacco votes in the Senate.

The popularity of the legal inebriants, of course, proves the deep craving people have for an inebriant. Cigarettes and alcohol are regularly used by 120 million Americans. Illegal drugs are regularly used by one-tenth that number, according to HHS. Cigarettes kill 450,000 Americans a year, alcohol kills 150,000, street drugs kill 6,000 and marijuana kills *zero*.[47] The hysteria about "drugs" is completely artificial. Bathroom accidents kill more people.

The popularity of cigarettes and alcohol is profoundly related to the unavailability of the safer and more calming herbal inebriants, like marijuana and coca leaf. Of the relatively few street drug deaths, a third were probably caused by combination with alcohol, and another third by poisonous adulterants. The 1995 Dutch drug-death figure is 42, which, adjusted to U.S. population, is about 700. That's 700:6000, the same ratio as all the other Dutch:U.S. crime and addiction figures.

According to the 1994 DAWN report of HHS, illegal drugs, adulterated or not, account for a grand total of one-half of one percent of U.S. emergency room admittances (500,000). Pot and hashish combined, according to these prohibitionists, account for less than a twelfth of that, and even that is an absurd exaggeration. Pot or hash is counted a "cause" or "contributing factor" if it was used at all, even if the admittance is for a broken nose. And pot is more different from hash than beer is from whiskey.

Nonetheless, even accepting these subterfuges, taking a shower, according to the Department of Health and Human Services, is considerably more dangerous than smoking pot or hash, which, I suppose, makes water a "substance."

In Holland, the Department of Alcohol, Drugs and Tobacco is part of the federal Ministry of Welfare, Health and Cultural Affairs. The Netherlands' top nark, isn't: "The Dutch do not rely heavily on criminal law and law enforcement in general. They prefer a policy of social control, adaptation, and integration to a policy of social exclusion through criminalization, punishment, and stigmatization," says Eddy Engelsman.

"I refer, for instance, to problems of highly priced drugs causing drug-related crimes, of prostitution and social ostracism, and of increased health risks such as AIDS. The effects of heroin and cocaine use are too often confused with the effects of their illegality."[48]

This anti-inquisitorial mentality has produced 15% of our addiction and crime rates, an efficient and humane criminal justice system that is neither overloaded nor corrupt, and the complete elimination of intravenous hepatitis and AIDS transmission.[49] The Dutch, in other words, with almost exactly the opposite policies advocated by American Prohibitionists, have achieved most of the strategic goals the Prohibitionists *say* they want to achieve.

Possession of pot, in quantities of less than an ounce, has been *de facto* legal in Holland since 1975, although technically punishable by 30 days in the slammer. Many Amsterdam coffee shops openly sell marijuana as a regular item on the menu. Kids, over 16, are intentionally allowed to rock out without incurring the hostility of the police. They are made to understand that this tolerance is conditional on their respect for their neighbors.[50]

Personal cocaine, heroin and amphetamine use is also legally tolerated, although technically punishable by up to a year in jail. Importation and large-scale dealing are severely punished, by Dutch standards: 12 years for isolates, 4 for pot, maximum. The spectacular result, according to the Dutch Ministry of Welfare, Health and Cultural

Affairs, is "virtually no young people under 20 using heroin or cocaine."

By making the safe herb available, the alkaloid's drawbacks become obvious. Where there is no legal and propaganda equation, there is no equation among users. According to the 1995 Ministry report, there are 25,000 heroin addicts in Holland, 1.6 tenths of one percent of the population of 15.1 million. That compares to 2.1-2.7 million heroin addicts reported by the U.S. Public Health Service's 1994 National Household Survey on Drug Abuse - about 1% of the population. That's 16:100. The USPHS adds that the 1% figure is probably a gross underestimation because the using population has been driven underground. Why is the U.S. rate of heroin use at least seven times higher than the Dutch? Why aren't we falling all over ourselves to adopt their policies? Again, we see that what is causative here is public policy, not pharmacology.

Since the Netherlands' few addicts don't fear public health workers, they can be weaned from alkaloids or stabilized with love and understanding, the only medicine that works. People addicted to pain killers are in *pain*, and people who insist on ecstatic use of concentrated compounds will continue to insist. The Ministry of Health actually finances "junkie unions" that encourages them to coalesce around newsletters advertising health and prevention related activities. 75% of Holland's heroin users are reached by government outpatient clinics, and most of those are on "methadone maintenance," a substitute palliative. "Heroin maintenance" would work just as well, but at least the lack of legal opprobrium allows the users to "live relatively normal lives," according to the Ministry of Health - that is, not to drive everyone crazy with their criminality. The clinics also offer free needle exchange, psychotherapy, group therapy and job placement. More stable older addicts are often simply seen along with their physician's other patients, and fill their methadone prescriptions at the local pharmacy.

Many cities throughout Western Europe have adopted this strategy with either methadone or heroin, thus bankrupting the local black market and eliminating crime. British policy has been leaning toward the use of formal cautions for drug users, rather than indictment, referring them to treatment instead of court.

Although the Criminal Justice Act of December, 1994, has expanded criminal penalties, the Department of Health remains more influential than the Home Office, so that addicts continue to have available to them clean needles, easy diversion from custody, detached work, and a variety of therapy and prescription options, including methadone and heroin maintenance.[51] These policies, in place since the late 60's, resulted in a 1994 HIV positivity rate near zero in Liverpool addicts. At this time the rate of HIV positivity in New York City addicts was 60%.[52] Volunteer needle exchange programs in NYC have since dropped that rate to about 35%.

In 1989, Sweden, debating the recommendation of the Council of Europe's Ministers Committee that needle exchange programs be adopted throughout Europe, decided to make free needles experimentally available only in Malmo and Lund, and unavailable throughout the rest of Sweden. The extraordinary result was a 60% rate of HIV positivity among Stockholm's addicts, and a 1% rate in Malmo and Lund, almost exactly the same difference as between New York and Liverpool. In Hong Kong, where needles are legal and cheap, there is no heroin-related AIDS at all.

Dutch addicts can actually exchange dirty needles for clean at the local police station. By not making addicts hysterical, Dutch police don't waste time chasing hysterical addicts. Since Dutch policy doesn't drive addicts to theft or start turf wars, Holland, in 1989, had 175 murders in the entire country, which would translate to less than 3,000 murders for U.S. population.[53] The actual U.S. figure was 20,000.[54]

Chicago Tribune:11/2/95: "Although drugs and violent crime often are linked in America, the violent crime rate in the Netherlands is far lower than in the U.S., despite the Netherlands' more liberal drug policies. There were 1.9 homicides in Holland per 100,000 people in 1993. The U.S. rate was 9.5 homicides per 100,000." "The effects of heroin and cocaine use are too often confused with the effects of their illegality."

Holland's pot decriminalization, according to the Ministry of Health, has produced a slight decrease in occasional pot use among the young. The Dutch figure wavers from year to year between 5 and 15% of 18 year-olds, half the U.S. figure, which wavers between 10 and 30%. Actually, none of these figures seem very reliable, given the enormous year-to-year fluctuations. But the generally lower Dutch figures indicate the same sort of calm adaptation that sociologists have been demonstrating in prescribing cultures for years. "We succeeded in making pot boring" explains Engelsman.

Holland's adult pot-use figures are about the same as the U.S. Pot is still popular in Holland, with 675,000 regular users, which translates to 11,500,000 for U.S. population - only 10% higher than the 1994 HHS estimate for the U.S.

In 1991 NIDA said 68,000,000 Americans had tried pot, so whether the 1994 HHS estimate is skewed downward is open to question. These are prohibitionist estimates based on samples of less than 5,000 people in a hostile legal atmosphere. The DEA's own Administrative Law Judge, Francis Young, in the 1988 ruling that recommended allowing medical marijuana, wrote that "20 to 50 million Americans routinely…smoke marijuana…" Nobody knows. Given the spectacular U.S. drug arrest rate, it is obvious that the "lower use" figures of the prohibitionists are like Westmoreland's "lower VC" figures - pure propaganda. That was the official conclusion of the 1998 American Bar Association study released on 2/4/99.

In any case, even according to current official figures, Holland's twenty-five year decriminalization of pot has produced almost exactly the same pot use rate the U.S. has with total criminalization, but one-seventh the alkaloid use rate. And, since it prefers to finance physicians rather than drug-gangs, Holland has virtually eliminated drug-related crime.

The Centre For Drug Research, University of Amsterdam; www.frw.uva.nl/cedro

So, if strategic success in the Drug War can be so easily demonstrated, why aren't we simply copying the successful model? Why can't rationality rule? Because the inquisitorial neurosis, upon which almost all our drug propaganda is based, is unconscious. Neurosis, emotional compulsion ruling conscious behavior, isn't susceptible to rationality. Sounds pompous, but it's true.

There is hardly an old Vietnam-era war-hawk today who wouldn't agree that we could have *bought* the Vietminh for a tenth of the price we paid to lose to them, because 20-20 hindsight is empirical, rational, unemotional. It's not hard to see now that buying them would have achieved the hawk goals as well as the dove. We could have had a base *and* a friend. But to make that suggestion in 1968, when American troops were under fire, was to risk getting your head busted - despite the fact that buying them would have saved thousands of American lives. Instead, in the name of Mom and Apple Pie, we "searched and destroyed" our way to complete defeat - destroying millions of lives in the process.

Who waved the flag of Mom and Apple Pie in 1966? Who insisted that the Vietminh were 5% of the population when it knew damn well they were 85%? Military intelligence. McCaffrey's Apple Pie propaganda is so emotionally compelling, such effective hysteria, that rationality hasn't got a political chance.

The extraordinary, ecstatic 60's threw the fascist power structures into their present inquisitorial mania, the worst, the most dangerous, in American history. The Drug War is a propaganda-fed neurotic repeat of the medieval Inquisition. I don't mean that metaphorically. The most common evidentiary bust of the medieval Inquisition was "the possession of prohibited substances." In fact, the legal phrase "prohibited substance" can be found in the *Malleus Maleficarum* of 1484 in relation to the "witches medicines" of the *curanderas*. "Possession," one of the premier *indicia* of "witchcraft," was the most common evidentiary bust of the Inquisition.

Today's propaganda barrage is a technologically-updated *duplicate* of that propaganda. History - the *psychology* of contemporary politics - moves much more slowly than technology.

The despicable Partnership For A Drug-Free America, financed by Big Tobacco and Alcohol, assures us that "This is not the 60's. There is no such thing as a safe drug," and that "60% of all rape victims are under the age of 18." We are then shown two teenage girls, dressed up as hippies, laughingly sharing a joint - amidst the libidinous stares of menacing bikers in the seediest part of town. And if the bikers don't get you, then the narks will, *in loco parentis*.

That the parental ostracism of partying teenagers drives them to rebellion and criminality was painfully obvious to the Dutch. The rape threat is an exact repeat of medieval inquisitorial propaganda, the medieval Devil wielding a joint even bigger than that of a hulking Biker.

The fixation on "sobriety" is as sick and manipulative as the fixation on celibacy or witchcraft. By "witchcraft" the medievals usually meant pharmacoshamanism, the essence of the spiritual spontaneity of pre-industrial cultures. Tribal cultures have always valued occasional spiritual intercourse with the "parental hermaphrodite," as the Greek Gnostics put it, that's why they called it "sacred marriage." When one is "in the spirit" in church, one is "drunk on God," not sober. Because of the social support, there is nothing dangerous about this state, but one would be insane to get behind the wheel of car. Not everything we do is an industrial activity, Bismark to the contrary notwithstanding.

Iasius, the healer, arises from Demeter's sacramental cauldron, amidst floating mushrooms and vines; from a Greek sacramental vase, c.500 BC; Cook

The Blood of Christ is only slightly less potent than the Blood of Dionysos, the ancient Cretan flower wine - spiked with entheogenic herbs. Mary, as Christian Gnostics have insisted since the dawn of Christianity, is Demeter.

The healer as the sacramental ram, from a Greek sacramental vase, c. 500 BC; Hill

But, of course, the early Greek Gnostics were heretical to the Church of Constantine the Slaver. By exterminating all traditional cultural knowledge of pharmacoshamanism, the traditional wisdom regarding its dangers is obliterated right along with the evolved wisdom regarding its correct usage. Nonetheless, thanks to its Greek roots, Christianity can't help but remember the herbal sacramentalism at the heart of its mystery.

An Attic sacramental vase, c.450 BC, depicting Dionysos as the tree from which the priestesses brew the entheogenic potion; Naples' Museo Archeologico

Obsessive fear of spiritual inebriation leads to an infantilized adult population that can't consciously contact its own inner being, its own automatic creativity, it's dream-genius. This infantilization leads to a political culture of conformist parrots. The traditional sacramental herbs are essential to social vision, since non-pharmacological methods of achieving deep subjectivity - musical, artistic, intellectual, athletic, therapeutic, sexual, karmic, religious - usually require an enormous amount of time and energy most people can't invest.

Such contact, however achieved, releases a torrent of healing creativity. That's why Plato would have made Eleusis' "fear-inducing potion" mandatory for Senators,[54a] and why Jung advocated "making contact with the psyche," which included not only psychoanalysis, but sophisticated psychopharmacology.

Marijuana is illegal, as Rasta shamans still insist, precisely because it is sacred to tribal peoples. The ancient Herb is a true sacrament capable of helping to call up the Holy Spirit of Jah. It is a connection to, real magic of, Holy Mother Earth - biological magic. But it simply is not legal anymore to be an Mbuti from the Ituri forest. It is no longer permissible to be part of the ecstatic forest, because that mitigates *against* industrial values. The forest, we are told, is no longer our awesome Holy Mother, but just so many board-feet of lumber, and the Mbuti, well, they can be made to haul the lumber. Slaver law - assembly line law - Suharto law - prevails.

It is perfectly reasonable for any employer to demand sobriety and concentration on the work at hand, especially if honest wages are being paid. Both the employment contract and the dignity of labor demand sobriety on the job. But to insist that the employee's free time belongs to the employer, that sobriety *off* the job is a condition of employment, is to outlaw traditional divinatory shamanism. People *need* socially-sanctioned methods of achieving deep subjectivity, just as they need love, and the social sanction itself prevents their widespread abuse.

As alcohol Prohibition abundantly proved, Prohibition *causes* alienated inebriative behaviors. It also, unquestionably, institutionalizes organized crime, military fascism, the driving engine of both the medieval Inquisition and today's Drug War. To allow the likes of the BIA, the WCTU, Wiley, Hoover, Anslinger, Bennett, Califano and McCaffrey to dictate medical and *pharmakon* law to our culture is precisely the equivalent of allowing the sadistic Kramer and Sprenger, authors of the *Malleus Maleficarum*, to control medical and *pharmakon* law in sixteenth-century Germany. It was done, but it triggered endemic bloodletting that drove the culture mad.

Jung: "Much, that is to say, that proves to be abysmally evil in its ultimate effects does not come from man's wickedness but from his stupidity and unconsciousness. One has only to think of the devastating effects of Prohibition in America or of the hundred thousand autos-da-fé in Spain, which were all caused by a praiseworthy zeal to save people's souls. One of the toughest roots of all evil is unconsciousness, and I could wish that the saying of Jesus, 'Man, if thou knowest what thou doest, thou art blessed, but if thou knowest not, thou art accursed, and a transgressor of the law,' were still in the gospels, even though it has only one authentic source. It might well be the motto for a new morality."[55]

That authentic source was Gnostic Christian, not Orthodox. Orthodox Christianity is too intentionally unconscious, building fascist political hysteria, a scapegoat, into its canon, as the Gnostics, who claimed descent from the Essenes, the *Iassai*, the "Healers," Jesus' Hebrew sect, did not. The difference between Christian *gnosis*, or for that matter any other kind of *gnosis*, and Orthodox Christianity is the difference between Christ, an Israeli war shaman who abhorred Roman slavery as the very definition of evil, and Augustine, a Roman slaver, who extolled slavery as the height of divine wisdom.[56]

It is the difference between Crazy Horse and Custer, between the Essene *Dead Sea Scrolls* and the Pauline *New Testament*. Although Paul's Greek was based on the Essene Hebrew, a whole hell of a lot was lost in translation (see *Shamanism and the Drug Propaganda*). Paul was not Jesus, however hysterically he and his followers confuse *eidolon* with *pharmakon*. *Iasius* ("The Healer") didn't say he was the *eidolon*; he said he was the *pharmakon*, what the Essenes, the *Iassai*, the "Jesuses," on Dead Sea scrolls we have, called "the plant of truth."

Despite its ethos of free speech - its great saving grace, instituted by Rosicrucian alchemists and radicals - this culture strongly prefers industrial servitude to personal art, and for the most part only industrial, public, values are taught and respected. This is a deeply ingrained historical characteristic of industrial Christian culture.

Protestantism changed the dogmatic Catholic image of Christ, which included a sacramental apprehension of the Mother of God. Mary was an image that Catholicism, the last great syncretism of the ancient world, was very careful to nurture. Evangelical Protestantism, a Renaissance German religion, instituted a more patriarchal Jesus, who stressed community and business ethics, and abhorred all mysticism.

Protestantism suppresses the ancient feminine imagery completely, burying the inherently pharmacoshamanic, the inherently ecstatic and sacramental, image of the Holy Mother. But the psychic pull of the feminine can't be so easily manipulated, since we are all born of the womb and first drink at the breast.[57]

Holy Mother Churches are powerful political institutions precisely because that's where many people, snug within the sanctioned confines of their adopted tribe, come closest to shamanic emotions. Shamanic analogues are the way inside the mind. Many churches, of course, are far more concerned with helping their communicants call up the Holy Spirit than with politics, and music is a fine substitute for pharmacology. Pan played the pipes. But it's good to remember that Pan was a Goat, not a Lamb.

Music is obviously a genuine shamanic technique with which innumerable communicants call up, or attempt to call up, the Holy Spirit every week. It is the fascist extrapolation of this, that, since we do it one way, all other ways ought to be illegal, that is the problem. That extrapolation, unfortunately, is built into Orthodox Christian theology. The fascist error is political, not necessarily religious, if such a distinction can be made within the confines of Pauline theology.

Inlay from the Soundbox Harp of Ur, c.3000 BC: "On meeting Gilgamesh as he searched for the land of the magical fruit trees, the scorpion-man says to his wife, 'The body of him who has come to us is flesh of the gods.'"

Buzz-word disinformation - constant, effective association of the archetypal herbal imagery with social chaos and stress - can manipulate a culture like a puppet on a string.

Theban sacramental vase, c. 700 BC; Harrison:1

Drug War

That is, sacramental herbal imagery - the Burning Bush, the Tree of Life, the Cross, the Blood of Christ, the contents of the Chalice - the *Kalyx*, the "Flower-Cup" - the Golden Apples, the Golden Flower - is instinctive. Like animal imagery, plant imagery comes up automatically in dreams.

The archetypal mammalian imagery is understood emotionally, unconsciously, leaving its recipients susceptible to authoritarian suggestion. Hitler used the wheel of life, the swastika, and the Star of David, both ancient shamanic images, to great effect with this technique. The Theban sacramental vase above dates to 700 BC. The swastikas have nothing to do with Hitler, but everything to do with the sacramental contents of the vase. If Christ is the Fish, then He is in the right place. That is a flower out of which His Mother arises.

Persephone and Demeter adore the Sacred Mushroom, from the temple wall at Eleusis, c. 450 BC

As Carl Jung puts it, "The conscious psyche is certainly of a personal nature, but it is by no means the whole of the psyche. The foundation of consciousness, the psyche *per se*, is unconscious, and its structure, like that of the body, is common to all, its individual features being only insignificant variants."[58]

The body, and its automatic imagery, are the sea we swim in. In a climate of legal industrial terrorism, the prohibitionist argument that sacramental herbs must be equated with social chaos makes perfect emotional sense because the target assumes that the planted axioms, rooted in its own dream imagery, are its own. It is the dream imagery that is sacred, not its demonization.

Social chaos, conducive to the militarization of culture, is also created by the legal equation of the ancient sacramental herbs with amateurishly produced street alkaloids and poisons - sort of like legally equating Judaism with treason and pedophilia, a classic technique Hitler got from the medievals. Below, North Africa's favorite sacramental herb, khat, with which untold generations of Yemenis have gone personally to sit with the Prophet.

Asia, c.1928

We have the politically sanctioned symbolic *pharmakos*, the *eidolon* Jesus Invictus, and its demonized *pharmakon*, any ancient sacramental herb, especially marijuana, the most gentle and accessible of the shamanic herbs.

Explained Quanah: "The White man goes into his church and talks *about* Jesus; the Indian goes into his tepee and talks *to* Jesus." As the Gnostic *Gospel of Philip* put it, 1800 years before: "You saw the spirit, you became spirit. You saw Christ, you became Christ....For this person is no longer a Christian, but a Christ" - or a Persephone, or a Miriam, as some Gnostic texts have it.[59]

To *become* the *pharmakos*, Quanah ate the *pharmakon*, not the *eidolon*. The *pharmakon* breaks Lucifer's spell; the *eidolon* is Lucifer's spell. That's what *Iasius*, the *pharmakon*, had to say. Like any powerful rabbi, he would have been nauseated to have been turned into a Roman *eidolon*: "Why do you call me good? No one is good but God alone. You know the commandments..."[60] He was teaching yoga, not posing for sculpture.

An ecstatic mind, in a state of blissful conscious harmony with its own unconscious, is hard to lie to and hard to sell, because it is the *inventor* of symbology and language, not its recipient. It is drawing directly from the universal font. It sees the future in terms of its evolutionary memory, its flesh-and-bone connection to the plants, animals and stars.

It achieves the sacred marriage between mammalian instinct and the conscious mind, leaving it in control of numinous powers.[61] Those powers reside in the Earth, the mother of our evolution - the pillow on which we dream.

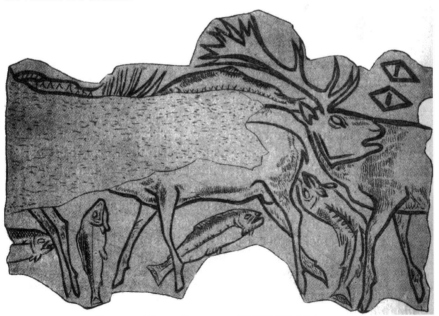

Engraved Bone, France, c. 13,000 BC; Mainage

That stag, and the floating-eyed shaman who carved him into bone, lived in France, 15,000 years ago. Should the Inquisition end, values other than industrial will pervade the culture. The thoughts of the animals will once again become visible. *Nektar* will again flow from the breast. Flowers will again reveal the respiration of the Earth. The "demographics," as they did in the 60's, will go haywire for the promulgators of the Official Faith. That's the peril the Bismark heads see in sophisticated adult shamanism. The assembly line would cease to be the official state religion. Mother Earth would be remembered.

By refusing to accept its animal nature, the culture can't rise above it. By not finding a place for Thoth, the ecstatic baboon, in heaven, the culture has condemned itself to hell, forever rolling the stone, on which it once rode in ecstacy, up Moloch's mountain.

An ecstatic Greek priestess holding the sacred herb carrier, the *thyrsos*, and the jaguar, symbol of her ferocity. She wears the magical snake in her hair - not a bringer of evil fruit, but symbol of her vegetal power to heal or destroy. The Brygos painter, c.490 BC.

Preparing the Sacramental Kava, Samoa, 1925; *Asia*

Preparing the Sacramental Kava, Samoa, 1925; *Asia*

Bibliography

Abel,Ernest L.:*Marihuana*:Plenum Press,1980
Achterberg,Jeanne:1:*Imagery In Healing*:New Science Libary,1985
  2:*Woman As Healer*:Shambhala,1990
Aeschylus:*Collected Works*:Herbert Weir Smyth,tr.,Harvard University
  Press,1922
Allegro,John:1:*The Sacred Mushroom and The Cross*:Doubleday &
  Company,1970
  2:*The Dead Sea Scrolls*:Penguin Books,1964
AMA:*The American Medical Association Encyclopedia of Medicine*:Random
  House,1989
Anderson,Edgar:*Plants,Man & Life*:University of California Press,1969
Anderson,Scott & Anderson,Jon Lee:*Inside The League*:Dodd,Mead &
  Company.1986
Andrews,George & Solomon,David:*The Coca Leaf And Cocaine Papers*:Harcourt
  Brace Jovanovich,1975
Apollodorus:*The Library*:Sir J.G.Frazer,tr.,Harvard University Press,1989
Apollonius Rhodius:*TheArgonautica*:R.C.Seaton,tr.,G.P. Putnam's Sons,1921
Ardrey,Robert:1:*African Genesis*:Dell Publishing Co.,1961
  2:*The Territorial Imperative*:Dell Publishing Co.,1966
  3:*The Social Contract*:Dell Publishing Co.,1970
Aristotle:*The Athenian Constitution*:P.J.Rhodes,tr.,Penguin Books,1984
Arms,Suzanne:*Immaculate Deception*:Bantam Books,1977
Artaud,Antonin:1:*Artaud Anthology*:City Lights Books,1965
  2:*The Peyote Dance*:Helen Weaver,tr.,Farrar,Strauss and Giroux,1976
  3:*The Theater and its Double*:Grove Press,1958
Ashley,Richard:*Cocaine*:St.Martin's Press,1975
Athanassakis,Apostolos N.:*The Homeric Hymns*:The Johns Hopkins
  University Press,1976
Augustine,Saint:*The City of God Against The Pagans*:David S.Wiesen,tr.,Harvard
  University Press,1968
The Badianus Manuscript:Emily Walcott Emmart,tr.,The Johns Hopkins
  Press,1940
Bailyn,Bernard,et al:*The Great Republic*:D.C.Heath and Company,1977
Bakalar,James B. & Grinspoon,Lester:*Drug Control In A Free Society*:
  Cambridge University Press,1988
Barber,Elizabeth Wayland:*Women's Work*:W.W.Norton & Company,1994
Barnstone,Willis:*Sappho*:New York University Press,1965
Barrett,Leonard:*The Rastafarians*:Beacon Press,1977
Baum,Dan:*Smoke and Mirrors*:Little,Brown and Co.,1996
Beowulf:Michael Alexander,tr.,Penguin Books,1973
Beschloss,Michael R.:*Taking Charge*:Simon & Schuster,1997
Boardman,John, Griffin,Jasper & Murray,Oswyn:1:*Greece and the Hellenistic
  World*:Oxford University Press,1989

2:*The Roman World*:Oxford University Press,1989
Bordin,Ruth:*Woman and Temperance*:Temple University Press,1981
Bourke,John Gregory:*On the Border with Crook*:Charles Scribner's Sons,1891
Brecher,Edward M.,ed.:*Licit & Illicit Drugs*:Little,Brown and Company,1972
Brewton,Pete:*The Mafia,CIA & George Bush*:S.P.I. Books,1992
Broun,Heywood & Leech,Margaret:*Anthony Comstock*:Albert & Charles
　　Boni,1927
Brown,Dee:*Bury My Heart At Wounded Knee*:Henry Holt and Company,1970
Brown,Peter:*Augustine of Hippo*:Faber & Faber,1967
Brunton,T.Lauder:*Pharmacology,Therapeutics and Materia Medica*:Lea Brothers
　　& Co.,1889
Budge,E.A. Wallis:1:*The Mummy*:Collier Macmillan Publishers,1974
　　2:*The Egyptian Book Of The Dead*:Dover Publications,1967
　　3:*Egyptian Magic*:Dover Publications,1971
　　4:*The Divine Origin Of The Craft Of The Herbalist*:Culpeper House,1928
Burroughs,William & Ginsberg,Allen:*The Yaje Letters*:City Lights Books,1971
Butler,Smedley D.:*War Is A Racket*:Round Table Press,1935
CAH:*The Cambridge Ancient History*:The Cambridge University Press
　　1:1:*Prolegomena and Prehistory*
　　1:2:*Early History of the Middle East*
　　2:1:*The Middle East and the Aegean Region, c.1800-1380 BC*
　　2:2:*The Middle East and the Aegean Region, c.1380-1000 BC*
　　3:1:*The Prehistory of the Balkans, The Middle East and the Aegean*
　　3:3:*The Expansion of the Greek World, Eighth to Sixth Centuries BC*
　　4:*The Persian Empire and the West*
　　5:*Athens: 478-401 BC*
　　6:*Macedon: 401-301 BC*
　　7:1:*The Hellenistic World*
　　8:*Rome and the Mediterranean, 218-133 BC*
　　9:*The Roman Republic, 133-44 BC*
　　10:*The Augustan Empire, 44 BC-AD 70*
　　11:*The Imperial Peace, AD 70-192*
　　12:*The Imperial Crisis and Recovery, AD 193-324*
Califano,Joseph A.Jr.:*Radical Surgery*:Random House,1994
Canfield,Michael&Weberman,Alan J.:*Coup d'etat In America*:The Third
　　Press,1975
Cantor,Norman F.:*The Civilization of the Middle Ages*:Harper Collins
　　Publishers,1993
Carter,Howard:*The Tomb of Tutankhamen*:E.P. Dutton & Co.,1972
Carthy,J.D. & Ebling,F.J.,eds.:*The Natural History of Aggression*:Academic
　　Press,1964
Castillo,Celerino III & Harmon,Dave:*Powderburns*:Mosaic Press,1994
Chomsky,Noam:1:*The Chomsky Reader*:Pantheon Books,1987
　　2: *Rethinking Camelot*:South End Press,1993
　　3: *Deterring Democracy*:South End Press,1991

Churchland,Patricia Smith:*Neurophilosophy*:The MIT Press,1989

Clark,W.E.LeGros:*History of the Primates*:The University of Chicago Press,1965

Cockburn,Alexander&St.Clair,Jeffrey:*Whiteout*:Verso,1998

Cockburn,Leslie:1:*Out of Control*:The Atlantic Monthly Press,1987
    2:& Alexander Cockburn:*Dangerous Liaison*:Harper Collins,1991

Cocteau,Jean:*Opium*:Peter Owen Ltd.,1968

Cohn,Norman:*Europe's Inner Demons*:Basic Books,1975

Cook,Arthur Bernard:*Zeus*:Cambridge University Press,1925

Copenhaver,Brian P.:*Hermetica*:Cambridge University Press,1992

Corson, William R,:*The Armies of Ignorance*:The Dial Press, 1977

Coulter,Harris L.:*Divided Legacy*:Wehawken Book Co.,1975

Coulter,Merle C. & Dittmer,Howard J.:*The Story Of The Plant Kingdom*:The
    University of Chicago Press,1972

Churchill,Ward & Vander Wall,Jim:*Agents of Repression*:South End Press,1988

The Creel Report:Da Capo Press,1972

Crystal,David:*The Cambridge Encyclopedia of Language*:Cambridge
    University Press,1987

Cultural Survival:*Coca and Cocaine*:Cultural Survival,1986

Cumont,Franz:*The Mysteries of Mithra*:Dover Publications,1956

Daniel,Glyn:*The First Civilizations*:Thomas Y.Crowell Company,1968

Darrow,Clarence & Yarros,Victor S.:*The Prohibition Mania*:Boni and
    Liveright,1927

Dart,Raymond A.:*Adventures With The Missing Link*:The Institutes Press,1967

Dartmouth:*The Dartmouth Bible*:Houghton Mifflin Company,1961

Davies,David:*The Centenarians Of The Andes*:Anchor Press,1975

Davis,John H.:*Mafia Kingfish*:McGraw-Hill,1989

DeKorne,Jim:*Psychedelic Shamanism*:Loompanics Unlimited,1994

Deno,Richard A., Rowe,Thomas D., Brodie,Donald C.:*The Profession of
    Pharmacy*: J.P. Lippincott Company,1966

Detienne,Marcel and Vernant,Jean-Pierre:*The Cuisine Of Sacrifice Among The
    Greeks*:The University of Chicago Press,1989

Dio Cassius:*Dio's Roman History*:Earnest Cary,tr.,MacMillan Company,1914

The Dispensatory of the United States of America,13th Edition:J.B. Lippincott
    And Co.,1874

The Dispensatory of the United States of America,20th Edition:J.B. Lippincott
    Company,1918

Dobkin de Rios,Marlene:*Visionary Vine*:Waveland Press,1984

Dodds,E.R.:1:*The Greeks and the Irrational*:University of CaliforniaPress,1951
    2:*Pagan And Christian In An Age Of Anxiety*:W.W.Norton & Company,1965

Drake,William Daniel Jr.:*The Connoisseur's Handbook of Marijuana*:Straight
    Arrow Books,1971

Drug Facts and Comparisons:J.B. Lippincott,1989

Dubois,W.E.B.:*The Suppression of the African Slave Trade to the U.S.A.,1638-
    1870*:Dover Publications,1970

Duke,Steven B. & Gross,Albert C.:*America's Longest War*:G.P.Putnam's

Sons,1993

Eisenberg,Dennis; Dan,Uri; Landau,Eli:*Meyer Lansky*:PaddingtonPress,1979

Eisler,Riane:*The Chalice & the Blade*:Harper & Row,1987

Eliade,Mircea:*Shamanism*:Princeton University Press,1974

Ellis,William T.:*Billy Sunday*:The John C.Winston Co.,1914

Ellul,Jacques:*Propaganda*:Random House,1973

Engelmann,Larry:*Intemperance*:The Free Press,1979

Epstein,Edward Jay:*Agency Of Fear*:G.P.Putnam's Sons,1977

Erman,Adolf,ed.:*The Ancient Egyptians*:Harper & Row,1966

Euripides:*Collected Works*:Arthur S.Way,tr.,Harvard University Press,1912

Euripides:*The Bacchae*:Michael Cacoyannis,tr.,New American Library,1982

Eusebius:*The History of the Church*:G.A.Williamson,tr.,Dorset Press,1965

Evans,Sir Arthur:*The Palace Of Minos At Knossos*:Macmillan And Co.,1921-1935

Evans-Wentz,W.Y.:*The Tibetan Book Of The Dead*:OxfordUniversity Press,1968

Finegan,Jack:*Light From The Ancient Past*:Princeton University Press,1959

Fleming,Paula Richardson & Luskey,Judith:*The North American Indians*:Dorset Press,1986

Fontenrose,Joseph:*The Delphic Oracle*:University of California Press,1978

Forbes,Thomas R.:*The Midwife and the Witch*:Yale University Press,1966

Fort,Charles F.:*Medical Economy During The Middle Ages*:Augustus M. Kelley,1973

Fowden,Garth:*The Egyptian Hermes*:Princeton University Press,1986

Frazier,Jack:*The Marijuana Farmers*:Solar Age Press,1974

Frend,W.H.C.:1:*The Rise of Christianity*:Fortress Press,1984

2:*Martyrdom and Persecution in the Early Church*:NewYork University Press,1967

3:*Religion Popular and Unpopular in the Early Christian Centuries*: Variorum Reprints, 1976

4:*The Early Church*:Fortress Press,1982

Freud,Sigmund:*Cocaine Papers*:Robert Byck,ed.,Stonehill Publishing Company,1974

Friedman,Milton & Szasz,Thomas S.:*On Liberty And Drugs*:The Drug Policy Foundation Press,1992

Furnas,J.C.:*The Late Demon Rum*:G.P.Putnam's Sons,1965

Furst,Peter:1:*Hallucinogens and Culture*:Chandler & Sharp Publishers,1988

2:*Mushrooms*:Chelsea House Publishers,1986

Gaskell,G.A.:*Dictionary Of All Scriptures And Myths*:The Julian Press,1973

Gaskin,Stephen:*Jurisdictional Statement*:The Farm,1973

Gelb,I.J.:*A Study of Writing*:The University of Chicago Press,1963

Gervais,C.H.:*The Rumrunners*:Firefly Books,1980

Gibson,J.C.L.:*Canaanite Myths And Legends*:T.&T.Clark,1978

Gimbutas,Marija:1:*The Goddesses and Gods Of Old Europe*:University of California Press,1982

2:*The Language Of The Goddess*:Harper Collins Publishers,1989

3:*The Civilization Of The Goddess*:Harper Collins Publishers,1991
Ginger,Ray:*Eugene V. Debs*:Macmillan,1949
Ginsberg,Allen:*Allen Verbatim*:Gordon Ball,ed.,McGraw-Hill Book
  Company,1974
Goldman,Eric F.:*Rendezvous With Destiny*:Vintage Books,1956
Gordon,Cyrus H.:1:*The Common Background of Greek and Hebrew
  Civilization*:W.W.Norton & Company,1965
  2:*Ugarit And Minoan Crete*:W.W.Norton,1966
Gosch,Martin A. & Hammer,Richard:*The Last Testament of Lucky Luciano*:Little
  Brown and Company,1975
Goshen,Charles E.:*Drinks,Drugs,and Do-Gooders*;The Free Press,1973
Goodall,Jane:*In The Shadow Of Man*:Houghton Mifflin Company,1988
Graves,Robert:1:*The Greek Myths*,George Braziller,Inc.,1959
  2:*The White Goddess*:Vintage Books,1959
  3:*Apuleius' The Golden Ass*:Farrar,Strauss & Giroux,1951
Gray,Mike:*Drug Crazy*:Random House,1998
The Great Geographical Atlas:Rand McNally:1989
Grieve,M.:*A Modern Herbal*:Dover Publications,1971
Griggs,Barbara:*Green Pharmacy*:The Viking Press,1981
Grinspoon,Lester:1:*Marihuana Reconsidered*:Harvard University Press,1971
  2:& Bakalar,James B.:*Psychedelic Drugs Reconsidered*:Basic Books,1979
Grossinger,Richard:1:*Planet Medicine*:Anchor Books,1980
  2:*Embryogenesis*:North Atlantic Books,1986
Guignebert,Charles:*The Jewish World in the Time of Jesus*:University Books,1965
Gutman,Roy:*Banana Diplomacy*:Simon & Schuster,1988
Haard,Richard & Karen:1:*Poisonous & Hallucinogenic Mushrooms*:Cloudburst
  Press,1975
  2:*Foraging for Edible Wild Mushrooms*:Cloudburst Press,1974
Haggard,Howard W.:*Devils,Drugs and Doctors*:Halcyon House,1929
Haller,John S.Jr.:*American Medicine in Transition,1840-1910*:University
  of Illinois Press,1981
Hand,Wayland D.,ed.:*American Folk Medicine:A Symposium*:University
  Of California Press,1976
Harner,Michael J.:1:*The Jivaro*:Anchor Books,1973
  2:ed.:*Hallucinogens and Shamanism*:Oxford University Press,1973
  3:*The Way of the Shaman*:Bantam Books,1986
Harris,Bob:*Growing Wild Mushrooms*:Wingbow Press,1976
Harrison,Jane Ellen:1:*Prolegomena to the Study of Greek Religion*:Cambridge
  University Press,1908
  2:*Epilegomena to the Study of Greek Religion*:Cambridge University
  Press,1921
  3:*Themis*:Cambridge University Press,1912
Hass,Hans:*The Human Animal*:Dell Publishing Co.,1970
Hawkes,Jacquetta:*The Atlas of Early Man*:St.Martin's Press,1993
Hawkins,Gerald S.:*Stonehenge Decoded*:Dell Publishing Co.,1965

Helmer,John:*Drugs and Minority Oppression*:The Seabury Press,1975
Herer,Jack:*The Emperor Wears No Clothes*:Hemp Publishing,1993
Herman,Edward S.:*The Real Terror Network*:South End Press,1982
Herodotus:*The History*:David Grene,tr.,The University of Chicago Press,1987
Hesiod:*The Collected Works,The Homeric Hymns and Homerica*:Hugh G.Evelyn-White,tr.,G.P.Putnam's Sons,1914
Hersh,Seymour M.:*The Dark Side of Camelot*:Little,Brown and Company,1997
High Times:1:*High Times Greatest Hits*:St. Martin's Press,1994
   2:*High Times Encyclopedia*:Stonehill Publishing Company,1978
Hill,G.F.:*Illustrations Of School Classics*:Macmillan and Co.,1903
Hinckle,Warren & Turner,William W.:*The Fish Is Red*:Harper & Row,1981
Hoffer,A. & Osmond,H.:*The Hallucinogens*:Academic Press,1967
Hofmann,Abbie with Silvers,Jonathan:*Steal This Urine Test*:Penguin Books, 1987
Hofmann,Albert:*LSD,My Problem Child*:J.P.Tarcher,1983
Hogshire,Jim:*Opium For the Masses*:Loompanics,1994
Holbrook,Stewart H.:*The Golden Age of Quackery*:The Macmillan Company, 1959
The Holy Bible:King James Version:Tyndale House Publishers,1979
The Holy Bible:Revised Standard Version:Meridian,1974
Homer:1:*The Iliad*:Richmond Lattimore,tr.,The University of Chicago Press,1967
   2:*The Odyssey*,Robert Fitzgerald,tr.,Doubleday and Company,1963
Howell,F.Clark & Bourliere,Francois,eds.:*African Ecology And Human Evolution*:Aldine Publishing Company,1966
Hughes,Muriel Joy:*Women Healers in Medieval Life and Literature*:Books For Libraries Press,1968
Huxley,Aldous:*The Doors of Perception*:Harper & Row,1954
Hyams,Edward:*Dionysus*:The Macmillan Company,1965
Inglis,Brian:*The Forbidden Game*:Charles Scribner's Sons,1975
James,Wharton:*Learning from the Indians*:Running Press,1974
Jayne,Walter Addison:*The Healing Gods of Ancient Civilizations*:University Books,1962
Jonas,Susanne:*The Battle for Guatemala*:Westview Press,1991
Josephson,Emanuel:*Merchants in Medicine*:Chedney Press,1941
Josephus:1:*The Essential Writings*:Paul L. Maier,tr.,Kregel Publications,1988
   2:*The Jewish War*:Penguin Books,1967
Jung,C.G.:*The Collected Works*:Princeton University Press,1956
   5:*Symbols Of Transformation*
   10:*Civilization In Transition*
   11:*Psychology And Religion:West And East*
   12:*Psychology And Alchemy*
   13:*Alchemical Studies*
   14:*Mysterium Coniunctionis*
   15:*The Spirit In Man,Art,And Literature*

Kahin,George McTurnan, & Lewis,John W.:*The United States In Vietnam*:Dell Publishing Co.,1969

Kaplan,John:*Marijuana-The New Prohibition*:Thomas Y.Crowell Company,1975

Karnow,Stanley:*Vietnam*:The Viking Press,1983

Karlsen,Carol F.:*The Devil in the Shape of a Woman*:W.W.Norton,1987

Kennedy,David M.:*Birth Control In America*:Yale University Press,1976

Kennedy,Jospeh:*Coca Exotica*:Fairleigh Dickinson University Press,1985

Kerenyi,Karl:1:*Dionysos*:Princeton University Press,1976

    2:*Asklepios*:Pantheon Books,1959

    3:*Eleusis*:Pantheon Books,1967

    4:*Prometheus*:Thames And Hudson,1963

    5:*The Religion Of The Greeks And Romans*:E.P.Dutton & Co.,1962

    6:*Athene*:Spring Publications,1978

    7:*Hermes*:Spring Publications,1976

Kerr,K.Austin:*Organized For Prohibition*:Yale University Press,1985

King,Rufus:*The Drug Hang-Up*:W.W. Norton & Company,1972

Kluver,Heinrich:*Mescal And Mechanisms Of Hallucinations*:The University of Chicago Press,1971

Kramer,Samuel Noah:1:*The Sumerians*:The University of Chicago Press,1963

    2:*Sumerian Mythology*:Harper & Row,1961

Krauss,Melvyn B. & Lazear,Edward P.:*Searching For Alternatives*:Hoover Institution Press,1991

Krippner,Stanley & Rubin,Daniel:*The Kirlian Aura*:Anchor Books,1974

Krout,John Allen:*The Origins of Prohibition*:Alfred A. Knopf,1925

Kruger,Henrik:*The Great Heroin Coup*:South End Press,1980

Kwitny,Jonathan:*Vicious Circles*:W.W.Norton & Co.,1979

LaBarre,Weston:*The Peyote Cult*:Archon Books,1975

Lacey,Robert:*Little Man*:Little,Brown and Company,1991

Lader,Lawrence:*The Margaret Sanger Story*:Doubleday & Company,1955

Lajoux,Jean-Dominique:*The Rock Paintings of Tassili*:Thames and Hudson,1963

Landels,J.G.:*Engineering in the Ancient World*:University of California Press,1978

Lane,Earle:*Electrophotography*:And/Or Press,1975

Lane,Mark:*Plausible Denial*:Thunder's Mouth Press,1991

Latimer,Dean & Goldberg,Jeff:*Flowers in the Blood*:Franklin Watts,1981

Lea,Henry Charles:*The Inquisition*:Russell & Russell,1958

Leakey,L.S.B.:*Adam's Ancestors*:Harper & Row,1960

Leaney,A.R.C.:*The Jewish And Christian World, 200 BC To AD 200*: Cambridge University Press,1984

Leary,Timothy, Metzner,Ralph, & Alpert,Richard:*The Psychedelic Experience*: University Books,1964

Lee,Martin A.& Schlain,Bruce:*Acid Dreams*:Grove Press,1985

Léons,Madeline Barbara&Sanabria,Harry:*Coca, Cocaine,and the Bolivian Reality*:State University of New York Press,1997

Levine,Michael with Kavanau-Levine,Laura:*The Big White Lie*: Thunder's

Mouth Press,1993

Levy,G.Rachel:*Religious Conceptions of the Stone Age*:Harper & Row,1963

Linder,Amnon:*The Jews In Roman Imperial Legislation*:Wayne State University Press,1987

Lindesmith,Alfred R.:*Addiction And Opiates*:Aldine Publishing Company,1968

Linklater,Magnus, Hilton,Isabel, Ascherson,Neal:*The Nazi Legacy*:Holt, Rinehart & Winston,1984

Loehr,Franklin:*The Power Of Prayer On Plants*:New American Library,1959

Long,James W.:*The Essential Guide To Prescription Drugs*: Harper & Row,1977

Lorenz,Konrad Z.:*King Solomon's Ring*:Thomas Y. Crowell Company,1952

Lyons,Albert S. & Petrucelli,Joseph R.:*Medicine*:Abradale Press,1987

The Mabinogion:Jeffrey Gantz,tr.,Penguin Books,1976

Maccoby,Hyam:1:*Revolution in Judaea*:Orbach and Chambers,1973
   2:*The Sacred Executioner*:Thames and Hudson,1982
   3:*The Myth-Maker*:Harper Collins Publishers,1987
   4:*Judas Iscariot and the Myth of Jewish Evil*:The Free Press,1992

MacMullen,Ramsay:*Paganism in the Roman Empire*:Yale University Press,1981

Mainage,Th.:*Les Religions De La Préhistoire:L'Age Paléolithique*:Desclée,De Brouwer & Cie.,1921

The Malleus Maleficarum Of Heinrich Kramer and James Sprenger:Dover Publications,1971

Mangelsdorf,Paul C.:*Corn*:Harvard University Press,1974

Marks,Geoffrey and Beatty,William K.:*The Story of Medicine in America*:Charles Scribner's Sons,1973

Marks,John:*The Search for the Manchurian Candidate*:Dell,1988

Marshack,Alexander:*The Roots Of Civilization*:McGraw-Hill Book Company,1972

McKenna,Terence:1:*Food Of The Gods*:Bantam Books,1993
   2:*The Archaic Revival*:Harper Collins Publishers,1991

McCoy,Alfred W.:1:*The Politics of Heroin in Southeast Asia*:Harper & Row,1972
   2:*The Politics of Heroin*:Lawrence Hill Books,1991

McCoy,Alfred W. & Block,Alan A.:*War on Drugs*:Westview Press,1992

McIlvaine,Charles & Macadam,Robert K.:*One Thousand American Fungi*:Dover Publications,1973

Mead,G.R.S.:1:*Fragments of a Faith Forgotten*:University Books,1960
   2:*Apollonius of Tyana*:University Books,1966

Meek,Theophile James:*Hebrew Origins*:Harper & Row,1960

Mellaart,James:1:*Catal Huyuk*:McGraw-Hill Book Company,1967
   2:*Earliest Civilizations of the Near East*:McGraw-Hill Book Company,1965

Mertz,Henriette:*Pale Ink*:The Swallow Press,1972

Merz,Charles:*The Dry Decade*:Doubleday,Duran & Co.,1931

Messick,Hank:*Syndicate Abroad*:Macmillan,1969

Mezzrow,Mezz & Wolfe,Bernard:*Really the Blues*:Doubleday & Company,1972

Mikuriya,Tod H.,ed.:*Marijuana:Medical Papers*:Medi-Comp Press,1973

Mills,James:*The Underground Empire*:Doubleday & Company,1986
Millspaugh,Charles R.:*American Medicinal Plants*:Dover Publications,1974
Milt,Harry:*The Revised Basic Handbook on Alcoholism*:Scientific Aids Publications,1977
Minucius,Marcus:*The Octavius*:G.W.Clarke,tr.,Newman Press,1974
The Mishnah:Jacob Neusner,tr.,Yale University Press,1988
Mizruchi,Ephraim H.,ed.:*The Substance of Sociology*:Meredith Corporation, 1973
Moldea,Dan E.:1:*Dark Victory*:Viking Penguin,1986
  2:*The Hoffa Wars*:Paddington Press,1978
Morales,Edmundo:*Cocaine*:The University of Arizona Press,1989
Moran,William L.:*The Amarna Letters*:The Johns Hopkins University Press,1992
Morgan,Lewis H.:*Ancient Society*:Harvard University Press,1878/1964
Morris,Desmond:*The Naked Ape*:Dell Publishing Co.,1973
Mortimer,W.Golden:*History Of Coca*:J.H.Vail & Company,1901
Murray,Margaret A.:1:*The God of the Witches*:Oxford University Press,1970
  2:*The Witch-Cult in Western Europe*:Oxford University Press,1971
Musto,David F.:*The American Disease*:Yale University Press,1973
Myerhoff,Barbara G.:*Peyote Hunt*:Cornell University Press,1976
Nadelmann,Ethan A.:*Cops Across Borders*:The Pennsylvania State University Press,1993
National Formulary XIV:American Pharmaceutical Association,1975
Neeley,Bill:*The Last Comanche Chief*:John Wiley & Sons
Neihardt,John G.:1:*Black Elk Speaks*:University of Nebraska Press,1961
  2:*The Splendid Wayfaring*:University of Nebraska Press,1970
Neumann,Erich:*The Great Mother*:Ralph Manheim,tr.,Princeton University Press,1974
The New English Bible:Oxford University Press,1971
NHL:*The Nag Hammadi Library*:James M. Robinson,ed.,Harper Collins Publishers,1990
Nilsson,Martin P.:1:*The Mycenaean Origin of Greek Mythology*:University of California Press,1972
  2:*The Dionysiac Mysteries Of The Hellenistic And Roman Age*:Arno Press,1975
  3:*Imperial Rome*:Schocken Books,1967
Nonnos:*Dionysiaca*:W.H.D.Rouse,tr.,Harvard University Press,1952
Oakley,Kenneth P.:*Man The Tool-Maker*:The University of Chicago Press,1959
Origen:*Contra Celsum*:Henry Chadwick,tr.,Cambridge University Press,1965
Osler,William,ed.:*Modern Medicine*:Lea & Febiger,1925
Oss,O.T. & Oeric,O.N.:*Psilocybin*:And/Or Press,1976
Ott,Jonathan:*Hallucinogenic Plants of North America*:Wingbow Press,1976
  2:*Pharmacophilia*: Jonathan Ott Books
  3:*Pharmacotheon*: Jonathan Ott Books
  4:*The Age of Entheogens*:Jonathan Ott Books
Ovid:*Metamorphoses*:Frank Justus Miller,tr.,Harvard University Press,1916

The Oxford Book Of Food Plants:Oxford University Press,1973
The Oxford Dictionary of English Etymology:Oxford University Press,1966
Pagels,Elaine:1:*The Gnostic Gospels*:Vintage Books,1989
2:*The Gnostic Paul*:Fortress Press,1975
3:*Adam,Eve,And The Serpent*:Random House,1988
Palmer,Leonard R.:*Mycenaeans and Minoans*:Alfred A. Knopf,1965
Pantaleone,Michele:*The Mafia and Politics*:Coward-McCann,1966
Parvati,Jeannine:*Hygieia:A Woman's Herbal*:Freestone Collective,1983
2:*Conscious Conception*:Freestone Publishing Co.
Patai,Raphael:*The Hebrew Goddess*:Ktav Publishing House,1967
Paterculus,Velleius:*Res Gestae Divi Augusti*:Frederick W.Shipley,tr., Harvard University Press,1924
Pausanias:*Guide To Greece*:Peter Levi,tr.,Penguin Books,1988
PDR:*Physicians Desk Reference:1989*:Edward R. Barnhart
Pei,Mario:*The Story of Language*:The New American Library,1965
Perowne,Stewart:*Caesars & Saints*:Barnes & Noble,1992
Peters,Edward:1:*Heresy and Authority in Medieval Europe*:University of Pennsylvania Press,1989
2:*Torture*:Basil Blackwell,1986
3:*Inquisition*:The Free Press,1988
Plato:*The Dialogues*:Harold North Fowler,tr.,Harvard University Press,1914
Plato:*Laws*:R.G.Bury,tr.,G.P.Putnam's Sons,1926
Pliny:*Natural History*:H.Rackham,tr.,Harvard University Press,1942
2:*A Selection of His Letters*:Clarence Greig,tr.,Cambridge University Press,1978
Polybius:*The Histories*;W.R.Paton,tr.,G.P.Putnam's Sons,1922
Porter,Joseph C.:*Paper Medicine Man*:University of Oklahoma Press,1986
Porphyry:1:*On the Cave of the Nymphs*:Thomas Taylor,tr.,Phanes Press,1991
2:*Letter To His Wife Marcella*:Alice Zimmern,tr.,Phanes Press,1986
Pritchard,James B.,ed.,:*The Ancient Near East*:Princeton University Press,1971
Prouty,L.Fletcher:1:*The Secret Team*:Prentice-Hall,1973
2:*JFK*:Carol Publishing Group,1996
Rappleye,Charles & Becker,Ed:*All American Mafioso*:Doubleday,1991
Rank,Otto:*Art and Artist*:Agathon Press,1968
Reed,Terry & Cummings,John:*Compromised*:Clandestine Publishing,1995
Reichel-Dolmatoff,G.:*The Shaman and the Jaguar*:Temple University Press,1975
Riebling,Mark:*Wedge*:Alfred A. Knopf,1994
Riedlinger,Thomas J.,ed.:*The Sacred Mushroom Seeker*:Dioscorides Press,1990
The Revised English Bible:Oxford and Cambridge University Presses,1989
Richardson,Cyril C.,tr.:*Early Christian Fathers*:The Westminster Press,1953
Riddle,John M.:*Dioscorides on Pharmacy and Medicine*:University of Texas Press,1985
Riis,Jacob A.:*How The Other Half Lives*:Dover Publications,1971
Robbins,Rosell Hope:*The Encyclopedia of Witchcraft and Demonology*:Crown Publishers,1959

Rodriguez,Felix I. & Weisman,John:*Shadow Warrior*:Simon & Schuster,1989
Roe,Derek:*Prehistory*:University of California Press,1970
Rorabaugh,W.J.:*The Alcoholic Republic*:Oxford University Press,1979
Rose,Jeanne:*Herbs & Things*:Grosset & Dunlap,1975
Rosenthal,Franz:*The Herb*:E.J.Brill,1971
Rotella,Sebastian:*Twilight on the Line*:W.W. Norton & Company,1998
Rothenberg,Jerome,ed.:1:*Shaking the Pumpkin*:Doubleday & Company,1972
    2:& Quasha,George:*America a Prophesy*:Random House,1974
    3:*Technicians of the Sacred*:Doubleday & Company,1969
Rowland,Beryl:*Medieval Woman's Guide To Health*:The Kent State University
    Press,1981
Ruck:2:See Wasson:2
    3:See Wasson:3
Ruspoli,Mario:*The Cave of Lascaux*:Harry N.Abrams,Inc.,1983
Sandoz,Mari:*Crazy Horse*:University of Nebraska Press,1961
Sanger,Margaret:*An Autobiography*:W.W.Norton & Company,1938
Sauer,Carl O.:1:*Seeds,Spades,Hearths and Herds*:The MIT Press,1969
    2:*Northern Mists*,Turtle Island Foundation,1968
Schlieffer,Hedwig,ed.:*Sacred Narcotic Plants Of The New World Indians*:Hafner
    Press,1973
Schlesier,Karl H.('S'):*The Wolves of Heaven*:University of Oklahoma Press,1987
Schlesinger,Arthur M.:1:*A Thousand Days*:Houghton Mifflin Company,1965
    2:*The Age of Jackson*:Little,Brown & Company,1946
Schlesinger,Stephen & Kinzer,Stephen:*Bitter Fruit*:Doubleday & Company,
    1982
Schonfield,Hugh J.:*The Passover Plot*:Bantam Books,1971
Schultes,Richard Evans:*Where the Gods Reign*:Synergetic Press,1988
Schultes,Richard Evans & Hofmann,Albert:1:*The Botany and Chemistry of
    Hallucinogens*:Charles C Thomas,1980
    2:*Plants of the Gods*:Healing Arts Press,1992
Scott,Peter Dale:*Deep Politics and the Death of JFK*: University of California
    Press,1993
Scott,Peter Dale & Marshall,Jonathan:*Cocaine Politics*:University of
    California Press,1991
Sered,Susan Starr:*Priestess,Mother,Sacred Sister*:Oxford University Press,1994
Shannon,Elaine:*Desperados*:Viking,1988
Siegel,Ronald K.:*Intoxication*:E.P Dutton,1989
Simpson,Christopher:*Blowback*:Weidenfeld & Nicolson,1988
Sloman,Larry:*Reefer Madness*;The Bobbs-Merrill Company
Slotkin,J.S.:*The Peyote Religion*:Farrar,Strauss and Giroux,1975
Smallwood,E.Mary:*The Jews Under Roman Rule*:E.J.Brill,1976
Smith,R.Harris:*OSS*:University of California Press,1972
Snyder,Charles R.:*Alcohol and the Jews*:The Free Press,1958
Snyder,Solomon H. & Matthysse,Steven:*Opiate Receptor Mechanisms*:The MIT
    Press,1975

Soren,David,Ben Abed,Aicha & Slim,Hedi:*Carthage*:Simon & Schuster,1990

Spuhler,J.N.ed.:*The Evolution of Man's Capacity For Culture*:Wayne State University Press,1965

Stafford,Peter:*Psychedelics Encyclopedia*:And/Or Press,1977

Starr,Paul:*The Social Transformation Of American Medicine*:Basic Books,1982

Stein,Philip L. & Rowe,Bruce M.:*Physical Anthropology*:McGraw-Hill Book Company,1989

Steinmetz,E.F.:*Kava Kava*:Level Press

Streuver,Stuart,ed.:*Prehistoric Agriculture*:The Natural History Press,1971

Sturtevant,Edward Lewis:*Sturtevant's Edible Plants of the World*:U.P. Hedrick,ed.,Dover Publications,1972

Summers,Anthony:*Conspiracy*:McGraw-Hill,1980

Swain,Tony,ed.:*Plants in the Development of Modern Medicine*:Harvard University Press,1972

Szasz,Thomas:1:*Our Right To Drugs*:Praeger,1992

2:*Ceremonial Chemistry*:Anchor Books,1975

3:*The Manufacture of Madness*:Dell Publishing,1970

4:*Ideology and Insanity*:Anchor Books,1970

5:*The Myth of Mental Illness*:Harper & Row,1974

Szent-Gyorgi,Albert:*The Crazy Ape*:Philosophical Library,1970

Tacitus:*The Histories*:Clifford H.Moore,tr.,G.P.Putnam's Sons,1925

Taussig,Michael:*Shamanism,Colonialism,and the Wild Man*:The University of Chicago Press,1987

Taylor,Arnold H.:*American Diplomacy and the Narcotics Traffic,1900-1939*:Duke University Press,1969

Taylor,Colin F. & Sturtevant,William C:*The Native Americans*:Smithmark Publishers,1991

Taylor,Norman:*Plant Drugs That changed The World*:Dodd,Mead & Company,1965

Telushkin,Rabbi Joseph:*Jewish Literacy*:William Morrow And Company,1991

Theoharis,Athan G. & Cox,John Sturat:*The Boss*:Temple University Press,1988

Thomas,Lee:*The Billy Sunday Story*:Zondervan Publishing House,1961

Thompson, C.J.S.:*The Mystic Mandrake*:Rider & Co.,1934

Thucydides:*The Peloponnesian War*:Thomas Hobbes,tr.,The University of Chicago Press,1989

Trebach,Arnold:*The Heroin Solution*:Yale University Press,1982

Tuchman,Barbara W.:*A Distant Mirror*:Alfred A.Knopf,1978

Turnbull,Colin M.:*The Forest People*:Simon & Schuster,1962

Ucko,Peter J. and Rosenfeld,Andree:*Palaeolithic Cave Art*:McGraw-Hill Book Company,1967

USDA:*Common Weeds of the United States*:Dover Publications,1971

The United States Dispensatory,26th Edition:J.B.Lippincott Company,1967

Utley,Robert M.:*The Lance And The Shield*:Henry Holt and Company,1993

Vallance,Theodore R.:*Prohibition's Second Failure*:Praeger Publishers,1993

Vaughn,J.W.:*The Reynolds Campaign On Powder River*:University of

Oklahoma Press,1961

Veninga,Louise:*The Ginseng Book*:Ruka Publications,1973

Vermes,G.:1:*The Dead Sea Scrolls in English*:Penguin Books,1987

2:*Jesus the Jew*:Fortress Press,1981

Vogel,Virgil J.:*American Indian Medicine*:University of Oklahoma Press,1982

Waley,Arthur:*The Opium War Through Chinese Eyes*:Stanford University Press,1968

Washburn,Sherwood L.,ed.:*Social Life Of Early Man*:Aldine Publishing Company,1961

Wasson,R.Gordon:1:*Soma:Divine Mushroom of Immortality*:Harcourt Brace Jovanovich,1968

2:with Ruck,Carl A.P. & Hofmann,Albert:*The Road To Eleusis*:Harcourt Brace Jovanovich, 1978

3:with Kramrisch,Stella, Ott,Jonathan & Ruck,Carl A.P.:*Persephone's Quest*:Yale University Press,1986

4:*The Wondrous Mushroom*:McGraw-Hill Book Company,1980

Watts,Alan W.:*The Joyous Cosmology*:Random House,1963

Webb,Gary:*Dark Alliance*:Seven Stories Press,1998

Webster's Third New International Dictionary:G.&C.Merriam Company,1968

Weil,Andrew:*The Natural Mind*:Houghton Mifflin Company:1972

Weil,Andrew and Rosen,Winifred:*Chocolate To Morphine*:Houghton Mifflin Company,1983

Wesley,John:*Primitive Remedies*:Woodbridge Press Publishing Company,1973

Whorf,Benjamin Lee:*Language,Thought & Reality*:The M.I.T. Press,1964

Willetts,R.F.:1:*The Civilization Of Ancient Crete*;University of California Press,1977

2:*Cretan Cults And Festivals*:Barnes & Noble,1962

Williams,Selma R.:*Riding The Nightmare*:Atheneum,1978

Williams,Terry:*The Cocaine Kids*:Addison-Wesley Publishing Company,1989

Wood,Michael:*In Search of the Dark Ages*:Facts on File Publications,1987

Woolley,C.Leonard:1:*The Sumerians*:W.W.Norton & Co.,1965

2:*Ur of the Chaldees*:W.W.Norton & Company,1965

Young,James Harvey:*The Toadstool Millionaires*:Princeton University Press, 1961

Zimmer,Lynn:*Marijuana Myths, Marijuana Facts*:The Open Center Institute,1997

Journals, pamphlets, reports, plays, magazines, newspaper articles and web sites mentioned in the text or the notes have not been individually listed.

Notes

Euroamerica

[1] Wesley:Preface
[2] Vogel:114
[3] Marks:14;44
[4] Bailyn:157
[5] Chomsky:1:128
[6] Marks:219
[7] Starr:48
[8] Rorabaugh:44
[9] Bailyn:411;414
[10] Marks:66
[11] Coulter:3:40;20;29;49
[12] Vogel:115
[13] Marks:145
[14] Haller:86
[15] Coulter:3:16;39;50;62
[16] Haller:48
[17] Haller:49;Coulter:1:223
[18] Haller:50
[19] Marks:240
[20] Coulter:3:59
[21] Vogel:101
[22] Vogel:226
[23] Vogel:227
[24] Vogel:117
[25] Vogel:50
[26] Vogel:215
[27] Vogel:11
[28] Vogel:116
[29] Dunlop in Vogel:121
[30] Stone in Vogel:120
[31] Vogel:255
[32] Vogel:261
[33] Vogel:133
[34] Marks:185
[35] Starr:51
[36] Starr:96;Coulter:3:6;92
[37] Vogel:134
[38] Goldman:98
[39] Jung:10:45-49
[40] Bourke:133
[41] Bourke:37
[42] Bourke:134
[43] Porter:8
[44] Taylor:78
[45] Taylor:54
[46] Slotkin:83
[47] Neely:90
[48] Brown:131-140
[49] Bourke:273
[50] Bourke:277
[51] Taylor:113
[52] Bourke:312
[53] Porter:60
[54] Bourke:415
[55] Porter:85
[56] Porter:67
[57] Porter:66
[58] Slotkin:87
[59] Morgan:7
[60] Morgan:22;33;41;42;51;57;59
[61] Morgan:42
[62] Bourke:484
[63] *Survey*:5/13/1916
[64] Hesiod:*Theogony*:53
[65] Cartier in Vogel:4;249; Lacourciere in Hand:204
[66] Vogel:10
[67] Schultes in Swain: 105
[68] Riddle:132
[69] Crystal:6;407
[70] Whorf:134-159
[71] Crystal:4
[72] Haller:134
[73] Bailyn:993
[74] Porter:65
[75] Porter:61
[76] Bourke:427
[77] Porter:69
[78] Bourke:217;437
[79] Porter:144
[80] Bourke:459
[81] Porter:170
[82] Porter:153
[83] Bourke:468
[84] Porter:308
[85] Fleming:72
[86] Fleming:74;Churchill:111

[87] Slotkin:89
[88] Slotkin:93
[89] Fleming:181
[90] Porter:264
[91] Neihardt:262
[92] Brown:431-445;170;Utley:269-314

Mescal

[1] Brecher:338
[2] Kluver:8
[3] Myerhoff
[4] Schultes & Hofmann:1:27
[5] Vogel:166;Emboden in Hand; Myerhoff
[6] NHL:147
[7] *Heresies*:1:5:4;in Pagels:1:144
[8] Slotkin:112
[9] Vermes:1:187
[10] Rothenberg:1:363
[11] Goldstein in Krauss:402
[12] Churchland:67-69
[13] Vermes:1:187
[14] Schultes & Hofmann:1:25-27
[15] AMA:405
[16] Snyder & Matthysse
[17] Hogshire:49
[18] Slotkin:36-50
[19] LaBarre:15
[20] Slotkin:106
[21] Slotkin:126
[22] Minucius:*Octavius*:9
[23] *Commonweal*:4/24/29
[24] LaBarre:23;Ott:4:21
[25] *Malleus*:2:1:16
[26] Allen in Cultural Survival:42
[27] Reichel-Dolmatoff in Schlieffer:74
[28] Taussig
[29] *JAMA*:4/9/1921
[30] Robbins:93
[31] *New York Times*:1/6/23
[32] *New York Times*:1/14/23
[33] *Commonweal*:4/24/1929
[34] Brown:437
[35] Slotkin:52;125;129

Inquisition

[1] Myerhoff in Hand:107
[2] Jung:13:85;305
[3] Jung:13:161
[4] Williams:139
[5] Artaud:2:10
[6] Vogel:50
[7] Vogel:231
[8] Vogel:232:238-44
[9] Haller:51
[10] Coulter:3:40
[11] Haller:76
[12] Haller:166
[13] Haller:162
[14] Haller:166
[15] Haller:164
[16] Haller:164-75
[17] Gebhard in Hand:91
[18] Haller:85
[19] Haller:49
[20] Coulter:3:69
[21] Haller:36
[22] Haller:64
[23] Haller:99
[24] Haller:91
[25] Haller:98
[26] Young:193
[27] Holbrook:214
[28] Holbrook:105
[29] Marks:158
[30] Cook:91
[31] Cook:88;Holbrook:59
[32] Vogel;Millspaugh;Grieve;Rose
[33] Holbrook:65
[34] Harner:1;Murray:1;Forbes:121
[35] *Disp*:20:427
[36] Wasson:2
[37] Haller:150
[38] Forbes:121
[39] Robbins:364;511
[40] Murray:1:91
[41] Broun:143
[42] 42nd Congress: Sess.III: Ch.258:

1873
[43] Lader:48
[44] *Malleus Maleficarum*:1:6;11
[45] Robbins:178
[46] Robbins:178
[47] *Malleus Maleficarum*:3
[48] Augustine:*Concerning Heresies*:46 in Peters:1:35
[49] *Malleus Maleficarum*:2:1:2
[50] Broun:155
[51] Lader:48
[52] Sanger:109
[53] Lader:57
[54] Sanger:112
[55] Broun:249
[56] Kennedy:43
[57] Sanger:111
[58] Broun:169
[59] Lader:55
[60] Sanger:81
[61] Jonas:179
[62] Lader:43
[63] Lader:45
[64] Lader:36;45
[65] Furnas:235;252;277;Bordin:39
[66] Bordin:3
[67] Furnas:281;284
[68] Kerr:48
[69] Furnas:284
[70] Bordin:9
[71] Bordin:94
[72] Bordin:57
[73] Bordin:54
[74] Bordin:109
[75] Kerr:49
[76] Furnas:193
[77] Furnas:189
[78] Kerr:127
[79] Engelmann:37
[80] Kerr:98
[81] Kerr:154
[82] Thomas:106
[83] Engelmann:2
[84] Furnas:305
[85] Engelmann:11

Monopoly

[1] Ashley:63
[2] *New York Times*:6/12/1918
[3] *Disp*:20:110-12
[4] *JAMA*:2/6/1915
[5] *Good Housekeeping*:10/1912
[6] *Disp*:20:820
[7] *Disp*:20:280
[8] 59th Congress:Sess.I: Ch.3915:1906
[9] Bailyn:930
[10] Gaskin:B-7
[11] *Harper's*:4/17/1915
[12] Coulter:3:262-271
[13] Haller:126
[14] Haller:201
[15] Haller:213
[16] Coulter:3:446
[17] Starr:121
[18] Coulter:3:447
[19] Haller:176
[20] Haller:178
[21] Haller:178
[22] Haller:186
[23] Starr:127
[24] Arms
[25] Deno:11
[26] Josephson
[27] Josephson;Starr:132
[28] Coulter:1:348
[29] Coulter:1:350-380
[30] *A.J.Pharm*:11/1902
[31] Shannon:76
[32] Ames:*Science*:221:1256(9/23/83)
[33] Carter in Cultural Survival:7;8
[34] Mortimer in Cultural Survival
[35] Davies
[36] Freud:47
[37] Freud:261
[38] Freud:77
[39] Musto:7;Andrews & Solomon:247
[40] *A.J.Pharm*:10/1903
[41] King:40-46
[42] Szasz:1:53
[43] *Sat.Eve.Post*:2/16/29

Black Fiends

[1] Barrett in Hand:297
[2] *Sci.Amer*:8/1/1891
[3] *Lit.Dig*:1/18/1920
[4] Schultes & Hofmann:1:238;Ott:4:24
[5] Speyrer in *Primal Feelings Newsletter*:11:Winter 95-96
[6] Bordin:104
[7] Hobson:2:28
[8] Musto:277

White Hope

[1] Musto:289;291
[2] Brecher:46;Ott:personal communication
[3] Taylor,Arnold:126
[4] Trebach:167;McCoy:2:382
[5] Brecher:22;34
[6] *Science*:7/18/96;Baum:220
[7] Gimbutas:3:196
[8] Palmer:205
[9] Pliny:*NH*:23:159;24:50;21:126
[10] McCoy:2:3
[11] McCoy:2:78
[12] McCoy:2:148;Ott:personal communication
[13] McCoy:2:97
[14] *Disp*:20:651
[15] Brecher:46
[16] McCoy:2:271
[17] Snyder:3
[18] Snyder:188;Milt:81-85
[19] Snyder:202
[20] Schultes & Hofmann:349;Drug Facts:575
[21] *JAMA*:6/1/94:1642
[22] Rosenthal in Krauss:228
[23] Achterberg:1:9
[24] Achterberg:1:99
[25] Duke & Gross:300
[26] Eliade:215
[27] *JAMA*:v.271#21:6/1/94:1648

[28] *JAMA*:v.271#21:6/1/94:1647
[29] Helmer:40
[30] Brecher:62
[31] Ostrowski in Krauss:312

Propaganda

[1] 63rd Congress:Sess.III:Ch.I:1914
[2] Musto:43
[3] Musto:255
[4] 63rd Congress:Sess.III:Ch.I:1914
[5] *Deterring Democracy*:Noam Chomsky:Ch.4
[6] Musto:267
[7] Musto:264
[8] Sanger:74
[9] Bailyn:970
[10] Schlesinger & Kinzer:80
[11] Scott:156
[12] Rappleye:74
[13] *High Times*:1:128
[14] *Popular Mechanics*:12/1941
[15] *High Times*:1:124
[16] Frazier:49-71
[17] *The Nation*:3/12/30
[18] Musto:207;Lacey:60
[19] Herer:1-40
[20] *Literary Digest*:2/6/1937; Theoharis:119
[21] Eisenberg:167; Theoharis:148; McCoy:2:27
[22] Scott:146
[23] Bailyn:1023
[24] Goldman:222
[25] Bailyn:1026
[26] Ginger:421;428
[27] Bailyn:1058
[28] Theoharis:52;58
[29] *Harper's*:1/16/1915
[30] Young:234
[31] *NYT*:4/27/52;5/6/52;11/24/53;7/18/54;8/29/54;*Am. Mercury*:9/53; *Reader's Dig.*:2/55
[32] McCoy:222
[33] Kruger:16;Scott:167

[34] *Lit.Dig*:2/1/30
[35] *Sci.Am*:1/31
[36] *New York Times*:1/16/32
[37] *New York Times*:10/10/33
[38] *Time*:1/13/36
[39] *Sci.Nws.Ltr*:12/21/40
[40] *Sci.Nws.Ltr*:2/23/57
[41] Califano:113
[42] Califano:98
[43] Califano:99
[44] Duke & Gross:105
[45] *New York Times Magazine*:1/29/95:41
[46] Califano:119
[47] *New York Times Magazine*:1/29/95:41
[48] Califano:120
[49] Califano:93
[50] Califano:119
[51] Morgan in Krauss:411
[52] Califano:124
[53] NORML:Spring 1995
[54] www.drugtext.com:2/23/96
[55] NPR:1/30/96
[56] NPR:1/30/96
[57] *JAMA*:6/1/94:1636
[58] *JAMA*:6/1/94: Skolnick: "Collateral Casualties Climb in the Drug War"
[59] Baum:268
[60] Califano in *NYT*:1/29/95:40
[61] *JAMA*:6/1/94:Skolnick:"Collateral Casualties Climb in the Drug War"
[62] Ostrowski in Krauss:314
[63] *New York Times Magazine*:1/29/95:40
[64] *NORML*:Spring/95
[65] Freud:47
[66] Mortimer
[67] Califano:126
[68] Krauss:314
[69] Califano:128
[70] *The Narcotic Peril*:Hobson:Int'l. Narcotic Ed. Ass.:23
[71] Musto:322;159:
[72] Epstein:44;Baum:70
[73] Trebach:259
[74] King:39
[75] Musto:107
[76] Musto:174
[77] Goshen:43
[78] Kerr:269
[79] *1998 Marijuana Crop Report*:Jon Gettman,Paul Armentano:10/98: NORML Foundation

Neocolonialism

[1] Duke & Gross:216
[2] 1 kilo of Southeast Asian heroin wholesales for about $110,000, according to the DEA, 1997. That's nearly $3,000 per ounce. Cut into bags for street retail, that's about $30,000 per ounce. Legal value, about $500. per ounce, retail.
[3] Reuters:10/4/95
[4] McCoy & Block:5
[5] *Excelsior* (Mexico):10/14/94;in Chomsky:"Rollback,"*Z Magazine*:2/95
[6] Scott:178
[7] Nadelmann:113
[8] Nadelmann:114
[9] Nadelmann:115
[10] Jonas:23
[11] Jonas:26
[12] Jonas:1
[13] Schlesinger & Kinzer:55
[14] Jonas:20
[15] Jonas:18
[16] Schlesinger & Kinzer:62
[17] Schlesinger:1:143
[18] Schlesinger & Kinzer:84
[19] Jonas:19
[20] Schlesinger & Kinzer:71-77
[21] Schlesinger & Kinzer:82
[22] Schlesinger & Kinzer:83
[23] Schlesinger & Kinzer:106
[24] Hinckle:79
[25] Corson:352

26 *Newsweek*:12/14/98:p.48
27 Smith:169;204-241
28 Prouty:2:25
29 Simpson:45
30 Simpson:7
31 Simpson:65
32 Simpson:56
33 Simpson:96ff;Cockburn,A:135
34 Simpson:145
35 Simpson:146
36 Simpson:179
37 Simpson:181
38 Simpson:132
39 Simpson:92
40 Anderson & Anderson:39
41 Simpson:185
42 Anderson & Anderson:43
43 Simpson:204
44 Smith:243
45 Robbins:44
46 McCoy & Block:254;McCoy:2:266; Cockburn,A:221
47 Mills:48
48 Smith:254;265
49 Smith:183
50 *Intelligence Connection*:Letter of the Month:10/96:From Burt Wilson
51 Smith:270;Cockburn,A:222
52 Smith:282
53 Anderson & Anderson:47
54 Kruger:131;Robbins:85ff; McCoy:2:165
55 Corson:322;McCoy:2:173; Cockburn,A:215;225
56 London *Weekend Telegraph*:3/10/67,p.25
57 McCoy & Block:255
58 Schlesinger & Kinzer:91
59 Hinckle:41
60 Schlesinger & Kinzer:88
61 Gutman:101
62 Schlesinger & Kinzer:184
63 Hinckle:33
64 Corson:382
65 Rappleye:179
66 Summers:355
67 Corson:367
68 Jonas:38
69 Schlesinger:274
70 McCoy:2:300;344;Cockburn,A:228; 247
71 Jonas:41
72 Schlesinger & Kinzer:234
73 Rappleye:149
74 Scott:110
75 Rappleye:169
76 Rappleye:163
77 Rappleye:150
78 Rappleye:152
79 Schlesinger & Kinzer:239
80 Rappleye:150
81 Jonas:70
82 Schlesinger & Kinzer:247
83 Anderson 7 Anderson:167
84 Chomsky:1:365
85 Schlesinger & Kinzer:247; Anderson & Anderson:185
86 Anderson & Anderson:189ff
87 Levine:80
88 Kruger:16;Lane:252
89 McCoy:2:352
90 Anderson & Anderson:137
91 Scott:109;Davis:160;168
92 Anderson & Anderson:23;37
93 Linklater:187
94 Anderson & Anderson:31
95 Hersh:158
96 Anderson & Anderson:168
97 Jonas:78
98 Jonas:78
99 Jonas:79
100 Jonas:95
101 Jonas:177ff
102 Jonas:95
103 Jonas:2
104 Jonas:90

Assassination

1 Lacey:121
2 McCoy:2:35

[3] Moldea:2:42;63;Cockburn,A:128-129

[4] Pantaleone:85;133;Kruger:14

[5] Scott:166;174ff

[6] Pantaleone:184-193

[7] McCoy:2:41

[7a] Cockburn,A:140

[8] Nadelmann:137;Cockburn,A:131

[9] *Foreign Relations of the United States:1952-54*:Department of State, Washington,D.C.:in Prouty:2:51

[10] McCoy:118;2:153

[11] Smith:352

[12] Kruger:129

[13] McCoy:2:131

[14] Kruger:133

[15] McCoy:126;2:197

[16] Scott & Marshall:4

[17] Gosch:159

[18] Hersh:134ff

[19] Rappleye:205

[20] Summers:285

[21] Davis:114

[22] Davis:317

[23] Davis:69

[24] Schlesinger:1:207

[25] Prouty:2:134

[26] Hinckle:100

[27] Corson:383

[28] Prouty:2:xxxii;130ff

[29] Lane:100

[30] Prouty:2:167-172

[31] Hersh:260

[32] Prouty:115-121

[33] Corson:391

[34] Corson:392

[35] Hersh:284

[36] Hersh:285

[37] Corson:399

[38] Hinckle:113-117

[39] Scott:196

[40] Theoharis:322

[41] Theoharis:326

[42] Kwitny:53

[43] Kwitny:83

[44] Kwitny:141;161ff

[45] Prouty:2:xxiv

[46] Scott:34

[47] *U.S.News*:4/6/56

[48] Scott:275

[49] Schlesinger:1:670

[50] Lane:102

[51] Scott:228

[52] Prouty2:148

[53] Lane:xiv

[54] Robbins:124

[55] Corson:402

[56] Prouty:258;Corson:349

[57] Schlesinger:1:357

[58] Prouty:43;100;104

[59] Prouty:2:100;124ff

[60] Prouty:109;111;409

[61] Corson:445

[62] Prouty:120;411;110

[63] Prouty:260

[64] Prouty:109;111;409

[65] Prouty:2:215

[66] Chomsky:2:Chapter 1:note 95

[67] Karnow:252

[68] Prouty:2:255

[69] Prouty:410;Schlesinger:1:284

[70] Chomsky:2:Chapter 1:note 91

[71] Chomsky:2:Chapter 1:note 91

[72] McCoy:2:140

[73] Smith:330

[74] Smith:354

[74a] Cockburn,A:97

[75] Chomsky:2:Chapter 1:note 95

[76] Chomsky:2:Chapter 1:note 60

[77] Karnow:268

[78] Lane:103

[79] Prouty:2:xxxiii

[80] Chomsky:2:Chapter 1:note 56

[81] Lane:103

[82] Lane:XV

[83] Davis:172

[84] Scott:260;Summers:92

[85] Summers:296

[86] Summers:172

[87] Summers:155

[88] Lane:32;Summers:222ff

[89] Hinckle:209

[90] Scott:79
[91] Scott:202
[92] Scott:207
[93] Brewton:193;Summers:248
[94] Summers:509
[95] Brewton:195
[96] Theoharis:311
[97] Theoharis:296
[98] Lane:332
[99] Hinckle:339
[100] Davis:401
[101] Scott:87
[102] Summers:300ff;Canfield:40
[103] Summers:304
[104] Summers:311
[105] Davis:119
[106] Davis:124;128
[107] Davis:90
[108] Rappleye:238
[109] Summers:326
[110] Davis:85
[111] Hinckle:205
[112] Anderson & Anderson:xvi
[113] Summers:329
[114] Summers:334
[115] Davis:131
[116] Summers:497;Davis:195
[117] Summers:337
[118] Davis:132
[119] Davis:187
[120] Summers:483;Davis:186
[121] Hinckle:204;Canfield:80
[122] Summers:332
[123] Lane:131;Summers:447
[124] Scott:265
[125] Davis:338
[126] Summers:321
[127] Kruger:145
[128] Rappleye:182
[129] Rappleye:183
[130] Rappleye:188
[131] Rappleye:198
[132] Hinckle:124
[133] Corson:362
[134] Corson:287
[135] Davis:400
[136] Rappleye:146
[137] Rappleye:223
[138] Rappleye:224
[139] Rappleye:225
[140] Scott:113
[141] Rappleye:268
[142] Rappleye:274
[143] Rappleye:271
[144] Lane:3
[145] Summers:460
[146] Scott:178
[147] Rappleye:177
[148] *The Inspector General's Report:An Introduction*:Peter Dale Scott:12/20/94
[149] Riebling:172
[150] Summers:437
[151] Summers:411ff;450; Canfield:125ff
[152] Summers:126
[153] Rappleye:245
[154] Lane:300
[155] Lane:152;167
[156] Lane:320
[157] Canfield:60
[158] *NYT*:4/11/68;Canfield:121
[159] Lane:82
[160] Summers:502
[161] Moldea:276
[162] Rappleye:8
[163] Hinckle:337
[164] Summers:505
[165] Scott:223
[166] Hersh:352
[167] Hersh:377
[168] Hinckle:167
[169] Lane:34
[170] Riebling:171;Hinckle:217; Summers:284
[171] Rappleye:238
[172] Scott:100
[173] Scott:103
[174] Scott:98
[175] Scott:100
[176] Scott:99
[177] Davis:58
[178] Messick:202

[179] Davis:34;266
[180] Theoharis:128
[181] Theoharis:252
[182] Rappleye:154
[183] Schlesinger:1:833
[184] Theoharis:395
[185] Summers:441
[186] Davis:368;Canfield:47
[187] Summers:356
[188] Summers:361
[189] Summers:261
[190] Summers:271;Canfield:96
[191] Summers:332
[192] Summers:350
[193] Summers:426
[193a] Prouty:2:24;Cockburn,A:155
[194] Summers:348
[195] Schlesinger:759
[196] Summers:419
[197] Summers:431
[198] Hinckle:196
[199] Lane:105
[200] Summers:434
[201] Lane:107;Hinckle:218
[202] Scott:296
[203] Davis:245
[204] Davis:249
[205] Rappleye:239
[206] Davis:263
[207] Davis:234
[208] Davis:280
[209] Summers:264
[210] Summers:427
[211] Summers:429
[212] Scott:119
[213] Lane:56
[214] Davis:153
[215] Summers:397
[216] Summers:506
[217] Scott:61
[218] Summers:363
[219] Summers:370
[220] Summers:369ff
[221] Lane:62
[222] Davis:150
[223] Hinckle:226;*High Times*: "Oswald and the CIA":Dick Russell:3/96
[224] Lane:64;Summers:386
[225] Davis:395
[226] Davis:247
[227] Summers:385
[228] Summers:392
[229] Scott:44
[230] Lane:68
[231] Lane:312
[232] Lane:69
[233] Davis:339
[234] Davis:343
[235] Scott:321
[236] Summers:63
[237] Lane:17
[238] Davis:191
[239] Summers:56
[240] Summers:54
[241] Davis:175
[242] Summers:476;Canfield:85
[243] Davis:190
[244] Summers:492
[245] Summers:111;Davis:189; Canfield:143
[246] Davis:387
[247] Canfield:145
[248] Summers:105
[249] Summers:77
[250] Scott:250
[251] *London Sunday Times*:6/3/74
[252] Davis:243
[253] Scott:248
[254] Lane:15
[255] Summers:240
[256] Summers:48
[257] Summers:14
[258] Scott:55;Summers:47
[259] *California Monthly*:9/95
[260] *Rolling Stone*:10/20/77
[261] Scott:128
[262] Davis:140
[263] Davis:142
[264] Scott:131
[265] Summers:492
[266] Canfield:158
[267] Summers:493

[268] Summers:466
[269] Scott:151
[270] Summers:458;Moldea:2:167
[271] Brewton:26;27;Kwitny:159ff
[272] Kwitny:52
[273] Rappleye:236
[274] Summers:286;Davis:360
[275] Scott:219
[276] Rappleye:238
[277] Riebling:171;Hinckle:217; Summers:284
[278] Hinckle:222
[279] Scott:174
[280] Moldea:2:91
[281] Brewton:315;Davis:319
[282] Scott:200
[283] Scott:181;201;Hinckle:288
[284] Scott:64
[285] Rappleye:246;Moldea:2:155
[286] Hinckle:216;Davis:144
[287] Scott:160
[288] Summers:490
[289] Scott:272
[290] Lane:17
[291] *The Nation*:7/16/88;8/13/88
[292] Lane:333
[293] Davis:139
[294] Schlesinger:1:833
[295] Brewton:20;297;Hinckle:47;325
[296] Messick:225ff

LSD

[1] Lee & Schlain:4
[2] Simpson:34;Cockburn,A:151
[3] Lee & Schlain:27-35
[4] Wasson:2
[5] Schultes & Hofmann:1:19;25
[6] *High Times*:1:167
[7] Kruger:162
[8] Lee & Schlain:27
[9] Corson:440
[10] *From The Wilderness*:1:4:6/21/98:www.copvcia.com;Marks:Ch.4
[11] Lee & Schlain:20
[12] Lee & Schlain:21
[13] Marks:Ch.4
[14] Lee & Schlain:24;Cockburn,A:200
[15] Marks:Ch.4
[16] Lee & Schlain:38
[17] Lee & Schlain:32;Cockburn,A:207
[18] Lee & Schlain:50
[19] *Tomorrow*:Spring 1961:"Peyote Night"
[20] Huxley:18
[21] Lee & Schlain:64
[22] Riebling, Mark:"Tinker, Tailor, Stoner, Spy":*Osprey Productions/Grand Royal*,1994
[23] Hofmann:ch.5
[24] Lee & Schlain::81
[25] Lee & Schlain:82
[26] Lee & Schlain:80
[27] Lee & Schlain:240
[28] Lee & Schlain:188
[29] Chuchill:189
[30] Lee & Schlain:250;281
[31] Lee & Schlain:225

CIA/Syndicate

[1] Prouty:120;411;110
[2] Prouty:2:326
[3] Prouty:120
[4] Prouty:11;14
[5] Scott:306; Hinckle:342
[6] Prouty:3
[7] Chomsky:2:Chapter 1:note 86
[8] Prouty:11;14
[9] Kruger:146
[10] Cockburn:101
[11] Cockburn:221
[12] Chomsky:131
[13] McCoy:2:x
[14] Kruger:147
[15] McCoy & Block:150
[16] Corson:413
[17] Kruger:124
[18] Kruger:125;McCoy:2:259;283;Cockburn,A:240-246

[19] McCoy:2:288
[20] McCoy:2:197
[21] Baum:72
[22] McCoy:2:219
[23] Karnow:426
[24] McCoy:2:250-254
[25] Kruger:93;McCoy:2:67;377
[26] Linklater:237;Cockburn,A:177
[27] Linklater:228
[28] McCoy:2:68
[29] Kruger:115
[30] McCoy & Block:263ff
[31] Kruger:121;McCoy & Block:13
[32] Moldea:2:351-2;Cockburn,A:239
[33] Hinckle:335
[34] Kruger:164;181
[35] Kruger:2
[36] Davis:370
[37] Lane:111;Canfield:87
[38] Davis:369
[39] *NY Post*:6/21/73
[40] Hinckle:300
[41] Davis:350
[42] Permission to reprint from Celerino Castillo and Michael C. Ruppert, *From the Wilderness@* www.copvcia.com
[43] Summers:522
[44] Hinckle:293
[45] Hinckle:306
[46] Moldea:2:104;155
[47] Davis:274
[48] Canfield:84
[49] Hinckle:28
[50] Rappleye:280
[51] Hinckle:279
[52] Hinckle:283
[53] Hinckle:325;McCoy:2:470
[54] *Wall Street Journal*:4/18/80
[55] Hinckle:287
[56] *National Times*:2/21/82;McCoy:2:461ff

Propaganda Due

[1] Kruger:173
[2] Nadelmann:116
[3] Kruger:165;Nadelmann:119
[4] Nadelmann:152
[5] Prouty:2:233;Cockburn,A:175
[6] Hinckle:310
[7] Cockburn:98
[8] Hinckle:293;Cockburn,A:294
[9] Brewton:304
[10] Kruger:8;Scott & Marshall:42
[11] Linklater:210;Cockburn,A:183
[12] Anderson & Anderson:101
[13] Kruger:10
[14] Hinckle:320
[15] Hinckle:324
[16] Kruger:14
[17] Brewton:307
[18] Brewton:183
[19] Brewton:182
[20] Brewton:184
[21] Nadelmann:182
[22] Reuters:"Interpol Chief Urges Drug Decriminalization";*The Boston Globe*:"Police Chiefs Appeal for Drugs Review";*The Independent*:6/9/94
[23] Reuters:10/4/95
[24] Levine:81
[25] Levine:4
[26] Levine:54
[27] Levine:160
[28] *High Times*:6/96
[29] Chomsky:3:Chapter 7:note 31
[30] Scott & Marshall:43
[31] Kruger:165
[32] Kruger:113
[33] Scott & Marshall:44
[34] Léons:10;Cockburn,A:181
[35] Linklater:267;Cockburn,A:179
[36] Levine:75
[37] Linklater:269
[38] Levine:57
[39] Levine:46
[40] Levine:59;Scott & Marshall:46;Linklater:289;Léons:13;119
[41] Levine:76
[42] Scott & Marshall:45

[43] Levine:79

SETCO

[1] Moldea:83;Rappleye:119
[2] Rappleye:48
[3] Rappleye:54
[4] Rappleye:70
[5] Rappleye:72
[6] Theoharis:255
[7] Moldea:141
[8] Moldea:116
[9] Moldea:342
[10] Moldea:290
[11] Moldea:299
[12] *Time*:8/8/77;Moldea:2:320
[13] Kwitny:154;Moldea:2:417
[14] Moldea:321
[15] Kwitny:252;288ff
[16] Kwitny:175
[17] Kwitny:152
[18] Moldea:319
[19] Moldea:302
[20] Moldea:331
[21] Brewton:198
[22] Brewton:45;393
[23] Brewton
[24] *From The Wilderness*:2:3:5/21/99@www.copvcia.com
[25] Fitts:Solari Memorandum Re:Welfare & Housing Reform:7/20/99:To Michael J.McManus,Esq. @www.solarivillage.com
[26] *Rolling Stone*:5/14/98:p37
[27] Szasz:1:113
[28] Duke & Gross:198; *NYT*:10/4/90:B6
[29] McCoy & Block:7
[30] Peterson in Krauss:274; Baum:256
[31] drugtext.com:2/26/96
[32] Cockburn,A:77
[33] Baum:250;Cockburn,A:77
[34] Bureau of Justice Statistics: "Prisoners in 1994," 1995
[35] Duke & Gross:170;Dr.Jerome Miller in *U.S. Catholic*:6/96; Bureau of Justice Statistics
[36] Webb:299
[37] Moldea:294
[38] Butler:1
[39] Chomsky:320
[40] *New York Times Magazine*:4/28/85
[41] *Z Magazine*:3/90:"The Decline of the Democratic Ideal":Chomsky: Note 21
[42] Hinckle:15
[43] Anderson & Anderson:176
[44] Anderson & Anderson:175
[45] Jonas:198
[46] Chomsky:365
[47] Jonas:149
[48] Congressional Record:5/7/98: H2970-H2978;Webb:482
[49] Jonas:150
[50] Anderson & Anderson:197
[51] Anderson & Anderson:194
[52] Anderson & Anderson:201
[53] Scott & Marshall:48
[54] Scott:111
[55] Webb:48
[56] Cockburn:7
[57] Gutman:267
[58] Cockburn:111
[59] Cockburn:71
[60] AP:7/15/93:"U.S. Officials Misleading On '81 Massacre In El Salvador"
[61] Chomsky:328
[62] Gutman:277
[63] Gutman:178
[64] Gutman:312
[65] Gutman:309
[66] *The Senate Committee Report on Drugs, Law Enforcement and Foreign Policy*, United States Senate,1989, S. Prt. 100-165; Senator John F. Kerry; McCoy & Block:205
[67] Shannon:61;Mills:1150
[68] Scott & Marshall:55
[69] Webb:52;159
[70] Gutman:46

[71] Scott & Marshall:55
[72] Webb:70;165
[73] Webb:120;197
[74] Anderson & Anderson:228
[75] McCoy & Block:128
[76] Scott & Marshall:28
[77] Levine:123;Cockburn,A:283
[78] *The Senate Committee Report on Drugs, Law Enforcement and Foreign Policy*, United States Senate,1989, S. Prt. 100-165; Senator John F. Kerry; Brewton:301;Scott & Marshall:56
[79] Scott & Marshall:59
[80] Brewton:6
[81] *New York Times*:11/2/84
[82] Scott & Marshall:62; Webb:346;Cockburn,A:293
[83] Scott & Marshall:61
[84] *The Nation* :"Contras, Crack, the C.I.A.":10/21/96
[85] Brewton:159;Shannon:152; Webb:262ff;469;Cockburn,A:318
[86] *Penthouse Magazine*:7/95:"The Crimes of Mena"
[87] Gutman:338
[88] Reed:252
[89] *The Washington Weekly*:8/18/97
[90] *The Washington Weekly*:8/18/97
[91] Reed:309
[92] Reed:102;124
[93] *The Nation*:2/24/92; Cockburn, A:330
[94] *Portland Free Press*:1-2/97
[95] Reed:428ff
[96] Secord v.Cockburn:Civ. A. No. 88-0727-GHR.United States District Court,District of Columbia:8/27/90
[97] *From The Wilderness*:1:9:11/25/98,@www.copvcia.com
[98] *Washington Post*:12/7/87;in Scott & Marshall:63
[99] McCoy & Block:128
[100] *Esquire*:3/91:136
[101] McCoy & Block:129;Webb:117
[102] Levine:123
[103] Cockburn:126
[104] Cockburn:162
[105] Webb:241-243
[106] McCoy & Block:147
[107] McCoy & Block:141
[108] Cockburn:178
[109] Brewton:118
[110] Associated Press:7/22/89;Costa Rican Legislative Assembly:*Special Commission on Drug Trafficking*:7/10/89, in Webb:210

Castillo

[1] McCoy & Block:154;Webb:253ff
[2] Castillo:70
[3] Castillo: 102-104
[4] Permission to reprint from Celerino Castillo and Michael C. Ruppert, *From the Wilderness*@www.copvcia.com; Castillo:151
[5] Response by Celerino Castillo III, Ex-DEA Special Agent in Guatemala, To The Intelligence Oversight Board Report on Guatemala of 6/28/96
[6] Castillo:208;124;132
[7] Webb:259;256; Castillo:166
[8] Robert Parry at Fairness & Accuracy in Reporting:3/28/93
[9] Cockburn:225;Cockburn:2:256; Webb:267
[10] *Final Report*:8/93:V. I,p.xxi
[11] Permission to reprint from Celerino Castillo and Michael C. Ruppert, *From the Wilderness*@ www.copvcia.com
[12] Response by Celerino Castillo III, Ex-DEA Special Agent in Guatemala, To The Intelligence Oversight Board Report on Guatemala of 6/28/96; Written Statement of Celerino Castillo III (D.E.A. Retired) for the House Permanent Select Committee on Intelligence,

April 27, 1998
[13] *Cerigua Weekly Briefs*:8/24/95
[14] *New York Times*:11/20/93;AP Wire:1/14/97:"Venezuela Pol Faces Drug Charge";Cockburn,A:95
[15] *The Shadow*:April/June 1994: "Haiti's Nightmare";*Los Angeles Times*:3/8/97:A:9; Cockburn,A:109
[16] *Christian Science Monitor*:1/29/95
[17] *Christian Science Monitor*:4/8/97
[18] Reed:375
[19] Anderson & Anderson:260; Cockburn:2:232
[20] Gutman:309
[21] McCoy & Block:329
[22] *Mother Jones*:11/12/93:"A Gift For George"
[23] McCoy & Block:332;*The Nation*:11/14/88;McCoy:2:450;Cockburn,A:264
[24] *Washington Post*:5/13/90
[25] McCoy & Block:340
[26] McCoy:2:454
[27] McCoy & Block:334
[28] McCoy & Block:347
[29] McCoy:2:444
[30] Gutman:320
[31] McCoy & Block:330
[32] *The New York Times*:2/27/96
[33] CIABASE:7/97;*Foreign Policy Magazine*:3/97
[34] *The Washington Post*:1/23/97:"Turkey Blasts German Court's Drug Claim"
[35] *Covert Action Quarterly*:Summer 1997:"Turkey:Trapped in a Web of Covert Killers":Ertugrul Kurkcu

Burma:8/8/88

[1] McCoy:2:432
[2] www.aiipowmia.com/gritz.html; Webb:348
[3] McCoy & Block:283
[4] *New York Times*:5/3/98 Sun, 3 May 1998
[5] *The Nation* :People of the Opiate:12/16/96
[6] *Covert Action Quarterly*:#58:Fall 1996
[7] McCoy & Block:308
[8] McCoy & Block:309
[9] *The Nation* :People of the Opiate:12/16/96
[10] *New York Times*:4/19/98
[11] *The Nation* :People of the Opiate:12/16/96;*Time*:11/7/94;McCoy:2:351;Cockburn,A:231
[12] "Conditions in Burma and U.S. Policy Toward Burma," For the period March 28, 1997 - September 28, 1997, Plan for Implementation of Section 570 of Public Law 104-208 (Omnibus Appropriations Act, Fiscal Year 1997) Submitted to the U.S. Congress, December 2, 1997, Released by the Bureau of East Asian and Pacific Affairs, December 5, 1997, U.S. Department of State
[13] *The Nation* :"People of the Opiate": 12/16/96;Cockburn,A:230
[14] *The Nation* :"People of the Opiate":12/16/96
[15] McCoy:2:185
[16] "Rim Lessons of History For The Indonesian Revolution":John Tully
[17] "Hostage Crisis And Separatist Fight Drag On":Pratap Chatterjee; Jayapura, Indonesia:IPS:2/5/96
[18] A. Barbedo de Magalhaes:*East Timor: Land of Hope*, in Peter Dale Scott, "Two Indonesias, Two Americas": 6/9/98, The Consortium
[19] *Human Rights Watch/ Asia*:vol.9,no.10:12/97
[20] *International Narcotics Control Strategy Report*, 1997, Released by the Bureau for International Narcotics and Law Enforcement Affairs, U.S. Department of State, Washington, DC, March 1998

[21] McCoy:2:413
[22] *Christian Science Monitor*:12/12/96;McCoy:2:180
[23] Mills:203
[24] *High Times*:9/8/97

Leopards

[1] Léons:22;Shannon:361
[2] Léons:22;McCoy & Block:4
[3] Cultural Survival:110
[4] Léons:19
[5] Cultural Survival:140
[6] Cultural Survival:78
[6a] Castillo:85
[7] Cultural Survival:90;Léons:3
[8] International Narcotics Control Strategy Report, 1996,Released by the Bureau for International Narcotics and LawEnforcement Affairs, U.S. Department of State, Washington,DC,3/1997;McCoy & Block:11
[9] McCoy & Block:4
[10] McCoy & Block:95
[11] *The Christian Science Monitor*:9/5/96
[12] Henman, Anthony Richard: "Coca: an Alternative to Cocaine?"Drug Policy 1989-90: A Reformer's Catalogue:164-176
[13] Duke & Gross:202;Léons:51;61;65
[14] *The Observer* (UK):7/11/99;Carter in Cultural Survival:7;8;Duke & Gross:66;Léons:68;76
[15] Léons:141
[16] Léons:152-161
[17] Léons:15;Cultural Survival:114-123;Shannon:76
[18] International Narcotics Control Strategy Report, 1996,Released by the Bureau for International Narcotics and LawEnforcement Affairs, U.S. Department of State, Washington,DC,3/1997

[19] Léons:182;255;257;264
[20] Léons:261
[21] Human Rights Watch/Americas:Vol. 8, No. 4 (D), May 1996:"Bolivia Under Pressure: Human Rights Violations and Coca Eradication"
[22] Léons:12;24;42;205;255
[23] Léons:37
[24] *Human Rights Watch Americas*:7-8:7/95; Léons:136
[25] Associated Press:3/3/98

Viva Zapata

[1] Anderson & Anderson:145; Cockburn,A:180
[2] Scott & Marshall:35
[3] Scott & Marshall:171;Webb:207
[4] McCoy & Block:199;Mills:1157
[5] Anderson & Anderson:74ff
[6] Anderson & Anderson:138
[7] Shannon:202
[8] McCoy & Block:183;Cockburn,A:352
[9] Mills:344
[10] Shannon:187;Mills:102
[11] *Time*:3/17/88;Shannon:186;Scott & Marshall:40
[12] Shannon:179
[13] Scott:167
[14] Mills:1142
[15] Mills:76
[16] Scott:110
[17] Mills:285
[18] Kruger:178
[19] Shannon:180;McCoy & Block:180
[20] McCoy & Block:181
[21] Scott:105;Mills:1157
[22] McCoy & Block:200
[23] Shannon:180
[24] McCoy & Block:181
[25] Shannon:62
[26] Scott & Marshall:38
[27] Kruger:180;Shannon:65

[28] Scott & Marshall:38
[29] Scott & Marshall:38; Shannon:67-69;*Newsweek*:12/16/85
[30] Scott & Marshall:39
[31] Shannon:293
[32] Shannon:194
[33] *New York Times*:11/23/84;Scott & Marshall:37
[34] *The Sinsemilla Technique* by Kayo;Shannon:293
[35] Mills:1154
[36] Permission to reprint from Celerino Castillo and Michael C. Ruppert, *From the Wilderness* @www.copvcia.com;Webb:205
[37] McCoy & Block:186
[38] *Oakland Tribune*:2/26/85;in Scott & Marshall:37
[39] Shannon:9
[40] Levine:121
[41] Mills:128
[42] Shannon:70
[43] McCoy & Block:189
[44] McCoy & Block:192
[45] Latimer:"Citibank and Your Drug War Dollars," *High Times*:1/97
[46] Cockburn, A:357
[47] US DISTRICT COURT/DISTRICT OF SOUTHERN TEXAS/HOUS-TON DIVISION/CIVIL CASE No H-95-3182
[48] Rotella:135
[49] Rotella:217ff
[50] *TIME*:8/12/96: "Good Guys Gone Bad?"
[51] Associated Press:2/19/97:"Mexico Drug Czar Arrested"
[52] *Newsweek*:3/10/97
[53] Susan E. Reed in *The New Republic*:3/17/97
[54] *Newsweek*:3/3/97:"A Defector in the Drug War"
[55] Susan E. Reed in *The New Republic*:3/17/97;Cockburn,A:375
[56] *New York Times*:4/23/98
[57] *New York Times*:12/24/97
[58] *From The Wilderness*:1:5:7/25/98
[59] *New York Times*:2/27/98

S.I.N.

[1] *The New York Times*:8/5/96
[2] McCoy & Block:104
[3] Henman, Anthony Richard:"Coca: an Alternative to Cocaine?"*Drug Policy 1989-1990*: A Reformer's Catalogue:164-176
[4] Human Rights Watch/Americas: 7/21/95:"Two Faces of Justice in Peru"
[5] *Current History*:2/92
[6] *La Vanguardia*:11/05/92
[7] *Covert Action Quarterly*:Summer 1994:"The Betrayal of Peru's Deomcracy" by Gustavo Gorriti
[8] *New York Review of Books*:5/25/92
[9] *Covert Action Quarterly*:2/97
[10] *Miami Herald*:5/30/92
[11] *Miami Herald*:4/18/92
[12] *El País*:5/22/92; Reuters:12/12/92
[13] *Newsweek*:5/10/93;Scott & Marshall:191;*Time*:8/7/95
[14] *El País*(Spain):5/22/92
[15] *The Christian Science Monitor*:5/18/93
[16] www.blythe.org/peru-pcp
[17] *The Geopolitical Drug Dispatch*:#39: 1/95. "Peru: Soldiers Against the Army"
[18] *The New Flag*:7/96
[19] *New York Times*:11/25/96:"American Drug Aid Goes South"
[20] *Gestion*:10/25/96
[21] Andes@www.calyx.com:2/26/96
[22] *El Comercio*(Peru):7/3/96;*Caretas*: 6/20/96

The Active Army

[1] Cockburn:2:254
[2] Peterson in Krauss:275

[3] Scott & Marshall:73;Shannon:165
[4] *Rolling Stone*:10/90
[5] Taubman in Kraus:96
[6] "Autopsy Shows How Marine Fire Killed Teen":Eduardo Montes: *Austin American-Statesman*:6/24/97
[7] 18 U.S.C. Section 1385
[8] *NORML Reports*:6/23/94;2/16/95
[9] Law #100-456;*Justicia*:12/92
[10] Solomon in The House of Representatives:4/6/95
[13] McCoy & Block:3
[14] Levine:462
[15] *1996 National Drug Control Strategy*:Office of National Drug Control Policy
[16] *Rolling Stone*:10/30/97,p.44
[17] *The Washington Post*:2/13/97: "Clinton Plans Ad Blitz In Domestic Drug War"
[18] Baum:5
[19] Baum:52-71
[20] Nadelmann:273
[21] (London) *Independent on Sunday*:1/25/98
[22] Chomsky:3:Chapter 4:note 17
[23] Mills:1146
[24] Cockburn:2:264;Shannon:141
[25] Robin Lloyd "Caught in the Crossfire:Women are Taking a Stand in Colombia's Struggle Between Corruption and Justice." The Drug Policy Letter #35, Winter 1998
[26] *New York Times*:2/28/98
[26a] *El Tiempo*(Colombia):2/29/99
[27] *New York Times*:2/28/98
[28] *New York Times*:2/28/98
[29] *Time*:2/5/96
[30] Associated Press:2/14/97:"Colombia Urges U.S. Aid Renewal"
[31] *Christian Science Monitor*:11/21/97
[32] *New York Times*:2/27/98
[33] *NY Times: CyberTimes*:5/96:V.8,#2:"Silencing The Net"
[34] *Observer*:10/189
[35] Andes@drugtext.com:2/26/96

[36] Herer:49
[37] *Time*:1/29/79

Interdiction

[1] *New York Times*:2/24/95
[2] *Toronto Sun*:4/12/98;
[3] Associated Press:4/18/98
[4] Shannon:56
[5] Shannon:72
[6] (London)*Independent on Sunday*:1/25/98
[7] Shannon:322
[8] McCoy & Block:3
[9] *Christian Science Monitor*:6/17/97
[10] Susan E. Reed in *The New Republic*:3/17/97
[11] *The Washington Post*:1/30/97: "Latin Drugs Flow North Via Pacific"
[12] International Narcotics Control Strategy Report, 1996,Released by the Bureau for International Narcotics and LawEnforcement Affairs, U.S. Department of State, Washington,DC,3/1997
[13] *New York Times*:2/28/98
[17] *The Christian Science Monitor*:7/15/96
[18] *Syr.Herald-American*:8/27/95
[19] Frank Mangan, senior trial attorney for Federal Defenders of San Diego, in *Rolling Stone*:4/16/98:p.92
[20] Zeese in Krauss:259; McCoy:2:408
[21] Zeese in Krauss:259

Fake Science

[1] *The Marihuana Problem in the City of New York*: Sociological, Medical, Psychological, and Pharmacological Studies by the Mayor's Committee on Marihuana: The Jaques Cattell Press: Lancaster, PA: 1944: p.25

[2] *The Journal of the International Hemp Association*:12/19/95
[3] DEA Docket No. 86-22:pp 57-59; Duke & Gross:184
[4] *APHA Public Policy Statements:Resolution #7014*
[5] *JAMA*:V.271#21:6/1/94:1647
[6] Grinspoon in Krauss:379
[7] Grinspoon in Krauss:382; *JAMA*:6/21/95;V.273,N.23
[8] *AMA*:113
[9] *U.S. Dispensatory*:26:296;Kaplan & Sadock:*Synopsis of Psychiatry*:6th Ed.
[10] Szasz:1:125
[11] *PDR*:1989:1571
[12] Grinspoon in Krauss:381
[13] *The Lancet*:V.346,N.8985:11/11/95,p.1241
[14] Glasser in Krauss:272
[15] Reuter in Krauss:138
[16] Chomsky:1:126
[17] *New York Times*:1/29/95; *NORML*:Spring/95
[18] Zimmer
[19] *Rolling Stone*:1/26/95;Herer:80;81;Playboy:5/87:149
[20] Lee & Schlain:154
[21] *The Journal of Psychoactive Drugs*:Vol.24:Apr-Jun 1992:"Marijuana and Immunity":Leo E Hollister,MD
[22] *JAMA*:6/1/94:1647
[23] Nahas:fax:8/95
[24] *Drug Alcohol Review*:1994:13:209-216
[25] *Maintenant*:10/93
[26] *New York Times*:1/29/95:40;Califano:123
[27] Baum:298
[28] *N Engl Med.*:1991:361-365
[29] *Science*:12/15/89:1381;*Vogue*:3/90:354
[30] *U.S. Catholic*:6/96
[31] Califano:XV
[32] *JAMA*:6/1/94:1639

The Cure

[1] Prouty:418;425
[2] 1990 Address to the Colorado Bar Association, "Is The Bill of Rights A Casualty of the Drug War?"
[3] Nadelmann:193;196;Baum:178-205
[4] Title 21, U.S. Code 841
[5] *Harper's Magazine*:7/96
[6] Schneider & Flaherty in *The Pittsburgh Press*,1991
[7] Schneider & Flaherty in *The Pittsburgh Press*,1991
[8] Schneider & Flaherty in *The Pittsburgh Press*,1991
[9] Duke & Gross:136
[10] Duke & Gross:136
[11] USA Today, July 11, 1995
[12] Duke & Gross:137
[13] *Washington Post Weekly Edition*:4/19/91:"Turning Drug Busts into a Profit Center"
[14] Duke & Gross:138
[15] Duke & Gross:129
[16] Duke & Gross:129;Baum:293
[17] Duke & Gross:136
[18] Schneider & Flaherty in *The Pittsburgh Press*:1991
[19] *The Independent Review*:Fall 1996:"Predatory Public Finance and the Origins of the War on Drugs, 1984-1989":Benson & Rasmussen
[20] *Washington Post Weekly Edition*:4/19/91:"Turning Drug Busts into a Profit Center"
[21] Szasz:1:23
[22] Duke & Gross:140
[23] *Cod.Th*:16:1:2;16:8:1;16:8:7; 16:8:19; 16:10:3;*Code*:1;12;16;48;54; Peters: 1:45;Linder:81;258
[24] *The NORML Leaflet*:6/91;9/91
[25] Zeese in Krauss:254
[26] Duke & Gross:124;Baum:216;278
[26a] *Progressive Review*:6/99
[27] Glasser in Krauss:277

[28] Bureau of Justice Statistics, Prisoners in 1996, 1997
[29] Bureau of Justice Statistics Special Report: Survey of State Prison Inmates, 1991; issued Feb. 1997
[30] Glasser in Krauss:275;McNamara in Krauss:293
[31] *San Francisco Examiner*:4/9/95
[32] Epstein:106
[33] McCoy & Block:56
[33a] Webb:381
[34] Stanford University's *Campus Report*:5/17/95
[35] *Ratification Handbook*;Merz:83
[36] Califano:111
[37] McCoy & Block:59
[38] *Rolling Stone*:5/5/94:33;Bureau of Prisons testimony:6/93
[39] *Rolling Stone*:5/5/94:33
[40] *Rolling Stone*:5/5/94:33
[41] Federal Bureau of Prisons:9/96:"Quick Facts"
[42] New York State Penal Law (P.L.) §220.39 (Criminal Sale of a Controlled Substance in the Third Degree); P.L. §160.15 (Robbery in the First Degree); P.L. §130.35 (Rape in the First Degree), and P.L. §120.10 (Assault in the First Degree)
[43] Duke & Gross:179
[44] Sweet in Krauss:356
[45] Friedman in Krauss:57
[46] *Oakland Tribune*:2/16/96
[47] Duke & Gross:77
[48] Engelsman in Krauss:170
[49] Duke & Gross:199
[50] *Amsterdam Drug Policy*:City of Amsterdam,1996
[51] Turner in Krauss:184;Fleming, Philip M:"Prescribing Policy in the UK:A Swing Away from Harm Reduction?" International Journal of Drug Policy:Vol. 6, No. 3, 1995:173-177
[52] Morgan in Krauss:409
[53] Engelsman in Krauss:173
[54] Zeese in Krauss:260
[54a] Plato:*The Laws*:1:648
[55] Jung:11:197
[56] Augustine:*City of God Against the Pagans*:19:15
[57] Jung:14:361
[58] Jung:13:347
[59] NHL:147
[60] Mark:10:18;Luke:18:18
[61] Jung:13:185

Index

X

Y

Z

Sometimes, instead of catching young sharks—man-eaters or the thick-headed variety at the right—the Quelpart fisherman goes up into the mountains after mushrooms. There he wears greased dogskin and spends the night in a cave of the extinct volcano

SHAMANISM
AND THE
DRUG
PROPAGANDA

Patriarchy and
The Drug War

"A magnificent production."
Prof. Richard Evans Schultes

Dan Russell

"A magnificent production. I find it not only brilliant, but beautifully organized and, of course, something that needs to be. It is a tremendous work and, by nature, a tremendous volume." Professor Richard Evans Schultes, Director Emeritus, Botanical Museum of Harvard University

"I had to write in appreciation of the invaluable contribution you've made to realizing the possible human. Immediately, I was impressed with the multi-perspectives through which you see the classics. I find your book a major ally in delivering truth today." Jeannine Parvati, author of *Hygieia, Conscious Conception, Prenatal Yoga*

"Dan Russell's book, *Shamanism and the Drug Propaganda* starts with questions of basic importance to ethnobotany. Anyone working in this discipline is aware of the profond and ancient relationship between man and plant.... Using studies such as my own among the Maku in the northwest Amazon, ethnobotany can demonstrate the relationship between psychoactive plants and the tribal roots of human religion."

"But if the psychoative plants are so deeply rooted in our evolved sense of the sacred, why are they so viciously banned in contemporary industrial cultures? Dan Russell's book answers this question."

"*Shamanism and the Drug Propaganda* traces the cultural evolution of our species from shamanism to the mass media religions. It is an important book, very well written, a must for anyone interested in psychoative plants and the cultural evolution of humankind. It is also a very pleasing volume to read, the kind of book that will keep you holding your breath until the end. I strongly recommend this heavily illustrated, original, yet rigorously empirical historical vision." Anthropologist and Ethnobotanist Pedro Fernandes Leite da Luz

"Beginning with the evolution of Paleolithic proto-hominids, Russell presents one example after another in support of his thesis that the Drug War is a psychological inheritance from ancient times, one which is now deeply embedded in and, in some cases, the driving force of our culture of power and profits. Russell draws extensively from archeological evidence, presenting object after object engraved with archetypal symbols of shamanic travels, and he deconstructs countless ancient stories and myths to show that many of them alluded to visionary states elicited by the ingestion of psychoactive plants and potions. Russell, building upon the seemingly impenetrable work of John Allegro, even presents evidence that the Bible is riddled with cryptic stories and word-play bestowing the importance of shamanic inebriation.

"*Shamanism and Drug Propaganda* is so detail rich that a summary does it an injustice. In essence, however, Russell argues that over time, the stories told by ancient people (culminating in the New Testament), have been co-opted, corrupted, and manipulated by forces bent on producing a conformist culture. Modern industrial culture, argues Russell, is dependent upon the active eradication of the conscious knowledge of entheogens." Richard Glen Boire, Esq., Executive Director, The Alchemind Society, *Journal of Cognitive Liberties*, Vol.1, Issue 1, Winter 1999/2000

Drug War

Dan Russell entered the University of Buffalo in 1963. His anthropological historiography was learned in the wildly creative 60's, as was his interest in the archaic techniques of ecstacy and automatic creativity. This interest was politicized by the fascists who have engineered the current Inquisition, which he has chosen to deconstruct. He is a 1970 graduate of the City College of New York, and a 1972 graduate of the streets of New York. Since then he has sold books in Pittsburgh and manufactured candy bars in North Central New York State, where he currently lives with his wife and three children.

Dan and his son Josh are retailers of **Frontier Herbs**. Frontier's full line, drop-shipped direct from the Frontier warehouse, is available from their website, **www.kalyx.com**.

Dan is also the author-publisher of *Shamanism and the Drug Propaganda*, an illustrated summary of which is up, along with a summary of this book, at **www.drugwar.com**.